Lecture Notes in Artificial In

Subseries of Lecture Notes in Computer Science

LNAI Series Editors

Randy Goebel
  University of Alberta, Edmonton, Canada
Yuzuru Tanaka
  Hokkaido University, Sapporo, Japan
Wolfgang Wahlster
  DFKI and Saarland University, Saarbrücken, Germany

LNAI Founding Series Editor

Joerg Siekmann
  DFKI and Saarland University, Saarbrücken, Germany

João Leite   Tran Cao Son
Paolo Torroni   Leon van der Torre
Stefan Woltran (Eds.)

Computational Logic in Multi-Agent Systems

14th International Workshop, CLIMA XIV
Corunna, Spain, September 16-18, 2013
Proceedings

 Springer

Volume Editors

João Leite
Universidade Nova de Lisboa, 2829-516 Caparica, Portugal
E-mail: jleite@fct.unl.pt

Tran Cao Son
New Mexico State University, Las Cruces, NM 88003, USA
E-mail: tson@cs.nmsu.edu

Paolo Torroni
University of Bologna, 40136 Bologna, Italy
E-mail: paolo.torroni@unibo.it

Leon van der Torre
University of Luxembourg, 1359 Luxembourg, Luxembourg
E-mail: leon.vandertorre@uni.lu

Stefan Woltran
Vienna University of Technology, 1040 Vienna, Austria
E-mail: woltran@dbai.tuwien.ac.at

ISSN 0302-9743   e-ISSN 1611-3349
ISBN 978-3-642-40623-2   e-ISBN 978-3-642-40624-9
DOI 10.1007/978-3-642-40624-9
Springer Heidelberg New York Dordrecht London

Library of Congress Control Number: 2013946306

CR Subject Classification (1998): I.2.11, F.4.1, D.2, D.3.1-2, I.2.4, F.3

LNCS Sublibrary: SL 7 – Artificial Intelligence

Typesetting: Camera-ready by author, data conversion by Scientific Publishing Services, Chennai, India

Printed on acid-free paper

Springer is part of Springer Science+Business Media (www.springer.com)

Preface

These are the proceedings of the 14th International Workshop on *Computational Logic in Multi-Agent Systems* (CLIMA XIV), held during September 15–18, 2013, in Corunna, Spain, and co-located with the 22nd International Conference Logic Programming and Non-Monotonic Reasoning (LPNMR) and with the 7th International Workshop on Modular Ontologies (WoMO 2013).

Multi-agent systems are systems of interacting autonomous agents or components that can perceive and act upon their environment to achieve their individual goals as well as joint goals. Research on such systems integrates many technologies and concepts in artificial intelligence and other areas of computing as well as other disciplines. Over recent years, the agent paradigm gained popularity, due to its applicability to a full spectrum of domains, from search engines to educational aids to electronic commerce and trade, e-procurement, recommendation systems, simulation and routing, to mention only some.

Computational logic provides a well-defined, general, and rigorous framework for studying syntax, semantics and procedures for various tasks by individual agents, as well as interaction amongst agents in multi-agent systems, for implementations, environments, tools, and standards, and for linking together specification and verification of properties of individual agents and multi-agent systems.

The purpose of the CLIMA workshops is to provide a forum for discussing techniques, based on computational logic, for representing, programming and reasoning about agents and multi-agent systems in a formal way.

Former CLIMA editions have mostly been conducted in conjunction with major computational logic and artificial intelligence events such as CL in 2000, ICLP in 2001 and 2007, FLoC in 2002, LPNMR and AI-Math in 2004, JELIA in 2004 and 2008, AAMAS in 2006, MATES in 2009, ECAI in 2010 and 2012, and IJCAI in 2011. In 2005, CLIMA VI was organized as a stand-alone event.

CLIMA XIV closely followed the format established by its predecessors, with regular proceedings and two special sessions: Argumentation Technologies, organized by Paolo Torroni and Stefan Woltran, and Norms and Normative Multi-Agent Systems, organized by Leon van der Torre.

Argumentation is an important and exciting topic in artificial intelligence, where uses of argumentation have increased in recent years, throughout a variety of subdisciplines. Research activities range from theory to applications. The Special Session on Argumentation Technologies was intended to be a forum to discuss concepts, theories, methodologies, and applications of computational models of argumentation.

Norms are pervasive in everyday life and influence the conduct of the entities subject to them. One of the main functions of norms is to regulate the behavior and relationships of agents. Norms have been proposed in multi-agent systems and computer science to deal with coordination issues, to deal with security issues of multi-agent systems, to model legal issues in electronic institutions and electronic commerce, to model multi-agent organizations, etc.

This 14th edition of CLIMA received an exceptionally high number of submissions. The 23 papers presented at CLIMA XIV were selected from 44 submissions, on average of very high quality, after two rounds of reviewing, resulting in a final acceptance rate of circa 50%, in line with the high standards of previous editions. Many of those involved in the revision and selection process acknowledged the high quality of the program. In many instances the authors expressed their satisfaction with very informative and constructive reviews, for which CLIMA is renown.

The Program Committee consisted of 63 top-level researchers from 44 institutions located in five continents and 18 countries; 16 additional reviewers helped in the process. The papers in this book have been authored by 62 researchers worldwide.

Besides the presentation of the regular papers contained in this book, CLIMA XIV featured four invited talks delivered by George Vouros (University of Piraeus, Greece), Pietro Baroni (Università degli Studi di Brescia, Italy), Gerhard Brewka (University of Leipzig, Germany), and Sven Ove Hansson (Royal Institute of Technology, Sweden), whose abstracts can be found after this preface.

Further information about CLIMA XIV is available from the website `http://centria.di.fct.unl.pt/events/climaXIV/`. General information about the workshop series, with links to past and future events, can be found on the CLIMA workshop series home page, `http://centria.di.fct.unl.pt/~clima/`.

We thank all the authors of papers submitted to CLIMA XIV, the invited speakers, the members of the Program Committee, and the additional reviewers for ensuring that CLIMA keeps up to its high standards. Additionally, we acknowledge Sintelnet for financially supporting the invited talk of George Vouros, LPNMR for supporting the invited talk of Gerhard Brewka, and *AI Journal* for financially supporting the invited talk of Pietro Baroni and the discounts in student registrations. A special thank you goes to Pedro Cabalar, the Co-chair of LPNMR 2013, and the local organizers in Corunna, for all their help and support.

September 2013

João Leite
Tran Cao Son
Paolo Torroni
Leon van der Torre
Stefan Woltran

Organization

Workshop Chairs

João Leite   New University of Lisbon, Portugal
Tran Cao Son   New Mexico State University, USA

Special Session Chairs

Paolo Torroni   University of Bologna, Italy
Leon van der Torre   University of Luxembourg
Stefan Woltran   Vienna University of Technology, Austria

Program Committee

Thomas Ågotnes   University of Bergen, Norway
Natasha Alechina   University of Nottingham, UK
José Júlio Alferes   New University of Lisbon, Portugal
Katie Atkinson   University of Liverpool, UK
Stefano Bistarelli   University of Perugia, Italy
Liz Black   King' College London, UK
Guido Boella   Università degli Studi di Torino, Italy
Elise Bonzon   Univ. Paris Descartes - Paris 5, France
Rafael Bordini   Fed. University of Rio Grande do Sul, Brazil
Gerhard Brewka   University of Leipzig, Germany
Jan Broersen   Utrecht University, The Netherlands
Nils Bulling   Clausthal University of Technology, Germany
Federico Cerutti   University of Aberdeen, UK
Stefania Costantini   University of L'Aquila, Italy
Mehdi Dastani   Utrecht University, The Netherlands
Louise Dennis   The University of Liverpool, UK
Frank Dignum   Utrecht University, The Netherlands
Juergen Dix   Technical University of Clausthal, Germany
Sylvie Doutre   University of Toulouse, France
Phan Minh Dung   Asian Institute of Technology, Vietnam
Wolfgang Dvorák   University of Vienna, Austria
Michael Fisher   The University of Liverpool, UK
Nicoletta Fornara   University of Lugano, Switzerland
Sarah Gaggl   Technische Universität Dresden, Germany
Chiara Ghidini   University of Trento, Italy
Massimiliano Giacomin   Università di Brescia, Italy

Lluís Godo	IIIA-CSIC, Spain
Davide Grossi	University of Amsterdam, The Netherlands
Stella Heras	Technical University of Valencia, Spain
Koen Hindriks	Delft University, The Netherlands
Wiebe van der Hoek	The University of Liverpool, UK
Katsumi Inoue	National Insitute of Informatics, Japan
Wojtek Jamroga	University of Luxembourg, Luxembourg
Jérôme Lang	Université Paris-Dauphine, France
Brian Logan	University of Nottingham, UK
Alessio Lomuscio	Imperial College London, UK
Emiliano Lorini	Université Paul Sabatier, France
Peter McBurney	King's College London, UK
John-Jules Meyer	Utrecht University, The Netherlands
Mehmet Orgun	Macquarie University, Australia
Fabio Paglieri	ISTC-CNR Roma, Italy
Maurice Pagnucco	University of New South Wales, Australia
Xavier Parent	University of Luxembourg, Luxembourg
Simon Parsons	Brooklyn College CUNY, USA
Célia da Costa Pereira	University of Nice Sophia Antipolis, France
Jeremy Pitt	Imperial College London, UK
Enrico Pontelli	New Mexico State University, USA
Henry Prakken	University of Utrecht, The Netherlands
Franco Raimondi	Middlesex University, UK
Chris Reed	University of Dundee, UK
Chiaki Sakama	Wakayama University, Japan
Fariba Sadri	Imperial College London, UK
Guillermo Simari	Universidad Nacional del Sur, Argentina
Martin Slota	New University of Lisbon, Portugal
Christian Strasser	University of Gent, Belgium
Michael Thielscher	University of New South Wales, Australia
Francesca Toni	Imperial College London, UK
Paolo Turrini	University of Luxembourg, Luxembourg
Wamberto Vasconcelos	University of Aberdeen, UK
Srdjan Vesic	CRIL, France
Serena Villata	INRIA Sophia Antipolis, France
Marina De Vos	University of Bath, UK
Cees Witteveen	Delft University, The Netherlands

Additional Reviewers

Leila Amgoud	IRIT University of Toulouse, France
Marco Baioletti	University of Perugia, Italy
Pietro Baroni	University of Brescia, Italy
Antonis Kakas	University of Cyprus
Matthias Knorr	New University of Lisbon, Portugal
Robert Kowalski	Imperial College London, UK

Beishui Liao   Zhejiang University, China
João Marques-Silva   Technical University of Lisbon, Portugal
Felipe Meneguzzi   PUC Rio Grande do Sul, Brazil
Sanjay Modgil   King's College London, UK
Julien Rossit   Université Paris Descartes, France
Francesco Santini   INRIA-Rocquencourt, Paris, France
Luciano Serafini   Fondazione Bruno Kessler, Italy
Bas Testerink   University of Utrecht, The Netherlands
Mirek Truszczynski   University of Kentucky, USA
Yi N. Wáng   Bergen University College, Norway

CLIMA Steering Committee

Thomas Ågotnes   University of Bergen, Norway
Michael Fisher   University of Liverpool, UK
Katsumi Inoue   National Institute of Informatics, Japan
João Leite   New University of Lisbon, Portugal
Leon van der Torre   University of Luxembourg, Luxembourg

Mind the Gap: Abstract vs. Applied Argumentation
–Invited Talk–

Pietro Baroni

Dip. di Ingegneria dell'Informazione, University of Brescia
via Branze 38, 25123 Brescia, Italy
baroni@ing.unibs.it

Using examples taken from the literature, the talk discusses gaps and links between formal notions and models in abstract argumentation and actual applications of argumentation technologies, with a twofold perspective. On one hand, it analyses the risks inherent in direct jumps from concrete examples to completely abstract formalisms. On the other hand, it examines the practical counterparts and potential utility of some abstract notions in actual application contexts.

Towards Reactive Multi-Context Systems
–Invited Talk–

Gerhard Brewka

Leipzig University, Informatics Institute
Postfach 100920, 04009 Leipzig, Germany
brewka@informatik.uni-leipzig.de

Among the challenges faced by the area of knowledge representation (KR) are the following ones: (1) knowledge represented in different knowledge representation languages needs to be integrated, and (2), certain applications, e.g. assisted living, have specific needs not typically fulfilled by standard KR systems. What we have in mind are applications where reasoners, rather than answering specific user calls, run online and have to deal with a continuous stream of information.

We argue that multi-context systems (MCS) are adequate tools for both challenges. The basic idea underlying MCS is to leave the diverse formalisms and knowledge bases untouched, and to equip each reasoning context with a collection of so-called bridge rules in order to model the necessary information flow among contexts. Bridge rules are similar to logic programming rules (including default negation), with an important difference: they allow to access other contexts in their bodies. The semantics of MCS is defined in terms of equilibria: a belief state assigns a belief set to each context C_i. A belief state is an equilibrium whenever the belief set selected for each C_i is acceptable for C_i's knowledge base *augmented by the heads of C_i's applicable bridge rules.*

Although this covers the flow of information, it does not capture other operations one may want to perform on context KBs. For instance, rather than simply *adding* a formula ϕ, we may want to delete some information, or to *revise* the KB with ϕ to avoid inconsistency in the context's belief set. To provide this additional functionality MCS were later generalized to so called managed MCS (mMCS).

The possibility to have arbitrary operators is what, as we believe, makes mMCS suitable tools for online applications. The systems we have in mind are *reactive* in the sense that they modify themselves to keep system performance up and to respond adequately to potential emergencies. In the talk we discuss what is needed to turn the managed MCS approach into a framework for online reasoning. In particular,

- we need to admit contexts which are connected to the real world through sensors,
- we need to identify operations on KBs which allow us to forget irrelevant information and to focus on potential emergencies. Ideally such operations also take the current system performance into account and are able to restrict recomputations to relevant parts,

- we need sophisticated preference handling techniques, as preferences will play an essential role to handle inconsistencies among different sensors, to deal with more important emergencies first, and to mediate between what's in the current focus and the goal not to overlook important events,
- we need to come up with notions describing the behavior of a system over time, e.g. that of a *system run*.

A lot remains to be done in KR to meet the challenges of online reasoning. Nevertheless, promising ideas are around and addressing these problems will definitely be worth it.

Intuition Pumps for Deontic Logic
–Invited Talk–

Sven Ove Hansson

Royal Institute of Technology, Sweden
`soh@kth.se`

In deontic logic as well as several other areas of logic, intuitions are applied not only to the representation of the actual subject-matter but also to various constructions such as possible worlds, maximal subsets not applying a certain sentence, etc. To what extent can intuitions related to such constructions help us determine the validity of logical principles for the actual subject-matter? In this talk we investigate the efficiency of different types of intuition pumps used in deontic logic and related fields.

Combing Ontologies in Settings with Multiple Agents
–Invited Talk–

George Vouros

Department of Digital Systems,
University of Piraeus, Greece
georgev@unipi.gr

Abstract. Combining knowledge and beliefs of autonomous peers in distributed settings, is a major challenge. In this talk we consider agents that combine their ontologies and reason jointly with their coupled knowledge using the E-SHIQ representation framework. We motivate the need for a representation framework that allows agents to combine their knowledge in different ways, maintaining the subjectivity of their own knowledge and beliefs, and to reason collaboratively, constructing a tableau that is distributed among them. The talk presents the $E - \mathcal{SHIQ}$ representation framework and the tableau reasoning algorithm. It presents the implications to the modularization of ontologies for efficient reasoning, implications to coordinating agents' subjective beliefs, as well as challenges for reasoning with ontologies in open and dynamic multi-agent systems.

1 Combining Ontologies with $E - \mathcal{SHIQ}$

To combine knowledge and beliefs of autonomous agents in open and inherently distributed settings, we need special formalisms that take into account the complementarity and heterogeneity of knowledge in multiple interconnected contexts. Agents may have different, subjective beliefs concerning "bridging" heterogeneity and coupling their knowledge with the knowledge of others. The subjectivity of beliefs plays an important role in such a setting, as agents may inherently (i.e. due to restrictions of their task environment) have different views of the knowledge possessed by others, or they may not agree on the way they may jointly shape knowledge.

On the other hand, large ontologies need to be dismantled so as to be evolved, engineered and used effectively during reasoning. The process of taking an ontology to possibly interdependent ontology units is called ontology modularization, and specifically, ontology partitioning. Each such unit, or module, provides a specific context for performing ontology maintenance, evolution and reasoning tasks, at scales and complexity that are smaller than that of the initial ontology. Therefore, in open and inherently distributed settings (for performing either ontology maintenance, evolution or reasoning tasks), several such ontology modules may co-exist in connection with each other. Formally, it is required that any axiom that is expressed using terms in the signature of a module and it is entailed by the ontology must be entailed by the module, and vise-versa. The partitioning task requires that the union of all the modules, together with the set of correspondences/relations between modules, is semantically equivalent to the original ontology. This later property imposes hard restrictions to the modularization task: Indeed, to maintain it, a method must do this with respect to the expressiveness of the language used for specifying correspondences/relations between modules' elements, to the local (per ontology module) interpretation of constructs, and to the restrictions imposed by the setting where modules are deployed.

The expressivity of knowledge representation frameworks for combining knowledge in multiple contexts, and the efficiency of distributed reasoning processes, depend on the language(s) used for expressing local knowledge and on the language used for connecting different contexts.

While our main goal is to provide a rich representation framework for combining and reasoning with distinct ontology units in open, heterogeneous and inherently distributed settings, we propose the $E-\mathcal{SHIQ}$ representation framework and a distributed tableau algorithm [1] [2].

The representation framework $E-\mathcal{SHIQ}$:

- Supports subjective concept-to-concept correspondences between concepts in different ontology units.
- In conjunction to subjective concept-to-concept correspondences, $E-\mathcal{SHIQ}$ supports relating individuals in different units via link relations, as well as via subjective individual correspondence relations. While correspondence relations represent equalities between individuals, from the subjective point of view of a specific unit, link relations may relate individuals in different units via domain-specific relations.
- Supports distributed reasoning by combining local reasoning chunks in a peer-to-peer fashion. Each reasoning peer with a specific ontology unit holds a part of a distributed tableau, which corresponds to a distributed model.
- Finally, $E-\mathcal{SHIQ}$ inherently supports subsumption propagation between ontologies, supporting reasoning with concept-to-concept correspondences in conjunction to link relations between ontologies.

2 Constructing $E-\mathcal{SHIQ}$ Distributed Knowledge Bases via Modularization

To distribute knowledge among different agents, we need to partition monolithic ontologies to possibly interconnected modules. In this part of the talk we describe efforts towards constructing $E-\mathcal{SHIQ}$ distributed knowledge bases by modularizing ontologies: Our aim is to make ontology units as much self-contained and independent from others as possible, so as to increase the efficiency of the reasoning process. We discuss the flexibility offered by $E - \mathcal{SHIQ}$ itself, and different modularization options available (a first attempt towards this problem has been reported in [3]).

3   Challenges towards Reasoning with Multiple Ontologies

Towards reasoning with ontology units in open and dynamic settings with multiple agents, this talk presents and discusses the following major challenges:

Reaching Agreements to correspondences: Agents in inherently distributed and open settings can not be assumed to share an agreed ontology of their common task environment. To interact effectively, these agents need to establish semantic correspondences between their ontology elements. As already pointed out, the correspondences computed by two agents may differ due to (a) different mapping methods used, to (b) different information one makes available to the other, or (c) restrictions imposed by their task environment. Although semantic coordination methods have already been proposed for the computation of subjective correspondences between agents, we need methods for communities, groups and arbitrarily formed networks of interconnected agents to reach semantic agreements on subjective ontology elements' correspondences [4].

Exploitation of ontology units in open and dynamic settings: In open settings where agents may enter or leave the system at will, we need agents to dynamically combine their knowledge and re-organize themselves, so as to form groups that can serve specific information needs successfully. There are several issues that need to be addressed here: Agents (a) must share information about their potential partners and must learn the capabilities, effectiveness, trustworthiness etc. of their peers, (b) must locate the potential partners, and (c) must decide for the "best" groups to be formed in an ad-hoc manner, towards serving the specific information needs. Reaching complete and optimal solutions in such a setting is a hard problem: we discuss the computation of approximate solutions [5].

Acknowledgements. Thanks to Georgios Santipantakis for his contributions to various parts of this work, especially the one concerning $E - \mathcal{SHIQ}$. The major part of the research work referenced in this talk is being supported by the project IRAKLITOS II" of the O.P.E.L.L. 2007 - 2013 of the NSRF (2007 - 2013), co-funded by the European Union and National Resources of Greece.

References

1. Vouros, G.A., Santipantakis, G.M.: Distributed reasoning with $e^{DDL}_{HQ+}\mathcal{SHIQ}$. In: Modular Ontologies: Proc. of the 6th International Workshop (WoMo 2012). (July 2012)
2. Santipantakis, G.M., Vouros, G.A.: The e-shiq contextual logic framework. In: AT. (2012) 300–301
3. Santipantakis, G.M., Vouros, G.A.: Modularizing owl ontologies using $e^{DDL}_{HQ+}\mathcal{SHIQ}$. In: ICTAI. (2012) 411–418
4. Vouros, G.A.: Decentralized semantic coordination via belief propagation. In: AAMAS. (2013) 1207–1208
5. Karagiannis, P., Vouros, G.A., Stergiou, K., Samaras, N.: Overlay networks for task allocation and coordination in large-scale networks of cooperative agents. Autonomous Agents and Multi-Agent Systems **24**(1) (2012) 26–68

CLIMA Publications

Special Issues

- **Journal of Logic and Computation**, Special issue on Computational Logic and Multi-Agent Systems, guest edited by João Leite, Tran Cao Son, Paolo Torroni, Leon van der Torre, and Stefan Woltran. Expected, 2015.
- **Journal of Logic and Computation**, Special issue on Computational Logic and Multi-Agent Systems, guest edited by Michael Fisher, Leon van der Torre, Mehdi Dastani, and Guido Governatori. Expected, 2014.
- **Journal of Logic and Computation**, Special issue on Computational Logic and Multi-Agent Systems, guest edited by João Leite, Paolo Torroni, Thomas Ågotnes, Guido Boella, and Leon van der Torre. Expected, 2013.
- **Annals of Mathematics and Artificial Intelligence**, 62(1-2), 2011. Special issue on Computational Logic and Multi-Agent Systems, guest-edited by Jürgen Dix and João Leite.
- **Journal of Autonomous Agents and Multi-Agent Systems**, 16(3), 2008. Special Issue on Computational Logic-Based Agents, guest-edited by Francesca Toni and Jamal Bentahar.
- **Annals of Mathematics and Artificial Intelligence**, 42(1-3), 2004. Special issues on Computational Logic and Multi-Agent Systems, guest-edited by Jürgen Dix Dix, João Leite, and Ken Satoh.
- **Annals of Mathematics and Artificial Intelligence**, 37(1-2), 2003. Special issue on Computational Logic and Multi-Agent Systems, guest-edited by Jürgen Dix, Fariba Sadri and Ken Satoh.
- **Electronic Notes in Theoretical Computer Science**, 70(5), 2002. Special Issue on Computational Logic and Multi-Agency, guest-edited by Jürgen Dix Dix, João Leite, and Ken Satoh.

Proceedings

- **Computational Logic in Multi-Agent Systems XIV, Proceedings**. Vol. 8143 of Lecture Notes in Artificial Intelligence, edited by João Leite, Tran Cao Son, Paolo Torroni, Leon van der Torre, and Stefan Woltran. Springer-Verlag Berlin Heidelberg 2013.
- **Computational Logic in Multi-Agent Systems XIII, Proceedings**. Vol. 7486 of Lecture Notes in Artificial Intelligence, edited by Michael Fisher, Leon van der Torre, Mehdi Dastani, and Guido Governatori. Springer-Verlag Berlin Heidelberg 2012.
- **Computational Logic in Multi-Agent Systems XII, Proceedings**. Vol. 6814 of Lecture Notes in Artificial Intelligence, edited by João Leite,

Paolo Torroni, Thomas Ågotnes, Guido Boella, and Leon van der Torre. Springer-Verlag Berlin Heidelberg 2011.
- **Computational Logic in Multi-Agent Systems XI, Proceedings**. Vol. 6245 of Lecture Notes in Artificial Intelligence, edited by Jürgen Dix, João Leite, Guido Governatori and Wojtek Jamroga. Springer-Verlag Berlin Heidelberg 2010.
- **Computational Logic in Multi-Agent Systems X, Revised Selected and Invited Papers**. Vol. 6214 of Lecture Notes in Artificial Intelligence, edited by Jürgen Dix, Michael Fisher, and Peter Novák. Springer-Verlag Berlin Heidelberg 2010.
- **Computational Logic in Multi-Agent Systems IX, Revised Selected and Invited Papers**. Vol. 5405 of Lecture Notes in Artificial Intelligence, edited by Michael Fisher, Fariba Sadri, and Michael Thielscher. Springer-Verlag Berlin Heidelberg 2009.
- **Computational Logic in Multi-Agent Systems VIII, Revised Selected and Invited Papers**. Vol. 5056 of Lecture Notes in Artificial Intelligence, edited by Fariba Sadri and Ken Satoh. Springer-Verlag Berlin Heidelberg 2008.
- **Computational Logic in Multi-Agent Systems VII, Revised Selected and Invited Papers**. Vol. 4371 of Lecture Notes in Artificial Intelligence, edited by Katsumi Inoue, Ken Satoh, and Francesca Toni. Springer-Verlag Berlin Heidelberg, Germany, 2007.
- **Computational Logic in Multi-Agent Systems VI, Revised Selected and Invited Papers**. Vol. 3900 of Lecture Notes in Artificial Intelligence (State-of-the-art Survey), edited by Francesca Toni and Paolo Torroni, Springer-Verlag Berlin Heidelberg, Germany, 2006.
- **Computational Logic in Multi-Agent Systems V, Revised Selected and Invited Papers**. Vol. 3487 of Lecture Notes in Artificial Intelligence, edited by João Leite Leite and Paolo Torroni. Springer-Verlag Berlin Heidelberg, Germany, 2005.
- **Computational Logic in Multi-Agent Systems IV, Revised Selected and Invited Papers**. Vol. 3259 of Lecture Notes in Artificial Intelligence, edited by Jürgen Dix and João Leite. Springer-Verlag Berlin Heidelberg, Germany, 2004.

Early Editions

- Proceedings of the **5th International Workshop on Computational Logic in Multi-Agent Systems** (CLIMA V), edited by João Leite Leite and Paolo Torroni. Lisbon, Portugal, ISBN: 972-9119-37-6, September 2004. http://centria.di.fct.unl.pt/~jleite/climaV/climaV-preprocs.pdf
- Proceedings of the **4th International Workshop on Computational Logic in Multi-Agent Systems** (CLIMA IV), edited by Jürgen Dix and João Leite. ITZ Bericht 1(5). Papierflieger Verlag, Clausthal-Zellerfeld, Germany, ISBN 3-89720-688-9, 2003. http://centria.di.fct.unl.pt/~jleite/climaIV/climaIV-TR.pdf

- Pre-proceedings of the **3rd International Workshop on Computational Logic in Multi-Agent Systems** (CLIMA III), edited by Jürgen Dix Dix, João Leite, and Ken Satoh. Datalogiske Skrifter 93, Roskilde University, Denmark, ISSN 0109-9779, 2002.
  http://centria.di.fct.unl.pt/jleite/papers/clima02_procs.pdf
- **ICLP'01 Workshop on Computational Logic in Multi-Agent Systems** (CLIMA II), held in association with ICLP'01, Paphos, Cyprus, December 1, 2001. Organized by Ken Satoh and Jürgen Dix.
  http://research.nii.ac.jp/~ksatoh/clima01.html
- **CL-2000 Workshop on Computational Logic in Multi-Agent Systems** (CLIMA I), held in association with the International Conference on Computational Logic, Imperial College London, UK, July 24-25, 2000. Organized by Ken Satoh and Fariba Sadri.
  http://research.nii.ac.jp/~ksatoh/clima00.html
- **Workshop on Multi-Agent Systems in Logic Programming** (MAS-LP), held in conjunction with the 16th International Conference on Logic Programming, Las Cruces, NM, November 30, 1999. Organized by Stephen Rochefort, Fariba Sadri, and Francesca Toni.
  http://www.cs.sfu.ca/news/conferences/MAS99/

Table of Contents

From Discourse Analysis to Argumentation Schemes and Back: Relations and Differences

Elena Cabrio[1], Sara Tonelli[2], and Serena Villata[1]

[1] INRIA Sophia Antipolis, France
`firstname.lastname@inria.fr`
[2] FBK Trento, Italy
`satonelli@fbk.eu`

Abstract. In argumentation theory, argumentation schemes are abstract argument forms expressed in natural language, commonly used in everyday conversational argumentation. In computational linguistics, discourse analysis have been conducted to identify the discourse structure of connected text, i.e. the nature of the discourse relationships between sentences. In this paper, we propose to couple these two research lines in order to (i) use the discourse relationships to automatically detect the argumentation schemes in natural language text, and (ii) use argumentation schemes to reason over natural language arguments composed by premises and a conclusion. In particular, we analyze how argumentation schemes fit into the discourse relations in the Penn Discourse Treebank and which are the argumentation schemes which emerge from this natural language corpus.

1 Introduction

Argumentation theory [25] has been proposed to tackle a variety of problems in Artificial Intelligence (AI). In particular, reasoning systems have to interact not only with intelligent agents but also with humans. This means that they should be able to reason not only in a purely deductive monotonic way, but they need to carry out presumptive, defeasible reasoning. Moreover, the arguments behind this reasoning must be expressed in a dialogical form such that they can be consumed by humans too. Argumentation schemes [33] have been introduced to capture reasoning patterns which are both non-deductive and non-monotonic as used in everyday interactions. In computational linguistics, the issue of representing the structure of the arguments used by humans in everyday interactions has been analyzed in particular in *discourse analysis*, that aims at identifying the discourse structure of connected text, i.e. the nature of the discourse relationships between sentences [18]. However, despite the common points in the goal of these two research lines, a clear analysis of their similarities and differences is still missing, which is a required step towards the definition of computational models of natural language arguments. The research question we answer in this paper is:

– How to bridge the argument patterns proposed in argumentation schemes, and in discourse analysis towards a better account of natural language arguments?

This question breaks down into the following subquestions:

J. Leite et al. (Eds.): CLIMA XIV, LNAI 8143, pp. 1–17, 2013.

1. What is the connection between argumentation schemes and discourse relations detected in discourse analysis?

2. Do discourse relations bring to light new argumentation schemes not considered so far?

The reference corpus for discourse relations is the Penn Discourse Treebank (PDTB) [23]. We choose to ground our experimental analysis on this corpus because it is a standard reference in the natural language processing (NLP) research field, and it is currently the largest collection of documents manually annotated with discourse relations. It contains 34,683 relations annotated over the 1 million words Wall Street Journal Corpus, divided into *explicit* (i.e. signaled by an overt connective) and *implicit* relations (for more details, see Section 3). Each relation has also been annotated with a sense label, following a hierarchical classification scheme (see Fig.1). The PDTB adopts a theory-neutral approach to the annotation, making no commitments to what kinds of high-level structures may be created from the low-level annotations of relations and their arguments. This approach has the appeal of allowing the corpus to be useful for researchers working within different frameworks, while at the same time providing a resource to validate the various existing theories of discourse structure. For all these reasons, it is the most suitable resource for our study.

The comparison we perform is composed of two steps. First, we select five argumentation schemes, namely *Example, Cause to Effect and Effect to Cause, Practical Reasoning, Inconsistency*, and we map these patterns to the categories used to characterize the discourse relations in the PDTB. We highlight which relations can be annotated with the corresponding scheme, and we extract the connectives characterizing each scheme in this natural language (NL) data. Finally, we explain why certain discourse relations are not considered in the present analysis.

Second, we start from the discourse relations used in the PDTB and we show which of them can be adopted to define new argumentation schemes that emerge from this annotated corpus. In particular, we introduce two additional argumentation schemes which *emerge* from such corpus: *Argument from Equivalence*, and *Argument from Specification*. These two additional argumentation schemes support reasoning when a certain situation occurs, and they conclude, by equivalence or by specification, which other situation may also occur. We point out the differences with the existing schemes and we instantiate the new schemes with examples extracted from the PDTB.

The advantage of this analysis is threefold. First, the dataset resulting from this investigation, where the categories of the PDTB are annotated with the schemes they are associated with, represents a rich training corpus fundamental for the improvement of the state of research in argumentation in computational linguistics, as highlighted by Feng and Hirst [9]. Second, this dataset represents a first step towards the definition of a benchmark for the argumentation research community, where the actual arguments' structures used in everyday argumentation can be used to test the next generation of systems grounded on argumentation schemes and able to automatically deal with natural language arguments. Third, this mapping between argumentation schemes and PDTB relations can be fruitfully used to support automated classification [9] or argument processing [3].

In this paper, we do not use NL semantics for a better understanding of critical questions in argumentation schemes [35], and we do not present a classification framework to automatically detect the argumentation schemes in the corpus.

The layout of the paper is as follows. In Section 2 we provide the basic ideas underlying the definition of argumentation schemes, as well as the description of the schemes we consider. In Section 3 we introduce the basic notions of discourse analysis and the Penn Discourse Treebank. Section 4 presents our analysis on how argumentation schemes are represented in the PDTB, and which schemes emerge from it. In Section 5, we summarize the related research comparing it with the proposed approach. We conclude discussing some future perspectives.

2   Argumentation Schemes

Argumentation schemes [33] are argument forms that represent inferential structures of arguments used in everyday discourse. In particular, argumentation schemes are exploited in contexts like legal argumentation [12], inter-agent communication [28,19], and pedagogy [30]. They are motivated by the observation that most of the schemes that are of central interest in argumentation theory are forms of plausible reasoning that do not fit into the traditional deductive and inductive argument forms [25]. Each scheme is associated with a set of so called *critical questions* (CQ), which represent standard ways of critically probing into an argument to find aspects of it that are open for criticism. In particular, the combination of an argumentation scheme and critical questions is used to *evaluate* the argument in a particular case: the argument is evaluated by judging if all the premises are supported by some weight of evidence. In this case, the weight of acceptability is shifted towards the conclusion of the argument which is further subject to a rebuttal by means of the appropriate critical question. In the literature, some works have distinguished different types of critical questions that cover *rebuttals, assumptions* and *exceptions*, which are important when argumentation schemes are used in procedural or dialogical contexts, in particular when we deal with the notion of burden of proof [11]. Let us consider the following argumentation scheme.

Argument from Example

Premise: In this particular case, the individual a has property F and also property G.
Conclusion: Therefore, generally, if x has property F, then it also has property G.

This scheme is one of the most common types of reasoning in debates [16] since it is used to support some kinds of generalization. The *Argument from Example* is a weak form of argumentation that does not confirm a claim in a conclusive way, nor associates it with a certain probability, but it gives only a small weight of presumption to support the conclusion. Three examples of critical questions for the *Argument from Example* scheme are the following:

CQ1: Is the proposition presented by the example in fact true?
CQ2: Does the example support the general claim it is supposed to be an instance of?
CQ3: Is the example typical of the kinds of cases that the generalization ranges over?

For the purpose of this paper, we do not consider all the 65 argumentation schemes presented by Walton and colleagues [33] since some of them, like for instance the *Argument from Position to Know* deal with argument patterns which involve the information sources. Reasoning about the information sources using argumentation schemes [20] is out of the scope of this paper. Beside the above presented *Argument from Example*, the following argumentation schemes will be the focus of the analysis we carry out in this paper.

Argument from Cause to Effect

Major Premise: Generally, if A occurs, then B will (might) occur.
Minor Premise: In this case, A occurs (might occur).
Conclusion: Therefore, in this case, B will (might) occur.

Argument from Effect to Cause

Major Premise: Generally, if A occurs, then B will (might) occur.
Minor Premise: In this case, B did in fact occur.
Conclusion: Therefore, in this case, A also presumably occured.

Practical Reasoning

Major Premise: I have a goal G.
Minor Premise: Carrying out action A is a means to realize G.
Conclusion: Therefore, I ought (practically speaking) to carry out this action A.

Argument from Inconsistency

Premise: If a is committed to proposition A (generally, or in virtue of what she has said in the past)
Premise: a is committed to proposition $\neg A$, which is the conclusion of the argument α that a presently advocates.
Conclusion: Therefore, a's argument α should not be accepted.

Argumentation schemes have been used in the Araucaria system [29] to mark instantiations of such schemes explicitly, providing in this way an online repository of arguments.[1] This annotated corpus contains approximately 600 arguments, manually annotated, extracted from various sources such as the US Congress Congressional Record, and the New York Times. Although, up to our knowledge, Araucaria is the best argumentation corpus available to date, it still has some drawbacks. First, Araucaria is rather small if compared for instance with the PDTB. Moreover, given that the final aim of this paper is to bridge discourse in NLP and argumentation schemes, we need a corpus like the PDTB, which is a well-established, standard reference in NLP and where the discourse relations are already annotated.

---

[1] http://araucaria.computing.dundee.ac.uk/

3   Discourse Analysis and the Penn Discourse Treebank

In Linguistics, discourse analysis is a broad term used to cover linguistic phenomena occurring beyond the sentence boundary, usually emerging from corpus evidence. Several paradigms have been proposed to approach discourse analysis from a computational point of view, from Hobb's theory on inference types [17] to Grosz and Sidner's [15] recursively defined relations between units of structure called *discourse segments*. A discourse theory which has gained popularity in the natural language processing community is the Rhetorical Structure Theory [18], which represents texts as trees whose leaves are elementary discourse units and whose nodes specify how these and larger units are linked to each other by rhetorical relations (e.g. contrast, elaboration, etc.). In the Penn Discourse Treebank project [23], instead, no assumption is made about the hierarchy of the relations and the overall structure of a text, and the analysis is focused on the single relations holding between two text spans. Given the simplicity of the annotation scheme, the availability of a large annotated corpus and the attempt to be as much theory-independent as possible, we select the PDTB for our comparison to argumentation schemes. It is a resource built on top of the Wall Street Journal corpus (WSJ) consisting of a million words annotated with discourse relations by human annotators. Discourse connectives are seen as discourse predicates taking two text spans as arguments, that correspond to propositions, events and states.

In the PDTB, relations can be explicitly signaled by a set of lexically defined connectives (e.g. "because", "however", "therefore", etc.). In these cases, the relation is overtly marked, which makes it relatively easy to detect using NLP techniques [21]. A relation between two discourse arguments, however, does not necessarily require an explicit connective, because it can be inferred also if a connective expression is missing. These cases are referred to as *implicit relations*, and in the PDTB they are annotated only between adjacent sentences within paragraphs. In case the connective is not overt, PDTB annotators were asked to insert a connective to express the inferred relation.

The abstract objects involved in a discourse relation are called `Arg1` and `Arg2` according to syntactic criteria and each relation can take two and only two arguments. Example 1 (a)-(b) represents sentences connected, respectively, by an explicit and an implicit relation. `Arg1` and `Arg2` are reported in italics and in bold respectively.

Example 1

(a) Explicit: *The federal government suspended sales of U.S. savings bonds* <u>because</u> **Congress hasn't lifted the ceiling on government debt.**

(b) Implicit: *The projects already under construction will increase Las Vegas's supply of hotel rooms by 11,795, or nearly 20%, to 75,500.* **By a rule of thumb of 1.5 new jobs for each new hotel room, Clark County will have nearly 18,000 new jobs.**

While in Example 1(a) the connective "because" explicitly signals a causal relation holding between `Arg1` and `Arg2`, in (b) no connective was originally expressed. A consequence relation is inferred between '*the increase in the number of rooms*' and '*the increase in the number of jobs*', though no *explicit* connective expresses this relation.

Each discourse relation is assigned a sense label based on a three-layered hierarchy of senses. The top-level, or *class level*, includes four major semantic classes, namely

TEMPORAL, CONTINGENCY, COMPARISON and EXPANSION. For each class, a more fine-grained classification has been specified at *type* level, as shown in Figure 1. For instance, the relation in Example 1(a) belongs to the CONTINGENCY class and the *Cause* type. A further level of *subtype* has been introduced to specify the semantic contribution of each argument. *Cause*, for instance, comprises the *reason* and the *result* subtypes. The former applies when the situation described in Arg2 is the cause of the situation in Arg1, like in Example 1 (a), while the latter indicates that the situation in Arg2 is the result of the situation in Arg1. The annotation scheme was developed and refined by the PDTB group in a bottom-up fashion, following a lexically grounded approach to annotation.

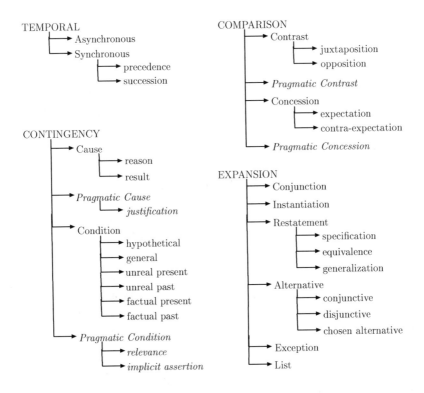

Fig. 1. Sense tags [The PDTB Research Group, 2008]

While in the PDTB they avoid considering the arguments as "logical arguments", for convention in our work we represent them in the standard format of a logical argument, where Arg1 is a (set of) premise(s), and Arg2 is the conclusion.

4   From Argumentation Schemes to Discourse Relations and Back

In this section, we position and analyze the work carried out in the computational linguistics field on discourse analysis, under the perspective of argumentation schemes.

We rely on the Penn Discourse Treebank (Section 3) as the reference resource of natural language text annotated with discourse relations. In particular, in Section 4.1 we start from the argumentation schemes, and we analyze how they fit into the categories of the discourse relations in PDTB. Examples in natural language support us in bringing to light the similarities and the discrepancies between the classifications sketched by the two research fields. From the opposite perspective, in Section 4.2, we first account for the PDTB categories of relations that we have not included in our analysis, and we further highlight the emergence of additional argumentation schemes from such natural language data.

4.1 From Argumentation Schemes to PDTB

In the following, we investigate how the argumentation schemes described in [33] and detailed in Section 2 fit into the discourse relations in PDTB.

We start our analysis from a theoretical viewpoint, comparing the definitions of the argumentation schemes as provided in [33], with the definitions of the discourse relations as provided in [The PDTB Research Group, 2008], to build our mapping hypothesis. We then randomly choose 10 examples for each (or each group of) discourse relation we associate with an argumentation scheme according to their definitions, to create a dataset of 50 examples to evaluate our mapping assumptions. Two annotators with skills in linguistics independently annotated the whole set of examples, according to the following tags: *i)* YES, if the structure and the reasoning type of the argument extracted from the PDTB correspond to the argumentation scheme to which they were previously associated in our working hypothesis (e.g. if the argument from the category EXPANSION:*Restatement*:"generalization" represents an instantiation of the argumentation scheme *Argument from Example*); *ii)* NO, if the structure and the reasoning type of the argument extracted from the PDTB do not correspond to the argumentation scheme to which they were previously associated; *iv)* INCORRECT, in case the argument extracted from the PDTB is incomplete and not understandable when out of context. To assess the validity of the annotation task (and therefore the reliability of our argumentation scheme/PDTB relations mapping), we compute the *inter-annotator agreement*, based on the annotations separately provided by the two annotators on the same sample of 50 argument pairs. The statistical measure usually used in NLP to calculate the inter-rater agreement for categorical items is Cohen's kappa coefficient [6], that is generally thought to be a more robust measure than simple percent agreement calculation since κ takes into account the agreement occurring by chance. More specifically, Cohen's kappa measures the agreement between two raters who each classifies N items into C mutually exclusive categories. The equation for κ is:

$$\kappa = \frac{\Pr(a) - \Pr(e)}{1 - \Pr(e)} \tag{1}$$

where Pr(a) is the relative observed agreement among raters, and Pr(e) is the hypothetical probability of chance agreement, using the observed data to calculate the probabilities of each observer randomly saying each category. If the raters are in complete agreement then $\kappa = 1$. If there is no agreement among the raters other than what would be expected by chance (as defined by Pr(e)), $\kappa = 0$. For NLP tasks, the inter-annotator agreement is considered as significant when $\kappa > 0.6$. Applying the formula (1) to our data, the inter-annotator agreement results in 0.71 (while the percentage of agreement between the two annotators is 88%). As a rule of thumb, this is a satisfactory agreement, confirming the reliability of the obtained resource, and the validity of the task.

The examples extracted from the PDTB for some categories of discourse relations perfectly represent instantiations of the argumentation schemes (e.g., the discourse relation EXPANSION:*Restatement*:"generalization" fits into the argumentation scheme *Argument from Example*). On the contrary, for some other schemes the mappings with discourse relations are much less straightforward, even if the relation definitions in the PDTB and the provided schemes are similar (see the PDTB Manual [31]).

Argument from Example. As introduced before, such argumentation scheme is used to support some kinds of generalization. Its definition shows high similarity with the discourse relation EXPANSION:*Restatement*:"generalization". More specifically, "generalization" applies when the connective indicates that Arg2 (i.e. the conclusion) summarizes Arg1 (the premises), or in some cases expresses a conclusion based on Arg1 (as in Example 2). Differently from the argumentation schemes, where the standard format allows *therefore* as the only connective used to introduce the conclusion, in natural language different connectives can be used with the same goal, and can vary according to the discourse relations they express. For instance, typical connectives for generalization are *in sum, overall, finally*.

Example 2 (generalization)

PREMISE: (Arg1) While the network currently can operate freely in Budapest, so can others
CONCLUSION: **indeed** (Arg2) Hungary is in the midst of a media explosion.

Example 2 can be considered as a good instantiation of the *Argument from Example* scheme, since given the property defined in the premise for a town (i.e. the good quality of the network status), the conclusion is inferred generalizing such property to the whole country. On the contrary, several PDTB examples for this relation, i.e. EXPANSION:*Restatement*:"generalization" were annotated as negative examples by the annotators, due to the fact that in many cases the conclusion is a sort of motto, as in Example 3, or a metaphor.

Example 3 (generalization)

PREMISE: (Arg1) It's time to take some risks if you want the kind of returns that will buy your toddler a ticket to Prestige U. in 18 years
CONCLUSION: **in short** (Arg2) throw away the passbook and go for the glory.

In general, both for this argumentation scheme, and for the following (i.e. *Argument from Cause to Effect* and *Argument from Effect to Cause*), the mappings with the categories of the discourse relations detected in the PDTB are straightforward (on the *Argument from Example* scheme, the agreement between annotators is 100%), and the positive examples collected can be fruitfully considered as examples of naturally occurring schemes in texts, as opposed to ad-hoc examples that can be found in most of the literature on argumentation theory.

Argument from Cause to Effect and from Effect to Cause. These two argumentation schemes are reported here in the same paragraph, since the underlying reasoning steps address, in a sense, opposite perspectives. More precisely, the *Argument from Cause to Effect* is a predictive form of reasoning that reasons from the past to the future, based on a probabilistic generalization. On the contrary, the *Argument from Effect to Cause* is based on a retroduction, from the observed data to a hypothesis about the presumed cause of the data (abductive reasoning) [33]. Comparing these definitions with the definitions provided for the discourse relations in the PDTB, we can note that they are highly similar with the discourse relation: CONTINGENCY:*cause*, identified when the situations described in Arg1 and Arg2 are causally influenced, and the two are not in a conditional relation. Directionality is specified at the level of subtype: "reason" $((\|\text{Arg2}\|<\|\text{Arg1}\|^2$, see Example 4) and "result" ($\|\text{Arg1}\|<\|\text{Arg2}\|$, see Example 5) specifying which situation is the cause and which is the effect. Both subtypes can be respectively mapped to the argumentation schemes *Argument from Effect to Cause*, and *Argument from Cause to Effect*. In the former (i.e."reason") the connective indicates that the situation described in Arg2 is the cause, and the situation described in Arg1 is the effect. The typical connective for such relation is indeed *because*. On the contrary, for the latter (i.e. "result") , the connective indicates that the situation described in Arg1 is the reason, and the situation described in Arg2 is the result. Typical connectives are *so that, thefore, as a result*.

Example 4 (reason)

CONCLUSION: (Arg1) She pleaded guilty.
PREMISE: **because** (Arg2) she was afraid of further charges

Example 5 (result)

PREMISE: (Arg1) Producers were granted the right earlier this year to ship sugar and the export licenses were expected to have begun to be issued yesterday
CONCLUSION: **as a result** (Arg2) it is believed that little or no sugar from the 1989-90 crop has been shipped yet

Note that, due to the variability of language, the sequence of premises and conclusion in NL arguments does not always follow the order defined in the standard structure (where premises always come first), as e.g. in Example 4, where the conclusion is expressed at the beginning of the sentence. In the same example, the reasoning is carried out from effect to cause (i.e. the fact that she was afraid of further charges, generates the woman's reaction of declaring herself guilty). On the contrary, in Example 5, the reasoning is carried out from cause to effect (i.e. the fact that licenses were expected

---

[2] The symbol $<$ used in the PDTB categories means "causes".

to have been issued the day before - but it did not happen - let to conclude that the sugar has not been shipped yet). In our dataset, 80% of the examples collected from the PDTB relations *Reason* and *Result* are annotated as positive instantiations of the *Argument from Cause to Effect* and *from Effect to Cause* schemes.

So far so good. As introduced before, the mapping of the above described types of argumentation schemes is pretty straightforward, and the examples collected in the PDTB generally fall within the definitions of such schemes provided in [33]. In the following, we enter into a grey area, where the mapping between the argumentation schemes and the categories of the discourse relations is more blurry, and the examples collected in the PDTB do not always represent correct instantiations of such schemes. But since the goal of our work is to investigate all the possible connections between the two research fields, we force the hand of the mapping, allowing us some simplifications.

Practical Reasoning. This argumentation scheme involves the general human capacity for resolving, through reflection, the question of what one is to do, given the goal that one has in mind. To fit such scheme into one discourse category, we need therefore to consider a relation that relies on some kind of pragmatic reasoning, and on common background knowledge. For this reason, we think that the most appropriate relation annotated in the PDTB is the CONTINGENCY:*Pragmatic condition*, used for instances of conditional constructions whose interpretation deviates from that of the semantics of *Condition*. In all cases, Arg1 holds true independently of Arg2. The conditional clause in the "relevance" conditional (Arg2, i.e. the premise) provides the context in which the description of the situation in Arg1, i.e. the conclusion, is relevant (see Example 6). There is no causal relation between premises and conclusion.

Example 6 (relevance)

PREMISE (Arg1): here's the monthly sum you will need to invest to pay for four years at Yale, Notre Dame and University of Minnesota
PREMISE : **if** (Arg2) you start saving for your child's education on Jan. 1, 1990

In Example 6 the major premise, i.e. the goal, is implicit (i.e., enthymeme [33]), and concerns the child education (in other words, the goal is to send the child to one of the best U.S. universities). The other two premises (i.e. Arg2 and Arg1) describe the action to be carried out to obtain the goal (i.e. given the amount of money you need, you can have it if you start saving from the beginning of 1990). Following the scheme's structure, also the conclusion is left implicit (i.e. *therefore, if you want to reach your goal, you should start saving*). Another interesting observation emerging from naturally occurring data is the fact that in human linguistic interactions a lot is left implicit, following [14]'s conversational *Maxim of Quantity* (i.e. do not make your contribution more informative than is required).

The tag "implicit assertion" applies in special rhetorical uses of if-constructions when the interpretation of the conditional construction is an implicit assertion.

Example 7 (implicit assertion)

PREMISE: **if** (Arg2) you want to keep the crime rates high
CONCLUSION (Arg1): O'Connor is your man

In Example 7 the conclusion, i.e. *O' Connor is your man*, is not a consequent state that will result if the condition expressed in the premise holds true. Instead, the conditional construction in this case implicitly asserts that O'Connor will keep the crime rates high (enthymeme), and requires a pragmatic reasoning step. For both subtypes, the typical connective expressing the discourse relation is *if*. In our dataset, 70% of the examples collected from the PDTB relation CONTINGENCY:*Pragmatic condition* are annotated as positive instantiations of the *Practical reasoning* argumentation scheme.

Argument from Inconsistency. The last argumentation scheme we consider in our inspection is the *Argument from Inconsistency*, where the inconsistency can be detected in an arguer's commitment set. Even if the mapping of such scheme with one of the discourse categories is far from being straightforward, after a careful analysis of both the definitions and the examples in the PDTB, we consider that the relation COMPARISON:*concession*, that applies when one of the arguments describes a situation A which causes C, while the other asserts (or implies) ¬C, seems to fall within such scheme. Alternatively, the same relation can apply when one premise denotes a fact that triggers a set of potential consequences, while the other denies one or more of them, and still in this case it fits with the definition of the above mentioned argumentation scheme. Formally, we have $A < C \wedge B \rightarrow \neg C$, where A and B are drawn from $\|Arg1\|$ and $\|Arg2\|$ ($\neg C$ may be the same as B, where $B \rightarrow B$ is always true). Two *concession* subtypes are defined in terms of the argument creating an expectation and the one denying it. Specifically, when Arg2 creates an expectation that Arg1 denies ($A = \|Arg2\|$ and $B = \|Arg1\|$), it is tagged as *expectation* (see Example 8). When Arg1 creates an expectation that Arg2 denies ($A = \|Arg1$ and $B = \|Arg2\|$), it is tagged as *contra-expectation* (see Example 9).

Example 8 (expectation)

PREMISE (Arg1): Attorneys for the two sides apparently began talking again yesterday in attempt to settle the matter before Thursday
PREMISE: **although** (Arg2) settlement talks had been dropped

Example 9 (contra-expectation)

CONCLUSION: (Arg1) The demonstrators have been non-violent
PREMISE: **but** (Arg2) the result of their trespasses has been to seriously impair the rights of others unconnected with their dispute

In Example 8 we start from the evidence provided by the premise according to which the settlement talks between the attorneys have started, and we are pushed to conclude that they are still going on, while the conclusion provided by the arguer is inconsistent (i.e. settlement talks had been dropped). With the same reasoning step, in Example 9 we expect that no bad consequences are caused by the demonstrators thanks to their pacific attitude, but our expectation is wrong. In our dataset, 60% of the examples collected from the PDTB relation *expectation* and *contra-expectation* are annotated as positive instantiations of the *Argument from Inconsistency* scheme. In general, the 12% of the examples of the dataset (i.e. 6/50) were annotated as INCORRECT by the annotators (i.e. incomplete arguments, and/or not understandable when out of context).

We report in Table 1 some statistics on the PDTB relations considered in our study. We extract them from the PDTB and report the total number of examples both of *implicit* and *explicit* relations (the 50 examples of our dataset were extracted from the explicit relations only, the analysis of implicit relations is left for future work). Since PDTB annotators were allowed to assign more than one relation label, we report only the relations whose *first* label is the one reported in the first column. Also, we consider only the examples in which Arg2 is not embedded in Arg1 (more than 90% of the overall examples), because we want to avoid that premises and conclusions according to argumentation schemes are expressed by discontinuous arguments. Next to each discourse subtype, we also list the three most-frequent connectives occurring in the *explicit* relations (for *Relevance*, only two connectives are found in the examples). This confirms that, although *therefore* is the only connective usually employed in argumentation schemes to introduce the conclusion, corpus-based analysis shows a higher variability and a much richer repository of admissible connectives.

Table 1. Statistics about the extracted examples

Relation class.Type *Subtype* ('most-frequent connectives')	Num. Expl.	Num. Impl.
Expansion.Restatement		
Generaliz. ('in short', 'in other words')	16	190
Contingency.Cause		
Reason ('because', 'as', 'since')	1,201	2,434
Result ('so', 'thus', 'as a result')	617	1,678
Contingency.Pragm.Condition		
Relevance ('if', 'when')	21	1
ImplicitAssertion ('if', 'when', 'or')	46	0
Comparison.Concession		
Expectation ('although', 'though', 'while')	386	31
ContraExpectation ('but', 'still', 'however')	798	182

Notice that we do not tackle the issue of dealing with enthymemes and implied assertions. Whilst human annotators can deal with this problem to an acceptable extent, identifying suitable markers to indicate the occurrence of such instances is a problem. Similar issues are reported in those works in which natural language texts are analyzed to produce instantiations of an argumentation scheme for an e-Participation tool. For instance, Pulfrey-Taylor et al. [24] report upon the instantiation of a scheme for practical reasoning with values, based upon responses to an EU green paper, and discourse indicators have also been used to annotate text to instantiate argumentation schemes in an e-Commerce corpus by Wyner et al. [36].

4.2 From PDTB to Argumentation Schemes

We have not included other PDTB relations in our analysis, either because they do not fall within the definition of arguments as provided in argumentation theory, or because no argument scheme accounts for them.

As introduced before, in our work we consider the set of discourse relations that better fall into the structure defined for the argumentation schemes. Other categories of discourse relations, e.g. the EXPANSION:*Alternative*, or *List* are not considered because they do not fall within the definition of arguments as provided in argumentation theory (i.e. they do not allow us to carry out a reasoning step), and can be more considered as claims or statements.

We propose now two additional argumentation schemes which emerge from the discourse relations in the PDTB. In particular, concerning the PDTB relations EXPANSION:*Restatement*:"equivalence", and EXPANSION:*Restatement*:"specification" we do not find an argumentation scheme actually fitting the argument pattern expressed by these relations. Even if the *Argument from Analogy* scheme [33] seems close to the equivalence relation, their semantics is slightly different: the former expresses that two cases are similar and that if A is found true in one case, then it is true also in the other case. The latter expresses that if a situation occurs, and this situation is known as equivalent to another one, then the second situation occurs too. The *Argument from Equivalence* is formalized below.

Argument from Equivalence

Premise: A occurs.
Premise: A is equivalent to B.
Conclusion: Therefore, also B occurs.

This argumentation scheme is instantiated in Example 10 extracted from the PDTB, where the premise provides an evidence about a fact (i.e. price augmentation), while in the conclusion the same fact is considered from a different viewpoint, showing the consequent currency depreciation.

Example 10 (equivalence)

PREMISE (Arg1): On average, something that cost $100 30 years ago now costs $425
CONCLUSION: **or** (Arg2) a wage that was $100 30 years ago would buy only $23.53 worth of stuff today

The second argumentation scheme we introduce is called *Argument from Specification* and it is formalized below. It specifies a kind of abductive reasoning such that a situation A occurs, and in the particular case of interest this means that a more specific situation B is a subclass of A, therefore more precisely B occurs. The basic idea here is that a particular situation is a specification of another situation, and it is in fact this more specific situation which occurred.

Argument from Specification

Premise: Generally, A occurs.
Premise: In this particular case, B is a subclass of A.
Conclusion: Therefore, more precisely, B occurs.

This argumentation scheme is instantiated in Example 11. In the premise, the general economical situation is not seen as rosy, while an implicit premise provides an evidence to support the fact that the steelmakers are part of the economic world and are influenced from its trend. An inferential step about the bad economical forecasts is further specified for that specific category in the conclusion.

Example 11 (specification)

PREMISE (Arg1): It doesn't bode well for coming quarters
CONCLUSION: **in fact** (Arg2) several steelmakers will report actual losses through the third quarter of 1990

In this section we have proposed two additional argumentation schemes, namely *Argument from Equivalence* and *Argument from Specification*, which emerge from the discourse relations highlighted in the PDTB. The rationale behind this kind of additional schemes is that two discourse relations as the EXPANSION:*Restatement*:"equivalence", and the EXPANSION:*Restatement*:"specification" cannot be mapped with the existing argumentation schemes as done for the schemes we presented in the previous section, but they lead to a reasoning step. We are aware that new argument schemes should be proposed only as a last resort since there is already a proliferation of such patterns, which often impairs their practical usefulness. However, it is actually the practical usefulness which guides the introduction of such new schemes which are *existing* schemes emerging from a real world corpus of natural language arguments. To conclude, we underline the importance of more "practical" argumentation schemes like those which could emerge from large corpora of NL arguments, even if we are aware of the remark about the proliferation of new schemes. To this concern, we may align the new argumentation schemes with existing ones (e.g., *Argument from Equivalence* aligned with *Argument from Definition*) even if the alignment may not be consistent in all real world examples concerning the above mentioned discourse relations.

5   Related Work

The need for coupling argumentation theory and NLP is becoming more and more important in the latest years, as shown by the increasing number of online debate systems like Debategraph[3] and Debatepedia[4]. The need for a machinery leading to arguments being automatically generated is underlined also by Grasso and colleagues [13,26].

Some approaches have been proposed to address this issue in the two research communities. For instance, Chasnevar and Maguitman [7] propose a defeasible argumentation system to provide recommendations on language patterns to assist the language usage assessment. The indices they use are computed from Web corpora.

---

[3] http://debategraph.org
[4] http://dbp.idebate.org/

Gilbert [10] addresses the problem of characterizing human/computer argumentation, where the ability to identify and classify various locutions as facts, values and goals is discussed, and the author chooses Toulmin's argumentation model [32] for his analysis.

Wyner and van Engers [34] propose to couple NLP and argumentation to support policy makers. The NLP module guides the user in writing the input text using Attempt to Controlled English allowing for a restricted grammar and vocabulary, and after a parsing step, the sentences are translated to First Order Logic. In this paper, we do not look for a translation in formal logic of NL arguments, but we are interested in the structure of the arguments such as in argumentation schemes, where the relation among the premises and the conclusion is represented through the discourse relations of the PDTB.

Cabrio and Villata [4] propose to use the NLP framework of textual entailment to extract from Debatepedia the arguments in NL and the relations among them. Then, the arguments are composed in a Dung-like [8] abstract argumentation framework to select the acceptable arguments. The authors look only at the relations among the arguments, while here we are most interested in the relation among premises and conclusion in NL arguments.

Carenini and Moore [5] present a computational framework for generating evaluative arguments. We use a different model of arguments, i.e., argumentation schemes, and we do not provide an automatic system for argument generation.

Amgoud and Prade [1] start from a model of argumentation presented in linguistics [2] and try to formalize it using formal argumentation. They envisage a comparison with argumentation schemes as future work. In this paper, we consider only such schemes to provide the parallel with NLP.

The difference with respect to this line of works is that they do not consider arguments as composed by a set of premises and a conclusion as done in argumentation schemes where the relation among these two kinds of elements is characterized in terms of *practical reasoning*, etc. In this paper, we address the problem of coupling two distinct research areas, namely discourse analysis in NLP and argumentation schemes in informal logic to better understand, over a real world set of examples (the PDTB), how discourse relations can be used towards the automatic detection of argumentation schemes in natural language texts.

The work which is most related to this paper is the following. Feng and Hirst [9] present an automatic system for classifying the argumentation schemes of NL arguments with the aim to infer enthymemes. The data set they use is the Araucaria one. Our analysis can be used to support this kind of automated classification task thanks to the mapping with the discourse relations we provide, and the resulting annotated arguments corpus can be used for training. Using automated approaches to classify argumentation schemes and infer enthymemes is the next step in our work.

6   Concluding Remarks

We presented an analysis of the connections between two distinct research areas, namely discourse analysis in natural language processing, and argumentation schemes in argumentation. Following the idea of focusing first on models of natural language schemes and then building formal systems [27], the rationale behind this kind of analysis is to provide a first, but compulsory step towards the development of automatic techniques able to deal with the complexities present in natural language arguments. Even if recent approaches like [26,4,35,1] provide a first attempt to tackle the open problem of natural language argumentation, they show that a satisfiable result is still far beyond. As demonstrated in this paper, the development of automated systems going beyond applications like the one proposed by Cabrio and Villata [4], where only two relations among the arguments are considered and arguments are abstract, is much more complex.

Our future work includes the design and implementation of an automated framework able to detect not only the abstract arguments from natural language text, but also their internal structure [27,22] with the aim to verify the coherence of such arguments before considering the (eventual) relations with the other arguments. The bridge with discourse analysis, enables us to carry out an in-depth study of the argument structures, relying on the data previously annotated with discourse relations, and now annotated also with the corresponding argumentation schemes. As an additional outcome of our work, we will soon release the annotation of the PDTB examples with the considered argumentation schemes, that can be fruitfully exploited as a training corpus in NLP applications.

References

1. Amgoud, L., Prade, H.: Can AI models capture natural language argumentation? Int. J. of Cognitive Informatics and Natural Intelligence (2013)
2. Apotheloz, D.: The function of negation in argumentation. J. of Pragmatics, 23–38 (1993)
3. Bex, F., Reed, C.: Dialogue templates for automatic argument processing. In: Procs. of COMMA 2012, pp. 366–377 (2012)
4. Cabrio, E., Villata, S.: Natural language arguments: A combined approach. In: Procs. of ECAI 2012. Frontiers in Artificial Intelligence and Applications, vol. 242, pp. 205–210 (2012)
5. Carenini, G., Moore, J.D.: Generating and evaluating evaluative arguments. Artif. Intell. 170(11), 925–952 (2006)
6. Carletta, J.: Assessing agreement on classification tasks: the kappa statistic. Comput. Linguist. 22(2), 249–254 (1996)
7. Chesñevar, C.I., Maguitman, A.: An argumentative approach to assessing natural language usage based on the web corpus. In: Procs. of ECAI 2004, pp. 581–585 (2004)
8. Dung, P.: On the acceptability of arguments and its fundamental role in nonmonotonic reasoning, logic programming and n-person games. Artif. Intell. 77(2), 321–358 (1995)
9. Feng, V.W., Hirst, G.: Classifying arguments by scheme. In: Procs. of ACL 2012, pp. 987–996 (2011)
10. Gilbert, M.: Getting good value. facts, values, and goals in computational linguistics. In: Procs. of ICCS 2010, pp. 989–998 (2001)
11. Gordon, T.F., Prakken, H., Walton, D.: The carneades model of argument and burden of proof. Artif. Intell. 171(10-15), 875–896 (2007)
12. Gordon, T.F., Walton, D.: Legal reasoning with argumentation schemes. In: ICAIL 2009, pp. 137–146. ACM (2009)
13. Grasso, F., Cawsey, A., Jones, R.B.: Dialectical argumentation to solve conflicts in advice giving: a case study in the promotion of healthy nutrition. Int. J. Hum.-Comput. Stud. 53(6), 1077–1115 (2000)

14. Grice, H.P.: Logic and conversation. In: Cole, P., Morgan, J.L. (eds.) Syntax and Semantics: Speech Acts, vol. 3, pp. 41–58. Academic Press (1975)
15. Grosz, B., Sidner, C.: Attention, Intentions and the Structure of Discourse. Computational Linguistics (1986)
16. Hastings, A.C.: A reformulation of the models of reasoning in argumentation. Ph.D. thesis, Evanstone, Illinois (1963)
17. Hobbs, J.: On the Coherence and Structure of Discourse. Tech. rep., Stanford University (1985)
18. Mann, W., Thompson, S.: Rhetorical structure theory: Toward a functional theory of text organization. Text 8(3), 243–281 (1988)
19. McBurney, P., Parsons, S.: Risk agoras: Dialectical argumentation for scientific reasoning. In: Procs. of UAI 2000, pp. 371–379 (2000)
20. Parsons, S., Atkinson, K., Haigh, K.Z., Levitt, K.N., McBurney, P., Rowe, J., Singh, M.P., Sklar, E.: Argument schemes for reasoning about trust. In: Procs. of COMMA 2012, pp. 430–441 (2012)
21. Pitler, E., Nenkova, A.: Using syntax to disambiguate explicit discourse connectives in text. In: Procs. of ACL 2009 (2009)
22. Prakken, H.: An abstract framework for argumentation with structured arguments. Argument & Computation 1, 93–124 (2010)
23. Prasad, R., Dinesh, N., Lee, A., Miltsakaki, E., Robaldo, L., Joshi, A., Webber, B.: The Penn Discourse TreeBank 2.0. In: Procs. of LREC 2008 (2008)
24. Pulfrey-Taylor, S., Henthorn, E., Atkinson, K., Wyner, A., Bench-Capon, T.J.M.: Populating an online consultation tool. In: Atkinson, K. (ed.) JURIX. Frontiers in Artificial Intelligence and Applications, vol. 235, pp. 150–154. IOS Press (2011)
25. Rahwan, I., Simari, G. (eds.): Argumentation in Artificial Intelligence. Springer (2009)
26. Reed, C., Grasso, F.: Recent advances in computational models of natural argument. Int. J. Intell. Syst. 22(1), 1–15 (2007)
27. Reed, C., Walton, D.: Towards a formal and implemented model of argumentation schemes in agent communication. Autonomous Agents and Multi-Agent Systems 11(2), 173–188 (2005)
28. Reed, C.: Dialogue frames in agent communication. In: Procs. of ICMAS 1998, pp. 246–253. IEEE Computer Society (1998)
29. Reed, C., Rowe, G.: Araucaria: Software for argument analysis, diagramming and representation. International Journal on Artificial Intelligence Tools 13(4), 983–1003 (2004)
30. Reed, C., Walton, D.: Applications of argumentation schemes. In: Procs. of OSSA 2001 (2001)
31. The PDTB Research Group: The PDTB 2.0. Annotation Manual. Tech. Rep. IRCS-08-01, Institute for Research in Cognitive Science, University of Pennsylvania (2008)
32. Toulmin, S.: The Uses of Argument. Cambridge University Press (1958)
33. Walton, D., Reed, C., Macagno, F.: Argumentation Schemes. Cambridge University Press (2008)
34. Wyner, A., van Engers, T.: A framework for enriched, controlled on-line discussion forums for e-government policy-making. In: Procs. of eGov 2010 (2010)
35. Wyner, A.: Questions, arguments, and natural language semantics. In: Procs. of CMNA 2012 (2012)
36. Wyner, A., Schneider, J., Atkinson, K., Bench-Capon, T.J.M.: Semi-automated argumentative analysis of online product reviews. In: Procs. of COMMA 2012, pp. 43–50 (2012)

Analyzing the Equivalence Zoo
in Abstract Argumentation

Ringo Baumann and Gerhard Brewka

University of Leipzig, Informatics Institute, Germany
lastname@informatik.uni-leipzig.de

Abstract. Notions of equivalence which are stronger than standard equivalence in the sense that they also take potential modifications of the available information into account have received considerable interest in nonmonotonic reasoning. In this paper we focus on equivalence notions in argumentation. More specifically, we establish a number of new results about the relationships among various equivalence notions for Dung argumentation frameworks which are located between strong equivalence [1] and standard equivalence. We provide the complete picture for this variety of equivalence relations (which we call the *equivalence zoo*) for the most important semantics.

1 Introduction

Notions of equivalence which are stronger than standard equivalence in the sense that they also take potential modifications of the available information into account have received considerable interest in nonmonotonic reasoning, and in particular in logic programming [2,3]. In this paper we focus on equivalence notions in argumentation. Formal argumentation has developed into a highly active field within Artificial Intelligence over the last decades. For a very good overview see [4]. Dung's abstract argumentation frameworks (AFs) [5] play a dominant role in the area. In AFs arguments and attacks among them are treated as abstract entities. The focus is on conflict resolution and argument acceptability. Various semantics for AFs have been defined, each of them specifying acceptable sets of arguments, so-called *extensions*, in a particular way. In a nutshell, the typical use of AFs can be characterized as follows: starting from some knowledge base expressed in a potentially rich KR language, one constructs arguments, that is structures containing a proposition together with reasons for accepting them, and conflicts among them (so-called attacks). The arguments, viewed as abstract entities, are then evaluated using an AF. The accepted propositions then are those which are supported by an argument which is accepted under the chosen AF semantics.

Argumentation is an inherently dynamic process. It is thus apparent that equivalence notions which guarantee mutual replaceability of two AFs - without any loss of information - in specific dynamic argumentation scenarios, that is, even under potential expansions of the current AF, are highly significant. For this reason, the study of various such equivalence notions has become an active and fruitful research line over the last years. Standard equivalence of two AFs $\mathcal{F}$ and $\mathcal{G}$, i.e. both possess the same extensions, guarantees that all queries w.r.t. credulously or skeptically accepted arguments

J. Leite et al. (Eds.): CLIMA XIV, LNAI 8143, pp. 18–33, 2013.

are answered identically. Strong equivalence [1], in contrast, even guarantees that both AFs possess the same extensions under arbitrary expansions. In [6] the middle ground between these two extremes was investigated, i.e. various intermediate equivalence notions taking into account specific anticipated types of expansions reflecting the very nature of argumentation were defined and characterized. Furthermore, in [7] the notion of minimal change equivalence between two AFs was introduced which guarantees that the minimal effort needed to convince the participants of a certain opinion E (a set of arguments) is identical.

In this paper we present a number of new results about the relationships among the mentioned equivalence notions. Our results provide a complete picture about the relationships among these notions for two of the most relevant semantics of Dung-style AFs, namely stable and preferred semantics. It turns out that minimal change equivalence naturally fits into this equivalence zoo, although its definition includes a graph-theoretical distance function and therefore an arithmetic aspect in contrast to standard or strong equivalence as well as the considered intermediate variants. Furthermore we clarify an open question concerning the characterization for preferred semantics and weak expansions.

The rest of the paper is organized as follows. Sect. 2 reviews the necessary background. Sect. 3 presents our results regarding various equivalence notions. Sect. 4 concludes the paper.

2   Background

An *argumentation framework* $\mathcal{F}$ is a pair (A, R), where A is a non-empty finite set whose elements are called *arguments* and $R \subseteq A \times A$ a binary relation, called the *attack relation*. The set of all AFs is denoted by $\mathscr{A}$. If $(a, b) \in R$ holds we say that a *attacks* b, or b is *defeated* by a in $\mathcal{F}$. An argument $a \in A$ is *defended* by a set $A' \subseteq A$ in $\mathcal{F}$ if for each $b \in A$ with $(b, a) \in R$, b is defeated by some $a' \in A'$ in $\mathcal{F}$. Furthermore, we say that a set $A' \subseteq A$ is *conflict-free* in $\mathcal{F}$ if there are no arguments $a, b \in A'$ such that a attacks b. The set of all conflict-free sets of an AF $\mathcal{F}$ is denoted by $cf(\mathcal{F})$. For an AF $\mathcal{F} = (B, S)$ we use $A(\mathcal{F})$ to refer to B and $R(\mathcal{F})$ to refer to S. Finally, we introduce the union of two AFs as usual, namely $\mathcal{F} \cup \mathcal{G} = (A(\mathcal{F}) \cup A(\mathcal{G}), R(\mathcal{F}) \cup R(\mathcal{G}))$.

Semantics determine acceptable sets of arguments for a given AF $\mathcal{F}$, so-called *extensions*. The set of all extensions of $\mathcal{F}$ under semantics σ is denoted by $\mathcal{E}_\sigma(\mathcal{F})$. Due to limited space we consider stable (st) and preferred (pr) semantics only [5].

Definition 1 (Semantics). *Given an AF $\mathcal{F} = (A, R)$ and $E \subseteq A$. E is a*

1. *stable extension ($E \in \mathcal{E}_{st}(\mathcal{F})$) iff*
   $E \in cf(\mathcal{F})$ *and each $a \in A \backslash E$ is defeated by some $e \in E$,*
2. *admissible set ($E \in \mathcal{E}_{ad}(\mathcal{F})$) iff*
   $E \in cf(\mathcal{F})$ *and each $e \in E$ is defended by E in $\mathcal{F}$,*
3. *preferred extension ($E \in \mathcal{E}_{pr}(\mathcal{F})$) iff*
   $E \in \mathcal{E}_{ad}(\mathcal{F})$ *and for each $E' \in \mathcal{E}_{ad}(\mathcal{F})$, $E \notin E'$ and*

Note that any stable extension is a preferred one. The converse do not hold in general but if the considered AFs are SCC-symmetric and self-loop-free stable and preferred semantics coincide (compare [8]).

Expansions were introduced by [9]. They will be our object of investigation since they represent reasonable types of dynamic argumentation scenarios.

Definition 2 (Expansions). *An AF $\mathcal{F}^*$ is an* expansion *of AF $\mathcal{F} = (A, R)$ (for short, $\mathcal{F} \leq_E \mathcal{F}^*$) iff $\mathcal{F}^* = (A \cup A^*, R \cup R^*)$ where $A^* \cap A = R^* \cap R = \emptyset$. An expansion is*

1. *normal ($\mathcal{F} \leq_N \mathcal{F}^*$) iff $\forall ab \, ((a,b) \in R^* \rightarrow a \in A^* \vee b \in A^*)$,*
2. *strong ($\mathcal{F} \leq_S \mathcal{F}^*$) iff $\mathcal{F} \leq_N \mathcal{F}^*$ and $\forall ab \, ((a,b) \in R^* \rightarrow \neg(a \in A \wedge b \in A^*))$,*
3. *weak ($\mathcal{F} \leq_W \mathcal{F}^*$) iff $\mathcal{F} \leq_N \mathcal{F}^*$ and $\forall ab \, ((a,b) \in R^* \rightarrow \neg(a \in A^* \wedge b \in A))$,*
4. *local ($\mathcal{F} \leq_L \mathcal{F}^*$) iff $A^* = \emptyset$.*

For short, normal expansions add new arguments and possibly new attacks which concern at least one of the fresh arguments. Strong (weak) expansions are normal and only add *strong (weak) arguments*, i.e. the added arguments never are attacked by (attack) former arguments. Normal expansions naturally occur in case of instantiation-based argumentation. If one adds a new piece of information to the underlying knowledge base, then only new arguments which may interact with the previous ones arise.

As usual $\mathcal{F} <_X \mathcal{F}^*$ for $X \in \{E, N, S, W, L\}$ stands for $\mathcal{F} \leq_X \mathcal{F}^*$ and $\mathcal{F} \neq \mathcal{F}^*$. To simplify notation we will later on often use X to refer to $\leq_X$. Whenever infix notation is used we stick to $\leq_X$, though.

The *minimal change problem* [7] is the problem of determining the minimal effort needed to transform a given argumentation framework, using a particular type of modifications, into a framework that possesses an extension containing a specific set of arguments C. The effort is characterized by the (σ, Φ)-*characteristic*:

Definition 3 (Characteristic). *Given a semantics σ, a binary relation $\Phi \subseteq \mathscr{A} \times \mathscr{A}$ and an AF $\mathcal{F}$. The (σ, Φ)-characteristic of a set $C \subseteq A(\mathcal{F})$ is a natural number or infinity defined by the following function*

$$N^{\mathcal{F}}_{\sigma, \Phi} : \mathscr{P}(A(\mathcal{F})) \rightarrow \mathbb{N}_\infty$$

$$C \mapsto \begin{cases} 0, & \exists C' : C \subseteq C' \text{ and } C' \in \mathcal{E}_\sigma(\mathcal{F}) \\ k, & k = \min\{d(\mathcal{F}, \mathcal{G}) \mid (\mathcal{F}, \mathcal{G}) \in \Phi, N^{\mathcal{G}}_{\sigma, \Phi}(C) = 0\} \\ \infty, & \text{otherwise.} \end{cases}$$

Here $d(\mathcal{F}, \mathcal{G})$ is the number of added or removed attacks needed to transform $\mathcal{F}$ to $\mathcal{G}$, i.e. $d(\mathcal{F}, \mathcal{G}) = |R(\mathcal{F}) \triangle R(\mathcal{G})|$ where $\triangle$ is the well-known symmetric difference.

The following notions of equivalence have been studied in the literature [1,6,7]:

Definition 4 (Equivalence). *Given a semantics σ. Two AFs $\mathcal{F}$ and $\mathcal{G}$ are*

1. *standard equivalent w.r.t. σ ($\mathcal{F} \equiv^\sigma \mathcal{G}$) iff they possess the same extensions under σ, i.e. $\mathcal{E}_\sigma(\mathcal{F}) = \mathcal{E}_\sigma(\mathcal{G})$ holds,*
2. *strongly equivalent w.r.t. σ ($\mathcal{F} \equiv^\sigma_E \mathcal{G}$) iff for each AF $\mathcal{H}$, $\mathcal{F} \cup \mathcal{H} \equiv^\sigma \mathcal{G} \cup \mathcal{H}$ holds,*
3. *normal expansion equivalent w.r.t. σ ($\mathcal{F} \equiv^\sigma_N \mathcal{G}$) iff for each AF $\mathcal{H}$, s.t. $\mathcal{F} \leq_N \mathcal{F} \cup \mathcal{H}$ and $\mathcal{G} \leq_N \mathcal{G} \cup \mathcal{H}$, $\mathcal{F} \cup \mathcal{H} \equiv^\sigma \mathcal{G} \cup \mathcal{H}$ holds,*
4. *strong expansion equivalent w.r.t. σ ($\mathcal{F} \equiv^\sigma_S \mathcal{G}$) iff for each AF $\mathcal{H}$, s.t. $\mathcal{F} \leq_S \mathcal{F} \cup \mathcal{H}$ and $\mathcal{G} \leq_S \mathcal{G} \cup \mathcal{H}$, $\mathcal{F} \cup \mathcal{H} \equiv^\sigma \mathcal{G} \cup \mathcal{H}$ holds,*

5. *weak expansion equivalent w.r.t. σ ($\mathcal{F} \equiv^{\sigma}_W \mathcal{G}$) iff*
   for each AF $\mathcal{H}$, s.t. $\mathcal{F} \leq_W \mathcal{F} \cup \mathcal{H}$ and $\mathcal{G} \leq_W \mathcal{G} \cup \mathcal{H}$, $\mathcal{F} \cup \mathcal{H} \equiv^{\sigma} \mathcal{G} \cup \mathcal{H}$ holds,
6. *local expansion equivalentw.r.t. σ ($\mathcal{F} \equiv^{\sigma}_L \mathcal{G}$) iff*
   for each AF $\mathcal{H}$, s.t. $A(\mathcal{H}) \subseteq A(\mathcal{F} \cup \mathcal{G})$, $\mathcal{F} \cup \mathcal{H} \equiv^{\sigma} \mathcal{G} \cup \mathcal{H}$ holds,
7. *minimal change equivalent ($\mathcal{F} \equiv^{\sigma,MC}_{\Phi} \mathcal{G}$) w.r.t. σ and a binary relation $\Phi \subseteq \mathscr{A} \times \mathscr{A}$*
   iff for any E, s.t. $E \subseteq A(\mathcal{F})$ or $E \subseteq A(\mathcal{G})$, $N^{\mathcal{F}}_{\sigma,\Phi}(E) = N^{\mathcal{G}}_{\sigma,\Phi}(E)$.

3 Analyzing the Equivalence Zoo

In the recent literature many new equivalence relations were discussed (see Def. 4). Each of them captures different conditions for mutual replaceability in certain dynamic scenarios. In this section we want to shed light on the equivalence zoo by providing a complete analysis w.r.t. ten different notions of equivalence, namely those introduced in Def. 4 where the relation Φ in the definition of minimal change equivalence is instantiated by arbitrary, normal, weak and strong expansions. Besides the general case, i.e. considering arbitrary AFs, we also provide results for two special cases, namely the case where the AFs do not contain self-loops, i.e. attacks of the form (a, a) for some argument a, and the case where two AFs have the same arguments.

In the interest of readability we present our results not only in terms of propositions, but also graphically. Our graphics will contain boxes connected by directed arrows. The boxes contain the names of equivalence notions, separated by +. Notions within the same box are equivalent: if, say, a box contains e and e', then 2 argumentation frameworks $\mathcal{F}$ and $\mathcal{G}$ are e-equivalent iff they are e'-equivalent. Links between two boxes represent implication: if box B_1 is connected via a directed link to box B_2 and the former contains e, the latter e', then whenever $\mathcal{F}$ and $\mathcal{G}$ are e-equivalent they are also e'-equivalent. Note that whenever there is a link representing an implication, the converse implication does *not* hold.

3.1 Stable Semantics: The Full Picture

The following proposition characterizes stable semantics in general.

Proposition 1. *For stable semantics and arbitrary argumentation frameworks the following relationships hold:*

- *strong equivalence = normal expansion equivalence = strong expansion equivalence,*
- *MC equivalence with arbitrary expansion = MC equivalence with normal expansion = MC equivalence with strong expansion,*
- *strong equivalence $\subsetneqq$ local expansion equivalence $\subsetneqq$ weak expansion equivalence $\subsetneqq$ standard equivalence,*
- *strong equivalence $\subsetneqq$ MC equivalence with arbitrary expansion $\subsetneqq$ MC equivalence with weak expansion $\subsetneqq$ weak expansion equivalence.*

Fig. 1 describes the results for stable semantics graphically. In case of stable semantics only local expansion equivalence and the family of minimal change equivalence relations are unrelated. For any other two equivalence relations we have at least one implication chain. In particular, the different forms of minimal change equivalence *are shown to be intermediate forms between strong expansion and weak expansion equivalence.*

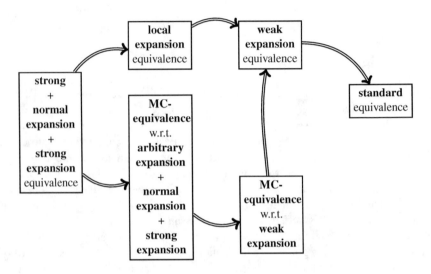

Fig. 1. Stable semantics in general

Proof. In [6] (Theorem 13) it was already shown that $\mathcal{F} \equiv_E^{st} \mathcal{G} \Leftrightarrow \mathcal{F} \equiv_N^{st} \mathcal{G} \Leftrightarrow \mathcal{F} \equiv_S^{st} \mathcal{G} \Rightarrow \mathcal{F} \equiv_L^{st} \mathcal{G} \Rightarrow \mathcal{F} \equiv_W^{st} \mathcal{G} \Rightarrow \mathcal{F} \equiv^{st} \mathcal{G}$. Since stable semantics satisfy regularity, i.e. strong equivalent AFs have to share the same arguments (compare Definition 3, Theorem 1 in [1]) we conclude that $\mathcal{F} \equiv_E^{st} \mathcal{G} \Rightarrow \mathcal{F} \equiv_E^{st,MC} \mathcal{G}$ (Theorem 14 [7]). Furthermore, by applying Theorem 9, Definition 10 [7] we deduce $\mathcal{F} \equiv_E^{st,MC} \mathcal{G} \Leftrightarrow \mathcal{F} \equiv_N^{st,MC} \mathcal{G} \Leftrightarrow \mathcal{F} \equiv_S^{st,MC} \mathcal{G}$.

We will show now that $\mathcal{F} \equiv_S^{st,MC} \mathcal{G} \Rightarrow \mathcal{F} \equiv_W^{st,MC} \mathcal{G}$. Assume $\mathcal{F} \equiv_S^{st,MC} \mathcal{G}$ and $\mathcal{F} \not\equiv_W^{st,MC} \mathcal{G}$. Note that the first assumption implies that $A(\mathcal{F}) = A(\mathcal{G})$. The second assumption means that there is a set E, s.t. $N_{st,W}^{\mathcal{F}}(E) \neq N_{st,W}^{\mathcal{G}}(E)$. W.l.o.g. we assume $N_{st,W}^{\mathcal{F}}(E) = \infty$ and $N_{st,W}^{\mathcal{G}}(E) = 0$ (Theorem 6, Definition 10 in [7]). Since the characteristic w.r.t. strong expansions does not exceed the characteristic w.r.t. weak expansions we have $N_{st,S}^{\mathcal{G}}(E) = 0$ (Proposition 10 [7]). Consequently (first assumption), $N_{st,S}^{\mathcal{F}}(E) = 0$ in contradiction to $N_{st,W}^{\mathcal{F}}(E) = \infty$ which proves the claimed implication.

We show now that $\mathcal{F} \equiv_W^{st,MC} \mathcal{G} \Rightarrow \mathcal{F} \equiv_W^{st} \mathcal{G}$. Assume $\mathcal{F} \equiv_W^{st,MC} \mathcal{G}$ and $\mathcal{F} \not\equiv_W^{st} \mathcal{G}$. First, minimal change equivalence implies $A(\mathcal{F}) = A(\mathcal{G})$. In [10] (Proposition 3) it was shown that two AFs are weak expansion equivalent w.r.t. stable semantics iff i) $A(\mathcal{F}) = A(\mathcal{G})$ and $\mathcal{E}_{st}(\mathcal{F}) = \mathcal{E}_{st}(\mathcal{G})$ or ii) $\mathcal{E}_{st}(\mathcal{F}) = \mathcal{E}_{st}(\mathcal{G}) = \emptyset$. Consequently, $\mathcal{E}_{st}(\mathcal{F}) \neq \mathcal{E}_{st}(\mathcal{G})$. Let $E \in \mathcal{E}_{st}(\mathcal{F})$ and $E \notin \mathcal{E}_{st}(\mathcal{G})$. Hence, $N_{st,W}^{\mathcal{F}}(E) = 0$. Since minimal change equivalence is assumed, $N_{st,W}^{\mathcal{G}}(E) = 0$. Since we assumed $E \notin \mathcal{E}_{st}(\mathcal{G})$ there has to be a proper superset E' of E, s.t. $E' \in \mathcal{E}_{st}(\mathcal{G})$. Consequently,

$N_{st,W}^{\mathcal{G}}(E') = 0$ and therefore $N_{st,W}^{\mathcal{F}}(E') = 0$. This means there is a superset E'' of E', s.t. $E'' \in \mathcal{E}_{st}(\mathcal{F})$. This means, there are two stable extensions E, E'' of $\mathcal{F}$, s.t. $E \subset E''$. This is impossible because stable semantics satisfies the I-maximality principle [11]. Altogether, the claimed implications are shown.

Now we present some counter-examples showing that the converse directions do not hold. It suffices to consider the following four cases. The other non-relations can be easily obtained by using the already shown relations presented in Figure 1.

1. $\mathcal{F} \equiv^{st} \mathcal{G} \not\Rightarrow \mathcal{F} \equiv_W^{st} \mathcal{G}$.

We have $\mathcal{E}_{st}(\mathcal{F}) = \mathcal{E}_{st}(\mathcal{G}) = \{\{a_2\}\} \neq \varnothing$ and obviously, $A(\mathcal{F}) \neq A(\mathcal{G})$. In [10] (Proposition 3) it was shown that two AFs are weak expansion equivalent w.r.t. stable semantics iff i) $A(\mathcal{F}) = A(\mathcal{G})$ and $\mathcal{E}_{st}(\mathcal{F}) = \mathcal{E}_{st}(\mathcal{G})$ or ii) $\mathcal{E}_{st}(\mathcal{F}) = \mathcal{E}_{st}(\mathcal{G}) = \varnothing$. Consequently, $\mathcal{F} \not\equiv_W^{st} \mathcal{G}$ and obviously, $\mathcal{F} \equiv^{st} \mathcal{G}$.

2. $\mathcal{F} \equiv_\Phi^{st,MC} \mathcal{G} \not\Rightarrow \mathcal{F} \equiv_L^{st} \mathcal{G}$ for each $\Phi \in \{E, N, S\}$.

Both AFs share the same arguments. Furthermore, $\mathcal{E}_{st}(\mathcal{F}) = \mathcal{E}_{st}(\mathcal{G}) = \{\{a_1, a_3\}\}$. Applying Definition 8 and Theorem 9 in [7] we conlude: First, for any $E \subseteq \{a_1, a_3\}$, we have $N_{st,S}^{\mathcal{F}}(E) = N_{st,S}^{\mathcal{G}}(E) = 0$. Second, $N_{st,S}^{\mathcal{F}}(\{a_1\}) = N_{st,S}^{\mathcal{G}}(\{a_1\}) = 1$ and third, for all not mentioned subsets C of $A(\mathcal{F})$, $N_{st,S}^{\mathcal{F}}(C) = N_{st,S}^{\mathcal{G}}(C) = \infty$ because they contain at least one conflict. This verifies $\mathcal{F} \equiv_\Phi^{st,MC} \mathcal{G}$ for each $\Phi \in \{E, N, S\}$ (Theorem 9, Theorem 13 in [7]). Consider the AFs $\mathcal{H} = (\{a_2, a_3\}, \{(a_2, a_3)\})$. We observe that $\mathcal{E}_{st}(\mathcal{F} \cup \mathcal{H}) = \{\{a_1, a_3\}, \{a_2\}\} \neq \{\{a_1, a_3\}\} = \mathcal{E}_{st}(\mathcal{G}) = \mathcal{E}_{st}(\mathcal{G} \cup \mathcal{H})$. Thus, $\mathcal{F} \not\equiv_L^{st} \mathcal{G}$.

3. $\mathcal{F} \equiv_W^{st,MC} \mathcal{G} \not\Rightarrow \mathcal{F} \equiv_\Phi^{st,MC} \mathcal{G}$ for each $\Phi \in \{E, N, S\}$.

Both AFs share the same arguments and $\mathcal{E}_{st}(\mathcal{F}) = \mathcal{E}_{st}(\mathcal{G}) = \{\{a_2\}\}$. Thus, $N_{st,W}^{\mathcal{F}}(\varnothing) = N_{st,W}^{\mathcal{G}}(\varnothing) = N_{st,W}^{\mathcal{F}}(\{a_2\}) = N_{st,W}^{\mathcal{G}}(\{a_2\}) = 0$. Furthermore, for any other subset C of $A(\mathcal{F})$, $N_{st,W}^{\mathcal{F}}(C) = N_{st,W}^{\mathcal{G}}(C) = \infty$ because they are not contained in an extension (Definition 7, Theorem 6 in [7]). Consequently, $\mathcal{F} \equiv_W^{st,MC} \mathcal{G}$. On the other hand, $N_{st,S}^{\mathcal{F}}(\{a_1\}) = 1 \neq 2 = N_{st,S}^{\mathcal{G}}(\{a_1\})$ (compare Definition 8, Theorem 9 in [7]). This means, $\mathcal{F} \not\equiv_\Phi^{st,MC} \mathcal{G}$ for each $\Phi \in \{E, N, S\}$.

4. $\mathcal{F} \equiv_L^{st} \mathcal{G} \not\Rightarrow \mathcal{F} \equiv_W^{st,MC} \mathcal{G}$.

Since minimal change equivalence implies sharing the same arguments we state $\mathcal{F} \not\equiv_W^{st,MC} \mathcal{G}$. Furthermore, it can be easily checked that for any AF $\mathcal{H}$, s.t. $A(\mathcal{H}) \subseteq \{a_1, a_2\}$, we have $\mathcal{E}_{st}(\mathcal{F} \cup \mathcal{H}) = \mathcal{E}_{st}(\mathcal{G} \cup \mathcal{H})$. Hence, $\mathcal{F} \equiv_L^{st} \mathcal{G}$.

How does the situation change if we restrict our considerations to AFs possessing the same arguments? It turns out that the equivalence zoo collapses to only 3 distinct classes, and in contrast to the general case local expansion equivalence and the different forms of minimal change equivalence become comparable.

Proposition 2. *For stable semantics and argumentation frameworks with the same arguments the following relationships hold:*

- *strong equivalence = normal expansion equivalence = strong expansion equivalence = local expansion equivalence,*
- *MC equivalence with arbitrary expansion = MC equivalence with normal expansion = MC equivalence with strong expansion,*
- *weak expansion equivalence = standard equivalence = MC equivalence with weak expansion,*
- *strong equivalence $\subsetneq$ MC equivalence with arbitrary expansion $\subsetneq$ weak expansion equivalence.*

Here is the graphical representation of the result:

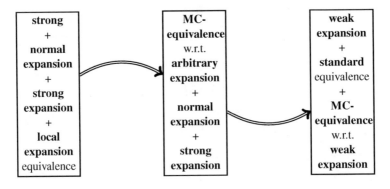

Fig. 2. Stable semantics in case of $A(\mathcal{F}) = A(\mathcal{G})$

Proof. For this proof we consider AFs sharing the same arguments, i.e. $A(\mathcal{F}) = A(\mathcal{G})$. Using the results presented in Figure 1 it suffices to show the following three implications.

At first we will show that $\mathcal{F} \equiv_L^{st} \mathcal{G} \Rightarrow \mathcal{F} \equiv_E^{st} \mathcal{G}$. In [1] (Theorem 9) it is proven that two AFs are local expansion equivalent iff i) $\mathcal{F} \equiv_E^{st} \mathcal{G}$ or ii) $\mathcal{E}_{st}(\mathcal{F}) = \mathcal{E}_{st}(\mathcal{G})$ and there is an argument $a \in (A(\mathcal{F}) \backslash A(\mathcal{G})) \cup (A(\mathcal{F}) \backslash A(\mathcal{G}))$ satisfying certain properties. Since $A(\mathcal{F}) = A(\mathcal{G})$ is assumed, $\mathcal{F} \equiv_E^{st} \mathcal{G}$ follows because there are no arguments in $(A(\mathcal{F}) \backslash A(\mathcal{G})) \cup (A(\mathcal{F}) \backslash A(\mathcal{G}))$.

We will show now that $\mathcal{F} \equiv^{st} \mathcal{G} \Rightarrow \mathcal{F} \equiv_W^{st} \mathcal{G}$. In [10] (Proposition 3) it was shown that two AFs are weak expansion equivalent w.r.t. stable semantics iff i) $A(\mathcal{F}) = A(\mathcal{G})$ and $\mathcal{E}_{st}(\mathcal{F}) = \mathcal{E}_{st}(\mathcal{G})$ or ii) $\mathcal{E}_{st}(\mathcal{F}) = \mathcal{E}_{st}(\mathcal{G}) = \varnothing$. Consequently, standard equivalence, i.e. $\mathcal{E}_{st}(\mathcal{F}) = \mathcal{E}_{st}(\mathcal{G})$ together with the assumption $A(\mathcal{F}) = A(\mathcal{G})$ implies weak expansion equivalence, i.e. $\mathcal{F} \equiv_W^{st} \mathcal{G}$ is shown.

Finally, we show that $\mathcal{F} \equiv_W^{st} \mathcal{G} \Rightarrow \mathcal{F} \equiv_W^{st,MC} \mathcal{G}$. Assume $\mathcal{F} \equiv_W^{st} \mathcal{G}$ and $\mathcal{F} \not\equiv_W^{st,MC} \mathcal{G}$. Using the characterization theorem in [10] (Proposition 3) we deduce $\mathcal{E}_{st}(\mathcal{F}) = \mathcal{E}_{st}(\mathcal{G})$. Since we assumed that $\mathcal{F}$ and $\mathcal{G}$ are not minimal change equivalent we deduce $N_{st,W}^{\mathcal{F}}(E) \neq N_{st,W}^{\mathcal{G}}(E)$ for some $E \subseteq A(\mathcal{F})(= A(\mathcal{G}))$. W.l.o.g. we assume $N_{st,W}^{\mathcal{F}}(E) = 0$ and $N_{st,W}^{\mathcal{G}}(E) = \infty$ (Theorem 6, Definition 10 in [7]). This means there is a superset E' of E, s.t. $E' \in \mathcal{E}_{st}(\mathcal{F})$. Consequently, $E' \in \mathcal{E}_{st}(\mathcal{G})$ in contradiction to $N_{st,W}^{\mathcal{G}}(E) = \infty$.

In consideration of the counter-examples 2 and 3 it follows that the converse directions do not hold because the considered AFs share the same arguments.

The role of self-loops is somewhat controversial in the literature. It is sometimes argued such self-attacks are necessary as they model paradoxical statements. On the other hand, it was shown (see Theorem 4.13 in [12]) that self-attacking arguments do not occur if Dung-style AFs are considered as instantiations of classical logic-based frameworks. At least in such contexts investigating AFs without self-loops is of interest. For this reason we present the equivalence zoo restricted to self-loop-free AFs. In contrast to the general case, local expansion equivalence coincides with strong, normal expansion and strong expansion equivalence and thus, the equivalence zoo becomes totally ordered.

Proposition 3. *For stable semantics and argumentation frameworks without self-loops the following relationships hold:*

- *strong equivalence = normal expansion equivalence = strong expansion equivalence = local expansion equivalence,*
- *MC equivalence with arbitrary expansion = MC equivalence with normal expansion = MC equivalence with strong expansion,*
- *strong equivalence $\subsetneq$ MC equivalence with arbitrary expansion $\subsetneq$ MC equivalence with weak expansion $\subsetneq$ weak expansion equivalence $\subsetneq$ standard equivalence.*

Here is again the graphical representation of the result:

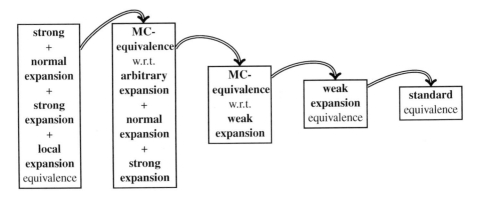

Fig. 3. Stable semantics in case of self-loop-free AFs

Proof. In consideration of the counter-examples given in the proof for stable semantics without restrictions we observe that only the fourth example showing that $\mathcal{F} \equiv_L^{st} \mathcal{G} \not\Rightarrow \mathcal{F} \equiv_W^{st,MC} \mathcal{G}$ contains self-loops. This is not a coincidence because local expansion equivalence coincides with strong equivalence in case of self-loop-free AFs. This follows immediately by Theorem 13 in [1] and Proposition 4 in [6].

Finally, we present a counter-example showing that $\mathcal{F} \equiv_W^{st} \mathcal{G} \not\Rightarrow \mathcal{F} \equiv_W^{st,MC} \mathcal{G}$.

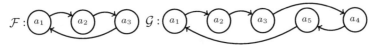

Two AFs are weak expansion equivalent w.r.t. stable semantics iff i) $A(\mathcal{F}) = A(\mathcal{G})$ and $\mathcal{E}_{st}(\mathcal{F}) = \mathcal{E}_{st}(\mathcal{G})$ or ii) $\mathcal{E}_{st}(\mathcal{F}) = \mathcal{E}_{st}(\mathcal{G}) = \varnothing$ [10, Proposition 3]. The second conditions holds for the considered AFs. Furthermore, they are not minimal change equivalent w.r.t. weak expansions since they do not share the same arguments.

3.2 Preferred Semantics: The Full Picture

How does the equivalence zoo look if we turn to the more relaxed notion of preferred semantics? To answer this question we first prove a characterization theorem for preferred semantics in case of weak expansions. It turns out that two AFs are weak expansion equivalent iff they share the same arguments, possess the same preferred extensions and furthermore, for any extension E the set of arguments which are not in the extension without being refuted has to coincide in both AFs.

Theorem 1. *For any two AFs $\mathcal{F},\mathcal{G}$ we have $\mathcal{F} \equiv_W^{pr} \mathcal{G}$ iff $A(F) = A(G)$, $\mathcal{E}_{pr}(\mathcal{F}) = \mathcal{E}_{pr}(\mathcal{G})$ and for each $E \in \mathcal{E}_{pr}(\mathcal{F}) : U_E^{\mathcal{F}} = U_E^{\mathcal{G}}$ where $U_E^{\mathcal{A}} = \{a \in A(\mathcal{A}) \mid a \notin E \wedge (E, a) \notin R(\mathcal{A})\}$.*

Proof. ($\Leftarrow$) Given an AF $\mathcal{H}$, s.t. $\mathcal{F} \leq_W \mathcal{F} \cup \mathcal{H}$ and $\mathcal{G} \leq_W \mathcal{G} \cup \mathcal{H}$. We have to show that $\mathcal{E}_{pr}(\mathcal{F} \cup \mathcal{H}) = \mathcal{E}_{pr}(\mathcal{G} \cup \mathcal{H})$. If $\mathcal{F} = \mathcal{F} \cup \mathcal{H}$, then $\mathcal{G} = \mathcal{G} \cup \mathcal{H}$ since $A(\mathcal{F}) = A(\mathcal{G})$ is assumed. In consideration of $\mathcal{E}_{pr}(\mathcal{F}) = \mathcal{E}_{pr}(\mathcal{G})$ the assertion follows. Assume now that $\mathcal{F} \neq \mathcal{F} \cup \mathcal{H}$. Using splitting results (Theorem 2 in [10]) one may easily show that $E \in \mathcal{E}_{pr}(\mathcal{F} \cup \mathcal{H})$ implies $E \in \mathcal{E}_{pr}(\mathcal{G} \cup \mathcal{H})$ (and vice versa).

($\Rightarrow$) We will show the contrapositive, i.e. if $A(F) \neq A(G)$ or $\mathcal{E}_{pr}(\mathcal{F}) \neq \mathcal{E}_{pr}(\mathcal{G})$ or there exists an $E \in \mathcal{E}_{pr}(\mathcal{F})$, s.t. $U_E^{\mathcal{F}} \neq U_E^{\mathcal{G}}$, then $\mathcal{F} \neq_W^{pr} \mathcal{G}$. Consider $E \in \mathcal{E}_{pr}(\mathcal{F})$ and $E \notin \mathcal{E}_{pr}(\mathcal{G})$. Consequently, $E \cup \{d\} \in \mathcal{E}_{pr}(\mathcal{F} \cup \mathcal{H})$ and $E \cup \{d\} \notin \mathcal{E}_{pr}(\mathcal{G} \cup \mathcal{H})$ where $\mathcal{H} = (\{d\}, \varnothing)$ and d is a fresh argument, i.e. $d \notin A(\mathcal{F}) \cup A(\mathcal{G})$. Assume now $A(F) \neq A(G)$ and $\mathcal{E}_{pr}(\mathcal{F}) = \mathcal{E}_{pr}(\mathcal{G})$. W.l.o.g. let $a \in A(F) \backslash A(G)$. Consequently, there is no preferred extension E, s.t. $a \in E$. If $\mathcal{H} = (\{a\}, \varnothing)$, then $\mathcal{F} \cup \mathcal{H} = \mathcal{F}$ and thus, there is no $E \in \mathcal{E}_{pr}(\mathcal{F} \cup \mathcal{H})$, s.t. $a \in E$. On the other hand, since a is unattacked in $\mathcal{G} \cup \mathcal{H}$ we deduce that a is contained in the grounded extension of $\mathcal{G} \cup \mathcal{H}$. Thus, $\mathcal{E}_{pr}(\mathcal{F} \cup \mathcal{H}) \neq \mathcal{E}_{pr}(\mathcal{G} \cup \mathcal{H})$ is shown. Finally, we consider $A(F) = A(G)$ and $\mathcal{E}_{pr}(\mathcal{F}) = \mathcal{E}_{pr}(\mathcal{G})$ but there exists an $E \in \mathcal{E}_{pr}(\mathcal{F})$, s.t. $U_E^{\mathcal{F}} \neq U_E^{\mathcal{G}}$. W.l.o.g. let $a \in U_E^{\mathcal{G}} \backslash U_E^{\mathcal{F}}$. This means, $a \notin E$, $(E, a) \notin R(\mathcal{G})$ and $(E, a) \in R(\mathcal{F})$, i.e. a is attacked by E in $\mathcal{F}$. Consider now $\mathcal{H} = (\{a, b\}, \{(a, b)\})$ where b is a fresh argument. One can easily see that $E \cup \{b\} \in \mathcal{E}_{pr}(\mathcal{F} \cup \mathcal{H})$ (b is defended by E) but $E \cup \{b\} \notin \mathcal{E}_{pr}(\mathcal{G} \cup \mathcal{H})$ (b is not defended by E). Altogether, $\mathcal{F} \neq_W^{pr} \mathcal{G}$ is shown.

Now we are prepared to tackle preferred semantics. The following result presents the interrelations if we put no restriction on the considered AFs. We observe that as in the case of stable semantics there is no total ordering of the equivalence relations in the equivalence zoo. In particular, weak expansion equivalence is not comparable with strong expansion equivalence and minimal change equivalence w.r.t. arbitrary, normal and strong expansions. Furthermore, members of the family of minimal change equivalence relations *are shown to be intermediate forms between strong expansion and standard equivalence.* Interestingly, weak expansion equivalence and minimal change equivalence w.r.t. weak expansions change their position in comparison to stable semantics.

Proposition 4. *For preferred semantics and arbitrary argumentation frameworks the following relationships hold:*

- *strong equivalence = normal expansion equivalence = local expansion equivalence,*
- *MC equivalence with arbitrary expansion = MC equivalence with normal expansion = MC equivalence with strong expansion,*
- *strong equivalence $\subsetneq$ strong expansion equivalence $\subsetneq$ MC equivalence with arbitrary expansion $\subsetneq$ MC equivalence with weak expansion $\subsetneq$ standard equivalence,*
- *strong equivalence $\subsetneq$ weak expansion equivalence $\subsetneq$ MC equivalence with weak expansion.*

Here is again the graphical representation of the result:

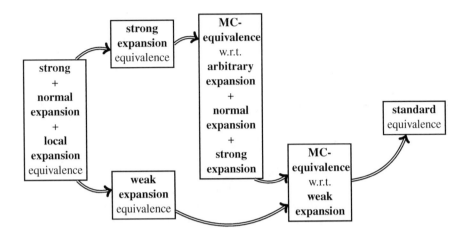

Fig. 4. Preferred semantics in general

Proof. In [6, Theorem 13] it was already shown that $\mathcal{F} \equiv_E^{pr} \mathcal{G} \Leftrightarrow \mathcal{F} \equiv_N^{pr} \mathcal{G} \Leftrightarrow \mathcal{F} \equiv_L^{pr}$ $\mathcal{G} \Rightarrow \mathcal{F} \equiv_S^{pr} \mathcal{G}, \mathcal{F} \equiv_W^{pr} \mathcal{G} \Rightarrow \mathcal{F} \equiv^{pr} \mathcal{G}$.

First, we will show that weak expansion equivalence implies minimal change equivalence w.r.t. weak expansions, i.e. $\mathcal{F} \equiv_W^{pr} \mathcal{G} \Rightarrow \mathcal{F} \equiv_W^{pr,MC} \mathcal{G}$. Applying Theorem 1 we deduce $A(F) = A(G)$ and $\mathcal{E}_{pr}(\mathcal{F}) = \mathcal{E}_{pr}(\mathcal{G})$. If $\mathcal{F} \not\equiv_W^{pr,MC} \mathcal{G}$, then there is a set $E \subseteq A(F)$, s.t. $N_{pr,W}^{\mathcal{F}}(E) \neq N_{pr,W}^{\mathcal{G}}(E)$. W.l.o.g. we assume $N_{pr,W}^{\mathcal{F}}(E) = 0$ and $N_{pr,W}^{\mathcal{G}}(E) = \infty$ (compare [7, Definition 7, Theorem 6]). Hence, there is a superset E' of E, s.t. $E' \in \mathcal{E}_{pr}(\mathcal{F})$ and $E' \notin \mathcal{E}_{pr}(\mathcal{G})$ in contradiction to $\mathcal{E}_{pr}(\mathcal{F}) = \mathcal{E}_{pr}(\mathcal{G})$.

Since preferred semantics satisfies I-maximality [11], i.e. no extension can be a proper subset of another one, we conclude $\mathcal{F} \equiv_W^{pr,MC} \mathcal{G} \Rightarrow \mathcal{F} \equiv^{pr} \mathcal{G}$ ([7, Theorem 15]).

We show now that $\mathcal{F} \equiv_S^{pr} \mathcal{G}$ implies $\mathcal{F} \equiv_\Phi^{pr,MC} \mathcal{G}$ for each $\Phi \in \{E, N, S\}$. We have already shown that minimal change equivalence w.r.t. arbitrary, normal and strong expansions coincide [7, Definition 10, Theorem 6]. Hence, it suffices to prove that $\mathcal{F} \equiv_S^{pr} \mathcal{G}$ and $\mathcal{F} \not\equiv_S^{pr,MC} \mathcal{G}$ yields a contradiction. Since strong expansion equivalence implies sharing the same arguments [6, Definition 7, Theorem 6] it follows the existence of a subset $E \subseteq A(\mathcal{F}) = A(\mathcal{G})$, s.t. $\mathcal{F} \not\equiv_S^{pr,E} \mathcal{G}$. Consequently, $N_{pr,S}^{\mathcal{F}}(E) \neq N_{pr,S}^{\mathcal{G}}(E)$. Let $N_{pr,S}^{\mathcal{F}}(E) = k_1 < k_2 = N_{pr,S}^{\mathcal{G}}(E)$ where $k_1, k_2 \in \mathbb{N}_\infty$. Note that $k_1 = 0$ yields a contradiction because strong expansion equivalence implies standard equivalence, i.e. $\mathcal{E}_{pr}(\mathcal{F}) = \mathcal{E}_{pr}(\mathcal{G})$ (Proposition 3 in [6]). Assume $k_1 \neq 0$. Consequently, there are an AF $\mathcal{H}$ and a set $E' \subseteq A(\mathcal{H})$, s.t. $\mathcal{F} \leq_S \mathcal{H}$, $d(\mathcal{F}, \mathcal{H}) = k_1$ and $E \subseteq E' \in \mathcal{E}_{pr}(\mathcal{H})$. W.l.o.g. there exists an AF $\mathcal{H}'$, s.t. $R(\mathcal{F}) \cap R(\mathcal{H}') = \varnothing$ and any attack in $R(\mathcal{H}')$ contains at least one fresh argument and $\mathcal{H} = \mathcal{F} \cup \mathcal{H}'$ (compare Definition 2). Since $\mathcal{F} \equiv_S^{pr} \mathcal{G}$ is assumed and $A(\mathcal{F}) = A(\mathcal{G})$ is already shown we conlude $\mathcal{G} \leq_S \mathcal{G} \cup \mathcal{H}'$ and therefore $E' \in \mathcal{E}_{pr}(\mathcal{G} \cup \mathcal{H}')$. It can be easily seen that $d(\mathcal{G}, \mathcal{G} \cup \mathcal{H}') = k_1$. Thus, $k_2 = N_{pr,S}^{\mathcal{G}}(E) = k_1$ in contradiction to $k_1 < k_2$. Consequently, $\mathcal{F} \equiv_S^{pr} \mathcal{G} \Rightarrow \mathcal{F} \equiv_\Phi^{pr,MC} \mathcal{G}$ for each $\Phi \in \{E, N, S\}$ is shown.

Finally, we will show that $\mathcal{F} \equiv_{\Phi}^{pr,MC} \mathcal{G} \Rightarrow \mathcal{F} \equiv_{W}^{pr,MC} \mathcal{G}$ for each $\Phi \in \{E, N, S\}$. Again, it suffices to show that $\mathcal{F} \equiv_{S}^{pr,MC} \mathcal{G}$ and $\mathcal{F} \not\equiv_{W}^{pr,MC} \mathcal{G}$ yields a contradiction [7, Theorem 9, Definition 10]. The first assumption implies $A(\mathcal{F}) = A(\mathcal{G})$. The second assumption means that there is a set E, s.t. $N_{pr,W}^{\mathcal{F}}(E) \neq N_{pr,W}^{\mathcal{G}}(E)$. Let $N_{pr,W}^{\mathcal{F}}(E) = \infty$ and $N_{pr,W}^{\mathcal{G}}(E) = 0$ [7, Theorem 6, Definition 10]. Recalling that the characteristic w.r.t. strong expansions does not exceed the characteristic w.r.t. weak expansions [7, Proposition 10] we conclude $N_{pr,S}^{\mathcal{G}}(E) = 0$. Hence, applying the minimal change equivalence w.r.t. strong expansions we deduce $N_{st,S}^{\mathcal{F}}(E) = 0$. This means, there is a superset E' of E, s.t. $E' \in \mathcal{E}_{pr}(\mathcal{F})$. Consequently, $N_{st,W}^{\mathcal{F}}(E) = \infty$ is impossible concluding the proof.

For the sake of completeness we will present some counterexamples showing that the converse directions do not hold. It suffices to check the following four cases. The other non-relations can be easily obtained by using the already shown relations depicted in Figure 4.

1. $\mathcal{F} \equiv^{pr} \mathcal{G} \not\Rightarrow \mathcal{F} \equiv_{W}^{pr,MC} \mathcal{G}$.

Obviously, $\mathcal{E}_{pr}(\mathcal{F}) = \mathcal{E}_{pr}(\mathcal{G}) = \{\{a_1\}\}$. Furthermore, $\mathcal{F} \not\equiv_{W}^{pr,MC} \mathcal{G}$ since minimal change equivalence guarantees sharing the same arguments (compare Definition 10 in [7]) but $A(\mathcal{F}) \neq A(\mathcal{G})$.

2. $\mathcal{F} \equiv_{\Phi}^{pr,MC} \mathcal{G} \not\Rightarrow \mathcal{F} \equiv_{S}^{pr} \mathcal{G}$ for each $\Phi \in \{E, N, S\}$.

It can be checked (Definition 8, Theorem 9 in [7]) that $N_{pr,S}^{\mathcal{F}}(\{a_1\}) = N_{pr,S}^{\mathcal{G}}(\{a_1\}) = N_{pr,S}^{\mathcal{F}}(\{a_3\}) = N_{pr,S}^{\mathcal{G}}(\{a_3\}) = 1$ and $N_{pr,S}^{\mathcal{F}}(\{a_2\}) = N_{pr,S}^{\mathcal{G}}(\{a_2\}) = N_{pr,S}^{\mathcal{F}}(\varnothing) = N_{pr,S}^{\mathcal{G}}(\varnothing) = 0$ and for any other $E \subseteq A(\mathcal{F}) = A(\mathcal{G})$ (thus, $E \notin cf(\mathcal{F}) = cf(\mathcal{G})$), we have $N_{pr,S}^{\mathcal{F}}(E) = N_{pr,S}^{\mathcal{G}}(E) = \infty$. Hence, $\mathcal{F} \equiv_{S}^{pr,MC} \mathcal{G}$. Furthermore, $\mathcal{F} \not\equiv_{S}^{pr} \mathcal{G}$ because $\mathcal{F}$ and $\mathcal{G}$ are self-loop-free but not syntactically identical (compare Proposition 4 in [6]).

3. $\mathcal{F} \equiv_{W}^{pr} \mathcal{G} \not\Rightarrow \mathcal{F} \equiv_{\Phi}^{pr,MC} \mathcal{G}$ for each $\Phi \in \{E, N, S\}$.

Since $A(\mathcal{F}) = A(\mathcal{G})$, $\mathcal{E}_{pr}(\mathcal{F}) = \mathcal{E}_{pr}(\mathcal{G}) = \{\{a_2\}\}$ and $U_{\{a_2\}}^{\mathcal{F}} = \varnothing = U_{\{a_2\}}^{\mathcal{G}}$ we conclude $\mathcal{F} \equiv_{W}^{pr} \mathcal{G}$ (Theorem 9). Furthermore, $N_{pr,S}^{\mathcal{F}}(\{a_1\}) = 1 \neq 2 = N_{pr,S}^{\mathcal{G}}(\{a_1\})$ (compare Definition 8, Theorem 9 in [7]). Consequently, $\mathcal{F} \not\equiv_{S}^{pr,MC} \mathcal{G}$.

4. $\mathcal{F} \equiv_S^{pr} \mathcal{G} \not\Rightarrow \mathcal{F} \equiv_W^{pr} \mathcal{G}.$

Since $\mathcal{F}$ and $\mathcal{G}$ possess identical admissible-*-kernels, namely $\mathcal{F} = \mathcal{F}^{k^*(ad)} = \mathcal{G}^{k^*(ad)}$ we deduce $\mathcal{F} \equiv_S^{pr} \mathcal{G}$ (compare Definition 7, Theorem 6 in [6]). Furthermore, $\mathcal{E}_{pr}(\mathcal{F}) = \mathcal{E}_{pr}(\mathcal{G}) = \{\{a_1\}\}$ but $U_{\{a_1\}}^{\mathcal{F}} = \{a_2\} \neq \varnothing = U_{\{a_1\}}^{\mathcal{G}}$. Hence, $\mathcal{F} \not\equiv_W^{pr} \mathcal{G}$ (Theorem 1).

Restricting our considerations to AFs sharing the same arguments does not have a big effect in comparison to the general case. We state a slight difference only, namely standard equivalence of two AFs becomes sufficient for their minimal change equivalence w.r.t. weak expansions.

Proposition 5. *For preferred semantics and argumentation frameworks with the same arguments the following relationships hold:*

- *strong equivalence = normal expansion equivalence = local expansion equivalence,*
- *MC equivalence with arbitrary expansion = MC equivalence with normal expansion = MC equivalence with strong expansion,*
- *standard equivalence = MC equivalence with weak expansion,*
- *strong equivalence $\subsetneq$ strong expansion equivalence $\subsetneq$ MC equivalence with arbitrary expansion $\subsetneq$ standard equivalence,*
- *strong equivalence $\subsetneq$ weak expansion equivalence $\subsetneq$ standard equivalence.*

Graphically:

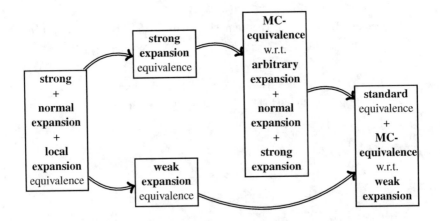

Fig. 5. Preferred semantics in case of $A(\mathcal{F}) = A(\mathcal{G})$

Proof. Consider again the counter-examples given in the proof before showing that some relations do not hold. We observe that only the first counter-example (showing that $\mathcal{F} \equiv^{pr} \mathcal{G} \not\Rightarrow \mathcal{F} \equiv_W^{pr,MC} \mathcal{G}$) deals with AFs which do not share the same arguments. This is not a coincidence as the following proof shows.

We assume $A(\mathcal{F}) = A(\mathcal{G})$ and $\mathcal{F} \equiv^{pr} \mathcal{G}$. Standard equivalence of two AFs, i.e. $\mathcal{E}_{pr}(\mathcal{F}) = \mathcal{E}_{pr}(\mathcal{G})$ together with the assumption guarentees that for any set $E \subseteq A(\mathcal{F})$, either $N_{pr,W}^{\mathcal{F}}(E) = N_{pr,W}^{\mathcal{G}}(E) = 0$ or $N_{pr,W}^{\mathcal{F}}(E) = N_{pr,W}^{\mathcal{G}}(E) = \infty$ (compare [7, Definition 7]). Consequently, $\mathcal{F} \equiv_W^{pr,MC} \mathcal{G}$ is shown [7, Theorem 6].

Finally, we consider the class of self-loop-free AFs. It turns out that in this case stable and preferred semantics behave in a very similar manner. The only difference is the role (or better, position) of weak expansion equivalence and minimal change equivalence w.r.t. weak expansions.

Proposition 6. *For preferred semantics and argumentation frameworks without self-loops the following relationships hold:*

- *strong equivalence = normal expansion equivalence = strong expansion equivalence = local expansion equivalence,*
- *MC equivalence with arbitrary expansion = MC equivalence with normal expansion = MC equivalence with strong expansion,*
- *strong equivalence $\subsetneq$ MC equivalence with arbitrary expansion $\subsetneq$ weak expansion equivalence $\subsetneq$ MC equivalence with weak expansion $\subsetneq$ standard equivalence.*

Graphically:

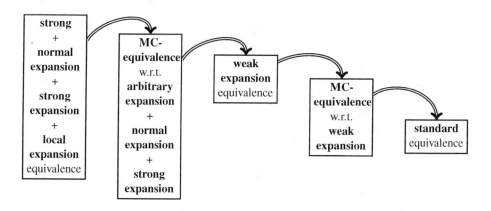

Fig. 6. Preferred semantics in case of self-loop-free AFs

Proof. In this proof we assume that the considered AFs do not possess self-loops. Consequently, in consideration of the results presented in Figure 4 it suffices to show the following two relations. First, $\mathcal{F} \equiv_S^{pr} \mathcal{G} \Rightarrow \mathcal{F} \equiv_N^{pr} \mathcal{G}$ (already shown in [6, Proposition 4]) and second, $\mathcal{F} \equiv_S^{pr,MC} \mathcal{G} \Rightarrow \mathcal{F} \equiv_W^{pr} \mathcal{G}$. Due to space limitations we omit this proof.

Consider again the counter-examples given in the proof of the relations depicted in Figure 6. We observe that the counter-examples 1-3 do not possess self-loops. Hence, these (non)-relations do not hold here either. A counter-example remains to be given for $\mathcal{F} \equiv_W^{pr,MC} \mathcal{G} \not\Rightarrow \mathcal{F} \equiv_W^{pr} \mathcal{G}$.

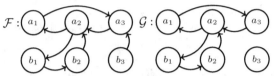

One may check that $\mathcal{E}_{pr}(\mathcal{F}) = \mathcal{E}_{pr}(\mathcal{G}) = \{\{b_3\}\}$. Furthermore, $A(\mathcal{F}) = A(\mathcal{G})$. Consequently, for any set $E \subseteq A(\mathcal{F})$, either $N_{pr,W}^{\mathcal{F}}(E) = N_{pr,W}^{\mathcal{G}}(E) = 0$ or $N_{pr,W}^{\mathcal{F}}(E) = N_{pr,W}^{\mathcal{G}}(E) = \infty$ (compare Definition 7 in [7]). Hence, $\mathcal{F} \equiv_W^{pr,MC} \mathcal{G}$ is shown (Theorem 6 in [7]). On the other hand, $U_{\{b_3\}}^{\mathcal{F}} = \{a_1, a_2, b_1, b_2\} \neq \{a_1, a_2, a_3, b_1, b_2\} = U_{\{b_3\}}^{\mathcal{G}}$. Thus, $\mathcal{F} \not\equiv_W^{pr} \mathcal{G}$ (Theorem 1).

4   Conclusions

In this paper we continued earlier work of the first author [6]. We fully clarified the relationship among all equivalence notions for AFs so far discussed in the literature for stable and preferred semantics. We provided an analysis for the whole class of AFs as well as for two important subclasses, namely AFs sharing the same arguments and self-loop-free AFs. The most relevant "take home" message following from our results is that the different notions of minimal change equivalence fit nicely into the global picture of other equivalence notions in the sense that they constitute alternative notions in between strong and standard equivalence.

Our results are not only of theoretical interest, they can also be very useful in practice. For instance, it is easy to decide (in linear time) whether two AFs are strong expansion equivalent. In cases where strong expansion equivalence is established, minimal change equivalence - which is much more difficult to decide in general - immediately follows, as shown in this paper. Furthermore, since argument and attack construction is monotonic, adding a new piece of information to the underlying knowledge base does not rule out old arguments and attacks. Thus, notions like normal expansion equivalence allow us to simplify AFs adequately as they reflect this kind of dynamic scenarios. In brief, abstract equivalence notions can *detect* redundant attacks no matter what the underlying KR-language is. An equivalence notion for the special case where classical logic is used is defined in [13].

Some obvious further work remains to be done, in particular we plan to extend our analysis to further argumentation semantics (like admissible, grounded or complete semantics [5]). Instead of considering a certain semantics one may alternatively look at general criteria sufficient and/or necessary for beeing in a particular interrelation. Examples of such criteria are *regularity* and *I-maximality* as it was shown in [7, Theorems 14,15]. A further direction is the generalization of existing equivalence notions concerning AFs to ADFs firstly introduced in [14].

Acknowledgements. The authors acknowledge support by Deutsche Forschungsgemeinschaft (DFG) under grant BR 1817/7-1.

References

1. Oikarinen, E., Woltran, S.: Characterizing strong equivalence for argumentation frameworks. Artificial Intelligence 175(14-15), 1985–2009 (2011)
2. Lifschitz, V., Pearce, D., Valverde, A.: Strongly equivalent logic programs. ACM Trans. Comput. Log. 2(4), 526–541 (2001)
3. Eiter, T., Fink, M., Tompits, H., Woltran, S.: Strong and uniform equivalence in answer-set programming: Characterizations and complexity results for the non-ground case. In: Proc. AAAI 2005, pp. 695–700 (2005)
4. Bench-Capon, T.J.M., Dunne, P.E.: Argumentation in artificial intelligence. Artificial Intelligence 171(10-15), 619–641 (2007)
5. Dung, P.M.: On the acceptability of arguments and its fundamental role in nonmonotonic reasoning, logic programming and n-person games. Artificial Intelligence 77(2), 321–357 (1995)
6. Baumann, R.: Normal and strong expansion equivalence for argumentation frameworks. Artificial Intelligence 193, 18–44 (2012)
7. Baumann, R.: What does it take to enforce an argument? Minimal change in abstract argumentation. In: ECAI, pp. 127–132 (2012)
8. Baroni, P., Giacomin, M.: Characterizing defeat graphs where argumentation semantics agree. In: Simari, G.P.T. (ed.) 1st International Workshop on Argumentation and Non-Monotonic Reasoning, pp. 33–48 (2007)
9. Baumann, R., Brewka, G.: Expanding argumentation frameworks: Enforcing and monotonicity results. In: Proc. COMMA 2010, pp. 75–86. IOS Press (2010)
10. Baumann, R.: Splitting an argumentation framework. In: Delgrande, J.P., Faber, W. (eds.) LPNMR 2011. LNCS, vol. 6645, pp. 40–53. Springer, Heidelberg (2011)
11. Baroni, P., Giacomin, M.: On principle-based evaluation of extension-based argumentation semantics. Artificial Intelligence 171(10-15), 675–700 (2007)
12. Besnard, P., Hunter, A.: A logic-based theory of deductive arguments. Artificial Intelligence 128(1-2), 203–235 (2001)
13. Amgoud, L., Vesic, S.: On the equivalence of logic-based argumentation systems. In: Benferhat, S., Grant, J. (eds.) SUM 2011. LNCS, vol. 6929, pp. 123–136. Springer, Heidelberg (2011)
14. Brewka, G., Woltran, S.: Abstract dialectical frameworks. In: Proceedings KR 2010, pp. 102–111 (2010)

On the Instantiation of Knowledge Bases in Abstract Argumentation Frameworks

Adam Wyner[1], Trevor Bench-Capon[2], and Paul Dunne[2]

[1] Department of Computing Science, University of Aberdeen, Aberdeen, United Kingdom
azwyner@abdn.ac.uk
[2] Department of Computer Science, University of Liverpool, Liverpool, United Kingdom
tbc,sq12@liverpool.ac.uk

Abstract. Abstract Argumentation Frameworks (AFs) provide a fruitful basis for exploring issues of defeasible reasoning. Their power largely derives from the abstract nature of the arguments within the framework, where arguments are atomic nodes in an undifferentiated relation of attack. This abstraction conceals different conceptions of argument, and concrete instantiations encounter difficulties as a result of conflating these conceptions. We distinguish three distinct senses of the term. We provide an approach to instantiating AF in which the nodes are restricted to literals and rules, encoding the underlying theory directly. Arguments, in each of the three senses, then emerge from this framework as distinctive structures of nodes and paths. Our framework retains the theoretical and computational benefits of an abstract AF, while keeping notions distinct which are conflated in other approaches to instantiation.

1 Introduction

Abstract Argumentation Frameworks (AFs) ([1,2,3], among others) provide a fruitful basis for exploring issues of defeasible reasoning.[1] Their power largely derives from the abstract nature of the arguments within the framework, where arguments are atomic nodes in an undifferentiated relation of attack; such AFs provide a very clean acceptability semantics, e.g. [5].

While abstract approaches facilitate the study of arguments and the relations between them, it is necessary to instantiate arguments to apply the theory. In instantiated argumentation, arguments are premises and rules from which conclusions are derived. The objective of such instantiated argumentation is to be able to reason about inconsistency of a knowledge base (KB) and derive consistent subsets of the KB. Methods for instantiation have been proposed which combine AFs with Logic Programs [2,6,7,3,8,9]. Such systems generally have three steps as in Figure 1 (from [10]), though for this paper we focus on the formalisation of ASPIC+ [8]. We start with an inconsistent knowledge base (KB) comprised of facts and rules, where the rules typically may include both strict (*SI*) and defeasible (*DI*) inference rules. In Step 1, we construct arguments (nodes) and attacks (arcs) from this KB, resulting in an AF; formalisations differ in just how arguments are constructed from the KB and how attacks between arguments are determined.

---

[1] Corresponding author: Adam Wyner. This paper is a revision of an unpublished paper [4]. Thanks to Federico Cerutti for comments. Errors and misunderstandings rest with the authors.

J. Leite et al. (Eds.): CLIMA XIV, LNAI 8143, pp. 34–50, 2013.
© Springer-Verlag Berlin Heidelberg 2013

In Step 2, we evaluate the AF according to a variety of semantics, resulting in extensions (sets) of arguments. In Step 3, we extract the conclusions from the arguments, resulting in extensions of conclusions. Thus, from a KB that is initially inconsistent (or derives inconsistency), we can nonetheless identify consistent sets of propositions.

Fig. 1. Three Steps of Argumentation

While such an approach to instantiated argumentation is attractive, it is not without issues. We discuss these briefly by way of motivation, then develop them over the course of the paper. Arguments in ASPIC+ are constructed from the KB as premises and a rule from which a conclusion is inferred; they may be *compounds* of strict and defeasible subarguments [8]. Thus, many arguments with some of the same elements of the KB may be constructed. An argument may attack a subargument of another argument. Successful attacks (*defeat*) are defined relative to a preference ordering amongst the arguments and used to determine AF extensions. In these respects, ASPIC+ differs from [1], where arguments are atomic, there is a uniform attack relation between arguments, and a preference ordering plays no role in determining successful attack. As well, the use of subarguments and attacks between arguments and subarguments gives rise to some *descriptive* unclarity in the commonly uses "senses" of the term "argument" [11]. More essentially, ASPIC+ must ensure that over the course of the three steps, the *rationality postulates* of *direct consistency*, *closure*, and *indirect consistency* of [3] are satisfied. For ASPIC+ to satisfy the rationality postulates, auxiliary definitions are required and only *restricted rebut* is available [8], though this seems limited [10]. Stepping back from the particulars of ASPIC+, there is a general question of whether all three steps are required to attain the goal of extensions of conclusions; after all, Step 1 "packs" a portion of the KB into arguments that have to be "unpacked" in Step 3. In this way, reasoning with respect to the KB is handled indirectly, with arguments standing as intermediaries. Finally, we cannot reason with *partial information* in KBs, where premises of a rule are missing, for no inference can be drawn, so no argument can be constructed.

In this paper, we provide a novel, two step approach to *instantiating the arguments of an* AF (see Figure 2), where arguments AF are atomic, there are no attacks on subarguments, and preferences are not used. It intuitively satisfies the rationality postulates *without restricted rebut* while addressing a key, problematic example. The AF "wears the logic on its sleeve": the KB, mainly classical logic with strict and defeasible *modus ponens* to use the rules along with the principles of *ex falso quodlibet* and *tertium non datum*, is directly constructed as an AF with literals and rules as the nodes of the AF, i.e. the arguments of the AF, with arcs, i.e. the attacks of the AF, specified between them. Once given the AF so constructed, evaluation proceeds as usual, though the extensions correlate with *models* of consistent subsets of the KB. We show how we can represent and reason with partial, incomplete, and inconsistent KBs. Our approach addresses a benchmark example of the ASPIC approach. In addition, in our approach, the various descriptive senses of *argument* such as found in ASPIC+ and elsewhere emerge from the framework as distinct structures in an AF; keeping them distinct avoids the confusions that can arise when these different senses are conflated. Our approach retains the appeal of AFs, evaluates the AF with the well understood semantics, allows reasoning with respect to knowledge bases, retains the appropriate level of abstraction of the nodes of the AF, and reasons with partial KBs.

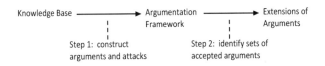

Fig. 2. Two Steps of Argumentation

The structure of the paper is as follows. In Section 2 we outline AFs [1] and characterise the types of knowledge base we are working with. We then show how a knowledge base is represented in a derived AF in Section 3. We illustrate the approach with basic examples of the definitions, a simple example of a combination of strict and defeasible rules, a partial KB, and the relationship of extensions to classical logic models. In Section 4, we discuss the approach to KB instantiation of [3,8] along with a key example and the problems it raises. We show how our approach addresses the problems of the example. The different senses of *argument* are then characterised in terms of particular structures within the AF as presented in Section 5. We end in Section 6 with some concluding remarks and future work.

2   Argumentation Frameworks

An *Argumentation Framework* AF is defined as follows [1].

Definition 1. *An argumentation framework* AF *is a pair* $\langle \mathcal{L}^A, \mathcal{R}^A \rangle$*, where* $\mathcal{L}^A$ *is a finite set of* arguments*,* $\{p_1, p_2, \ldots, p_n\}$ *and* $\mathcal{R}^A$ *is an* attack *relation between elements of* $\mathcal{L}^A$*. For* $\langle p_i, p_j \rangle \in \mathcal{R}^A$ *we say the argument* p_i *attacks argument* p_j*. We assume that no object attacks itself.*

The relevant auxiliary definitions are as follows, where S is a subset of $\mathcal{L}^A$:

Definition 2. *We say that* $p \in \mathcal{L}^A$ *is acceptable with respect to* S *if for every* $q \in \mathcal{L}^A$ *that attacks* p *there is some* $r \in S$ *that attacks* q*. A subset,* S*, is conflict-free if no argument in* S *is attacked by any other argument in* S*. A conflict-free set* S *is admissible if every* $p \in S$ *is acceptable to* S*. A preferred extension is a maximal (w.r.t.*

$\subseteq$) *admissible set. The argument* $p \in \mathcal{L}^A$ is credulously accepted *if it is in at least one* *preferred extension, and* sceptically accepted *if it is in* every *preferred extension.*

There are a variety of other semantics, e.g. *grounded, stable,* and others, but considering preferred extensions serves our purposes in this paper.

As we clarify the notion of *argument* itself and do not want to introduce presumptions about them, we sometimes prefer to refer to arguments as *objects* or graph-theoretic *nodes* (denoted by $\mathcal{L}^A$) and their attack relations as *arcs* (denoted by $\mathcal{R}^A$). Context makes it clear what is being referred to.

3   Representing a Theory as an AF

The approach has two basic parts (the presentation is a revision of [4]). In the first part, we represent a Theory Base $\mathcal{T}$, which represents the KB. Then, we construct an AF from the KB, following Step 1 of Figure 2, where the nodes of an AF are labeled with respect to the literals and inference rules of the Theory Base, while the attack relation is partitioned with respect to the nodes. In the second part, we impose conditions on the assertion of literals with respect to the AF. Following the theoretical presentation, we provide basic examples, carrying out Step 2 of Figure 2 to evaluate an AF according to Definitions 1 and 2.

3.1   Theory Base $\mathcal{T}$

Definition 3. *A Theory Base,* $\mathcal{T}$, *comprises a pair* $(\mathcal{L}, \mathcal{R})$ *in which*

$$\mathcal{L} = \{x_1, \ldots, x_n\} \cup \{\neg x_1, \ldots, \neg x_n\}$$

is a set of literals over a set of propositional variables $\{x_1, \ldots, x_n\}$. *We use* y_i *to denote an arbitrary literal from* $\{x_i, \neg x_i\}$.

We have a set of proper names *of rules* $\{r_1, r_2, \ldots, r_n\}$. *Rules are either strict (*$r \in \mathcal{R}_{str}$*) or defeasible (*$r \in \mathcal{R}_{dfs}$*), and* $\mathcal{R}_{str} \cap \mathcal{R}_{dfs} = \emptyset$. $\mathcal{R} = \mathcal{R}_{str} \cup \mathcal{R}_{dfs}$ *where*

$$\mathcal{R} = \{r_1, r_2, \ldots, r_n\}$$

in which $r \in \mathcal{R}$ *has a body,* $bd(r) \subseteq \mathcal{L}$, *and a head,* $hd(r) \in \mathcal{L}$.

We refer to the literals in $bd(r)$ as *premises* and the literal in $hd(r)$ as the *claim*.

For easy reference to the "content" of the rule, we assume each rule has an associated *definite description* as follows. For $r \in \mathcal{R}_{str}$, the definite description of r has the form $r : bd(r) \rightarrow hd(r)$, where $hd(r) \in \mathcal{L}$ and $bd(r) \subseteq \mathcal{L}$. Similarly, the definite description for $r \in \mathcal{R}_{dfs}$, has the form $r : bd(r) \Rightarrow hd(r)$. Where a rule has an empty body, $bd(r) = \emptyset$, we have $r :\rightarrow hd(r)$ or $r :\Rightarrow hd(r)$, which are *strict* and *defeasible* assertions, respectively. To refer distinctly to the set of rules with non-empty bodies and those with empty bodies (*assertions*), we have $\mathcal{R}$ = TRules $\cup$ ARules, where TRules = $\{r \mid r \in \mathcal{R} \wedge bd(r) \neq \emptyset\}$ and ARules = $\{r \mid r \in \mathcal{R} \wedge bd(r) = \emptyset\}$.

We constrain a Theory Base, which we refer to as a *Well-formed Theory*.

Definition 4. *A* Well-formed Theory, $\mathcal{W}$, *is a Theory Base*, $\mathcal{T}$, *abiding Constraints 1-4.*

First, the relationship between literals of strict and defeasible rules is constrained:

Constraint 1 *For Theory Base* $(\mathcal{L}, \mathcal{R})$, $\forall r \in \mathcal{R}_{str}$, *there is no rule*, $r' \in \mathcal{R}_{dfs}$ *with* $hd(r) = hd(r')$ *and* $bd(r) \subseteq bd(r')$.

Furthermore, no literal and its negation can both be strictly asserted.

Constraint 2 *For Theory Base* $(\mathcal{L}, \mathcal{R})$, *if* $r \in \mathcal{R}$, *where* $r :\rightarrow hd(r)$, *then* $r' \notin \mathcal{R}$, *where* $r' :\rightarrow \neg hd(r)$.

In addition, every literal appears in some rule.

Constraint 3 *For Theory Base* $(\mathcal{L}, \mathcal{R})$, *if* $y \in \mathcal{L}$, *then* $\exists\, r \in \mathcal{R}$, $y \in bd(r) \vee y = hd(r)$.

Finally, every rule has a claim.

Constraint 4 *For Theory Base* $(\mathcal{L}, \mathcal{R})$, *if* $r \in \mathcal{R}$, *then* $\exists\, y \in \mathcal{L}$, $y = hd(r)$.

Semantically, a rule $r \in \mathcal{R}_{str}$ represents the notion that $hd(r)$ holds if *all* of the literals in $bd(r)$ simultaneously hold; with respect to the rule, we say the $bd(r)$ strictly implies the $hd(r)$. We assume standard notions of *truth* and *falsity* of literals along with the truth-tables of Propositional Logic for material implication which are models under which the rule is *true* or *false*. Semantically, a rule $r \in \mathcal{R}_{dfs}$ represents the notion that $hd(r)$ "usually" holds if *all* of the literals in $bd(r)$ simultaneously hold, but there are circumstances where $\neg hd(r)$ holds though *all* of the literals in $bd(r)$ simultaneously hold. With respect to the rule, we say the $bd(r)$ defeasibly implies the $hd(r)$.

While the clauses are similar to the *Horn Clauses* of logic programming, the head literal can be in a positive or negative form. We only have classical negation, not negation as failure; we do not allow iterated negation. The rationale for this choice of clauses is that it naturally supports our analysis of the senses of *argument*.

3.2 Deriving an AF from a Theory Base

A core element of our approach is the concept of the AF derived from a Theory Base. The AF uses a set of labels for the nodes in the graph: $\{x_1,\ldots,x_n\} \cup \{\neg x_1,\ldots,\neg x_n\} \cup \{r_1,\ldots,r_n\}$ (or for clarity, the definite description of the rule name). Thus, we can see how elements of a Theory Base, $\mathcal{T}$, correspond to but are distinct from elements of the derived AF, indexing the AF to the $\mathcal{T}$.

Definition 5. *Let* $\mathcal{T} = (\mathcal{L}, \mathcal{R})$ *be a Theory Base with*

$$\mathcal{L} = \{x_1, \ldots, x_n\} \cup \{\neg x_1, \ldots, \neg x_n\}$$
$$\mathcal{R} = \mathcal{R}_{str} \cup \mathcal{R}_{dfs}$$

The derived framework *from* $\mathcal{T}$, *is the* AF, $\langle \mathcal{L}_{\mathcal{T}}^A, \mathcal{R}_{\mathcal{T}}^A \rangle$ *in which,*

$$\mathcal{L}_{\mathcal{T}}^A = \{ \mathbf{x}, \neg\mathbf{x} : x, \neg x \in \mathcal{L}\}$$
$$\cup \{ r : bd(r) \to hd(r) : r \in \mathcal{R}_{str}\}$$
$$\cup \{ r : bd(r) \Rightarrow hd(r) : r \in \mathcal{R}_{dfs}\}$$

Furthermore,

$$\forall \mathbf{x} \in \mathcal{L}_{\mathcal{T}}^A, x \in \mathcal{L}, \text{ and}$$
$$\forall r \in \mathcal{L}_{\mathcal{T}}^A, r \in \mathcal{R}$$

In an AF, the nodes have no internal content.

The attack set $\mathcal{R}_{\mathcal{T}}^A$ comprises three disjoint sets which describe: attacks by nodes labeled with names for literals on other nodes labeled with names for literals; attacks by nodes labeled with names for literals on nodes labeled with names for rules; and attacks by nodes labeled with names for rules on nodes labeled with names for literals. We recall that $y_i \in \{x_i, \neg x_i\}$ so that $\neg y_i$ is the complementary literal to y_i.

Definition 6. *In the* AF $\langle \mathcal{L}_{\mathcal{T}}^A, \mathcal{R}_{\mathcal{T}}^A \rangle$, $\mathcal{R}_{\mathcal{T}}^A = \mathcal{R}_{ll}^A \cup \mathcal{R}_{lr}^A \cup \mathcal{R}_{rl}^A$ *where:*

$$\mathcal{R}_{ll}^A = \{\langle \mathbf{y}_i, \neg\mathbf{y}_i \rangle, \langle \neg\mathbf{y}_i, \mathbf{y}_i \rangle : 1 \le i \le n$$
$$\text{and } \mathbf{y}_i, \neg\mathbf{y}_i \in \mathcal{L}_{\mathcal{T}}^A\}$$
$$\mathcal{R}_{lr}^A = \{\langle \neg\mathbf{y}_i, r_j \rangle : y_i \in bd(r_j) \text{ and } \neg\mathbf{y}_i, r_j \in \mathcal{L}_{\mathcal{T}}^A\}$$
$$\cup \{\langle \neg\mathbf{y}_i, r_j \rangle : r_j \in \mathcal{R}_{dfs} \text{ and } hd(r_j) = y_i$$
$$\text{and } \neg\mathbf{y}_i \in \mathcal{L}_{\mathcal{T}}^A\}$$
$$\mathcal{R}_{rl}^A = \{\langle r_j, \neg\mathbf{y}_i \rangle : hd(r_j) = y_i \text{ and } \neg\mathbf{y}_i, r_j \in \mathcal{L}_{\mathcal{T}}^A\}$$

The following hold for an AF derived from a $\mathcal{T}$:

1. Each literal y in $\mathcal{L}$ of Theory Base $\mathcal{T}$ corresponds to a node labeled $\mathbf{y}$ in $\mathcal{L}^A$ of the derived AF; $\mathcal{L}^A$ of the derived AF contains, in addition, the node labeled $\neg\mathbf{y}$. Nodes labeled for literals of opposite polarity are mutually attacking.
2. Each rule in r in $\mathcal{R}$ of a Theory Base $\mathcal{T}$ corresponds one-to-one to a node label r in $\mathcal{L}^A$ of the derived AF. Whereas a rule in $\mathcal{R}$ is true (or false) in the Theory Base, in the derived AF we say it *has been applied* relative to the admissible set where it appears and otherwise *has not been applied*. In the AF, a rule node is attacked by the nodes which correspond to the negation of the body literals and, in addition, attacks the node which corresponds to the negation of the head literal.
3. For *strict* rules, if a node which corresponds to the negation of a body literal of a rule is in an admissible set, we say the rule node has not been applied relative to that set. In this case, the node which corresponds to the head literal is only credulously admissible. If all the nodes which correspond to the body literals are in an admissible set, then the rule node has been applied and the node which corresponds to head literal is admissible in that set.

4. For *defeasible* rules, if a node which corresponds to the negation of a body literal or if the node which corresponds to the negation of the head literal of the rule is in an admissible set, we say the rule node has not been applied relative to that set. In both instances, the node corresponding to the literal attacks the rule node. Even if all nodes which correspond to the body literals of a rule are in an admissible set, the rule node or the node which corresponds to the head literal may not be in that set, for they can be defeated.

We evaluate the derived AFs only following the definitions of extensions relative to the standard AF $\langle \mathcal{L}_\mathcal{T}^A, \mathcal{R}_\mathcal{T}^A \rangle$; that is, while the partitions of nodes or arcs are important for deriving the AF from $\mathcal{T}$, they are ignored for the purposes of the standard AF evaluation, so that we have a standard abstract framework. Thus, the fundamental semantics of abstract AFs are maintained.

For our purposes and relative to our classical logic context, the set of extensions provided by Dungian AFs must be *filtered*. In our approach, AFs are derived from a Theory Base, and the resulting extensions are *not* homogeneous, for they may contain both literals and rules. More importantly, we must ensure that the extensions also serve to satisfy classical logic properties such as *closure* under strict implication. With these points in mind, we have the following.

Constraint 5 *Consider: a, an admissible set of the derived AF* $\langle \mathcal{L}_\mathcal{T}^A, \mathcal{R}_\mathcal{T}^A \rangle$; $\mathcal{A}$, *the set of admissible sets a; and* $\mathcal{R}_{str} \subseteq \mathcal{L}_\mathcal{T}^A$. *For every* $r \in \mathcal{R}_{str}$ *and every* $a \in \mathcal{A}$, *if* $r \in a$ *and every* $bd(r) \in a$, *then* $hd(r) \in a$.

Definition 7. *An admissible set of the derived AF* $\langle \mathcal{L}_\mathcal{T}^A, \mathcal{R}_\mathcal{T}^A \rangle$ *is a* Well-formed Admissible Set *(WFAS) iff it satisfies Constraint 5.*

The implication is that relative to WFASs, the hd(r) of a rule r is *sceptically acceptable* relative to the derived AF. On the other hand, for $r' \in \mathcal{R}_{dfs}$, hd(r') is *credulously acceptable* relative to the derived AF. We emphasise that we change nothing about Dungian AFs or evaluations, but we do provide a justification to select amongst the resulting extensions. These points are illustrated with respect to Figure 6.

To this point, we have Theory Bases, corresponding derived AFs, and a constraint on extensions. Fundamental observations of our approach are:

Observation 1 *For the literals and the rules which are* true *of every model for the Theory Base* $\mathcal{T}$, *the corresponding nodes of the WFAS extensions of the derived AF are sceptically acceptable, otherwise they are credulously acceptable.*

Observation 2 *For the literals and the rules which are* false *in any model of a Theory Base* $\mathcal{T}$, *the corresponding nodes of the WFAS extensions of the derived AF* $\langle \mathcal{L}_\mathcal{T}^A, \mathcal{R}_\mathcal{T}^A \rangle$ *are not an element of any admissible set.*

Both of these follow by the evaluation of a derived framework $\langle \mathcal{L}_\mathcal{T}^A, \mathcal{R}_\mathcal{T}^A \rangle$ relative to a $\mathcal{T}$. Thus, the derived AF is *information-preserving* with respect to the Theory Base. The derived AF is an instantiation of the corresponding Theory Base, and the preferred extensions of the AF correspond to models of the Theory Base.

3.3   Examples of the Definitions

We now give some examples of the basic definitions, discuss defeasibility, provide a simple combination of strict and defeasible rules, illustrate reasoning with an assertion in a partial KB, and comment on the connection between the extensions and the classical models. In Section 4, we give a more complex, problematic example from the literature is used to illustrate the advantages of this approach over an ASPIC-type approach. First, we provide a Theory Base $\mathcal{T}_1$ with just one strict rule, the derived AF, a graphic representation of the derived AF, and then the preferred extensions. Since it is always clear in context where we have literals and rules (in a Theory Base) and where we have labels (in an AF), we use one typographic form without confusion.

Example 1. Let $\mathcal{T}_1$ be the pair with $(\mathcal{L}_1, \mathcal{R}_1)$, where

$$\mathcal{L}_1 = \{x_1, x_2\} \cup \{\neg x_1, \neg x_2\}$$
$$\mathcal{R}_1 = \{r_1\}, \ where \ r_1 \ has \ rule \ name \ r_1 : x_1 \rightarrow x_2$$

The *derived framework* from $\mathcal{T}_1$ is $\langle \mathcal{L}_{\mathcal{T}_1}^A, \mathcal{R}_{\mathcal{T}_1}^A \rangle$ in which,

$$\mathcal{L}_{\mathcal{T}_1}^A = \{x_1, x_2\} \cup \{\neg x_1, \neg x_2\} \cup \{r_1\}$$

and in which $\mathcal{R}_{\mathcal{T}_1}^A$ comprises the union of three disjoint sets:

$$\mathcal{R}_{ll}^A = \{\langle x_1, \neg x_1 \rangle, \langle \neg x_1, x_1 \rangle, \langle x_2, \neg x_2 \rangle, \langle \neg x_2, x_2 \rangle\}$$
$$\mathcal{R}_{lr}^A = \{\langle \neg x_1, r_1 \rangle\}$$
$$\mathcal{R}_{rl}^A = \{\langle r_1, \neg x_2 \rangle\}$$

We graphically represent $\langle \mathcal{L}_{\mathcal{T}_1}^A, \mathcal{R}_{\mathcal{T}_1}^A \rangle$ as in Figure 3.

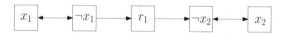

Fig. 3. AF of $x_1 \rightarrow x_2$

In $\langle \mathcal{L}_{\mathcal{T}_1}^A, \mathcal{R}_{\mathcal{T}_1}^A \rangle$, the preferred extensions are:

$$\{x_1, r_1, x_2\}, \{\neg x_1, x_2\}, \{\neg x_1, \neg x_2\}$$

Each of the nodes is *credulously accepted* and none is *sceptically* accepted. The interpretation of the presence of a rule node in a preferred extension is that the rule *has been applied*. Moreover, the rule is not *defeated* in the sense that where the premises hold, the conclusion *must* hold. No admissible set contains both x_1 and $\neg x_2$: if x_1 is in the set, then r_1 is in the set; r_1 attacks $\neg x_2$, leaving x_2 in the set; if $\neg x_2$ is in the set, then r_1 must be attacked; r_1 can only be attacked by $\neg x_1$, which also attacks x_1, leaving $\neg x_1$ in the set.

There are three related points about the extensions. First, we can provide extensions in an AF *with respect to a rule per se*; that is, it is not necessary to provide *asserted* premises along with the rule from which we draw the inferred conclusion. By the same token, we can provide extensions where only some of the premises are asserted, e.g. the KB has partial, incomplete information of what holds. Suppose a Theory Base with only the following two rules: $\rightarrow x_1$ and $r_4:x_1, x_3 \rightarrow x_2$. The extensions are:

$$\{x_1, x_3, r_1, x_2\}, \{x_1, \neg x_3, x_2\}, \{x_1, \neg x_3, \neg x_2\}$$

In this respect, our approach differs markedly from approaches to instantiated AFs that rely on KBs where inferences are essential to the construction of well-formed arguments. Third, we see that the preferred extensions with respect to an AF correlate with the models of the Theory Base; in this respect, the AF and Step 2 of Figure 2 can be viewed as a means to build models for the Theory Base. These three points apply to strict and defeasible rules alike.

The following is an example of a *defeasible* rule.

Example 2. Let $\mathcal{T}_2$ be the pair with $(\mathcal{L}_2, \mathcal{R}_2)$, where

$$\mathcal{L}_2 = \{x_1, x_2\} \cup \{\neg x_1, \neg x_2\}$$
$$\mathcal{R}_2 = \{r_2\}, \text{ where } r_2 \text{ has rule name } r_2:x_1 \Rightarrow x_2$$

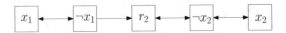

Fig. 4. AF of $x_1 \Rightarrow x_2$

We graphically represent the derived AF $\langle \mathcal{L}_{\mathcal{T}_2}^A, \mathcal{R}_{\mathcal{T}_2}^A \rangle$ as: In $\langle \mathcal{L}_{\mathcal{T}_2}^A, \mathcal{R}_{\mathcal{T}_2}^A \rangle$, the preferred extensions are as follows, where we see that each of the nodes is *credulously accepted* and none is *sceptically* accepted.

$$\{x_1, r_2, x_2\}, \{\neg x_1, x_2\}, \{\neg x_1, \neg x_2\}, \{x_1, \neg x_2\}$$

The first three preferred extensions are similar to SI. In the last extension, $\neg x_2$ itself attacks the rule node r_2; consequently, either x_1 or $\neg x_1$ are in a preferred extension along with $\neg x_2$. This contrasts with the preferred extension of a derived AF with just a SI. While defeasible implication might be construed as the trivial logical tautology $[x_1 \rightarrow [x_2 \vee \neg x_2]]$, here we see a key difference, which highlights the utility of some semantic content to the extensions. To make use of a defeasible rule, one must provide the means to *choose between extensions*, for example, by selecting the extension which maximises the number of applicable defeasible rules, or which uses some notion of priority or entrenchment on the rules. Different ways of making this choice give rise to different varieties of non-monotonic logic [12,13]). Circumscription [14] could be used by including additional designated nodes such as $ab(r_1)$ which attack the rule r_1 and attack and are attacked by $notab(r_1)$. We then choose the extension containing the most $notab(r_1)$ nodes. Using DeLP defeaters [6], we can specify circumstances where the rule is not applied.

In our third example, we show the interaction of defeasible and strict rules, which was the root of several of the problems identified in [3].

Example 3. Suppose $\mathcal{T}_3$ with rules r_2: $x_1 \Rightarrow x_2$ and r_3: $x_2 \rightarrow x_3$ which has derived AF $\langle \mathcal{L}_{\mathcal{T}_3}^A, \mathcal{R}_{\mathcal{T}_3}^A \rangle$ graphically represented as in Figure 5.

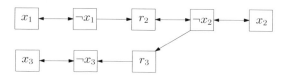

Fig. 5. AF derived from $\mathcal{T}$ with $x_1 \Rightarrow x_2$ and $x_2 \rightarrow x_3$

AF $\langle \mathcal{L}_{\mathcal{T}_3}^A, \mathcal{R}_{\mathcal{T}_3}^A \rangle$ has the following six preferred extensions:

$$1.\{x_1, r_2, x_2, r_3, x_3\} \quad 4.\{\neg x_1, x_2, r_3, x_3\}$$
$$2.\{x_1, \neg x_2, x_3\} \quad\quad 5.\{\neg x_1, \neg x_2, x_3\}$$
$$3.\{x_1, \neg x_2, \neg x_3\} \quad 6.\{\neg x_1, \neg x_2, \neg x_3\}$$

Given a strict assertion that x_1, we would normally choose the preferred extension (1) from among (1)-(3), maximising the number of defeasible rules. Thus, normally, we say that x_1 implies x_3. However, we are not obliged to make this choice. In particular, if $\neg x_2$ is strictly asserted, r_2 and r_3 are inapplicable, and x_3 is credulously acceptable ((2) and (3)); thus, in this AF, a strict assertion of x_1 does not imply that x_3 necessarily holds as well. Where the claim of a defeasible rule is a premise of a strict rule (x_2), we cannot use the defeasibly inferred claim to draw strict inferences about the claim of the strict rule (x_3). Similarly, the defeasible rule is inapplicable where either the claim of the rule ($\neg x_2$) is false ((2), (3), (5), and (6)) or the claim of the strict rule ($\neg x_3$) is false ((3) and (6)). Whereas in e.g. [12], the defeasible rule is inapplicable only where the claim of the defeasible rule itself is asserted to be false, here the falsity of any consequences of that claim, however remote, will also block the application of the rule.

4   Comparison to ASPIC with a Base-Case Example

In this section, we briefly review the key components of the benchmark argument instantiation method of [3,8], compare it to our proposal, provide one of the key examples which showed a flaw in the instantiation method as well as motivated the *Rationality Postulates*. We then show how such problems do not arise in our approach.

In constructing arguments, several functions are introduced: `Prem` is the set of premisese of the argument, `Conc` returns the last conclusion of an argument, `Sub` returns all the subarguments of an argument, `DefRules` returns all the defeasible rules used in an argument, and `TopRule` returns the last inference rule used in the argument. Theory Bases $\mathcal{T}$ are comprised of strict and defeasible implications. Arguments have a deductive form and are constructed recursively from the rules of the Theory Base. To distinguish strict or defeasible rules from the deductive form of arguments, we use *short* arrows, $\rightarrow$ and $\Rightarrow$, for the former and *long* arrows, $\longrightarrow$ and $\Longrightarrow$ for the latter. For brevity, we only provide the clauses for the construction of strict arguments as the clauses for the construction of defeasible arguments are analogous (including among the DefRules the TopRule(A) that is defeasible) [8].

Definition 8. *(Argument) Suppose a* Theory Base, $\mathcal{T}$, *with strict and defeasible rules. An argument* A *is:*
$A_1, \ldots, A_n \longrightarrow \psi$ *if* $A_1, \ldots, A_n$, *with* $n \geq 0$, *are arguments such that there exists a strict rule* $Conc(A_1), \ldots, Conc(A_n) \rightarrow \psi$.
$Prem(A) = Prem(A_1) \cup \ldots \cup Prem(A_n)$,
$Conc(A) = \psi$,
$Sub(A) = Sub(A_1) \cup \ldots \cup Sub(A_n) \cup \{A\}$,
$DefRules(A) = DefRules(A_1) \cup \ldots \cup DefRules(A_n)$
$TopRule(A) = Conc(A_1), \ldots, Conc(A_n) \rightarrow \psi$

Consider a Theory Base with strict and defeasible rules from which we construct arguments according to this definition (see Example 5 [3]).

Example 4. Let $\mathcal{T}_4$ be a Theory Base with the following rules:
$r_{21}: \rightarrow x_1; r_{22}: \rightarrow x_2; r_{23}: \rightarrow x_3; r_{24}: x_4, x_5 \rightarrow \neg x_3; r_{25}: x_1 \Rightarrow x_4; r_{26}: x_2 \Rightarrow x_5$.
We construct the following arguments:
$A_1: [[\rightarrow x_1] \Rightarrow x_4]; A_2: [[\rightarrow x_2] \Rightarrow x_5]; A_3: [\rightarrow x_3]$;
$A_4: [\rightarrow x_1]; A_5: [\rightarrow x_2]$;
$A_6: [[\rightarrow x_1] \Rightarrow x_4], [[\rightarrow x_2] \Rightarrow x_5] \rightarrow \neg x_3$.

We see clearly that arguments can have subarguments: A_6 has a subargument A_1, and A_1 has a subargument A_4.

Several additional elements are needed to define *justified conclusions*. An argument is strict if it has no defeasible subargument, otherwise it is defeasible (non-strict). An argument A_i rebuts an argument A_j where the conclusion of some subargument of A_i is the negation of the conclusion of some non-strict subargument of A_j; rebuttal is one way an argument defeats another argument. Admissible argument orderings specify that a strict argument (containing premises that are axioms and rules that are strict) can defeat a defeasible argument, but not vice versa. Moreover, one argument can defeat another argument with respect to subarguments; in effect, defeat of a part is inherited as defeat of a whole. With respect to our example, the undefeated arguments are A_1, A_2, A_3, A_4, and A_5. A_3, which is a strict argument, defeats A_6 but not vice versa since A_6 is a non-strict argument in virtue of having a defeasible subargument. Given the arguments and defeat relation between them, we can provide an AF and the different extensions. The `Output` of an AF, understood as the *justified conclusions* of the AF, is given as the sceptically accepted conclusions of the arguments of the AF.

With respect to the example, [3] claim that the justified conclusions are x_1, x_2, x_3, x_4, and x_5 since these are all conclusions of arguments which are not attacked (it appears not to be an example analysed in [8]). However, $\neg x_3$ is *not* a justified conclusion, even though it is the conclusion of a strict rule in which all the premises are justified conclusions. This is so since the argument A_6 of which $\neg x_3$ is the conclusion is defeated by but does not defeat A_3 because A_6 has a *subargument* which is a non-strict argument (namely A_1 or A_2), so making A_6 a non-strict argument, while A_3 is a strict argument. Yet, given the antecedents of the strict rule are justified conclusions, it would seem intuitive that the claim of a strict rule should also be a justified conclusion. This, they claim, shows that justified conclusions are not closed under strict rules or could even be inconsistent.

In our view, these notions of argument and defeat are problematic departures from [1], which has no notion of subargument or of defeat in terms of subarguments. In addition, they give rise to the problems with justified conclusions: what is a strict rule in the Theory Base can appear in the AF as a non-strict argument in virtue of subarguments; what cannot be false in the Theory Base without contradiction is defeated in the AF; thus, what "ought" to have been a justified conclusion is not. In addition, the notion of justified conclusion leads to some confusion: on the one hand, it only holds for sceptically accepted arguments, which presumably implies that the propositions which constitute them are sceptically accepted; on the other hand, there is no reason to expect that $\neg x_3$ is sceptically accepted, given that it only follows from defeasible antecedents. Clearly the anomaly arises because of the way that arguments can have defeasible subarguments, that the defeat of the whole can be determined by the defeat of a part, and that justified conclusions depend on these notions.

In our approach, the results are straightforward and without anomaly; we do not make use of arguments with subarguments, inheritance of defeasiblity, or problematic notions of justified conclusions. We consider a key example from [3] as the two other problematic examples cited in [3] follow suit. The Theory Base of Example 4 appears as in Figure 6, for which all the preferred extensions for the AF are given. For clarity and discussion, we include undefeated strict and defeasible rules.

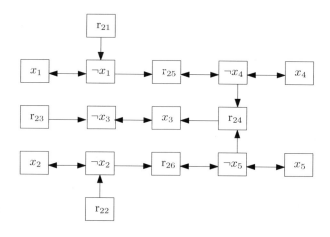

Fig. 6. Graph of Problem Example

$$1. \{x_1, r_{21}, r_{25}, x_2, r_{22}, x_3, x_4, r_{25}, \neg x_5\}$$
$$2. \{x_1, r_{21}, r_{23}, x_2, r_{22}, x_3, \neg x_4, x_5, r_{26}\}$$
$$3. \{x_1, r_{21}, r_{23}, x_2, r_{22}, x_3, \neg x_4, \neg x_5\}$$
$$4. \{x_1, r_{21}, r_{23}, r_{25}, x_2, r_{22}, r_{24}, r_{26}, x_4, x_5\}$$

Notice that extensions (1)-(3) are unproblematic with respect to *consistency* and *closure*. They also satisfy Definition 7, so are the *relevant* extensions to consider. In contrast, extension (4) is problematic in an argumentation theory *without* Definition 7 since the conclusions of strict rules are missing, thus violating *closure*. Yet, (4) does not satisfy Constraint 5: the premises and rule nodes of strict rules are present, but the conclusions are not. With respect to those extensions that satisfy Definition 7, x_1, x_2, x_3 are all sceptically accepted, while x_4 and x_5 are credulously accepted. $\neg x_3$ is not credulously accepted given that x_3 is strictly asserted. Note that every literal which is strictly asserted is sceptically acceptable. Therefore, the rule node r_{24} must be defeated where one or both of $\neg x_4$ and $\neg x_5$ hold. There is, in our view, no reason to expect $\neg x_3$ to hold in any extension since we have no preferred extension in which both x_4 and x_5 are justified conclusions. Given admissible sets, we satisfy the *consistency* rationality postulate; *closure*, which is relevant only of strict rules where all the body literals hold, is not relevant to this problem. Moreover, we can provide machinery to meet Definition 7 in that we can examine the extensions relative to the rules of the AF to determine if Constraint 5 is satisfied. The analysis also corresponds well with model-building for classical logic.

We have considered a widely adopted approach to instantiating Theory Bases in AFs [8] along with the problems that arise. There are other approaches to instantiating a KB in an AF that may avoid problems with the Rationality Postulates such as Assumption-based [2] or Logic-based [7] argumentation. We leave further comparison and contrast to future work. However, these approaches, like the ASPIC approach, follow the three step structure of Figure 1.

5   Three Senses of Argument

In this section, we discuss the auxiliary point about the various conflated *senses* of the term *argument* as found in the literature. We show how these senses can be formally articulated in our framework as distinct structures [4] . The term *argument* is ambiguous [11]. It can mean the reasons for a claim given in one step (an *Argument*); or it can mean a train of reasoning leading towards a claim (a *Case*), that is, a set of linked *Arguments*; or it can be taken as reasons for and against a claim (a *Debate*), that is, a *Case* for the claim and a *Case* against the claim. An additional structure is where the intermediate claims of the *Debate* are also points of dispute, but we will not consider this further here. In the following, we formally define these three senses of *argument* as structures in the argumentation framework, starting with *Arguments*, then providing *Cases*, and finally *Debates*. We provide a graphic, examples, and then definitions for the three different kinds of attack: *Rebuttal*, *Undercut*, and *Premise Defeat*.

We provide a recursive, pointwise definition of a graph which is constructed relative to an AF. Since the sets are constructed relative to an AF, we can infer the attack relations which hold among them. The different senses of *argument* are defined as subgraphs.

Definition 9. *Suppose there is a derived* AF $= \langle \mathcal{L}^A, \mathcal{R}^A \rangle$, *where y and z are arbitrary literals from* $\mathcal{L}^A$ *and r and r' are arbitrary rules from* $\mathcal{L}^A$. $\mathcal{F}$ *abbreviates* $\{r : r$ *added in* $\rho_{2k-1}\}$.

$$
\begin{aligned}
\rho_0(y) &= \{y, \neg y\} \\
\rho_1(y) &= \rho_0(y) \cup \bigcup_{\{r: hd(r)=y\}} \{r\} \\
\rho_{2k}(y) &= \rho_{2k-1}(y) \cup \bigcup_{\{r \in \mathcal{F}\}} \{z, \neg z : z \in bd(r)\} \\
\rho_{2k+1}(y) &= \rho_{2k}(y) \cup \bigcup_{\{r \in \mathcal{F}\}} \{r' : z \in hd(r') \cap bd(r)\} \\
\rho_{2k+2}(y) &= \rho_k(y)
\end{aligned}
$$

$\rho_0(y)$ provides the basis for the construction, which are nodes labeled by literals in an AF that attack one another with respect to the node labeled y. At $\rho_1(y)$, we add to the previous set of rules which have y as their head; depending on whether we have a strict or a defeasible rule, the rule node attacks and may be attacked by the literal which is the negation of the head. At $\rho_{2k}(y)$, we add the positive and negative literals relative to the body of the rules; each of the negative literals associated with literals of the body of the rule attacks the rule node. At $\rho_{2k+1}(y)$, we link rules: the literals in the body of a rule added at $\rho_1(y)$ serve as the heads of other rules. At $\rho_{2k+2}(y)$, we have iterated the steps $\rho_1(y)$-$\rho_{2k+1}(y)$ until there is no further change. Constructions for negations of literals are similarly defined.

Supposing a derived AF, Arg_{S1} and Arg_{S2} are subgraphs of that AF. An *Argument for y*, $Arg_{S1}(y)$, is defined at $\rho_{2k}(y)$: it is the nodes and their attacks defined at this step relative to the derived AF. A graph defined as $Arg_{S1}(y)$ can *only have one rule in the set of nodes*, namely a rule of the Theory Base with y as head (other rules with y as head will give rise to distinct arguments for y in sense 1). In $Arg_{S1}(y)$, y is the *claim* of $Arg_{S1}(y)$ and the literals in the body of the rule are the *premises*. A *Case for y*, $Arg_{S2}(y)$, is defined where $\rho_{k+1}(y) = \rho_k(y)$. $Arg_{S2}(y)$ is comprised of $Arg_{S1}(y)$ along with graphs of form Arg_{S1} for the literals that are bodies of every rule constructed relative to $Arg_{S1}(y)$. In other words, a Case links together all those graphs of Arguments for a particular y where the claim of one rule is the premise of another rule.

Definition 10. *Suppose an* AF *derived from Theory Base* $\mathcal{T}$, $\langle \mathcal{L}_{\mathcal{T}}^A, \mathcal{R}_{\mathcal{T}}^A \rangle$. *We define* Arg_{S1}-Arg_{S2} *as subgraphs of a derived* AF:

An Argument for y is $Arg_{S1}(y) = \langle \mathcal{L}_{S_1y}^A, \mathcal{R}_{S_1y}^A \rangle$,
where $\mathcal{L}_{S_1y}^A \subseteq \mathcal{L}_{\mathcal{T}}^A$ *and* $\mathcal{R}_{S_1y}^A \subseteq \mathcal{R}_{\mathcal{T}}^A$,
$\forall r, r' \in \mathcal{L}_{S_1y}^A \ r = r'$, *is a subgraph at* $\rho_{2k}(y)$.

A Case for y is $Arg_{S2}(y) = \langle \mathcal{L}_{S_2y}^A, \mathcal{R}_{S_2y}^A \rangle$,
where $\mathcal{L}_{S_2y}^A \subseteq \mathcal{L}_{\mathcal{T}}^A$ *and* $\mathcal{R}_{S_2y}^A \subseteq \mathcal{R}_{\mathcal{T}}^A$, *is a subgraph*
at $\rho_{k+1}(y) = rho_k(y)$.

Where we have $Arg_{S2}(y)$ and $Arg_{S2}(\neg y)$, we have a *Single-point Debate about y*, $Arg_{S3}(y)$. The two graphs share only the literals $\{y, \neg y\}$, and no other rules or literals.

Definition 11. *Suppose two derived* AFs, $Arg_{S2}(y) = \langle \mathcal{L}^A_{S_2\neg y}, \mathcal{R}^A_{S_2\neg y} \rangle$ *and* $Arg_{S2}(y) =$ $\langle \mathcal{L}^A_{S_2 y}, \mathcal{R}^A_{S_2 y} \rangle$:

$$A\ Single - point\ Debate\ about\ y\ is$$
$$Arg_{S3}(y) = \langle \mathcal{L}^A_{S_2 y} \cup \mathcal{L}^A_{S_2\neg y}, \mathcal{R}^A_{S_2 y} \cup \mathcal{R}^A_{S_2\neg y} \rangle,$$
$$where\ \mathcal{L}^A_{S_2\neg y} \cap \mathcal{L}^A_{S_2 y} = \{y, \neg y\}$$
$$and\ \mathcal{R}^A_{S_2\neg y} \cap \mathcal{R}^A_{S_2 y} = \emptyset.$$

Clearly a debate with subsidiary debates can be constructed to argue pro and con about other literals in the base debate; we start with a $Arg_{S2}(y)$, then add further *Single-point Debates* about some literal in the graph other than y.

Example 5 shows the senses in a derived AF only with SI rules since they restrict the available preferred extensions.

Example 5. Suppose a Theory Base comprised of the rules (and related literals): r_7 : $x_6 \rightarrow \neg x_8, r_{10} : x_5, x_7 \rightarrow x_8, r_{11} : \neg x_3, x_4 \rightarrow x_7$. Figure 7 graphically represents the various senses of *argument* in an AF derived from this Theory Base.

In Figure 7, we have three subgraphs which represent an Argument; each Argument is derived from the corresponding rule of the Theory Base. For example $Arg_{S1}(\neg x_8)$, the argument for $\neg x_8$, is the graph comprised of nodes $\{\neg x_8, x_8, r_7, \neg x_6, x_6\}$ with the relations among them as given; the graph is derived from the rule of the Theory Base which corresponds to $r_7 : x_6 \rightarrow \neg x_8$. The other two rules of the Theory Base are also represented in the graph as subgraphs that represent an Argument. Figure 7 presents two Cases. The Case $Arg_{S2}(x_8)$ is derived from the following rules: r_{10} : $x_5, x_7 \rightarrow x_8, r_{11} : \neg x_3, x_4 \rightarrow x_7$. We see how the Arguments in the Case are linked; for instance, the graph of $r_{11} : \neg x_3, x_4 \rightarrow x_7$ has as claim x_7, which is the premise of $r_{10} : x_5, x_7 \rightarrow x_8$. The Case $Arg_{S2}(\neg x_8)$ is derived from the following rule (recall that an Argument can also be a Case): $r_7 : x_6 \rightarrow \neg x_8$. The Single-point Debate for x_8, $Arg_{S3}(x_8)$, is comprised of the Cases $Arg_{S2}(x_8)$ and $Arg_{S2}(\neg x_8)$.

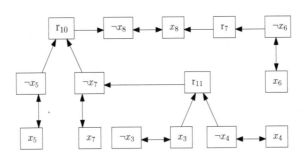

Fig. 7. Arguments, Cases, and Single-point Debates

In [4], there are some auxiliary definitions for *rebuttal, premise defeat,* and *undercutting* in this framework. However, space precludes presenting them here.

6 Concluding Remarks and Future Work

We have discussed in some detail comparison on one developed approach to argument instantiation [8] and noted other that remain to be compared in depth [7,2] though they share substantive similarities in terms of the Three Steps of Figure 1. Here we comment briefly on the somewhat different approach of *Abstract Dialectical Frameworks* (ADF) [9], which is presented as a generalisation of Dungian AFs but also as a means to represent instantiated arguments, e.g. logic programs [9]. Broadly, we may distinguish between approaches based on [1] that make use of nodes (arguments) and arcs (attacks) alone to determine extensions and those which use *auxiliary conditions to specify extensions with respect to successful attacks* such as preferences [8] or values [15]. The approach of [9] is a generalisation of the latter approach: in addition to nodes (which can be statements or literals) and links (generalised from arcs as attacks), there are acceptance conditions, which are functions for each statement from its parents (those nodes in a single link) to {*in,out*}. Given this generic approach to acceptance conditions, many complex aspects of argumentation can be accommodated. On the other hand, this emphasises reasoning with the (presumably correct) acceptance conditions rather than on the graph per se, which was one of the main advantages of the Dungian abstraction. For example, ADF remains to demonstrate that it abides by the Rationality Postulates or can generically reconstruct KBs. It adds the complexity of the acceptance conditions to the existing complexity of the graph [9]. On the other hand, our approach is compatible with ADF in the sense that given an AF derived from a KB, we can add auxiliary ADF acceptance conditions for other aspects of reasoning. In future, we plan to examine the advantages and disadvantages of the more specific approach to KB representation proposed here in comparsion with the more generic appoach of [9].

We have presented a method of instantiating a Theory Base which contains strict and defeasible rules in a Dung-style abstract argumentation framework, building on and refining [4]. The Theory Base is directly represented in the framework, and the conclusions of the Theory Base can be computed as extensions of that framework. Our method avoids the logic dependent step of generating arguments from the Theory Base and then organising them in a framework for evaluation. It does not introduce preferences or auxiliary means to determine successful arguments. The sceptically acceptable arguments of the framework are the consequences of the Theory Base under classical logic, assuming that the Theory Base is consistent: the consequences under a variety of non-monotonic logics can be identified as credulously acceptable arguments, with different non-monotonic logics corresponding to different ways of choosing between preferred extensions. We believe that this method provides a very clear way of instantiating Theory Bases as abstract argumentation frameworks. By separating the notion of a node from the ambiguous notion of argument, we have clear criteria for what constitutes a node in the framework. We can explain our reasoning in terms of arguments of the appropriate granularity. In addition, the variety of senses of "argument" emerge as structures within the framework, and can be used to explain the consequences.

In future work we will demonstrate the formal properties of our approach. In addition, we will further compare and contrast approaches to Theory Base instantiation in AFs. An important avenue of exploration and development is to add values, preferences, and weights to the KB, which then appear in the graph. In a different vein, we will explore the potential for improved explanation offered by our distinction between various senses of the term "argument".

References

1. Dung, P.M.: On the acceptability of arguments and its fundamental role in nonmonotonic reasoning, logic programming and n-person games. Artificial Intelligence 77(2), 321–358 (1995)
2. Bondarenko, A., Dung, P.M., Kowalski, R.A., Toni, F.: An abstract, argumentation-theoretic approach to default reasoning. Artificial Intelligence 93, 63–101 (1997)
3. Caminada, M., Amgoud, L.: On the evaluation of argumentation formalisms. Artificial Intelligence 171(5-6), 286–310 (2007)
4. Wyner, A., Bench-Capon, T., Dunne, P.: Instantiating knowledge bases in abstract argumentation frameworks. In: Proceedings of the Uses of Computational Argumentation, AAAI Fall Symposium (2009)
5. Dunne, P.E., Bench-Capon, T.J.M.: Coherence in finite argument systems. Artificial Intelligence 141(1), 187–203 (2002)
6. García, A.J., Simari, G.R.: Defeasible logic programming: An argumentative approach. Theory and Practice of Logic Programming 4(1), 95–137 (2004)
7. Besnard, P., Hunter, A.: Elements of Argumentation. MIT Press (2008)
8. Prakken, H.: An abstract framework for argumentation with structured arguments. Argument and Computation 1(2), 93–124 (2010)
9. Brewka, G., Woltran, S.: Abstract dialectical frameworks. In: Proceedings of the Twelfth International Conference on the Principles of Knowledge Represetnation and Reasoning (KR 2010), pp. 102–211 (2010)
10. Caminada, M., Wu, Y.: On the limitations of abstract argumentation. In: Causmaecker, P.D., Maervoet, J., Messelis, T., Verbeeck, K., Vermeulen, T. (eds.) Proceedings of the 23rd Benelux Conference on Artificial Intelligence, Ghent, Belgium, pp. 59–66 (November 2011)
11. Wyner, A.Z., Bench-Capon, T.J.M., Atkinson, K.: Three senses of "Argument". In: Casanovas, P., Sartor, G., Casellas, N., Rubino, R. (eds.) Computable Models of the Law. LNCS (LNAI), vol. 4884, pp. 146–161. Springer, Heidelberg (2008)
12. Reiter, R.: A logic for default reasoning. Artificial Intelligence 13(1-2), 81–132 (1980)
13. Prakken, H., Sartor, G.: Argument-based extended logic programming with defeasible priorities. Journal of Applied Non-Classical Logics 7(1) (1997)
14. McCarthy, J.: Circumscription - a form of non-monotonic reasoning. Artificial Intelligence 13, 27–39 (1980)
15. Bench-Capon, T.J.M.: Persuasion in practical argument using value-based argumentation frameworks. Journal of Logic and Computation 13(3), 429–448 (2003)

Rewriting Rules for the Computation of Goal-Oriented Changes in an Argumentation System

Dionysios Kontarinis[1], Elise Bonzon[1], Nicolas Maudet[2], Alan Perotti[3],
Leon van der Torre[4], and Serena Villata[5]

[1] LIPADE, Université Paris Descartes
{dionysios.kontarinis,elise.bonzon}@parisdescartes.fr
[2] LIP6, Université Pierre et Marie Curie
nicolas.maudet@lip6.fr
[3] Turin University
perotti@di.unito.it
[4] University of Luxembourg
leon.vandertorre@uni.lu
[5] INRIA, Sophia Antipolis
serena.villata@inria.fr

Abstract. When several agents are engaged in an argumentation process, they are faced with the problem of deciding how to contribute to the current state of the debate in order to satisfy their own goal, ie. to make an argument under a given semantics accepted or not. In this paper, we study the minimal changes (or target sets) on the current state of the debate that are required to achieve such a goal, where changes are the addition and/or deletion of attacks among arguments. We study some properties of these target sets, and propose a Maude specification of rewriting rules which allow to compute all the target sets for some types of goals.

1 Introduction

Debates are pursued with the aim to obtain at the end a set of *accepted arguments*. As in [1–3], we assume that such debates are represented by a central, dynamic argumentation system which is modified by the agents' locutions. During these debates, each agent tries to argue in such a way that his own *argumentative goals* belong to the final set of accepted arguments in the central system. Given the number of participants and of proposed arguments, it is a challenging task to identify the part of the debate to focus on and to compute possible modifications which can affect the current state of the debate, in order to achieve a given argumentative goal.

We assume in this work, as it is done in [1–3], that the participating agents may disagree on the existence of binary attacks between some pairs of arguments. But what can cause such a disagreement? First, in the framework of value-based argumentation [4], a *defeat* relation between two arguments holds if there is a conflict between those arguments, and if the value promoted by the attacking argument is higher than the value promoted by the other argument. Therefore, if two agents order these values differently, they may disagree on the existence of this defeat relation. A similar type of reasoning

J. Leite et al. (Eds.): CLIMA XIV, LNAI 8143, pp. 51–68, 2013.

is applied in preference-based argumentation [5]. Second, a usual phenomenon in everyday argumentation is the disagreement on the existence of a conflict between some pairs of arguments. Often, the claim of an argument does not explicitly contradict one of the premises of another argument (nor its claim), but it may still be considered that it is attacking the latter. This is due to the use of enthymemes (arguments whose internal structures are not fully defined), as stated in [6].

In this work, for the sake of simplicity, we consider that the set of arguments and some attacks between those arguments are fixed in the debate. This can be done, for example, as follows. In the first phase of the debate, agents (following a given protocol) put forward all the arguments and attacks they consider relevant to the subject of the debate. Then follows a voting phase on the arguments and attacks which have been proposed by the agents. Afterwards, we assume, as it is done in [2], that all the arguments approved by a majority (for example) of agents are fixed and considered in the debate, as well as all the attacks on which a quasi-unanimity of agents have agreed. From that point on, the debate focuses on the attacks which have caused disagreement among the agents.

In our context, a *move* modifies the current state of the debate by either adding or removing attacks. A *successful move* brings about the acceptance or rejection of a particular argumentative goal, that is, ensures that a designated argument belongs (or not) to some (all) extension(s). Here we shall focus on (subset-)minimal successful moves, called *target sets* [7].

We acknowledge that, in some cases, focusing on minimal change may not be the best strategy for a debating agent. For example, if an agent is uncertain whether he will be able to assert additional moves during the debate, then it may be preferable for him to assert all the moves he can, as soon as possible. Also, if we consider a framework where the agents' personal beliefs are dynamic, a non-minimal move by an agent may be preferable for him, if it provokes some wished changes to the beliefs of the other agents. However, we believe that minimality is a useful notion in the study of argumentation dynamics. An agent may be motivated to find a minimal change satisfying his goal, because this would be the easiest, fastest way to do it. Moreover, it can be a good strategy for agents in a debate, as it minimizes their commitments.

Our first contribution in this paper is to provide some general properties of such (minimal) successful moves. We then put forward a set of rewriting rules for the Maude system [8], which exploit the recent attack semantics of [9] to compute target sets, and provide some properties of the resulting procedure.

Our work is inspired by proof theories for abstract argumentation frameworks, as in the work of [10], which treat the problem of how to prove the acceptance (or non-acceptance) of an argument under some semantics. The main new elements introduced here are the following. First, we consider dynamic systems where (several) attacks can be added and removed. Second, we focus on minimal change required to achieve acceptance (or non-acceptance) of an argument and we analyze the properties of minimal change.

Recently, the question of the *dynamics of argumentation systems* has been studied by several authors [11–15]. Baumann [14] studies different types of *expansions*, that is, different ways to modify the current system. For instance the most general kind, *arbitrary modifications*, allows the addition of new arguments, as well as the addition/removal of attacks. Formally, the problem studied is as follows: given a current argumentation system (AS), given a "goal set" E, find a minimal expansion such that E belongs to at least one extension of the modified AS. The notion of minimality differs from ours, since it relies on a pseudometric measuring the distance (in terms of number of differences between AS). Another key difference is that our modifications are typically constrained, and also restricted to adding/removing attacks. Most importantly, our work focuses on the design of a procedure which returns the target sets in a given situation. The recent work of [16, 17] is also closely related. They share with us the view that the possible modifications of the system may be constrained, and also investigate practical computation techniques to enforce argumentative goals. In theory, their model caters for *sequences* of basic modifications of the system (and allows addition and removal of arguments as well). One important difference is that they do not focus on minimal changes. In practice, they design a tool which relies on characterization results for the dynamics of argumentation systems studied in [16]. The current implementation is restricted to single modifications [17].

The paper is organized as follows. Section 2 provides some basic background on abstract argumentation theory [18] and the notion of acceptability. Section 3 formalizes the notions of *successful moves* and of *target sets*, and highlights some important properties that they exhibit. In Section 4 we give the specification of rewriting rules to be used with the Maude system. We study some key properties that can (or cannot) be guaranteed with our approach. Finally, Section 5 concludes.

2 Background

In this section, we provide the basic concepts of abstract argumentation frameworks, as proposed by Dung [18], in which the exact content of arguments is left unspecified. In the definition of argumentation system we provide here, the difference compared to [18] is that we do not only have the standard attack relation (here denoted R), but we also have a relation R^+ which denotes the attacks which can be added to the system, and a relation R^- which denotes the attacks which can be removed from the system.

Definition 1. *We define an* **argumentation system** *as a tuple* $AS = \langle A, R, R^+, R^- \rangle$, *where A is a finite set of arguments, $R \subseteq A \times A$ is a binary attack relation between arguments, $R^+ \subseteq A \times A$, with $R^+ \cap R = \{\}$, contains the pairs of arguments which can be added in R, and $R^- \subseteq R$ contains the pairs of arguments which can be removed from R.*

As stated in the introduction, we assume that the arguments of such a system have been fixed on a previous phase where the agents have put forward the arguments they thought were pertinent for the debate, and have then voted on the arguments. Moreover, attacks in $R \setminus R^-$ are supposed to be attacks on which a quasi unanimity of agents have agreed (these attacks are not questioned anymore), whereas the validity of attacks in R^+ and R^- is still debated. For convenience, we will denote $At = R \cup R^+$ the set of attacks which are either on the system, or can be added to it. Note that we will only consider systems having a finite number of arguments, so $|A|$ is finite.

From now on, we will focus on the attack relations more than on the arguments. We will then need the following definition.

Definition 2. *Let $AS = \langle A, R, R^+, R^- \rangle$, and $x = (a,b) \in At$. We refer to the argument a as the* **tail of the attack** *x, denoted by $tail(x) = a$, and we refer to the argument b as the* **head of the attack** *x, denoted by $head(x) = b$.*
Let $x, y \in At$. We will say that x **hits** *y, denoted by $hits(x,y)$, if $head(x) = tail(y)$.*

Example 1. Let $AS = \langle A, R, R^+, R^- \rangle$ be an argumentation system such that $A = \{a,b,c,d,e\}, R = \{(a,b),(b,a),(c,d),(e,d)\}, R^+ = \{(a,c),(b,c)\}, R^- = \{(c,d),(e,d)\}$. This system can be represented as follows:

Non-removable attacks are represented by thick arrows, removable attacks by simple arrows, and addable attacks by dotted arrows. For the sake of convenience, we will denote an attack $(a,b) \in At$ simply as ab. We have that $tail(ba) = b$, $head(ba) = a$ and also $hits(ab, ba)$, as well as $hits(ba, ab)$.

In Dung's framework, the *acceptability of an argument* depends on its membership to some sets, called extensions.

Definition 3. *Let $AS = \langle A, R, R^+, R^- \rangle$ and $C \subseteq A$. The set C is* **conflict-free** *iff $\nexists x \in R$ such that $tail(x) \in C$ and $head(x) \in C$. An argument $a \in A$ is* **acceptable w.r.t.** *C iff $\forall x \in R$: if $head(x) = a$, then $\exists y \in R$ such that $hits(y,x)$ and $tail(y) \in C$.*

Several types of extensions have been defined by Dung [18].

Definition 4. *Let $C \subseteq A$ be conflict-free. C is an* **admissible extension** *iff each argument of C is acceptable w.r.t. C. C is a* **preferred extension** *iff it is a maximal (w.r.t. $\subseteq$) admissible extension. C is a* **complete extension** *iff every argument in C is acceptable w.r.t. C, and $\forall x \in A$: if x is acceptable w.r.t. C, then $x \in C$. C is a* **grounded extension** *iff it is the minimal (w.r.t. $\subseteq$) complete extension. Admissible, preferred, complete and grounded semantics are from now on denoted Adm, Pref, Comp and Gr, respectively.*

The next question is to decide, given a semantics, which arguments are acceptable.

Definition 5. *Let $AS = \langle A, R, R^+, R^- \rangle$ and $a \in A$. Argument a is said* **credulously accepted** *w.r.t. system AS under semantics $S \in \{Adm, Pref, Comp, Gr\}$, denoted $S_\exists(a, AS)$, iff a belongs to at least one extension of AS under the S semantics. Argument a is said* **sceptically accepted** *w.r.t. AS under semantics $S \in \{Adm, Pref, Comp, Gr\}$, denoted $S_\forall(a, AS)$, iff a belongs to all the extensions of AS under the S semantics.*

As $\{\}$ is always an admissible extension, $Adm_\forall(a, AS)$ does not hold for any $a \in A$. So, sceptical acceptability under admissible semantics is not an interesting notion, and we will not refer to it anymore. As there always exists a unique grounded extension, there is no difference between credulous and sceptical acceptability for grounded semantics. If $a \in A$ is accepted under the grounded semantics, we simply denote this by $Gr(a, AS)$. Moreover, as stated in [18], an argument $a \in A$ belongs to the grounded extension if and only if it is sceptically accepted under the complete semantics (thus,

$Gr(a,AS) \Leftrightarrow Comp_\forall(a,AS))$. We will use this latter notation to refer to the grounded extension.

In the rest of the paper, we will denote by $Sem = \{Adm, Pref, Comp\}$ the set of admissible, preferred and complete semantics. Moreover, for the sake of readability, if there is no danger of confusing which argumentation system we refer to, we will simply write $\forall S \in Sem$, $S_\exists(a)$, or $S_\forall(a)$, without mentioning the AS.

The following property states that the set of arguments credulously accepted under the admissible semantics are the same as those accepted under the preferred, or the complete semantics.

Property 1. [18] Let $AS = \langle A, R, R^+, R^- \rangle$ be an argumentation system, and $a \in A$. It holds that $Adm_\exists(a,AS) \Leftrightarrow Pref_\exists(a,AS) \Leftrightarrow Comp_\exists(a,AS)$.

The case of sceptical acceptability is a bit different. Every argument sceptically accepted under complete semantics is also sceptically accepted under preferred semantics, but the inverse does not hold in the general case.

Property 2. [18] Let $AS = \langle A, R, R^+, R^- \rangle$ be an argumentation system, and $a \in A$. It holds that $Comp_\forall(a,AS) \Rightarrow Pref_\forall(a,AS)$. The inverse does not necessarily hold.

As we have just seen, Dung's semantics [18] are stated in terms of sets of arguments, but it is also possible to express them using argument *labeling* [19, 20]. Roughly, an argument is *in* if all its attackers are *out*, it is *out* if it has at least an attacker *in*, otherwise it is *undec*. Villata et al. [9] introduce *attack semantics* where arguments are accepted when there are no *successful* attacks on them. An attack x is '1' when $tail(x)$ is *in*, '?' when $tail(x)$ is *undec*, and '0' when $tail(x)$ is *out*. An attack is called *successful* when it is '1' or '?', and *unsuccessful* when it is '0'.

Example 2. Let $AS = \langle A, R, R^+, R^- \rangle$ be an argumentation system, with $A = \{a,b,c\}$, $R = \{(a,b), (b,c), (c,b)\}$, $R^+ = R^- = \{\}$.

In argument semantics, an extension for a semantics $S \in Sem$ contains a and c. Thus, b is rejected (*out*) whereas a and c are accepted (*in*). In attack semantics, the attacks $(a,b) \in R$ and $(c,b) \in R$ are successful, whereas $(b,c) \in R$ is unsuccessful.

Boella et al. [7] propose a new kind of labelling, called *conditional labelling*. The idea is to provide the agents with a way to discover the arguments they should attack to get a particular argument accepted or rejected. Given a conditional labelling, the agents have complete knowledge about the consequences of the attacks they may raise on the acceptability of each argument without having to recompute the labelling for each possible set of attacks they may raise.

3   Argumentative Goals and Target Sets

In this work, we consider that attacks are the core components of an argumentation system and thus prefer to commit to the attack semantics. As said before, we assume that the arguments of a system cannot change (neither new arguments can be added, nor arguments can be removed). Instead, we consider that the only change that can happen is the addition of new attacks and the removal of some attacks already in the system. A central notion, related to this type of change, is the following notion of atom.

Definition 6. *Let $AS = \langle A, R, R^+, R^- \rangle$ be an argumentation system, $x \in At = R \cup R^+$ be an attack, and $d \in A$ be an argument. An **atom** of AS is defined as follows:*

$$Atom(AS) ::= \top \mid \perp \mid (x,+,\#) \mid (x,-,\#) \mid (x,1,\#) \mid (x,0,\#) \mid (x,?,\#) \mid$$
$$(x,1,*) \mid (x,0,*) \mid (x,?,**) \mid (x,?,*) \mid PRO(d) \mid CON(d)$$

*Atoms $\top$, $\perp$, $(x,+,\#)$, $(x,-,\#)$, $(x,1,\#)$, $(x,0,\#)$ and $(x,?,\#)$ are called **closed atoms**, whereas atoms $(x,1,*)$, $(x,0,*)$, $(x,?,**)$, $(x,?,*)$, PRO(d) and CON(d) are called **open atoms**.*

The atom $(x,+,\#)$ (resp. $(x,-,\#)$) indicates the action of adding (resp. removing) the attack x from the system. The atom $(x,1,*)$ (resp. $(x,?,*)$, resp. $(x,0,*)$) indicates that we must find a way for attack x to become '1' (resp. '?', resp. '0'). [1] On the other hand, the atom $(x,1,\#)$ (resp. $(x,?,\#)$, resp. $(x,0,\#)$), indicates that we have already found a way for attack x to become '1' (resp. '?', resp. '0'). PRO(d) and CON(d) are two specific atoms regarding the acceptability status of d. Their exact meaning will be explained later. Finally, the atom $\perp$ indicates failure, whereas $\top$ indicates success.

By using the atoms $(x,+,\#)$ and $(x,-,\#)$, we define the notion of move on a system:

Definition 7. *Let $AS = \langle A, R, R^+, R^- \rangle$ and $m = \{(x,s,\#) \mid x \in At, s \in \{+,-\}\}$ be a set of atoms. m is called **move** on AS iff $\forall (x,+,\#) \in m$, $x \in R^+$, and $\forall (x,-,\#) \in m$, $x \in R^-$. The **resulting system** of playing move m on AS is the argumentation system $\Delta(AS,m) = \langle A, R_m, R_m^+, R_m^- \rangle$, such that: (1) $x \in R_m$ iff either $x \in R$ and $(x,-,\#) \notin m$, or $(x,+,\#) \in m$. (2) $x \in R_m^+$ iff either $x \in R^+$ and $(x,+,\#) \notin m$, or $(x,-,\#) \in m$. (3) $x \in R_m^-$ iff either $x \in R^-$ and $(x,-,\#) \notin m$, or $(x,+,\#) \in m$.*

Example 1, cont. The move $m = \{(ed,-,\#),(ac,+,\#)\}$ on AS will lead to the following system $\Delta(AS,m)$:

If we are able to play a move on $AS = \langle A, R, R^+, R^- \rangle$, we may be motivated to play it by the desire to satisfy a specific goal. Let us formally define this notion of goal.

Definition 8. *Let Systems be a set of argumentation systems, and Props be a set of properties, such that each property can refer to any $AS \in Systems$. We define the function $f: Props \times Systems \to \{true, false\}$, such that $\forall P \in Props, \forall AS \in Systems$, it holds that $f(P,AS) = true$ iff P, when referring to AS, holds; otherwise $f(P,AS) = false$. A property P may be chosen as a **positive goal**: we say that goal P is satisfied in AS iff $f(P,AS) = true$. A negated property $\neg P$ may be chosen as a **negative goal**: we say that goal $\neg P$ is satisfied in AS iff $f(P,AS) = false$ (that is iff $f(\neg P,AS) = true$).*

---

[1] The atom $(x,?,**)$ is similar to $(x,?,*)$, their difference is explained later.

If a specific (positive or negative) goal is not satisfied in AS, then we search for possible moves m on AS leading to a modified system $\Delta(AS,m)$ in which that goal is satisfied. Any move on AS which achieves this is called a *successful move*. Such a succesful move is called a *target set* if the changes induced by it on AS are minimal.

Definition 9. *Let $AS = \langle A, R, R^+, R^- \rangle$, and Props be a set of properties. Let m be a move on AS, $P \in Props$, and g be a goal, that is P or $\neg P$. m is called* **successful move for goal** *g iff goal g is satisfied in $\Delta(AS,m)$, that is if $f(g, \Delta(AS,m)) = true$. m is called* **target set for goal** *g iff m is minimal w.r.t. $\subseteq$ among all the successful moves for g.*

Let us now describe the types of goals that we focus on. Let $AS = \langle A, R, R^+, R^- \rangle$, m be a move on AS, $X \in \{\exists, \forall\}$ and $S \in Sem$. We focus on the acceptance of a single argument $d \in A$ called the *issue*, and we consider these two types of goals: (1) $S_X(d)$ is a positive goal, with $\mathbb{M}_X^S = \{m \mid S_X(d)$ is satisfied in $\Delta(AS,m)\}$. (2) $\neg S_X(d)$ is a negative goal, with $\mathbb{M}_{\neg X}^S = \{m \mid \neg S_X(d)$ is satisfied in $\Delta(AS,m)\}$.

Example 1, cont. Let $d \in A$ be the issue.
d does not belong to any admissible extension of AS. The goal $S_\exists(d)$ consisting in placing d in some admissible (or preferred, or complete) extension has three target sets: $\mathbb{T}_\exists^S = \{\{(ed, -, \#), (cd, -, \#)\}, \{(ed, -, \#), (ac, +, \#)\}, \{(ed, -, \#), (bc, +, \#)\}\}$. Moreover, we have $\{(ed, -, \#), (bc, +, \#), (ac, +, \#)\} \in \mathbb{M}_\exists^S$: this move is successful for $S_\exists(d)$, but it is not a target set, as it is not minimal. Now, regarding sceptical preferred semantics, it holds that $\mathbb{T}_\forall^{Pref} = \{\{(ed, -, \#), (cd, -, \#)\}, \{(ed, -, \#), (bc, +, \#), (ac, +, \#)\}\}$. Finally, as far as grounded semantics is concerned, $\mathbb{T}_\forall^{Comp} = \{\{(ed, -, \#), (cd, -, \#)\}\}$.

We now provide some properties of succesful moves and of target sets.

Property 3. It holds that

$$\mathbb{M}_\forall^{Comp} \subseteq \mathbb{M}_\forall^{Pref} \subseteq \mathbb{M}_\exists^S \text{ and } \mathbb{M}_{\neg \exists}^S \subseteq \mathbb{M}_{\neg \forall}^{Pref} \subseteq \mathbb{M}_{\neg \forall}^{Comp}$$

Proof. Let us begin with the case of the positive goals. If move $m \in \mathbb{M}_\forall^{Comp}$, then d is accepted in $AS' = \Delta(AS,m)$ under complete semantics (using sceptical acceptability), so d belongs in all the complete extensions of AS', therefore in all the preferred extensions of AS'. So, it holds that $m \in \mathbb{M}_\forall^{Pref}$. Thus, we have proved that $\mathbb{M}_\forall^{Comp} \subseteq \mathbb{M}_\forall^{Pref}$. Moreover, if $m \in \mathbb{M}_\forall^{Pref}$, then d belongs in all the preferred extensions of AS', therefore d belongs in at least one preferred extension of AS' (so, it also belongs in at least one admissible, and in at least one complete extension of AS'). Thus, it holds that $m \in \mathbb{M}_\exists^S$, and we have proved that $\mathbb{M}_\forall^{Pref} \subseteq \mathbb{M}_\exists^S$. As a result, $\mathbb{M}_\forall^{Comp} \subseteq \mathbb{M}_\forall^{Pref} \subseteq \mathbb{M}_\exists^S$. The proof is similar in the case of negative goals. It is omitted due to the lack of space.

Property 4. If m is a move such that $m \in \mathbb{T}_\forall^{Comp}$ and $m \in \mathbb{T}_\exists^S$, then $m \in \mathbb{T}_\forall^{Pref}$ (1)
Moreover, if m is a move such that $m \in \mathbb{T}_{\neg \exists}^S$ and $m \in \mathbb{T}_{\neg \forall}^{Comp}$, then $m \in \mathbb{T}_{\neg \forall}^{Pref}$ (2)

Proof. (1) By contradiction, let $m \in \mathbb{T}_\forall^{Comp}$, $m \in \mathbb{T}_\exists^S$ and assume that $m \notin \mathbb{T}_\forall^{Pref}$. Now, $m \in \mathbb{T}_\forall^{Comp}$ implies that $m \in \mathbb{M}_\forall^{Comp}$ (as m is minimal w.r.t. $\subseteq$ among the moves in

$\mathbb{M}_\forall^{Comp}$). Then, from $m \in \mathbb{M}_\forall^{Comp}$ it follows that $m \in \mathbb{M}_\forall^{Pref}$ (from Property 3). Moreover, we assumed that $m \notin \mathbb{T}_\forall^{Pref}$, so there must exist another move $m' \subset m$, such that $m' \in \mathbb{T}_\forall^{Pref}$ (and, of course, $m' \in \mathbb{M}_\forall^{Pref}$). From $m' \in \mathbb{M}_\forall^{Pref}$, we get that $m' \in \mathbb{M}_\exists^S$ (from Property 3). Finally, from $m' \in \mathbb{M}_\exists^S$ and $m \in \mathbb{T}_\exists^S$, it follows that $m \subseteq m'$. Contradiction, since above we had $m' \subset m$. Therefore, $m \in \mathbb{T}_\forall^{Pref}$.

(2) Similar proof for the case of negative goals. It is omitted due to the lack of space.

Figure 1 graphically represents the links between the set of succesful moves and the target sets for the positive and the negative goals. The meaning of the sets $\mathcal{M}^{PRO}$ and $\mathcal{M}^{CON}$ will be explained in Section 4.

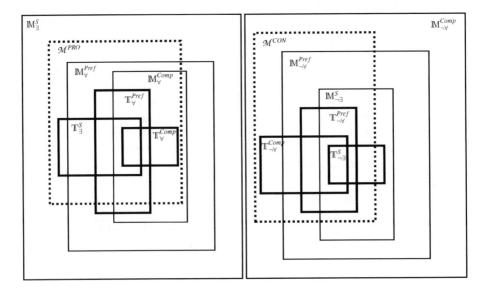

Fig. 1. On the left: The sets of successful moves and target sets for the positive goals, and $\mathcal{M}^{PRO}$. On the right: The sets of successful moves and target sets for the negative goals, and $\mathcal{M}^{CON}$.

Having highlighted some properties of the successful moves and of the target sets, we define in the following section our rewriting procedure which computes target sets.

4   Computing Target Sets and Successful Moves

In this section we provide a set of rewriting rules which help us to compute, for any system $AS = \langle A, R, R^+, R^- \rangle$, all the target sets for some types of goals. In order to do this, we have used the Maude [2] system [8] which is based on rewriting logic. This section is arranged as follows: we start by explaining what Maude is and why it is useful for the type of computations we want to make. Then, we analyze the core component of our program, its set of rules. Afterwards, we explain the rewriting procedure of Maude, in the context of our program. Finally, we prove some important properties.

---

[2] http://maude.cs.uiuc.edu

4.1   The Maude Rewriting System and the Intuition behind Our Program

Maude is both a declarative programming language and a system. It is based on rewriting logic and it can model systems and the actions within those systems. Maude is a high-level, expressive language, which can model from biological systems to programming languages, including itself. A program in Maude is a logical theory, and a computation made by that program is logical deduction using the axioms of the theory.

Our Maude program, presented in Appendix A, is given as input a term which describes an argumentation system $AS = \langle A, R, R^+, R^- \rangle$ and contains either $PRO(d)$ or $CON(d)$, with $d \in A$. If we want to ensure the (positive) goal of accepting argument d under some semantics, we start with $PRO(d)$. Otherwise, if we want to ensure the (negative) goal of rejecting d, we start with $CON(d)$. Maude starts from these atoms and, based on a set of rewriting rules and equations, rewrites the initial term, thus producing new terms, which are, in turn, rewritten. The system stops when all the computed terms are non-rewritable. We will see that every term of the output corresponds to a move on the initial system AS. Their connection with the status of d is detailed in Property 6.

4.2   The Rewriting Rules

Before explaining the rules of our program, we must provide two more basic definitions. The notion of atom is central in what follows. The connectors $\wedge$ and $\vee$ are used in order to link atoms, forming conjuncts and formulas.

Definition 10
Conjunct ::= Atom | (Conjunct ∧ Conjunct);
Formula ::= Conjunct | (Formula ∨ Formula)
Let Conjuncts denote the set of all possible conjuncts, and let Formulas denote the set of all possible formulas. A conjunct which contains at least one open atom is called **open conjunct**. *Otherwise, it is called* **closed conjunct**. *A formula which contains at least one open conjunct is called* **open formula**. *Otherwise, it is called* **closed formula**.

We now proceed to the analysis of the program's rules. There exist two types of rules: **Atom expansions**, or **rewriting rules**, indicated by '=>', and **atom simplifications**, or **equations**, indicated by '='. In our program, an atom expansion replaces two atoms appearing in an open conjunct by some other atoms, whereas an atom simplification replaces two atoms found in the same conjunct by a single atom.

Let us briefly explain the intuition behind the expansion rules. Depending on whether we want to accept or reject the issue, we start from it and we navigate the attacks backwards, while adding and removing attacks, trying to enforce the status of the attacks relevant to the issue. When there exist more than one choice to achieve our goal, we try to explore all the possibilities (combinations of additions and removals). Very roughly, if at some point of the computation, the left side of an expansion rule appears, Maude replaces it with the right side of that rule. The same principle holds for equations.

So, when the initial goal is $PRO(d)$, we want to see the issue d accepted. To do so, we have to take each attack against d, one at the time, and either remove it (if it belongs to R^-), or make it '0' by making an attack which attacks it become '1'. On the other hand, when the initial goal is $CON(d)$, and we want to see d rejected, we have to either make one attack against d become '1', add such an attack if it is in R^+ (and ensure its succesfulness), or to make one attack against d become '?'. Let us see the rules in more detail:

Rules 1-3 say that if an attack is '1', then for every attack against it, either that attack is '0' (rule 1), or it is removed (rule 2), or (if it belongs to R^+) we introduce an atom $(x,0,\#)$ which will lead to a simplification if we later add this attack (rule 3), thus it can never become successful. Rules 4-5 say that if an attack is '0', then there exists an attack against it which is '1'. That attack is either already in the system (rule 4), or it is added to it (rule 5). Rules 6-12 say that if an attack is '?', then two things hold: first, there exists at least one attack against it which is also '?' (rules 6 and 7). [3] Also, the rest of the attacks set against it are either '?', or '0', or removed (rules 8-10), or (if they belong to R^+) we introduce $(x,0,\#)$ and $(x,?,\#)$, which will lead to simplifications if we later add these attack and try to make them '1' (rules 11-12). Rules 13-15 say that in the PRO case every attack against the issue is either '0' (rule 13), is removed (rule 14), or (if it belongs to R^+) we introduce an atom $(x,0,\#)$ for the same reason as explained above (rule 15). Rules 16-19, finally, say that in the CON case there exists one attack against the issue which is either '1' (rules 16 and 17) or '?' (rules 18 and 19).

Now, as far as the simplification rules (equations) are concerned: Equation 1 says that if two identical atoms appear in the same conjunct, then one of them is deleted. Equation 2 performs a simplification related to the '?' status of an attack. Equation 3 says that if an open atom and a closed atom (which are otherwise identical) appear in the same conjuct, then the open atom is deleted. Equations 4-6 say that if two atoms referring to the same attack, but indicating different status, appear in the same conjunct, then $\perp$ is introduced. Equations 7-8 say that if an attack which cannot be attacked is set to be '?' or '0', then $\perp$ is introduced. Equations 9-10 are applied in case there exist no potential attacks against d. Equation 11, finally, says that the atom $\perp$ once it appears in a conjunct, it reduces that conjunct into $\perp$.

Also, notice the **and** operator in the program (corresponding to the $\wedge$ sign) which is declared as associative and commutative. This makes the firing of expansion and simplification rules easy, regardless of the position of the atoms in a conjunct.

Finally, we explain how an argumentation system is represented and passed as input to our program. We define the attacks of the system by using the following conventions. The name of an attack must be preceded by '. If attack $x \in R^+$ (resp. $x \in R^-$) then its name starts with '+' (resp. '−'). Also, by using the *hits*, *isNotHit* and *hitsArg* operators, we define how the attacks are related to each other (and to the issue). For example ('-cd hitsArg d) means that $head(-cd) = d$. Moreover, ('+bc hits '-cd) means that $hits(+bc, -cd)$. Finally, (isNotHit '-ed) means there is no attack against the attacked.

4.3 The Rewriting Procedure (*RP*)

Now we explain how the rewriting procedure of Maude works, not in general, but in the specific case of our program. Informally, its input is an argumentation system *AS*,

---

[3] Note that if we only had atoms of the type $(x,?,*)$, but not of the type $(x,?,**)$, there would exist a possible rewriting making *all* the the attacks against x become '0' (for example), thus not achieving to make x become '?'.

Data: A system $AS = \langle A, R, R^+, R^- \rangle$, $init F = PRO(d)$ or $init F = CON(d)$, with $d \in A$,
a set of expansion rules, a set of simplification rules.　　　　　　　　　 -
Result: A set of moves $\mathcal{M}_d$.
Initialise formula $currF := init F$;
while $currF$ *has an expandable conjunct* **do**
　　Let Exp denote the set of all the expandable conjuncts of $currF$;
　　foreach *conjunct* $C \in Exp$ **do**
　　　　Initialise the set of conjuncts $repl_C := \{\}$;
　　　　foreach *applicable rewriting rule rl on C* **do**
　　　　　　if *rule rl applied on C gives* C' **then**
　　　　　　　　while *a simplification can be applied on* C' **do**
　　　　　　　　　　Choose such a simplification, and apply it on C' ;
　　　　　　　　Add C' into the set $repl_C$;
　　　　Replace C with $C'_1 \vee C'_2 \vee \cdots \vee C'_m$ in $currF$, s.t. $\forall i \in [1\ldots m], C'_i \in repl_C$;
Initialise the set of moves $\mathcal{M}_d := \{\}$;
foreach *conjunct* C *of* $currF$ **do**
　　if $C \neq \perp$ **then**
　　　　$m := \{(x,s,\#) \mid (x,s,\#) \text{ appears in } C, \text{ and } s \in \{+,-\}\}$; Add m into the set $\mathcal{M}_d$;
return $\mathcal{M}_d$;

Algorithm 1. Maude's rewriting procedure, in the context of our program

either the atom $PRO(d)$ or the atom $CON(d)$, a set of expansion rules and a set of
simplification rules. The rewriting procedure starts from $PRO(d)$ or $CON(d)$. All the
applicable expansion rules are considered, one-by-one. For every applicable expansion
rule, that rule is applied, and a set of new conjuncts is computed. In every new conjunct,
simplification rules are applied repeatedly, until no more simplification rules are applicable. Once an "expansion-simplification" step is finished, all the conjuncts computed
in the previous step are considered (one by one) and there follows another "expansion-
simplification" step. These steps are repeated until, at some point, there are no conjuncts
which can be further expanded. Finally, from every non-expandable conjunct computed,
just the $(x, +, \#)$ and $(x, -, \#)$ atoms are filtered. The formal definition of Maude's rewriting procedure, in the context of our program, is given in Algorithm 1.

In the rest of the paper, the set of returned moves will be denoted $\mathcal{M}_d^{PRO}$ if $init F = PRO(d)$, and $\mathcal{M}_d^{CON}$ if $init F = CON(d)$.

Example 1, cont. In order to represent the system AS of this example, we must run the
Maude program with the following input:
> **search** PRO(d) and ('-cd hitsArg d) and ('-ed hitsArg d) and ('+bc hits
'-cd) and ('+ac hits '-cd) and ('ba hits '+ac) and ('ba hits 'ab) and
('ab hits '+bc) and ('ab hits 'ba) and (isNotHit '-ed) =>! C:Conjunct .

Two important remarks: first, the "search" keyword tells Maude that whenever more
than one rewriting rules are applicable, it must consider them all, one at a time, in a
Breadth-First-Search way. This is essential in order to find all the possible rewritings.
Second, by using =>! C:Conjunct, we tell Maude to continue the rewritings, until the
obtained terms are non-rewritable conjuncts.

Once this computation finishes, we obtain three conjuncts which correspond to moves on AS, as well as a fourth conjunct $\perp$. The moves corresponding to the three conjuncts are: $\mathcal{M}_d^{PRO} = \{\{(ed, -, \#), (cd, -, \#)\}, \{(ed, -, \#), (bc, +, \#)\}, \{(ed, -, \#), (ac, +, \#)\}\}$.

Now, let us highlight some properties of the RP procedure.

Property 5. The procedure RP always terminates.

Proof. RP starts with a conjunct containing $PRO(d)$ or $CON(d)$. It finds all the applicable expansion rules, therefore it computes a number of new conjuncts. We can see the initial conjunct as the root of a tree and the new conjuncts as the children of the root. Gradually, RP will compute a tree whose nodes are conjuncts. We will prove that this tree has obligatorily a finite number of nodes. First, from the expansion rules it follows that every conjunct computed by RP has a finite number of atoms. Moreover, there is a finite number of applicable rules on every conjunct, so the branching factor of the tree is finite. Finally, we must prove that the depth of the tree is finite. From the set of rewriting rules, it follows that a conjunct will be expandable (that is not a leaf node), if it contains an open atom and an atom of the form (x hits y), or of the form (x hitsArg d). [4] Notice that every conjunct contains a finite number of (x hits y) and (x hitsArg d) atoms, because the number of arguments and attacks of AS is finite. Also, after the application of any expansion rule, the newly created conjunct contains one less (x hits y) or (x hitsArg d) atom than its parent-node. As a result, the depth of the tree cannot be greater than the initial number of (x hits y) and (x hitsArg d) atoms, which is finite. So, we have proved that RP always terminates.

At this point, we underline that the "search" keyword ensures that, after a simplification step, Maude tries every applicable rewriting rule. Therefore, the order in which the rules are checked (Maude uses an internal strategy to decide on the order) does not affect the results.

We now analyze the output of the rewriting procedure w.r.t. the different argumentative goals. We shall say that: (1) the procedure is *correct* for *successful moves* (resp. *target sets*) for goal g if every move it returns is successful (resp. a target set) for g ; (2) the procedure is *complete* for *successful moves* (resp. *target sets*) for goal g if it returns *all* the successful moves (resp. the target sets) for g.

As shown by Figure 1, correctness for target sets is not satisfied: the procedure returns, for PRO or CON, some moves that are not target sets for any of the semantics. But in some cases we can ensure that the procedure is correct for successful moves—in that case moves only fail on the minimality criterion. In the same way, the completeness for successful moves is not satisfied: RP does not give all the successful moves for any semantics (in the general case). However, completeness for target sets can be obtained in some cases. Of course, the most interesting lines are those for which we have "Yes" in both columns: only successful moves are returned, and all the target sets are.

Property 6. The following table illustrates for which goals the rewriting procedure is correct for successful moves and/or complete for target sets.

---

[4] This means that it is quite possible for an open atom to be non-expandable. This is the case when no relevant (x hits y) or (x hitsArg d) atom is found in the same conjunct as the open atom.

Goal	Correctness for successful moves	Completeness for target sets
$S_\exists(d)$	Yes	Yes
$Pref_\lor(d)$	No	No
$Comp_\lor(d)$	No	Yes
$\neg S_\exists(d)$	No	No
$\neg Pref_\lor(d)$	No	?
$\neg Comp_\lor(d)$	Yes	Yes

Note that the completeness regarding the goal $\neg Pref_\lor(d)$ is left open so far. However, for the sake of readability, we draw Figure 1 assuming that the answer is "Yes".

Proof. There are counter-examples for the "No" entries of the table, omitted due to the lack of space. As far as the "Yes" cases are concerned, we only provide the proofs of completeness and correctness for $S_\exists(d)$.

Correctness of *RP* for $S_\exists(d)$: That is $\mathcal{M}_d^{PRO} \subseteq \mathbb{M}_\exists^S$. Let $m \in \mathcal{M}_d^{PRO}$. The move m correponds to some conjunct, denoted c_m, computed by *RP*. From c_m we can construct the set of arguments $D = \{x \mid (xy, 1, s)$ is an atom of $c_m\}$. We will now prove that in $\Delta(AS, m) = \langle A, R_m, R_m^+, R_m^- \rangle$, it holds that D is an admissible set of arguments which defends argument d. First, let us assume that in $\Delta(AS, m)$ the set D is not conflict-free. In that case there exist two arguments $x_1, x_2 \in D$, such that $x_1 x_2 \in R_m$. Now, $x_1, x_2 \in D$ implies that $\exists x_3, x_4 \in A$ such that $(x_1 x_3, 1, s)$ and $(x_2 x_4, 1, s)$ are atoms of c_m. Given that $(x_2 x_4, 1, s)$ appears in c_m, and that $x_1 x_2 \in R_m$, it follows that atom $(x_1 x_2, 0, s)$ must also appear in c_m (from expansion rule 1). In turn, this means that $\exists x_5 \in A$ such that $(x_5 x_1, 1, s)$ also appears in c_m (from expansion rules 4,5). Similarly, given that $(x_1 x_3, 1, s)$ appears in c_m, it holds that $(x_5 x_1, 0, s)$ also appears in c_m. But, it is impossible for both $(x_5 x_1, 1, s)$ and $(x_5 x_1, 0, s)$ to appear in the same conjunct (as they would have been simplified into $\bot$). Therefore, we have proved that D is conflict-free. Second, let us assume that in the system $\Delta(AS, m)$, the set D does not defend all its elements. In that case $\exists x_1 \in D$ and $\exists x_2 \notin D$ such that $x_2 x_1 \in R_m$, and no argument of D attacks x_2. $x_1 \in D$ implies that $\exists x_0 \in A$ such that atom $(x_1 x_0, 1, s)$ appears in c_m. So, it follows that atom $(x_2 x_1, 0, s)$ also appears in c_m (from expansion rule 1), and as a result, $\exists x_3 \in A$ such that atom $(x_3 x_2, 1, s)$ also appears in c_m. By definition of the set D, notice that $x_3 \in D$. Impossible, since we assumed that no argument of D attacks x_2 in $\Delta(AS, m)$. Therefore, we have proved that D defends all its elements. Given that D is conflict-free and it defends all its elements, it follows that D is an admissible set of arguments. Finally, since for every attack $xd \in R_m$ against the issue d, it holds that atom $(xd, 0, s)$ appears in c_m (because of expansion rule 13), it holds that argument d is defended by the set D. From this, and from the fact that D is admissible in $\Delta(AS, m)$, it follows that $D \cup \{d\}$ is admissible in $\Delta(AS, m)$. Thus, $m \in \mathbb{M}_\exists^S$, and we have proved that $\mathcal{M}_d^{PRO} \subseteq \mathbb{M}_\exists^S$.

Completeness of *RP* for $S_\exists(d)$ (sketch of proof): We want to prove that $\mathbb{T}_\exists^S \subseteq \mathcal{M}_d^{PRO}$. Let $t \in \mathbb{T}_\exists^S$. We will prove that *RP* constructs a tree which has a leaf node containing all the atoms of t, and no additional $(x, +, \#)$, or $(x, -, \#)$ atoms. Let the set $\{x_1, \dots, x_n\}$ contains the arguments attacking d in AS. Let $P = \{(x_1 d, -, \#), \dots, (x_n d, -, \#)\}$. t contains a subset of atoms $P' \subseteq P$, and cannot contain any atoms of the form $(xd, +, \#)$. Moreover, it is not difficult to prove that the tree has a node n (not a leaf, in the general case) which contains all the atoms of P', and no other $(x, +, \#)$ or $(x, -, \#)$ atoms.

Let $\{x_k,\ldots,x_l\} \subseteq \{x_1,\ldots,x_n\}$ denote the arguments whose attacks against d remain in $\Delta(AS,t)$. According to the expansion rules for $PRO(d)$, the node n also contains the atoms $(x_k d, 0, *)$, $\ldots$, $(x_l d, 0, *)$. Thus t contains the atoms of P' and some additional atoms, resulting from the expansions of $(x_k d, 0, *)$, $\ldots$, $(x_l d, 0, *)$, so it can be denoted $t = P' \cup Q$. Note that every atom of Q refers to an attack necessarily "connected" to an argument of $\{x_k,\ldots,x_l\}$. Let us focus on the attacks against d which are not removed. Those attacking arguments must get attacked back, in order for d to be reinstated. At this point, it is not difficult to prove that, for every argument $x_i \in \{x_k,\ldots,x_l\}$: (1) It is impossible for any $(yx_i, -, \#)$ atom to appear in t. (2) It is impossible for two atoms $(y_1 x_i, +, \#)$ and $(y_2 x_i, +, \#)$ to appear in t. As a result, for every argument $x_i \in \{x_k,\ldots,x_l\}$, t can only contain 0 or 1 atoms of the type $(yx_i, +, \#)$. Now we must make sure that RP computes all these possible combinations of attack additions reinstating d. When RP expands the node n, it creates a node for every possible combination of attack additions reinstating d. Thus, there will be below the node n a number of nodes which contain either 0 or 1 atoms of the type $(yx_i, +, \#)$ for every $x_i \in \{x_k,\ldots,x_l\}$. One of these nodes will obligatorily contain exactly the atoms of t which indicate attack additions against the arguments $\{x_k,\ldots,x_l\}$. Moreover, if such a node contains atom $(yx_i, +, \#)$, then it also contains atom $(yx_i, 1, *)$, as the added attacks must be '1'. RP continues to search the graph backwards, considering the indirect attackers (and defenders) of d, using the expansion rules for the $(yx_i, 1, *)$ atoms. Therefore, after a finite number of expansions, the procedure will compute a node which contains exactly the $(x, +, \#)$ and $(x, -, \#)$ atoms found in t. This last statement is true only if the simplification rules which produce $\perp$ cannot lead to the "loss of a target set". Two simplification rules can introduce $\perp$ here: the first one says that if there is a node n containing $(xy, 0, *)$, and no potential attacker of x in the system, $\perp$ is introduced. Having $(xy, 0, *)$ in n means that all the target sets found in the subtree below n must lead to a modified system where there is an attack against x. Since x has no potential attackers this can never happen. The second rule says that if node n contains both $(xy, 0, s)$ and $(xy, 1, s)$, $\perp$ is introduced. Let n a node containing both $(xy, 0, s)$ and $(xy, 1, s)$. Every eventual target set found in the subtree below n leads to a modified system in which some admissibe extension: (a) attacks the argument x (because of $(xy, 0, s)$), and (b) contains argument x (because of $(xy, 1, s)$). This is impossible.

5   Conclusion

The dynamics of argumentation systems is a central and compelling notion to address when debates are to be considered among users or agents. However, the task of computing which move to make in order to reach a given argumentative goal is difficult. In this paper we focus on complex simultaneous moves involving addition and retraction of attacks. We first proved a number of results related to the relation which holds among sets of successful moves and target sets. Then we described an approach based on a dedicated rewriting procedure within the Maude system, and proposed rules inspired from the attack semantics [9]. This approach provides the advantage of being relatively easy to design and interpret. This is an important feature if we consider a context where such moves are suggested to a user, since for instance traces can provide human-readable explanations of the result of the procedure. We then presented a number of results regarding the procedure (together with our rules): regarding positive goals, it is correct for successful moves and complete for target sets for *any* credulous semantics; while it is complete for target sets for the complete semantics, regardless of the type of goal considered (we recall that grounded semantics are included as a special case).

As far as potential extensions of this work are concerned, there are a number of possibilities. First, the efficiency of our rewriting procedure requires further investigation. We also plan to make some modifications of the procedure, in order to be correct and/or complete for more semantics. At this point, we note that adding the possibility to explicitly add/remove arguments from a system would require the definition of some additional rules, but it would not significantly change the procedure. Finally, we will study the use of target sets in protocols for multi-agent debates. We wish to analyze the properties of such protocols, as well as the possible strategic considerations of the agents.

References

1. Bonzon, E., Maudet, N.: On the outcomes of multiparty persuasion. In: Proc. of AAMAS 2011, pp. 47–54 (2011)
2. Kontarinis, D., Bonzon, E., Maudet, N., Moraitis, P.: Picking the right expert to make a debate uncontroversial. In: Proc. of COMMA 2012, pp. 486–497 (2012)
3. Egilmez, S., Martins, J., Leite, J.: Extending social abstract argumentation with votes on attacks. In: Proc. of TAFA 2013 (to appear, 2013)
4. Bench-capon, T.J.M., Doutre, S., Dunne, P.E.: Value-based argumentation frameworks. In: Artificial Intelligence, pp. 444–453 (2002)
5. Amgoud, L., Cayrol, C.: On the acceptability of arguments in preference-based argumentation. In: Proc. of UAI 1998, pp. 1–7 (1998)
6. Modgil, S.: Revisiting abstract argumentation frameworks. In: Proc. of TAFA 2013 (to appear, 2013)
7. Boella, G., Gabbay, D.M., Perotti, A., van der Torre, L., Villata, S.: Conditional labelling for abstract argumentation. In: Modgil, S., Oren, N., Toni, F. (eds.) TAFA 2011. LNCS, vol. 7132, pp. 232–248. Springer, Heidelberg (2012)
8. Clavel, M., Durán, F., Eker, S., Lincoln, P., Martí-Oliet, N., Meseguer, J., Quesada, J.F.: The maude system. In: Narendran, P., Rusinowitch, M. (eds.) RTA 1999. LNCS, vol. 1631, pp. 240–243. Springer, Heidelberg (1999)
9. Villata, S., Boella, G., van der Torre, L.: Attack semantics for abstract argumentation. In: Walsh, T. (ed.) Proc. of IJCAI 2011, IJCAI/AAAI, pp. 406–413 (2011)
10. Modgil, S., Caminada, M.: Proof theories and algorithms for abstract argumentation frameworks. In: Argumentation in Artificial Intelligence, pp. 105–129. Springer US (2009)
11. Cayrol, C., de Saint-Cyr, F.D., Lagasquie-Schiex, M.C.: Change in abstract argumentation frameworks: Adding an argument. J. Artificial Intelligence Research (JAIR) 38, 49–84 (2010)
12. Baumann, R., Brewka, G.: Expanding argumentation frameworks: Enforcing and monotonicity results. In: COMMA 2010, pp. 75–86 (2010)
13. Liao, B., Jin, L., Koons, R.C.: Dynamics of argumentation systems: A division-based method. Artificial Intelligence 175(11), 1790–1814 (2011)
14. Baumann, R.: What does it take to enforce an argument? minimal change in abstract argumentation. In: ECAI 2012, pp. 127–132 (2012)

15. Coste-Marquis, S., Konieczny, S., Mailly, J.G., Marquis, P.: On the revision of argumentation systems: Minimal change of arguments status. In: Proc. of TAFA 2013 (to appear, 2013)

16. Bisquert, P., Cayrol, C., de Saint-Cyr, F.D., Lagasquie-Schiex, M.C.: Characterizing change in abstract argumentation systems. Technical report, IRIT-UPS (2013)

17. Bisquert, P., Cayrol, C., de Saint-Cyr, F.D., Lagasquie-Schiex, M.C.: Changements guidés par les buts en argumentation: Cadre théorique et outil. In: MFI 2013 (2013)

18. Dung, P.M.: On the acceptability of arguments and its fundamental role in nonmonotonic reasoning, logic programming and n-persons games. Artificial Intelligence 77, 321–357 (1995)

19. Jakobovits, H., Vermeir, D.: Robust semantics for argumentation frameworks. J. Log. Comput. 9(2), 215–261 (1999)

20. Caminada, M.: On the issue of reinstatement in argumentation. In: Fisher, M., van der Hoek, W., Konev, B., Lisitsa, A. (eds.) JELIA 2006. LNCS (LNAI), vol. 4160, pp. 111–123. Springer, Heidelberg (2006)

A   Maude's Listing

```
mod RP_PROCEDURE is
protecting QID .
******************** SORTS AND SUBSORTS
sorts Attack Argument Sign Atom Conjunct .
subsort Atom < Conjunct . subsort Qid < Attack .
******************** CONSTANTS
ops top btm : -> Atom [ctor] .
ops + - 1 ? 0 * ** # : -> Sign [ctor] .
ops d : -> Argument [ctor] .
******************** VARIABLES
vars X Y : Attack .
vars S T : Sign .
var At : Atom .
******************** OPERATORS
op ___ : Attack Sign Sign -> Atom [ctor] .
op PRO_ : Argument -> Atom [ctor] .
op CON_ : Argument -> Atom [ctor] .
op _hits_ : Attack Attack -> Atom [ctor] .
op _hitsArg_ : Attack Argument -> Atom [ctor] .
op isNotHit_ : Attack -> Atom [ctor] .
op isNotHitArg_ : Argument -> Atom [ctor] .
op _and_ : Conjunct Conjunct -> Conjunct [ctor assoc comm] .
******************** EQUATIONS - SIMPLIFICATION RULES
eq (X S T) and (X S T) = (X S T) .    *** Eq. 1
eq (X S **) and (X S *) = (X S *) .    *** Eq. 2
eq (X S *) and (X S #) = (X S #) .    *** Eq. 3
eq (X 0 S) and (X 1 T) = btm .    *** Eq. 4
eq (X 0 S) and (X ? T) = btm .    *** Eq. 5
eq (X ? S) and (X 1 T) = btm .    *** Eq. 6
eq (X 0 *) and isNotHit(X) = btm .    *** Eq. 7
eq (X ? S) and isNotHit(X) = btm .    *** Eq. 8
eq PRO(d) and isNotHitArg(d) = top .    *** Eq. 9
eq CON(d) and isNotHitArg(d) = btm .    *** Eq. 10
eq At and btm = btm .    *** Eq. 11
******************** REWRITING RULES - EXPANSION RULES
--------- Expansion rules for (X 1 *) atoms (rules 1, 2 and 3) ---------
*** RULE 1: The attack Y is on the system.
crl [expand_X1*_with_Y0*] : (X 1 *) and (Y hits X) =>
(X 1 *) and (Y 0 *) if not (substr(string(Y),0,1) == "+") .
*** RULE 2: The attack Y is removable.
crl [expand_X1*_with_Y-#_Y0#] : (X 1 *) and (Y hits X) =>
(X 1 *) and (Y - #) and (Y 0 #) if (substr(string(Y),0,1) == "-") .
*** RULE 3: The attack Y is addable.
crl [expand_X1*_with_Y0#] : (X 1 *) and (Y hits X) =>
(X 1 *) and (Y 0 #) if (substr(string(Y),0,1) == "+") .
--------- Expansion rules for (X 0 *) atoms (rules 4 and 5) ---------
*** RULE 4: The attack Y is on the system.
```

```
crl [expand_X0*_with_Y1*] : (X 0 *) and (Y hits X) =>
(X 0 #) and (Y 1 *) if not (substr(string(Y),0,1) == "+") .
```
*** *RULE 5: The attack Y is addable.*
```
crl [expand_X0*_with_Y+#_Y1*] : (X 0 *) and (Y hits X) =>
(X 0 #) and (Y + #) and (Y 1 *) if (substr(string(Y),0,1) == "+") .
```
--------- Expansion rules for (X ? **),(X ? *) atoms (rules 6-12) ---------
*** *RULE 6: Sign **, the attack Y is on the system.*
```
crl [expand_X?**_with_Y?**] : (X ? **) and (Y hits X) =>
(X ? *) and (Y ? **) if not (substr(string(Y),0,1) == "+") .
```
*** *RULE 7: Sign **, the attack Y is addable.*
```
crl [expand_X?**_with_Y+#_Y?**] : (X ? **) and (Y hits X) =>
(X ? *) and (Y + #) and (Y ? **) if (substr(string(Y),0,1) == "+") .
```
*** *RULE 8: Sign *, the attack Y is on the system.*
```
crl [expand_X?*_with_Y?**] : (X ? *) and (Y hits X) =>
(X ? *) and (Y ? **) if not (substr(string(Y),0,1) == "+") .
```
*** *RULE 9: Sign *, the attack Y is on the system.*
```
crl [expand_X?*_with_Y0*] : (X ? *) and (Y hits X) =>
(X ? *) and (Y 0 *) if not (substr(string(Y),0,1) == "+") .
```
*** *RULE 10: Sign *, the attack Y is removable.*
```
crl [expand_X?*_with_Y-#_Y0#] : (X ? *) and (Y hits X) =>
(X ? *) and (Y - #) and (Y 0 #) if (substr(string(Y),0,1) == "-") .
```
*** *RULE 11: Sign *, the attack Y is addable.*
```
crl [expand_X?*_with_Y0#] : (X ? *) and (Y hits X) =>
(X ? *) and (Y 0 #) if (substr(string(Y),0,1) == "+") .
```
*** *RULE 12: Sign *, the attack Y is addable.*
```
crl [expand_X?*_with_Y?#] : (X ? *) and (Y hits X) =>
(X ? *) and (Y ? #) if (substr(string(Y),0,1) == "+") .
```
--------- Expansion rules for PRO, CON atoms (rules 13-19) ---------
*** *RULE 13: PRO, and the attack Y is on the system.*
```
crl [expand_PRO_with_Y0*] : PRO(d) and (Y hitsArg d) =>
PRO(d) and (Y 0 *) if not (substr(string(Y),0,1) == "+") .
```
*** *RULE 14: PRO, and the attack Y is removable.*
```
crl [expand_PRO_with_Y-#_Y0#] : PRO(d) and (Y hitsArg d) =>
PRO(d) and (Y - #) and (Y 0 #) if (substr(string(Y),0,1) == "-") .
```
*** *RULE 15: PRO, and the attack Y is addable.*
```
crl [expand_PRO_with_Y0#] : PRO(d) and (Y hitsArg d) =>
PRO(d) and (Y 0 #) if (substr(string(Y),0,1) == "+") .
```
*** *RULE 16: CON, and the attack Y is on the system.*
```
crl [expand_CON_with_Y1*] : CON(d) and (Y hitsArg d) =>
(Y 1 *) if not (substr(string(Y),0,1) == "+") .
```
*** *RULE 17: CON, and the attack Y is addable.*
```
crl [expand_CON_with_Y+#_Y1*] : CON(d) and (Y hitsArg d) =>
(Y + #) and (Y 1 *) if (substr(string(Y),0,1) == "+") .
```
*** *RULE 18: CON, and the attack Y is on the system.*
```
crl [expand_CON_with_Y?**] : CON(d) and (Y hitsArg d) =>
(Y ? **) if not (substr(string(Y),0,1) == "+") .
```
*** *RULE 19: CON, and the attack Y is addable.*
```
crl [expand_CON_with_Y+#_Y?**] : CON(d) and (Y hitsArg d) =>
(Y + #) and (Y ? **) if (substr(string(Y),0,1) == "+") .
endm
```

A Sequent-Based Representation of Logical Argumentation

Ofer Arieli

School of Computer Science, The Academic College of Tel-Aviv, Israel
oarieli@mta.ac.il

Abstract. In this paper we propose a new presentation of logic-based argumentation theory through Gentzen-style sequent calculi. We show that arguments may be represented by Gentzen-type *sequents* and that attacks between arguments may be represented by *sequent elimination rules*. This framework is logic-independent, i.e., it may be based on arbitrary languages and consequence relations. Moreover, the usual conditions of minimality and consistency of support sets are relaxed, allowing for a more flexible way of expressing arguments, which also simplifies their identification. This generic representation implies that argumentation theory may benefit from incorporating techniques of proof theory and that different non-classical formalisms may be used for backing up intended argumentation semantics.

1 Introduction

Argumentation is the study of how mutually acceptable conclusions can be reached from a collection of arguments. A common dialectical approach for analyzing and evaluating arguments is based on Dung-style abstract argumentation frameworks [22], which can be seen as a diagramming of arguments and their interactions [6, 7, 32]. Logic-based formalization of argumentation frameworks (sometimes called *logical* (or *deductive*) *argumentation*; see reviews in [20, 30]) have also been extensively studied in recent years. One of the better-known approaches in this respect is Besnard and Hunter's logic-based counterpart of Dung's theory [12, 13], in which arguments are represented by classically valid entailments whose premised are consistent and minimal with respect to set inclusion (see also [3, 24, 27]).

Our purpose in this paper is to show that deductive argumentation theory can be described and represented in terms of *sequents*. The latter are logical expressions that have been introduced by Gerhard Gentzen in order to specify his famous sequent calculi [26]. We show that sequents are useful for representing logical arguments since they can be regarded as specific kinds of judgments, and that their interactions (the attack relations) can by represented by Gentzen-style rules of inference. The outcome is a general and uniform approach to deductive argumentation based on manipulations of sequents.

The introduction of sequent-based formalism in the context of logical argumentation has some important benefits. Firstly, well-studied sequent calculi may

J. Leite et al. (Eds.): CLIMA XIV, LNAI 8143, pp. 69–85, 2013.
© Springer-Verlag Berlin Heidelberg 2013

be incorporated for producing arguments in an automated way. Secondly, some restrictions in previous definitions of logical arguments, like minimality and consistency of support sets, may now be lifted. Finally, the sequent-based approach is general enough to accommodate different logics, including non-classical ones. This enables the use of different substructural logics, including paraconsistent logics [21] that support robust methods of handling conflicts among arguments.

The rest of this paper is organized as follows: in the next section we briefly review the basics of abstract and logical argumentation theory. In Section 3 we introduce a sequent-based representation of logical argumentation frameworks, and in Section 4 we show how argumentation semantics may be computed in this context in terms of entailment relations. In Section 5 we discuss some further advantages of using sequent calculi for argumentation frameworks, and in Section 6 we conclude.

2   Preliminaries: Abstract and Logical Argumentation

We start by recalling the terminology and some basic concepts behind Dung-style argumentation [22].

Definition 1. An *argumentation framework* [22] is a pair $\mathcal{AF} = \langle Args, Attack \rangle$, where *Args* is an enumerable set of elements, called *arguments*, and *Attack* is a binary relation on $Args \times Args$ whose instances are called *attacks*. When $(A, B) \in Attack$ we say that A *attacks* B (or that B is *attacked by* A).

The study of how to evaluate arguments based on the structures above is usually called *abstract argumentation*. Given an argumentation framework $\mathcal{AF} = \langle Args, Attack \rangle$, a key question is what sets of arguments (called *extensions*) can collectively be accepted. Different types of extensions have been considered in the literature (see, e.g., [17, 18, 22, 23]), some of them are listed below.

Definition 2. Let $\mathcal{AF} = \langle Args, Attack \rangle$ be an argumentation framework, and let $\mathcal{E} \subseteq Args$. We say that $\mathcal{E}$ *attacks* an argument A if there is an argument $B \in \mathcal{E}$ that attacks A (i.e., $(B, A) \in Attack$). The set of arguments that are attacked by $\mathcal{E}$ is denoted $\mathcal{E}^+$. We say that $\mathcal{E}$ *defends* A if $\mathcal{E}$ attacks every argument B that attacks A. The set $\mathcal{E}$ is called *conflict-free* if it does not attack any of its elements, $\mathcal{E}$ is called *admissible* if it is conflict-free and defends all of its elements, and $\mathcal{E}$ is *complete* if it is admissible and contains all the arguments that it defends.

Let $\mathcal{E}$ be a complete subset of *Args*. We say that $\mathcal{E}$ is a *grounded extension* (of $\mathcal{AF}$) iff it is the minimal complete extension of $\mathcal{AF}$,[1] a *preferred extension* iff it is a maximal complete extension of $\mathcal{AF}$, an *ideal extension* iff it is a maximal complete extension that is a subset of each preferred extension of $\mathcal{AF}$, a *stable extension* iff it is a complete extension of $\mathcal{AF}$ that attacks every argument in $Args \setminus \mathcal{E}$, a *semi-stable extension* iff it is a complete extension of $\mathcal{AF}$ where $\mathcal{E} \cup \mathcal{E}^+$ is maximal among all complete extensions of $\mathcal{AF}$, and an *eager extension* iff it is a maximal complete extension that is a subset of each semi-stable extension of $\mathcal{AF}$.

---

[1] In this definition the minimum and maximum are taken with respect to set inclusion.

In the context of abstract argumentation, then, the arguments themselves are usually considered as atomic objects, and argument acceptability is based on the interactions among these objects, depicted in terms of the attack relation. Acceptability of arguments (with respect to semantics like those considered above) is now defined as follows:

Definition 3. We denote by $\mathcal{E}_{\mathsf{Sem}}(\mathcal{AF})$ the set of all the Sem-extensions of an argumentation framework $\mathcal{AF} = \langle Args, Attack \rangle$, where Sem is one of the extension-based semantics considered previously. Now,

- An argument A is *skeptically accepted* by $\mathcal{AF}$ according to Sem, if $A \in \mathcal{E}$ for *every* $\mathcal{E} \in \mathcal{E}_{\mathsf{Sem}}(\mathcal{AF})$,
- An argument A is *credulously accepted* by $\mathcal{AF}$ according to Sem, if $A \in \mathcal{E}$ for *some* $\mathcal{E} \in \mathcal{E}_{\mathsf{Sem}}(\mathcal{AF})$.

Example 1. Consider the argumentation framework $\mathcal{AF}$, represented by the directed graph of Figure 1, where arguments are represented by nodes and the attack relation is represented by arrows.

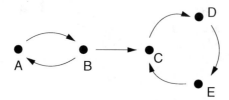

The admissible sets of $\mathcal{AF}$ are $\emptyset$, $\{A\}$, $\{B\}$ and $\{B, D\}$, its complete extensions are $\emptyset$, $\{A\}$, and $\{B, D\}$, the grounded extension is $\emptyset$, the preferred extensions are $\{A\}$ and $\{B, D\}$, the ideal extension is $\emptyset$, the stable extension is $\{B, D\}$, and this is also the only semi-stable extension and eager extension of $\mathcal{AF}$. Thus, e.g., B is credulously accepted by $\mathcal{AF}$ according to the preferred semantics and it is skeptically accepted by $\mathcal{AF}$ according to the stable semantics.

A wealth of research has been conducted on formalizing deductive argumentation, in which arguments can be expressed in terms of formal languages and acceptance of arguments can be determined by logical entailments. This is usually called *logical argumentation*. One of the better-known works in this context is that of Besnard and Hunter [12], sketched below.

Definition 4. Let $\mathcal{L}$ be a standard propositional language, Σ a finite set of formulas in $\mathcal{L}$, and $\vdash_{cl}$ the consequence relation of classical logic (for $\mathcal{L}$). An *argument in the sense of Besnard and Hunter* [12] (BH-argument, for short), formed by Σ, is a pair $A = \langle \Gamma, \psi \rangle$, where ψ is a formula in $\mathcal{L}$ and Γ is a minimally consistent subset of Σ (where minimization is with respect to set inclusion), such that $\Gamma \vdash_{cl} \psi$. Here, Γ is called the *support set* of the argument A and ψ is its *consequent*.[2]

---

[2] A similar definition of arguments for defeasible reasoning goes back to [33]; We refer, e.g., to [13] for a comparison between the two approaches.

Different attack relations have been considered in the literature for logical argumentation frameworks. Below we recall those that are considered in [27] (see also [1, 2, 12, 28, 29]).

Definition 5. Let $A_1 = \langle \Gamma_1, \psi_1 \rangle$ and $A_2 = \langle \Gamma_2, \psi_2 \rangle$ be two BH-arguments.

- A_1 is a *defeater* of A_2 if $\psi_1 \vdash_{cl} \neg \bigwedge_{\gamma \in \Gamma_2} \gamma$.
- A_1 is a *direct defeater* of A_2 if there is $\gamma \in \Gamma_2$ such that $\psi_1 \vdash_{cl} \neg\gamma$.
- A_1 is an *undercut* of A_2 if there is $\Gamma_2' \subseteq \Gamma_2$ such that ψ_1 is logically equivalent to $\neg \bigwedge_{\gamma \in \Gamma_2'} \gamma$.
- A_1 is a *direct undercut* of A_2 if there is $\gamma \in \Gamma_2$ such that ψ_1 is logically equivalent to $\neg\gamma$.
- A_1 is a *canonical undercut* of A_2 if ψ_1 is logically equivalent to $\neg \bigwedge_{\gamma \in \Gamma_2} \gamma$.
- A_1 is a *rebuttal* of A_2 if ψ_1 is logically equivalent to $\neg\psi_2$.
- A_1 is a *defeating rebuttal* of A_2 if $\psi_1 \vdash_{cl} \neg\psi_2$.

Let $Args_{\mathsf{BH}}(\Sigma)$ be the (countably infinite) set of BH-arguments formed by Σ. Each condition in Definition 5 induces a corresponding attack relation *Attack* on $Args_{\mathsf{BH}}(\Sigma)$. For instance, one may define that $(A_1, A_2) \in Attack$ iff A_1 is a defeater of A_2. In turn, Σ and *Attack* induce the (abstract) argumentation framework $\mathcal{AF}(\Sigma) = \langle Args_{\mathsf{BH}}(\Sigma), Attack \rangle$. By this, one may draw conclusions from Σ with respect to each of the abstract argumentation semantics considered in Definition 2, by incorporating Definition 3:

Definition 6. Let $\mathcal{AF}(\Sigma) = \langle Args_{\mathsf{BH}}(\Sigma), Attack \rangle$ be a logical argumentation framework and Sem one of the extension semantics considered in Definition 2.

- A formula ψ is *skeptically entailed* by Σ according to Sem, if there is an argument $\langle \Gamma, \psi \rangle \in Args_{\mathsf{BH}}(\Sigma)$ that is skeptically accepted by $\mathcal{AF}(\Sigma)$ according to Sem.
- A formula ψ is *credulously entailed* by Σ according to Sem, if there is an argument $\langle \Gamma, \psi \rangle \in Args_{\mathsf{BH}}(\Sigma)$ that is credulously accepted by $\mathcal{AF}(\Sigma)$ according to Sem.

3   Sequent-Based Logical Argumentation

The setting described in the previous section is a basis of several works on logical argumentation (e.g., [1, 2, 3, 12, 13, 14, 24, 27]). In this section we re-examine some of its basic concepts.

3.1   Arguments as Sequents

First, we consider the notion of a logical argument. We argue that the minimality and consistency requirements in Definition 4 not only cause complications in the evaluation and the construction of arguments, but also may not be really necessary for capturing the intended meaning of this notion.

- **Minimality.** Minimization of supports is not an essential principle for defining arguments. For instance, mathematical proofs are usually not required
  to be minimal in order to validate their claim. For a more specific example, consider a framework in which supports are expressed only by literals
  (atomic formulas or their negation). Then $\langle \{p, q\}, p \vee q \rangle$ is excluded due to
  minimality considerations, although one may consider $\{p, q\}$ as a *stronger*
  support for $p \vee q$ than, say, $\{p\}$. Indeed, the former contains *several* pieces of
  evidence for $p \vee q$ (this may be relevant when, e.g., majority votes or other
  quantitative considerations are taken into account).[3]

- **Consistency.** The requirement that the support set Γ of an argument $\langle \Gamma, \psi \rangle$
  should be consistent may be irrelevant for some logics, at least when con-
  sistency is defined by satisfiability. Indeed, in logics such as Priest's LP [31]
  or Belnap's four-valued logic [10], *every* set of formulas in the language of
  $\{\neg, \vee, \wedge\}$ is satisfiable. What really matters in these cases is the consequence
  relation of the underlying logic. Thus, e.g., in opposed to classical logic, when
  intuitionistic logic is concerned, $\langle \{\neg\neg\psi\}, \psi \rangle$ shouldn't be considered as a legitimate argument, although $\neg\neg\psi \in \Gamma$ is (minimally) consistent in Γ when
  ψ is consistent.

- **Complexity.** From a more pragmatic point of view, the involvement of
  minimally consistent subsets of the underlying knowledge-base poses serious
  questions on the computational viability of identifying arguments and generating them. Indeed, deciding the existence of a minimal subset of formulas
  that implies the consequent is already at the second level of the polynomial
  hierarchy (see [25]).

Our conclusion, then, is that what really matters for an argument, is that
(i) its consequent would logically follow, according to the underlying logic, from
the support set, and that (ii) there would be an effective way of constructing
and identifying it. In what follows we therefore adhere the following principles:

1. Supports and consequents of arguments are solely determined by the *logic*.
2. Arguments are syntactical objects that are *effectively computable* by a formal
   system that is related to the logic, and are *refutable* by the attack relation
   of the argumentation system.

For the first item we indicate what a logic is (Definition 7). The first part of the
second item corresponds to the primary goal of proof theory, so notations and
machinery are borrowed from that area (Definitions 8 and 9).

---

[3] Another argument that is sometimes pleaded for set-inclusion minimization is that
it reduces the number of attacks. Again, it is disputable whether set-inclusion minimization is the right principle for assuring this property, since, for instance, the
singletons $S_1 = \{p_1\}$ and $S_2 = \{p_2 \wedge \ldots \wedge p_n\}$, supporting (e.g., in classical logic) the
claim $p_1 \vee \ldots \vee p_n$, are incomparable w.r.t. set-inclusion (and moreover they even
do not share any atomic formula), but it is obvious that as n becomes larger S_2
becomes more exposed to attacks than S_1.

Definition 7. Let $\mathcal{L}$ be a propositional language. A (propositional) *logic* for $\mathcal{L}$ is a pair $\mathfrak{L} = \langle \mathcal{L}, \vdash \rangle$, where $\vdash$ is a (Tarskian) consequence relation for $\mathcal{L}$, i.e., a binary relation between sets of formulas and formulas in $\mathcal{L}$, satisfying the following conditions:

Cautious Reflexivity: $\psi \vdash \psi$.
Monotonicity: if $\Gamma \vdash \psi$ and $\Gamma \subseteq \Gamma'$, then $\Gamma' \vdash \psi$.
Transitivity: if $\Gamma \vdash \psi$ and $\Gamma', \psi \vdash \varphi$ then $\Gamma, \Gamma' \vdash \varphi$.

Definition 8. Let $\mathcal{L}$ be a propositional language, and let $\Rightarrow$ be a symbol that does not appear in $\mathcal{L}$. An $\mathcal{L}$-*sequent* (or just a sequent) is an expression of the form $\Gamma \Rightarrow \Delta$, where Γ and Δ are finite sets of formulas in $\mathcal{L}$.

Proof systems that operate on sequents are called *sequent calculi* [26]. We shall say that a logic $\mathfrak{L}$ is *effective*, if it has a sound and complete sequent calculus. For an effective logic $\mathfrak{L} = \langle \mathcal{L}, \vdash \rangle$, then, there is an effective way of drawing entailments: $\Gamma \vdash \psi$ iff there is a proof of the sequent $\Gamma \Rightarrow \psi$ in the corresponding sequent calculus. In what follows we shall always assume that the underlying logics are effective.

Definition 9. Let $\mathfrak{L} = \langle \mathcal{L}, \vdash \rangle$ be an effective logic with a corresponding sequent calculus $\mathfrak{C}$, and let Σ be a set of formulas in $\mathcal{L}$. An $\mathfrak{L}$-*argument* based on Σ is an $\mathfrak{L}$-sequent of the form $\Gamma \Rightarrow \psi$, where $\Gamma \subseteq \Sigma$, that is provable in $\mathfrak{C}$. The set of all the $\mathfrak{L}$-arguments that are based on Σ is denoted $\mathsf{Arg}_{\mathfrak{L}}(\Sigma)$.

In the notation of Definition 9, we have that:

Proposition 1. *Let* $\mathfrak{L} = \langle \mathcal{L}, \vdash \rangle$ *be an effective propositional logic. Then* $\Gamma \Rightarrow \psi$ *is in* $\mathsf{Arg}_{\mathfrak{L}}(\Sigma)$ *iff* $\Gamma \vdash \psi$ *for* $\Gamma \subseteq \Sigma$.

Example 2. When the underlying logic is classical logic $\mathfrak{CL}$, one may use Gentzen's well-known sequent calculus LK, which is sound and complete for $\mathfrak{CL}$ [26]. In this case we have, for instance, that the sequent $\psi \supset \phi \Rightarrow \neg \psi \vee \phi$ is derivable in LK and so it belongs to $\mathsf{Arg}_{\mathfrak{CL}}(\Sigma)$ whenever Σ contains the formula $\psi \supset \phi$. Note, however, that this sequent is not derivable by any sequent calculus that is sound and complete for intuitionistic logic $\mathfrak{IL}$ (e.g., Gentzen's LJ), thus it is not in $\mathsf{Arg}_{\mathfrak{IL}}(\Sigma)$ for any Σ.

Proposition 2. *For every effective logic* $\mathfrak{L} = \langle \mathcal{L}, \vdash \rangle$ *and a finite set* Σ *of formulas in* $\mathcal{L}$*, the set* $\mathsf{Arg}_{\mathfrak{L}}(\Sigma)$ *is closed under the following rules:*[4]

Σ-*Reflexivity:*   *For every* $\Gamma \subseteq \Sigma$ *and* $\psi \in \Gamma$ *it holds that* $\Gamma \Rightarrow \psi \in \mathsf{Arg}_{\mathfrak{L}}(\Sigma)$.
Σ-*Monotonicity:* *If* $\Gamma \Rightarrow \psi \in \mathsf{Arg}_{\mathfrak{L}}(\Sigma)$ *and* $\Gamma \subseteq \Gamma' \subseteq \Sigma$ *then* $\Gamma' \Rightarrow \psi \in \mathsf{Arg}_{\mathfrak{L}}(\Sigma)$
Σ-*Transitivity:*   *If* $\Gamma \Rightarrow \psi \in \mathsf{Arg}_{\mathfrak{L}}(\Sigma)$ *and* $\Gamma', \psi \Rightarrow \phi \in \mathsf{Arg}_{\mathfrak{L}}(\Sigma)$ *then also*
          $\Gamma, \Gamma' \Rightarrow \phi \in \mathsf{Arg}_{\mathfrak{L}}(\Sigma)$.

---

[4] Following the usual convention we use commas in a sequent for denoting the union operation.

Proof. By Proposition 1, Σ-Reflexivity follows from the cautious reflexivity and the monotonicity of $\vdash$, Σ-Transitivity follows from the transitivity of $\vdash$, and Σ-monotonicity follows from the monotonicity of $\vdash$. $\square$

Note 1. The set $Args_{\mathsf{BH}}(\Sigma)$ of the BH-arguments is not closed under any rule in Proposition 2. To see this consider for instance the set $\Sigma = \{p, q, \neg p \vee q, \neg q \vee p\}$. Then $\langle\{p, \neg p \vee q\}, q\rangle \in Args_{\mathsf{BH}}(\Sigma)$ and $\langle\{q, \neg q \vee p\}, p\rangle \in Args_{\mathsf{BH}}(\Sigma)$, however $\langle\{p, \neg p \vee q, \neg q \vee p\}, p\rangle \notin Args_{\mathsf{BH}}(\Sigma)$, since its support set is not minimal. Thus $Args_{\mathsf{BH}}(\Sigma)$ is not Σ-transitive. The fact that $\langle\{p, \neg p \vee q, \neg q \vee p\}, p\rangle \notin Args_{\mathsf{BH}}(\Sigma)$ (while $\langle\{p\}, p\rangle \in Args_{\mathsf{BH}}(\Sigma)$) also shows that $Args_{\mathsf{BH}}(\Sigma)$ is not Σ-monotonic and that it is not Σ-reflexive.[5]

Note 2. Let $\mathfrak{L} = \langle \mathcal{L}, \vdash \rangle$ be an effective logic and Σ a finite set of formulas in $\mathcal{L}$. Then Σ-Transitivity can be strengthened as follows:

$$\text{If } \Gamma \Rightarrow \psi \in \mathsf{Arg}_{\mathfrak{L}}(\Sigma) \text{ and } \Gamma', \psi \vdash \phi \text{ for } \Gamma' \subseteq \Sigma, \text{ then } \Gamma, \Gamma' \Rightarrow \phi \in \mathsf{Arg}_{\mathfrak{L}}(\Sigma).$$

This rule implies that for generating $\mathfrak{L}$-arguments based on Σ it is enough to consider only formulas in Σ.

3.2   Attacks as Sequent Elimination Rules

In order to represent attack relations we introduce rules for excluding arguments (i.e., sequents) in the presence of counter arguments. We call such rules *sequent elimination rules*, or *attack rules*. The obvious advantage of representing attacks by sequent elimination rules is that the form of such rules is similar to that of the construction rules, and both types of rules are expressed by the same syntactical objects. This allows us to uniformly identify and generate arguments and attacks by the same sequent-manipulation systems.

Since the underlying logic may not be classical and its language may not be the standard propositional one, we shall have to make the following assumptions on the availability of particular connectives in the language:

- To generalize attack relations that are defined by the classical conjunction, we assume that the underlying language contains a $\vdash$-conjunctive connective $\wedge$, for which $\Gamma \vdash \psi \wedge \phi$ iff $\Gamma \vdash \psi$ and $\Gamma \vdash \phi$. In these cases we shall denote by $\wedge\Gamma$ the conjunction of all the elements in Γ.
- To generalize attack relations that are defined by logical equivalence, we assume that in addition to the $\vdash$-conjunctive connective, the underlying language also contains a $\vdash$-deductive implication $\supset$, for which $\Gamma, \psi \vdash \phi$ iff $\Gamma \vdash \psi \supset \phi$. In these cases we shall abbreviate the formula $(\psi \supset \phi) \wedge (\phi \supset \psi)$ by $\psi \leftrightarrow \phi$.

Let us now show how the attack relations in Definition 5 can be described in terms of corresponding sequent elimination rules. Typical conditions of such

---

[5] Note that $Args_{\mathsf{BH}}(\Sigma)$ is *cautiously Σ-reflexive*: $\langle\{\psi\}, \psi\rangle \in Args_{\mathsf{BH}}(\Sigma)$ for a consistent formula $\psi \in \Sigma$.

rules consist of three sequents: the attacking argument, the attacked argument, and the condition for the attack. Conclusions of sequent elimination rules will be the elimination of the attacked argument. In the sequel, we denote by $\Gamma \not\Rightarrow \psi$ the elimination of the argument $\Gamma \Rightarrow \psi$.

In what follows we say that a sequent elimination rule $\mathcal{R}$ is *applicable* with respect to a logic $\mathfrak{L}$, if all of its conditions are valid for $\mathfrak{L}$, that is, every condition of $\mathcal{R}$ is provable in a corresponding sound and complete sequent calculus for $\mathfrak{L}$.[6]

Attacks by defeaters: In terms of an arbitrary logic $\mathfrak{L} = \langle \mathcal{L}, \vdash \rangle$ and $\mathfrak{L}$-arguments in $\mathsf{Arg}_{\mathfrak{L}}(\Sigma)$, an argument $\Gamma_1 \Rightarrow \psi_1$ is an $\mathfrak{L}$-defeater of an argument $\Gamma_2 \Rightarrow \psi_2$ if $\psi_1 \vdash \neg \bigwedge \Gamma_2$. In the presence of a $\vdash$-deductive implication $\supset$ in $\mathcal{L}$, this means that $\vdash \psi_1 \supset \neg \bigwedge \Gamma_2$, and so $\Rightarrow \psi_1 \supset \neg \bigwedge \Gamma_2$ is an $\mathfrak{L}$-argument in $\mathsf{Arg}_{\mathfrak{L}}(\Sigma)$. It follows that attacks by defeaters may be represented by the following sequent elimination rule (relative to $\mathfrak{L}$):

$$\text{Defeat:} \quad \frac{\Gamma_1 \Rightarrow \psi_1 \qquad \Rightarrow \psi_1 \supset \neg \bigwedge \Gamma_2 \qquad \Gamma_2 \Rightarrow \psi_2}{\Gamma_2 \not\Rightarrow \psi_2}$$

In the particular case where the underlying logic is classical logic $\mathfrak{CL}$, this rule is a sequent-based encoding of a defeater attack in the sense of Definition 5:

Proposition 3. *Let $A_1 = \langle \Gamma_1, \psi_1 \rangle$ and $A_2 = \langle \Gamma_2, \psi_2 \rangle$ be two BH-arguments. Then A_1 is a defeater of A_2 in the sense of Definition 5 iff the Defeat rule $\mathcal{R}$, in which $\Gamma_2 \Rightarrow \psi_2$ is attacked by $\Gamma_1 \Rightarrow \psi_1$, is $\mathfrak{CL}$-applicable.*

Proof. Since A_i is a BH-argument it holds that $\Gamma_i \Rightarrow \psi_i$ is $\mathfrak{CL}$-valid ($i = 1, 2$). Moreover, since A_1 is a defeater of A_2, the attack condition of $\mathcal{R}$ is also $\mathfrak{CL}$-valid. It follows that $\mathcal{R}$ is $\mathfrak{CL}$-applicable. Conversely, suppose that $A_1 = \langle \Gamma_1, \psi_1 \rangle$ and $A_2 = \langle \Gamma_2, \psi_2 \rangle$ are BH-arguments so that the Defeat rule in which $\Gamma_2 \Rightarrow \psi_2$ is attacked by $\Gamma_1 \Rightarrow \psi_1$ is $\mathfrak{CL}$-applicable. Then the attacking condition of this rule is $\mathfrak{CL}$-valid, and so A_1 is a defeater of A_2 in the sense of Definition 5.   □

Note 3. The following sequent elimination rule may be viewed as a generalized form of Defeat, which moreover does not assume the availability of a deductive implication in the language.

$$\text{Strong Defeat:} \quad \frac{\Gamma_1 \Rightarrow \neg \bigwedge \Gamma_2 \qquad \Gamma_2 \Rightarrow \psi_2}{\Gamma_2 \not\Rightarrow \psi_2}$$

Proposition 4. *Strong Defeat implies Defeat.*

Proof. Assume that the three conditions of Defeat hold. Since $\Rightarrow \psi_1 \supset \neg \bigwedge \Gamma_2$ is derivable and $\mathfrak{L}$ is effective, it holds that $\vdash \psi_1 \supset \neg \bigwedge \Gamma_2$. Thus, since $\supset$ is a $\vdash$-deductive implication, $\psi_1 \vdash \neg \bigwedge \Gamma_2$. This, together with the assumption that $\Gamma_1 \Rightarrow \psi_1$ is derivable (and so it is an argument in $\mathsf{Arg}_{\mathfrak{L}}(\Sigma)$), imply by Note 2 that $\Gamma_1 \Rightarrow \neg \bigwedge \Gamma_2$ is an argument in $\mathsf{Arg}_{\mathfrak{L}}(\Sigma)$, and so it is derivable in the underlying sequent calculus. By Strong Defeat, then, $\Gamma_2 \not\Rightarrow \psi_2$, which is also the conclusion of Defeat.   □

---

[6] Semantically, this usually means that for every condition $\Gamma \Rightarrow \psi$ of $\mathcal{R}$, any $\mathfrak{L}$-model of (all the formulas in) Γ is an $\mathfrak{L}$-model of ψ.

Attacks by direct defeaters: Direct defeat with respect to an arbitrary logic $\mathfrak{L} = \langle \mathcal{L}, \vdash \rangle$ and a set $\mathsf{Arg}_{\mathfrak{L}}(\Sigma)$ of $\mathfrak{L}$-arguments based on Σ, means that $\Gamma_1 \Rightarrow \psi_1$ is an $\mathfrak{L}$-direct defeater of $\Gamma_2 \Rightarrow \psi_2$ if $\psi_1 \vdash \neg\gamma$ for some $\gamma \in \Gamma_2$. Thus, a direct defeat attack may be expressed by the following sequent elimination rule:

$$\text{Direct Defeat:} \quad \frac{\Gamma_1 \Rightarrow \psi_1 \qquad \Rightarrow \psi_1 \supset \neg\phi \qquad \Gamma_2, \phi \Rightarrow \psi_2}{\Gamma_2, \phi \not\Rightarrow \psi_2}$$

Thus, an argument should be withdrawn in case that the negation of an element in its support set is implied by a consequent of another argument.

As in the case of attacks by defeaters, we have the following relation between attacks by direct defeaters in classical logic (Definition 5) and the above sequent-based formalization:

Proposition 5. *Let $A_1 = \langle \Gamma_1, \psi_1 \rangle$ and $A_2 = \langle \Gamma_2, \psi_2 \rangle$ be BH-arguments. Then A_1 is a direct defeater of A_2 in the sense of Definition 5 iff the Direct Defeat sequent elimination rule, in which $\Gamma_2 \Rightarrow \psi_2$ is attacked by $\Gamma_1 \Rightarrow \psi_1$, is $\mathfrak{CL}$-applicable.*

Proof. Similar to that of Proposition 3. □

Note 4. Again, it is possible to express a stronger form of the rule above, which does not mention an implication connective:

$$\text{Strong Direct Defeat:} \quad \frac{\Gamma_1 \Rightarrow \neg\phi \qquad \Gamma_2, \phi \Rightarrow \psi_2}{\Gamma_2, \phi \not\Rightarrow \psi_2}$$

Proposition 6. *Strong Direct Defeat implies Direct Defeat.*

Proof. As in the proof of Proposition 4, by Note 2 and the fact that $\supset$ is a $\vdash$-deductive implication, the availability of $\Gamma_1 \Rightarrow \psi_1$ and $\Rightarrow \psi_1 \supset \neg\phi$ implies that $\Gamma_1 \Rightarrow \neg\phi$ is an element in $\mathsf{Arg}_{\mathfrak{L}}(\Sigma)$. Thus, Strong Direct Defeat may be applied to conclude that $\Gamma_2, \phi \not\Rightarrow \psi_2$, which is also the conclusion of Direct Defeat. □

Attacks by undercuts: For expressing undercuts with respect to a logic $\mathfrak{L} = \langle \mathcal{L}, \vdash \rangle$ we first have to define logical equivalence in $\mathfrak{L}$. A natural way to do so is to require that ψ and ϕ are logically equivalent in $\mathfrak{L}$ iff $\psi \vdash \phi$ and $\phi \vdash \psi$. Using a $\vdash$-deductive implication $\supset$ and a $\vdash$-conjunctive connective $\wedge$, this means that $\vdash (\psi \supset \phi) \wedge (\phi \supset \psi)$, i.e., that $\psi \leftrightarrow \phi$ is a theorem of $\mathfrak{L}$. It follows that attacks by undercuts are represented by the following sequent elimination rule:

$$\text{Undercut:} \quad \frac{\Gamma_1 \Rightarrow \psi_1 \qquad \Rightarrow \psi_1 \leftrightarrow \neg \bigwedge \Gamma_2 \qquad \Gamma_2, \Gamma_2' \Rightarrow \psi_2}{\Gamma_2, \Gamma_2' \not\Rightarrow \psi_2}$$

Again, one may show that an attack by undercuts in the sense of Definition 5 is a particular case, for classical logic, of the rule above (cf. Propositions 3 and 5).

Proposition 7. *Let $A_1 = \langle \Gamma_1, \psi_1 \rangle$ and $A_2 = \langle \Gamma_2, \psi_2 \rangle$ be BH-arguments. Then A_1 is an undercut of A_2 iff the Undercut rule in which $\Gamma_2 \Rightarrow \psi_2$ is attacked by $\Gamma_1 \Rightarrow \psi_1$ is $\mathfrak{CL}$-applicable.*

Attacks by direct and canonical undercuts: Using the same notations as those for attacks by undercuts, and under the same assumptions on the language, attacks by direct undercuts may be represented by the following elimination rule:

$$\text{Direct Undercut:} \quad \frac{\Gamma_1 \Rightarrow \psi_1 \qquad \Rightarrow \psi_1 \leftrightarrow \neg\gamma_2 \qquad \Gamma_2, \gamma_2 \Rightarrow \psi_2}{\Gamma_2, \gamma_2 \nRightarrow \psi_2}$$

Similarly, attacks by canonical undercuts may be represented as follows:

$$\text{Canonical Undercut:} \quad \frac{\Gamma_1 \Rightarrow \psi_1 \qquad \Rightarrow \psi_1 \leftrightarrow \neg\bigwedge\Gamma_2 \qquad \Gamma_2 \Rightarrow \psi_2}{\Gamma_2 \nRightarrow \psi_2}$$

The rules above may be justified by propositions that are similar to 3, 5, and 7.

Attacks by rebuttal and defeating rebuttal: By the discussion above it is easy to see that attacks by rebuttal and defeating rebuttal are also represented by sequent elimination rules. Indeed, these two attacks are represented as follows:

$$\text{Rebuttal:} \quad \frac{\Gamma_1 \Rightarrow \psi_1 \qquad \Rightarrow \psi_1 \leftrightarrow \neg\psi_2 \qquad \Gamma_2 \Rightarrow \psi_2}{\Gamma_2 \nRightarrow \psi_2}$$

$$\text{Defeating Rebuttal:} \quad \frac{\Gamma_1 \Rightarrow \psi_1 \qquad \Rightarrow \psi_1 \supset \neg\psi_2 \qquad \Gamma_2 \Rightarrow \psi_2}{\Gamma_2 \nRightarrow \psi_2}$$

Again, these rules are justifiable by propositions that are similar to 3, 5, and 7.

As the next proposition shows, the relations between the attacks in Definition 5, indicated in [27], carry on to our sequent elimination rules.

Proposition 8. *Let $\mathfrak{L} = \langle \mathcal{L}, \vdash \rangle$ be an effective propositional logic and suppose that $\mathcal{L}$ has a $\vdash$-conjunction $\wedge$ and a $\vdash$-deductive implication $\supset$. Then: (a) Defeating Rebuttal implies Rebuttal, (b) Undercut implies Canonical Undercut and Direct Undercut, (c) Direct Defeat implies Direct Undercut.*

Proof. Part (a) follows from the fact that the conditions of Rebuttal are stronger than those of Defeating Rebuttal. More specifically, suppose that the conditions of Rebuttal hold, i.e., $\Gamma_1 \Rightarrow \psi_1$ and $\Rightarrow \psi_1 \leftrightarrow \neg\psi_2$ and $\Gamma_2 \Rightarrow \psi_2$ are derivable in the underlying sequent calculus. Since $\mathfrak{L}$ is effective, it holds that $\vdash \psi_1 \leftrightarrow \neg\psi_2$, i.e., $\vdash (\psi_1 \supset \neg\psi_2) \wedge (\neg\psi_2 \supset \psi_1)$. Since $\wedge$ is a $\vdash$-conjunction, $\vdash \psi_1 \supset \neg\psi_2$, thus by the effectiveness of $\mathfrak{L}$ again, the sequent $\Rightarrow \psi_1 \supset \neg\psi_2$ is derivable in the calculus. By Defeating Rebuttal, $\Gamma_2 \nRightarrow \psi_2$, which is also the conclusion of Rebuttal.

Part (b) follows from the fact that Undercut holds in particular when Γ_2 is a singleton (in which case Direct Undercut is obtained) and when Γ_2 is the whole support set of the sequent (in which case Canonical Undercut is obtained).

To see Part (c), note that the conditions of Direct Undercut are stronger than those of Direct Defeat (taking $\gamma_2 = \phi$). □

Note 5. Further relations between the elimination rules introduced above may be obtained under further assumptions on the underlying logics. For instance, when $\mathfrak{L}$ is classical logic, Defeat implies Direct Defeat, since in LK the sequent $\Rightarrow \psi \supset \neg\bigwedge\Gamma$ is derivable from $\Rightarrow \psi \supset \neg\gamma$ for any $\gamma \in \Gamma$. Similar considerations show that in this case Defeat also implies Undercut and Defeating Rebuttal.

4   Argumentation by Sequent Processing

In light of the previous section, a logical argumentation framework for a set of formulas Σ, based on a logic $\mathfrak{L}$, consists of a set of arguments $\mathsf{Arg}_{\mathfrak{L}}(\Sigma)$ and a set of sequent elimination rules *Attack*. The arguments in $\mathsf{Arg}_{\mathfrak{L}}(\Sigma)$ may be constructed by a sequent calculus which is sound and complete for $\mathfrak{L}$, while the rules in *Attack* allow to discard arguments that are attacked according to some attacking policy. Semantics of such a logical framework $\mathcal{AF}_{\mathfrak{L}}(\Sigma)$ are therefore determined by a process involving constructions and eliminations of sequents (logical arguments). Below, we describe and exemplify this process.

Definition 10. We say that an argument $\Gamma \Rightarrow \psi$ is *discarded* by an argument $\Gamma' \Rightarrow \psi'$, if there is a rule $\mathcal{R} \in Attack$ in which $\Gamma' \Rightarrow \psi'$ attacks $\Gamma \Rightarrow \psi$, that is, $\Gamma \Rightarrow \psi$ and $\Gamma' \Rightarrow \psi'$ appear in the conditions of $\mathcal{R}$ and $\Gamma \not\Rightarrow \psi$ is the conclusion of $\mathcal{R}$.

Note 6. If $\mathfrak{L}$ is a logic in which any formula follows from a contradiction (in particular, if $\mathfrak{L} = \mathfrak{CL}$), *any* sequent is discarded when Σ is contradictory. It follows that either the consistency requirement from support sets of arguments should be restored, or the underlying logic should be paraconsistent [21]. Since our goal here is to avoid the first option, in what follows we consider argumentation frameworks that are based on paraconsistent logics.[7] Here we chose Priest's three-valued logic $\mathcal{LP}$ [31], which is one of the most famous and simplest paraconsistent logics in the literature. A sound and complete sequent calculus for $\mathcal{LP}$ is given in Figure 1 (see also [4]).

Example 3. Consider the argumentation framework for the set $\Sigma = \{\neg p, p, q\}$, based on $\mathcal{LP}$, in which attacks are by Undercut. Then, while $q \Rightarrow q \vee p$ is not discarded by any argument in $\mathsf{Arg}_{\mathcal{LP}}(\Sigma)$, the argument $q, p \Rightarrow q \vee p$ is discarded by, e.g., $\neg p \Rightarrow \neg p$. The intuition behind this is that the support set of the argument $q, p \Rightarrow q \vee p$, unlike that of the argument $q \Rightarrow q \vee p$, contains a formula (p) which is controversial in Σ (because it is contradictory).

   The arguments that are not discarded by any argument are those that are not attacked according to the attack rules in *Attack*. This conflict-free set of arguments may define a semantics for $\mathcal{AF}_{\mathfrak{L}}(\Sigma)$ as follows:

Definition 11. Let $\mathcal{AF}_{\mathfrak{L}}(\Sigma) = \langle \mathsf{Arg}_{\mathfrak{L}}(\Sigma), Attack \rangle$ be a logical argumentation framework for a set of formulas Σ based on a logic $\mathfrak{L}$. We denote $\mathsf{Arg}_{\mathfrak{L}}(\Sigma) \Vdash_{\mathsf{ND}} \psi$ if there is a set of formulas $\Gamma \subseteq \Sigma$ such that $\Gamma \Rightarrow \psi$ is an argument in $\mathsf{Arg}_{\mathfrak{L}}(\Sigma)$ that is not discarded by any argument in $\mathsf{Arg}_{\mathfrak{L}}(\Sigma)$ according to the rules in *Attack*.

---

[7] Paraconsistent logics may also be helpful in preventing contamination in defeasible argumentation (see, for instance, [16, 18]). This is beyond the scope of the current paper.

Axioms: $\psi \Rightarrow \psi$ $\Rightarrow \psi, \neg\psi$

Structural Rules:

Weakening: $\dfrac{\Gamma \Rightarrow \Delta}{\Gamma, \Gamma' \Rightarrow \Delta, \Delta'}$

Cut: $\dfrac{\Gamma_1, \psi \Rightarrow \Delta_1 \qquad \Gamma_2 \Rightarrow \Delta_2, \psi}{\Gamma_1, \Gamma_2 \Rightarrow \Delta_1, \Delta_2}$

Logical Rules:

$[\neg\neg\Rightarrow] \dfrac{\Gamma, \phi \Rightarrow \Delta}{\Gamma, \neg\neg\phi \Rightarrow \Delta}$ $[\Rightarrow\neg\neg] \dfrac{\Gamma \Rightarrow \Delta, \phi}{\Gamma \Rightarrow \Delta, \neg\neg\phi}$

$[\wedge\Rightarrow] \dfrac{\Gamma, \phi, \psi \Rightarrow \Delta}{\Gamma, \phi \wedge \psi \Rightarrow \Delta}$ $[\Rightarrow\wedge] \dfrac{\Gamma \Rightarrow \Delta, \phi \qquad \Gamma \Rightarrow \Delta, \psi}{\Gamma \Rightarrow \Delta, \phi \wedge \psi}$

$[\neg\wedge\Rightarrow] \dfrac{\Gamma, \neg\phi \Rightarrow \Delta \qquad \Gamma, \neg\psi \Rightarrow \Delta}{\Gamma, \neg(\phi \wedge \psi) \Rightarrow \Delta}$ $[\Rightarrow\neg\wedge] \dfrac{\Gamma \Rightarrow \Delta, \neg\phi, \neg\psi}{\Gamma \Rightarrow \Delta, \neg(\phi \wedge \psi)}$

$[\vee\Rightarrow] \dfrac{\Gamma, \phi \Rightarrow \Delta \qquad \Gamma, \psi \Rightarrow \Delta}{\Gamma, \phi \vee \psi \Rightarrow \Delta}$ $[\Rightarrow\vee] \dfrac{\Gamma \Rightarrow \Delta, \phi, \psi}{\Gamma \Rightarrow \Delta, \phi \vee \psi}$

$[\neg\vee\Rightarrow] \dfrac{\Gamma, \neg\phi, \neg\psi \Rightarrow \Delta}{\Gamma, \neg(\phi \vee \psi) \Rightarrow \Delta}$ $[\Rightarrow\neg\vee] \dfrac{\Gamma \Rightarrow \Delta, \neg\phi \qquad \Gamma \Rightarrow \Delta, \neg\psi}{\Gamma \Rightarrow \Delta, \neg(\phi \vee \psi)}$

Fig. 1. A sequent calculus for $\mathcal{LP}$

By Definition 11, ψ is a $\Vdash_{\mathsf{ND}}$-consequence of $\mathcal{AF}_{\mathfrak{L}}(\Sigma)$ if it is a consequent of an unattacked (and so, non-discarded) argument in $\mathcal{AF}_{\mathfrak{L}}(\Sigma)$. Thus, the set of these arguments is clearly admissible (and in particular conflict-free).

In what follows, when the underlying logical framework is fixed and known, we shall abbreviate $\mathsf{Arg}_{\mathfrak{L}}(\Sigma) \Vdash_{\mathsf{ND}} \psi$ by $\Sigma \Vdash_{\mathsf{ND}} \psi$.

Example 4. By Example 3, in an argumentation framework based on $\mathcal{LP}$ and Undercut, $\{\neg p, p, q\} \Vdash_{\mathsf{ND}} q \vee p$. It is easy to see that in the same framework $\{\neg p, p, q\} \Vdash_{\mathsf{ND}} q$ but $\{\neg p, p, q\} \not\Vdash_{\mathsf{ND}} p$ and $\{\neg p, p, q\} \not\Vdash_{\mathsf{ND}} \neg p$.

Example 5. As indicated, e.g., in [19], abstract argumentation frameworks face difficulties in handling n-ary conflicts for $n \geq 3$. As far as consequences are defined by entailment relations, such conflicts are easily maintained in logical argumentation frameworks. Using the canonical example from [19], it holds that in an argumentation framework for $\Sigma = \{p, q, \neg p \vee \neg q\}$ that is based, for instance, on $\mathcal{LP}$ and Undercut, the argument $p \Rightarrow p$ is discarded, e.g., by the argument $q, \neg p \vee \neg q \Rightarrow \neg p$. Similarly, the arguments $q \Rightarrow q$, and $\neg p \vee \neg q \Rightarrow \neg p \vee \neg q$ are discarded by other arguments based on Σ, and so neither of the consequents of these arguments is derivable from Σ according to $\Vdash_{\mathsf{ND}}$.[8]

---

[8] Assertions that are not related to the inconsistency in Σ are still inferrable, though. For instance, $\Sigma' \Vdash_{\mathsf{ND}} r$ when $\Sigma' = \Sigma \cup \{r\}$.

Some interesting properties of $\Vdash_{\mathsf{ND}}$ are considered next.

Proposition 9. *Let ψ be a theorem of a logic $\mathfrak{L} = \langle \mathcal{L}, \vdash \rangle$. Then for every set Σ of formulas and every set Attack of elimination rules considered in Section 3.2, $\mathsf{Arg}_{\mathfrak{L}}(\Sigma) \Vdash_{\mathsf{ND}} \psi$.*

Proof. Since ψ is an $\mathfrak{L}$-theorem, we have that $\vdash \psi$, and so $\Rightarrow \psi$ is an element in $\mathsf{Arg}_{\mathfrak{L}}(\Sigma)$. Since the support set of this argument is empty, it is not discarded by an argument in $\mathsf{Arg}_{\mathfrak{L}}(\Sigma)$ according to a rule in *Attack*, thus $\mathsf{Arg}_{\mathfrak{L}}(\Sigma) \Vdash_{\mathsf{ND}} \psi$.   □

Proposition 10. $\Vdash_{\mathsf{ND}}$ *is nonmonotonic in the size of the underlying knowledge-bases: Let $\mathcal{AF}_{\mathfrak{L}}(\Sigma) = \langle \mathsf{Arg}_{\mathfrak{L}}(\Sigma), Attack \rangle$ and $\mathcal{AF}_{\mathfrak{L}}(\Sigma') = \langle \mathsf{Arg}_{\mathfrak{L}}(\Sigma'), Attack \rangle$ be two argumentation frameworks such that $\Sigma \subseteq \Sigma'$ and Attack contains (at least) one of the elimination rules considered in Section 3.2. Then the fact that $\mathsf{Arg}_{\mathfrak{L}}(\Sigma) \Vdash_{\mathsf{ND}} \psi$ does* not *necessarily imply that $\mathsf{Arg}_{\mathfrak{L}}(\Sigma') \Vdash_{\mathsf{ND}} \psi$ as well.*

Proof. Consider, for instance, $\Sigma = \{p\}$. Since $\mathfrak{L}$ is a logic, $p \Rightarrow p \in \mathsf{Arg}_{\mathfrak{L}}(\Sigma)$, and so $\mathsf{Arg}_{\mathfrak{L}}(\{p\}) \Vdash_{\mathsf{ND}} p$. From the same reason, $\neg p \Rightarrow \neg p \in \mathsf{Arg}_{\mathfrak{L}}(\Sigma')$ where $\Sigma' = \Sigma \cup \{\neg p\}$. It follows that every argument in $\mathsf{Arg}_{\mathfrak{L}}(\Sigma')$ whose consequent is p, is discarded by $\neg p \Rightarrow \neg p$, and so $\mathsf{Arg}_{\mathfrak{L}}(\{p, \neg p\}) \not\Vdash_{\mathsf{ND}} p$.   □

Note 7. An interesting property of $\Vdash_{\mathsf{ND}}$ is that arguments that hold in a stronger logic cannot be discharged by weaker logics. This may be useful in agent nego-tiation as described below: Consider two agents G_1 and G_2, relying on the same knowledge-base Σ and referring to the same attack rules, but using different logics $\mathfrak{L}_1 = \langle \mathcal{L}, \vdash_1 \rangle$ and $\mathfrak{L}_2 = \langle \mathcal{L}, \vdash_2 \rangle$, respectively. In this case each agent has its own logical argumentation framework, which can be represented, respectively, by $\mathcal{AF}_{\mathfrak{L}_1}(\Sigma) = \langle \mathsf{Arg}_{\mathfrak{L}_1}(\Sigma), Attack \rangle$ and $\mathcal{AF}_{\mathfrak{L}_2}(\Sigma) = \langle \mathsf{Arg}_{\mathfrak{L}_2}(\Sigma), Attack \rangle$. Now, sup-pose that the logic used by G_2 is at least as strong as the logic used by G_1, i.e., $\vdash_1 \subseteq \vdash_2$. Then $\Gamma \vdash_1 \psi$ implies that $\Gamma \vdash_2 \psi$ and so $\mathsf{Arg}_{\mathfrak{L}_1}(\Sigma) \subseteq \mathsf{Arg}_{\mathfrak{L}_2}(\Sigma)$. Sup-pose now that $\mathsf{Arg}_{\mathfrak{L}_2}(\Sigma) \Vdash_{\mathsf{ND}} \psi$. Then there is an argument $\Gamma \Rightarrow \psi$ in $\mathsf{Arg}_{\mathfrak{L}_2}(\Sigma)$ that is not discarded by any argument in $\mathsf{Arg}_{\mathfrak{L}_2}(\Sigma)$. In particular, this sequent is not discarded by any argument in $\mathsf{Arg}_{\mathfrak{L}_1}(\Sigma)$. It follows that in this case G_2 has an argument in favor of ψ, which may not be producible by G_1 (since ψ may not follow from any subset of Σ according to $\vdash_1$), yet it cannot be discharged by G_1. In this setting, then, claims of agents with stronger logical sources may not be verified but cannot be dismissed by agents with weaker sources.

Other entailment relations, similar to $\Vdash_{\mathsf{ND}}$, may be defined by other semantics just like in Definition 3, provided that the underlying semantics is computable in terms of the rules in *Attack*. For instance, the grounded extension of $\mathcal{AF}_{\mathfrak{L}}(\Sigma)$, denoted by $\mathsf{GE}(\mathcal{AF}_{\mathfrak{L}}(\Sigma))$, contains all the arguments which are not attacked as well as the arguments which are directly or indirectly defended by non-attacked arguments. Thus, $\mathsf{GE}(\mathcal{AF}_{\mathfrak{L}}(\Sigma))$ is computable as follows: First, the non-attacked arguments in $\mathsf{Arg}_{\mathfrak{L}}(\Sigma)$ are added to $\mathsf{GE}(\mathcal{AF}_{\mathfrak{L}}(\Sigma))$. Then, the rules in *Attack* are applied on $\mathsf{Arg}_{\mathfrak{L}}(\Sigma)$ and the discarded arguments are removed. Denote the modified set of arguments by $\mathsf{Arg}_{\mathfrak{L}}^1(\Sigma)$. Again, the non-attacked arguments in $\mathsf{Arg}_{\mathfrak{L}}^1(\Sigma)$ are added to the set $\mathsf{GE}(\mathcal{AF}_{\mathfrak{L}}(\Sigma))$ and those that are discarded by rules in *Attack* are removed. This defines a new set, $\mathsf{Arg}_\mathfrak{L}^2(\Sigma)$, and so forth. Now, entailment by grounded semantics is defined by: $\mathcal{AF}_\mathfrak{L}(\Sigma) \Vdash_{\mathsf{GE}} \psi$ if there is an argument of the form $\Gamma \Rightarrow \psi$ in $\mathsf{GE}(\mathcal{AF}_\mathfrak{L}(\Sigma))$ for some $\Gamma \subseteq \Delta$.

We conclude this section with some simple observations regarding the general entailment relations that are obtained in our framework.

Definition 12. Let $\mathcal{AF}_\mathfrak{L}(\Sigma) = \langle \mathsf{Arg}_\mathfrak{L}(\Sigma), Attack \rangle$ be a logical argumentation framework for a set of formulas Σ based on an effective logic $\mathfrak{L} = \langle \mathcal{L}, \vdash \rangle$. Let Sem be one of the extension-based semantics considered in Definition 2 and $\mathcal{E}_{\mathsf{Sem}}(\mathcal{AF}_\mathfrak{L}(\Sigma))$ the corresponding Sem-extensions (Definition 3).

- We denote $\Sigma \Vdash_{\mathsf{Sem}} \psi$ if there is an argument $\Gamma \Rightarrow \psi$ in $\mathsf{Arg}_\mathfrak{L}(\Sigma)$ that is an element of every $\mathcal{E} \in \mathcal{E}_{\mathsf{Sem}}(\mathcal{AF}_\mathfrak{L}(\Sigma))$.
- We denote $\Sigma \vdash_{\mathsf{Sem}} \psi$ if every Sem-extension $\mathcal{E} \in \mathcal{E}_{\mathsf{Sem}}(\mathcal{AF}_\mathfrak{L}(\Sigma))$ contains an argument in $\mathsf{Arg}_\mathfrak{L}(\Sigma)$ whose consequent is ψ.

Proposition 11. *In the notations of Definition 12 we have that:*

1. *If $\Sigma \Vdash_{\mathsf{Sem}} \psi$ then $\Sigma \vdash_{\mathsf{Sem}} \psi$.*
2. *If $\Sigma \Vdash_{\mathsf{Sem}} \psi$ or $\Sigma \vdash_{\mathsf{Sem}} \psi$ then $\Sigma \vdash \psi$.*
3. *If $\vdash$ is paraconsistent, so are $\Vdash_{\mathsf{Sem}}$ and $\vdash_{\mathsf{Sem}}$.*
4. *If $\vdash$ has the variable sharing property,[9] so do $\Vdash_{\mathsf{Sem}}$ and $\vdash_{\mathsf{Sem}}$.*

Proof. Item 1 holds because the condition defining $\Vdash_{\mathsf{Sem}}$ is stronger than the one defining $\vdash_{\mathsf{Sem}}$. The condition of Item 2 assures that there is an argument of the form $\Gamma \Rightarrow \psi$ in $\mathsf{Arg}_\mathfrak{L}(\Sigma)$ and so by Proposition 1, $\Gamma \vdash \psi$ for some $\Gamma \subseteq \Sigma$. Since $\vdash$ is monotonic (because $\mathfrak{L}$ is a logic), also $\Sigma \vdash \psi$. For Item 3, note that if $p, \neg p \nvdash q$ then by Item 2 $p, \neg p \nVdash_{\mathsf{Sem}} q$ and $p, \neg p \nvdash_{\mathsf{Sem}} q$. Similar argument holds for Item 4: if $\Sigma \nvdash \psi$ whenever Σ and ψ do not share any atomic formula, so by Item 2 we have that in this case $\Sigma \nVdash_{\mathsf{Sem}} \psi$ and $\Sigma \nvdash_{\mathsf{Sem}} \psi$ either. $\square$

5   Further Utilizations of Arguments as Sequents

Apart of the obvious benefits of viewing arguments as sequents, such as the ability to incorporate well-established and general methods for representing arguments and automatically generating new arguments from existing ones, the use of sequents also allows to make some further enhancements in the way arguments are traditionally captured. Below, we mention two such enhancements.

- We used Gentzen-type systems which employ finite sets of formulas. However, one could follow Gentzen's original formulation and use *sequences* instead. This would allow, for instance, to encode *prefenrences* in the arguments, where the order in a sequence represents priorities. In this way one would be able to argue, for example, that $\Gamma \Rightarrow p$ for any sequence Γ

---

[9] That is, $\Sigma \nvdash \psi$ unless Σ and ψ share some atomic formula.

of literals that contains p and in which the first appearance of p precedes any appearance of $\neg p$. Another possibility is to employ *multisets* in the sequents, e.g. for representing majority considerations. Thus, one may state that $\Gamma \Rightarrow p$ holds whenever the number of appearances of p in a multiset Γ of literals is strictly bigger than the number of appearances of $\neg p$ in the same multiset. Of-course, the opposite may also be stated when incorporating mathematical objects other than (finite) sets. That is, it is possible to explicitly indicate that the order and/or the number of appearances of formulas do *not* matter, by introducing (either of) the following standard structural rules:

$$\text{Permutation:} \quad \frac{\Gamma_1, \psi, \varphi, \Gamma_2 \Rightarrow \Delta}{\Gamma_1, \varphi, \psi, \Gamma_2 \Rightarrow \Delta} \quad \frac{\Gamma \Rightarrow \Delta_1, \psi, \varphi, \Delta_2}{\Gamma \Rightarrow \Delta_1, \varphi, \psi, \Delta_2}$$

$$\text{Contraction:} \quad \frac{\Gamma_1, \psi, \psi, \Gamma_2 \Rightarrow \Delta}{\Gamma_1, \psi, \Gamma_2 \Rightarrow \Delta} \quad \frac{\Gamma \Rightarrow \Delta_1, \psi, \psi, \Delta_2}{\Gamma \Rightarrow \Delta_1, \psi, \Delta_2}$$

- The incorporation of more complex forms of sequents, such as nested sequents [15] or hypersequents [5], allows to express more sophisticated forms of argumentation, such as argumentation by counterfactuals or case-based argumentation. For instance, the nested sequent $\Gamma_1 \Rightarrow (\Gamma_2 \Rightarrow \psi)$ may be intuitively understood by "if Γ_1 were true, one would argue that $\Gamma_2 \Rightarrow \psi$" and the hypersequent $\Gamma_1 \Rightarrow \psi_1 \mid \Gamma_2 \Rightarrow \psi_2$ may be understood (again, intuitively) as a disjunction, at the meta-level, of the arguments $\Gamma_1 \Rightarrow \psi_1$ and $\Gamma_2 \Rightarrow \psi_2$.

6   Conclusion and Further Work

The contribution of this paper is mainly conceptual. It raises some basic questions on the definition of arguments in the context of logic-based argumentation, and claims that sequent-based representation and reasoning is an appropriate setting for logic-based modeling of argumentation systems. Among others, this approach enables a general and natural way of expressing arguments and implies that well-studied techniques and methodologies may be borrowed from proof theory and applied in the context of argumentation theory.

The starting point of this paper is Besnard and Hunter's approach to logical argumentation, which we believe is a successful way of representing deductive reasoning in argumentation-based environments (Comparisons to other logic-based approaches, such as those that are based on defeasible logics [30, 33], can be found e.g. in [13]). Our work extends this approach in several ways: first, the usual conditions of minimality and consistency of supports are abandoned. This offers a simpler way of producing arguments and identifying them (also for systems that are not formulated in a Gentzen-type style). Second, arguments are produced and are withdrawn by rules of the same style, allowing for a more uniform way of representing the frameworks and computing their extensions. What is more, as noted previously, the representation of arguments as inferences suggests that techniques of proof theory may be incorporated.[10] Third, our approach

---

[10] Other techniques for generating arguments are considered, e.g., in [11] and [24].

is logic-independent. This allows in particular to rely on a classical as well as on a non-classical logic, and so, for instance, paraconsistent formalisms may be used for improving consistency-maintenance. Logic independence also implies that our approach is appropriate for multi-agent environments, involving different logics for different agents.

Much is still need to be done in order to tighten the links between abstract and logical argumentation theories. For instance, it would be interesting to investigate what *specific* logics and attack relations yield useful frameworks, and whether the argumentation semantics that they induce give intuitively acceptable solutions to practical problems. Another important issue for further exploration is the computational aspect of our approach, which so far remains mainly on the representation level. This requires an automated machinery that not only produces sequents, but is also capable of eliminating them, as well as their consequences. Here, techniques like those used in the context of dynamic proof theory for adaptive logics may be useful (see, e.g., [8, 9]).

References

[1] Amgoud, L., Besnard, P.: Bridging the gap between abstract argumentation systems and logic. In: Godo, L., Pugliese, A. (eds.) SUM 2009. LNCS, vol. 5785, pp. 12–27. Springer, Heidelberg (2009)

[2] Amgoud, L., Besnard, P.: A formal analysis of logic-based argumentation systems. In: Deshpande, A., Hunter, A. (eds.) SUM 2010. LNCS, vol. 6379, pp. 42–55. Springer, Heidelberg (2010)

[3] Amgoud, L., Besnard, P., Vesic, S.: Identifying the core of logic-based argumentation systems. In: Proc. ICTAI 2011, pp. 633–636. IEEE (2011)

[4] Arieli, O., Avron, A.: The value of the four values. Artificial Intelligence 102(1), 97–141 (1998)

[5] Avron, A.: A constructive analysis of RM. J. Symbolic Logic 52, 939–951 (1987)

[6] Baroni, P., Caminada, M.W.A., Giacomin, M.: An introduction to argumentation semantics. The Knowledge Engineering Review 26(4), 365–410 (2011)

[7] Baroni, P., Giacomin, M.: Semantics for abstract argumentation systems. In: Rahwan, Simary (eds.) [32], pp. 25–44

[8] Batens, D.: Dynamic dialectical logics. In: Priest, G., Routely, R., Norman, J. (eds.) Paraconsistent Logic. Essay on the Inconsistent, pp. 187–217. Philosophia Verlag (1989)

[9] Batens, D.: A survey on inconsistency-adaptive logics. In: Batens, D., Mortensen, C., Priest, G., Van Bendegem, J. (eds.) Frontiers of Paraconsistent Logic. Studies in Logic and Computation, vol. 8, pp. 69–73. Research Studies Press (2000)

[10] Belnap, N.D.: A useful four-valued logic. In: Dunn, M., Epstein, G. (eds.) Modern Uses of Multiple-Valued Logics, pp. 7–37. Reidel Publishing (1977)

[11] Besnard, P., Grégoire, É., Piette, C., Raddaoui, B.: MUS-based generation of arguments and counter-arguments. In: Proc. IRI 2010, pp. 239–244. IEEE (2010)

[12] Besnard, P., Hunter, A.: A logic-based theory of deductive arguments. Artificial Intelligence 128(1-2), 203–235 (2001)

[13] Besnard, P., Hunter, A.: Argumentation based on classical logic. In: Rahwan, Simary (eds.) [32], pp. 133–152

[14] Besnard, P., Hunter, A., Woltran, S.: Encoding deductive argumentation in quantified boolean formulae. Artificial Intelligence 173(15), 1406–1423 (2009)
[15] Brünnler, K.: Nested Sequents. PhD thesis, Institut für Informatik und Angewandte Mathematik, Universität Bern (2010)
[16] Caminada, M.W.A.: Contamination in formal argumentation systems. In: Proc. BNAIC 2005, pp. 59–65 (2005)
[17] Caminada, M.W.A.: Semi-stable semantics. In: Dunne, P.E., Bench-Capon, T.J.M. (eds.) Proc. COMMA 2006, pp. 121–130. IOS Press (2006)
[18] Caminada, M.W.A., Carnielli, W.A., Dunne, P.E.: Semi-stable semantics. Journal of Logic and Computation 22(5), 1207–1254 (2012)
[19] Caminada, M.W.A., Vesic, S.: On extended conflict-freeness in argumentation. In: Uiterwijk, J., Roos, N., Winands, M. (eds.) Proc. BNAIC 2012, pp. 43–50 (2012)
[20] Chesñevar, C.I., Maguitman, A.G., Loui, R.P.: Logical models of argument. ACM Computing Surveys 32(4), 337–383 (2000)
[21] da Costa, N.C.A.: On the theory of inconsistent formal systems. Notre Dame Journal of Formal Logic 15, 497–510 (1974)
[22] Dung, P.M.: On the acceptability of arguments and its fundamental role in non-monotonic reasoning, logic programming and n-person games. Artificial Intelligence 77, 321–357 (1995)
[23] Dung, P.M., Mancarella, P., Toni, F.: Computing ideal sceptical argumentation. Artificial Intelligence 171(10-15), 642–674 (2007)
[24] Efstathiou, V., Hunter, A.: Algorithms for generating arguments and counterarguments in propositional logic. Journal of Approximate Reasoning 52(6), 672–704 (2011)
[25] Eiter, T., Gottlob, G.: The complexity of logic-based abduction. Journal of the ACM 42, 3–42 (1995)
[26] Gentzen, G.: Investigations into logical deduction (1934) (in German); An English translation appears in 'The Collected Works of Gerhard Gentzen', edited by M. E. Szabo. North-Holland (1969)
[27] Gorogiannis, N., Hunter, A.: Instantiating abstract argumentation with classical logic arguments: Postulates and properties. Artificial Intelligence 175(9-10), 1479–1497 (2011)
[28] Pollock, J.L.: Defeasible reasoning. Cognitive Science 11(4), 481–518 (1987)
[29] Pollock, J.L.: How to reason defeasibly. Artificial Intelligence 57, 1–42 (1992)
[30] Prakken, H., Vreeswijk, G.: Logical systems for defeasible argumentation. In: Gabbay, D., Guenthner, F. (eds.) Handbook of Philosochical Logic, vol. 14, pp. 219–318. Kluwer Academic Publishers (2002)
[31] Priest, G.: Reasoning about truth. Artificial Intelligence 39, 231–244 (1989)
[32] Rahwan, I., Simari, G.R.: Argumentation in Artificial Intelligence. Springer (2009)
[33] Simari, G.R., Loui, R.P.: A mathematical treatment of defeasible reasoning and its implementation. Artificial Intelligence 53(2-3), 125–157 (1992)

Instantiating Knowledge Bases in Abstract Dialectical Frameworks*

Hannes Strass

Computer Science Institute, Leipzig University

Abstract. We present a translation from defeasible theory bases to abstract dialectical frameworks, a recent generalisation of abstract argumentation frameworks. Using several problematic examples from the literature, we first show how our translation addresses important issues of existing approaches. We then prove that the translated frameworks satisfy the rationality postulates closure and direct/indirect consistency. Furthermore, the frameworks can detect inconsistencies in the set of strict inference rules and cyclic (strict and defeasible) supports amongst literals. We also show that the translation involves at most a quadratic blowup and is therefore effectively and efficiently computable.

1 Introduction

Abstract argumentation frameworks (AFs) [1] are a formalism that is widely used in argumentation research. Such an AF consists of a set of arguments and an attack relation between these arguments. Their semantics determines which sets of arguments of a given AF can be accepted according to specific criteria. A common way to employ Dung's AFs is as abstraction formalism. In this view, expressive languages are used to model concrete argumentation scenarios, and translations into Dung AFs provide these original languages with semantics. The advantage of translating into an argumentation formalism is that the resulting semantics can be given a dialectical interpretation, which can be used to inform humans how a particular conclusion was inferred.

However, the approach is not without its problems. Caminada and Amgoud [2] reported some difficulties they encountered when defining an abstract argumentation-based semantics for defeasible theory bases. Defeasible theory bases are simple logic-inspired formalisms working with inference rules on a set of literals. Inference rules can be strict, in which case the conclusion of the inference (a literal) must necessarily hold whenever all antecedents (also literals) hold. Inference rules can also be defeasible, which means that the conclusion *usually* holds whenever the antecedents hold. Here, the word "usually" suggests that there could be exceptional cases where a defeasible rule has not been applied.

In response to the problems they encountered, Caminada and Amgoud [2] stated general rationality postulates for AFs based on defeasible theories. The intention of these postulates is to mathematically capture what humans perceive

---

* This research has been partially supported by DFG under project BR-1817/7-1.

as rational behaviour from the semantics of defeasible theory bases. First of all the *closure* postulate says that whatever model or extension the target formalism (the AF) produces, it must be closed under application of strict rules, meaning that all applicable strict rules have been applied. Direct and indirect *consistency* postulates express that any model or extension of the target formalism must be internally consistent with respect to the literals of the defeasible theory base (directly) and even with respect to application of strict rules (indirectly).

Later, Wyner et al. [3] criticised Caminada and Amgoud's definition of arguments on ontological grounds and gave an alternative translation. We are agnostic with respect to Wyner et al.'s criticism, but use their translation as a starting point for our own work. Such a further refinement is necessary since the translation of Wyner et al. [3] still yields unintuitive results on benchmark examples and does not satisfy the closure and indirect consistency postulates.

The basis of our solution to the aforementioned problems is a shift in the target language. While until now abstract argumentation frameworks were the formalism of choice, we will use the more general abstract *dialectical* frameworks (ADFs) [4]. Where AFs allow only attacks between arguments, ADFs can also represent support relations and many more. More specifically, in an AF an argument is accepted if none of its attackers is accepted. The same can be expressed in an ADF. But ADFs can also express that an argument is only accepted if all of its supporters are accepted, or the argument is accepted if *some* of its supporters are accepted, or it is accepted if some *attacker* is *not* accepted or . . .

The expressiveness of ADFs in comparison to AFs – which we studied in [5,6] – enables us to give a direct and straightforward translation from defeasible theory bases to abstract dialectical frameworks. We will show that this translation – the main contribution of this paper – treats the benchmark examples right and satisfies the rationality postulates of Caminada and Amgoud [2]. We consider this further important evidence that abstract dialectical frameworks are useful tools for representing and reasoning about argumentation scenarios. We also perform a complexity analysis of our translation; this is significant in that we are not aware of complexity analyses of the mentioned previous approaches.

The availability of support in ADFs (in contrast to AFs) as a target formalism will be of fundamental importance to our translation. Among other things, it will allow us to resolve cyclic dependencies among literals in a defeasible theory base in a straightforward way. The treatment of such support cycles is built into ADF standard semantics, which can be considered a product of decades of research into nonmonotonic knowledge representation languages.

In the rest of the paper, we first recall the necessary background on defeasible theory bases, abstract argumentation frameworks and abstract dialectical frameworks. In Section 3 we look at the translations of Caminada and Amgoud [2] and Wyner et al. [3], discuss some problems of these, and introduce generalised versions of the rationality postulates. In Section 4 we then define our own translation. We show how it treats the problematic examples, prove that it satisfies the (generalised versions of the) rationality postulates and analyse its computational complexity. We conclude with a discussion of related and future work.

2 Background

Defeasible Theories. Following Caminada and Amgoud [2], we use a set *Lit* of literals that are built using syntactical negation ¬· and define a semantic negation function ⁻ such that for an atom p we have $\overline{p} = \neg p$ and $\overline{\neg p} = p$. Throughout the paper, we assume that *Lit* is closed under negation in the sense that $\psi \in Lit$ implies $\overline{\psi} \in Lit$. A set $S \subseteq Lit$ of literals is *consistent* iff there is no literal $\psi \in Lit$ such that both $\psi \in S$ and $\neg\psi \in S$. For literals $\phi_1, \ldots, \phi_n, \psi \in Lit$, a *strict rule* over *Lit* is of the form $r : \phi_1, \ldots, \phi_n \rightarrow \psi$; a *defeasible rule* over *Lit* is of the form $r : \phi_1, \ldots, \phi_n \Rightarrow \psi$. (The only difference is the arrows.) Here r is the unique *rule name*, the literals $\phi_1, \ldots, \phi_n$ constitute the *rule body* and ψ is the *rule head* or *conclusion*. Intuitively, a strict rule says that the rule head is necessarily true whenever all body literals are true; a defeasible rule says that the head ψ is *usually* true whenever all body literals are true. In definitions, we use the symbol $\Rightarrow$ as meta-level variable for $\rightarrow$ and $\Rightarrow$.

For a set $M \subseteq Lit$ of literals and a set *StrInf* of strict rules over *Lit*, we say that M is *closed under StrInf* iff $r : \phi_1, \ldots, \phi_n \rightarrow \psi \in StrInf$ and $\phi_1, \ldots, \phi_n \in M$ imply $\psi \in M$. Accordingly, the *closure of M under StrInf* is the smallest set $Cl_{StrInf}(M)$ that contains M and is closed under *StrInf*. A *defeasible theory* or *theory base* is a triple $(Lit, StrInf, DefInf)$ where *Lit* is a set of literals, *StrInf* is a set of strict rules over *Lit* and *DefInf* is a set of defeasible rules over *Lit*. The semantics of theory bases is usually defined via a translation to abstract argumentation frameworks, which will be introduced next.

Abstract Argumentation Frameworks. Dung [1] introduced argumentation frameworks as pairs $\Theta = (A, R)$ where A is a set and $R \subseteq A \times A$ a relation. The intended reading of an AF Θ is that the elements of A are arguments whose internal structure is abstracted away. The only information about the arguments is given by the relation R encoding a notion of attack: a pair $(a, b) \in R$ expresses that argument a attacks argument b in some sense.

The purpose of semantics for argumentation frameworks is to determine sets of arguments (called *extensions*) which are acceptable according to various standards. We will only be interested in so-called *stable* extensions, sets S of arguments that do not attack each other and attack all arguments not in the set. More formally, a set $S \subseteq A$ of arguments is *conflict-free* iff there are no $a, b \in S$ with $(a, b) \in R$. A set S is a *stable extension* for (A, R) iff it is conflict-free and for all $a \in A \setminus S$ there is a $b \in S$ with $(b, a) \in R$.

Abstract Dialectical Frameworks. Brewka and Woltran [4] introduced abstract dialectical frameworks as a powerful generalisation of Dung AFs that are able to capture not only attack and support, but also more general notions such as joint attack and joint support.

Definition 1. *An* abstract dialectical framework *is a triple* $\Xi = (S, L, C)$ *where*

- S *is a set of* statements,
- $L \subseteq S \times S$ *is a set of* links, *where* $par(s) \overset{\text{def}}{=} \{r \in S \mid (r, s) \in L\}$

– $C = \{C_s\}_{s \in S}$ *is a set of total functions* $C_s : 2^{par(s)} \to \{in, out\}$.

Intuitively, the function C_s for a statement s determines the acceptance status of s, which naturally depends on the status of its parent nodes. Any such function C_s can alternatively be represented by a propositional formula φ_s over the vocabulary $par(s)$. The understanding here is that for $M \subseteq par(s)$, $C_s(M) = in$ iff M is a model of φ_s (written $M \models \varphi_s$), where an interpretation is identified with the set of atoms that are evaluated to true.

Brewka and Woltran [4] introduced several semantic notions for ADFs. First, for an ADF $\Xi = (S, L, C)$ where C is given by a set of propositional formulas φ_s for each $s \in S$, a set $M \subseteq S$ is a *model for* Ξ iff for all statements s we have: $s \in M$ iff $M \models \varphi_s$.

Example 1 (Abstract dialectical framework). Consider the ADF $D = (S, L, C)$ with statements $S = \{a, b, c, d\}$, links $L = \{(a, c), (b, b), (b, c), (b, d)\}$ and acceptance functions given by the formulas $\varphi_a = \top$, $\varphi_b = b$, $\varphi_c = a \wedge b$ and $\varphi_d = \neg b$. Intuitively, these acceptance conditions express that (1) a is always accepted, (2) b supports itself, (3) c needs the joint support of a and b, and (4) d is attacked by b. The two models of D are $M_1 = \{a, b, c\}$ and $M_2 = \{a, d\}$.

In recent work [6], we redefined several standard ADF semantics and defined additional ones. In this paper, we are only interested in two-valued semantics, that is, models and stable models. The definition of the latter is based on the notion of a reduct and an operator originally introduced by Brewka and Woltran [4].

The operator Γ_Ξ takes two sets A, R of statements, where the intuition is that all statements in A are accepted and those in R are rejected. (So those in $S \setminus (A \cup R)$ are undecided.) According to these acceptance statuses, the operator evaluates all acceptance formulas and decides which statements can be definitely accepted or rejected.

The reduct implements the intuition that whatever is false in a stable model can be assumed false, but whatever is true in a stable model must be constructively provable. The next definition combines all of this.

Definition 2. *Let* $\Xi = (S, L, C)$ *be an abstract dialectical framework. Define an operator by* $\Gamma_\Xi(A, R) = (acc(A, R), rej(A, R))$ *for* $A, R \subseteq S$, *where*

$$acc(A, R) = \{s \in S \mid \text{for all } A \subseteq Z \subseteq (S \setminus R), \text{ we have } Z \models \varphi_s\}$$
$$rej(A, R) = \{s \in S \mid \text{for all } A \subseteq Z \subseteq (S \setminus R), \text{ we have } Z \not\models \varphi_s\}$$

For a set $M \subseteq S$, *define the reduced ADF* $\Xi_M = (M, L_M, C_M)$ *by the set of links* $L_M = L \cap M \times M$ *and for each* $s \in M$ *we set* $\varphi_{M,s} = \varphi_s[r/\bot : r \notin M]$. *A model* M *for* Ξ *is a* stable model *of* Ξ *iff the least fixpoint of the operator* Γ_{Ξ_M} *is given by* (M, R) *for some* $R \subseteq S$.

Example 1 (Continued). Of the two models M_1, M_2 we have seen earlier, only M_2 is a stable model. Intuitively, the statement $b \in M_1$ cyclically supports itself.

It is clear that ADFs are a generalisation of AFs: for an argumentation framework $\Theta = (A, R)$, its *associated abstract dialectical framework* is $\Xi(\Theta) = (A, R, C)$

with $C_a(B) = in$ iff $B = \emptyset$ for each $a \in A$. But this is not just syntactical; Brewka and Woltran [4] showed that their semantical notions for ADFs are generalisations of Dung's respective AF notions; likewise, in [5,6] we proved correspondence results for all of the newly defined semantics. Brewka and Woltran [4] defined a particular subclass of ADFs called *bipolar*. Intuitively, in bipolar ADFs each link is supporting or attacking (or both). It will turn out that ADFs resulting from our automatic translation from defeasible theory bases are all bipolar.

3   Instantiations to Abstract Argumentation Frameworks

The general approach to provide a semantics for defeasible theories is to translate the defeasible theory into an argumentation formalism and then let the already existing semantics for that argumentation formalism determine the semantics of the defeasible theory. In the literature, the target formalism of choice are Dung's abstract argumentation frameworks. They abstract away from everything except arguments and attacks between them, so to define a translation to AFs one has to define arguments and attacks. We now review two particular such approaches.

3.1   The Approach of Caminada and Amgoud [2]

Caminada and Amgoud [2] define a translation from defeasible theories to argumentation frameworks. They create arguments in an inductive way by applying one or more inference rules. The internal structure of the arguments reflects how a particular conclusion was derived by applying an inference rule to the conclusions of subarguments, and allows arguments to be nested. So the base case of the induction takes into account rules with empty body, that is, rules of the form $\to \psi$ (or $\Rightarrow \psi$) for some literal ψ. Each such rule leads to an argument $A = [\to \psi]$ (or $[\Rightarrow \psi]$), and the conclusion of the rule becomes the conclusion of the argument. For the induction step, we assume there are arguments $A_1, \ldots, A_n$ with conclusions $\phi_1, \ldots, \phi_n$, respectively. If there is a strict rule $\phi_1, \ldots, \phi_n \to \psi$, we can build a new argument $A = [A_1, \ldots, A_n \to \psi]$ with conclusion ψ. (Likewise, from a defeasible rule $\phi_1, \ldots, \phi_n \Rightarrow \psi$ we can build a new argument $A = [A_1, \ldots, A_n \Rightarrow \psi]$.) Similar to rules, arguments can be strict or defeasible, where application of at least one defeasible rule makes the whole argument defeasible. (So strict arguments exclusively use strict rules.)

Caminada and Amgoud [2] then define two different kinds of attacks between arguments, rebuts and undercuts. An argument a rebuts another argument b if a subargument of a concludes some literal ψ, while there is a defeasible subargument of b that concludes $\overline{\psi}$. An argument a undercuts another argument b if the latter has a subargument that results from applying a defeasible rule and the applicability of that rule is disputed by a subargument of a.[1] In any case, we see that only defeasible arguments can be attacked.

---

[1] We will focus on rebuts in this paper since they are sufficient for our main points.

Example 2 (Married John, [2, Example 4]). Consider the following vocabulary with intended natural-language meaning: $w \ldots$ John wears something that looks like a wedding ring, $g \ldots$ John often goes out late with his friends, $m \ldots$ John is married, $b \ldots$ John is a bachelor, $h \ldots$ John has a wife. There are several relationships between these propositions, which are captured in the following theory base: the literals are $Lit = \{w, g, h, m, b, \neg w, \neg g, \neg h, \neg m, \neg b\}$, the strict rules are given by $StrInf = \{r_1 :\to w, \ r_2 :\to g, \ r_3 : b \to \neg h, \ r_4 : m \to h\}$ and the defeasible rules $DefInf = \{r_5 : w \Rightarrow m, \ r_6 : g \Rightarrow b\}$.

In the ASPIC system of Caminada and Amgoud [2], all the literals in the set $S = \{w, g, m, b\}$ are sceptical consequences of the constructed AF. Caminada and Amgoud observe that this is clearly unintended since the natural-language interpretation would be that John is a married bachelor. Moreover, the closure of S under $StrInf$ is $Cl_{StrInf}(S) = \{w, g, m, b, h, \neg h\}$, which is inconsistent. So not only are there applicable strict rules that have not been applied in S, but their application would lead to inconsistency.

To avoid anomalies such as the one just seen, Caminada and Amgoud [2] went on to define three natural rationality postulates for rule-based argumentation-based systems which are concerned with the interplay of consistency and strict rule application. Our formulation of them is slightly different for various reasons:

- We are concerned with argumentation frameworks as well as with abstract dialectical frameworks in this paper, so we made the postulates parametric in the target argumentation formalism.
- We removed the respective second condition on the sceptical conclusions with respect to all extensions/models. Propositions 4 and 5 in [2] show that they are redundant in their case.
- We are not constrained to formalisms and semantics where there are only finitely many extensions/models.
- For the sake of readability, we assume that the literals Lit of the defeasible theory are contained in the vocabulary of the target formalism.[2]

The first postulate requires that the set of conclusions for any extension should be closed under application of strict rules.

Postulate 1 (Closure) *Let* $(Lit, StrInf, DefInf)$ *be a defeasible theory. Its translation satisfies* closure *for semantics* σ *iff for any* σ*-model* M*, we find that* $Cl_{StrInf}(Lit \cap M) \subseteq Lit \cap M$.

Naturally, the notion of consistency is reduced to consistency of a set of literals of the underlying logical language. Note that consistency only concerns the local consistency of a given single model/extension of the target formalism. It may well be that the formalism is globally inconsistent in the sense of not allowing for any model with respect to a particular semantics. The latter behaviour can be desired, for example if the original theory base is inconsistent already.

---

[2] This is not a proper restriction since reconstruction of conclusions about the original defeasible theory is one of the goals of the whole enterprise and so there should be at least a translation function from argumentation models to theory models.

Postulate 2 (Direct Consistency) *Let* $(Lit, StrInf, DefInf)$ *be a defeasible theory with translation* X *and* σ *a semantics.* X *satisfies* direct consistency *iff for all* σ-*models* M *we have that* $Lit \cap M$ *is consistent.*

Caminada and Amgoud [2] remark that it is usually easy to satisfy direct consistency, but much harder to satisfy the stronger notion of indirect consistency. For this to hold, for each model its closure under strict rules must be consistent.

Postulate 3 (Indirect Consistency) *Let* $(Lit, StrInf, DefInf)$ *be a defeasible theory with translation* X *and* σ *a semantics.* X *satisfies* indirect consistency *iff for all* σ-*models* M *we have that* $Lit \cap Cl_{StrInf}(Lit \cap M)$ *is consistent.*

As a counterpart to Proposition 7 of Caminada and Amgoud [2], we can show that closure and direct consistency together imply indirect consistency.

Proposition 1. *Let* $(Lit, StrInf, DefInf)$ *be a defeasible theory with translation* X *and* σ *a semantics. If* X *satisfies closure and direct consistency, then it satisfies indirect consistency.*

Proof. Let X satisfy closure and direct consistency, and let M be a σ-model for X. We have to show that $Lit \cap Cl_{StrInf}(Lit \cap M)$ is consistent. Since X satisfies closure, $Cl_{StrInf}(Lit \cap M) \subseteq Lit \cap M$. Thus $Lit \cap Cl_{StrInf}(Lit \cap M) \subseteq Lit \cap M$. Now since X satisfies direct consistency, $Lit \cap M$ is consistent. Hence its subset $Lit \cap Cl_{StrInf}(Lit \cap M)$ is consistent and X satisfies indirect consistency. $\square$

3.2   The Approach of Wyner et al. [3]

Wyner et al. [3] identified some problems of the approach of Caminada and Amgoud [2] and proposed an alternative translation from theory bases to argumentation frameworks. We do not necessarily support or reject their philosophical criticisms, but rather find the translation technically appealing. They create an argument for each literal in the theory base's language and additionally an argument for each rule. Intuitively, the literal arguments indicate that the literal holds, and the rule arguments indicate that the rule is applicable. Furthermore, the defined conflicts between these arguments are straightforward:

(1) opposite literals attack each other; (2) rules are attacked by the negations of their body literals; (3) defeasible rules are attacked by the negation of their head; (4) all rules attack the negation of their head.

Definition 3 ([3, Definitions 4,5]). *Let* $TB = (Lit, StrInf, DefInf)$ *be a defeasible theory. Define an argumentation framework* $\Theta(TB) = (A, R)$ *as follows.*

$$A = \quad Lit \cup \{r \mid r : \phi_1, \ldots, \phi_n \Rightarrow \psi \in StrInf \cup DefInf\}$$

$$R = \quad \{(\psi, \overline{\psi}) \mid \psi \in Lit\}$$
$$\cup \; \{(\overline{\phi_i}, r) \mid r : \phi_1, \ldots, \phi_n \Rightarrow \psi \in StrInf \cup DefInf, 1 \leq i \leq n\}$$
$$\cup \; \{(\overline{\psi}, r) \mid r : \phi_1, \ldots, \phi_n \Rightarrow \psi \in DefInf\}$$
$$\cup \; \{(r, \overline{\psi}) \mid r : \phi_1, \ldots, \phi_n \Rightarrow \psi \in StrInf \cup DefInf\}$$

Let us look at one of their own examples which they adapted from [2].

Example 3 ([3, Example 5]). Consider the following theory base.

$$Lit = \{x_1, x_2, x_3, x_4, x_5, \neg x_1, \neg x_2, \neg x_3, \neg x_4, \neg x_5\}$$
$$StrInf = \{r_1 :\to x_1, \quad r_2 :\to x_2, \quad r_3 :\to x_3, \quad r_4 : x_4, x_5 \to \neg x_3\}$$
$$DefInf = \{r_5 : x_1 \Rightarrow x_4, \quad r_6 : x_2 \Rightarrow x_5\}$$

We can see that x_1, x_2, x_3 are strictly asserted and thus should be contained in any extension. The AF translation is depicted below.

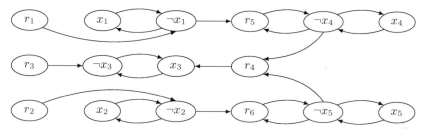

The stable extensions of this AF are as follows:

$$S_1 = \{x_1, x_2, x_3, \neg x_4, \neg x_5, r_1, r_2, r_3\} \quad S_2 = \{x_1, x_2, x_3, \neg x_4, x_5, r_1, r_2, r_3, r_6\}$$
$$S_3 = \{x_1, x_2, x_3, x_4, \neg x_5, r_1, r_2, r_3, r_5\} \quad S_4 = \{x_1, x_2, x_4, x_5, r_1, r_2, r_3, r_4, r_5, r_6\}$$

While the first three extensions can be considered intended, S_4 is not closed under strict rules and indirectly inconsistent: r_3 is applicable but x_3 does not hold, r_4 is applicable but $\neg x_3$ does not hold.

A similar observation can be made in Example 2: the AF translation according to Wyner et al. [3] has a stable extension $\{w, g, m, b, r_1, r_2, r_3, r_4, r_5, r_6\}$ where John is a married bachelor.

4   Instantiations to Abstract Dialectical Frameworks

In this section, we extend the theory base to AF translation of Wyner et al. [3] to ADFs. Due to the availability of support, this is straightforward. Indeed, support and attack are sufficient for our purposes.

4.1   From Theory Bases to ADFs

As in the approach of Wyner et al. [3], we directly use the literals from the theory base as statements that express whether the literal holds. We also use rule names as statements indicating that the rule is applicable. Additionally, for each rule r we create a statement $-r$ indicating that the rule has not been applied. Not applying a rule is acceptable for defeasible rules, but unacceptable for strict rules since it would violate the closure postulate. This is enforced via

integrity constraints saying that it may not be the case in any model that the
rule body holds but the head does not hold. Defeasible rules offer some degree of
choice, whence we leave it to the semantics whether or not to apply them. This
choice is modelled by a mutual attack cycle between r and $-r$. The remaining
acceptance conditions are equally straightforward:

- Opposite literals attack each other.
- A literal is accepted whenever some rule deriving it is applicable, that is, all
  rules with head ψ support statement ψ.
- A strict rule is applicable whenever all of its body literals hold, that is, the
  body literals of r are exactly the supporters of r.
- Likewise, a defeasible rule is applicable whenever all of its body literals hold,
  and additionally the negation of its head literal must not hold.

In particular, literals cannot be accepted unless there is some rule deriving them.

Definition 4. *Let* $TB = (Lit, StrInf, DefInf)$ *be a theory base. Define an ADF*
$\Xi(TB) = (S, L, C)$ *by* $S = Lit \cup \{r, -r \mid r : \phi_1, \ldots, \phi_n \Rightarrow \psi \in StrInf \cup DefInf\}$;
the acceptance functions of statements s *can be parsimoniously represented by*
propositional formulas φ_s.[3] *For a literal* $\psi \in Lit$, *we define*

$$\varphi_\psi = \neg[\overline{\psi}] \wedge \bigvee_{r:\phi_1,\ldots,\phi_n \Rightarrow \psi \in StrInf \cup DefInf} [r]$$

For a strict rule $r : \phi_1, \ldots, \phi_n \to \psi \in StrInf$, *we define*

$$\varphi_r = [\phi_1] \wedge \ldots \wedge [\phi_n] \qquad and \qquad \varphi_{-r} = [\phi_1] \wedge \ldots \wedge [\phi_n] \wedge \neg[\psi] \wedge \neg[-r]$$

For a defeasible rule $r : \phi_1, \ldots, \phi_n \Rightarrow \psi \in DefInf$, *we define*

$$\varphi_r = [\phi_1] \wedge \ldots \wedge [\phi_n] \wedge \neg[\overline{\psi}] \wedge \neg[-r] \qquad and \qquad \varphi_{-r} = \neg[r]$$

Finally, there is a link $(s', s) \in L$ *iff* $[s']$ *occurs in the acceptance formula* φ_s.

For strict rules with name r, the self-attack of $-r$ does not materialise whenever
either the rule body is not satisfied or the rule head holds; otherwise the strict
rule is applicable but has not been applied and the constraint $-r$ prevents this
undesirable state of affairs from getting included in a model. (For the formulas
defined above, the empty disjunction leads to $\bot$ – logical falsity – and the empty
conjunction to $\top$ – logical truth.)

Let us see how our translation treats the examples seen earlier.

---

[3] In these formulas, we write ADF statements in brackets, to avoid confusion between
negation being applied inside a statement name – as in $[\neg x]$ – and negation being
applied in the formula outside of the statement's name – as in $\neg[-r]$. Thus $[\neg x]$ and
$\neg[x]$ are syntactically different literals in the language of acceptance formulas; their
meaning is intertwined via the semantics of ADFs.

Example 3 (Continued). Definition 4 yields the following acceptance formulas.

$$\varphi_{x_1} = \neg[\neg x_1] \wedge [r_1] \qquad \varphi_{x_2} = \neg[\neg x_2] \wedge [r_2] \quad \varphi_{x_3} = \neg[\neg x_3] \wedge [r_3]$$
$$\varphi_{x_4} = \neg[\neg x_4] \wedge [r_5] \qquad \varphi_{x_5} = \neg[\neg x_5] \wedge [r_6]$$
$$\varphi_{\neg x_1} = \bot \quad \varphi_{\neg x_2} = \bot \qquad \varphi_{\neg x_3} = \neg[x_3] \wedge [r_4] \quad \varphi_{\neg x_4} = \bot \quad \varphi_{\neg x_5} = \bot$$
$$\varphi_{r_1} = \top \quad \varphi_{r_2} = \top \qquad \varphi_{r_3} = \top \qquad \varphi_{r_4} = [x_4] \wedge [x_5]$$
$$\varphi_{r_5} = [x_1] \wedge \neg[\neg x_4] \wedge \neg[-r_5] \quad \varphi_{r_6} = [x_2] \wedge \neg[\neg x_5] \wedge \neg[-r_6]$$
$$\varphi_{-r_1} = \neg[x_1] \wedge \neg[-r_1] \qquad \varphi_{-r_2} = \neg[x_2] \wedge \neg[-r_2] \quad \varphi_{-r_3} = \neg[x_3] \wedge \neg[-r_3]$$
$$\varphi_{-r_4} = [x_4] \wedge [x_5] \wedge \neg[\neg x_3] \wedge \neg[-r_4] \qquad \varphi_{-r_5} = \neg[r_5] \quad \varphi_{-r_6} = \neg[r_6]$$

Statements with an acceptance condition of the form $\neg p_1 \wedge \ldots \wedge \neg p_n$ behave like AF arguments. So in particular r_1, r_2, r_3 are always *in* since these rules have an empty body. Similarly, $-r_1, -r_2, -r_3$ are self-attacking arguments. The statements $\neg x_1, \neg x_2, \neg x_4, \neg x_5$ are always *out* since there are no rules deriving these literals. The remaining acceptance conditions are clear from the definitions: literals are supported by the rules deriving them and rules in turn are supported by their body literals.

For illustration, we also provide the ADF in form of a labelled graph, where the labels + and − indicate supporting and attacking links. Several statements have constant truth values as acceptance conditions, in the picture this is indicated via a link from the surroundings.[4]

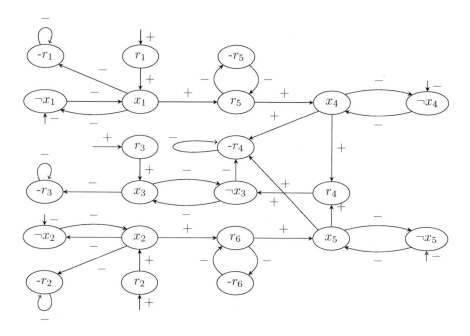

---

[4] This is inspired by conventions from automata theory, where initial states are indicated likewise.

For this ADF, models and stable models coincide, and there are three of them:

$$M_1 = \{x_1, x_2, x_3, r_1, r_2, r_3, \text{-}r_5, \text{-}r_6\} \qquad M_2 = \{x_1, x_2, x_3, x_4, r_1, r_2, r_3, r_5, \text{-}r_6\}$$
$$M_3 = \{x_1, x_2, x_3, x_5, r_1, r_2, r_3, \text{-}r_5, r_6\}$$

Roughly, in M_1 none of the defeasible rules r_5, r_6 has been applied – indicated by -r_5 and -r_6 –, while in M_2 and M_3 either one of them has been applied. As intended, there is no model where both defeasible rules have been applied, as this would lead to a set that contains both x_4 and x_5; this in turn would make rule r_4 applicable, allowing to conclude $\neg x_3$ in contradiction to x_3 being strictly true according to rule r_3.

We can furthermore see that all of the models are closed under strict rule application (they contain x_1, x_2, x_3 and no other strict rule is applicable) and directly consistent, thus also indirectly consistent.

A similar observation can be made for John (not) being married (Example 2); our ADF translation has three (stable) models: $M_1 = \{w, g, r_1, r_2, \text{-}r_5, \text{-}r_6\}$, $M_2 = \{w, g, h, m, r_1, r_2, r_4, r_5, \text{-}r_6\}$ and $M_3 = \{w, g, b, \neg h, r_1, r_2, r_3, \text{-}r_5, r_6\}$. Again, the argumentation translation of the theory base satisfies closure and direct and indirect consistency. We will later prove that the satisfaction of the postulates is not a coincidence in our approach. But first of all let us consider another problem which often arises in knowledge representation and reasoning.

4.2   Support Cycles in Theory Bases

When logical, rule-based approaches are used for knowledge representation, a recurring issue is that of cyclic dependencies between propositions of the knowledge base. If such support cycles are carelessly overlooked or otherwise not treated in an adequate way, they can lead to counterintuitive conclusions. Consider this famous example from Denecker et al. [7].

Example 4 (Gear Wheels [7]). There are two interlocked gear wheels x and y that can be separately turned and stopped. Let x_0 and y_0 denote whether x (resp. y) turns at time point 0, and likewise for a successive time point 1. At any one time point, whenever the first wheel turns (resp. stops), it causes the second one to turn (resp. stop), and vice versa. This is expressed by strict rules r_1 to r_8. Without a cause for change, things usually stay the way they are from one time point to the next, which is expressed by the defeasible rules r_a to r_d.

$$Lit = \{x_0, y_0, x_1, y_1, \neg x_0, \neg y_0, \neg x_1, \neg y_1\}$$
$$StrInf = \{r_1 : x_0 \to y_0, \quad r_2 : y_0 \to x_0, \quad r_3 : \neg x_0 \to \neg y_0, \quad r_4 : \neg y_0 \to \neg x_0,$$
$$r_5 : x_1 \to y_1, \quad r_6 : y_1 \to x_1, \quad r_7 : \neg x_1 \to \neg y_1, \quad r_8 : \neg y_1 \to \neg x_1\}$$
$$DefInf = \{r_a : x_0 \Rightarrow x_1, \quad r_b : \neg x_0 \Rightarrow \neg x_1, \quad r_c : y_0 \Rightarrow y_1, \quad r_d : \neg y_0 \Rightarrow \neg y_1\}$$

For later reference, we denote this theory base by $TB_{GW} = (Lit, StrInf, DefInf)$. To model a concrete scenario, we add the rules $StrInf' = \{r_i :\to \neg x_0, r_j :\to \neg y_0\}$

expressing that both wheels initially stand still. We denote the augmented theory base for this concrete scenario by $TB'_{GW} = (Lit, StrInf \cup StrInf', DefInf)$. It is clearly unintended that there is some model for TB'_{GW} where the gear wheels magically start turning with one being the cause for the other and vice versa.

Example 5. Consider the following defeasible rules saying that *rain* and *wet* grass usually go hand in hand: $Lit = \{rain, wet, \neg rain, \neg wet\}$, $StrInf = \emptyset$ and $DefInf = \{r_1 : rain \Rightarrow wet, r_2 : wet \Rightarrow rain\}$. The intended meaning is that one is usually accompanied by the other, not that both may appear out of thin air.

To see how argumentation translations of theory bases treat such cycles, let us look at a simplified version of the gear wheels example.

Example 6. Consider a theory base with two literals mutually supporting each other through strict rules: $Lit = \{x_1, x_2, \neg x_1, \neg x_2\}$, the strict rules are given by $StrInf = \{r_1 : x_1 \rightarrow x_2, \quad r_2 : x_2 \rightarrow x_1\}$ and $DefInf = \emptyset$. Our ADF translation of this example yields the acceptance formulas

$$\varphi_{x_1} = [r_2] \qquad \varphi_{\neg x_1} = \bot \qquad \varphi_{r_1} = [x_1] \qquad \varphi_{-r_1} = [x_1] \wedge \neg[x_2] \wedge \neg[-r_1]$$
$$\varphi_{x_2} = [r_1] \qquad \varphi_{\neg x_2} = \bot \qquad \varphi_{r_2} = [x_2] \qquad \varphi_{-r_2} = [x_2] \wedge \neg[x_1] \wedge \neg[-r_2]$$

The ADF has two models, $M_1 = \{x_1, x_2, r_1, r_2\}$ and $M_2 = \emptyset$. Only M_2 is a stable model due to the cyclic self-support of the statements in M_1. Note that not only do x_1 and x_2 not hold in M_2, neither do $\neg x_1$ and $\neg x_2$ (there are no rules possibly deriving them). In contrast, the translation of Wyner et al. [3] yields the AF

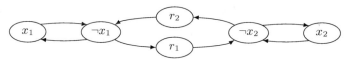

with two stable extensions $S_1 = \{x_1, r_1, x_2, r_2\}$ and $S_2 = \{\neg x_1, \neg x_2\}$. In S_1, x_1 and x_2 hold due to self-support while in S_2 they are "guessed" to be false.

In our view, this is problematic since it is not made clear to the user that these different extensions arise due to self-support. Even if we grant that for some application domains, cyclic self-support of literals might be intended or at least not unintended, the user should be able to distinguish whether different models/extensions arise due to present or absent self-support on the one hand, or due to conflicts between defeasible conclusions on the other hand. ADFs provide this important distinction, since cycles are allowed in models and disallowed in stable models, while both semantics are identical in their treatment of conflicts between defeasible conclusions.

In the approach of Caminada and Amgoud [2], treatment of cycles is built into the definition of the set of arguments in the resulting argumentation framework. The arguments are created using structural induction, where rules with empty bodies form the induction base and all other rules form the induction step. For the general gear wheel domain TB_{GW} of Example 4, and for Examples 5 and

6, their translation would not create any arguments (there are no assertions in the theory bases), and the approach could not draw any conclusions about these examples. The concrete scenario of the interlocked gear wheel domain TB'_{GW} in Example 4, where both wheels initially stand still, would be treated correctly by the approach of Caminada and Amgoud [2]. But note that the well-foundedness of the treatment of cyclic dependencies is built into the syntax of the resulting argumentation framework – there are no arguments that could conclude that any of the wheels is turning, although there are (strict and defeasible) rules with such conclusions. Consequently, a part of the semantics of the theory base is already fixed by the translation, irrespective of the argumentation semantics that is used later on.

4.3   Inconsistent Theory Bases

Example 7 (Inconsistent Theory Base). Consider the following (obviously inconsistent) theory base in which both a literal and its negation are strictly asserted: $Lit = \{x, \neg x\}$, $StrInf = \{r_1 :\to x,\ r_2 :\to \neg x\}$ and $DefInf = \emptyset$. Our ADF translation yields the acceptance formulas

$$\varphi_x = \neg[\neg x] \wedge [r_1] \qquad \varphi_{r_1} = \top \qquad \varphi_{\text{-}r_1} = \neg[x] \wedge \neg[\text{-}r_1]$$
$$\varphi_{\neg x} = \neg[x] \wedge [r_2] \qquad \varphi_{r_2} = \top \qquad \varphi_{\text{-}r_2} = \neg[\neg x] \wedge \neg[\text{-}r_2]$$

This ADF has no models, and so the theory base's inconsistency is detected.

On the other hand, the associated argumentation framework due to Wyner et al. [3] is given by the set of arguments $A = \{x, \neg x, r_1, r_2\}$ and the attacks $R = \{(x, \neg x), (\neg x, x), (r_1, \neg x), (r_2, x)\}$. In the only stable extension $\{r_1, r_2\}$ both rules are applicable but none of the head literals hold due to immanent conflict.

In the approach of Caminada and Amgoud [2], we can construct two strict arguments that conclude x and $\neg x$, respectively. There are no attacks between these arguments since they are both strict. The resulting AF has a stable extension from which both x and $\neg x$ can be concluded, which detects the inconsistency.

4.4   Properties of the Translation

In this section, we analyse some theoretical properties of our translation. First we show that it satisfies (our reformulations of) the rationality postulates of Caminada and Amgoud [2]. Then we analyse the computational complexity of translating a given theory base and show that the blowup is at most quadratic.

Postulates. It is elementary to show that the ADFs resulting from our translation satisfy direct consistency. This is because the statements ψ and $\overline{\psi}$ mutually attack each other.

Proposition 2. *For any theory base* $TB = (Lit, StrInf, DefInf)$, *its associated ADF* $\Xi(TB)$ *satisfies direct consistency with respect to the model semantics.*

Proof. Let M be a model for $\Xi(TB)$ and assume to the contrary that $M \cap Lit$ is inconsistent. Then there is a $\psi \in Lit$ such that $\psi \in M$ and $\neg\psi \in M$. Since $\neg\psi \in M$, the acceptance condition of $\neg\psi$ yields $\psi \notin M$. Contradiction. □

We can also prove that they satisfy closure: by construction, the (acceptance conditions of) statements -r for strict rules r guarantee that the rule head is contained in any model that contains the rule body.

Proposition 3. *For any theory base $TB = (Lit, StrInf, DefInf)$, its associated ADF $\Xi(TB)$ satisfies closure with respect to the model semantics.*

Proof. Let M be a model of $\Xi(TB)$ and $r : \phi_1, \ldots, \phi_n \to \psi \in StrInf$ such that we find $\phi_1, \ldots, \phi_n \in M$. We have to show $\psi \in M$. By definition, $\Xi(TB)$ has a statement -r with parents $par(-r) = \{\phi_1, \ldots, \phi_n, \psi, -r\}$. We next show that $-r \notin M$: assume to the contrary that $-r \in M$. Then by the acceptance condition of -r we get $-r \notin M$, contradiction. Thus $-r \notin M$. Now the acceptance condition of -r yields $\phi_1 \notin M$ or $\ldots$ or $\phi_n \notin M$ or $\psi \in M$ or $-r \in M$. By assumption, we have $\phi_1, \ldots, \phi_n \in M$ and $-r \notin M$, thus we get $\psi \in M$. □

By Proposition 1 the translation satisfies indirect consistency.

Corollary 1. *For any theory base $TB = (Lit, StrInf, DefInf)$, its associated ADF $\Xi(TB)$ satisfies indirect consistency with respect to the model semantics.*

Since any stable model is a model, our translation also satisfies the postulates for the stable model semantics.

Corollary 2. *For any theory base $TB = (Lit, StrInf, DefInf)$, its associated ADF $\Xi(TB)$ satisfies closure and direct and indirect consistency with respect to the stable model semantics.*

It should be noted that defeasible rules may or may not be applied – the approach is not eager to apply defeasible rules.

Complexity. For a theory base $TB = (Lit, StrInf, DefInf)$, we define the size of its constituents as follows. Quite straightforwardly, the size of a set of literals is just its cardinality, the size of a rule is the number of literals in it, the size of a set of rules is the sum of the sizes of its elements and the size of a theory base is the sum of the sizes of its components.

We want to analyse the size of its ADF translation $\Xi(TB) = (S, L, C)$ according to Definition 4. Clearly, the number of statements is linear in the size of the theory base, since we have one statement for each literal and two statements for each rule: $|S| = |Lit| + 2 \cdot (|StrInf| + |DefInf|)$. Since $L \subseteq S \times S$, the number of links in L is at most quadratic in the cardinality of S: $|L| \leq |S|^2$. Finally, we have seen in Definition 4 that the acceptance conditions of statements can be parsimoniously represented by propositional formulas. It can be checked that the size of each one of these formulas is at most linear in the size of the theory base. Since there are linearly many statements with one acceptance formula each, the acceptance conditions can be represented in quadratic space. So overall, the resulting ADF $\Xi(TB) = (S, L, C)$ can be represented in space which is at most quadratic in the size of the original theory base. In particular, in our approach a finite theory base always yields a finite argumentation translation. This is in contrast to the definition of Caminada and Amgoud [2], where the strict rule set $StrInf = \{r_0 :\to a, r_1 : a \to b, r_2 : b \to a\}$ allows to construct infinitely many arguments $A_1 = [\to a], A_2 = [A_1 \to b], A_3 = [A_2 \to a], A_4 = [A_3 \to b], \ldots$[5]

5   Conclusion

We presented a translation from theory bases to abstract dialectical frameworks. The translated frameworks satisfy the rationality postulates closure and direct/indirect consistency, which we generalised to make them independent of a specific target formalism. Furthermore, the translated frameworks can detect inconsistencies in the rule base and cyclic supports amongst literals. We also showed that the translation involves at most a quadratic blowup and is therefore effectively computable. Furthermore, our translation produces a number of statements which is linear in the size of the theory base and can be considered efficient in this regard. (In the approach of [2] the number of produced arguments is unbounded in general.) In terms of desired behaviour, we compared our translation to previous approaches from the literature [2,3] and demonstrated how we avoid common problems.

In earlier work, Brewka and Gordon [8] translated Carneades [9] argument evaluation structures (directly) to ADFs. They extended the original Carneades formalism by allowing cyclic dependencies among arguments. Meanwhile, Van Gijzel and Prakken [10] also translated Carneades into AFs (via ASPIC+ [11], that extends and generalises the definitions of Caminada and Amgoud [2]). They can deal with cycles, but there is only one unique grounded, preferred, complete, stable extension. Thus the semantic richness of abstract argumentation is not used, and the user cannot choose whether they want to accept or reject circular justifications of arguments. In contrast, in the approach of Brewka and Gordon [8] the user can decide whether cyclic justifications should be allowed or disallowed, by choosing models or *stable* models as ADF semantics.

We regard this work as another piece of evidence that abstract dialectical frameworks are well-suited as target formalisms for translations from less directly accessible languages such as theory bases. A natural next step would be to consider as input the specification language of ASPIC+ [11]. A recent approach to preferences between statements [6] might be a good starting point for this. Further work could also encompass the study of additional ADF semantics, like complete or preferred models [6], and whether the approach can be modified such that it is eager to apply defeasible rules. Finally, we can compare existing approaches to cycles in AFs [12,13] with the treatment of cycles in ADFs.

---

[5] Even if we exclude cycles in rules, there are rule sets which allow for exponentially many arguments: Set $D_0 = \{\Rightarrow p_0, \Rightarrow \neg p_0\}$, $D_1 = D_0 \cup \{p_0 \Rightarrow p_1, \neg p_0 \Rightarrow p_1\}$ and for $i \geq 1$, $D_{i+1} = D_i \cup \{p_0, p_i \Rightarrow p_{i+1}, \neg p_0, p_i \Rightarrow p_{i+1}\}$. For any $n \in \mathbb{N}$, the size of D_n is linear in n and D_n leads to 2^{n+1} arguments, among them 2^n arguments for p_n.

Acknowledgements. The author is grateful to Gerhard Brewka for informative discussions. He also thanks Leila Amgoud and Martin Caminada for clarifying some aspects of the ASPIC framework.

References

1. Dung, P.M.: On the Acceptability of Arguments and its Fundamental Role in Nonmonotonic Reasoning, Logic Programming and n-Person Games. Artificial Intelligence 77, 321–358 (1995)
2. Caminada, M., Amgoud, L.: On the evaluation of argumentation formalisms. Artificial Intelligence 171(5-6), 286–310 (2007)
3. Wyner, A., Bench-Capon, T., Dunne, P.: Instantiating knowledge bases in abstract argumentation frameworks. In: Proceedings of the AAAI Fall Symposium – The Uses of Computational Argumentation (2009)
4. Brewka, G., Woltran, S.: Abstract Dialectical Frameworks. In: Proceedings of the Twelfth International Conference on the Principles of Knowledge Representation and Reasoning (KR), pp. 102–111 (2010)
5. Strass, H.: Approximating operators and semantics for Abstract Dialectical Frameworks. Technical Report 1, Institute of Computer Science, Leipzig University (January 2013)
6. Brewka, G., Ellmauthaler, S., Strass, H., Wallner, J.P., Woltran, S.: Abstract Dialectical Frameworks Revisited. In: Proceedings of the Twenty-Third International Joint Conference on Artificial Intelligence. AAAI Press (to appear, August 2013)
7. Denecker, M., Theseider-Dupré, D., Van Belleghem, K.: An Inductive Definition Approach to Ramifications. Linköping Electronic Articles in Computer and Information Science 3(7), 1–43 (1998)
8. Brewka, G., Gordon, T.F.: Carneades and Abstract Dialectical Frameworks: A Reconstruction. In: Computational Models of Argument: Proceedings of COMMA 2010, Desenzano del Garda, Italy, September 8-10. Frontiers in Artificial Intelligence and Applications, vol. 216, pp. 3–12. IOS Press (2010)
9. Gordon, T.F., Prakken, H., Walton, D.: The Carneades model of argument and burden of proof. Artificial Intelligence 171(10-15), 875–896 (2007)
10. Van Gijzel, B., Prakken, H.: Relating Carneades with Abstract Argumentation. In: Proceedings of the Twenty-Second International Joint Conference on Artificial Intelligence, vol. 2, pp. 1113–1119. AAAI Press (2011)
11. Prakken, H.: An abstract framework for argumentation with structured arguments. Argument & Computation 1(2), 93–124 (2010)
12. Baroni, P., Giacomin, M., Guida, G.: SCC-recursiveness: A general schema for argumentation semantics. Artificial Intelligence 168(1-2), 162–210 (2005)
13. Baroni, P., Dunne, P.E., Giacomin, M.: On the resolution-based family of abstract argumentation semantics and its grounded instance. Artificial Intelligence 175(3-4), 791–813 (2011)

Admissibility in the Abstract Dialectical Framework

Sylwia Polberg, Johannes Peter Wallner, and Stefan Woltran

Vienna University of Technology,
Institute of Information Systems,
Favoritenstraße 9-11, 1040 Vienna, Austria

Abstract. The aim of this paper is to study the concept of admissibility in abstract dialectical frameworks (ADFs). While admissibility is well-understood in Dung-style frameworks, a generalization to ADFs is not trivial. Indeed, the original proposal turned out to behave unintuitively at certain instances. A recent approach circumvented this problem by using a three-valued concept. In this paper, we propose a novel two-valued approach which more directly follows the original understanding of admissibility. We compare the two approaches and show that they behave differently on certain ADFs. Our results imply that for generalizations of Dung-style frameworks, establishing a precise correspondence between two-valued (i.e. extension-based) and three-value (i.e. labeling-based) characterizations of argumentation semantics is not easy and requires further investigations.

Keywords: abstract argumentation, abstract dialectical framework, admissible semantics.

1 Introduction

Dung's abstract argumentation frameworks [1] have proven successful in many applications related to multi-agent systems (see, e.g. [2]). These frameworks are conceptually simple and appealing: arguments are viewed only on an abstract level and a binary attack relation models conflicts between arguments. In several domains this simplicity however leads to certain limitations. Therefore, several enrichments of Dung's approach were proposed [3–9], with abstract dialectical frameworks (ADFs) [10] being one of the most general of these concepts.[1] Simply speaking, in ADFs it is not only the arguments that are abstract but also the relations between them. This is achieved by associating a propositional formula with each argument describing its relation to the other arguments. A common problem in applications of abstract argumentation concerns instantiation. Preliminary results on this matter in the case of ADFs can be found in this

---

[1] A different approach to model relations between arguments which are beyond attack is meta-argumentation [11]. Here additional (artificial) arguments are added together with certain gadgets to capture the functioning of relations which cannot be modeled with binary attacks.

J. Leite et al. (Eds.): CLIMA XIV, LNAI 8143, pp. 102–118, 2013.
© Springer-Verlag Berlin Heidelberg 2013

volume [12]. Moreover, the application of ADFs in the context of the Carneades system [13] and proof standards [10] have been studied in the literature, advising that ADFs might also be applicable to certain problems from the domain of multi-agent systems.

One of the most central concepts in Dung's frameworks is the notion of admissibility which is based on defense. In a nutshell, an argument a is defended (in a given framework) by a set S of arguments if all arguments attacking a are counter-attacked by S. A (conflict-free) set S of arguments is called admissible if each $a \in S$ is defended by S. In fact, many semantics for abstract argumentation are based on admissibility, and in the context of instantiation-based argumentation, admissibility plays an important role w.r.t. rationality postulates, see e.g. [14].

While the concept of admissibility is very intuitive in the Dung setting it is not easy to be generalized to extensions of the Dung–style framework where relations between arguments are not restricted to attacks. As a minimal requirement for such generalized notions of admissibility one would first state "downward-compatibility". Basically speaking, if a given object F in an extended formalism corresponds to a standard Dung framework F', then the admissible (in its generalized form) sets of F should match the admissible sets of F'. In the world of ADFs, the original proposal for admissibility, albeit satisfying this minimal requirement, turned out to behave unintuitively at certain instances. A recent approach first presented in [15] and slightly simplified in [16] is based on (post) fixed points in three–valued interpretations. However, the original intuition that arguments in the set have to "stand together" against the arguments outside the set is somehow lost in that approach (nonetheless, there is a certain correspondence to the characteristic function of Dung-style frameworks).

In this work, we propose a novel two–valued approach which more directly follows the original understanding of admissibility. We call our approach the decisive outing formulation, reflecting its definition which iteratively decides of the status of the arguments. We compare our approach with the three–valued approach from [16] and show that the two semantics can consider different sets of arguments admissible. Since both approaches are downward–compatible, they clearly coincide on Dung-style ADFs; in the paper, we define another class of ADFs where this relation is also preserved. Finally, we further elaborate on these two approaches by showing that each decisive outing admissible extension has a counterpart in the three–valued setting, but not vice versa.

Our results not only show that admissibility can be naturally generalized in different ways, they also imply that for descendants of Dung–style frameworks, establishing one–to–one correspondences between two–valued (i.e. extension–based) and three–valued (i.e. labeling–based) characterizations of argumentation semantics is not necessarily granted. This could stipulate further investigations towards a better understanding of admissibility for more expressive formalisms taking into account also the work of Kakas et al. [17] in logic programming.

The structure of this paper is as follows. In Section 2 we present the theoretical background and notations. Section 3 is dedicated to describing and comparing the three formulations of admissibility and Section 4 is focused on discussion and some pointers for future work.

2   Background

2.1   Dung's Abstract Argumentation Frameworks

The argumentation framework developed by Phan Minh Dung is the simplest, yet quite powerful, formalism for abstract argumentation [1].

Definition 1. *A **Dung abstract argumentation framework**, or a **Dung Framework** is a pair (A, R), where A is a set of arguments and $R \subseteq A \times A$ represents the attack relation.*

Due to the great interest it has received, many semantics have been developed. Semantics define the properties or methods of obtaining framework extensions, i.e. sets of arguments we can accept. Nevertheless, it is generally agreed that any rational opinion should be consistent. This minimal property is expressed with the conflict–free semantics, a common root for all other developed approaches.[2]

Definition 2. *Let $AF = (A, R)$ be a Dung framework. A set $S \subseteq A$ is a **conflict–free extension** of AF, if for each $a, b \in S, (a, b) \notin R$.*

Admissibility is another fundamental requirement in argumentation. It comes from the fact that regardless of the presented point of view, we should be able to defend it. In the Dung setting, due to only one type of relation, it boils down to the following definitions.

Definition 3. *Let $AF = (A, R)$ be a Dung framework. An argument $a \in A$ is **defended** by a set S in AF, if for each $b \in A$ s.t. $(b, a) \in R$, there exists $c \in S$ s.t. $(c, b) \in R$. A conflict–free extension S is an **admissible extension** of AF if each $a \in S$ is defended by S in AF.*

With this at hand, we can start describing the stronger semantics. They can be roughly grouped by varying concepts of maximality or skepticism. Prominent examples are the stable and preferred semantics.

Definition 4. *Let $AF = (A, R)$ be a Dung framework. A conflict–free extension S is a **stable extension** of AF iff for each $a \in A \setminus S$ there exists an argument $b \in S$ s.t. $(b, a) \in R$.*

---

[2] Conflict–freeness and admissibility can also be treated as some basic properties, rather than very weak semantics. Due to the fact that in some approaches of argumentation frameworks additional types of conflict–freeness have been introduced, we have chosen the latter.

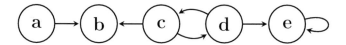

Fig. 1. Sample Dung framework

Definition 5. *Let $AF = (A, R)$ be a Dung framework. A* **preferred extension** *of AF is a maximal admissible extension of AF w.r.t. subset inclusion.*

We close the list with a semantics belonging to the unique–state approach class, i.e. a semantics producing only a single extension. To this end, we first need to introduce the characteristic function of a framework.

Definition 6. *Let $AF = (A, R)$ be a Dung framework. Its characteristic function $F_{AF} : 2^A \to 2^A$ is defined as follows:*

$$F_{AF}(S) = \{a \mid a \text{ is defended by } S \text{ in } AF\}$$

Definition 7. *Let $AF = (A, R)$ be a Dung framework. The* **grounded extension** *of AF is the least fixed point of F_{AF}.*

Please note that further semantics can be described via the characteristic function [1,15]. For our purposes, the most important is the alternative formulation of admissibility as already presented in [1].

Lemma 1. *Let $AF = (A, R)$ be a Dung framework and F_{AF} its characteristic function. A set $S \subseteq A$ is an* **admissible extension** *of AF iff it is conflict–free and $S \subseteq F_{AF}(S)$.*

Example 1. Consider the Dung framework $AF = (A, R)$ with $A = \{a, b, c, d, e\}$ and the attack relation $R = \{(a, b), (c, b), (c, d), (d, c), (d, e), (e, e)\}$, as depicted in Figure 1. It has eight conflict–free extensions in total, namely $\{a, c\}, \{a, d\}$, $\{b, d\}, \{a\}, \{b\}, \{c\}, \{d\}$ and $\emptyset$. As b is attacked by an unattacked argument, it cannot be defended against it and will not be in any admissible extension. We end up with two preferred extensions, $\{a, c\}$ and $\{a, d\}$. However, only $\{a, d\}$ is stable, and $\{a\}$ is the grounded extension.

2.2   Abstract Dialectical Frameworks

The main goal of abstract dialectical frameworks (ADFs) [10] is to overcome the limitations of the pure attack relation in the Dung frameworks and its descendants. They assume some predefined set of connection types – attacking, attacking or supporting, and so on – which affects what can be expressed in a framework naturally, and what requires some semantics–dependent modifications. In ADFs relation abstractness is achieved by the introduction of the acceptance conditions instead of adding new elements to the set of relations. They define what (sets of) arguments related to a given argument should be present for it to be included/excluded from an extension.

Definition 8. *An **abstract dialectical framework** (ADF) is a tuple (S, L, C), where S is a set of abstract **arguments** (nodes, statements), $L \subseteq S \times S$ is a set of **links** (edges) and $C = \{C_s\}_{s \in S}$ is a set of **acceptance conditions**, one condition per each argument.*

Originally, the acceptance conditions were defined in terms of functions:

Definition 9. *Let (S, L, C) be an ADF. The set of **parents** of an argument s, denoted par(s), consists of those $p \in S$ for which $(p,s) \in L$. An **acceptance condition** is given by a total function $C_s : 2^{par(s)} \to \{in, out\}$.*

Alternatively, one can also use the propositional formula representation, described in detail in [18]. These two forms are equivalent, and we will be referring to both of them in the rest of this paper.

Definition 10. *Let (S, L, C) be an ADF. **Propositional acceptance conditions** are formulas of the form:*

$$\varphi ::= a \in S \mid \bot \mid \top \mid \neg\varphi \mid (\varphi \wedge \varphi) \mid (\varphi \vee \varphi) \mid (\varphi \to \varphi)$$

All and only parents of an argument appear as atoms in the acceptance condition of this argument. In what follows, we use $a : \varphi$ as shorthand for $C_a = \varphi$.

Note that the set L of links can be extracted from the acceptance conditions (more on this matter can be found in [18]). Hence, making it explicit is not necessary. We have decided to keep L in its current form in order to have a consistent representation when weights or more advanced relation properties are added to ADFs.

In the original setting, the truth value of a formula is based on the standard propositional valuation function (i.e. truth tables). However, in [16] Kleene's strong three–valued logic has been used. We will come back to this approach in Section 3.

Due to the abstractness of ADFs, redefining the semantics in an intuitive manner is still an ongoing work and one of the main topics of this paper. In order to take the research step by step, a subclass of ADFs called bipolar was identified in the original paper [10]:

Definition 11. *Let $D = (S, L, C)$ be an ADF. A link $(r, s) \in L$ is*

1. ***supporting**: for no $R \subseteq par(s)$ we have $C_s(R) = in$ and $C_s(R \cup \{r\}) = out$,*
2. ***attacking**: for no $R \subseteq par(s)$ we have $C_s(R) = out$ and $C_s(R \cup \{r\}) = in$.*

*D is **bipolar** iff all links in L are supporting or attacking and we can write it as $D = (S, (L^+ \cup L^-), C)$. The links L^+ denote the supporting links and L^- denote the attacking links. The set of **parents supporting** an argument x is defined as $supp_D(x) = \{y \mid (y, x) \in L^+\}$. The set of **parents attacking** an argument x is defined as $att_D(x) = \{y \mid (y, x) \in L^-\}$.*

Along with the support relations came the problem of the support cycles. We will discuss it further in Section 4.

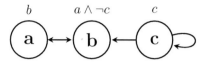

Fig. 2. Example of support cycles

Definition 12. *Let $D = (S, (L^+ \cup L^-), C)$ be a bipolar ADF. D is a bipolar ADF **without support cycles** if L^+ is acyclic.*

Example 2. Let us look at the ADF depicted in Figure 2: $D = (\{a, b, c, \}, \{(a, b), (b, a), (c, b), (c, c)\}, \{a : b, b : a \wedge \neg c, c : c\})$. In this case c self–supports itself, and a and b exchange supports.

We continue with several semantics that have already been developed for the general class of ADFs.

Definition 13. *Let $D = (S, L, C)$ be an ADF. $M \subseteq S$ is a **conflict–free extension** of D if for all $s \in M$ we have $C_s(M \cap par(s)) = in$.*

The model semantics follows the 'what can be accepted, should be accepted' intuition. It coincides with the stable semantics in the Dung setting.

Definition 14. *Let $D = (S, L, C)$ be an ADF. $M \subseteq S$ is a **model** of D if M is conflict–free and $\forall s \in S, \; C_s(M \cap par(s)) = in$ implies $s \in M$.*

Finally, we also have the grounded semantics (here referred to as well–founded). Just like in the Dung framework, it is obtained by the means of a special function:

Definition 15. *Let $D = (S, L, C)$ be an ADF. Consider the operator*

$$\Gamma_D^W(A, R) = (acc(A, R), reb(A, R))$$

where:

$$acc(A, R) = \{r \in S \mid A \subseteq S' \subseteq (S \backslash R) \Rightarrow C_r(S' \cap par(s)) = in\}$$
$$reb(A, R) = \{r \in S \mid A \subseteq S' \subseteq (S \backslash R) \Rightarrow C_r(S' \cap par(s)) = out\}$$

Γ_D^W *is monotonic in both arguments and thus has a least fix–point. E is the **well–founded model** of D iff for some $E' \subseteq S, (E, E')$ is the least fix–point of Γ_D^W.*

Example 3. Let us transform the Dung framework $F = (A, R)$ from Example 1 into an ADF $D = (S, L, C)$. The set of arguments does not change: $A = S$. The same goes for the set of links, please note however, that L loses its meaning – it now represents the connections only, without any information as to their nature. Argument a is unattacked and can always be accepted, hence its acceptance condition is $\top$. b can only be accepted when both a and c are not present ($\neg a \wedge \neg c$). Next, c and d mutually exclude one another (respectively $\neg d$ and $\neg c$). Finally, e is attacked not only by d, but also by itself, and its acceptance condition is $\neg d \wedge \neg e$. Therefore in total we obtain an abstract dialectical framework $D = (A, R, \{a : \top, b : \neg a \wedge \neg c, c : \neg d, d : \neg c, e : \neg d \wedge \neg e\})$.

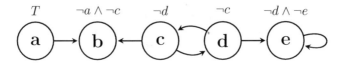

Fig. 3. Sample Dung–style ADF

2.3   Kleene's Three–Valued Logic and Interpretations

In order to be able to explain one of the approaches to the admissibility in ADFs, we need to provide a short recap on the three–valued interpretations and lattices. A more detailed background can be found in [16].

Given a set of arguments S, a three–valued interpretation is a mapping $v : S \to \{\mathbf{t}, \mathbf{f}, \mathbf{u}\}$. The truth tables for the basic connectives are given in Figure 4.

$\neg$	
$\mathbf{t}$	$\mathbf{f}$
$\mathbf{f}$	$\mathbf{t}$
$\mathbf{u}$	$\mathbf{u}$

$\vee$	$\mathbf{t}$	$\mathbf{u}$	$\mathbf{f}$
$\mathbf{t}$	$\mathbf{t}$	$\mathbf{t}$	$\mathbf{t}$
$\mathbf{u}$	$\mathbf{t}$	$\mathbf{u}$	$\mathbf{u}$
$\mathbf{f}$	$\mathbf{t}$	$\mathbf{u}$	$\mathbf{f}$

$\wedge$	$\mathbf{t}$	$\mathbf{u}$	$\mathbf{f}$
$\mathbf{t}$	$\mathbf{t}$	$\mathbf{u}$	$\mathbf{f}$
$\mathbf{u}$	$\mathbf{u}$	$\mathbf{u}$	$\mathbf{f}$
$\mathbf{f}$	$\mathbf{f}$	$\mathbf{f}$	$\mathbf{f}$

$\to$	$\mathbf{t}$	$\mathbf{u}$	$\mathbf{f}$
$\mathbf{t}$	$\mathbf{t}$	$\mathbf{u}$	$\mathbf{f}$
$\mathbf{u}$	$\mathbf{t}$	$\mathbf{u}$	$\mathbf{u}$
$\mathbf{f}$	$\mathbf{t}$	$\mathbf{t}$	$\mathbf{t}$

Fig. 4. Truth tables for the three–valued logic of Kleene

Let us assume the following partial order $\leq_i$ according to information content: $\mathbf{u} <_i \mathbf{t}$ and $\mathbf{u} <_i \mathbf{f}$. The pair $(\{\mathbf{t}, \mathbf{f}, \mathbf{u}\}, \leq_i)$ forms a complete meet–semilattice with the meet operation $\sqcap$ assigning values in the following way: $\mathbf{t} \sqcap \mathbf{t} = \mathbf{t}$, $\mathbf{f} \sqcap \mathbf{f} = \mathbf{f}$ and $\mathbf{u}$ in all other cases. Given two valuations v and v', we say that v' **contains more information** than v, denoted $v \leq_i v'$ iff $\forall_{s \in S}\ v(s) \leq_i v'(s)$; in case v is three–valued and v' two–valued, then we say that v' **extends** v. This means that elements mapped originally to $\mathbf{u}$ are now assigned either $\mathbf{t}$ or $\mathbf{f}$. The set of all two–valued interpretations extending v is denoted $[v]_2$.

Given a set A, we say that an interpretation v is **partial** if it is defined for a nonempty $B \subseteq A$. Let v' be some interpretation on A. We define a shorthand $v \sqsubseteq v'$ meaning that $\forall b \in B,\ v(b) = v'(b)$. We say that v' is **completion** of v to A. v' is respectively a $\mathbf{t}/\mathbf{f}/\mathbf{u}$–**completion**, if it maps all elements from $A \setminus B$ to respectively $\mathbf{t}/\mathbf{f}/\mathbf{u}$.

It is often very handy to be able to talk about the set of arguments mapped to a certain value by a given interpretation:

Definition 16. *Let v be an interpretation. Then $v^x = \{s \mid v(s) = x\}$ for $x \in \{\mathbf{t}, \mathbf{f}\}$ in case v is two–valued and $x \in \{\mathbf{t}, \mathbf{f}, \mathbf{u}\}$ if v is three–valued.*

When it comes to the two–valued setting, we can use interpretations and sets of accepted arguments as extensions interchangeably as they uniquely define one another. Unfortunately, this is not the case with the three–valued interpretations. In order to compare both of these settings we need to focus on arguments accepted in both of them. Therefore, sometimes we may refer to a family of the three–valued interpretations using a set of arguments they map to **t**. Finally, we define a shorthand $v(\varphi)$ for evaluation of a propositional formula φ under an interpretation v.

3   Admissible Semantics for ADFs

In this section we will recall some work on argumentation semantics and discuss several approaches to defining the admissibility for ADFs. We will start with the original definition from [10] and recall some objections raised on it. Then, we introduce two recent formulations (one from [16] and our own novel approach) that are different both in spirit and resulting extensions. At the end of this section we will compare the two in a formal way.

3.1   Related Work on Semantics Rationalities

Throughout the time, many different argumentation semantics have been developed [19]. Very often a new semantics is an improvement of an already existing one by introducing further restrictions on the set of accepted arguments or possible attackers. One of the most important semantical problems is concerned with the cycles in a framework. A thorough study of attack cycles and self–attackers in the Dung setting can be found in [20]. In the bipolar setting, the situation is not yet analyzed this well and approaches differ between available frameworks [5, 9, 21]. The moment we introduce a new type of relation, the situation gets more complicated and every Dung semantics gives rise to several further specializations. Currently, our focus is on whether arguments taking part in support cycles can be in an extension and if they should be considered valid attackers. We will discuss the validity of support cycles further in Section 4. The two recent definitions of admissibility we are going to present differ in the treatment of cycles. The explanation will be provided in Section 3.5.

3.2   Original Formulation

The main motivation behind the original formulation of admissibility in [10] was to create a definition that would not explicitly use the notion of defense. Unfortunately, it was only applicable for the bipolar ADFs. The admissible extensions were obtained via the stable models as proposed in [10].

Definition 17. *Let $D = (S, L, C)$ be a bipolar ADF. A model M of D is a **stable model** of D if M is the least model of the reduced ADF D^M obtained from D by:*

1. *eliminating all nodes not contained in M together with all links in which any of these nodes appear,*
2. *eliminating all attacking links,*
3. *replacing in each acceptance condition C_s of a node s in D^M each occurrence of a statement $t \notin M$ with $\perp$.*

With this at hand, admissible semantics are defined as follows.

Definition 18. *Let $D = (S, L, C)$ be a bipolar ADF. $M \subseteq S$ is **admissible** in D iff there is $R \subseteq S$ such that no element in R attacks an element in M and M is a stable model of $D \setminus R$.*

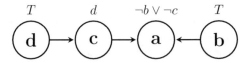

Fig. 5. Counterexample for the original formulation of admissibility

However, this definition has been proved to give undesired extensions [16]. Take for example the framework depicted in Figure 5. In this setting we have the following admissible extensions: $\emptyset$, $\{b\}$, $\{d\}$, $\{b, d\}$, $\{a, b\}$, $\{c, d\}$, $\{c, b, d\}$. $\{a, b\}$ is not a desired answer as we have no way of preventing our opponent from uttering c since the acceptance condition of d is always *in*. Therefore, the need for a more appropriate definition arises.

3.3 Lattice Formulation

In abstract argumentation, semantics can usually be described in more than one way. The main idea behind it is to provide a relatively constructive formulation that would give us a hint on how to create extensions in a more systematic manner. For example, in case of Dung's frameworks grounded and admissible extensions can be obtained via the characteristic function (see Section 2.1). For ADFs, the original definition has been revised and a new, constructive variant, based on (post) fixed-points, is presented in [15]. A simplified approach published in [16] is based on three–valued interpretations, which we will use in this paper.

The semantics are defined via the following operator, which is similar to the characteristic function of Dung's frameworks. Based on a three-valued interpretation a new one is returned by the function, which accepts or rejects arguments based on the given interpretation. For convenience we will slightly abuse our notation and identify *in* with **t** and *out* with **f**.

Definition 19. *Let $D = (S, L, C)$ be an ADF, v a three–valued interpretation defined over S, $s \in S$ and $\Gamma_D : (S \to \{\mathbf{t}, \mathbf{f}, \mathbf{u}\}) \to (S \to \{\mathbf{t}, \mathbf{f}, \mathbf{u}\})$ a function from three-valued interpretations to three-valued interpretations. Then $\Gamma_D(v) = v'$ with*

$$v'(s) = \bigsqcap_{w \in [v]_2} C_s(par(s) \cap w^{\mathbf{t}})$$

That is, given a three-valued v interpretation a new one is returned by Γ_D for an ADF D. The new truth value for each argument s is given by considering all two-valued interpretations that extend v, i.e. all interpretations that assign either **t** or **f** to an argument, which is assigned **u** by v. Now we evaluate the acceptance condition of each argument under all these two–valued interpretations. If all of them agree on the truth value, i.e. all of them evaluate to *in* (**t**) or respectively *out* (**f**) , then this is the result or the overall consensus. Otherwise, if there is a disagreement, i.e. we have **t** for one evaluation and **f** for another, then the result is undecided, i.e. **u**.

The new definition of admissibility resembles the one for AFs. We apply Γ_D similarly as the characteristic function and just use the information ordering instead of the subset relation. Please note that conflict–freeness is already incorporated in this definition.

Definition 20. *A three-valued interpretation v for an ADF D* $= (S, L, C)$ *is* **admissible** *in D iff* $v \leq_i \Gamma_D(v)$.

The following example illustrates this definition.

Example 4. Let us go back to the framework in Figure 5. The following three-valued interpretations are then admissible $v_1 = \{d \mapsto \mathbf{u},\ b \mapsto \mathbf{u},\ c \mapsto \mathbf{u},\ a \mapsto \mathbf{u}\}$, $v_2 = \{d \mapsto \mathbf{t},\ b \mapsto \mathbf{u},\ c \mapsto \mathbf{u},\ a \mapsto \mathbf{u}\}$, $v_3 = \{d \mapsto \mathbf{t},\ b \mapsto \mathbf{u},\ c \mapsto \mathbf{t},\ a \mapsto \mathbf{u}\}$, $v_4 = \{d \mapsto \mathbf{u},\ b \mapsto \mathbf{t},\ c \mapsto \mathbf{u},\ a \mapsto \mathbf{u}\}$, $v_5 = \{d \mapsto \mathbf{t},\ b \mapsto \mathbf{t},\ c \mapsto \mathbf{u},\ a \mapsto \mathbf{u}\}$, $v_6 = \{d \mapsto \mathbf{t},\ b \mapsto \mathbf{t},\ c \mapsto \mathbf{t},\ a \mapsto \mathbf{u}\}$, $v_7 = \{d \mapsto \mathbf{t},\ b \mapsto \mathbf{t},\ c \mapsto \mathbf{t},\ a \mapsto \mathbf{f}\}$.

Let us inspect closer why v_7 is admissible in this ADF. The three-valued interpretation v_7 is already two–valued, i.e. no argument is assigned the value **u**. This means that $[v_7]_2 = \{v_7\}$. Now if we evaluate for each argument its acceptance condition under v_7, then the result is the same as the assigned value by v_7. Consider for instance argument a with the acceptance condition $\neg b \vee \neg c$ as a propositional formula. This formula evaluates to **f** under v_7, which is the same value assigned by v_7, i.e. $v_7(a) = C_a(par(a) \cap v_7^t) = \mathbf{f}$.

Considering a slightly more complex example, let us look at v_6. Here $[v_6]_2 = \{v, v'\}$ with $v = \{d \mapsto \mathbf{t},\ b \mapsto \mathbf{t},\ c \mapsto \mathbf{t},\ a \mapsto \mathbf{t}\}$ and $v' = \{d \mapsto \mathbf{t},\ b \mapsto \mathbf{t},\ c \mapsto \mathbf{t},\ a \mapsto \mathbf{f}\}$. This means we have to consider both evaluations, one assigning the argument a true and one false. Now the acceptance condition of a evaluates under both v and v' to **f**. This means that $\Gamma_D(v_6) = v_6'$ and $v_6(a) = \mathbf{u} \leq_i v_6'(a) = \mathbf{f}$, since $\mathbf{f} \sqcap \mathbf{f} = \mathbf{f}$. Similarly for the other arguments and hence v_6 is admissible.

Let us check if there exists an admissible three–valued interpretation v, which assigns **f** to d, i.e. $v(d) = \mathbf{f}$. Since the acceptance condition of d always evaluates to true, we know that for any two-valued interpretation w we have $C_a(par(a) \cap w^t) = \mathbf{t}$. This in particular holds for for all $v' \in [v]_2$. Hence $\Gamma_D(v) = v'$, with $v(d) = \mathbf{f} \not\leq_i \mathbf{t} = v'(d)$ and v is not admissible.

3.4   Decisive Outing Formulation

We now introduce an alternative definition of admissibility that comes back to the intuition behind the semantics. An admissible extension is supposed to be able to 'stand on its own' [22], i.e. discard any argument that would render any of the set's elements unacceptable. In the Dung setting, a set defends an argument if it attacks all of its attackers. In the ADF setting, which is more abstract, this is not enough. We can discard an argument in more ways than just a direct attack

– overall we want to make sure that the acceptance of a different argument will not make the 'bad' one acceptable via a chain reaction. Moreover, due to the various types of relations available in ADF, it might be the case that to discard one argument, more counterarguments may be required (in the Dung case, one 'attacker' per 'attacker' was sufficient).

This intuition is enough to create a definition of admissibility that does not make use of the notion of attack or defense, which is quite appropriate for this abstract setting. Our approach is based on iteratively building a set of arguments that our candidate for admissibility has the power to permanently set to *out*. Important in this construction is the notion of decisiveness:

Definition 21. *Let* $D = (S, L, C)$ *be an ADF and* $s \in S$. *Let* v_Z *be a two or three–valued interpretation defined on a set* $Z \subseteq par(s)$, *We say that* v_Z *is **decisive** for* s *iff for any two (respectively two or three–valued) completions* $v_{par(s)}$ *and* $v'_{par(s)}$ *of* v *to* $par(s)$, *it holds that* $v_{par(s)}(C_s) = v'_{par(s)}(C_s)$.
We say that s *is **decisively out/in/undecided** wrt* v_Z *if* v_Z *is decisive and all of its completions map* s *to respectively* $out, in, undec$.

Example 5. The idea behind this formulation is to identify the partial interpretations that are "enough" to know the final value of an acceptance condition. Assume an ADF $D = (\{a, b\}, \{(a, a), (a, b), (b, a), (b, b)\}, \{a : a \rightarrow b, b : a \wedge b\})$. Let v be a partial two–valued interpretation s.t. $v(b) = \mathbf{t}$. Then $a \rightarrow b$ will always evaluate to $\mathbf{t}$ no matter the assignment of a and we can say that a is decisively in wrt to v. It is of course not decisive for b.

With this at hand, we can define the set of arguments permanently excluded by a given set. The idea behind it corresponds to identifying all the arguments attacked by an extension E in the Dung setting and is known as the E^+ set. Due to its abstractness, ADFs also give us indirect ways of discarding an argument and such a straightforward check would be inadequate.

Definition 22. *Let* $D = (S, L, C)$ *be an ADF and* $A \subseteq S$ *a conflict–free extension of* D. *Let* v *be a partial two–valued interpretation built as follows:*

1. *Let* $M = A$. *For every* $a \in M$ *set* $v(a) = \mathbf{t}$.
2. *For every argument* $b \in S \setminus M$ *that is decisively out in* v, *set* $v(b) = \mathbf{f}$ *and add* b *to* M.
3. *Repeat the previous step until there are no new elements added to* M.

By A^+ *we understand the set of arguments* $v^{\mathbf{f}}$. *The **range** of* A, *denoted* A^R *is defined as* $A \cup A^+$. *We refer to* v *as **range interpretation** of* A.[3]

We can now naturally proceed to admissibility:

Definition 23. *Let* $D = (S, L, C)$ *be an ADF,* $A \subseteq S$ *a conflict–free extension of* D *and* A^+ *its discarded set.* A *is **admissible** in* D *iff for any* $F \subseteq S \setminus A$ *($F \neq \emptyset$), if there exists an* $a \in A$ *s.t.* $C_a(par(a) \cap (F \cup A)) = out$ *then* $F \cap A^+ \neq \emptyset$.

---

[3] Please note that although these notions were originally defined for arbitrary sets, in practice they were always used for at least conflict–free ones and this assumption allowed us to create a cleaner formulation.

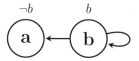

Fig. 6. Example of nonequivalence between the formulations of admissibility

Example 6. Let us come back to the counterexample from Figure 5. Clearly $\emptyset, \{b\}, \{d\}, \{b, d\}, \{c, d\}$ and $\{b, c, d\}$ are admissible; they are not attacked in any way and hence implication is always true. Let us now check $\{a\}$: its discarded set is empty, while the set $\{c, d\}$ has the power to out the acceptance condition of a. The same situation can be observed for $\{a, c, d\}$ and $\{a, b\}$: the discarded sets are both empty, while we need to be able to counter $\{b\}$ and $\{c\}$ respectively. Thus, none of these sets is admissible.

3.5   Comparison

Moving from the two–valued to the three–valued approach is more than just a structural change. This was the case also in the Dung setting, even though both approaches were strongly related [19]. When computing classical extensions, we focus on what arguments we can accept. In the three–valued setting, a discarded argument is also important and **f** means something more than just a lack of acceptance. In this setting **u** represents the lack of either a proper reason to accept or discard an argument or will to commit to a value (i.e. we decide not to assign **t** or **f** even though we have sufficient basis for that). As a result, a semantics truly exploiting a three–valued setting has naturally different assumptions than a two–valued one. For example it would rather maximize on the arguments that are not left undecided, rather than just on the ones we are ready to accept. Therefore if one decides to treat the three–valued setting as the means of computing extensions in the two–valued one, he or she should take special care when choosing semantics.

Let us compare the decisive outing and lattice formulations of admissibility. The main difference lies in the treatment of the self–support and support cycles. The first one admits both and treats attacks generated by them as valid. The latter also admits both, however, attacks coming from them do not need to be defended from. Take the framework depicted in Figure 6. According to the outing formulation, $\emptyset$ and $\{b\}$ are the only admissible extensions. This comes from the fact that if we were to utter $\{a\}$, an opponent could always respond with $\{b\}$, which we cannot counter. In the lattice setting, if we collect just the arguments set to **t**, i.e. the arguments accepted in an admissible three-valued interpretation, then we obtain the following sets: $\emptyset$, $\{a\}$ and $\{b\}$.

The fact that the outing definition admits arguments forming support cycles as valid attackers has some side effects. Most importantly, it breaks the relation between the stable and the admissible semantics – in this example $\{a\}$ is a stable extension, but not (outing) admissible. This does not occur in the lattice approach.

As we have mentioned before, there is a difference in motivation behind the two and three–valued semantics. Take for example the preferred extensions, which in general do not have to agree even if their admissible bases do. Let us assume a framework consisting of a single self–supporting argument $D = (\{a\}, \{(a, a)\}, \{a : a\})$. If we were to follow the standard set inclusion maximality definition then $\{a\}$ would be the preferred extension according to the outing formulation. However, the lattice version follows information maximality and both $\emptyset$ and $\{a\}$ would be considered preferred.

Let us close this section with some formal results on how and when can extensions under both approaches coincide. We will start with the outing to lattice direction. Please note that it recreates the relation between extensions from the two to three–valued setting that held in the Dung framework [19].

Theorem 1. *Let $D = (S, L, C)$ be an ADF. For any (decisive outing) admissible extension E of D there exists a lattice admissible three–valued interpretation v_3 s.t. $v_3^t = E$.*

Proof. We will prove this theorem by constructing an appropriate interpretation (please note there may be more than one per extension). Let v_3 be a u–completion to S of the range interpretation v of E. Assume that v_3 is not lattice admissible, i.e. it is not the case that $v_3 \leq_i \Gamma_D(v_3)$. This means that the new interpretation "loses" information, i.e. at least one element formerly mapped to $\mathbf{t}$ or $\mathbf{f}$ is now $\mathbf{u}$, or becomes incomparable (some element formerly mapped to $\mathbf{t}/\mathbf{f}$ goes to $\mathbf{f}/\mathbf{t}$).

Let us first take a look at the case when $v_3(a) = \mathbf{f}$ and $\Gamma_D(v_3)(a) \neq \mathbf{f}$. This means that for at least one $w \in [v_3]_2$, $w(C_a) = \mathbf{t}$. Consequently, a is not decisively out in v_3 and could not have been decisively out in v. Contradiction.

Now let us consider the case when $v_3(a) = \mathbf{t}$ and $\Gamma_D(v_3)(a) \neq \mathbf{t}$. From this follows that there is at least one $w \in [v_3]_2$ s.t. $w(C_a) = \mathbf{f}$. Let F be the set of all arguments originally mapped to $\mathbf{u}$ that are now assigned $\mathbf{t}$, i.e. $F = \{f \in S$ s.t. $v_3(f) = \mathbf{u}$ and $w(f) = \mathbf{t}\}$. If the set F is empty, then w is a $\mathbf{f}$–completion of v and therefore failure for a means E cannot be two–valued conflict–free. Contradiction. If set F is not empty, it means that $C_a(par(a) \cap E) = in$ (by conflict–freeness) and $C_a(par(a) \cap (E \cup F)) = out$ (coming from w). Moreover, $F \cap E^+ = \emptyset$ by construction – no element from E^+ is assigned $\mathbf{u}$, which is the requirement for adding to F. Conclusion is that E cannot be outing admissible. Contradiction.

In what follows we show that the two notions of admissibility, the lattice and decisive outing formulation, coincide on a special class of ADFs, namely the bipolar ADFs without support cycles. Although we do not claim that this class is the maximal one where the semantics agree, it appears natural to consider, since the semantics can differ when support cycles are present. Note that we assume finite ADFs, i.e. the set of arguments S is finite.

We prove a technical lemma, which intuitively states that every argument that is set to $\mathbf{f}$ in a three-valued admissible interpretation is rejected either because the set of accepted arguments together are enough reason to reject it, or it requires supporters, which are rejected.

Lemma 2. *Let $D = (S, L, C)$ be a bipolar ADF without support cycles and v a lattice admissible three-valued interpretation in D and $a \in v^{\mathbf{f}}$. Then at least one of the following statements is true.*

1. *For any $M \supseteq v^{\mathbf{t}}$ we have $C_a(par(a) \cap M) = out$, or*
2. *$supp_D(a) \neq \emptyset$ and for any $M \supseteq v^{\mathbf{t}}$ with $M \cap supp_D(a) \cap v^{\mathbf{f}} = \emptyset$ we have $C_a(par(a) \cap M) = out$.*

Proof. Assume that v is admissible in D and $a \in v^{\mathbf{f}}$. Assume that statement 1 does not hold. This means there exists a $M' \supseteq v^{\mathbf{t}}$ s.t. $C_a(par(a) \cap M') = in$. Since v is admissible we have that $C_a(par(a) \cap v^{\mathbf{t}}) = out$. This follows from the fact that there exists a $w \in [v]_2$ with $w^{\mathbf{t}} = v^{\mathbf{t}}$ and $w^{\mathbf{f}} = v^{\mathbf{f}} \cup v^{\mathbf{u}}$. Since v is admissible, it follows that $C_a(par(a) \cap w^{\mathbf{t}}) = out$, since otherwise $v(a) \not\leq_i w(a)$. Hence, there exists a $x \in (M' \setminus v^{\mathbf{t}})$ which is supporting a.

Now let $M \supseteq v^{\mathbf{t}}$ and $M \cap supp_D(a) \cap v^{\mathbf{f}} = \emptyset$. Let further $M^p = M \cap par(a)$, i.e. M^p is restricted to the parents of a. Suppose $C_a(M^p) = in$, let $X = (M^p \setminus (att_D(a) \setminus v^{\mathbf{t}}))$, i.e. X is a subset of M^p, without the attackers of a, which are not in $v^{\mathbf{t}}$. Then we have that also $C_a(X) = in$. Suppose the contrary, i.e. $C_a(X) = out$, but since $C_a(M^p) = in$ this means that there exists a $b \in (M^p \setminus X)$ with $b \in supp_D(a)$, which is a contradiction. This in turn implies $X \cap v^{\mathbf{f}} \cap par(a) = \emptyset$. This is a contradiction to admissibility of v, since also $(v^{\mathbf{t}} \cap par(a)) \subseteq X$ holds and admissibility requires that in this case $C_a(X) = out$, by a similar reasoning as above.

Now we can show the coincidence of the admissible semantics on the bipolar ADFs without support cycles.

Theorem 2. *Let $D = (S, L, C)$ be a bipolar ADF without support cycles and v a lattice admissible three-valued interpretation in D, then $A = v^{\mathbf{t}}$ is (decisive outing) admissible in D.*

Proof. Assume there exists a non-empty set $F \subseteq (S \setminus A)$ and $M = F \cup A$, s.t. there exists an argument $a \in A$ with $C_a(par(a) \cap M) = out$. We first show that $M \cap v^{\mathbf{f}} \neq \emptyset$. Suppose the contrary, i.e. $M \cap v^{\mathbf{f}} = \emptyset$. It is straightforward to see that $M \supsetneq v^{\mathbf{t}}$, since $C_a(par(a) \cap v^{\mathbf{t}}) = in$, otherwise v would not be admissible in D. Suppose all elements in M which are not in $v^{\mathbf{t}}$ are undecided in v, i.e. $(M \setminus v^{\mathbf{t}}) \subseteq v^{\mathbf{u}}$. But this implies that the corresponding two-valued interpretation of M, namely $v'(s) = \mathbf{t}$ if $s \in M$ and $v'(s) = \mathbf{f}$ otherwise, must be in $[v]_2$ and hence v would not be admissible, since then $\Gamma_D(v)(a) \neq \mathbf{t}$.

Now we show that for every $r \in v^{\mathbf{f}}$ it holds that $r \in A^+$, hence $v^{\mathbf{t}}$ is decisive outing admissible in D. Let L^+ and L^- be the supporting and attacking links of D and $L = L^+ \cup L^-$. Since the graph $G = (S, L^+)$ is an acyclic directed graph (DAG), we can construct a topological ordering, represented by the function $f : S \to \mathbb{N}$, on the vertices S such that if $(a, b) \in L^+$ we have $f(a) < f(b)$. This means if a supports b, then the former is ordered lower than the latter. We now show the claim by induction on $f(s)$ for arguments in S.

(IH): Let $r \in v^{\mathbf{f}}$, $f(r) = i$, if $\forall r' \in v^{\mathbf{f}}$, s.t. $f(r') < f(r)$ we have $r' \in A^+$, then $r \in A^+$.

(IB): The claim holds for all $s \notin v^{\mathbf{f}}$, hence we look at the smallest element in $r \in v^{\mathbf{f}}$ w.r.t. the ordering induced by f. We know that one of the two statements of Lemma 2 must hold for r. If the first one holds, then clearly $r \in A^+$. Otherwise we have $supp_D(r) \cap v^{\mathbf{f}} = \emptyset$, since r must be the minimal element of the order induced by f. But then we know that for any $M \supseteq A$ we have that $M \cap supp_D(r) \cap v^{\mathbf{f}} = \emptyset$ and thus $C_r(par(r) \cap M) = out$. Hence $r \in A^+$.

(IS): Let $r \in v^{\mathbf{f}}$ with $f(r) = i$. We assume that $\forall r' \in v^{\mathbf{f}}$ with $f(r') < f(r)$ it holds that $r' \in A^+$. Again, since $r \in v^{\mathbf{f}}$ we know that one of the statements of Lemma 2 is true. Furthermore, if the first one is true, then clearly $r \in A^+$. Suppose only the second statement is true. By assumption, we know that $\forall x \in supp_D(r) \cap v^{\mathbf{f}}$ we have that $x \in A^+$, since all of the elements in this set are in $v^{\mathbf{f}}$ and have a lower order w.r.t. f. This means $(supp_D(r) \cap v^{\mathbf{f}}) \subseteq A^+$. But then r must be in A^+, since r is decisively out for the partial two-valued interpretation v', which sets all elements in A^+, in particular $supp_D(r) \cap v^{\mathbf{f}}$ to $\mathbf{f}$ and all elements in A to true. Indeed for all $M \supseteq A$, s.t. $M \cap supp_D(r) \cap v^{\mathbf{f}} = \emptyset$ we have that $C_r(par(r) \cap M) = out$.

4   Discussion

Notes on defense. Strongly tied to the notion of admissibility is the concept of defense. Although we have managed to formulate admissibility without making the defense explicit, giving a proper account of it is required for redefining some of the stronger semantics. The current definition of the discarded set (A^+) can be a base for detecting defense known from the conflict–based setting (i.e. counterattacking) and one arising in the bipolar setting (e.g. cutting off the support of an attacker). However, in ADFs, one can defend in one more way. Due to the fact that the framework (mostly via disjunction in acceptance conditions) has the possibility to express some weak notion of preference between incoming relations, we have a case of *overpowering defense*. Instead of responding to a discard with another discard, we overpower it. A simple example of it would be an acceptance condition of the form $\neg a \vee b$. As long as b is present in the framework, accepting a has no effect. It does not require the "defender" and the "attacker" to be connected by a link, and hence cannot be detected by the discarded set. This type of defense in ADFs is also problematic as often a conflict–free extension possessing it simply does not "react" to incoming conflicts. Therefore, verifying whether a set has the power to defend an argument not belonging to it in this particular way is challenging.

Revisiting support cycles. From the point of view of ADFs, the ongoing research on bipolarity in argumentation is very important. A thorough overview can be found in [5]. Although the acceptance conditions allow us to express support in several ways, we do not yet take into account all of its side effects. In this section we would like to discuss the problem of support cycles in argumentation. Although discarded in logic programming and some frameworks [9], they do not always represent an error in our thinking. A very simple example, yet common in every day life and, for instance, game theory is the case of mutual agreement. An agent can decide to cooperate as long as his opponent agrees to do the same. This rule 'I play nice as long as you play nice' is not something irrational or rare. The 'good will' mutual agreement is in our opinion a very important example of reasoning that is not only defeasible (we just 'assume' everyone else is following their commitment, and this assumption can very well be withdrawn when it turns out it is not the case) but also has a support cycle in it. And yet, it is very reasonable and, be it good or not, unavoidable.

Nevertheless, there are support cycles that are clearly erroneous and need to be avoided. Unfortunately, there is not much intuition on how to distinguish between the 'good' and the 'bad' ones. For these reasons, in future we would like to admit the semantics both with and without the support cycles and use them according to a given situation. We hope that further research will shed more light on this case.

Future work. Throughout this paper we have mentioned several open questions and problems concerning not only the ADFs, but also argumentation overall. First, we see a need for a discussion on the rationality of arguments, i.e. how should self–attackers, self–supporters and support cycles be treated. Addressing the rationality issue would give rise to stricter notions of semantics. Another task for the future is moving the logic programming style acceptability [17] to ADFs. In order to give an intuitive definition, a proper account of support cycles in ADFs is required, which were so far informally described in Section 2.2.

Finally, we would like to formalize the concept of defense in ADFs and provide a tool for an efficient detection of overpowering. With this concept at hand, moving over to other well known semantics in this abstract framework is a next natural step. In particular, complete and preferred semantics can be based on our notion of admissibility. In case of the latter, this could circumvent certain problems of the formulation introduced in [16], where three–valued preferred extensions are not necessarily incomparable on the sets of accepted arguments.

5   Conclusion

In this paper we have reviewed the existing definitions of admissibility in abstract dialectical frameworks — one of the most general enhancements of Dung's abstract frameworks — and introduced a novel two–valued approach reflecting the original formulation of admissibility in a more direct way. Besides a thorough discussion on the conceptual level, we have also compared the approaches on a formal one. The results show that each new two–valued admissible extension is also admissible in the three–valued setting of [16], but that the other direction does not hold in general.

Acknowledgements. This work has been funded by FWF through project I1102. Sylwia Polberg is financially supported by the Vienna PhD School of Informatics. We would like to thank Martin Riener for his help and valuable suggestions.

References

1. Dung, P.M.: On the acceptability of arguments and its fundamental role in non-monotonic reasoning, logic programming and n-person games. Artif. Intell. 77, 321–357 (1995)
2. McBurney, P., Parsons, S., Rahwan, I. (eds.): ArgMAS 2011. LNCS, vol. 7543. Springer, Heidelberg (2012)
3. Amgoud, L., Vesic, S.: A new approach for preference-based argumentation frameworks. Annals of Mathematics and Artificial Intelligence 63, 149–183 (2011)
4. Baroni, P., Cerutti, F., Giacomin, M., Guida, G.: AFRA: Argumentation framework with recursive attacks. Int. J. Approx. Reasoning 52(1), 19–37 (2011)
5. Cayrol, C., Lagasquie-Schiex, M.C.: Bipolarity in argumentation graphs: Towards a better understanding. Int. J. Approx. Reasoning (in Press, 2013)
6. Bench-Capon, T.J.M.: Persuasion in practical argument using value-based argumentation frameworks. J. Log. Comput. 13(3), 429–448 (2003)
7. Modgil, S.: Reasoning about preferences in argumentation frameworks. Artif. Intell. 173(9-10), 901–934 (2009)
8. Nielsen, S.H., Parsons, S.: A generalization of Dung's abstract framework for argumentation: Arguing with sets of attacking arguments. In: Maudet, N., Parsons, S., Rahwan, I. (eds.) ArgMAS 2006. LNCS (LNAI), vol. 4766, pp. 54–73. Springer, Heidelberg (2007)
9. Nouioua, F., Risch, V.: Argumentation frameworks with necessities. In: Benferhat, S., Grant, J. (eds.) SUM 2011. LNCS, vol. 6929, pp. 163–176. Springer, Heidelberg (2011)
10. Brewka, G., Woltran, S.: Abstract Dialectical Frameworks. In: KR, pp. 102–111 (2010)
11. Boella, G., Gabbay, D.M., van der Torre, L., Villata, S.: Meta-argumentation modelling I: Methodology and techniques. Studia Logica 93(2-3), 297–355 (2009)
12. Strass, H.: Instantiating Knowledge bases in Abstract Dialectical Frameworks. In: Leite, J., Son, T.C., Torroni, P., van der Torre, L., Woltran, S. (eds.) CLIMA XIV. LNCS (LNAI), vol. 8143, pp. 86–101. Springer, Heidelberg (2013)
13. Brewka, G., Gordon, T.F.: Carneades and Abstract Dialectical Frameworks: A Reconstruction. In: COMMA, pp. 3–12. IOS Press (2010)
14. Caminada, M., Amgoud, L.: On the evaluation of argumentation formalisms. Artif. Intell. 171(5-6), 286–310 (2007)
15. Strass, H.: Approximating operators and semantics for Abstract Dialectical Frameworks. Technical Report 1, Institute of Computer Science, Leipzig University (2013)
16. Brewka, G., Ellmauthaler, S., Strass, H., Wallner, J.P., Woltran, S.: Abstract Dialectical Frameworks Revisited. In: IJCAI (in Press, 2013)
17. Kakas, A.C., Mancarella, P., Dung, P.M.: The acceptability semantics for logic programs. In: ICLP, pp. 504–519 (1994)
18. Ellmauthaler, S.: Abstract Dialectical Frameworks: Properties, Complexity, and Implementation. Master's thesis, Vienna University of Technology (2012)
19. Baroni, P., Caminada, M., Giacomin, M.: An introduction to argumentation semantics. Knowledge Eng. Review 26(4), 365–410 (2011)
20. Baroni, P., Giacomin, M., Guida, G.: SCC–recursiveness: a general schema for argumentation semantics. Artif. Intell. 168(12), 162–210 (2005)
21. Oren, N., Norman, T.J.: Semantics for evidence-based argumentation. In: COMMA, pp. 276–284 (2008)
22. Baroni, P., Giacomin, M.: Semantics of abstract argument systems. In: Simari, G., Rahwan, I. (eds.) Argumentation in Artificial Intelligence, pp. 25–44. Springer (2009)

Computing the Grounded Semantics in all the Subgraphs of an Argumentation Framework: An Empirical Evaluation

Pierpaolo Dondio

School of Computing, Dublin Institute of Technology,
Kevin Street 2, Dublin, Ireland
pierpaolo.dondio@dit.ie

Abstract. Given an argumentation framework $AF = (Ar, R)$ – with Ar a finite set of arguments and $R \subseteq Ar \times Ar$ the attack relation identifying the graph G – we study how the grounded labelling of a generic argument $a \in Ar$ varies in all the subgraphs of G. Since this is an intractable problem of above-polynomial complexity, we present two non-naïve algorithms to find the set of all the subgraphs where the grounded semantic assigns to argument a a specific label $l \in \{in, out, undec\}$. We report the results of a series of empirical tests over graphs of increasing complexity. The value of researching the above problem is two-fold. First, knowing how an argument behaves in all the subgraphs represents strategic information for arguing agents. Second, the algorithms can be applied to the computation of the recently introduced probabilistic argumentation frameworks.

Keywords: Argumentation Theory, Semantics, Algorithms.

1   Introduction

An abstract argumentation framework AF is a directed graph where nodes represent arguments and arrows represent the attack relation. AFs were introduced by Dung [2] to analyze properties of defeasible arguments.

The problem investigated in this paper is the following: given an argumentation framework $AF = (Ar, R)$ – with Ar a finite set of arguments and $R \subseteq Ar \times Ar$ the attack relation identifying the graph G – we study how the grounded labelling of a generic argument $a \in Ar$ varies in all the subgraphs of G. Since this is an intractable problem of above-polynomial complexity, we present two algorithms, one recursive and one modelled as a decision-tree, to find the set of all the subgraphs where the grounded semantic assigns to an argument a a specific label $l \in \{in, out, undec\}$.

The value of researching the above problem is two-fold. First, knowing how an argument behaves in all the subgraphs of an argumentation graph helps us to understand the sensitivity of the argument label to the removal of other arguments via further attacks. This represents strategic information for agents in pursuing a discussion, since they can identify which arguments should be attacked.

J. Leite et al. (Eds.): CLIMA XIV, LNAI 8143, pp. 119–137, 2013.
© Springer-Verlag Berlin Heidelberg 2013

However, the main motivation is represented by the recently introduced probabilistic argumentation frameworks. In such frameworks, the computation of the probability of acceptance of arguments requires the identification of all the subgraphs where a certain label for an argument holds (this is known as the *constellation approach* [6]).

This first work only presents algorithms and results for grounded semantics. This is mainly due to space limitations and the fact that the versions of our algorithms for other semantics have not been yet implemented and therefore an empirical evaluation cannot be made. However, the idea behind the algorithms proposed is general enough to be applied to other semantics. Our recursive algorithm is based on constraints valid for any complete semantics and we have already presented a version for preferred semantics in [11]. The core mechanism of our decision-tree algorithm, based on splitting subgraphs and removing irrelevant arguments, is valid for any complete semantics and it can be extended to specific semantics by modifying the treatments of cyclic subgraphs.

The paper is organized as follows: section 2 presents the required background of abstract argumentation; section 3 sets the problem with the required definitions and presents a brute-force algorithm; section 4 describes the recursive algorithm; section 5 describes our decision-tree algorithm; section 6 reports the results of our experimental evaluation before the description of related works in section 7 and conclusions.

2   Background Definitions

Definition 1 (Abstract Argumentation Framework). Let U be the universe of all possible arguments. An argumentation framework is a pair (Ar, R) where Ar is a finite subset of U and $R \subseteq Ar \times Ar$ is called attack relation. We define an argument a **initial** if $\nexists b \in Ar \mid R(b, a)$, i.e. the argument is not attacked.

Let's consider $AF = (Ar, R)$ and $Args \subseteq Ar$.

Definition 2 (defense). $Args$ defends an argument $a \subseteq Ar$ iff $\forall b \in Ar$ such that $R(b, a), \exists c \in Args$ such that $R(c, b)$. The set of arguments defended by $Args$ is denoted $F(Args)$.

Definition 3 (indirect attack/defense). Let $a, b \in Ar$ and the graph G defined by (Ar, R). Then (1) a indirectly attacks b if there is an odd-length path from a to b in the attack graph G and (2) a indirectly defends b if there is an even-length path (with non-zero length) from a to b in G.

Labelling. A semantics identifies a set of arguments that can survive the conflicts encoded by the attack relation R. In the labelling approach a semantics assigns a label to each argument. Following [4], the choice for the set of labels is: *in, out* or *undec*.

Definition 4 (Labelling/conflict free). Let $AF = (Ar, R)$ be an argumentation framework. A labelling is a total function $L : Ar \rightarrow \{in, out, undec\}$. We write $in(L)$ for $\{a \in Ar \mid L(a) = in\}$, $out(L)$ for $\{a \in Ar \mid L(a) = out\}$, and $undec(L)$ for $\{a \in Ar \mid L(a) = undec\}$. We say that a labelling is conflict-free if no *in*-labelled argument attacks an (other or the same) *in*-labelled argument.

Definition 5 (complete labelling). Let $AF = (Ar, R)$ be an argumentation framework. A complete labelling is a labelling that for every $a \in Ar$ holds that:

1. if a is labelled *in* then all attackers of a are labelled *out*
2. if all attackers of a are labelled *out* then a is labelled *in*
3. if a is labelled *out* then a has an attacker labelled *in*
4. if a has an attacker labelled *in* then a is labelled *out*
5. if a is labelled *undec* then it has at least one attacker labelled *undec* and it does not have an attacker labelled *in*.

Theorem 1, Grounded Labelling. (proved in [4]) Let $AF = (Ar, R)$ be an argumentation framework. L is the grounded labelling iff L is a complete labelling where $undec(L)$ is *maximal* (w.r.t. set inclusion) among all complete labellings of AF.

In figure 1 two argumentation graphs are depicted. The grounded semantics assigns the status of *undec* to all the arguments of (A) (always when there are no initial arguments), while in (B) it assigns *in* to a and c, and *out* to b. Note how a reinstates c.

Fig. 1. Two Argumentation Graphs (A) and (B)

3 Describing and Labelling Subgraphs

Given an argumentation framework $AF = (Ar, R)$ with $|Ar| = n$, and the graph G identified by Ar and R, we consider the set H of all the subgraphs of G. We focus on particular sets of subgraphs, i.e. elements of 2^H. Given $a \in Ar$, we define:

$$A = \{g \in H \mid a \in g\} \quad ; \quad \bar{A} = \{g \in H \mid a \notin g\}$$

that are respectively the set of subgraphs where argument a is present and the set of subgraphs where a is not present (note how we use $\bar{A}$ for the complementary set A^C). If $Ar = \{a_1, .., a_n\}$, a single subgraph g can be expressed by an intersection of n sets A_i or $\bar{A}_i$ ($0 < i \leq n$) depending on whether the ith argument a_i is or is not contained in g.

In general, we can express a set of subgraphs combining some of the sets $A_1, .., A_n, \bar{A}_1, .., \bar{A}_n$. with the connectives $\{\cup, \cap\}$. We write AB to denote $A \cap B$ and $A + B$ for $A \cup B$. For instance, in figure 1 the single subgraph with only b and c present is denoted with $\bar{A}BC$, while the expression AB denotes a set of two subgraphs where arguments a and b are present and c can be either present or not.

We call a *clause* φ a finite intersection (or conjunction) of sets A_i, $\bar{A}_i$. We consider expressions of sets of subgraphs in their *disjunctive normal form*, i.e. as a finite disjunction of clauses $\varphi_1 + \varphi_2 + .. + \varphi_m$. An expression is said to be in *standard form* if $\varphi_j \cap \varphi_i = \emptyset$, for each $i \leq m, j \leq m, j \neq i$. The standard form is made of disjoint sets of subgraphs and it is of particular interest for its applications to probabilistic argumentation. As an example, let's consider the argumentation graph in fig.1 left. The clause $A + B$ is not in standard form. It identifies six out of eight possible subgraphs (the two left out are the one where a, b and c are not present and the one with a and b not present and c present). A standard form is for instance $A + \bar{A}B$.

3.1   Grounded Labelling of Subgraphs

Given a subgraph $g \in H$, the labelling of g simply follows the rules of the chosen semantics. We therefore define a *subgraph labelling* $\mathcal{L}$ as a total function over the Cartesian product of arguments in Ar and subgraphs in H, therefore $\mathcal{L}: Ar \times H \rightarrow \{in, out, undec\}$. When labelling a subgraph, we follow this choice: an argument a is automatically labelled out in all the subgraphs where a is not present (since it does not promote any claim) *or* when it is present but it is labelled out by the semantics, representing the effect on a of the other arguments.

In the case of grounded semantics there is only one labelling per subgraph g, that we call $\mathcal{L}(g)$ (we omit Ar). We call $in(\mathcal{L}(g))$, $out(\mathcal{L}(g))$, $undec(\mathcal{L}(g))$ the sets of arguments labelled in, out, $undec$ in the labelling $\mathcal{L}(g)$. In order to study how an argument behaves across subgraphs in H, we define the following sets of subgraphs:

$$A_{IN} = \{g \in H: a \in in(\mathcal{L}(g))\} ; \quad A_{OUT} = \{g \in H: a \in out(\mathcal{L}(g))\}$$

$$A_U = \{g \in H: a \in undec(\mathcal{L}(g))\}$$

which represent all the subgraphs where argument a is labelled in, out or $undec$.

Example 1. Let's compute A_{IN} for the graph of figure 1 left. There are 3 arguments and 2^3 subgraphs; argument a is labelled in in all the subgraphs where it is present and b is not present (and c becomes irrelevant), i.e. the set of two subgraphs $A_{IN} = A\bar{B}$. It is $undec$ when all the arguments are present, the single subgraph $A_U = ABC$, while it is labelled out when it is not present or when b is present and c is not present, i.e. $A_{OUT} = \bar{A} + AB\bar{C}$ (the set of the remaining five subgraphs).

The following definition is needed in the presentation of our algorithms.

Definition 6 (Exclusively connected arguments). Given an argument a and an argumentation graph G, let's define $C_G(a)$ as the set of arguments connected to a, i.e. the set of all arguments x for which there is at least a path from x to a in G.

Given two arguments a and b, we also define the set of arguments *exclusively connected* to a via b, called $exC_{G,b}(a)$. $exC_{G,b}(a)$ is the set of arguments x for which there is no path from x to a when b is removed from graph G. Therefore, if G' is the subgraph of G obtained by removing b, $exC_{G,b}(a) = \{x \mid x \in C_G(a) \wedge x \notin C_{G'}(a)\}$

3.2   The Brute Force Approach

A brute force algorithm to solve our problem simply computes the grounded semantics in all the subgraphs of Ar and it assigns each subgraph to A_{IN}, A_{OUT} or A_U depending on the label of argument a in that subgraph.

Algorithm 1 – A brute force approach for computing A_{IN}, A_{OUT}, A_U
```
for each subgraph g of G = (Ar, R)
       for each argument a in g
          assign a label l(a) to a in g using the chosen semantics
          if  l(a) = in  add g to A_IN
          if  l(a) = out add g to A_OUT
          if  l(a) = undec add g to A_U
```

The complexity of the problem studied is above polynomial. There are 2^n possible subgraphs, and the computation of the grounded semantics in each subgraph requires a polynomial time, while other semantics such as the preferred are intractable (see [9]). The algorithms proposed in this paper aim to reduce the computational time by reducing the number of times the grounded semantics has to be computed, by identifying set of equivalent subgraphs in one step instead of individually.

The brute approach is not efficient in the computation of A_{IN} and it is not efficient in the way A_{IN} is expressed, that is a conjunction of single subgraphs. Let's consider the graph in figure 2 left. It can be computed that the expression of A_{IN} includes 56 subgraphs out of the potential 128 (in fact, there are 8 arguments and a total of 256 subgraphs, but we removed the 128 where a is not present).

In [11] we describe an alternative algorithm, which we optimize in the next section. The idea is that we do not need to consider all the subgraphs individually, but a set of subgraphs can be assigned to A_{IN}, A_{OUT} or A_U in a single step. For the graph of figure 2 left, the optimized algorithm of the next section produces the expression in standard form $A_{IN} = A\bar{B}\bar{D} + ABE\bar{D} + AB\bar{E}G\bar{D}$, composed of only three clauses.

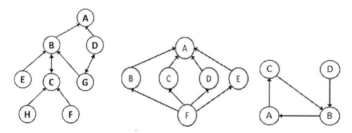

Fig. 2. Three Argumentation Graphs

4   Computing A_{IN}: A Recursive Algorithm

This section presents an algorithm to compute A_{IN}, A_{OUT} under grounded semantics. Given a starting argument a and a label $l \in \{in, out\}$, we need to find the set of subgraphs where argument a is legally labelled l. The idea is to traverse the transpose graph (a graph with reversed arrows) from a down to its attackers, propagating the constraints of the grounded labelling. While traversing the graph, the various paths correspond to a set of subgraphs. The constraints needed are listed in definition 5 and theorem 1. If argument a – attacked by n arguments x_n – is required to be labelled in, we impose the set A_{IN} to be:

$$A_{IN} = A \cap \left(X_{1_{OUT}} \cap X_{2_{OUT}} \cap \ldots \cap X_{n_{OUT}}\right) \qquad \text{condition (1)}$$

i.e. argument a can be labelled in in the subgraphs where:

1. a is present - set A and
2. all the attacking arguments x_i are labelled out (sets $X_{i_{OUT}}$).

If a is required to be labelled out, the set of subgraphs is:

$$A_{OUT} = \bar{A} \cup A \cap \left(X_{1_{IN}} \cup X_{2_{IN}} \cup \ldots \cup X_{n_{IN}}\right) \qquad \text{condition (2)}$$

i.e. a is labelled out in all the subgraphs where it is not present or at least one of the attackers is labelled in. Therefore we recursively traverse the graph, finding the subgraphs that are compatible with the starting label of a. The sets $X_{n_{OUT}}$ and $X_{n_{IN}}$ are found when terminal nodes are reached. When a terminal node x_T is reached the following conditions are applied:

1. if x_T is required to be *in* then $X_{T_{IN}} = X_T$
2. if node x_T is required to be *out* then $X_{T_{OUT}} = \overline{X_T}$

The way the algorithm treats cycles guarantees that only grounded complete labellings are identified. If a cycle is detected, the recursion path terminates, returning an empty set that also has the effect to discard all the sets of subgraphs linked with a logical *AND* (by condition 1) to the cyclic path. As described in [11], this treatment of cycles guarantees to discard *undec* arguments not contributing to A_{IN} or A_{OUT} and to identify grounded complete labellings. We present the pseudo-code of the algorithm, while Table 1 describes the steps for computing A_{IN} in the graph of figure 2 right.

Algorithm 2 - The Recursive FindSet(A,L,P) Algorithm

A is a node, L a label (IN or OUT), P is the list of parent nodes, Cset holds the partial result of the computation of conditions (1) and (2).

```
FindSet(A,L,P):
  if A in P:
    return empty_set // Cycle found
  if L = IN:
    if A terminal:
      return a // Terminal condition for IN Label
    else:
      add A to P
      for each child C of A
        Cset = Cset AND FindSet(C,OUT,P)
      return (a AND Cset)                    // condition 1
  if L = OUT:
    if A terminal:
      return NOT(a) // Terminal condition for OUT Label
    else
      add A to P
      for each child C of A
        Cset = Cset OR FindSet(C,IN,P)
      return (NOT(a) OR (a AND Cset))   //condition 2
```

4.1   Optimizations

Generating non-overlapping solutions. The *Recursive* algorithm generates solutions not in standard form, composed by potentially overlapping clauses. If – as in the probabilistic frameworks – sets of disjoint subgraphs are required, a costly Boolean simplification is needed. This is an inclusion-exclusion problem of combinatorial complexity. It is also inefficient in that the recursive steps need to carry expressions longer than necessary.

Table 1. Recursively applying Algorithm 2 on the graph of figure 2 right.

	Node, label	Constraint	Parent List	Comment
1↓	A_{IN}	$A_{IN} = A \cap B_{OUT}$	[]	a must exist and b=OUT
2↓	B_{OUT}	$B_{OUT} =$ $\bar{B} \cup (B \cap (C_{IN} \cup D_{IN}))$	[a]	b is out when b does not exist or b exists and c = in or d = in
3=	C_{IN}	$C_{IN} = C \cap A_{OUT}$	[a,b]	c=IN when c exists and a=OUT. Cycle with a, $C_{IN} = \emptyset$
4=	D_{IN}	$D_{IN} = D$	[a,b]	d is initial
5↑	B_{OUT}	$B_{OUT} = \bar{B} \cup (B \cap D)$		
6↑	A_{IN}	$A_{IN} = A \cap (\bar{B} \cup (B \cap D)) = A\bar{B} + ABD$		

A more efficient approach is to modify the algorithm so it produces solutions in a non-overlapping form by simplifying expressions during the computation. Let's analyse the two algorithm conditions:

1. $A_{IN} = A \cap \left(X_{1_{OUT}} \cap X_{2_{OUT}} \cap ... \cap X_{n_{OUT}}\right)$ condition (1)
2. $A_{OUT} = \bar{A} \cup A \cap \left(X_{1_{IN}} \cup X_{2_{IN}} \cup ... \cup X_{n_{IN}}\right)$ condition (2)

Condition 1 clearly generates disjoints sets if $X_{n_{OUT}}$ are expressed as disjoint sets. Regarding condition 2, since an expression such as $A + B + C + ..$ can be rewritten as disjoint sets in the form $A + \bar{A}B + \bar{A}\bar{B}C + ..$, we modify condition 2 as follows:

$$A_{OUT} = \bar{A} \cup A \cap \left(X_{1_{IN}} \cup \overline{X_{1_{IN}}}X_{2_{IN}} \cup \overline{X_{1_{IN}}}\,\overline{X_{2_{IN}}}X_{3_{IN}} \cup ... \cup \left(\overline{X_{1_{IN}}} ... \overline{X_{n-1_{IN}}}\right)X_{n_{IN}}\right) (2b)$$

In order to generate shorter expressions, the algorithm first computes $\overline{X_{1_{IN}}}$ for all the attackers, then it sorts the expressions of the set $\overline{X_{1_{IN}}}$ in ascending order by number of clauses contained in each expression and then it applies condition 2b.

Optimizing Condition 1: Returning Empty Set. When the *in*-set of an argument has to be computed, all its attackers x_i must be labelled *out* (condition 1). Therefore, if a recursion step returns $X_{i_{OUT}} = \emptyset$, the algorithm immediately returns $A_{IN} = \emptyset$.

Exploiting Rebuttals. Argument b is a rebuttal of argument a iff $R(a,b)$ and $R(b,a)$. Rebuttals can be used to terminate a recursion branch earlier. In fact, if a and b are rebuttals, under grounded semantics neither of them can defeat the other (see [14] pag. 8). Therefore it is $A_{OUT} = \bar{A}$ instead of $A_{OUT} = \bar{A} + AB_{IN}$ as condition 2 would suggest in the general case. Therefore in the presence of a rebuttal argument b the set A_{OUT} results independent from B_{IN} (that increments A_U by forming a cycle), and the algorithm can spare itself the recursive computation of AB_{IN}. This implies a new terminal condition: while we are visiting node a, if a has a rebutting attacker b then the general condition $A_{OUT} = \bar{A} + AB_{IN}$ can be replaced by the condition $A_{OUT} = \bar{A}$, that terminates the recursion branch. Note how without this optimization the algorithm would eventually return $AB_{IN} = \emptyset$ in a further (and unnecessary) recursion step when the cycle with a is detected.

Re-using Computations. Since an argumentation framework can be composed of an intricate set of links, the same node could be visited from different paths, and therefore the same label for the same argument may be computed more than once during the recursion. The idea is therefore to re-use the computed sets. However, this is not straightforward, since the expressions of X_{IN} (or X_{OUT}) might be different according to which path the recursion took before visiting x.

Let's presume we can reach node x with two computations 1 and 2, and we have already computed $X_{1_{IN}}$. We wonder when we can reuse the result sets $X_{1_{IN}}$ to compute $X_{1_{IN}}$. It is clearly $X_{1_{IN}} = X_{2_{IN}}$ if $C_1(x) = C_2(x)$, and the current version of the algorithm implements this simplification, by keeping a buffer of the previously solved recursion. Note how the condition $C_1(x) = C_2(x)$ is quite restrictive and it does not cover all the cases where previous computations, or part of them, can be reused. We leave further simplification for future research.

Example 2. We apply the recursive optimized algorithm to the graph of figure 2 left. Table 2 shows the computation performed. We comment on some of the differences with the baseline recursive algorithms of section 3. First, condition 1 splits the computation into two recursive steps. In step 1.1, the new condition $2b$ is applied to generate disjoints sets. The condition is further simplified by applying the rebuttals simplification that removes the term $B\overline{E_{IN}}\,\overline{G_{IN}}C_{IN}$ from the expression of B_{OUT}. Since c rebuts b, C_{IN} is irrelevant in the computation of B_{OUT} (note that would be relevant to the computation of B_{IN} or B_U, but these sets are not required by any recursive step).

Table 2. Computing A_{IN} using the optimized recursive algorithm for the graph of fig 2 left

1	$A_{IN} = AB_{OUT}D_{OUT}$	Condtion 1
1.1	$B_{OUT} = \overline{B} + BE_{IN} + B\overline{E_{IN}}G_{IN} + B\overline{E_{IN}}\overline{G_{IN}}C_{IN}$	Condition 2b (with reordering)
	$B_{OUT} = \overline{B} + BE_{IN} + B\overline{E_{IN}}G_{IN}$	2b after rebuttals detection. Since c rebuts b, c cannot label b *out*.
1.1.1	$E_{IN} = E$	Terminal node
1.1.2	$G_{IN} = G$	Terminal node
1.1	$B_{OUT} = \overline{B} + BE + B\overline{E}G$	Solution of the recursive step 1.1
1.2	$D_{OUT} = \overline{D} + DG_{IN}$	Condition 2b
	$D_{OUT} = \overline{D}$	Rebuttals optimization applied, g cannot defeat c
1	$A_{IN} = A(\overline{B} + BE + B\overline{E}G)\overline{D}$	Final Solution

5   *ADT*: Arguments Decision Tree Algorithm

In many cases, the recursive algorithm reduces the computational effort required to compute A_{IN} in comparison with the brute force approach, but it is still prone to combinatorial explosion. For instance, for the graph of figure 2 centre the algorithm produces $A_{IN} = (\overline{B} + BF)(\overline{C} + CF)(\overline{D} + DF)(\overline{E} + EF)$, an expression with an exponential number of terms equal to 2^{n-2}, where n is the number of nodes.

In this section we describe a new algorithm modelled as a decision-tree, where at each step a node x is selected and the computation of A_{IN} is split in two disjoint graphs, one containing the node and the other not containing it ($A_{IN} = A'_{IN}X + A''_{IN}\overline{X}$).

Our idea is to select a node that reduces the complexity of the remaining sub-graphs. We select the node x that makes the most number of nodes indifferent for the computation of A_{IN}, because these nodes are either (1) defeated by x in the subgraph containing x or (2) disconnected from a in the subgraph where x is not present. As an example, referring again to figure 2 centre, let's select node f for our tree split. In the subgraphs where node f is present, all the other nodes are defeated and a results labelled *in*. When f does not exist, the only possible subgraph is the one not containing all the attackers of a. Therefore $A_{IN} = F + \bar{F}\bar{B}\bar{C}\bar{D}\bar{E}$, which is a shorter and more manageable standard form expression.

The algorithm we present, called ADT, finds the sets A_{IN}, A_{OUT}, A_U in parallel; it is guaranteed to find disjoint sets and it works better than algorithm 2. First of all, we need to define the metric used to select the argument used for the split. We call this metric *dialectical strength*.

Definition 7. Given $G = (Ar, R)$ and an argument $a \in Ar$, the dialectical strength of an argument $x \in Ar$ w.r.t. a, called $DS_a(x)$, is defined as follows:

If x is initial, $DS_a(x)$ is the number of arguments that are defeated by x plus the arguments that result disconnected from a once the arguments defeated by x are removed from G. Therefore:

$$DS_a(x) = \left| \{x\} \cup A(x) \cup \bigcup_{y \in A(x)} exC_a(y) \right|$$

Where $A(x)$ is the set of all arguments attacked by x, i.e. $\forall x \in Ar, A(x) = \{a \in Ar | R(x, a)\}$. Note that, if x directly attacks a, then $DS_a(x) = |Ar|$. If x is not initial, $DS_a(x)$ is the number of arguments that are disconnected from a after x is removed. Therefore:

$$DS_a(x) = |\{x\} \cup exC_a(x)|$$

The argument with the highest DS_a is selected for the split. In the case of several arguments with the same DS_a, the node for the split is randomly selected.

In figure 2 centre, all the nodes have $DS_a = 1$, except argument f that has $DS_a(f) = 4$ (of course it is always $DS_a(a) = |Ar|$).

Once argument x is selected, the original graph G is split into $G_1 = GX$ and $G_2 = G\bar{X}$. For each subgraph the algorithm keeps a list of the nodes already used for the split and the constraint over each split node (i.e. if in the subgraph the argument is present or not present). At each step the algorithm removes the nodes defeated by argument x in G_1 and the nodes disconnected from a in G_2. Note how a chain effect can happen: by removing arguments, new initial nodes might be created that might defeat other arguments. Note how the number of nodes removed is equal to the dialectical strength DS Therefore, at each split ADT actually computes a set of 2^{DS-1} sub-graphs that, as proven at the end of this section, are all equivalent for the labelling of a. Moreover, the computational complexity of ADT will strongly depend on the average value of the dialectical strength.

Regarding terminal conditions, ADT stops when one of the following terminal conditions is met:

1. If argument a is defeated, the branch of the tree will contribute to A_{OUT}
2. If argument a is isolated, the branch of the tree will contribute to A_{IN}, since a has no attackers.
3. If there are no more arguments for the split and neither of the above two are verified, the branch contributes to A_U since a cycle is detected.

Figure 3 proposes an illustrative example of the *ADT* algorithm applied to the graph of figure 2 right, followed by the pseudo-code of the algorithm.

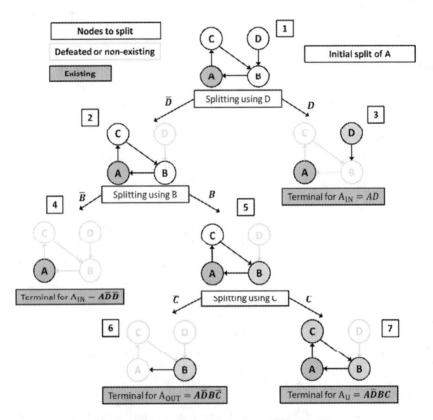

Fig. 3. Visual Representation of the *ADT* Algorithm

At the beginning (not shown), the set $\bar{A}$ is trivially assigned to A_{OUT}, and we start from the situation where a is present (set of subgraphs A), depicted in subgraph 1 of figure 3. First, the DS_a of each argument is computed. Arguments d and b have both $DS_a = 3$ while c has $DS_a(c) = 1$. Therefore d is chosen.

In the subgraph (3), obtained by set d to present, b is defeated, a becomes initial and defeats c. Therefore a is isolated, the terminal condition for A_{IN} is reached and the path AD is added to A_{IN}. In the subgraph with d non-existent (2), no other node is disconnected. Since no terminal condition is reached, a new split is needed. Now b is selected. In the subgraph with b not present (4), argument a becomes isolated, and therefore the path $A\overline{D}\overline{B}$ is added to A_{IN}, while in the graph with b present (5) no arguments are disconnected. Only c is left for the split.

When c is present (subgraph 7), the terminal condition 3 is reached so $A\overline{D}BC$ contributes to A_U. Subgraph 6, with c not present in the subgraph, contributes to A_{OUT} (set of subgraphs $A\overline{D}B\overline{C}$) since b becomes initial and defeats a.

Algorithm 3 - ADT (Arguments Decision Tree Algorithm).

<u>Inputs:</u> Graph G, argument a <u>Output:</u> (A_{IN}, A_{OUT}, A_U)

Initialize C to $\emptyset$. //C is the list of constraints on the split arguments

ADT(G, a, C)

   If C is $\emptyset$ then C = A

   remove from G all the nodes disconnected from node a

   compute I_G, the list of initial nodes of G

   while ($\exists x$ in I_G with X is in C)

      for each x in I_G with X in C

           remove form G all the arguments attacked by x

           update the initial list I_G

      remove form G all the arguments not connected to a

      If $\nexists b$ so that R(b,a) **then** add C to A_{IN} and **return**

      If $a \notin G$ **then** add C to A_{OUT} and **return**

      If no more nodes to split **then** add C to A_U and **return**

   for each x in G and not in C Compute the $DS_a(x)$

   select node x with highest $DS_a(x)$

   split the subgraph: $G_1 = G \cup X$ and $G_2 = G \cup \overline{X}$

   call ADT$(G_1, a, C \cup X)$

   call ADT$(G_2, a, C \cup \overline{X})$

Optimization. We optimized the ADT algorithm by keeping a buffer of the subgraphs that have already been computed. When, after a split, one of the remaining subgraph has been already encountered in the computation, its solution can be reused and joint with the constraints of the current branch. This operation is theoretically simpler than in the case of the *Recursive* algorithm. For instance, considering the graph of figure 2 left, after we split using node g, the subgraph where g is present is reduced to the nodes $\{a, c\}$, but the same subgraph is obtained in the branch where g is not present by further splitting, using node e and selecting the branch where node e is present. The first branch has constraints G (g is present in all the subgraphs) while the second has constraints $\overline{G}E$ (g is not present and e is present). A solution S for the subgraph $\{a, c\}$ is computed only the first time the subgraph is encountered (branch G in our example), generating the clause GS that is added to the ADT output. When the same subgraph is encountered in the branch $\overline{G}E$, the solution S is reused and joint with the constraints of the branch, obtaining the new solution $G\overline{E}S$ that is also added to the ADT output. For instance, referring to the computation of A_{IN}, the solution for the subgraph $\{a, c\}$ is $A\overline{C}$, and this set is used to add the two clauses $GA\overline{C} + \overline{G}EA\overline{C}$ to the output of ADT for the set A_{IN}.

ADT$_{fast}$**.** We implemented a version of the above *ADT* algorithm, called ADT_{fast}, where at each step the node used for the split is chosen randomly. The algorithm will be used to compare the impact of using the dialectical strength in the computation.

Soundness and Completeness. We end this section by proving the *soundness* and *completeness* of the *ADT* algorithm. Each of the clauses φ_j composing the output of the *ADT* algorithm identifies a set of subgraphs. We prove that all the subgraphs identified by a clause assign the same label to argument a and this label is correctly assigned under grounded semantics. The set of subgraphs associated with a clause φ_j have in common a subset of the arguments in Ar, the arguments present in the expression of φ_j. For instance, if $Ar = \{a, b, c, d, e\}$, the clause $AB\bar{C}$ identifies all the subgraphs having in common the presence of nodes a, b and the absence of node c. Nodes d and e are not specified, therefore their presence or absence is irrelevant and they identify a set of 4 different subgraphs associated with φ_j. We prove that these *irrelevant* arguments are actually irrelevant to the computation of the label of a and therefore all the subgraphs in φ_j assign the same label to a. *ADT* uses two conditions to identify irrelevant arguments. First, when the argument used for the split is removed, all the arguments resulting disconnected from a are irrelevant to the labelling of a. Second, in the subgraphs where an initial argument i is constrained to be present, all the arguments attacked by i are labelled *out*, and therefore they become irrelevant (as proven by [8], removing an *out* argument does not change the grounded extension). Therefore all the arguments marked as irrelevant do not alter the label of a and therefore we prove that all the subgraphs in φ_j assign the same label to a.

ADT also assigns the correct label under grounded semantics, since its second condition and the three terminal conditions described above actually implement the basic step of the algorithm for grounded labelling described by Modgil and Caminada in [14, page 8] and therefore *ADT* generates correct grounded labellings.

In order to prove *ADT completeness*, we observe that the *ADT* algorithm considers the entire problem space, since all the arguments that are not found irrelevant to the labelling of a are split. Therefore in all the 2^n subgraphs of G argument a is labelled by the *ADT* algorithm.

6   Evaluation

We implemented our algorithms in Python 2.7, and we performed a set of initial experiments on a *Windows* 7 machine with 3Gb RAM and *Core I3 Intel* processor. We implemented the following algorithms:

1. **Brute** – the brute force approach.
2. **ADT** – the decision-tree based algorithm using the dialectical strength as splitting criterion.
3. **ADT**$_{fast}$ – the *ADT* algorithm where splitting nodes are selected randomly.
4. **Rec** *(Recursive)* – the optimized recursive algorithm. All the optimization of section 4 were implemented.

Our first evaluation tests two aspects of the computation of A_{IN}: computational time and length of the output expression. The evaluation described in this paper does not claim to be exhaustive. It focuses on the generic case of random graphs; it does not study particular class of graphs nor does it test hybrid approaches.

Random Graphs Generation. We generate different acyclic and cyclic graphs of increasing complexity both in terms of number of nodes and density. Graph instances have been generated as follows. Given n arguments, we assign an incremental index i to each argument and we generate a tree with node a as root, to guarantee that for each argument there is at least a path to a. Then, in the case of acyclic graphs, random links are added until the required density is reached. In order to generate only acyclic graphs, the links are added only if they go from a node with a higher index to a node with a lower index. In the case of cyclic graph, links are added randomly with no restrictions. However, we require each random graph to at least contain a cycle. Note that the density for an acyclic graph is computed over $n(n-1)$ (instead of $\frac{n(n-1)}{2}$ used for the acyclic case) to take into consideration the presence of symmetric attacks.

6.1   Experimenting with the Length of A_{IN}

This set of experiments tests the ability of each algorithm to express a standard-form solution for A_{IN} in the most compact way. We use as a metric the length l of the expression of A_{IN}, defined as the number of clauses contained in its standard-form expression. Results reported are the average of a set of 1000 executions of each algorithm using graphs differentiated by number of nodes, density and type (cyclic or acyclic).

In the brute force approach, the length of the solution equates to the number of subgraphs in A_{IN}. Table 3 shows results for the brute force approach. No data for graphs with more than 15 nodes are available due to the long computational time needed by this algorithm (a single 15-node with a 0.3 density takes about 12 minutes).

Table 3. Length of A_{IN}, brute force approach

Nodes	6	7	8	9	10	11	12	13	14	15
Length of A_{IN}	12	23	44	85	158	335	618	1421	2219	4853

Graphs 1-4 show the behaviour of the other algorithms. We divide the analysis into cyclic and acyclic graphs. Overall, the *ADT* algorithm shows the best performance, even if its performance is not consistent with the type of graph (cyclic or acyclic). Graph 3 shows how the *ADT* algorithm is extremely efficient for acyclic graphs, and the gap with the other algorithm increases rapidly. For a 20-node graph, *ADT* output is on average 42.1 clauses against the 659.4 of the *Recursive* algorithm.

Again, Graphs 1 and 2 (left) show the ratio (by density and by number of nodes) between the length of the solution expressed by the *ADT* algorithm and the second best algorithm, the *Recursive* algorithm, for acyclic graphs.

Graph 1 left shows how the ratio by density increases almost linearly, showing how the *ADT* algorithm becomes more efficient with high density acyclic graphs. This could be explained by the fact that, when the number of links increases, each node is likely to attack a larger set of nodes, and therefore nodes' dialectical strength *DS* increases and the split subgraphs that result are smaller and easier to compute.

The introduction of the dialectical strength is also proved to be efficient, since the ADT_{fast} algorithm (i.e. that in which nodes for the split are randomly selected) produces much longer expressions, already 22 times longer for a 20-node graph.

However, the situation is different for cyclic graphs. The *Recursive* algorithm shows similar or better performance than *ADT*, as shown in Graph 4 and Graphs 1 and 2 right. Graphs 1 and 2 right now show an inverse ratio (*Recursive* algorithm over *ADT*). The presence of cycles and rebuttals increase the likelihood that some recursive branches quickly generate an empty return set, and consequently the length of the solution decreases. Moreover, when the number of cycles increases, the dialectical strength is no longer effective, since the number of initial arguments diminishes and the number of arguments disconnected from the root node a after the generic node x is removed – i.e. $|exC(x)|$ – diminishes as well or it could likely be empty.

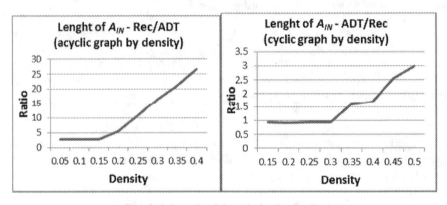

Graph 1. Length of the solution by density

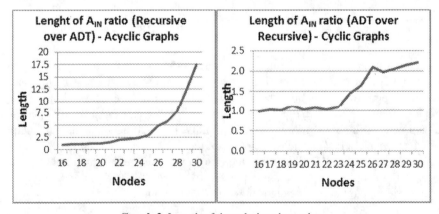

Graph 2. Length of the solutions by nodes

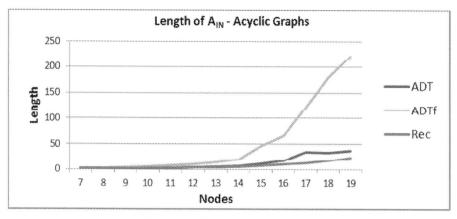

Graph 3. Length of the solutions – Acyclic Graphs

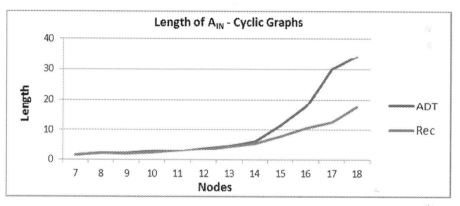

Graph 4. Length of the solutions – Cyclic Graphs

6.2 Computational Time

This second set of experiments tests the efficiency of the above algorithms in terms of computational time. Again, the brute force approach is by far the slowest. In a 14-node graph with 0.3 density, the average computing time is about 45 times longer than the *Recursive* algorithm, while it increases to 650 times for a 15-node graph.

The ADT_{fast} algorithm is also considerably slower than the others. For a 25-node acyclic graph it is on average 15 times slower than the ADT, while it is more than 200 times slower for a cyclic graph compared to the *Recursive* algorithm.

It is interesting to compare the performance of ADT versus ADT_{fast} in order to understand the impact of the dialectical strength as splitting criterion. Following a similar pattern encountered in the length-based experiment, the gap between ADT and ADT_{fast} is highly significant for both the acyclic graph and the cyclic graph with low density. ADT is already 10 times faster with a 23-node acyclic graph, while for a cyclic graph the computational time is comparable and it does not show a clear trend.

The reason for this is mainly because in an acyclic (or quasi-acyclic) graph, the dialectical strength DS of the arguments is high and this effectively reduces the complexity of the split subgraphs. In a cyclic graph, the set exC is small or empty and few nodes are removed during a split. Therefore the choice of a splitting node is less important and the overhead of computing the dialectical strength is not justified.

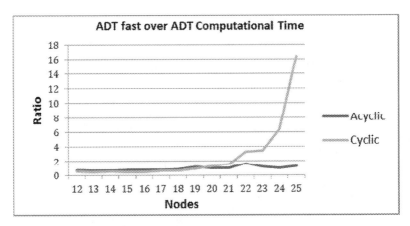

Graph 5. ADT versus ADT fast computational Time

ADT vs Recursive. For acyclic graphs, thanks to the high dialectical strength of the arguments, the *ADT* algorithm is faster. *ADT* is already 100 times faster for a 20-node graph. On our machine setting, the average computational time needed to compute an acyclic graph goes above 60 seconds between 50-55 nodes. Graph 6 shows the computational time in terms of number of nodes. The computational time grows with a quite constant slope after about 25 nodes.

For cyclic graphs, the *Recursive* algorithm takes advantage of the presence of rebuttals and cycles, which reduce some of the recursive steps. The *Recursive* algorithm is already 25 times faster for a 15-node and 60 times faster for a 25-node graph. The *ADT* algorithm remains better up to a density of 0.1.

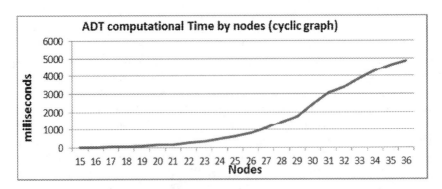

Graph 6. ADT Computational Time by number of nodes

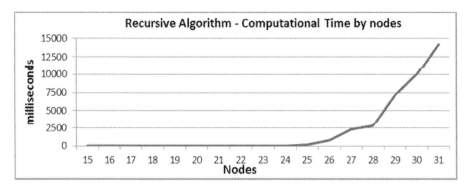

Graph 7. Recursive Algorithm computational time

The *Recursive* algorithm goes above the 60-second threshold at 38 arguments. Graph 7 shows the computational time of the *Recursive* algorithm by number of nodes. We notice how the algorithm has a rapid increase after 25 nodes, much faster than the *ADT* increase for acyclic graphs. An explanation could be that, since the *Recursive* algorithm is based on paths visited on the graph, it is sensitive to the number of links rather than to the number of nodes, and the number of links grows like n^2 rather than n. However, the experimental analysis calls for a theoretical complexity analysis that is at the top of our research agenda.

Overall, our results suggest defining a hybrid approach exploiting both the *ADT* (good for acyclic or quasi-acyclic graphs) and the *Recursive* algorithms (good for cyclic graphs), depending on the characteristics of the graph. Another observation is about the computation of the dialectical strength, which could be optimized and made more effective in the presence of cyclic graphs (for instance by considering the effect of removing a couple of nodes instead of a single node).

7   Related Works

The research presented in this paper is inspired by the recently introduced Probabilistic Argumentation Framework. The original paper by Li [3] introduces the formalism but it does not present any computational algorithm beyond the brute force approach. The author proposes an approximate method using a *Montecarlo* simulation for grounded semantic. Other papers in the field (Hunter [6], Trimm [7], Dung [2]) do not investigate computational aspects. This paper continues our research in [11], where we presented the baseline non-optimized recursive algorithm.

To the author's best knowledge, there is no other study that directly approaches the problem of subgraph-based computation in the context of probabilistic argumentation. Even for abstract argumentation in general, experimental evaluations of algorithms represents a small corpora. The work by Nofal at al. [13] represents one such work. As the author notes, "*although experimental analysis of algorithms is a well-established in other domains, such methodology is given a little attention in the context of AFs"* [13]. We mention also the experimental thesis by Charwat [10] based on tree-decomposition of *AFs*. Therefore, our paper contributes to the experimental analysis of abstract argumentation algorithms.

However, the algorithms proposed in this paper decompose the computation of the grounded semantic, and they can be described as a study on how an argument label behaves when arguments are added (or removed) from an argumentation graph. In particular we refer to the work by Boella [8], that studied how the grounded extension changes with the addition of a new argument. Indeed our algorithm – especially the *ADT* algorithm – relies on similar mechanisms and theoretical foundations. The work in [8] is extended by Cayrol [12] to the case of preferred semantics and the removing of arguments or attacking links.

In abstract argumentation there are works that employ similar techniques to ours. The work by Baumann [9] et al. provides an experimental evaluation of computing extensions semantics by splitting the argumentation graph into subparts that are then combined to obtain a final solution. Their systematic empirical evaluation shows that the performance of algorithms may drastically improve when splitting is applied.

8   Conclusions and Future Works

In this paper we initiated an investigation of how the label assignment of an argument varies in all the subgraphs of an argumentation framework. We presented a recursive algorithm and a tree-based computation. We started to evaluate the algorithms experimentally, showing how they drastically improve performance compared to a brute-force approach. We claim to have provided enough evidence to justify further investigations. In particular, the *ADT* algorithm is proven to be efficient in expressing solutions using the minimal number of clauses, and effective in computing acyclic and quasi-acyclic graphs. The *Recursive* algorithm shows the best computational efficiency for cyclic graphs, and on average it can compute cyclic graphs of up to 35/40 nodes. However, this last result might not fit all the applications, and the number of nodes could be small in some contexts. Interesting future research trajectories include the theoretical complexity analysis of the algorithms, which has not been addressed in this work. Regarding extensions to other semantics, we have already described an extension to preferred semantics for the recursive algorithms, while defining the preferred version of the *ADT* should not present difficulties. Moreover, we intend to focus on the definition of a hybrid approach that uses the *ADT* and the *Recursive* algorithms together. Specific classes of graphs have also to be studied. It appears reasonable to the author that natural argumentation graphs could show specific patterns in terms of density and type of cycles – mostly rebuttal cycles – that could differ from randomly-generated graphs. Finally, attention might also be devoted to the application of the above algorithms to probabilistic argumentation frameworks.

References

1. Dung, P.: On the acceptability of arguments and its fundamental role in nonmonotonic reasoning, logic programming and n-person games. Artificial Intelligence 77, 321–357 (1995)
2. Dung, P., Thang, P.: Towards (Probabilistic) Argumentation for Jury-based Dispute Resolution. In: COMMA 2010, pp. 171–182. IOS Press, Amsterdam (2010)
3. Li, H., Oren, N., Norman, T.J.: Probabilistic Argumentation Frameworks. In: 1st TAFA, JICAI 2011, Barcellona, Spain (2011)
4. Baroni, P., Caminada, M., Giacomin, M.: An introduction to argumentation semantics. Knowledge Eng. Review 26(4), 365–410 (2011)
5. Dunne, P.E., Wooldridge, M.: Complexity of abstract argumentation. In: Argumentation in Artificial Intelligence, pp. 85–104. Springer US (2009)
6. Hunter, A.: A probabilistic approach to modeling uncertain logical arguments. International Journal of Approximate Reasoning 54(1), 47–81 (2013)
7. Thimm, M.: Probabilistic Semantics for Abstract Argumentation. In: Proceedings. of 20th European Conference of Artificial Intelligence, pp. 750–755. IOS Press (2012)
8. Boella, G., Kaci, S., van der Torre, L.: Dynamics in argumentation with single extensions: Abstraction principles and the grounded extension. In: Sossai, C., Chemello, G. (eds.) ECSQARU 2009. LNCS, vol. 5590, pp. 107–118. Springer, Heidelberg (2009)
9. Baumann, R.: Splitting an argumentation framework. In: Delgrande, J.P., Faber, W. (eds.) LPNMR 2011. LNCS, vol. 6645, pp. 40–53. Springer, Heidelberg (2011)
10. Charwat, G.: Tree-Decomposition based Algorithms for Abstract Argumentation Frameworks. Thesis, Vienna University of Technology (February 2012)
11. Dondio, P.: Probabilistic Argumentation Frameworks: Basic Properties and Computation, Highlights on Practical Applications of Multi-Agent Systems, pp. 263–279. Springer (2013)
12. Cayrol, C., Dupin, F., Lagasquie-Schiex, M.: Change in abstract argumentation frameworks: adding an argument. Journal of Artificial Intellgence Research 38(1), 49–84 (2010)
13. Nofal, S., Dunne, P.E., Atkinson, K.: Towards Experimental Algorithms for Abstract Argumentation. In: COMMA, pp. 217–228 (2012)
14. Modgil, S., Caminada, M.: Proof theories and algorithms for abstract argumentation frameworks. In: Argumentation in Artificial Intelligence, pp. 105–129. Springer US (2009)

Advanced SAT Techniques
for Abstract Argumentation

Johannes Peter Wallner, Georg Weissenbacher, and Stefan Woltran

Institute of Information Systems, Vienna University of Technology,
Favoritenstraße 9-11, A-1040 Vienna, Austria

Abstract. In the area of propositional satisfiability (SAT), tremendous
progress has been made in the last decade. Today's SAT technology covers not only the standard SAT problem, but also extensions thereof,
such as computing a backbone (the literals which are true in all satisfying assignments) or minimal corrections sets (minimal subsets of clauses
which if dropped leave an originally unsatisfiable formula satisfiable). In
this work, we show how these methods can be applied to solve important problems from the area of abstract argumentation. In particular,
we present new systems for semi-stable, ideal, and eager semantics. Our
experimental results demonstrate the feasibility of this approach.

Keywords: Abstract Argumentation, Propositional Satisfiability, Argumentation Systems.

1 Introduction

Argumentation is an interdisciplinary subfield of Artificial Intelligence [4] with
links to psychology, linguistics, philosophy and legal theory. Formal methods
of argumentation are nowadays embedded in decision support systems [1], E-
Democracy tools [9], multi-agent systems [34], and many more. Dung's abstract
model of argumentation [13] (and variants thereof) plays a central role in many of
these applications providing a common core for diverse aspects of argumentation
formalisms. This clearly calls for efficient systems and significant progress and
variety in implementing Dung's argumentation semantics has been achieved over
the last years (for an overview, see [11]).

One central method is to reduce the argumentation problem at hand to a formula in propositional logic. Reductions of this kind make highly sophisticated
SAT solvers amenable for the field of argumentation. Using classical propositional logic to evaluate Dung-style argumentation frameworks was first advocated by Besnard and Doutre in [5] and later extended to quantified propositional
logic [22,2] in order to efficiently reduce abstract argumentation problems with
complexity beyond NP. However, these methods have not been implemented yet.

The goal of this paper is to demonstrate how modern SAT technology can be
used for solving such hard problems in the area of argumentation. In particular,
we consider two extensions of the SAT problem, namely *minimal correction sets*
(MCSes) [28,31] and *backbones* [32]. A minimal correction set is a minimal subset

J. Leite et al. (Eds.): CLIMA XIV, LNAI 8143, pp. 138–154, 2013.

of the clauses of an unsatisfiable SAT instance which, if dropped, results in a satisfiable formula. The backbone of a propositional formula ϕ is the set of all literals that evaluate to true in all interpretations that satisfy ϕ.

We demonstrate that these methods suit particular argumentation problems surprisingly well, simplifying the design of the actual procedures. The work which is closest to the methods we propose here is the CEGARTIX system [19], which relies on iterative calls of standard SAT-solvers. Our modular approach results in reduced engineering effort, allowing for rapid prototyping of abstract argumentation systems that immediately benefit from future improvements of SAT technology. Moreover, our results indicate that MCSes and backbones can be more broadly applied to reasoning problems in the AI domain since they directly treat typical features of such problems making the design of the reductions easier compared to reductions to standard (quantified) propositional logic.

Moreover, our experimental results are very promising and show that the proposed methods are competitive to the CEGARTIX system. We recall that experimental results in [19] show that CEGARTIX outperforms other reduction approaches like ASPARTIX [21], although the number of calls to the SAT engine is exponential (with respect to the instance size) in the worst case due to the high complexity of the problems. One reason for the good performance of CEGARTIX is that it performs certain semantic-specific optimizations between the SAT-calls while in monolithic reductions like the ASPARTIX approach, where the entire problem is reduced at once and given to a "black-box" solver, the domain specific short-cuts have to be identified by the underlying systems.

The structure of the paper and its main contribution are as follows: After reviewing abstract argumentation, we present SAT-based techniques to compute backbones and MCSes (Section 2.2). Section 3 contains our main results: we provide new proof procedures for semi-stable [8] and eager semantics [7] based on MCSes and backbones; and show how the ideal semantics [14] can be realized via a backbone. In Section 4 we present our experimental evaluation showing that for the ideal semantics we achieve a significant performance gain over existing systems, and that for semi-stable reasoning we outperform the CEGARTIX system.

Our new systems and test instances are freely available under the link `www.dbai.tuwien.ac.at/research/project/argumentation/sat-based`.

2   Background

2.1   Abstract Argumentation

In this section we introduce (abstract) argumentation frameworks [13] and recall the semantics we study in this paper.

Definition 1. *An* argumentation framework *(AF) is a pair $F = (A, R)$ where A is a set of arguments and $R \subseteq A \times A$ is the attack relation. The pair $(a, b) \in R$ means that a attacks b.*

Fig. 1. Example argumentation framework

An argumentation framework can be represented as a directed graph, as shown in the following example.

Example 1. Let $F = (A, R)$ be an AF with $A = \{a, b, c, d, e\}$ and $R = \{(a, b),$ $(b, a), (a, c), (b, c), (c, d), (e, e)\}$. The corresponding graph representation is depicted in Fig. 1.

A semantics for argumentation frameworks is given via a function σ which assigns to each AF $F = (A, R)$ a set $\sigma(F) \subseteq 2^A$ of extensions. In this paper we focus on the semi-stable [8], eager [7] and ideal [14] semantics. These are based on the stable and preferred semantics [13] and a fundamental notion underlying all of these is the concept of an admissible set. Hence we consider for σ the functions *adm, prf, stb, sem, ideal*, and *eager* which stand for admissible, preferred, stable, semi-stable, ideal, and eager extensions, respectively. We will introduce these concepts in the following.

The basic concept for all the semantics considered in this paper is the admissible set. Admissibility has two requirements, namely conflict-freeness and defense of all arguments in the set.

Definition 2. *Let $F = (A, R)$ be an AF. A set $S \subseteq A$ is conflict-free in F, if there are no $a, b \in S$, such that $(a, b) \in R$. We say that an argument $a \in A$ is defended by a set $S \subseteq A$ in F if, for each $b \in A$ such that $(b, a) \in R$, there exists a $c \in S$ such that $(c, b) \in R$.*

Admissible sets are then conflict-free sets of arguments, where each argument in the set is defended by the set.

Definition 3. *Let $F = (A, R)$ be an AF. A set $S \subseteq A$ is admissible in F, if S is conflict-free in F; and each $a \in S$ is defended by S in F.*

Maximal admissible sets, w.r.t. subset-inclusion are called preferred extensions and accept as many arguments as possible, without violating admissibility.

Definition 4. *Let $F = (A, R)$ be an AF. An admissible set $S \subseteq A$ is a preferred extension in F, if there is no admissible set $S' \subseteq A$ such that $S \subsetneq S'$.*

A basic property of the preferred semantics is that admissible sets and hence preferred extensions always exist for any given framework. A popular semantics for which this is not the case is the stable semantics. For the definition of the stable semantics and the closely related semi-stable semantics we make use of the concept of the range of a given set S of arguments, which is simply the set itself and everything it attacks, i.e. given an AF $F = (A, R)$ and $S \subseteq A$, then the range of S, denoted by S_R^+ is given by $S_R^+ \overset{\text{def}}{=} S \cup \{a \mid (b, a) \in R, b \in S\}$.

Definition 5. *Let $F = (A, R)$ be an AF. A conflict-free set $S \subseteq A$ in F is a stable extension in F, if $S_R^+ = A$. An admissible set E in F is a semi-stable extension in F if there does not exist a set T admissible in F, with $E_R^+ \subset T_R^+$.*

A basic property of these two semantics is that if an AF has stable extensions, then the semi-stable and stable semantics coincide [8]. The intuition is that semi-stable extensions should be "close" to stable extensions, in case no stable extensions exist.

Example 2. Consider the AF from Example 1. Then we have the following admissible sets, respectively extensions: $adm(F) = \{\emptyset, \{a\}, \{b\}, \{a, d\}, \{b, d\}\}$; $stb(F) = \{\{a, d\}\}$; $prf(F) = \{\{a, d\}, \{b, d\}\}$; and $sem(F) = \{\{a, d\}\}$. Note that if we would add a single isolated self-attacking argument to F, i.e. $F' = (A', R')$ with $A' = A \cup \{f\}$ and $R' = R \cup \{(f, f)\}$, then $stb(F') = \emptyset$, but the set of semi-stable extensions would remain the same, i.e. $sem(F') = sem(F)$.

Notice that all the semantics introduced until now in this paper may have multiple extensions. Reasoning tasks on AFs w.r.t. a semantics σ, apart from simple enumeration of all extensions, include the credulous and skeptical acceptance of arguments. An argument is credulously (skeptically) accepted for a semantics and an AF, if it is present in at least one extension (in all extensions) of the semantics.

Definition 6. *Given an AF $F = (A, R)$, a semantics σ and an argument $a \in A$ then we define the following reasoning tasks. The decision problem $\mathsf{Cred}_\sigma(a, F)$ answers yes if $a \in \bigcup \sigma(F)$ and no otherwise. The decision problem $\mathsf{Skept}_\sigma(a, F)$ answers yes if $a \in \bigcap \sigma(F)$ and no otherwise. Let $\mathsf{AllCred}_\sigma(F) \overset{\text{def}}{=} \bigcup \sigma(F)$ and $\mathsf{AllSkept}_\sigma(F) \overset{\text{def}}{=} \bigcap \sigma(F)$.*

Example 3. Applying the reasoning tasks to the AF in Example 1, we have for the preferred semantics the following credulously and skeptically accepted arguments: $\mathsf{AllCred}_{prf}(F) = \{a, b, d\}$ and $\mathsf{AllSkept}_{prf}(F) = \{d\}$.

The remaining two semantics we study in this paper are the ideal and eager semantics, which take a particular skeptical stance and are among the so-called unique-status semantics, i.e. always have a unique extension for any AF.

Definition 7. *Let $F = (A, R)$ be an AF. For an admissible set $S \in adm(F)$, it holds that*

- *$S \in ideal(F)$, if $S \subseteq \mathsf{AllSkept}_{prf}(F)$ and there is no $T \in adm(F)$ with $S \subset T \subseteq \mathsf{AllSkept}_{prf}(F)$;*
- *$S \in eager(F)$, if $S \subseteq \mathsf{AllSkept}_{sem}(F)$ and there is no $T \in adm(F)$ with $S \subset T \subseteq \mathsf{AllSkept}_{sem}(F)$.*

Table 1. Computational complexity of reasoning in AFs

σ	stb	adm	prf	sem	ideal	eager
Cred_σ	NP-c	NP-c	NP-c	Σ_2^P-c	in Θ_2^P	Π_2^P-c
Skept_σ	coNP-c	trivial	Π_2^P-c	Π_2^P-c	in Θ_2^P	Π_2^P-c

That is, the ideal and eager extensions are the maximal-admissible sets w.r.t. subset-inclusion, composed only of arguments skeptically accepted under preferred, respectively semi-stable semantics.

Example 4. Continuing the Example 2, based on the AF in Example 1, then $ideal(F) = \{\emptyset\}$; and $eager(F) = \{\{a, d\}\}$. Note that although $\text{AllSkept}_{prf}(F) = \{d\}$, the set $\{d\}$ is not admissible in F.

Given the set of skeptically accepted arguments w.r.t. preferred or semi-stable semantics to compute the unique subset-maximal admissible set composed only of the arguments skeptically accepted, we can make use of the following function, which we call restricted characteristic function [15].

Definition 8. *Let* $F = (A, R)$ *be an AF. Then* $\hat{\mathcal{F}}_F : 2^A \to 2^A$ *is the re-stricted characteristic function of* F *and is defined by* $\hat{\mathcal{F}}_F(S) \overset{\text{def}}{=} \{a \in S \mid a$ *is defended by* $S\}$.

This function iteratively removes arguments from S, which are not defended by S in F. Applying the function at most $|A|$ times for an AF $F = (A, R)$ yields the maximal admissible set $U \subseteq S$, w.r.t. subset-inclusion. Note that this function is not to be confused with the characteristic function, which one can use for defining semantics of AFs.

The computational complexity of all the semantics considered in this paper is high and in many cases "beyond" NP. The complexity of semi-stable has been investigated in [20], eager in [16] and ideal in [15]. See Table 1 for details. We briefly recall the complexity classes here. The class Σ_2^P contains decision problems that can be decided in polynomial time using a nondeterministic Turing machine with access to an NP-oracle, i.e. it can solve a problem in NP in one step. The class Π_2^P is defined as the complementary class of Σ_2^P. The class Θ_2^P contains decision problems that can be solved by a deterministic polynomial time algorithm which is allowed to make $O(n)$ non-adaptive calls to the NP-oracle.

2.2   Boolean Satisfiability

This section provides an overview of the propositional SAT problem, satisfiability solvers, and extensions of the SAT problem – in particular *minimal correction sets* [28,31] and *backbones* [32] – and iterative SAT-based algorithms for these problems. For an introduction we refer the reader to the tutorial paper [29].

Algorithm 1. Iterative Probing (computes the backbone of ϕ)

Require: ϕ is satisfiable
Ensure: returns $\{\ell \mid \ell \in \{a, \neg a \mid a \in A\} \wedge \forall I . I \models \phi \wedge \ell \vee I \models \neg\phi\}$
1: $S = \emptyset$
2: **let** $I : A \to \mathbb{B}$ be such that $I \models \phi$ $\triangleright$ I may be partial
3: **for all** $\ell \in \{a, \neg a \mid a \in A\}$ with $I \models \ell$ **do**
4:      **if** $\phi \wedge \neg\ell$ is unsatisfiable **then**
5:          $S = S \cup \{\ell\}$; $\phi = \phi \cup \{\ell\}$
6:      **else let** J be such that $J \models \phi \wedge \neg\ell$ **in**
7:          $I = \{a \mapsto v \mid a \in A, v \in \mathbb{B}, I(a) = v \wedge J(a) = v\}$
8:      **end if**
9: **end for**
10: *return* S

Propositional Logic. We work in the standard setting of propositional logic over a set $A \overset{\text{def}}{=} \{a, b, c, \ldots\}$ of propositional atoms, and the standard logical connectives $\wedge$, $\vee$, and $\neg$ (denoting conjunction, disjunction, and negation, respectively). A literal ℓ is an atom $a \in A$ or its negation $\neg a$. A clause C is a set of literals representing the disjunction $\bigvee_{\ell \in C} \ell$. A propositional formula in Conjunctive Normal Form (CNF) is a conjunction of clauses, also represented as a set of clauses. An interpretation $I : A \to \mathbb{B}$ maps atoms to boolean values $\mathsf{T}, \mathsf{F} \in \mathbb{B}$. An interpretation I satisfies a formula ϕ (denoted by $I \models \phi$) if ϕ evaluates to T under the (potentially partial) assignment determined by I. A formula ϕ is satisfiable if there exists an interpretation I such that $I \models \phi$, and unsatisfiable otherwise.

SAT Solvers. A satisfiability solver is a decision procedure which determines whether a given formula ϕ (in CNF) is satisfiable or not. Contemporary SAT solvers are capable of solving instances with hundreds of thousands of literals and clauses. SAT solvers largely owe their success to efficient search heuristics (e.g., [30]) and conflict-driven back-tracking [33]. The latter technique avoids the repeated exploration of similar portions of the search space by augmenting the original instance ϕ with conflict clauses C derived from ϕ (i.e., $\models \neg\phi \vee C$).

Modern SAT solvers operate in an iterative manner: conflict clauses derived from a previous instance ϕ can be retained in a subsequent run of the solver on a formula ψ if $\phi \subseteq \psi$. In addition, the back-tracking capabilities of SAT solvers make it possible to fix a tentative assignment (or *assumption*, respectively) for a subset S of A in form of a conjunction of literals over S. Assumptions can be discarded in subsequent calls. This capability to perform iterative calls is crucial to the performance of the SAT-based algorithms presented below.

Backbones. The backbone of a satisfiable propositional formula ϕ comprises the literals over A that are true in every interpretation I satisfying ϕ. To compute the backbone of a formula ϕ (with $I \models \phi$), the currently most efficient algorithms (according to [37,32]) iteratively "probe" each atom $a \in A$ by subsequently checking the satisfiability of $\phi \wedge \ell$ (with $\ell \overset{\text{def}}{=} \neg a$ if $I(a) = \mathsf{T}$, and

---

Algorithm 2. Minimal Correction Sets

Require: $\phi \overset{\text{def}}{=} \bigcup_i \{C_i\}$ is unsatisfiable
Ensure: returns set $\mathcal{M}$ of all minimal correction sets for ϕ
1: $\psi = \bigcup_i \{(a_i \vee C_i)\}$, with $L \overset{\text{def}}{=} \bigcup_i \{a_i\}$ a set of fresh atoms
2: $k = 1$
3: $\mathcal{M} = \emptyset$
4: **while** ψ is satisfiable **do**
5:     $\psi_k = \psi \wedge AtMost(k, L)$
6:     **while** ψ_k is satisfiable **do**
7:         **let** I be such that $I \models \psi_k$
8:         $\mathcal{M} = \mathcal{M} \cup \{\{C_i \mid a_i \in L \wedge I(a_i) = \mathsf{T}\}\}$
9:         **let** D be $\{\neg a_i \mid a_i \in L \wedge I(a_i) = \mathsf{T}\}$
10:        $\psi_k = \psi_k \wedge D$
11:        $\psi = \psi \wedge D$
12:    **end while**
13:    $k = k + 1$
14: **end while**
15: *return* $\mathcal{M}$

$\ell \overset{\text{def}}{=} a$ otherwise). Algorithm 1 illustrates the basic structure of such an implementation. Practical implementations incorporate techniques such as excluding variables with opposing values in subsequent satisfying assignments (line 7 of Algorithm 1), clause reuse, and variable filtering [37,32].

Minimal Correction Sets. Given an unsatisfiable formula ϕ, a *minimal correction set* is a minimal subset $\psi \subseteq \phi$ such that $\phi \setminus \psi$ is satisfiable. The constraints $\chi \subseteq \phi$ are *hard* if we require that $\psi \cap \chi = \emptyset$ (conversely, the clauses $\phi \setminus \chi$ are *soft*).

Numerous techniques to compute MCSes exist (e.g., [28,36,24,35]), and the field is still advancing: the algorithm presented in the upcoming publication [31], for instance, partitions ϕ into one satisfied and r unsatisfied subsets ($\mathcal{S}$ and $\mathcal{U}_1, \ldots, \mathcal{U}_r$) and computes MCSes by heuristically moving clauses from $\mathcal{U}_i$ to $\mathcal{S}$.

Our implementation for semi-stable and eager semantics (see Sections 3 and 4) does not inherently depend on the implementation details of the MCS algorithm. Algorithm 2 shows a simplified version of the algorithm in [28] that underlies our implementation. Each (soft) clause C is augmented up front with *relaxation literal* a that does not occur anywhere else in ϕ (line 1). (A common optimization is to instrument only clauses contained in an unsatisfiable subset of ϕ.) The effect of dropping C can now be simulated by choosing an interpretation which maps a to T. Given a set $L \subset A$ of relaxation literals, a cardinality constraint $AtMost(k, L) \overset{\text{def}}{=} |\{a \in L \mid I(a) = \mathsf{T}\}| \leq k$ (encoded as a propositional formula [12,3]) limits the number of clauses that can be dropped. Algorithm 2 derives *all* MCSes by *systematically* enumerating assignments of relaxation literals for increasingly larger values of k (cf. the outer loop starting in line 4). The inner loop (line 6) enumerates all MCSes of size k by incrementally *blocking* MCSes represented by a conjunction of relaxation literals $\neg D$.

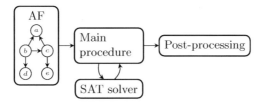

Fig. 2. Basic workflow for the algorithms based on iterative SAT procedures

3 Algorithms

In this section we will present algorithms to solve reasoning problems associated with three kinds of complex semantics on AFs, namely the semi-stable, eager and ideal semantics. The basic idea is to utilize state-of-the-art SAT solvers. Due to the high complexity it is unlikely that we can in general compactly answer the reasoning tasks within one propositional encoding and one invocation of a SAT solver. To tackle this problem we look at multiple calls to the SAT solver, in particular *iterative* calls.

The basic workflow of our algorithms is depicted in Fig. 2. We first translate the given AF to boolean constraints, i.e. into sets of boolean clauses. The main procedure now formulates queries to the SAT solver and iteratively adapts the calls depending on already computed calls. After the main procedure is finished we apply post-processing if needed.

On a more abstract level, we apply the MCS algorithm to solve reasoning tasks under the semi-stable semantics, in particular $\mathsf{AllSkept}_{sem}$, and the backbone algorithm to solve $\mathsf{AllCred}_{adm}$. Both approaches are based on iterative calls to a SAT solver.

The eager semantics is based on the semi-stable semantics and, given the skeptically accepted arguments under the semi-stable semantics from the MCS algorithm, one can compute the unique eager extension in polynomial time by means of a post-processing step. The algorithm behind the ideal semantics is more complicated and is taken from [16]. The difficult part of this algorithm from a computational point of view is to compute $\mathsf{AllCred}_{adm}$; the remainder can be done by a similar post-processing technique as for eager.

In the following we will show how this works in detail. In Section 3.1 we show how to use MCSes (Algorithm 2) to compute the semi-stable and eager extensions, and in Section 3.2 we show how to utilize backbones (Algorithm 1) to compute the ideal extensions of a given framework. In both cases we build on existing reductions to SAT [5] for the admissible and stable semantics.

We will first recall the propositional formula representing admissible sets of a given AF from [5], in form of sets of disjunctions of atoms, i.e. in CNF. The basic idea is that every atom represents an argument. By slightly abusing

our notation we use the set of arguments for a given AF and the set of propositional atoms of the constructed formula interchangeably.

$$adm_{A,R} \stackrel{\text{def}}{=} \bigcup_{(a,b)\in R} \{(\neg a \vee \neg b)\} \cup \bigcup_{(b,c)\in R} \{(\neg c \vee \bigvee_{(a,b)\in R} a)\} \qquad (1)$$

The first part of the formula (1) encodes the conflict-free property and the
second part the defense of arguments. Now using the result from [5] we have for
any AF $F = (A, R)$ that $adm(F) = \{S \mid I \models adm_{A,R}, S = \{a \mid I(a) = \mathsf{T}\}\}$, i.e.
the interpretations satisfying $adm_{A,R}$, projected to the atoms mapped to true,
directly correspond to the admissible sets of F.

3.1 MCS Algorithm for Semi-stable and Eager Semantics

Computing semi-stable extensions inherently requires to compute admissible
sets, which are subset-maximal w.r.t. the range. The MCS algorithm computes
subset-minimal sets of clauses of a formula in CNF, which if removed result in
a satisfiable formula. The idea to exploit the MCS algorithm for the semi-stable
semantics is to encode the range as satisfied clauses of a propositional formula
for a given interpretation and additionally requiring that the result is admissible.

For this to work we slightly adapt the formulas from [5] for the stable semantics. Given an AF $F = (A, R)$ we define the following formulas.

$$in\_range_{a,R} \stackrel{\text{def}}{=} (a \vee \bigvee_{(b,a)\in R} b) \qquad (2)$$

$$all\_in\_range_{A,R} \stackrel{\text{def}}{=} \bigcup_{a \in A} \{in\_range_{a,R}\} \qquad (3)$$

The formula $in\_range_{a,R}$ indicates whether the argument a is in the range
w.r.t. the atoms set to true in an interpretation. In other words, for an AF
$F = (A, R)$ and $a \in A$ we have, $I \models in\_range_{a,R}$ iff $a \in S_R^+$ for $S = \{b \mid$
$I(b) = \mathsf{T}\}$. The formula $all\_in\_range_{A,R}$ is satisfied if all arguments are in the
range. Taking the formulas $adm_{A,R}$ and $all\_in\_range_{A,R}$ together conjunctively,
denoted by $stb_{A,R}$, results in a formula equivalent to the stable formula in [5].

$$stb_{A,R} \stackrel{\text{def}}{=} adm_{A,R} \cup all\_in\_range_{A,R} \qquad (4)$$

An interpretation I which satisfies $adm_{A,R}$ for a given AF $F = (A, R)$ and
a *subset-maximal* set of clauses of $all\_in\_range_{A,R}$ corresponds to a semi-stable
extension of F. Consequently, we can derive semi-stable extensions from the
correction sets computed with the MCS algorithm, as long as no clause from
$adm_{A,R}$ is dropped. That is, we consider the clauses of the formula $adm_{A,R}$ as
hard constraints and the clauses in $all\_in\_range_{A,R}$ as *soft* constraints. Note also,
since any AF $F = (A, R)$ has at least one admissible set, we know that $adm_{A,R}$ is
always satisfiable. If $stb_{A,R}$ is satisfiable, meaning that F has stable extensions,
then immediately this computation yields the stable extensions, which are equal
to the semi-stable extensions.

The following proposition shows this result more formally. For a given propositional formula ϕ in CNF and an interpretation I, we define ϕ^I to be the set of clauses in ϕ, which are satisfied by I, i.e. $\phi^I \stackrel{\text{def}}{=} \{C \in \phi \mid I \models C\}$.

Proposition 1. *Let $F = (A, R)$ be an AF and $\mathcal{I}_{sem} = \{S \mid I \models adm_{A,R}, S = \{a \mid I(a) = \mathsf{T}\}, \nexists I' : I' \models adm_{A,R} \text{ s.t. } all\_in\_range^I_{A,R} \subset all\_in\_range^{I'}_{A,R}\}$. Then $sem(F) = \mathcal{I}_{sem}$.*

Proof. Let $F = (A, R)$ be an AF. Assume $E \in sem(F)$, then define the following interpretation I with $I(a) = \mathsf{T}$ iff $a \in E$. Then $I \models adm_{A,R}$, since E is admissible by definition and due to [5] we know that I satisfies $adm_{A,R}$. Suppose now there exists an interpretation I' such that $I' \models adm_{A,R}$ and $all\_in\_range^I_{A,R} \subset all\_in\_range^{I'}_{A,R}$. But then E would not be maximal w.r.t. the range and hence no semi-stable extension of F.

Assume $E \in \mathcal{I}_{sem}$, which implies $E \in adm(F)$ and as above let I be an interpretation with $I(a) = \mathsf{T}$ iff $a \in E$. Suppose there exists a set $S \in adm(F)$ with $E^+_R \subset S^+_R$. Then $all\_in\_range^I_{A,R} \subset all\_in\_range^{I'}_{A,R}$ for an interpretation I' defined as $I'(a) = \mathsf{T}$ iff $a \in S$, which is a contradiction. $\qquad\square$

The MCS algorithm can now be straightforwardly applied for the reasoning tasks for the semi-stable semantics we study in this paper, that is the algorithm can be easily adapted to yield an enumeration of all semi-stable extensions, answer credulous or skeptical queries or enumerate all arguments skeptically accepted. Since we need the set of skeptically accepted arguments for computation of the eager extension, we will present this variant in Algorithm 3.

Algorithm 3. MCS-AllSkept$_{sem}$

Require: AF $F \stackrel{\text{def}}{=} (A, R)$
Ensure: returns AllSkept$_{sem}(F)$

1: $\phi = \{a_i \vee C_i \mid C_i \in all\_in\_range_{A,R}\}$ with $L \stackrel{\text{def}}{=} \bigcup_i \{a_i\}$ a set of fresh atoms
2: $\psi = adm_{A,R} \cup \phi$
3: $k = 0$
4: $X = A$
5: **while** ψ is satisfiable and $k \leq |A|$ **do**
6:     $\psi_k = \psi \cup AtMost(k, L)$
7:     $X = X \cap Probing(\psi_k)$
8:     **while** ψ_k is satisfiable **do**
9:         **let** I be such that $I \models \psi_k$
10:        **let** D be $\{\neg a_i \mid a_i \in L \wedge I(a_i) = \mathsf{T}\}$
11:        $\psi_k = \psi_k \wedge D$
12:        $\psi = \psi \wedge D$
13:    **end while**
14:    $k = k + 1$
15: **end while**
16: *return* X

Algorithm 3 computes the set $\mathsf{AllSkept}_{sem}(F)$ for a given AF $F = (A, R)$. The formula ψ consists of the clauses for admissibility and the instrumented clauses of $all\_in\_range_{A,R}$, i.e. these clauses may be dropped during the running time. The idea is that if $I \models \psi_k$, then $E = \{a \mid I(a) = \mathsf{T}\}$ is an admissible set in F and $|E_R^+| = |A| - k$, since we allow to drop k clauses of $all\_in\_range_{A,R}$ and block previously computed MCSes. This means that E is a semi-stable extension of F, since there is no assignment I' which satisfies $adm_{A,R}$ and a superset of $all\_in\_range_{A,R}^I$. We need to slightly modify Algorithm 2 to incorporate our reasoning task. We utilize the backbone algorithm in line 7 to compute in X the set of skeptically accepted arguments. Since all satisfying interpretations of ψ_k are semi-stable extensions we compute the set of atoms set to true in all such interpretations by applying Algorithm 1. There exists alternatives and optimizations to compute MCSes and Algorithm 3 can be adapted to work with these as long as all satisfying assignments can be computed w.r.t. the formula reduced by each of its MCSes separately.

Using the Algorithm 3 for solving the $\mathsf{AllSkept}_{sem}$ problem, we can use its output to calculate the unique eager extension, since we just have to compute the subset-maximal admissible set within $\mathsf{AllSkept}_{sem}(F)$ for an AF F. For this we apply the restricted characteristic function a number of times bounded by the number of arguments in the framework, i.e. $\hat{\mathcal{F}}_F^{|A|}(\mathsf{AllSkept}_{sem}(F))$ results in the eager extension of F.

3.2   Backbone Algorithm for Ideal Semantics

For the ideal semantics we make use of a method proposed in [16], which we recall in Algorithm 4. The important point for our instantiation of this algorithm is that we essentially need to compute $\mathsf{AllCred}_{adm}$ and afterwards again, as before for the eager semantics, a post-processing with the function $\hat{\mathcal{F}}_F$. We define for an AF $F = (A, R)$ the auxiliary notion of adjacent arguments of an argument: $adj(a) \stackrel{\text{def}}{=} \{x \mid (x, a) \in R \text{ or } (a, x) \in R\}$. Additionally we define the restriction of an attack relation for a set S by $R_{|S} \stackrel{\text{def}}{=} \{(a, b) \in R \mid a \in S \text{ and } b \in S\}$.

Briefly put, Algorithm 4 computes first the credulously accepted arguments w.r.t. admissible sets and then a set X, which consists of all of the credulously accepted arguments, except those, which have an adjacent argument also credulously accepted. This set acts as a kind of approximation of the skeptically

---

Algorithm 4. Ideal-Extension [16]

Require: AF $F \stackrel{\text{def}}{=} (A, R)$
Ensure: returns $ideal(F)$
  1: $Cred = \mathsf{AllCred}_{adm}(F)$
  2: $Out = A \setminus Cred$
  3: $X = \{x \in Cred \mid adj(x) \subseteq Out\}$
  4: $F' = (X \cup Out, R_{|(X \cup Out)})$
  5: *return* $\hat{\mathcal{F}}_{F'}^{|A|}(X)$

---

accepted arguments w.r.t. the preferred semantics. Constructing then the new framework F' and computing the restricted characteristic function at most $|A|$ times in this new framework for X, suffices for computing the ideal extension.

Now it is straightforward to instantiate this with the help of a backbone algorithm. Given an AF $F = (A, R)$, we first simply compute the backbone of $adm_{A,R}$. Let S be the output of Algorithm 1 on this formula, then $O = \{a \mid \neg a \in S\}$ be the set of variables set to false in every satisfying interpretation of $adm_{A,R}$. Since we know that this formula is satisfiable, this means that $(A \setminus O) = \mathsf{AllCred}_{adm}(F)$. The rest of Algorithm 4 can be achieved with post-processing.

4   Experimental Evaluation

In this section we will present our concrete implementation of the presented algorithms and an experimental evaluation.

In our implementations the overall workflow from Fig. 2 is handled by Unix shell scripts and for the main procedures we utilize already implemented MCS and backbone solvers. For all our implementations we adopt the input language from the ASPARTIX system [21], a system capable of solving many problems on AFs, based on the answer-set programming (ASP) paradigm. The first step of the workflow, the translation of this language to a boolean formula, is handled by a parser implemented in C++.

Our instantiation of the presented algorithm for semi-stable semantics covers the reasoning tasks of enumerating all extensions, credulous and skeptical reasoning, as well as computing the set of all skeptically accepted arguments for a given AF. For the main procedure we utilize the CAMUS solver [28] in version 1.0.5, which we slightly modified to handle our reasoning tasks. The distinction between hard and soft constraints is implemented in CAMUS by the possibility to supply additional clauses for the relaxation literals. Based on this we implemented the necessary post-processing for computing the eager extension with an ASP call using the clingo ASP solver [26], version 3.0.4. Note that the post-processing step is inherently computable in polynomial time, the ASP solver for this step was used for its declarative and easy-to-use nature. The implementation for the ideal semantics to compute its unique extensions is based on the backbone solver JediSAT [37], version 0.2 beta. The post-processing step is again handled by an ASP call.

To show the feasibility of our approach, we conducted preliminary experiments for checking the performance of the presented algorithms. All tests were executed under OpenSUSE with Intel Xeon processors (2.33 GHz) and 49 GB memory. We note that this high amount of memory is not actually used by our algorithms, we set a hard limit of 4 GB memory usage on all runs, which was never reached.

Regarding test instances for our experiments, we note that, as identified in [17], there is still need for benchmark libraries for AFs. Without such standard libraries artificially generated AFs are the main source of test instances. Therefore, we follow the line of [19] for benchmarking and used randomly generated AFs for testing. For our random creation of AFs we fix a number of arguments

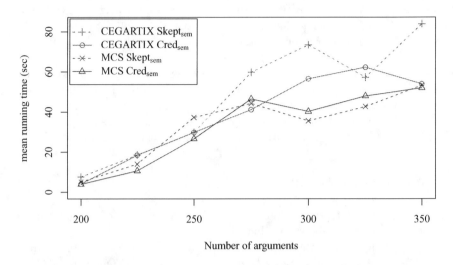

Fig. 3. Mean running time for CEGARTIX and the MCS-based algorithm

and insert for any pair of arguments (a, b) with $a \neq b$ the attack from a to b with a given probability $p \in \{0.1, 0.2, 0.3, 0.4\}$. For each parameter we created ten random AFs. We considered AFs (A, R) of size $|A| \in \{100, 150, 200, 225, 250, 275, 300, 325, 350\}$, which totaled in 360 AFs. We have chosen to use larger random AFs than in [19], since the SAT-based procedures appear to be able to handle small-sized AFs very well.

For all runs we enforced a timeout of five minutes and measure the whole time for the workflow from Fig. 2, i.e. combining parsing, solving and post-processing time. We tested the following reasoning tasks.

- Credulous and skeptical reasoning for semi-stable semantics
- Enumeration of all semi-stable extensions
- Computing the ideal extension
- Computing the eager extension

We compare credulous and skeptical reasoning for semi-stable semantics with CEGARTIX [19], a SAT-based system for reasoning tasks in abstract argumentation, which was shown to be a competitive solver. We chose version 0.1a of

Table 2. Number of solved instances for CEGARTIX and the MCS-based algorithm

reasoning task \ $|A|$	200	225	250	275	300	325	350	% solved overall
CEGARTIX Cred$_{sem}$	120	120	112	91	71	64	50	74.8%
CEGARTIX Skept$_{sem}$	120	120	104	84	69	60	48	72%
MCS Cred$_{sem}$	117	120	117	111	85	77	76	83.7%
MCS Skept$_{sem}$	117	120	116	102	79	73	73	81%

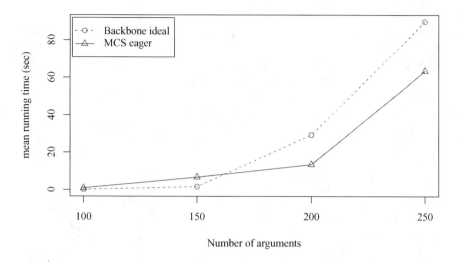

Fig. 4. Mean running time for computing the ideal respectively eager extension

CEGARTIX for our tests, since in this version CEGARTIX is able to utilize
incremental SAT-solving techniques and further versions of CEGARTIX mainly
feature capabilities to use different SAT solvers. We let both CEGARTIX and
the MCS-based approach compute the queries for three pre-specified arguments
for AFs with at least 200 arguments, i.e. credulous and skeptical acceptance with
three different arguments. This gives us 120 queries per AF size and in total 840
queries. The results are summarized in Fig. 3, where we show the mean running
time in seconds for both approaches, *excluding* timed out runs. We grouped together queries on AFs with the same number of arguments. We see that the
MCS-based approach is competitive and in cases even somewhat outperforming
CEGARTIX. Note that by excluding the timeouts, which are shown in Table 2,
the figures slightly favor CEGARTIX for large AFs.

It is interesting to note that the expected edge density, which we set between 0.1 and 0.4 appears to play an important role for the performance of the
SAT-based approaches. Out of the total 212 timeouts encountered for credulous
reasoning under semi-stable semantics for the solver CEGARTIX for all considered queries, 113 were on AFs with 0.1, 75 on AFs with 0.2 and 24 on AFs with
0.3 expected edge density. Showing a similar picture, the MCS-approach had 137
total timeouts and 105 of them with 0.1 and 32 with 0.2 expected edge density.
For skeptical reasoning the results are similar.

For comparing our MCS-approach w.r.t. the enumeration of all semi-stable
extensions we use an ASP approach [18] utilizing metasp for our performance
test. For this ASP approach we used gringo 3.0.5 and claspD 1.1.4 [26]. We
tested both approaches on the same AFs as for the credulous and skeptical
reasoning under semi-stable semantics and out of the 280 AFs we tested, the

MCS-approach solved (i.e. enumerated all semi-stable extensions) 172 instances while ASP with metasp solved only seven instances within the time limit of five minutes.

For ideal and eager semantics, we report the mean computation time for AFs of size $|A| \in \{100, 150, 200, 250\}$ in Fig. 4 to compute the unique extension. Hence we compute the ideal respectively eager extension for each AF separately, which gives us 40 computations per number of arguments and 160 such calls in total per semantics. We encountered one timeout for eager reasoning on AFs with size 200 and ten with AFs of size 250. For ideal reasoning we encountered 17 timeouts with AFs of size 250. Other systems capable of solving these tasks are e.g. ASPARTIX, but which could only solve instances with a low number of arguments, i.e. AFs with less than 30 arguments, which is the reason we excluded this system in a comparison with our implementations. For ideal reasoning AS-PARTIX uses a complex ASP encoding technique [23] for the DLV solver [27] (we used build BEN/Dec 16 2012 of DLV). The system ConArg [6], which is based on constraint satisfaction solvers, appears to be more competitive. ConArg is a visual tool, so more detailed performance comparisons are subject of future work. We tested some randomly generated AFs with 100 and 150 arguments and let ConArg compute the ideal extension, which it solved within ten seconds for the AFs with 100 arguments and took more than a minute for AFs with 150 arguments, but one has to factor in that a graphical representation of large graphs may consume a part of the resources needed for solving the problem.

5   Conclusion

In this paper, we presented new algorithms utilizing extensions of the SAT problem for hard tasks in abstract argumentation. In particular we showed how to solve reasoning tasks under the semi-stable and eager semantics using an MCS solver and based an algorithm for the ideal semantics on the computation of a backbone of a boolean formula. Reduction-based approaches for semantics in abstract argumentation include transformations to equational systems [25], propositional logic [5] and quantified boolean formulas [2,22]. Our approach differs from these in that we do not use a single encoding for the whole problem, but rather solving partial problems iteratively using solvers for extensions to the SAT problem. Preliminary experiments using our approaches are very promising, showing a good performance without much engineering effort. The benefit of applying SAT-solvers for abstract argumentation is also witnessed by a very recent related approach [10] for enumeration of preferred extensions. Our approach for semi-stable semantics can be adapted for preferred semantics and a performance comparison with the systems [10,19] is an interesting subject for future work. Further interesting directions are on one side incorporating optimizations developed in the SAT community for our approaches and on the other side applying the proposed methods to further hard problems in abstract argumentation and extensions thereof. Not in the least, this indicates that modern SAT technology might be well applicable to other hard problems in the areas of knowledge representation and AI.

Acknowledgements. This research has been supported by the Austrian Science Fund (FWF) through projects I1102 and P25518-N23, and the Austrian National Research Network S11403-N23 (RiSE), as well as the Vienna Science and Technology Fund (WWTF) through project VRG11-005.

References

1. Amgoud, L., Prade, H.: Using arguments for making and explaining decisions. Artif. Intell. 173(3-4), 413–436 (2009)
2. Arieli, O., Caminada, M.W.A.: A QBF-based formalization of abstract argumentation semantics. J. Applied Logic 11(2), 229–252 (2013)
3. Asín, R., Nieuwenhuis, R., Oliveras, A., Rodríguez-Carbonell, E.: Cardinality networks: a theoretical and empirical study. Constraints 16(2), 195–221 (2011)
4. Bench-Capon, T.J.M., Dunne, P.E.: Argumentation in Artificial Intelligence. Artif. Intell. 171(10-15), 619–641 (2007)
5. Besnard, P., Doutre, S.: Checking the acceptability of a set of arguments. In: NMR 2004, pp. 59–64 (2004)
6. Bistarelli, S., Santini, F.: Conarg: A constraint-based computational framework for argumentation systems. In: ICTAI 2011, pp. 605–612 (2011)
7. Caminada, M.W.A.: Comparing two unique extension semantics for formal argumentation: Ideal and eager. In: BNAIC 2007, pp. 81–87 (2007)
8. Caminada, M.W.A., Carnielli, W.A., Dunne, P.E.: Semi-stable Semantics. J. Log. Comput. 22(5), 1207–1254 (2012)
9. Cartwright, D., Atkinson, K.: Using computational argumentation to support e-participation. IEEE Intelligent Systems 24(5), 42–52 (2009)
10. Cerutti, F., Dunne, P.E., Giacomin, M., Vallati, M.: A SAT-based Approach for Computing Extensions on Abstract Argumentation. In: TAFA 2013 (2013)
11. Charwat, G., Dvořák, W., Gaggl, S.A., Wallner, J.P., Woltran, S.: Implementing Abstract Argumentation – A Survey. Technical Report DBAI-TR-2013-82, Vienna University of Technology (2013)
12. Codish, M., Zazon-Ivry, M.: Pairwise cardinality networks. In: Clarke, E.M., Voronkov, A. (eds.) LPAR-16 2010. LNCS, vol. 6355, pp. 154–172. Springer, Heidelberg (2010)
13. Dung, P.M.: On the acceptability of arguments and its fundamental role in non-monotonic reasoning, logic programming and n-person games. Artif. Intell. 77(2), 321–358 (1995)
14. Dung, P.M., Mancarella, P., Toni, F.: Computing ideal sceptical argumentation. Artif. Intell. 171(10-15), 642–674 (2007)
15. Dunne, P.E.: The computational complexity of ideal semantics. Artif. Intell. 173(18), 1559–1591 (2009)
16. Dvořák, W., Dunne, P.E., Woltran, S.: Parametric properties of ideal semantics. In: IJCAI 2011, pp. 851–856 (2011)
17. Dvořák, W., Gaggl, S.A., Szeider, S., Woltran, S.: Benchmark libraries for argumentation. In: Agreement Technologies, LGTS The Added Value of Argumentation, vol. 8, pp. 389–393. Springer (2013)
18. Dvořák, W., Gaggl, S.A., Wallner, J.P., Woltran, S.: Making use of advances in answer-set programming for abstract argumentation systems. In: INAP 2011, pp. 117–130 (2011)

19. Dvořák, W., Järvisalo, M., Wallner, J.P., Woltran, S.: Complexity-sensitive decision procedures for abstract argumentation. In: KR 2012, pp. 54–64 (2012)
20. Dvořák, W., Woltran, S.: Complexity of semi-stable and stage semantics in argumentation frameworks. Inf. Process. Lett. 110(11), 425–430 (2010)
21. Egly, U., Gaggl, S.A., Woltran, S.: Answer-set programming encodings for argumentation frameworks. Argument and Computation 1(2), 147–177 (2010)
22. Egly, U., Woltran, S.: Reasoning in argumentation frameworks using quantified boolean formulas. In: COMMA 2006. FAIA, vol. 144, pp. 133–144 (2006)
23. Faber, W., Woltran, S.: Manifold answer-set programs and their applications. In: Balduccini, M., Son, T.C. (eds.) LPNMR 2011. LNCS, vol. 6565, pp. 44–63. Springer, Heidelberg (2011)
24. Felfernig, A., Schubert, M., Zehentner, C.: An efficient diagnosis algorithm for inconsistent constraint sets. Artificial Intelligence for Engineering Design, Analysis and Manufacturing 26(1), 53–62 (2012)
25. Gabbay, D.M.: An equational approach to argumentation networks. Argument & Computation 3(2-3), 87–142 (2012)
26. Gebser, M., Kaminski, R., Kaufmann, B., Ostrowski, M., Schaub, T., Schneider, M.: Potassco: The Potsdam Answer Set Solving Collection. AI Communications 24(2), 105–124 (2011)
27. Leone, N., Pfeifer, G., Faber, W., Eiter, T., Gottlob, G., Perri, S., Scarcello, F.: The DLV system for knowledge representation and reasoning. ACM Trans. Comput. Log. 7(3), 499–562 (2006)
28. Liffiton, M.H., Sakallah, K.A.: Algorithms for computing minimal unsatisfiable subsets of constraints. J. Autom. Reasoning 40(1), 1–33 (2008)
29. Malik, S., Weissenbacher, G.: Boolean satisfiability solvers: techniques and extensions. In: Software Safety and Security - Tools for Analysis and Verification. NATO Science for Peace and Security Series. IOS Press (2012)
30. Malik, S., Zhao, Y., Madigan, C.F., Zhang, L., Moskewicz, M.W.: Chaff: Engineering an efficient SAT solver. In: DAC 2001, pp. 530–535 (2001)
31. Marques-Silva, J., Heras, F., Janota, M., Previti, A., Belov, A.: On computing minimal correction subsets. In: IJCAI 2013 (2013)
32. Marques-Silva, J., Janota, M., Lynce, I.: On computing backbones of propositional theories. In: ECAI 2010. FAIA, vol. 215, pp. 15–20. IOS Press (2010)
33. Marques-Silva, J., Sakallah, K.A.: GRASP – a new search algorithm for satisfiability. In: ICCAD 1996, pp. 220–227 (1996)
34. McBurney, P., Parsons, S., Rahwan, I. (eds.): ArgMAS 2011. LNCS, vol. 7543. Springer, Heidelberg (2012)
35. Nöhrer, A., Biere, A., Egyed, A.: Managing SAT inconsistencies with HUMUS. In: Workshop on Variability Modelling of Software-Intensive Systems, pp. 83–91. ACM (2012)
36. Rosa, E.D., Giunchiglia, E., Maratea, M.: Solving satisfiability problems with preferences. Constraints 15(4), 485–515 (2010)
37. Zhu, C.S., Weissenbacher, G., Sethi, D., Malik, S.: SAT-based techniques for determining backbones for post-silicon fault localisation. In: HLDVT, pp. 84–91 (2011)

Web Based System for Weighted Defeasible Argumentation

Alsinet Teresa[1], Béjar Ramón[1], Francesc Guitart[1], and Lluís Godo[2]

[1] Department of Computer Science – University of Lleida
Jaume II, 69 – 25001 Lleida, Spain
{tracy,ramon,fguitart}@diei.udl.cat
[2] Artificial Intelligence Research Institute (IIIA-CSIC)
Campus UAB - 08193 Bellaterra, Barcelona, Spain
godo@iiia.csic.es

Abstract. In a previous work we defined a recursive semantics for reasoning about which arguments should be warranted when extending Defeasible Argumentation with defeasibility levels for arguments. Our approach is based on a general notion of collective conflict among arguments and on the fact that if an argument is warranted it must be that all its sub-arguments also are warranted. An output of a program is a pair consisting of a set of warranted and a set of blocked arguments with maximum strength. Arguments that are neither warranted nor blocked correspond to rejected arguments. On this recursive semantics a program may have multiple outputs in case of circular definitions of conflicts among arguments and for these circular definitions of conflicts we define what output, called maximal ideal output, should be considered based on the claim that if an argument is excluded from an output, then all the arguments built on top of it should also be excluded from that output. In this paper we show a web based system we have designed and implemented to compute the output for programs with single and multiple outputs. For programs with multiple outputs the system also computes the maximal ideal output. An interesting feature of the system is that it provides not only both sets of warranted an blocked arguments with maximum strength but also useful information that allows to better understand why an argument is either warranted, blocked or rejected.

Keywords: weighted defeasible argumentation, recursive semantics, web based technologies.

1 Introduction and Motivation

The study of argumentation may, informally, be considered as concerned with how assertions are proposed, discussed, and resolved in the context of issues upon which several diverging opinions may be held [7].

Defeasible argumentation is a natural way of identifying relevant assumptions and conclusions for a given problem which often involves identifying conflicting information, resulting in the need to look for pros and cons for a particular conclusion [19]. This process may involve chains of reasoning, where conclusions are used in the assumptions for deriving further conclusions and the task of finding pros and cons may be decomposed recursively [8,20].

J. Leite et al. (Eds.): CLIMA XIV, LNAI 8143, pp. 155–171, 2013.

Defeasible Logic Programming (DeLP) [14] is a formalism that combines techniques of both logic programming and defeasible argumentation. As in logic programming, knowledge is represented in DeLP using facts and rules; however, DeLP also provides the possibility of representing defeasible knowledge under the form of weak (defeasible) rules, expressing reasons to believe in a given conclusion. In DeLP, a conclusion succeeds in a program if it is warranted, i.e., if there exists an argument (a consistent set of defeasible rules) that, together with non-defeasible rules and facts, entails the conclusion, and moreover, this argument is found to be undefeated by a warrant procedure. This builds a dialectical tree containing all arguments that challenge this argument, and all counterarguments that challenge those arguments, and so on, recursively. Actually, dialectical trees systematically explore the universe of arguments in order to present an exhaustive synthesis of the relevant chains of pros and cons for a given conclusion.

In [1] we defined a new recursive semantics for DeLP extended with weights for arguments and based on a general notion of collective (non-binary) conflict among arguments. In this framework, called *Recursive Possibilistic* DeLP (RP-DeLP for short), an output (or extension) of a program is a pair consisting of a set of warranted and a set of blocked formulas with maximum strength. Arguments for both warranted and blocked formulas are recursively based on warranted formulas but, while warranted formulas do not generate any collective conflict, blocked conclusions do. Formulas that are neither warranted nor blocked correspond to rejected formulas. The key feature that our warrant recursive semantics addresses is the *closure under subarguments postulate* recently proposed by Amgoud [6], claiming that if an argument is excluded from an output, then all the arguments built on top of it should also be excluded from that output. Then, in case of circular definitions of conflict among arguments, the recursive semantics for warranted conclusions may result in multiple outputs for RP-DeLP programs. Following the approach of Pollock [18], in [1] we characterized circular definitions of conflict among arguments by means of what we called *Warrant Dependency Graphs*, representing support and conflict relations between argument conclusions.

In [2] we considered the problem of deciding the set of conclusions that can be ultimately warranted in RP-DeLP programs with multiple outputs. The usual skeptical approach would be to adopt the intersection of all possible outputs. However, in addition to the computational limitation, as stated in [18], adopting the intersection of all outputs may lead to an inconsistent output. Intuitively, for a conclusion, to be in the intersection does not guarantee the existence of an argument for it, that is recursively based on ultimately warranted conclusions. With the aim of computing single outputs and based on the idea defined by Dung, Mancarella and Toni [11,12] as an alternative skeptical basis for defining collections of justified arguments in abstract argumentation frameworks, we characterized what we called *Maximal Ideal Output* for an RP-DeLP program based on a recursive definition considering the maximum set of conclusions based on warranted information and not involved in neither a conflict nor a circular definition of conflict.

In this paper we present a web based system we have designed and implemented to compute the set of conclusions that can be ultimately warranted in RP-DeLP programs. The system considers both types of programs: programs with single output and programs with multiple outputs. For programs with multiple outputs the system also computes the maximal ideal output. The reasoning algorithm of the system has been implemented based on two different formalisms: SAT based encodings and ASP based encodings. The web based system allows the user to select the implementation of the reasoning algorithm and allowing to compare the efficiency in terms of execution time.

An interesting feature of the system is that it provides not only both sets of warranted an blocked conclusions with maximum strength but also useful information that allows to better understand why a conclusion is either warranted, blocked or rejected. In particular the system shows the consistent part of the program that supports the set of warranted conclusions. This sub-program is an explanation of the reason why conclusions are warranted. For the set of blocked conclusions, the system also shows the part of the program that supports them. However, in this case the sub-program is inconsistent, this being the reason why conclusions are not warranted. Regarding the latter, the system provides the user with information on which parts of the program should be refined to reduce the set of blocked conclusions, which might imply either refining it with new information or assigning new defeasibility levels.

After this introduction, the rest of the paper is structured as follows. In Section 2 we recall the main definitions from RP-DeLP, we summarize the semantic differences between the set of multiple outputs for a program and its maximal ideal output, and we show how the strength of warranted and blocked conclusions spreads between defeasibility levels. In Section 3 we design an algorithm for computing the set of outputs for programs with multiple outputs when considering weights for defeasible facts and rules. The algorithm we present here is an extension of the one recently presented in [4], that worked only with programs with one defeasible level. In Section 4 we present the web based system architecture, and in Section 5 we explore its application to decision support environments. We end up with some concluding remarks.

2   Weighted Recursive Semantics of RP-DeLP

The *language* of RP-DeLP, denoted $\mathcal{L}$, is inherited from the language of logic programming, including the notions of atom, literal, rule and fact. Formulas are built over a finite set of propositional variables $\{p, q, \ldots\}$ which is extended with a new (negated) atom "$\sim p$" for each original atom p. Atoms of the form p or $\sim p$ will be referred as literals.[1] *Formulas* of $\mathcal{L}$ consist of rules of the form $Q \leftarrow P_1 \wedge \ldots \wedge P_k$, where $Q, P_1, \ldots, P_k$ are literals. A fact will be a rule with no premises. We will also use the name *clause* to denote a rule or a fact. The R-DeLP framework is based on the propositional logic $(\mathcal{L}, \vdash)$ where the inference operator $\vdash$ is defined by instances of the modus ponens rule of the form: $\{Q \leftarrow P_1 \wedge \ldots \wedge P_k, P_1, \ldots, P_k\} \vdash Q$. A set of clauses Γ will be deemed as *contradictory*, denoted $\Gamma \vdash \bot$, if , for some atom q, $\Gamma \vdash q$ and $\Gamma \vdash \sim q$.

An RP-DeLP *program* $\mathcal{P}$ is a tuple $\mathcal{P} = (\Pi, \Delta, \preceq)$ over the logic $(\mathcal{L}, \vdash)$, where $\Pi, \Delta \subseteq \mathcal{L}$, and $\Pi \nvdash \bot$. Π is a finite set of clauses representing strict knowledge (information we take for granted they hold true), Δ is another finite set of clauses representing the defeasible knowledge (formulas for which we have reasons to believe they

---

[1] For a given literal Q, we write $\sim Q$ as an abbreviation to denote "$\sim q$" if $Q = q$ and "q" if $Q = \sim q$.

are true). Finally, $\preceq$ is a total pre-order on $\Pi \cup \Delta$ representing levels of defeasibility: $\varphi \prec \psi$ means that φ is more defeasible than ψ. Actually, since formulas in Π are not defeasible, $\preceq$ is such that all formulas in Π are at the top of the ordering. For the sake of a simpler notation we will often refer in the paper to numerical levels for defeasible clauses and arguments rather than to the pre-ordering $\preceq$, so we will assume a mapping $N : \Pi \cup \Delta \to [0, 1]$ such that $N(\varphi) = 1$ for all $\varphi \in \Pi$ and $N(\varphi) < N(\psi)$ iff $\varphi \prec \psi$.[2] The notion of *argument* is the usual one. Given an RP-DeLP program $\mathcal{P} = (\Pi, \Delta, \preceq)$, an argument for a literal (conclusion) Q of $\mathcal{L}$ is a pair $\mathcal{A} = \langle A, Q \rangle$, with $A \subseteq \Delta$ such that $\Pi \cup A \not\vdash \bot$, and A is minimal (w.r.t. set inclusion) such that $\Pi \cup A \vdash Q$. If $A = \emptyset$, then we will call $\mathcal{A}$ a s-argument (s for strict), otherwise it will be a d-argument (d for defeasible). We define the *strength of an argument* $\langle A, Q \rangle$, written $s(\langle A, Q \rangle)$, as follows: (i) $s(\langle A, Q \rangle) = 1$ if $A = \emptyset$; and (ii) $s(\langle A, Q \rangle) = \min\{N(\psi) \mid \psi \in A\}$, otherwise.

The notion of *subargument* is referred to d-arguments and expresses an incremental proof relationship between arguments which is defined as follows. Let $\langle B, Q \rangle$ and $\langle A, P \rangle$ be two d-arguments such that the minimal sets (w.r.t. set inclusion) $\Pi_Q \subseteq \Pi$ and $\Pi_P \subseteq \Pi$ such that $\Pi_Q \cup B \vdash Q$ and $\Pi_P \cup A \vdash P$ verify that $\Pi_Q \subseteq \Pi_P$. Then, $\langle B, Q \rangle$ is a *subargument* of $\langle A, P \rangle$, written $\langle B, Q \rangle \sqsubset \langle A, P \rangle$, when either $B \subset A$ (strict inclusion for defeasible knowledge), or $B = A$ and $\Pi_Q \subset \Pi_P$ (strict inclusion for strict knowledge). A literal Q of $\mathcal{L}$ is called *justifiable conclusion* w.r.t. $\mathcal{P}$ if there exists an argument for Q, i.e., there exists $A \subseteq \Delta$ such that $\langle A, Q \rangle$ is an argument.

The warrant recursive semantics for RP-DeLP is based on the following notion of collective conflict in a set of arguments which captures the idea of an inconsistency arising from a consistent set of justifiable conclusions W together with the strict part of a program and the set of conclusions of those arguments. Let $\mathcal{P} = (\Pi, \Delta, \preceq)$ be an RP-DeLP program and let $W \subseteq \mathcal{L}$ be a set of conclusions. We say that a set of arguments $\{\langle A_1, Q_1 \rangle, \ldots, \langle A_k, Q_k \rangle\}$ *minimally conflicts* with respect to W iff the two following conditions hold: (i) the set of argument conclusions $\{Q_1, \ldots, Q_k\}$ is contradictory with respect to W, i.e. it holds that $\Pi \cup W \cup \{Q_1, \ldots, Q_k\} \vdash \bot$; and (ii) the set $\{\langle A_1, Q_1 \rangle, \ldots, \langle A_k, Q_k \rangle\}$ is minimal with respect to set inclusion satisfying (i), i.e. if $S \subsetneq \{Q_1, \ldots, Q_k\}$, then $\Pi \cup W \cup S \not\vdash \bot$.

This general notion of conflict is used to define an output for an RP-DeLP program $\mathcal{P} = (\Pi, \Delta, \preceq)$ as a pair (*Warr*, *Block*) of subsets of $\mathcal{L}$ of warranted and blocked conclusions respectively all of them based on warranted information but while warranted conclusions do not generate any conflict, blocked conclusions do. Since we are considering several levels of strength among arguments, the intended construction of the sets of conclusions *Warr* and *Block* is done level-wise, starting from the highest level and iteratively going down from one level to next level below. If $1 > \alpha_1 > \ldots > \alpha_p \geq 0$ are the strengths of d-arguments that can be built within $\mathcal{P}$, we define: *Warr* = *Warr*(1) $\cup \{\cup_{i=1,p} Warr(\alpha_i)\}$ and *Block* = $\cup_{i=1,p} Block(\alpha_i)$, where *Warr*(1) = $\{Q \mid \Pi \vdash Q\}$, and *Warr*(α_i) and *Block*(α_i) are respectively the sets of

---

[2] Actually, a same pre-order $\preceq$ can be represented by many mappings, but we can take any of them to since only the relative ordering is what actually matters.

the warranted and blocked justifiable conclusions of strength α_i and are required to satisfy the following recursive constraints:[3]

1. $Q \in Warr(\alpha_i) \cup Block(\alpha_i)$ iff there exists an argument $\langle A, Q \rangle$ of strength α_i satisfying the following three conditions:
   (V1) for each subargument $\langle E, P \rangle \sqsubset \langle A, Q \rangle$ of strength β, $P \in Warr(\beta)$;
   (V2) $Q \notin Warr(> \alpha_i) \cup Block(> \alpha_i)$;
   (V3) $\sim Q \notin Block(> \alpha_i)$ and $\Pi \cup Warr(> \alpha_i) \cup \{P \mid \langle E, P \rangle \sqsubset \langle A, Q \rangle\} \cup \{Q\} \nvdash \bot$.
   In this case we say that $\langle A, Q \rangle$ is *valid* with respect to the sets $Warr(\geq \alpha_i)$ and $Block(> \alpha_i)$.
2. For every valid argument $\langle A, Q \rangle$ of strength α_i we have that
   - $Q \in Block(\alpha_i)$ whenever there exists a set $\mathbb{G}$ of valid arguments of strength α_i such that
     (i) $\langle A, Q \rangle \not\sqsubseteq \mathbb{G}$, and
     (ii) $\mathbb{G} \cup \{\langle A, Q \rangle\}$ minimally conflicts with respect to the set $W = Warr(> \alpha_i) \cup \{P \mid \langle E, P \rangle \sqsubset \mathbb{G} \cup \{\langle A, Q \rangle\}\}$.
   - otherwise, $Q \in Warr(\alpha_i)$.

Intuitively, an argument $\langle A, Q \rangle$ is valid whenever (V1) it is based on warranted conclusions; (V2) there does not exist a valid argument for Q with greater strength; and (V3) Q is consistent with already warranted and blocked conclusions. Then, a valid argument $\langle A, Q \rangle$ becomes blocked as soon as it leads to some conflict among valid arguments of same strength and the set of already warranted conclusions, otherwise it is warranted.

Next we outline some relevant properties regarding warranted and blocked conclusions when considering stratified strengths of arguments:

1. If $Q \in Warr(\alpha) \cup Block(\alpha)$, then there exists an argument $\langle A, Q \rangle$ of strength α such that for all subargument $\langle E, P \rangle \sqsubset \langle A, \varphi \rangle$ of strength β, $\psi \in Warr(\beta)$.
2. If $Q \in Warr(\alpha) \cup Block(\alpha)$, then for any argument $\langle A, Q \rangle$ of strength β, with $\beta > \alpha$, there exists a subargument $\langle E, P \rangle \sqsubset \langle A, Q \rangle$ of strength γ and $P \notin Warr(\gamma)$.
3. If $Q \in Warr$, then $Q, \sim Q \notin Block$.
4. If $Q \notin Warr \cup Block$, then either $\sim Q \in Block$, or for all argument $\langle A, Q \rangle$ there exists a subargument $\langle E, P \rangle \sqsubset \langle A, Q \rangle$ such that $P \notin Warr$ or $\Pi \cup Warr(> \alpha_i) \cup \{P \mid \langle E, P \rangle \sqsubset \langle A, Q \rangle\} \cup \{Q\} \vdash \bot$.

In [1] we showed that, in case of some circular definitions of conflict among arguments, the output of an RP-DeLP program may be not unique, that is, there may exist several pairs $(Warr, Block)$ satisfying the above conditions for a given RP-DeLP program. Following the approach of Pollock [18], circular definitions of conflict were formalized by means of what we called *warrant dependency graphs*. A warrant dependency graph represents (i) support relations of almost valid arguments with respect to valid arguments and (ii) conflict relations of valid arguments with respect to almost valid arguments. An almost valid argument is an argument based on a set of valid arguments and whose status is warranted or blocked (but not rejected), whenever every valid

---

[3] In what follows we will also write $Warr(\geq \alpha_i)$ and $Warr(> \alpha_i)$ to denote $\cup_{\beta \geq \alpha_i} Warr(\beta)$ and $\cup_{\beta > \alpha_i} Warr(\beta)$, respectively, and analogously for $Block(> \alpha_i)$, assuming $Block(> \alpha_1) = \emptyset$.

argument in the set is warranted, and rejected, otherwise. Then, a cycle in a warrant dependency graph represents a circular definition of conflict among a set of arguments.

Based on warrant dependency graphs, in [2] we defined the characteristics to be met by an RP-DeLP program to have a single output. Moreover we considered the problem of deciding the set of conclusions that can be ultimately warranted in RP-DeLP programs with multiple outputs. The usual skeptical approach would be to adopt the intersection of all possible outputs. However, in addition to the computational limitation adopting the intersection of all outputs may lead to an inconsistent output (in the sense of violating the base of the underlying recursive warrant semantics) in case some particular recursive situation among conclusions of a program occurs. Intuitively, for a conclusion, to be in the intersection does not guarantee the existence of an argument for it that is recursively based on ultimately warranted conclusions.

For instance, consider the following situation involving three conclusions P, Q, and T, where P can be warranted whenever Q is blocked, and vice-versa. Moreover, suppose that T can be warranted when either P or Q are warranted. Then, according to the warrant recursive semantics, we would get two different outputs: one where P and T are warranted and Q is blocked, and the other one where Q and T are warranted and P is blocked. Then, adopting the intersection of both outputs we would get that T would be ultimately warranted, however T should be in fact rejected since neither P nor Q are ultimately warranted conclusions.[4]

According to this example, one could take then as the set of ultimately warranted conclusions of RP-DeLP programs those conclusions in the intersection of all outputs which are recursively based on ultimately warranted conclusions. However, as in RP-DeLP there might be different levels of defeasibility, this approach could lead to an incomplete solution, in the sense of not being the biggest set of ultimately warranted conclusions with maximum strength.

For instance consider the above example extended with two defeasibility levels as follows. Suppose P can be warranted with strength α whenever Q is blocked, and vice-versa. Moreover, suppose T can be warranted with strength α whenever P is warranted at least with strength α, and that T can be warranted with strength β, with $\beta < \alpha$, independently of the status of conclusions P and Q. Then, again we get two different outputs: one output warrants conclusions P and T with strength α and blocks conclusion Q, and the other one warrants conclusions Q and T with strengths α and β, respectively, and blocks P. Now, if we restrict ourselves to only those conclusions in the intersection which are recursively based on ultimately warranted conclusions, we get that conclusion T is finally rejected, since T is warranted with a different argument and strength in each output. However, as we are interested in determining the biggest set of warranted conclusions with maximum strength, it seems quite reasonable to reject T at level α but to warrant it at level β.

Therefore, we are led to define the *maximal ideal output* for an RP-DeLP program as a pair (*Warr*, *Block*) of respectively warranted and blocked conclusions, with a maximum strength, such that:

---

[4] Remember that our warrant recursive semantics is based on the fact that if an argument is excluded from an output, then all the arguments built on top of it should also be excluded from that output.

(i) the arguments of all conclusions in *Warr* ∪ *Block* are recursively based on war-
    ranted conclusions;
(ii) a conclusion is warranted (at level α) if does not generate any conflict with the set
     of already warranted conclusions (at a level $\beta > \alpha$) and it is not involved in any
     cycle of a warrant dependency graph; otherwise, it is blocked; and
(iii) a conclusion is rejected if it can be neither warranted nor blocked to any level.

Recently in [5] we have proved that the maximal ideal output for an RP-DeLP program is unique and we have characterized the relationship between the sets of warranted
and blocked conclusions for the maximal ideal output for an RP-DeLP program with
multiple outputs and the sets of warranted and blocked conclusions to each of these
outputs. In this context we have proved that if an RP-DeLP program has a single output
then it coincides with the maximal ideal output. Moreover, when we restrict ourselves
to the case of RP-DeLP programs with a single defeasibility level, we get the following
property of the maximal ideal output. Let $\mathcal{P} = (\Pi, \Delta, \preceq)$ be an RP-DeLP program
with a single defeasibility level for Δ and let $(Warr, Block)$ be the maximal ideal output for $\mathcal{P}$. Then, for each output $(Warr', Block')$ for $\mathcal{P}$, we have $Warr \subseteq Warr'$ and
$Block \subseteq Warr' \cup Block'$. Moreover, under this hypothesis of a single defeasibility level
for Δ, we have that the set of warranted conclusions satisfies closure with respect to the
strict part of the program Π and the inference operator $\vdash$; i.e., if $(Warr, Block)$ is the
maximal ideal output for $\mathcal{P}$ and $\Pi \cup Warr \vdash Q$, then $Q \in Warr$.

In case we consider multiple defeasibility levels, the set of conclusions that are warranted and blocked at each level is decisive for determining which arguments are valid
at lower levels. Then, since the maximal ideal output for an RP-DeLP program corresponds to a skeptical criterion regarding warranted conclusions, we get that a conclusion can be warranted for the maximal ideal output at some level α and, due to the set
of warranted conclusions at higher levels, rejected for each output (extension). Then,
under this general hypothesis of multiple defeasibility levels for Δ, we have the following result. Let $\mathcal{P} = (\Pi, \Delta, \preceq)$ be an RP-DeLP program with defeasibility levels
$1 > \alpha_1 > \ldots > \alpha_p > 0$, and let $(Warr, Block)$ be the maximal ideal output for $\mathcal{P}$.
If $\Pi \cup Warr(\geq \alpha_i) \vdash Q$ and $\Pi \cup Warr(> \alpha_i) \nvdash Q$, then either $Q \in Warr(\alpha_i)$, or
$Q \in Block(> \alpha_i)$, or $\sim Q \in Block(> \alpha_i)$.

Our maximal ideal output semantics is based on the idea that if a conclusion P is
warranted at level β so it could also be guaranteed in any higher level α. A different
approach could have been to consider that blocked conclusions at one level are not
propagated to lower levels. In such a case it could happen to have a conclusion Q
blocked at a given level α and to have P, with $\Pi \cup W(\geq \alpha) \cup \{P, Q\} \vdash \bot$, warranted at a
lower level β. We plan to consider such alternative semantics for our system, following
a similar line to the one in [17].

3   Computing the Set of Outputs for an RP-DeLP Program

From a computational point of view, the set of outputs for a recursive based semantics
can be computed by means of a recursive algorithm, starting with the computation of
warranted conclusions from strict clauses and recursively going from warranted conclusions to defeasible arguments based on them.

Recently, in [4] we have defined an algorithm for computing the set of outputs for programs with multiple outputs but with a single level for defeasible facts and rules. In this section we extend the algorithm in order to consider multiple defeasible levels which is achieved using a stack to store the set of partially computed outputs. For every level the algorithm must compute the sets of valid and almost valid arguments and has to check the existence of conflicts between valid arguments and cycles at some warrant dependency graph. When a cycle is found the algorithm explores all possible outputs and stores them at the top of the stack in order to be considered at the next level.

Algorithm RP-DeLP outputs
Input $\mathcal{P} = (\Pi, \Delta, \preceq)$: An RP-DeLP program
Output O: Set of outputs for $\mathcal{P}$
Variables
    (W, B): Current output for $\mathcal{P}$
    $S(W, B, \alpha)$: Stack of partially computed outputs for $\mathcal{P}$
Method
    $O := \emptyset$;
    $W := \{Q \mid \Pi \vdash Q\}$;
    $B := \emptyset$;
    $\alpha := 1$;
    Push$(S, (W, B, \alpha))$;
    while $(\neg$Empty_Stack$(S))$ **do**
        (W, B, α) = Top(S);
        Pop(S);
        while $(\alpha >$lower_level$(\preceq))$ **do**
            $\alpha :=$ next_level$(\preceq)$;
            level_computing(W, B, α, S, O)
        end while
    end while
end algorithm

The algorithm RP-DeLP outputs first computes the set of warranted conclusions form the set of strict clauses Π and uses the stack S to store the set of partially computed outputs. For every partially computed output and every defeasible level $1 > \alpha > 0$, the procedure level_computing determines the sets of warranted and blocked conclusions of the output with strength α: the procedure level_computing receives a partially computed output with a set of warranted conclusions $W(> \alpha)$ and a set of blocked conclusions $B(> \alpha)$, and computes $W(\geq \alpha)$ and $B(\geq \alpha)$ for every extension. Extensions are recursively computed and stored in the stack S by means of the procedure weighted_extension.

Procedure level_computing (**in_out** W, B, α, S, O)
Variable VA: Set of valid arguments
Method
    $VA := \{\langle A, Q\rangle$ with strength $\alpha \mid \langle A, Q\rangle$ is valid w.r.t. W and $B\}$;
    weighted_extension (W, B, α, VA, S, O);
    (W, B, α) = Top(S);
    Pop(S)
end procedure level_computing

The procedure `level_computing` first computes the set *VA* of valid arguments with respect to $W(> \alpha)$ and $B(> \alpha)$. Then, the procedure `weighted_extension` dynamically updates the set *VA* of valid arguments depending on new warranted and blocked arguments with strength α. When an RP-DeLP program has multiple outputs, every output is recursively computed by the procedure `weighted_extension` and new outputs are stored in the stack S. Procedure `level_computing` returns to the main program `RP-DeLP outputs` the last generated output which is used as starting point for the next defeasibility level at the main program `RP-DeLP outputs`.

Procedure `weighted_extension` (**in** W, B, α, *VA*; **in_out** S, O)

Variables
    W_{ext}: Extended set of warranted conclusions
    VA_{ext}: Extended set of valid arguments
    is_leaf: Boolean
Method
    is_leaf := `true`;
    while (*VA* $\neq \emptyset$ **and** *is_leaf* = `true`) **do**
        while $(\exists \langle A, Q \rangle \in VA \mid$
        $\neg$ `conflict`$(\langle A, Q \rangle, VA, W,$ `not_dependent`$(\langle A, Q \rangle,$ `almost_valid`$(VA, (W, B))))$
        and $\neg$ `cycle`$(\langle A, Q \rangle, VA, W,$ `almost_valid`$(VA, (W, B)))$ **do**
            $W := W \cup \{Q\}$;
            $VA := VA \backslash \{\langle A, Q \rangle\} \cup \{\langle E, P \rangle$ with strength $\alpha \mid \langle E, P \rangle$ is valid w.r.t. W and $B\}$
        end while
        $I := \{\langle A, Q \rangle \in VA \mid$ `conflict`$(\alpha, \langle A, Q \rangle, VA, W, \emptyset) \}$;
        $B := B \cup \{Q \mid \langle A, Q \rangle \in I\}$;
        $VA := VA \backslash I$;
        $J := \{\langle A, Q \rangle \in VA \mid$ `cycle`$(\alpha, \langle A, Q \rangle, VA, W,$ `almost_valid`$(\alpha, VA, W, B)) \}$;
        for each argument $(\langle A, Q \rangle \in J)$ **do**
            $W_{ext} := W \cup \{Q\}$;
            $VA_{ext} := VA \backslash \{\langle A, Q \rangle\} \cup \{\langle E, P \rangle$ with strength $\alpha \mid \langle E, P \rangle$ is valid w.r.t. W_{ext} and $B\}$;
            `weighted_extension` $(W_{ext}, B, \alpha, VA_{ext}, S, O)$
        end for
        if $(J \neq \emptyset)$ **then** *is_leaf* := `false`
    end while
    if $((W, B, \alpha) \notin S$ **and** *is_leaf* = `true`) **then**
            `Push`$(S, (W, B, \alpha))$;
            if $(\alpha = $ `lower_level`$(\preceq))$ **then** $O := O \cup \{(W, B)\}$
    end if
end procedure `weighted_extension`

The recursive procedure `weighted_extension` receives as input a partially computed output (W, B) at a level α and the set of valid arguments *VA* with respect to W and B and dynamically updates the set *VA* depending on new warranted and blocked conclusions and the appearance of cycles in some warrant dependence graph. When a cycle is found in a warrant dependence graph, each valid argument of the cycle can lead to a different output. Then, the procedure `weighted_extension` selects one valid argument of the cycle and recursively computes the resulting output by warranting the selected argument. The procedure finishes when the status for every valid argument is computed. If the recursive analysis leads to a new extension, it is stored in the stack S. Moreover, if the level computing α corresponds with the lower strength of the program arguments, each new output is added to the set of outputs O.

The function `almost_valid` computes the set of almost valid arguments based on some valid arguments in *VA*. The function `not_dependent` computes the set of almost valid arguments which do not depend on $\langle A, Q \rangle$. The function `conflict` has two different functionalities. On the one hand, the function `conflict` checks conflicts among the argument $\langle A, Q \rangle$ and the set *VA* of valid arguments, and thus, every valid argument involved in a conflict is blocked. On the other hand, the function `conflict` checks possible conflicts among the argument $\langle A, Q \rangle$ and the set *VA* of valid arguments extended with the set of almost valid arguments whose supports depend on some argument in $VA \backslash \{ \langle A, Q \rangle \}$, and thus, every valid argument with options to be involved in a conflict remains as valid. Finally, the function `cycle` checks the existence of a cycle in the warrant dependency graph for the set of valid arguments *VA* and the set of almost valid arguments based on some valid arguments in *VA*. In [2] we showed that whenever `cycle` returns true for $\langle A, Q \rangle$, then a conflict will be detected with the set of almost valid arguments which do not depend on $\langle A, Q \rangle$. Moreover, the set of valid arguments J computed by function `cycle` can also be computed by checking the stability of the set of valid arguments after two consecutive iterations, so it is not necessary to explicitly compute dependency graphs. Hence the `weighted_extension` procedure needs to compute two main queries during its execution: i) whether an argument is almost valid and ii) whether there is a conflict for a valid argument.

In [2] and [3] we proposed SAT and ASP encodings, respectively, for resolving both queries with a SAT and an ASP solver. In both cases, only programs with a single output and a single strength for defeasible arguments were considered. Recently, in [4] we have provided experimental results regarding the performance of the SAT based implementation for programs with multiple outputs but with a single strength for defeasible arguments. This is the first time that we consider programs with multiple outputs and multiple strengths for defeasible arguments. The web based system also allows us to compute the maximal ideal output for this programs.

4   Web System Architecture

In this section we describe the architecture of the web based system we have designed and implemented to process RP-DeLP programs [5] and which is available at http://arinf.udl.cat/rp-delp.

A web application is a software tool which is available through a network of computers, in most of the cases this software is being executed in a server and accessible by all the clients connected to the same network. That software provides a common interface which is supported by a web browser. One of the main features of a web application is ubiquity, that means that the application is ready as long as there is access to the network. Another advantage is that the only software required at the client part is a web browser. A key reason for its popularity is the fact that the software can be updated and maintained without the necessity of installing or disturbing the clients. There are

---

[5] We plan to deliver an open-source version as soon as we consider the system is sufficiently mature.

more advantages, such as the inherent cross-platform compatibility and the lack of high system requirements, because most of the processing tasks are executed in the server side.

However, there are also some inconveniences, as a web interface is not easily adaptable to other systems. To solve this drawback we designed a web system capable of solving both instances posted through a web interface and also instances received through HTTP requests. By using HTTP protocol, any client will be able to send a query without the necessity of filling a web interface.

Our system is allocated in a stand-alone server where all the required software is installed, including a web server to handle HTTP requests, the RP-DeLP algorithm to handle the user programs and the rest of the software required by the system, such as the ASP and SAT solvers. As said previously, the user can access to the server using a web browser through the web interface or by posting an HTTP request. The RP-DeLP algorithm is implemented with Python. In Figure 1 we show the web interface structure of the system.

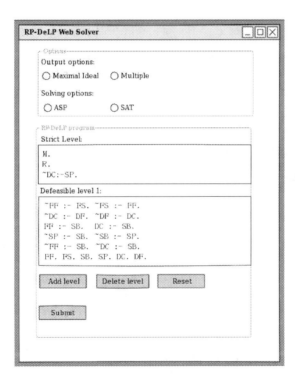

Fig. 1. Web interface form for submitting RP-DeLP programs

The web interface is divided into two main parts. The first part is devoted to choose the computation options. The *Maximal Ideal* radio button computes the maximal ideal output and the *Multiple* radio button computes the set of outputs. Remark that for RP-DeLP programs with a single output both options will compute the same output.

The *SAT* radio button encodes queries with SAT formulas and solves them with `minisat` solver [13]. The *ASP* radio button encodes queries with ASP formulas and solves them with `clingo` solver [16].

The second part of the web interface is devoted to define RP-DeLP programs. Each defeasible level is depicted by a text box. The strict part of the program is defined in the *Strict Level* text box. The defeasible part of the program can be defined using multiple levels of strength, starting from the highest level and going down from one level to the level below. The form is dynamically updated, so the user can add new levels by pressing the *Add level* button. The *Delete level* erases the last added level and the *Reset* button deletes all levels except the strict part and the first defeasible level. The *Submit* button starts the computation process.

Clauses are defined as follows:

- All clauses must end with a dot.
- A literal is an alphanumeric word starting with a letter.
- Negation is denoted with symbol $\sim$.
- Implication symbol is written with `:-` and conjunction symbol is a comma. For instance, $q \leftarrow p_1 \wedge \sim p_2$ is written in our formalism as: `q :- p1, ~p2`.

Regarding the system architecture, represented in Figure 2, the computation process starts with the translation of the RP-DeLP program and the set of computation options into an XML file. Then, appropriate Python structures are built from the XML file in order to be processed by the RP-DeLP algorithm. The RP-DeLP algorithm uses the ASP or the SAT implementation depending on the computation options. When the RP-DeLP algorithm finishes, outputs are stored in an XML file which allow us to provide an HTTP response or an HTML page.

One of the main features of our system is that provides not only sets of warranted and blocked conclusions, but also information to further understand the reasons why conclusions are warranted or blocked.

In Table 1 we show the information that the system provides to the user for every output. This information is divided in two parts. The first part shows the total number of outputs, a label of the computing order of the output, the set of warranted conclusions of the output and the time expended computing the output. For each warranted conclusion there is a list of conclusions which support it and the strength of the conclusion. The second part shows the set of blocked conclusions of the output and the set of conclusions which support them. For each blocked conclusion the system informs about the strength of the conclusion and the reason that leads to block it: a conflict or a cycle. For conflicts it shows the set of valid conclusions that minimally conflicts. For cycles it shows the set of valid conclusions of the cycle at some warrant dependency graph. Remark that a conclusion is blocked due to a cycle whenever we compute the maximal ideal output, otherwise conclusions are blocked due to conflicts.

5   A Running Example: Arguing about the Best Menu

In this section we consider the application of the RP-DeLP argumentation framework to the construction of suitable menus in a restaurant. Suppose we have two persons in the restaurant arguing about how to select the different menu items: Chicote (the chef) and

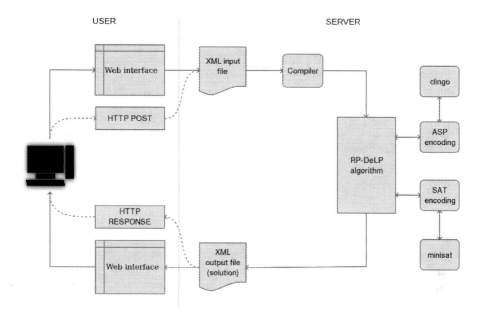

Fig. 2. RP-DeLP web system architecture

Luis (the restaurant manager). Chicote is more concerned about the quality of the menu, whereas Luis is more concerned about the price of the menu. However, both agree that for preparing the menu they should reach a consensus that considers the preferences of both.

The menu must contain appetizer, drink, first course, second course and dessert. For appetizer and drink they have already reach the conclusion that they will serve mussels (M) and red wine (R), respectively. But there is no a consensus about the other items.

For the first course, the options are Soup (FS) and Fish (FF). For the second course are Beef (SB) and pork (SP). And for the dessert are fruit (DF) and Sacher cake (DC).

First case. As we have said, they both agree on the selection for the appetizer and the drink. Also, they both agree that when pork is served, Sacher cake cannot be served. So, at the strict level we have the following hard constraints:

$$\Pi = \{M, R, \sim DC \leftarrow SP\}$$

The other conditions for the menu are not so clear, as both sides have some opposite preferences, or not any preferences between some options. First, regarding what option to select for each course and dessert, they do not have, a priori, any preference between the two options for each menu item. But it is clear that once one option is selected, the other should be avoided. So, at the defeasible level we have propositions for all the possible options for first and second course and dessert and rules that express the preference that once one option is selected for a course or for the dessert, the other should not be selected.

Table 1. Information provided by the system for an RP-DeLP program

Number of outputs	# output	Warranted conclusions	Time
n	i	$P_1 : \{P_{1,1}, \ldots, P_{1,h}\} \, [\alpha_{P_1}]$ $\vdots$ $P_r : \{P_{r,1}, \ldots, P_{r,u}\} \, [\alpha_{P_r}]$	t_n

# output	Blocked conclusions	Support of blocked conclusions
i	$Q_1 : conflict(Q_{1,1}, \ldots, Q_{1,j}) \, [\alpha_{Q_1}]$ $\vdots$ $Q_s : cycle(Q_{s,1}, \ldots, Q_{s,v}) \, [\alpha_{Q_s}]$	$Q_1 : \{P_{1,1}, \ldots, P_{1,k}\}$ $\vdots$ $Q_x : \{P_{x,1}, \ldots, P_{x,w}\}$

Secondly, regarding the preferred combinations of courses and dessert, Luis prefers not to serve the more expensive first course (fish) and the more expensive dessert (Sacher cake) when beef is the second course. By contrast, Chicote believes that when beef is served, the preferred options for first course and dessert are fish and Sacher cake. Then, all these conditions are encoded with a single defeasible level as follows: [6]

$$\Delta_{\alpha_1} = \{ \ FF, FS, SB, SP, DC, DF,$$
$$F1 : \sim FF \leftarrow FS, \qquad F2 : \sim FS \leftarrow FF,$$
$$S1 : \sim SP \leftarrow SB, \qquad S2 : \sim SB \leftarrow SP,$$
$$D1 : \sim DC \leftarrow DF, \qquad D2 : \sim DF \leftarrow DC,$$
$$C1 : FF \leftarrow SB, \qquad C2 : DC \leftarrow SB,$$
$$L1 : \sim FF \leftarrow SB, \qquad L2 : \sim DC \leftarrow SB \ \}$$

Given all these conditions, it turns out that there is an unique menu that we extract with our argumentation system, that corresponds with the unique output of our program shown in Table 2.

Table 2. Output of the system for our first running example

# of outputs	Warranted conclusions	Blocked conclusions	Support of blocked
1	$M : \{M\}[\Pi]$ $R : \{R\}[\Pi]$ $SB : \{SB\}[\alpha_1]$ $DF : \{DF\}[\alpha_1]$ $FS : \{FS\}[\alpha_1]$	$SP : conflict(SP, DC)[\alpha_1]$ $DC : conflict(SP, DC)[\alpha_1]$ $FF : conflict(FF, \sim FF)[\alpha_1]$ $\sim FF : conflict(FF, \sim FF)[\alpha_1]$	$\sim FF : \{SB\}$ $FF : \{FF\}$ $SP : \{SP\}$ $DC : \{DC\}$

The reasons for this unique output are as follows. First, observe that there is a conflict between valid arguments for SP and DC, so they are blocked and SB and DF can be warranted. Then given the warrant status of SB and the defeasible rule $L1$, $\sim FF$ becomes valid, but then there is a conflict between FF and $\sim FF$, so they are blocked. This allows to warrant FS. As we have an unique output, in this case this output coincides with the maximal ideal output of the program.

---

[6] The RP-DeLP program of Figure 1 corresponds with the set of facts and rules of this example.

Second case. Suppose now that after some deliberation between Luis and Chicote, they agree that the preference of Chicote of having fish and cake when we have beef should receive more consideration than the preference of Luis of not having fish and cake. But we still do not have a preference between fish and soup, so they are still in the same defeasible level. So, we have the same strict knowledge as before, but two defeasible levels α_1 and α_2 with $\alpha_1 > \alpha_2$. Then, the set of defeasible facts and rules is stratified as follows:

$$\Delta_{\alpha_1} = \{\ FF, FS, SB, SP, DC, DF$$
$$F1 : {\sim}FF \leftarrow FS, \qquad F2 : {\sim}FS \leftarrow FF,$$
$$S1 : {\sim}SP \leftarrow SB, \qquad S2 : {\sim}SB \leftarrow SP,$$
$$D1 : {\sim}DC \leftarrow DF, \qquad D2 : {\sim}DF \leftarrow DC,$$
$$C1 : FF \leftarrow SB, \qquad C2 : DC \leftarrow SB\ \}$$

$$\Delta_{\alpha_2} = \{\ L1 : {\sim}FF \leftarrow SB, \qquad L2 : {\sim}DC \leftarrow SB\ \}$$

Given the modified defeasible knowledge, we have that now two menus are possible, that correspond with the two outputs we have this time. We have two outputs because now the warrant status of SB does not create a conflict between FF and ${\sim}FF$. So, as both FF and FS are valid arguments at the defeasible level α_1, together with the defeasible rules $F1$ and $F2$ we have two conflicts with almost valid arguments that cannot be resolved because there is a cyclic dependence. To break this cycle, we have to consider two options: either to warrant FF or to warrant FS:

1. If we warrant FF, then ${\sim}FS$ becomes valid so we have to block FS and ${\sim}FS$. This gives our first output in Figure 3.
2. If we warrant FS, then ${\sim}FF$ becomes valid so we have to block FF and ${\sim}FF$. This gives our second output in Figure 3.

Number of outputs	Output	Warranted conclusions	Bolcked conclusions	Support of bolcked conclusions	Time
2	1	M:{M} [strict] R:{R} [strict] SB:{SB} [delta 1] DF:{DF} [delta 1] FF:{FF} [delta 1]	SP:conflict(SP,DC) [delta 1] DC:conflict(SP,DC) [delta 1] FS:conflict(FS,~FS) [delta 1] ~FS:conflict(FS,~FS) [delta 1]	~FS:{FF} FS:{FS} SP:{SP} DC:{DC}	time: 0.01 s.
2	2	M:{M} [strict] R:{R} [strict] SB:{SB} [delta 1] DF:{DF} [delta 1] FS:{FS} [delta 1]	SP:conflict(SP,DC) [delta 1] DC:conflict(SP,DC) [delta 1] FF:conflict(FF,~FF) [delta 1] ~FF:conflict(FF,~FF) [delta 1]	~FF:{FS} FF:{FF} SP:{SP} DC:{DC}	time: 0.01 s.

Fig. 3. Output of the system for our second running example

For this case, the maximal ideal output has content shown in Table 3. Remark that for our example the set of warranted conclusions for the maximal ideal output coincides with the intersection of the set of warranted conclusions for each output which indicates that Chicote and Luis coincide always at least on the second course and the dessert. [7]

Table 3. Maximal ideal output for the second running example

# of outputs	Warranted conclusions	Blocked conclusions	Support of blocked
1	$M : \{M\}[\Pi]$	$SP : conflict(SP, DC)[\alpha_1]$	$FF : \{FF\}$
	$R : \{R\}[\Pi]$	$DC : conflict(SP, DC)[\alpha_1]$	$FS : \{FS\}$
	$SB : \{SB\}[\alpha_1]$	$FF : cycle(FF, FS)[\alpha_1]$	$SP : \{SP\}$
	$DF : \{DF\}[\alpha_1]$	$FS : cycle(FF, FS)[\alpha_1]$	$DC : \{DC\}$

6   Concluding Remarks

In this paper we have presented a web system implementing an argumentation-based reasoner for general RP-DeLP programs (with multiple defeasibility levels), using two different encodings, one based on SAT techniques and another one based on ASP techniques. As it has been argued, having an available reasoner as a web application has many advantages, specially to be an easy-to-use tool for non-expert potential users, for instance as in [22,9]. On the other hand argumentation web services can also be used as part of bigger systems, like in the BDI system described in [21] where they use an available argumentation web system [15] for the DeLP argumentation framework [14]. It remains as future work to further develop the user interface to make it both more informative and easier to manage. As more concrete application domains, we have already started to consider the use of our system to encourage users to discuss political actions, through the use of argumentation structures, following the line of an existing tool for that purpose that is based also on argumentation structures: the Parmenides System [10].

Acknowledgments. The authors acknowledge the Spanish projects ARINF (TIN2009-14704-C03-01), TASSAT (TIN2010-20967-C04-03) and EdeTRI (TIN2012-39348-C02-01).

References

1. Alsinet, T., Béjar, R., Godo, L.: A characterization of collective conflict for defeasible argumentation. In: Proceedings of COMMA 2010. Frontiers in Artificial Intelligence and Applications, vol. 216, pp. 27–38. IOS Press (2010)

---

[7] The set of warranted conclusions for the maximal ideal output is not equal to the intersection of the set of warranted conclusions for each output for all RP-DeLP program with multiple outputs. However, the set of blocked conclusions for the maximal ideal output is different to the intersection of the set of warranted conclusions for each output for all RP-DeLP program with multiple outputs.

2. Alsinet, T., Béjar, R., Godo, L., Guitart, F.: Maximal ideal recursive semantics for defeasible argumentation. In: Benferhat, S., Grant, J. (eds.) SUM 2011. LNCS, vol. 6929, pp. 96–109. Springer, Heidelberg (2011)
3. Alsinet, T., Béjar, R., Godo, L., Guitart, F.: Using answer set programming for an scalable implementation of defeasible argumentation. In: ICTAI, pp. 1016–1021 (2012)
4. Alsinet, T., Béjar, R., Godo, L., Guitart, F.: On the implementation of a multiple outputs algorithm for defeasible argumentation. In: Proceedings of SUM 2013 (in press, 2013)
5. Alsinet, T., Béjar, R., Godo, L., Guitart, F.: RP-DeLP: A weighted defeasible argumentation framework based on a recursive semantics. Journal of Logic and Computation: Special Issue on Loops in Argumentation (submitted)
6. Amgoud, L.: Postulates for logic-based argumentation systems. In: Proceedings of the ECAI 2012 Workshop WL4AI, pp. 59–67 (2012)
7. Bench-Capon, T.J.M., Dunne, P.E.: Argumentation in artificial intelligence. Artif. Intell. 171(10-15), 619–641 (2007)
8. Besnard, P., Hunter, A.: Elements of Argumentation. The MIT Press (2008)
9. Bouyias, Y.N., Demetriadis, S.N., Tsoukalas, I.A.: iargue: A web-based argumentation system supporting collaboration scripts with adaptable fading. In: Proceedings of ICALT 2008, pp. 477–479 (2008)
10. Cartwright, D., Atkinson, K.: Using computational argumentation to support e-participation. IEEE Intelligent Systems 24(5), 42–52 (2009)
11. Minh Dung, P., Mancarella, P., Toni, F.: A dialectic procedure for sceptical, assumption-based argumentation. In: Proceedings of COMMA 2008. Frontiers in Artificial Intelligence and Applications, vol. 172, pp. 145–156. IOS Press (2006)
12. Minh Dung, P., Mancarella, P., Toni, F.: Computing ideal sceptical argumentation. Artif. Intell. 171(10-15), 642–674 (2007)
13. Eén, N., Sörensson, N.: An extensible SAT-solver. In: Giunchiglia, E., Tacchella, A. (eds.) SAT 2003. LNCS, vol. 2919, pp. 502–518. Springer, Heidelberg (2004)
14. García, A., Simari, G.: Defeasible Logic Programming: An Argumentative Approach. Theory and Practice of Logic Programming 4(1), 95–138 (2004)
15. García, A.J., Rotstein, N.D., Tucat, M., Simari, G.R.: An argumentative reasoning service for deliberative agents. In: Zhang, Z., Siekmann, J.H. (eds.) KSEM 2007. LNCS (LNAI), vol. 4798, pp. 128–139. Springer, Heidelberg (2007)
16. Gebser, M., Kaminski, R., Kaufmann, B., Ostrowski, M., Schaub, T., Schneider, M.: Potassco: The Potsdam answer set solving collection. AI Commun. 24(2), 107–124 (2011)
17. Governatori, G., Maher, M.J., Antoniou, G., Billington, D.: Argumentation semantics for defeasible logic. J. Log. Comput. 14(5), 675–702 (2004)
18. Pollock, J.L.: A recursive semantics for defeasible reasoning. In: Rahwan, I., Simari, G.R. (eds.) Argumentation in Artificial Intelligence, ch. 9, pp. 173–198. Springer (2009)
19. Prakken, H., Vreeswijk, G.: Logical Systems for Defeasible Argumentation. In: Gabbay, D., Guenther, F. (eds.) Handbook of Phil. Logic, pp. 219–318. Kluwer (2002)
20. Rahwan, I., Simari, G.R. (eds.): Argumentation in Artificial Intelligence. Springer (2009)
21. Schlesinger, F., Errecalde, M., Aguirre, G.: An approach to integrate web services and argumentation into a BDI system (extended abstract). In: van der Hoek, Kaminka, Lespérance, Luck, Sen (eds.) Proceedings of AAMAS 2010, pp. 1371–1372 (2010)
22. Tsai, C.Y., Jack, B.M., Huang, T.C., Yang, J.T.: Using the cognitive apprenticeship web-based argumentation system to improve argumentation instruction. Journal of Science Education and Technology 21, 476–486 (2012)

Coalitional Responsibility in Strategic Settings

Nils Bulling[1] and Mehdi Dastani[2]

[1] Clausthal University, Germany
bulling@in.tu-clausthal.de
[2] Utrecht University, The Netherlands
M.M.Dastani@uu.nl

Abstract. This paper focuses on the concept of group responsibility and presents a formal analysis of it from a strategic point of view. A group of agents is considered to be responsible for an outcome if the group can avoid the outcome. Based on this interpretation of group responsibility, different notions of group responsibility are provided and their properties are studied. The formal analysis starts with the semantics of different notions of group responsibility followed by their logical characterizations. The presented work is compared and related to the existing work on responsibility.

1 Introduction

Responsibility is a central concept in philosophy and social sciences. Various types of responsibility such as moral, legal, social, and organizational responsibility have been identified [10]. Moreover, responsibility is classified along different dimensions such as individual or collective, normative or descriptive, forward-looking or backward-looking, and action-based or state-based [16]. An example of an individual forward-looking responsibility is the obligation of an academic researcher to see to it that the outcome of his research is truthful, not plagiarized, original, etc. This responsibility can be moral, legal, social or organizational. In general, responsibility that is based on the obligation to see to it that a state of affairs is the case is often seen as a forward-looking responsibility. An example of a collective backward-looking responsibility is the responsibility for the low-ranked teaching quality of a university department. In such a case, the teaching members of the department can collectively be held responsible for the low teaching quality.

The attribution of responsibility to agents or groups of agents is often characterized by means of specific (fairness) conditions [11,15]. For example, the conditions that characterize accountability and blameworthiness, which are considered as two instances of backward-looking responsibility, are formulated as follows. Agents can be held accountable for a state of affairs (or an action) if they have intentionally, deliberately and actively been involved in realizing the state of affairs (or the action). On the other hand, agents can be blamed for a state of affairs (or an action) if they can be held accountable for it, and moreover, the involvement is based on free choice (agents were not enforced or compelled), and they know that the state of affairs (or the action) has negative consequences.

J. Leite et al. (Eds.): CLIMA XIV, LNAI 8143, pp. 172–189, 2013.
© Springer-Verlag Berlin Heidelberg 2013

Although the concept of responsibility has been studied for quite a long time, there is yet no consensus of what this concept exactly and formally means. Most formal work on responsibility is concerned with specific instantiation of this concept such as having moral (legal, social, or organizational) obligations and being accountable or blame-worthy for something. To our knowledge there is not much work on formalizing and analyzing the very abstract concept of responsibility without considering its instantiations. The abstract concept of responsibility that we have in mind captures the power dimension of responsibility as illustrated by the quote *"With great power, comes great responsibility"*. More specifically, this notion of responsibility can be used to hold a group of agents responsible for a state of affairs if they can ensure avoiding the state of affairs. In other words, agents can be held responsible for a state of affairs if they have the power to preclude the state of affairs.

This notion of responsibility is neither forward-looking nor backward-looking since it neither requires the agents to see to it that a state of affairs is the case nor implies that the agents are accountable because the state of affairs may not be realized. Moreover, most work on responsibility is concerned with individual agents, ignoring responsibility of coalitions of agents with a strategic flavor. A coalition of agents can be held responsible for some state of affairs due to strategic reasons. For example, two political parties that jointly have a majority in the parliament are responsible for the enactment of a law because they can form a coalition to block the enactment of the law. Note that the involved agents can also strategically reason and decide to be absent at the voting session in order to abdicate their responsibilities. Our proposed framework can be applied to analyze the responsibility of agent coalitions in multi-agent scenario's where different agents have different sets of actions/options available to them, e.g., elections and collective decision making, distributed problem solving and collaborative systems.

This paper aims at formalizing this abstract concept of state-based responsibility for coalitions of agents. We consider a coalition of agents as being responsible for some states of affairs if the coalition can preclude it. This abstract notion of responsibility is formalized in concurrent game structures where the strategic behavior of a set of agents can be represented and analyzed. The proposed framework allows defining various notions of this abstract concept of responsibility. It also allows reasoning about responsibilities of agents' coalitions and deciding which coalition of agents is responsible for specific states of the system.

The structure of this paper is as follows. Section 2 presents the formal framework in which the notion of responsibility is characterized. Section 3 provides a semantic analysis of various notions of group responsibility and study their properties. In Section 4 we show how a coalition logic with quantification can be used to characterize and to reason about group responsibility. The provided notion of group responsibility is put in the context of related work in Section 5. Finally, Section 6 concludes the paper and we point out some future work directions.

2   Preliminaries: Models and Power

In this paper, the behavior of a multi-agent system is modeled by concurrent game structures (CGS). A *concurrent game structure* [3] (CGS) is a tuple $\mathcal{M} = (N, Q, Act, d, o)$

which includes a nonempty finite set of all agents $N = \{1, \ldots, k\}$, a nonempty set of system states Q, and a nonempty finite set of (atomic) actions Act. The function $d : N \times Q \to \mathcal{P}(Act)$ defines sets of actions available to agents at each state, and o is a deterministic and partial transition function that assigns the outcome state $q' = o(q, \alpha_1, \ldots, \alpha_k)$ to state q and a tuple of actions $\alpha_i \in d(i, q)$ that can be executed by N in q. An action profile is a sequence $(\alpha_1, \ldots, \alpha_k)$ consisting of an action for each player. We require that if $o(q, \alpha_1, \ldots, \alpha_k)$ is undefined then $o(q, \alpha'_1, \ldots, \alpha'_k)$ is undefined for each action profile $(\alpha'_1, \ldots, \alpha'_k)$. We write $d_i(q)$ for $d(i, q)$ and $d_C(q) := \prod_{i \in C} d_i(q)$.

A *state of affairs* is defined as a set $S \subseteq Q$ of states. In the rest of this paper, we use $\bar{S}$ to denote the set $Q \backslash S$ of states. Let $\mathcal{M}$ be a CGS, q a state in it and S be a state of affairs. We say that:

– C can q-enforce S in $\mathcal{M}$ iff there is a joint action $\alpha_C \in d_C(q)$ such that for all joint actions $\alpha_{N \backslash C} \in d_{N \backslash C}(q)$ we have that $o(q, (\alpha_C, \alpha_{N \backslash C})) \in S$. That is, coalition C must have an action profile that guarantees to end up in a state from S, independent of what the agents outside C do.

– C q-controls S in $\mathcal{M}$ iff C can q-enforce S as well as $\bar{S}$ in $\mathcal{M}$.

– C can q-avoid S in $\mathcal{M}$ iff for all $\alpha_{N \backslash C} \in d_{N \backslash C}(q)$ there is $\alpha_C \in d_C(q)$ such that $o(q, (\alpha_{N \backslash C}, \alpha_C)) \in \bar{S}$.

In the following we shall omit "in $\mathcal{M}$" whenever $\mathcal{M}$ is clear from context. We note that the notions of enforcement and avoidance correspond to the game-theoretic notions of α-effectivity and β-effectivity, respectively (e.g. [13]). More, precisely, we have that C can q-enforce S in $\mathcal{M}$ iff C is α-effective for S in q; and C can q-avoid S in $\mathcal{M}$ iff C is β-effective for $\bar{S}$ in q[1].

In general, a coalition that q-controls S is not unique; that is, there is a CGS $\mathcal{M}$, state q, state of affairs S, and different coalitions C and C' that q-control S. In this case we have that $C \cap C' \neq \emptyset$. Moreover, if C can q-enforce $\bar{S}$ then C can q-avoid S.

It is often the case that agents have incomplete information about the world. In CGSs this is modeled by equivalence relations $\sim_a$, one for each $a \in N$. A *uniform* strategy for a player a is a function $s_a : Q \to Act$ such that $s_a(q) = s_a(q')$ for all $q \sim_a q'$. A collective uniform strategy for C is a tuple of strategies consisting of a uniform strategy for each member of C. Moreover, we defined the mutual knowledge relation $\sim_C$ as $\bigcup_{a \in C} \sim_a$. Consequently, we say that a coalition *knows* that it can q-enforce S in $\mathcal{M}$ if there is a collective joint uniform strategy s_C of C such that for all states q' with $q \sim_C q'$ and all actions $\alpha_{N \backslash C} \in d_{N \backslash C}(q')$ we have that $o(q', (\alpha_C, \alpha_{N \backslash C})) \in S$. Analogously, we say that C knows that it q-controls and can q-avoid S.

3   Coalitional Strategic Responsibility

This section provides a semantic analysis of various notions of group responsibility. The intuitive idea of responsibility that we have in mind is that a group of agents can be said to be responsible for some state of affairs if they have the preclusive power to prevent the state of affairs, regardless of what the other agents can do. Under this interpretation, a group of agents is responsible for a state of affairs in the sense that the state of affairs can only be realized if they allow the state of affairs to become the case.

---

[1] In this context, we consider the normal form game naturally associated to the state q in $\mathcal{M}$.

3.1 Basic Definitions of Responsibility

In the following let $\mathcal{M}$ be a CGS, q a state of $\mathcal{M}$ and S a state of affairs in $\mathcal{M}$. We consider two definitions of responsibility. Both notions are *preclusive* in the sense of [12]. The first notion assigns a coalition responsible for a state of affairs if it is the smallest coalition (provided it exists) that can prevent that state of affairs. Our concept of responsibility is local in the sense that it is defined regarding some origin state. A coalition can be responsible for a state of affairs from some state and not responsible from others.

Definition 1 (Responsibility). *We say that a group $C \subseteq N$ is q-responsible for S in $\mathcal{M}$ iff C can q-enforce $\bar{S}$ and for all other coalitions C' that can q-enforce $\bar{S}$ we have that $C \subseteq C'$.*

Again, we omit "in $\mathcal{M}$" if clear from context and proceed in the same way in the rest of the paper. This definition ensures that a coalition is q-responsible for S if there is no other coalition that does not contain the coalition and which can prevent S. This notion of responsibility has the property that a responsible coalition is unique.

Proposition 1. *If C_1 and C_2 are q-responsible for S in $\mathcal{M}$ then $C_1 = C_2$.*

The proposition shows that responsibility is a *very strong concept*. Often there is no smallest group of agents which can preclude a state of affairs. This is for example the case when there are agents with identical preclusive powers. The next definition captures this intuition. A coalition is *weakly responsible* for a state of affairs if it has the power to preclude it and if the coalition is minimal. We do not require, however, that it is the smallest coalition having such preclusive power. It is important to note that if there are some weakly responsible coalition but no responsible one that does *not* mean that there is not responsible coalition in the colloquial sense. It simply means that there are several coalitions that are responsible–again, in the colloquial sense–but no unique one.

Definition 2 (Weak Responsibility). *We say that a group $C \subseteq N$ is weakly q-responsible for S in $\mathcal{M}$ iff C is a minimal coalition that can q-enforce $\bar{S}$.*

We note that both notions of responsibility are based on *preclusive power* in terms of enforcement and not in terms of avoidance. Clearly, we have the following result.

Proposition 2. *If C is q-responsible for S then it is also weakly q-responsible for S and there is no other weakly q-responsible coalition for S. Also if $\emptyset$ is weakly q-responsible for S; then, $\emptyset$ is q-responsible for S.*

Proof. The first part of the proof is obvious. Suppose C' is a weakly q-responsible coalition for S with $C' \neq C$. We cannot have $C' \subsetneq C$ as this would contradict the minimality of C. Analogously, we cannot have $C \subsetneq C'$. Thus, we must have $C \not\subseteq C'$ which contradicts that C is q-responsible for S. Clearly, if $\emptyset$ is weakly q-responsible for S; then, it is the smallest such coalition. $\square$

Example 1. We consider the CGS shown in Figure 1^2. We refer to player 1 as "Driver 1", to 2 as "Driver 2", and to 3 as "family member of Driver 2". The story is as follows.

---

[2] We thank an anonymous CLIMA reviewer for this example.

Two drivers can decide to drive or to wait. If both chose to drive their cars will crash, with one exception: a family member of Driver 2 can poison Driver 2, making him/her unable to drive and thus avoids a crash. In this example the weakly q_0-responsible coalitions for $\{q_2\}$ are exactly $\{1\}$, $\{2\}$, and $\{3\}$. However, no coalition is q_0-responsible for $\{q_2\}$! Again, it is important to note that this does not mean that no coalition is responsible in the colloquial sense but simply that there are three (weakly) responsible coalitions.

Also note that our notion of responsibility is *free* of any moral connotation. The family member who has not poisoned the driver is as responsible for a crash (i.e. state $\{q_2\}$) as Driver 1 and Driver 2; although, intuitively poisoning should not be a serious alternative.

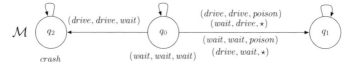

Fig. 1. The CGS $\mathcal{M}_1 = (\{1,2,3\}, \{q_0, q_1, q_2\}, \{drive, wait, poison\}, d, o)$ where $d_1(q_0) = d_2(q_0) = \{drive, wait\}$, $d_3(q_0) = \{poison, wait\}$ and $d_i(q) = \{wait\}$ for all $i \in \{1,2,3\}$ and $q \in \{q_1, q_2\}$. The outcome function o is shown in the figure, e.g. $o(q_0, (drive, drive, wait)) = q_2$. The star $\star$ represents any available action, i.e. $\star \in \{wait, poison\}$.

3.2 Degrees of Responsibility: Crucial and Necessary Coalitions

Responsible as well as weakly responsible coalitions have the preclusive power to prevent a specific state of affairs. A natural question is whether all members of a coalition are equally responsible or if it is possible to assign different degrees of responsibility to subcoalitions of agents.

Crucial Coalitions. Firstly, we consider subcoalitions of a responsible coalition which cannot be replaced by other coalitions without losing their status of being responsible. We call such responsible subcoalition the crucially responsible coalition, or simply, a crucial coalition.

Definition 3 (Crucial coalition). *Let C be (weakly) q-responsible for S in $\mathcal{M}$. We say that a (sub)coalition $\hat{C} \subseteq C$ is q-crucial for S in C and $\mathcal{M}$ iff for all coalitions $C' \subseteq N$, if $(C \backslash \hat{C}) \cup C'$ is weakly q-responsible for S then $\hat{C} \subseteq C'$.*

Example 2. Let $N = \{1,2,3,4\}$ and $\mathcal{M} = (N, \{q_0, q_1, q_2\}, \{1,2\}, d, o)$ with $d(q_0) = \{1,2\}$, $d_i(q_2) = d_i(q_1) = \{1\}$, and $d_i(q_1) = d_i(q_2) = \emptyset$ where $i \in N$. The transition function is defined as follows $o(q_0, (1,1,1,\star)) = o(q_0, (\star, 2, \star, 2)) = q_2$, and $o(q_0, \alpha) = q_1$ for $\alpha \in d_N(q_0) \backslash \{(1,1,1,\star), (\star, 2, \star, 2)\}$ where $\star \in \{1,2\}$. We have that $C_1 = \{1,2,3\}$ and $C_2 = \{2,4\}$ are the weakly q_0-responsible coalitions for $S = \{q_1\}$. We also have that all subsets of C_1 except $\{1,3\}$ and $\{1,2,3\}$ are q_0-crucial for S in C_1. For example, to see that $\hat{C} = \{2,3\}$ is q_0-crucial for S in C_1, we have to check if for all $C' \subseteq N$ it holds that if $(\{1,2,3\} \backslash \{2,3\}) \cup C'$ is weakly q_0-responsible for S in C_1 (i.e., if $\{1\} \cup C' \in \{C_1, C_2\}$), then $\hat{C} = \{2,3\} \subseteq C'$. Clearly, the antecedent is only true if C' equals $\{2,3\}$ or $\{1,2,3\}$. In both cases we have that $\hat{C} \subseteq C'$. As the previous case shows, we can replace $\hat{C}$ by $C' = \{2, 4\}$ in C_1 and the resulting coalition can q-enforce $\bar{S}$; though, it is not minimal. Moreover, note that $\hat{C}$ is not q_0-crucial for S in C_2 because it can be replaced by $\{2\}$. Similarly, we have that $\{1\}$, $\{2\}$, and $\{1, 2\}$ are q_0-crucial for S in C_1. $\{1\}$ and $\{2\}$ are q_0-crucial for S in C_2. To some extend one may argue that $\{2\}$ is more responsible than $\{2, 3\}$ as it is crucial in C_1 as well as in C_2. We will further discuss the latter statement.

Note that a weakly responsible coalition can have several crucial subcoalitions, i.e., in general a crucial coalition is not unique. In the following proposition we analyze some properties of crucial coalitions.

(i) The first property states that subcoalitions that are crucial for a weakly responsible coalition are characteristic for the weakly responsible coalition, i.e., they cannot be replaced to form a different weakly responsible coalition. (ii) The second property states that cruciality is closed under subset relation in the sense that crucial coalitions of one (weak) responsible coalition cannot have non-crucial subcoalitions. (iii) The third property states that the intersection of all weakly responsible coalitions is always crucial for all these weakly responsible coalitions. Note that the empty coalition is always crucial. (iv) The fourth property states that cruciality is not closed under union, i.e., the union of two crucial coalition is not necessarily crucial. (v) The fifth property states that the proper subsets of non-overlapping weakly responsible coalitions are crucial while the weakly responsible coalitions themselves are not crucial when there is more than one. (vi) Finally, the sixth property states that the subtraction of weakly responsible coalitions is not a crucial coalition.

Proposition 3 (Properties). *Let C be weakly q-responsible for S in $\mathcal{M}$ and $\hat{C}$ be q-crucial for S in C.*

1. *For any $C' \subseteq N$ such that $(C\backslash\hat{C}) \cup C'$ is weakly q-responsible for S we have that $\hat{C} \subseteq C' \subseteq C$; hence, $(C\backslash\hat{C}) \cup C' = C$.*
2. *Any subcoalition $\hat{C}' \subseteq \hat{C}$ is q-crucial for S in C. In particular, this shows that cruciality is closed under intersection and subtraction: if $\hat{C}_1$ and $\hat{C}_2$ are q-crucial for S in C; then, so is $\hat{C}_1 \cap \hat{C}_2$, $\hat{C}_1\backslash\hat{C}_2$, and $\hat{C}_2\backslash\hat{C}_1$.*
3. *Let W be the set of all weakly q-responsible coalitions for S. Then, $\bigcap W$ is q-crucial for S for all coalitions in W.*
4. *Given another q-crucial coalition $\hat{C}'$ for S in C the union $\hat{C}\cup\hat{C}'$ is not necessarily q-crucial for S in C.*
5. *Let W be the set of all weakly q-responsible coalitions for S such that for all $C_i, C_j \in W$ with $i \neq j$ it holds $C_i \cap C_j = \emptyset$. Then, every strict subcoalition $\hat{C} \subset C \in W$ is q-crucial for S in C. Moreover, if $|W| > 1$, then coalition $C \in W$ is not q-crucial for S in C.*
6. *If C_1 and C_2 are weakly q-responsible coalitions for S in $\mathcal{M}$ and $C_1 \setminus C_2 \neq \emptyset$ and $C_1 \neq \emptyset \neq C_2$, then $C_1 \setminus C_2$ is not q-crucial for S in C_1.*

Proof. **1.** By definition $\hat{C} \subseteq C'$. Now suppose that $C' \not\subseteq C$. Then, $Y := C'\backslash C \neq \emptyset$. We have $C = (C\backslash\hat{C}) \cup (C'\backslash Y) \subsetneq (C\backslash\hat{C}) \cup C'$. This shows that $(C\backslash\hat{C}) \cup C'$ is not a minimal coalition that can q-enforce S; hence, it is not weakly q-responsible for S. Contradiction! **2.** Clearly, this is the case for $\hat{C}' = \hat{C}$. Now, suppose there is a coalition

$\hat{C}' \subsetneq \hat{C}$ which is not q-crucial for S in C. Then, there is $C' \subseteq N$ such that $\hat{C}' \not\subseteq C'$ and $(C \backslash \hat{C}') \cup C'$ is weakly q-responsible for S in C. Let $Y := C' \backslash \hat{C}'$. We have that $Y \not\subseteq C$; for, if $Y \subseteq C$ then $(C \backslash \hat{C}') \cup C' \subsetneq C$. This would contradict the minimality of C. We define $D := (\hat{C} \backslash \hat{C}') \cup C'$. Because $Y \not\subseteq C$ we have $\hat{C} \not\subseteq D$. Moreover, $(C \backslash \hat{C}) \cup D = (C \backslash \hat{C}') \cup C'$ is weakly q-responsible for S. But this implies that $\hat{C}$ cannot be q-crucial for S in C. Contradiction! **3.** Suppose $\bigcap W$ is not q-crucial for S in $C \in W$. Then, there is $C' \subseteq N$, such that $(C \backslash \bigcap W) \cup C'$ is weakly q-responsible for S and $\bigcap W \not\subseteq C'$. But this contradicts $\bigcap W \subseteq (C \backslash \bigcap W) \cup C' \in W$. **4.** To see that consider the q_0-crucial coalitions $\{1,2\}$ and $\{2,3\}$ for S in C_1 from Example 2. The union equals $C_1 = \{1,2,3\}$ which is not q_0-crucial coalitions for S in C. **5.** Suppose $\hat{C} \subset C \in W$ is not q-crucial for S in C, i.e., for some $C' \subseteq N$ it holds that $(C \backslash \hat{C}) \cup C'$ is weakly q-responsible for S in C and $\hat{C} \not\subseteq C'$. We make the following case distinction: 1) $(C \backslash \hat{C}) \cup C' = C$ and 2) $(C \backslash \hat{C}) \cup C' = C^* \neq C$ for some $C^* \in W$. In the first case we have $\hat{C} \subseteq C'$. Contradiction. In the second case, we must have $\hat{C} = C$ and $C' = C^*$ because C^* and C are disjoint by assumption. This also yields a contradiction because we have assumed that $\hat{C} \subset C$. Now, let $C, C' \in W$ with $C \neq C'$ (note, by Proposition 2 no set can be empty). If C is q-crucial for S in C; then $C \subseteq C'$ because $C' = (C \backslash C) \cup C'$ is weakly q-responsible for S. But this is a contraction as C and C' are disjoint. **6.** Suppose $C_1 \setminus C_2$ were q-crucial for S in C_1. This implies that for all $C' \subseteq N$ it holds that if $(C_1 \setminus (C_1 \setminus C_2)) \cup C'$ is weakly q-responsible for S, then $(C_1 \setminus C_2) \subseteq C'$. Now take $C' = C_2$. By assumption $(C_1 \setminus (C_1 \setminus C_2)) \cup C_2 = C_2$ is weakly q-responsible for S in C_1. But we have $(C_1 \setminus C_2) \not\subseteq C_2$. Contradiction! □

The next lemma gives a characterization of responsible coalitions. As expected from Proposition 1 a responsible coalition consists only of crucial subcoalitions.

Lemma 1. *Coalition C is q-responsible for S in $\mathcal{M}$ iff every (sub)coalition $\hat{C} \subseteq C$ is q-crucial for S in C and $\mathcal{M}$.*

Proof. "⇒": Suppose C is q-responsible for S and there is a subcoalition $\hat{C} \subseteq C$ which is not q-crucial for S in C. Then, there is an C' with $\hat{C} \not\subseteq C'$ such that $(C \backslash \hat{C}) \cup C'$ is weakly q-responsible for S. This means that $(C \backslash \hat{C}) \cup C'$ can q-enforce $\bar{S}$ and that $(\star)$ $C \not\subseteq (C \backslash \hat{C}) \cup C'$ which contradicts the assumption that C is q-responsible for S. To see that $(\star)$ holds, we consider the following cases. (i) If $C' \subsetneq \hat{C}$ then $(C \backslash \hat{C}) \cup C' \subsetneq C$; hence, $(\star)$. (ii) Let $Y := C' \backslash \hat{C} \neq \emptyset$. If $Y \subseteq C$ then $(C \backslash \hat{C}) \cup C' \subsetneq C$; hence, $(\star)$; else, if $Y \not\subseteq C$ then $(C \backslash \hat{C}) \cup C' \not\subseteq C$. Hence, if it would be the case that $C \subseteq (C \backslash \hat{C}) \cup C'$ then also $C \subsetneq (C \backslash \hat{C}) \cup C'$. But this contradicts the minimality of $(C \backslash \hat{C}) \cup C'$ that has to hold because $(C \backslash \hat{C}) \cup C'$ is weakly q-responsible for S.

"⇐": Suppose every (sub)coalition $\hat{C} \subseteq C$ is q-crucial for S in C and that C is not q-responsible for S. Then, there is another coalition C' which can q-enforce $\bar{S}$ and $C \not\subseteq C'$. Let $C'' \subseteq C'$ be the coalition that is q-weakly responsible for S (it has to exist!). However, this means that C is not q-crucial for S in C, because $(C \backslash C) \cup C'' = C''$. This contradicts the assumption that every subset of C is crucial! □

Thanks to the previous lemma and Proposition 3.2 we obtain the following result relating responsible coalitions with crucial ones.

Proposition 4 (Characterization of responsibility). *A coalition C is q-responsible for S iff C is q-crucial for S in C.*

Proof. If C is q-responsible for S then C is q-crucial for S in C by Lemma 1. On the other hand, if C is q-crucial for S in C then any subcoalition is q-crucial for S in C by Proposition 3.2. Then, by Lemma 1 we can deduce that C is q-responsible for S. □

Necessary Coalitions. We consider subcoalitions of responsible coalitions with stronger properties. The notion of *necessary coalition* is stronger than the one of crucial coalitions in the sense that they are an indispensable part of any replacing coalition which maintains the preclusive power. This is realized by relaxing the condition of weak responsibility underlying the concept of cruciality.

Definition 4 (Necessary coalition). *Let C be (weakly) q-responsible for S. We say that a (sub)coalition $\hat{C} \subseteq C$ is q-necessary for S in C iff for all coalitions $C' \subseteq N$ it holds that if $(C \backslash \hat{C}) \cup C'$ can q-enforce $\bar{S}$ we have that $\hat{C} \subseteq C'$.*

Example 3. We continue Example 2. The coalition $\{2\}$ is q_0-necessary for S in C_1 as well as in C_2. Now, let C be any weakly q_0-responsible coalition for $\{q_2\}$ of Example 1. Then, the only q_0-crucial and q_0-necessary coalition of C is $\emptyset$. Intuitively, this shows that all coalitions are "equally responsible" in a colloquial sense.

Proposition 5 (Properties). *Let C be weakly q-responsible for S and $\hat{C}$ be q-necessary for S in C.*

1. *For any other coalition C' which is weakly q-responsible for S we have that $\hat{C} \subseteq C \cap C'$.*
2. *Let C' be another weakly q-responsible coalition for S. Then, $\hat{C}$ is q-necessary for S in C'.*
3. *$\hat{C}$ is q-crucial for S in C.*
4. *Given another q-necessary coalition $\hat{C}'$ for S in C the union $\hat{C} \cup \hat{C}'$ is also q-necessary for S in C.*

Proof. **1.** Let C and C' be two different weakly q-responsible coalitions for S as stated in the proposition. Any supercoalition of C' can q-enforce $\bar{S}$, in particular also $(C \backslash \hat{C}) \cup C'$. Because $\hat{C}$ is q-necessary for S in C we have $\hat{C} \subseteq C'$ which proves that $\hat{C} \subseteq C \cap C'$. **2.** By Proposition 5.1, $\hat{C} \subseteq C'$. Now suppose that $\hat{C}$ were not q-necessary for S in C'. Then, there is a coalition $C'' \subseteq N$, such that $\hat{C} \not\subseteq C''$ and $(C' \backslash \hat{C}) \cup C''$ can q-enforce $\bar{S}$. We have that $\hat{C} \not\subseteq (C' \backslash \hat{C}) \cup C''$. Moreover, $(C \backslash \hat{C}) \cup ((C' \backslash \hat{C}) \cup C'')$ can q-enforce $\bar{S}$. But this contradicts that $\hat{C}$ is q-necessary for S in C. **3.** Suppose $\hat{C}$ is not q-crucial for S in C. Then, there is an $C' \subseteq N$ such that $(C \backslash \hat{C}) \cup C'$ is weakly q-responsible for S and $\hat{C} \not\subseteq C'$. However, in particular $(C \backslash \hat{C}) \cup C'$ can q-enforce $\bar{S}$. This contradicts the assumption that $\hat{C}$ is q-necessary for S in C. **4.** Suppose that $\hat{C} \cup \hat{C}'$ were not q-necessary for S in C. Then, there is an $C' \subseteq N$ such that $(C \backslash (\hat{C} \cup \hat{C}')) \cup C'$ can q-enforce $\bar{S}$ and $\hat{C} \cup \hat{C}' \not\subseteq C'$. Then, $\hat{C} \not\subseteq C'$ or $\hat{C}' \not\subseteq C'$. Without loss of generality, assume that $\hat{C} \not\subseteq C'$. Because $(C \backslash (\hat{C} \cup \hat{C}')) \cup C'$ can q-enforce $\bar{S}$ we also have that $(C \backslash \hat{C}) \cup C'$ can q-enforce $\bar{S}$. But this means that $\hat{C}$ cannot be q-necessary for S in C. Contradiction! □

In particular, note that every necessary coalition is crucial and that necessary coalitions are closed under union which is not the case for crucial coalitions.

3.3   The Most Responsible Coalition

In this section we study a special type of necessary coalition, the *most responsible coalition*. In principle there can be many coalitions that are crucial or necessary for a weakly responsible coalition. In Proposition 5.2 we have shown that a coalition necessary for *some* weakly responsible coalition is necessary for *all* weakly responsible coalitions. In the next theorem we show that each weakly responsible coalition has a largest necessary coalition and that this is actually the largest necessary coalition in all weakly responsible coalitions. Hence, members of this coalition may be seen as more responsible than other members as they are part of all possible coalitions that can prevent a specific state of affairs.

Theorem 1 (Uniqueness). *Let coalition C be weakly q-responsible for S. Then, there is a unique maximal q-necessary coalition C^u for S in C and this coalition is also the unique maximal q-necessary coalition for S in any other coalition which is weakly q-responsible for S. In particular, if C is q-responsible for S then $C^u = C$.*

Proof. Let W be the set of all weakly q-responsible coalitions for S. By Proposition 5.4, each $C \in W$ has a largest q-necessary coalition for S in C. By Proposition 5.2 a q-necessary coalition for S for some coalition in W is q-necessary coalition for S for all coalitions in W. The claim follows.   □

Definition 5 (Most responsible coalition). *We call the coalition C^u from Theorem 1 the* most q-responsible coalition for S.

In Proposition 5.3 we have shown that every necessary coalition is also crucial. Note, that the reverse is not necessarily true. The following lemma is important for our Characterization Theorem and shows that a coalition that is crucial in *all* weakly responsible coalitions is also necessary.

Lemma 2. *Suppose $\hat{C}$ is q-crucial for S in all weakly q-responsible coalitions for S. Then, $\hat{C}$ is q-necessary for S in all weakly q-responsible coalitions for S.*

Proof. Suppose the claim is false; then there is a weakly q-responsible coalitions C for S such that $\hat{C}$ is not q-necessary for S in C. Hence, there is a coalition $C' \subseteq N$ such that $(C \backslash \hat{C}) \cup C'$ can q-enforce S and $\hat{C} \not\subseteq C'$. Then, there also is a weakly q-responsible coalition $C'' \subseteq (C \backslash \hat{C}) \cup C'$ with $\hat{C} \not\subseteq C''$. Contradiction, as $\hat{C}$ is q-crucial for S for all weakly q-responsible coalitions for S by assumption.   □

Finally, we show that exactly the agents that are part of all weakly responsible coalitions form the most responsible coalition which nicely matches with the intuition that these agents can be seen more responsible than others.

Theorem 2 (Characterization: most responsible coalition). *Let W be the set of all (weakly) q-responsible coalitions for S. The most q-responsible coalition C^u for S equals $\bigcap W$.*

Proof. Let C^u denote the most q-responsible coalition for S. "$C^u \subseteq \bigcap W$": By definition C^u is a member of any weakly q-responsible coalition $\overline{C \text{ for } S}$ which shows that $C^u \subseteq \bigcap W$. "$\bigcap W \subseteq C^u$": $\bigcap W$ is q-crucial for S in any $C \in W$ by Proposition 3.3. Thanks to Lemma 2 we have that $\bigcap W$ is also q-necessary for S. Then, because C^u is the largest q-necessary coalition in each weakly q-responsible coalition we have $\bigcap W \subseteq C^u$ by Theorem 2.   □

Example 4. We continue Example 3. The coalition $\{2\}$ is the most q-responsible coalition for S. In Example 1, the most q_0-responsible coalition for $\{s_2\}$ is $\emptyset$ (cf. Example 3).

3.4   Evidence Sets and Responsibility

If a coalition C is q-responsible for S and we collect some evidence A by either observing or being informed about some of the agents' actions in q, then we can ask whether C can be held responsible for S in q under the collected evidence A. Moreover, we can ask which particular agents in C can be held responsible for S in q under the collected evidence A. On the other hand, we can ask which (minimal set of) evidence needs to be collected to hold a coalition or particular agents responsible for S in q.

The intuition for *holding* a group of agents responsible under an evidence set is as follows. Suppose a group C of agents is (weakly) q-responsible for some states S in a model $\mathcal{M}$ because they have actions that prevent the state of affairs S, i.e., C can prevent S in state q of $\mathcal{M}$. In Example 2 the group $C_2 = \{2, 4\}$ is weakly q_0-responsible for $S = \{q_1\}$ as they can prevent S by performing action 2. Suppose we have evidence that some agents have performed some actions. For example, we have evidence that agent 4 has performed action 1. This evidence can be used to modify the model $\mathcal{M}$ by removing the transitions that are inconsistent with the evidence, i.e., those transitions that contradict the evidence are removed from $\mathcal{M}$. In our example, we can remove actions $(*, *, *, 2)$ from the model presented in Example 2.

Now, the idea is that if the group C of agents is not (weakly) q-responsible for the states S in the modified model any more, then some of the agents from which the evidence is collected have decided not to prevent S such that these agents can be held responsible for S. In our example, agent 4 has performed action 1 which does not ensure the prevention of q_2. It has to be emphasized that the statement "C can be held responsible for S in q under the collected evidence" should be interpreted as "the evidence suggests that C has acted irresponsibly or incautious" since C has not performed actions to prevent S. This interpretation is aligned with the following quote on responsibility: "*It is not only for what we do that we are held responsible, but also for what we do not do*". It should also be stressed that under this interpretation it is not necessarily the case that S is actually being realized such that C cannot be held accountable or blameworthy for S in q. In our example, the evidence that agent 4 has performed action 1 does not imply that state q_1 is realized. The collected evidence indicates that C_2 is not q-responsible for S any more which means that in q the agent group C_2 has no preclusive power for S any more.

Formally, we assume that we are given an *evidence set* $A \subseteq Q \times N \times Act$ of (occurred) events. A tuple (q, i, α_i) states that agent i has executed action α_i in state q. We assume that our information is correct; that is, for all states q and players i there is at most one tuple $(q, i, \alpha) \in A$ and if such a tuple exists that $\alpha \in d_i(q)$. Given an evidence set A, we use $\mathcal{M}|_A$ to denote the update of model $\mathcal{M}$ that is obtained by removing all transitions not consistent with A from $\mathcal{M}$. Note that the update operation here is considered as a meta-model operation.

Definition 6. *Let coalition C be (weakly) q-responsible for S in $\mathcal{M}$ and A be an evidence set. The coalition C can be held responsible for S in q under evidence A if C is not (weakly) q-responsible for S in $\mathcal{M}|_A$. Moreover, a subset $A' \subseteq A$ is said to be a relevant evidence set of A for coalition C with respect to S and $\mathcal{M}$ (i.e., C can be held responsible for S in $\mathcal{M}$ based on A') iff A' is a minimal subset of A such that C is not (weakly) q-responsible for S in $\mathcal{M}|_{A'}$ but it is (weakly) q-responsible for S in $\mathcal{M}|_{A \setminus A'}$.*

Let $\mathcal{A}$ be the set of all possible evidence sets and $Ag : \mathcal{A} \to 2^N$ be a function that determines the agents from which evidence is collected. The following proposition states that the evidence under which an agent can be held responsible should be about the agent's actions. The result follows directly from the fact that the loss of preclusive power of an agent group can only be due to their own actions, and not the actions of other agents.

Proposition 6. *Let coalition C be (weakly) q-responsible for S in $\mathcal{M}$ and A be an evidence set. (1) If C is not (weakly) q-responsible for S in $\mathcal{M}|_A$, then $Ag(A) \cap C \neq \emptyset$. (2) If $A' \subseteq A$ is a relevant evidence set for coalition C in $\mathcal{M}$, then $Ag(A') \subseteq C$.*

An implication of the above is that in order to hold a coalition responsible, one needs to collect evidence against at least one of the agents involved in the coalition. It should be noted that our aim was not to characterize the concept of "responsibility under evidence" in the proposed framework as it involves a meta-model update operation. Of course, our framework can be extended to make this possible, but we leave an elaboration on this concept for future work.

3.5 Reasoning about Responsibility
In the previous section we have introduced definitions of responsibility and the notions of crucial and necessary coalitions. How can we make use of these notations? Suppose that we have observed S–nothing more, nothing less–and would like to determine which coalition(s) is (are) responsible for S. As we have no more knowledge, we consider all states leading to S. These are all states in $X_S = \{q \mid \exists \alpha_N \in d_N(q) : o(q, \alpha_N) \in S\}$. We follow a conservative strategy and only consider a coalition (weakly) responsible for S if it is (weakly) responsible for any state in X_S. That is, a coalition is (weakly) responsible for S iff it is *(weakly) X_S-responsible for S* iff it is (weakly) q-responsible for S for all $q \in X_S$. Now, if there is a coalition C which is X-responsible for S we can say that C is responsible for S because at all states in X coalition C is the unique coalition that can prevent S. Similarly, we can interpret the notions of crucial, necessary and most responsible to sets of states X.

However, it might not be fair to assign responsibility to a coalition if the agents are not aware that they can prevent S. To model this, we have introduced incomplete information models and the concept of knowledge. Thus, we say that the coalition C *knows* that it is X-responsible for S if the coalition is responsible from all states it considers possible. For this purpose we replace "C is q-responsible" by "C knows it is q-responsible" etc. This means that responsibility is not only verified from X_S but from all states $\{q' \mid q \in X_S$ and $q \sim_C q'\}$ with the limitation that only uniform strategies are considered. Knowledge and responsibility are strongly interweaved and we would like to study the connection in more depth in our future research.

4 Logical Characterization

In this section we propose a logical characterization of responsibility. Therefore, we use a slight variant of the logic *coalition logic with quantification* (CLQ) proposed in [2, in the Proof of Theorem 8][3]. The logic is an extension of *coalition logic* [13,14] that allows to quantify over coalitions with specific properties. It is worth mentioning that the quantified versions are, in the finite case, not more expressive than coalition logic but often allow for an exponentially more succinct specification [2].

4.1 Preliminaries: Coalition Logic with Quantification

Formulae of *coalition logic* [13] (over $\mathcal{P}(N)$) are given by the following grammar: $\varphi ::= p \mid \neg\varphi \mid \varphi \vee \varphi \mid [A]\varphi$ where $A \in \mathcal{P}(N)$, $\mathsf{p} \in \Pi$. We define $\langle A \rangle \varphi$ as $\neg[A]\neg\varphi$ and Boolean connectives as usual. The semantics is defined over a CGS and a state q:

$\mathcal{M}, q \models [C]\varphi$ iff there is a joint action $\alpha_C \in d_C(q)$ such that for all joint actions $\alpha_{N\setminus C} \in d_{N\setminus C}(q)$ we have that $\mathcal{M}, o(q, (\alpha_C, \alpha_{N\setminus C})) \models \varphi$

Let $\mathcal{M}$ be a CGS and q a state in it. It is easy to verify that we have that: (i) C *can q-enforce* φ iff $\mathcal{M}, q \models [C]\varphi$; (ii) C *q-controls* φ iff $\mathcal{M}, q \models [C]\varphi \wedge [C]\neg\varphi$; and (iii) C *can q-avoid* φ iff $\mathcal{M}, q \models \langle N\setminus C \rangle \neg\varphi$.

We use an extension of coalition logic, introduced in [2], that allows to quantify over coalitions. Firstly, we introduce *coalitional predicates over* $\mathcal{P}(N)$: $P ::= \mathsf{sub}(C) \mid \mathsf{super}(C) \mid \neg P \mid P \vee P$ where $C \in \mathcal{P}(N)$ is a set of agents. The semantics of these predicates is defined over $A \subseteq N$ in a straight forward way: $A \models \mathsf{sub}(C)$ iff $A \subseteq C$ and $A \models \mathsf{super}(C)$ iff $A \supseteq C$. Negation and disjunction are treated as usual. We define equality between coalitions as macro: $\mathsf{eq}(C) \equiv \mathsf{sub}(C) \wedge \mathsf{super}(C)$. Note, we assume that the coalitional symbols C have their canonical semantic meaning—we do not discern between semantic and syntactic constructs in this paper.

Now let $\mathcal{V}$ be a set of coalitional variables. We define the logic *coalition logic with quantification*[4] (CLQ) [2, in the Proof of Theorem 8] as follows:

$$\varphi ::= \psi \mid \neg\varphi \mid \varphi \vee \varphi \mid \exists X|_P \, \varphi \mid \forall X|_P \, \varphi$$

where $X \in \mathcal{V}$, P is a coalitional predicate over $\mathcal{P}(N) \cup \mathcal{V}$, and ψ a coalition logic formula over $\mathcal{V}$. Moreover, we assume that all coalitional variables are bound. As for coalition logic the semantics is given over a CGS, a state in it, and a coalition valuation $\xi : \mathcal{V} \to \mathcal{P}(N)$. We define $\xi[X := C]$ as the valuation that equals ξ for all $Y \neq X$, i.e. $\xi[X := C](Y) = \xi(Y)$, and $\xi[X := C](X) = C$. We also define a special valuation ξ_0 with $\xi_0(X) = \emptyset$ for all $X \in \mathcal{V}$. We just give the semantics for the cooperation modality and the quantifiers, all other cases are standard:

$\mathcal{M}, q, \xi \models [X]\psi$ iff there is a joint action $\alpha_{\xi(X)} \in Act_{\xi(X)}$ such that for all joint actions $\alpha_{N\setminus\xi(X)} \in Act_{N\setminus\xi(X)}$ we have that $\mathcal{M}, o(q, (\alpha_{\xi(X)}, \alpha_{N\setminus\xi(X)})), \xi \models \varphi$

---

[3] Note, that CLQ is different from the better known logic Quantified Coalition Logic (QCL) also presented in [2].

[4] We would like to note that in comparison to [2] our definition of CLQ is somewhat more general as we allow coalitional variables within coalitional predicates.

$\mathcal{M}, q, \xi \models \exists X|_P \psi$ iff there is $C \subseteq N$ such that $C, \xi[X := C] \models P$ and $\mathcal{M}, q, \xi[X := C] \models \psi$

$\mathcal{M}, q, \xi \models \forall X|_P \psi$ iff for all $C \subseteq N$ with $C, \xi[X := C] \models P$ we have that $\mathcal{M}, q, \xi[X := C] \models \psi]$

where $C, \xi \models P$ is defined as $C \models P[\xi]$ and $P[\xi]$ is obtained from P where each coalitional variable Y occurring in P is replaced by $\xi(Y)$. We simply write $\mathcal{M}, q \models \varphi$ if φ is a closed formula. For a set of states $Q' \subseteq Q$ we write $\mathcal{M}, Q', \xi \models \varphi$ iff for all $q \in Q'$ we have $\mathcal{M}, q, \xi \models \varphi$. For a closed formula φ we define $[\![\varphi]\!]_{\mathcal{M}} = \{q \in Q \mid \mathcal{M}, q \models \varphi\}$. In [2] it was shown that model checking Quantified Coalition logic (QCL) is **PSPACE**-complete over compact models and can be done in polynomial time over an explicit representation based on effectivity functions. These results do not straight-forwardly transfer to our setting as we use (i) a different representation of models, and (ii) a slightly generalized version of CLQ–which is somewhat different from QCL. A detailed study in our setting is out of the scope of this paper and we leave it for future work.

4.2 Logical Characterization of Responsibility

Given a closed formula φ, $[\![\varphi]\!]_{\mathcal{M}}$ associates to it the set of states in which φ holds. Moreover, instead of writing "C is q-responsible for $[\![\varphi]\!]_{\mathcal{M}}$ in $\mathcal{M}$", we simply say "C is q-responsible for φ (in $\mathcal{M}$)" etc. In the following we show that our notions of responsibility can be formalized within *coalition logic with quantification*. We assume that $\mathcal{M}$ is a CGS, q a state in it, C a coalition and φ a closed formula. Again, we omit mentioning $\mathcal{M}$ whenever clear from context. Firstly, we define the following two formulae:

$$R^s_C \varphi \equiv \exists X|_{eq(C)}([X]\neg\varphi \wedge \forall Y|_{\neg super(X)} \neg[Y]\neg\varphi)$$
$$R^w_C \varphi \equiv \exists X|_{eq(C)}([X]\neg\varphi \wedge \forall Y|_{\neg eq(X)\wedge sub(X)} \neg[Y]\neg\varphi)$$

Proposition 7. *C is q-responsible (resp. weakly q-responsible) for φ in $\mathcal{M}$ iff $\mathcal{M}, q \models R^s_C \varphi$ (resp. φ iff $\mathcal{M}, q \models R^w_C \varphi$).*

Proof (Sketch). We only show the case for weak responsibility. We have that $\mathcal{M}, q, \xi \models R^w_C \varphi$ iff $\mathcal{M}, q, \xi \models \exists X|_{eq(C)}([X]\neg\varphi \wedge \forall Y|_{\neg eq(X)\wedge sub(X)} \neg[Y]\neg\varphi)$ iff $\mathcal{M}, q, \xi[X := C] \models [X]\neg\varphi$ and for all C' with $C' \neq C$ and $C' \subseteq C$ we have $\mathcal{M}, q, \xi[X := C, Y := C'] \not\models [Y]\neg\varphi$ iff C can q-enforce $\neg\varphi$ and all $C' \subset C$ cannot q-enforce $\neg\varphi$ iff C can q-enforce $\neg\varphi$ and there is no subcoalition of C that can q-enforce $\neg\varphi$ iff C is a minimal coalition that can q-enforce $\neg\varphi$ iff C is weakly q-responsible for φ. □

Now, we can simply express properties as given in Proposition 2 by $\models R^s_C \varphi \to R^w_C \varphi$. We can also easily define crucial coalitions, necessary coalitions, and the most responsible coalition:

$$\text{Crucial}_{\hat{C},C}\varphi \equiv (R^s_C\varphi \vee R^w_C) \wedge \exists X_C|_{eq(C)}\exists X_{\hat{C}}|_{eq(\hat{C})}\forall X|_{\neg super(X_{\hat{C}})}\neg R^w_{(X_C\setminus X_{\hat{C}})\cup X}\varphi$$

$$\text{Nec}_{\hat{C},C}\varphi \equiv (R^s_C\varphi \vee R^w_C) \wedge \exists X_C|_{eq(C)}\exists X_{\hat{C}}|_{eq(\hat{C})}\forall X|_{\neg super(X_{\hat{C}})}\exists Y|_{eq((X_C\setminus X_{\hat{C}})\cup X)}\neg[Y]\neg\varphi$$

$$\text{Most}_{C^u}\varphi \equiv \exists X|_{sub(N)}(\text{Nec}_{C^u,X}\varphi \wedge \forall Y|_{\neg sub(C^u)}\neg\text{Nec}_{Y,X}\varphi)$$

Proposition 8. *We have that $\hat{C}$ is q-crucial (resp. q-necessary and most q-responsible) for φ in the (weakly) q-responsible coalition C for φ iff $\mathcal{M}, q \models$ Crucial$_{\hat{C},C}\varphi$ (resp. $\mathcal{M}, q \models$ Nec$_{\hat{C},C}\varphi$ and $\mathcal{M}, q \models$ Most$_C\varphi$).*

Proof (Sketch). **Cruciality:** We have that $\mathcal{M}, q, \xi \models$ Crucial$_{\hat{C},C}\varphi$ iff C is q-responsible for φ or weakly q-responsible for φ (by Proposition 7) and for all $C' \not\supseteq \hat{C}$ we have that $(C\backslash\hat{C}) \cup C'$ is not weakly q-responsible for φ iff C is q-responsible for φ or weakly q-responsible for φ and for all $C' \subseteq N$ such that if $(C\backslash\hat{C})\cup C'$ is weakly q-responsible for φ then $\hat{C} \subseteq C'$ iff $\hat{C}$ is q-crucial for φ in C.

Necessary: We have that $\mathcal{M}, q, \xi \models$ Nec$_{\hat{C},C}\varphi$ iff C is q-responsible for φ or weakly q-responsible for φ (by Proposition 7) and for all $C' \not\supseteq \hat{C}$ we have that $(C\backslash\hat{C}) \cup C'$ cannot q enforce $\neg\varphi$ iff C is q-responsible for φ or weakly q-responsible for φ and for all $C' \subseteq N$ such that if $(C\backslash\hat{C})\cup C'$ can q-enforce $\neg\varphi$ then $\hat{C} \subseteq C'$ iff $\hat{C}$ is q-necessary for φ in C.

Most responsible: Now, let us consider the most responsible coalition. $\mathcal{M}, q, \xi \models$ Most$_{C^u}\varphi$ iff there is $C \subseteq N$ such that C^u is q-necessary for φ in C and for all $C' \not\subseteq C^u$ we have that C' is not q-necessary for φ in C iff there is $C \subseteq N$ such that C^u is the maximal coalition that is q-necessary for φ in C iff C^u is the most q-responsible coalition for φ by Theorem 1 and Definition 5. □

The logical formulation shows that our notions of responsibility are fully based on strategic ability; there are no other hidden concepts. Also, it provides a first step to reasoning about group responsibility. We leave a detailed study for future work, including a deeper analysis of epistemic concepts and meta logical properties.

5   Related Work

Existing work on formalizing responsibility can be categorized in two approaches. The first type of work considers backward-looking responsibility formalized in dynamic logic while the second type of work considers forward-looking responsibility formalized in deontic and STIT logics. In the following, we provide an example of each approach.

Grossi et al. [8] investigate the concept of responsibility in an organizational setting where role playing agents operate within organizational structures defined by power, coordination and control relations. They distinguish causal and task-based responsibility, and investigate when agents in an organization can be held accountable for or be blamed for some (undesirable) state of affairs. For example, an agent A who delegates a task to an agent B using its organizational power can be held responsible for the failure of performing the task even though agent B has actually failed in performing the task. In order to formalize these notions of responsibility, they propose a dynamic deontic logic framework in which agents' activities as well as the organizational setting are specified. In this framework, an agent is defined to be causally responsible for ϕ by performing action α if and only if ϕ is the necessary effect of α and moreover ϕ would not have been the case if α was not performed. An agent is then said to be causally blameworthy (backward-looking responsible) if the agent is casually responsible for a violation and the agent knows that his/her action would cause the violation which he could prevent by not performing the action. The task-based responsibility (forward-looking responsibil-'ity) is defined in terms of organizational tasks/plans that the agent is obliged to perform. Finally, an agent is said to be accountable for a violation caused by performing an action α if the agent is blameworthy for performing α causing the violation and moreover if the agent is task-responsible to perform α.

The characterizing feature of this approach is the formalization of different notions of responsibility in the context of organizational structures. The formalization of causal and task-based responsibility are defined with respect to individual agents and based on violation of an agent's obligations.

Another formal framework for analyzing the concept of (forward-looking) responsibility is proposed by Mastop [11]. The main focus of this work is the normative dimension of the "many hands problem", which is formulated as the problem of attributing the responsibility for the violation of a global norm to individual agents. This is a challenging problem because agents may not be responsible for the violation of a global norm even when they clearly violate their individual norms and thereby cause the violation of the global norm. The problem with attributing responsibility in such cases is argued to be the fairness issue. The fairness considered in this work is explained in terms of conditions such as "agents should be able to obey their individual norms", "agents should be aware of their individual norms", or "the violation of individual norms should be intentional and caused by some accidents". The framework is based on an extension of the XSTIT logic with intentions [5]. This logic is extended with, among other things, a set of designated constants denoting the responsibility of agents. The semantics of the extended XSTIT framework explicitly attributes to each agent a set of possibilities (history-state pairs) in which the agent fulfills all of its responsibilities (i.e., possibilities in which the agent's designated responsibility constant is true). An agent is defined to be responsible for ϕ if and only if the set of possibilities attributed to the agent satisfy ϕ. Based on this definition of forward-looking responsibility, the fairness conditions are formulated as axiom schemes. The author claims that the introduction of these axioms ensures that the responsibility of any violation of global norms can be attributed to some individuals that violate their individual norms.

In another work [7], Ciuni and Mastop, the XSTIT is used and extended to analyze the concept of distributed responsibility, i.e., the responsibility that is attributed to a group of agents. The basic problem considered in this work is to distinguish the responsibilities of individuals within a group to which a group responsibility is attributed. For example, if a group of two agents is responsible for $\phi \land \psi$, the presented framework can distinguish whether one of the agents or both are responsible for this composite fact. The characterizing feature of this approach is the explicit introduction of responsibility constants as well as their corresponding semantics counterparts, i.e., the sets of possibilities in which agents' responsibilities are fulfilled. In fact, the proposed framework is assumed to be informed about agents' responsibilities such that the main contribution of this paper is not to define the concept of responsibility itself, but the formalization of the fairness conditions in order to solve the "many hands problem".

We would like to mention three other papers in which responsibility is related to other notions such as emotions, causality, and morality. In the first paper [9], the authors use a STIT logic for counterfactual reasoning about emotions. Their characterizations are based on the group's potential power to *could have prevented* some state-of-affairs. In contrast to their setting, however, we do not assume that the state-of-affairs has actually been materialized as we do not model backward-looking responsibility. Moreover, our focus is on the inherent structure of the coalitions at hand rather than on their pure power to prevent some states of affairs. In [6] the authors argue that causality has mostly been studied as an all-or-nothing concept and propose an extension to capture the degree of responsibility and blame in causal relations. The proposed extension allows one to express that a phenomenon A is responsible (or blameworthy) for causing a phenomenon B to a certain degree depending on A's contribution in causing B. The contribution of A in causing B (the degree of A's responsibility) is determined based on some counterfactual reasoning and other factors relevant to B being caused. An obvious difference with our work is the central role of causality and the fact that responsibility and blame are directly defined in terms of causality, i.e., A is responsible for B iff A has caused B. In our work, however, a group of agents is responsible for some states, not because they have caused the states (as the states are not assumed to be materialized), but because they have the power to preclude the states. In our framework, it can even be the case that a group of agents has the power to ensure a certain outcome while a different group of agents is responsible for the outcome. In the last paper [4], the authors focus on moral responsibility and provide a set of conditions that are claimed to be necessary and sufficient for assigning moral responsibility for a certain outcome to individuals. These conditions require that an individual can be held responsible for an outcome if the individual is autonomous, has causal contribution to the outcome, and has the opportunity to avoid the outcome. Again, in contrast to our framework, this paper assumes that an outcome is materialized and that the responsible individual has causally contributed to the materialization of the outcome. Moreover, although the last condition seems to be related to our notion of precluding power for avoiding the outcome, it requires that the individual who has causally contributed to the outcome should have the power to avoid the outcome. This is different from our approach where responsible coalitions for an outcome may be unrelated to the coalition who can ensure the outcome. Finally, this paper considers only the responsibility of individuals as it aims to tackle 'the problem of many hands' while we investigate the responsibility of coalitions.

6 Conclusion and Future Work

In this paper, we provided an abstract notion of group responsibility that does not imply accountability or blameworthiness. The proposed notion of responsibility is based on the preclusive power of groups of agents and is defined as the responsibility to prevent some state of affairs. We have formalized this notion of responsibility in concurrent game structures, which model multi-agent system behaviors. Different notions of responsibility such as (weak) responsibility, crucial and necessary responsibility are formally defined and their properties are analyzed. We then presented the notion of "responsibility under evidence" according to which a group of agents can be held responsible for a state of affairs if there is evidence that they did not act to prevent the state of affairs. In this sense, it can be said that the agents have acted irresponsibly or incautiously (as they did not act to prevent the state of affairs) even if their performed actions do not cause the realization of the state of affairs that have to be prevented. The main results of this paper are formulated in the characterization theorems. Finally, we show how our notions of responsibility can be characterized as formulas of coalition logic with quantification [2].

We plan to extend this framework with different levels of agents' knowledge and intention in order to distinguish different levels of responsibilities. Such extension would also allow us to instantiate the presented abstract notion of responsibility to capture different types of responsibilities, for example accountability and blameworthiness. In such extensions, one would be able to determine if a group of agents is accountable or blameworthy for some state of affairs. We also aim at generalizing the notion of responsibility to a strategic setting as the current notion of responsibility is relativized to a specific state q such that it can only be expressed that a group of agents is q-responsible. Based on such an extension and given a realized state of affair, one would be able to reason about which agents at which states were responsible for the realization of the state of affairs. We aim at extending the framework such that group responsibility can be distributed to individual agents and elaborating on the logical characterization. Finally, it would be interesting to relate the concepts of crucial and necessary coalitions to the concept of power as discussed in [1].

References

1. Ågotnes, T., van der Hoek, W., Tennenholtz, M., Wooldridge, M.: Power in normative systems. In: AAMAS 2009: Proceedings of The 8th International Conference on Autonomous Agents and Multiagent Systems, Richland, SC, pp. 145–152. International Foundation for Autonomous Agents and Multiagent Systems (2009)
2. Ågotnes, T., van der Hoek, W., Wooldridge, M.: Quantified coalition logic. Synthese 165(2), 269–294 (2008)
3. Alur, R., Henzinger, T.A., Kupferman, O.: Alternating-time Temporal Logic. Journal of the ACM 49, 672–713 (2002)
4. Braham, M., van Hees, M.: An anatomy of moral responsibility. Mind 121(483), 601–634 (2012)
5. Broersen, J.: Deontic epistemic stit logic distinguishing modes of mens rea. Journal of Applied Logic 9(2), 137–152 (2011)
6. Chockler, H., Halpern, J.Y.: Responsibility and blame: A structural-model approach. Journal of Artificial Intelligence Research 22, 93–115 (2004)
7. Ciuni, R., Mastop, R.: Attributing distributed responsibility in stit logic. In: He, X., Horty, J., Pacuit, E. (eds.) LORI 2009. LNCS, vol. 5834, pp. 66–75. Springer, Heidelberg (2009)
8. Grossi, D., Royakkers, L.M.M., Dignum, F.: Organizational structure and responsibility. Artificial Intelligence and Law 15(3), 223–249 (2007)
9. Lorini, E., Schwarzentruber, F.: A logic for reasoning about counterfactual emotions. In: IJCAI, pp. 867–872 (2009)
10. Lucas, J.: Responsibility. Oxford University Press (1993)
11. Mastop, R.: Characterising responsibility in organisational structures: The problem of many hands. In: Governatori, G., Sartor, G. (eds.) Deontic Logic in Computer Science, 10th International Conference (DEON 2010), pp. 274–287 (2010)

12. Miller, N.R.: Power in game forms. In: Holler, M.J. (ed.) Power, Voting, and Voting Power, pp. 33–51. Physica-Verlag, Wuerzberg-Vienna (1982); Reprinted in Homo Oeconomicus 15(2), 219–243 (1999)
13. Pauly, M.: Logic for Social Software. PhD thesis, University of Amsterdam (2001)
14. Pauly, M.: A modal logic for coalitional power in games. Journal of Logic and Computation 12(1), 149–166 (2002)
15. van der Poel, I.: The relation between forward-looking and backward-looking responsibility. In: Vincent, N., van de Poel, I., van den Hoven, J. (eds.) Moral Responsibility: Beyond Free Will and Determinism, pp. 37–52. Springer (2011)
16. Vincent, N., van de Poel, I., van den Hoven, J. (eds.): Moral Responsibility: beyond free will and determinism. Library of Ethics and Applied Philosophy. Springer (2011)

Symmetries and Epistemic Reasoning

Jeffrey Kane and Pavel Naumov

Department of Mathematics and Computer Science
McDaniel College, Westminster, Maryland 21157, USA
{jmk001,pnaumov}@mcdaniel.edu

Abstract. The paper studies epistemic properties of symmetric communication protocols. It proposes a logical system describing properties common to all protocols with the same group of symmetries. This system is an extension of the standard epistemic logic S5 by a new axiom, capturing properties of symmetry in the modal language. The main results are soundness and completeness theorems for this logical system.

1 Introduction

In this paper we study epistemic properties of symmetric communication protocols. Consider, for example, a variation of the well-known telephone[1] game in which a designated player picks a word and whispers it to the player on her left. The remaining six players, in turn, whisper the word to their left neighbors, possibly modifying it, until the word comes back to the original player. Let us assume that players only use four-letter words and at most one letter is changed at each step. For this example, let us also assume that the original player announces that the word that came back is identical to the word that she sent through the circular communication chain. We are interested in describing what each player knows about the words whispered by the other players.

In this example, the first and the last words are the same, so one can simplify the setting by talking about only six players (excluding the designated player) and the six words whispered by these players. We will refer to such a six-word cyclic sequence $r = (a, b, c, d, e, f)$ as a "run" of the telephone game. Note that each two adjacent words in the run (including words f and a) differ by no more than one letter.

Let run r_1 be the sequence $(math, hath, hate, fate, date, mate)$, as shown in Figure 1. Note that each agent who knows the value of the word a on this run is able to conclude that word d is not $true$ because words a and d are only three steps apart in the circle and thus can not differ by more than three letters. We will denote this epistemic fact by

$$r_1 \Vdash \Box_a(d \neq word). \tag{1}$$

In this example and throughout the rest of the paper, we label the modality not by an agent, as common in epistemic logic, but by the information known to the agent. We have used this approach in an earlier work [1].

---

[1] This game is also known as Chinese Whispers, Grapevine, Broken Telephone, Whisper Down the Lane, and Gossip.

J. Leite et al. (Eds.): CLIMA XIV, LNAI 8143, pp. 190–205, 2013.

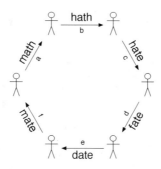

Fig. 1. Run r_1

Another example of a true epistemic property of run r_1 is

$$r_1 \Vdash \Box_b \Box_a (b \neq word), \tag{2}$$

which states that any agent who knows the value of b on this run is able to conclude that any agent who knows the value of a knows that b is not $word$. This property is true because the words $hath$ and $word$ differ by four letters.

In all prior examples, the atomic propositions were inequality statements. An example of a true epistemic property of run r_1, with a different type of atomic proposition, is

$$r_1 \Vdash \Box_b(\text{``Word } a \text{ contains at least one letter } h\text{.''}). \tag{3}$$

This property is true because the word $hath$ contains two letters h and any two adjacent words differ by no more than one letter.

Properties (1), (2), and (3) are specific to r_1. For instance, if $r_2 = (cars, caps, taps, tape, cape, care)$, then $r_2 \Vdash \Box_a (d \neq word)$ is false since any agent who knows only the value of a is not able to distinguish the run $(cars, caps, taps, tape, cape, care)$ from the run $(cars, card, cord, word, ward, wars)$. An example of an epistemic property which is true for each run of the telephone game is

$$\Vdash \Box_a(c \neq math) \rightarrow \Box_a(e \neq math). \tag{4}$$

This property is true on any run because of the symmetry in our setting. Namely, $(w_1, w_2, w_3, w_4, w_5, w_6)$ is a run of the telephone game iff $(w_1, w_6, w_5, w_4, w_3, w_2)$ is also such a run, see Figure 2. For a similar reason, the following property is true on any run of the telephone game:

$$\Vdash \Box_a \Box_b(f \neq math) \rightarrow \Box_a \Box_f(b \neq math).$$

Formally, by a symmetry of the telephone game we mean any bijection from the set $\{a, b, c, d, e, f\}$ into the same set that maps a run of the game into another run. In this paper, we will use graphical notations to describe symmetries. The symmetry τ that maps the run $(w_1, w_2, w_3, w_4, w_5, w_6)$ to the run $(w_1, w_6, w_5, w_4, w_3, w_2)$ is depicted

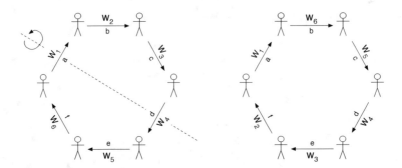

Fig. 2. Sequence $(w_1, w_2, w_3, w_4, w_5, w_6)$ is a run of the telephone game if and only if $(w_1, w_6, w_5, w_4, w_3, w_2)$ is also such a run

in Figure 3 (left). All symmetries of the telephone game protocol can be described as combinations of the rotation σ and the flip τ from Figure 3 (left). For example, symmetry μ depicted on the Figure 3 (right) is flip τ followed by rotation σ applied four times: $\sigma^4 \circ \tau$. In abstract algebra, the set of all symmetries of an object is commonly referred to as a group of symmetries of the object.

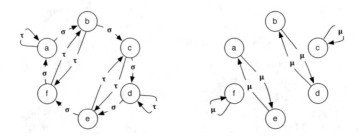

Fig. 3. Symmetries σ, τ, and μ of the telephone game, where $\mu = \sigma^4 \circ \tau$

The telephone game is just an example of what we refer to as a "protocol". Another example of a protocol is a variation of the telephone game in which any two adjacent words differ by no more than *two* letters. This protocol has the same group of symmetries as the telephone game. In this paper we investigate common epistemic properties of all protocols that have the same group of symmetries. A more general way to state property (4) for an arbitrary protocol is

$$\Vdash \Box_a p \rightarrow \Box_a q, \tag{5}$$

where p is a property of the value of c and q is a "symmetric" property of the value of e. The exact meaning of the word "symmetric" in the previous sentence will be given in Definition 3.

The main result of this work is a sound and complete axiomatization of such properties for any fixed group of symmetries. This axiomatization is an extension of a variation of the multi-modal version of epistemic logic S5 [2] by an additional axiom specific to a given group of symmetries.

Properties of symmetry in information [3] and especially in applications to model checking [4] have been studied before. The closest to our current contribution is probably our own article on symmetries and functional dependencies [5]. The setting of that work is similar to our current setting in the sense that we also studied properties of a communication protocol with a given group of symmetries and gave a sound and complete axiomatization of these properties. However, in [5] we studied properties expressible in terms of functional dependence relation and the resulting logical system has been an extension of Armstrong [6] axiomatization of functional dependence. Our current work focuses on properties expressible in an epistemic modal language and the resulting logical system is an extension of multi-modal version of S5.

2   Group Theory Terminology

In this section we review group theory vocabulary used throughout the rest of the paper.

In abstract algebra, a group is a pair $G = (A, \cdot)$, where A is an arbitrary set and $\cdot$ is an associative binary operation on A such that A contains an identity element and an inverse element for each element of Σ.

In this paper, for any fixed set X by a group acting on X we mean an arbitrary set of permutations G of X (bijections from X onto X) such that

1. G is closed with respect to composition $\circ$,
2. G contains identity function,
3. if $\sigma \in G$, then $\sigma^{-1} \in G$.

We assume $(\sigma \circ \tau)(x) = \sigma(\tau(x))$. By a stabilizer set G_x of an element x we mean the set $\{\sigma \in G \mid \sigma(x) = x\}$. In the telephone game example, G_a contains both the identity function and τ. Similarly, G_c contains the identity function and $\mu = \sigma^4 \circ \tau$. It is easy to see that G_x is itself a group. By the orbit $Orbit_G(x)$ of element $x \in X$ with respect to a group G we mean the set $\{\sigma(x) \mid \sigma \in G\}$. In the telephone game example, $Orbit_G(b)$ is the whole set $\{a, b, c, d, e, f\}$ and $Orbit_{G_a}(b)$ is the set $\{b, f\}$.

Given a set of bijections $\{\sigma_1, \ldots, \sigma_n\}$, by $\langle \sigma_1, \ldots, \sigma_n \rangle$ we mean the set of all possible finite combinations of bijections $\sigma_1, \ldots, \sigma_n$. For example, in the telephone game, $\langle \sigma, \tau \rangle$ is the entire group of symmetries of the telephone game.

If set X could be partitioned into sets Y and Z in such a way that each function in G maps Y onto Y and Z onto Z, then we say that group G acts on both Y and Z.

3   Syntax and Semantics

Definition 1. *A signature Σ is a triple $(S, \{P_a\}_{a \in S}, G)$ such that*

1. *S is an arbitrary set of variables,*
2. *$\{P_s\}_{s \in S}$ are disjoint sets of atomic propositions,*

3. G is a group acting on set S and on set $\bigcup_{s \in S} P_s$,
4. $\sigma(p) \in P_{\sigma(s)}$ for each $\sigma \in G$ and each $p \in P_s$,
5. $\sigma(p) = p$ for each $s \in S$, each $p \in P_s$, and each $\sigma \in G_s$.

For example, in the telephone game, the set S is $\{a, b, c, d, e, f\}$. Atomic propositions in the set P_a are meant to represent various statements about variable a. Examples of such statements for the telephone game are "word a contains at least one letter h" and $a \neq math$. Similarly, atomic propositions in set P_b meant to represent various statements about variable b such as "b contains two vowels" or even "b is a palindrome". Group G in the telephone game is $\langle \sigma, \tau \rangle$ and is known in abstract algebra as the dihedral group of order 12.

Next, for any signature Σ we define the set of formulas $\Phi(\Sigma)$. These formulas represent the properties of the protocols with signature Σ that we consider.

Definition 2. *For any signature Σ, let set $\Phi(\Sigma)$ be the smallest set such that*

1. $\perp \in \Phi(\Sigma)$,
2. $P_a \subseteq \Phi(\Sigma)$, *for each $a \in S$,*
3. $\varphi \to \psi \in \Phi(\Sigma)$, *for each $\varphi, \psi \in \Phi(\Sigma)$,*
4. $\Box_a \varphi \in \Phi(\Sigma)$, *for each $a \in S$ and each $\varphi \in \Phi(\Sigma)$.*

Definition 3. *A (symmetric) protocol over a signature $(S, \{P_a\}_{a \in S}, G)$ is any triple (V, R, Tr) such that*

1. $V(a)$ *is an arbitrary set of "possible values" of $a \in S$ such that if $a \in Orbit_G(b)$, then $V(a) = V(b)$,*
2. R *is an arbitrary set of functions (called "runs") such that any function $r \in R$ maps each $a \in S$ into an element of $V(a)$ and $r \circ \sigma \in R$ for each $\sigma \in G$,*
3. Tr *is an "atomic truth" predicate such that*
   (a) $Tr \subseteq \bigcup_{a \in S}(V(a) \times P_a)$ *and*
   (b) Tr *is symmetric in the sense that $(v, p) \in Tr$ if and only if $(v, \sigma(p)) \in Tr$, for each $a \in S$, $p \in P_a$, $\sigma \in G$, and $v \in V_a = V_{\sigma(a)}$.*

We will abbreviate $(v, p) \in Tr$ as $Tr(v, p)$. In the telephone game example, $V(a)$, $V(b)$, ..., $V(f)$ are all equal to the set of all four-letter words. Atomic truth predicate $Tr(v, p)$ specifies whether an atomic proposition $p \in P_a$ is true for a specific value v of variable a. For example, proposition $p = $ "word a is a palindrome" is true if $v = noon$ but is false if $v = noun$.

Definition 4. *For any run $r \in R$ of a protocol (V, R, Tr) over a signature $\Sigma = (S, \{P_a\}_{a \in S}, G)$ and any formula $\varphi \in \Phi(\Sigma)$, we define relation $r \Vdash \varphi$ recursively:*

1. $r \nVdash \perp$,
2. $r \Vdash p$ *for $p \in P_a$ if $Tr(r(a), p)$,*
3. $r \Vdash \varphi_1 \to \varphi_2$ *if $r \nVdash \varphi_1$ or $r \Vdash \varphi_2$,*
4. $r \Vdash \Box_a \psi$ *if $r' \Vdash \psi$ for all $r' \in R$ such that $r'(a) = r(a)$.*

Definition 5. *For any signature $\Sigma = (S, \{P_s\}_{s \in S}, G)$ and any $\sigma \in G$, we extend σ from acting on set S and set $\bigcup_{s \in S} P_s$ to acting on set S and set $\Phi(\Sigma)$ as follows:*

1. $\sigma(\bot) = \bot$,
2. $\sigma(\psi_1 \to \psi_2) = \sigma(\psi_1) \to \sigma(\psi_2)$,
3. $\sigma(\Box_a \psi) = \Box_{\sigma(a)} \sigma(\psi)$.

Furthermore, we assume that $\sigma \in G$ also acts on sets of formulas in $\Phi(\Sigma)$ in such a way that $\sigma(X) = \{\sigma(\psi) \mid \psi \in X\}$.

4   Axioms

1. Distributivity: $\Box_a(\varphi \to \psi) \to (\Box_a \varphi \to \Box_a \psi)$,
2. Reflexivity: $\Box_a \varphi \to \varphi$,
3. Transitivity: $\Box_a \varphi \to \Box_a \Box_a \varphi$,
4. Euclideanity: $\neg \Box_a \varphi \to \Box_a \neg \Box_a \varphi$,
5. Self-Awareness: $p \to \Box_a p$ if $p \in P_a$,
6. Stability: $\Box_a \sigma(\varphi) \to \Box_a \varphi$, where $\sigma \in G_a$.

We write $\vdash_\Sigma \varphi$ if $\varphi \in \Phi(\Sigma)$ is provable from the axioms above and propositional tautologies in the language $\Phi(\Sigma)$ using the Modus Ponens inference rule and the Necessitation inference rule:

$$\frac{\varphi}{\Box_a \varphi}.$$

We write $X \vdash_\Sigma \varphi$ if φ is provable from the *theorems* of our logical system using only Modus Ponens rule and the additional set of axioms X. We will omit the subscript Σ when its value is clear from the context.

Lemma 1. *For each $\varphi \in \Phi(\Sigma)$, each $X \subseteq \Phi(\Sigma)$ and each $\sigma \in G$, if $X \vdash \varphi$, then $\sigma(X) \vdash \sigma(\varphi)$.*

Proof. Induction on the length of the proof of φ. If φ is an axiom, then $\sigma(\varphi)$ is also an axiom. If φ is derived from ψ and $\psi \to \varphi$ by Modus Ponens rule, then $\sigma(\varphi)$ could be derived from $\sigma(\psi)$ and $\sigma(\psi \to \varphi)$ by Modus Ponens rule because $\sigma(\psi \to \varphi) = \sigma(\psi) \to \sigma(\varphi)$ due to Definition 5. $\qquad\Box$

5   Examples

Soundness and completeness of our logical system will be established later in this paper. In this section we give several examples of proofs in our logical system. We will start with property (5) from the introduction.

Proposition 1. *Let $p \in P_c$ and $q \in P_e$. If group $G = \langle \sigma, \tau \rangle$ is acting, as shown on Figure 3, on set $S = \{a, b, c, d, e, f\}$, and additionally $\tau(q) = p$, then*

$$\vdash \Box_a p \to \Box_a q.$$

Proof. Note that $\tau(a) = a$. Hence, $\tau \in G_a$. Thus, by the Stability axiom, $\Box_a \tau(q) \to \Box_a q$. Therefore, $\Box_a p \to \Box_a q$. $\qquad\Box$

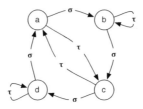

Fig. 4. Group $\langle \sigma, \tau \rangle$ acting on set $\{a, b, c, d\}$

Proposition 2. *Let* $p \in P_b$ *and* $q \in P_d$. *If group* $G = \langle \sigma, \tau \rangle$ *is acting, as shown on Figure 4, on set* $S = \{a, b, c, d\}$, *and additionally* $\sigma^2(q) = p$, *then*

$$\vdash \Box_a p \to \Box_a q.$$

Proof. Note that $\tau \circ \sigma^2 \in G_a$. Thus, by the Stability axiom,

$$\vdash \Box_a (\tau \circ \sigma^2) q \to \Box_a q.$$

Due to our assumptions, $\sigma^2(q) = p$. In addition, by part 5 of Definition 1, $\tau(p) = p$. Hence, $(\tau \circ \sigma^2) q = p$. Therefore, $\vdash \Box_a p \to \Box_a q$.   □

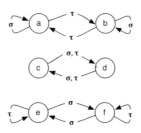

Fig. 5. Group $\langle \sigma, \tau \rangle$ acting on set $\{a, b, c, d, e, f\}$

Proposition 3. *Let* $p \in P_c$ *and* $q \in P_d$. *If group* $G = \langle \sigma, \tau \rangle$ *is acting, as shown on Figure 5, on set* $S = \{a, b, c, d, e, f\}$, *and additionally* $\sigma(q) = p$ *and* $\tau(p) = q$, *then*

$$\vdash \Box_a \Box_e p \to \Box_a \Box_f p.$$

Proof. Since $\sigma \in G_a$, by the Stability axiom,

$$\vdash \Box_a (\sigma(\Box_f q)) \to \Box_a \Box_f q.$$

In other words,

$$\vdash \Box_a \Box_e p \to \Box_a \Box_f q. \tag{6}$$

At the same time, $\tau \in G_f$. Thus, by the Stability axiom,

$$\vdash \Box_f(\tau(p)) \to \Box_f p.$$

Hence,

$$\vdash \Box_f q \to \Box_f p.$$

Thus, by the Necessitation rule,

$$\vdash \Box_a(\Box_f q \to \Box_f p).$$

By the Distributivity axiom,

$$\vdash \Box_a \Box_f q \to \Box_a \Box_f p.$$

Finally, taking into account Statement (6),

$$\vdash \Box_a \Box_e p \to \Box_a \Box_f p.$$

$\Box$

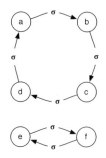

Fig. 6. Group $\langle \sigma \rangle$ acting on set $\{a, b, c, d, e, f\}$

Proposition 4. *Let $p \in P_a$ and $q \in P_c$. If group $G = \langle \sigma \rangle$ is acting, as shown on Figure 6, on set $S = \{a, b, c, d, e, f\}$, and, additionally, $\sigma^2(p) = q$ and $\sigma^2(q) = p$, then*

$$\vdash \Box_e \Box_b(p \vee q) \to \Box_d(p \vee q).$$

Proof. Since $\sigma^2 \in G_e$, by the Stability axiom,

$$\Box_e \sigma^2(\Box_d(q \vee p)) \to \Box_e \Box_d(q \vee p).$$

In other words,

$$\Box_e(\Box_b(p \vee q)) \to \Box_e \Box_d(q \vee p).$$

By the Reflexivity axiom,

$$\Box_e(\Box_b(p \vee q)) \to \Box_d(q \vee p). \tag{7}$$

Note now that $q \vee p \to p \vee q$ is a propositional tautology. Thus, by the Necessitation rule,

$$\Box_d(q \vee p \to p \vee q).$$

By the Distributivity axiom,

$$\Box_d(q \vee p) \to \Box_d(p \vee q).$$

Therefore, taking into account statement (7),

$$\Box_e(\Box_b(p \vee q)) \to \Box_d(p \vee q).$$

$\square$

6   Soundness

Soundness of propositional tautologies and the Modus Ponens inference rule is straightforward. We will prove soundness of the Necessitation rule and of the remaining six axioms as separate lemmas.

Lemma 2 (necessitation). *If $r \Vdash \varphi$ for any run r of any protocol over a signature Σ, then $r \Vdash \Box_a\varphi$ for any run r of any protocol over Σ.*

Proof. Consider any run r of a protocol over signature Σ. It will be sufficient to show that $r' \Vdash \varphi$ for each r' of the same protocol such that $r'(a) = r(a)$, which is true due to the assumption of the lemma. $\square$

Lemma 3 (distributivity). *For any run r of a protocol $\mathcal{P}$, if $r \Vdash \Box_a(\varphi \to \psi)$ and $r \Vdash \Box_a\varphi$, then $r \Vdash \Box_a\psi$.*

Proof. Let r' be any run of $\mathcal{P}$ such that $r'(a) = r(a)$. We will show that $r' \Vdash \psi$. Indeed, by the first assumption, $r' \Vdash \varphi \to \psi$. By the second assumption, $r' \Vdash \varphi$. Therefore, by Definition 4, $r' \Vdash \psi$. $\square$

Lemma 4 (reflexivity). *For any run r of a protocol $\mathcal{P}$, if $r \Vdash \Box_a\varphi$, then $r \Vdash \varphi$.*

Proof. The lemma follows from Definition 4 and the fact that $r(a) = r(a)$. $\square$

Lemma 5 (transitivity). *For any run r of a protocol $\mathcal{P}$, if $r \Vdash \Box_a\varphi$, then $r \Vdash \Box_a\Box_a\varphi$.*

Proof. Consider any run r' of the protocol $\mathcal{P}$ such that $r'(a) = r(a)$. It will be sufficient to show that $r' \Vdash \Box_a\varphi$. Consider now any run r'' of the same protocol such that $r''(a) = r'(a)$. We need to prove that $r'' \Vdash \varphi$, which is true due to the fact $r''(a) = r'(a) = r(a)$ and the assumption $r \Vdash \Box_a\varphi$. $\square$

Lemma 6 (Euclideanity). *For any run r of a protocol $\mathcal{P}$, if $r \nVdash \Box_a\varphi$, then $r \Vdash \Box_a\neg\Box_a\varphi$.*

Proof. By the assumption $r \not\Vdash \Box_a \varphi$, there exists a run r' of the protocol $\mathcal{P}$ such that $r'(a) = r(a)$ and $r' \not\Vdash \varphi$. Consider any run r'' of the protocol $\mathcal{P}$ such that $r''(a) = r(a)$. It will be sufficient to show that $r'' \not\Vdash \Box_a \varphi$, which follows from $r''(a) = r(a) = r'(a)$ and $r' \not\Vdash \varphi$. $\qquad\square$

Lemma 7 (self-awareness). *For any run r of a protocol $\mathcal{P}$ and any $p \in P_a$, if $r \Vdash p$, then $r \Vdash \Box_a p$.*

Proof. If $r \Vdash p$, then $Tr(r(a), p)$ by Definition 4. Thus, $Tr(r'(a), p)$ for each run r' of the protocol P such that $r'(a) = r(a)$. Hence, by Definition 4, $r' \Vdash p$ for each run r' of the protocol P such that $r'(a) = r(a)$. Therefore, again by Definition 4, $r \Vdash \Box_a p$. $\qquad\square$

Our proof of soundness for the Stability axiom relies on the following lemma. As we mentioned before, by $f \circ g$ we denote the composition of functions f and g such that $(f \circ g)(x) = f(g(x))$.

Lemma 8. *For any run r of a protocol $\mathcal{P}$ over a signature $(S, \{P_a\}_{a \in S}, G)$ and any $\sigma \in G$, if $r \Vdash \varphi$, then $(r \circ \sigma) \Vdash \sigma^{-1}(\varphi)$.*

Proof. Induction on structural complexity of formula φ.

1. If $\varphi \equiv \bot$, then $r \not\Vdash \bot$ by Definition 4.
2. Let $\varphi \equiv p$ for some $a \in S$ and some $p \in P_a$. If $r \Vdash p$, then by Definition 4, $Tr(r(a), p)$. Thus, $Tr(r(\sigma(\sigma^{-1}(a))), p)$. Hence, $Tr(r(\sigma(\sigma^{-1}(a))), \sigma^{-1}(p))$ by item 3b of Definition 3. Notice now that $\sigma^{-1}(p) \in P_{\sigma^{-1}(a)}$ due to Definition 1. Therefore, $(r \circ \sigma) \Vdash \sigma^{-1}(p)$ by Definition 4.
3. Let $\varphi \equiv \psi_1 \to \psi_2$. Assume $r \Vdash \psi_1 \to \psi_2$. Then by Definition 4, $r \not\Vdash \psi_1$ or $r \Vdash \psi_2$.
   First suppose $r \not\Vdash \psi_1$. In other words, $r \not\Vdash \sigma(\sigma^{-1}(\psi_1))$. Thus, $(r \circ \sigma \circ \sigma^{-1}) \not\Vdash \sigma(\sigma^{-1}(\psi_1))$. Then, $(r \circ \sigma) \not\Vdash \sigma^{-1}(\psi_1)$ by the contrapositive of the Induction Hypothesis for bijection σ^{-1}. Hence, by Definition 4, $(r \circ \sigma) \Vdash \sigma^{-1}(\psi_1) \to \sigma^{-1}(\psi_2)$. Therefore, by Definition 5, $(r \circ \sigma) \Vdash \sigma^{-1}(\psi_1 \to \psi_2)$.
   Next suppose $r \Vdash \psi_2$. Then, by the Induction Hypothesis, $(r \circ \sigma) \Vdash \sigma^{-1}(\psi_2)$. Thus, by Definition 4, $(r \circ \sigma) \Vdash \sigma^{-1}(\psi_1) \to \sigma^{-1}(\psi_2)$. Therefore, by Definition 5, $(r \circ \sigma) \Vdash \sigma^{-1}(\psi_1 \to \psi_2)$.
4. Let $\varphi \equiv \Box_a \psi$ for some $a \in S$. Let $r \Vdash \Box_a \psi$. We need to show $(r \circ \sigma) \Vdash \sigma^{-1}(\Box_a \psi)$. By Definition 5, this is equivalent to $(r \circ \sigma) \Vdash \Box_{\sigma^{-1}(a)} \sigma^{-1}(\psi)$. Consider any r' of the protocol $\mathcal{P}$ such that $r'(\sigma^{-1}(a)) = (r \circ \sigma)(\sigma^{-1}(a))$. It will be sufficient to show that $r' \Vdash \sigma^{-1}(\psi)$. Note that $r'(\sigma^{-1}(a)) = r(a)$. Thus, by the assumption $r \Vdash \Box_a \psi$ and Definition 4, $(r' \circ \sigma^{-1}) \Vdash \psi$. Then, by the Induction Hypothesis, $(r' \circ \sigma^{-1} \circ \sigma) \Vdash \sigma^{-1}(\psi)$. Therefore, $r' \Vdash \sigma^{-1}(\psi)$. $\qquad\square$

Lemma 9 (stability). *For any run r of a protocol $\mathcal{P}$ over a signature $(S, \{P_a\}_{a \in S}, G)$ and any $\sigma \in G_a$, if $r \Vdash \Box_a \sigma(\varphi)$, then $r \Vdash \Box_a \varphi$.*

Proof. Consider an arbitrary run r' of the protocol $\mathcal{P}$ such that $r'(a) = r(a)$. It will be sufficient to show $r' \Vdash \varphi$. By Lemma 8, $r \Vdash \Box_a \sigma(\varphi)$ implies $(r \circ \sigma) \Vdash \Box_{\sigma^{-1}(a)} \varphi$. Hence, $(r \circ \sigma) \Vdash \Box_a \varphi$ because $\sigma \in G_a$ and thus $\sigma^{-1} \in G_a$ as well. Notice that $(r \circ \sigma)(a) = r(a) = r'(a)$, because $\sigma \in G_a$ and due to the assumption $r'(a) = r(a)$. Therefore, by Definition 4, $r' \Vdash \varphi$. $\qquad\square$

7 Completeness

In this section, we will prove the completeness of our logical system. The completeness argument follows the standard outline of a modal logic completeness, with additional considerations for the symmetry of our setting.

Theorem 1. *Let* $\Sigma = (S, \{P_a\}_{a \in S}, G)$ *be an arbitrary signature and let* $\varphi \in \Phi(\Sigma)$. *If* $r \Vdash \varphi$ *for each run* $r \in R$ *of each protocol* (V, R, Tr) *over* Σ, *then* $\vdash_\Sigma \varphi$.

Proof. Suppose that $\nvdash_\Sigma \varphi$. We will construct a protocol $\mathcal{P} = (V, R, Tr)$ over Σ and a run $r \in R$ such that $r \nVdash \varphi$. Let X_0 be any maximal and consistent (in the sense $X_0 \nvdash_\Sigma \bot$) subset of $\Phi(\Sigma)$ such that $\neg \varphi \in X_0$. By $\mathbb{X}$ we mean the set of all maximal and consistent subsets of $\Phi(\Sigma)$. Thus, for instance $X_0 \in \mathbb{X}$.

Definition 6. *For any* $X, Y \in \mathbb{X}$ *let* $X \sim_a Y$ *mean that* $\Box_a \psi \in X$ *if and only if* $\Box_a \psi \in Y$ *for each* $\psi \in \Phi(S)$.

Lemma 10. *Relation* $\sim_a$ *is an equivalence relation on* $\mathbb{X}$, *for each* $a \in S$. $\Box$

By $\mathbb{X}_a$ we mean the set of equivalence classes with respect to the relation $\sim_a$, and by $[X]_a$ we mean the equivalence class of X. We will later use these classes to define the values in $V(a)$ of protocol $\mathcal{P}$. The next lemma is a standard lemma in the proofs of completeness for modal logics.

Lemma 11. *For any* $X \in \mathbb{X}$ *and any* ψ *such that* $\Box_a \psi \notin X$, *there is* $Y \in \mathbb{X}$ *such that* $Y \sim_a X$ *and* $\neg \psi \in Y$.

Proof. We will first show that the following set is consistent:

$$\{\Box_a \omega \mid \Box_a \omega \in X\} \cup \{\neg \Box_a \eta \mid \neg \Box_a \eta \in X\} \cup \{\neg \psi\}.$$

Towards a contradiction, let there be $\Box_a \omega_1, \ldots, \Box_a \omega_n, \neg \Box_a \eta_1, \ldots, \neg \Box_a \eta_k \in X$ such that

$$\vdash \Box_a \omega_1 \rightarrow (\cdots \rightarrow (\Box_a \omega_n \rightarrow (\neg \Box_a \eta_1 \rightarrow (\cdots \rightarrow (\neg \Box_a \eta_k \rightarrow \psi) \ldots))) \ldots).$$

By the Necessitation rule,

$$\vdash \Box_a (\Box_a \omega_1 \rightarrow (\cdots \rightarrow (\Box_a \omega_n \rightarrow (\neg \Box_a \eta_1 \rightarrow (\cdots \rightarrow (\neg \Box_a \eta_k \rightarrow \psi) \ldots))) \ldots)).$$

By multiple applications of the Distributivity axiom,

$$\vdash \Box_a \Box_a \omega_1 \rightarrow (\cdots \rightarrow (\Box_a \Box_a \omega_n \rightarrow (\Box_a \neg \Box_a \eta_1 \\ \rightarrow (\cdots \rightarrow (\Box_a \neg \Box_a \eta_k \rightarrow \Box_a \psi) \ldots))) \ldots).$$

By multiple applications of the Transitivity axiom,

$$\vdash \Box_a \omega_1 \rightarrow (\cdots \rightarrow (\Box_a \omega_n \rightarrow (\Box_a \neg \Box_a \eta_1 \\ \rightarrow (\cdots \rightarrow (\Box_a \neg \Box_a \eta_k \rightarrow \Box_a \psi) \ldots))) \ldots).$$

By multiple applications of the Euclideanity axiom,

$$\vdash \Box_a \omega_1 \to (\cdots \to (\Box_a \omega_n \to (\neg \Box_a \eta_1 \to$$
$$(\cdots \to (\neg \Box_a \eta_k \to \Box_a \psi) \dots))) \dots).$$

Hence, by multiple applications of the Modus Ponens rule,

$$\Box_a \omega_1, \dots, \Box_a \omega_n, \neg \Box_a \eta_1, \dots, \neg \Box_a \eta_k \vdash \Box_a \psi.$$

Thus, $X \vdash \Box_a \psi$, which is a contradiction with maximality of X and the assumption $\Box_a \psi \notin X$. Let Y be a maximal consistent set containing

$$\{\Box_a \omega \mid \Box_a \omega \in X\} \cup \{\neg \Box_a \eta \mid \neg \Box_a \eta \in X\} \cup \{\neg \psi\}.$$

We are only left to show that if $\Box_a \eta \in Y$, then $\Box_a \eta \in X$ for each $\Box_a \eta \in \Phi(\Sigma)$. Indeed, assume that $\Box_a \eta \notin X$. Then, $\neg \Box_a \eta \in X$ by the maximality of X. Hence, $\neg \Box_a \eta \in Y$ due to the choice of Y. Therefore, $\Box_a \eta \notin Y$ due to consistency of Y.   □

The following lemma shows that the symmetries which act on S and $\Phi(\Sigma)$ also could be viewed as acting on $\mathbb{X}$.

Lemma 12. $\sigma(X) \in \mathbb{X}$, for each $X \in \mathbb{X}$ and each $\sigma \in G$.

Proof. To prove maximality of the set $\sigma(X)$, consider any formula $\varphi \in \Phi(S)$. It will be sufficient to show that either $\varphi \in \sigma(X)$ or $(\varphi \to \bot) \in \sigma(X)$. Indeed, consider the formula $\sigma^{-1}(\varphi)$. Due to the assumption of maximality of the set X, either $\sigma^{-1}(\varphi) \in X$ or $\sigma^{-1}(\varphi \to \bot) \in X$. Therefore, either $\varphi \in \sigma(X)$ or $(\varphi \to \bot) \in \sigma(X)$ by Definition 5.

To prove consistency of the set $\sigma(X)$, suppose that $\sigma(X) \vdash \bot$. Thus, $\sigma^{-1}(\sigma(X)) \vdash \sigma^{-1}(\bot)$ by Lemma 1. Therefore, by Definition 5, $X \vdash \bot$, which is a contradiction with the assumption of consistency of the set X.   □

Lemma 13. If $X \sim_a Y$, then $\sigma(X) \sim_{\sigma(a)} \sigma(Y)$, for each $\sigma \in G$, each $X, Y \in \mathbb{X}$, and each $a \in S$.

Proof. Let $\Box_{\sigma(a)} \psi \in \sigma(X)$. Thus, $\sigma^{-1}(\Box_{\sigma(a)} \psi) \in X$. Hence, $\Box_a \sigma^{-1}(\psi) \in X$. Then, $\Box_a \sigma^{-1}(\psi) \in Y$ by the assumption $X \sim_a Y$. Hence, $\sigma(\Box_a \sigma^{-1}(\psi)) \in \sigma(Y)$. In other words, $\Box_{\sigma(a)} \psi \in \sigma(Y)$.   □

It follows from the previous lemma that symmetry σ now also can be viewed as acting on $\bigcup_{a \in S} \mathbb{X}_a$ in such a way that $\sigma([X]_a) = [\sigma(X)]_{\sigma(a)}$.

Lemma 14. For any $X \in \mathbb{X}$, any $a \in S$, and any $\sigma \in G_a$, $\sigma(X) \sim_a X$.

Proof. Suppose that $\Box_a \psi \in X$. Thus, $\sigma(\Box_a \psi) \in \sigma(X)$. Hence, $\Box_a \sigma(\psi) \in \sigma(X)$, by the assumption $\sigma \in G_a$. Therefore, $\Box_a \psi \in \sigma(X)$, by the Stability axiom and maximality of $\sigma(X)$.

Assume now that $\Box_a \psi \in \sigma(X)$. Thus, $\sigma^{-1}(\Box_a \psi) \in X$. Hence, $\Box_a \sigma^{-1}(\psi) \in X$, because $\sigma \in G_a$ and thus $\sigma^{-1} \in G_a$. Therefore, $\Box_a \psi \in X$ by the Stability axiom and due to maximality of X.   □

Recall that by the orbit $Orbit_G(a)$ of element $a \in S$ with respect to group G we mean the set $\{\sigma(a) \mid \sigma \in G\}$. Orbits partition set S into disjoint subsets. We pick a unique representative from each orbit. If $a \in S$, then the unique representative of $Orbit_G(a)$ is denoted by $\hat{a}$. For each $a \in S$ we also pick any $\mu_a \in G$ such that $\mu_a(\hat{a}) = a$. We are now ready to define the protocol $\mathcal{P} = (V, R, Tr)$.

Definition 7. *For any $a \in S$, let $V(a) = \mathbb{X}_{\hat{a}}$.*

The following lemma verifies that $\mathcal{P}$ satisfies condition 1 from Definition 3.

Lemma 15. $V(a) = V(\sigma(a))$ *for each $a \in S$ and each $\sigma \in G$.*

Proof. Note that $\hat{a} = \widehat{\sigma(a)}$ because the elements a and $\sigma(a)$ belong to the same orbit. Thus, $V(a) = \mathbb{X}_{\hat{a}} = \mathbb{X}_{\widehat{\sigma(a)}} = V(\sigma(a))$. $\square$

Definition 8. *Let set R contain all functions $r(s)$ on the set S such that*

1. *$r(a) \in V(a)$ for each $a \in S$,*
2. *$\bigcap_{a \in S} \mu_a(r(a)) \neq \varnothing$.*

The first condition of the above definition mirrors Definition 3. Informally, the second condition requires the values of the same run to be "consistent" with each other. The technical lemma below shows that the intersection of a family of sets is not dependent on the indexing of the family.

Lemma 16. *If $\{Y_a\}_{a \in S}$ is an arbitrary family of sets and f is any bijection of S onto S, then*

$$\bigcap_{a \in S} Y_a = \bigcap_{a \in S} Y_{f(a)}.$$

Proof. Since f is a bijection, the left side and the right side of the equality intersect the same family of sets (indexed differently). $\square$

The next lemma demonstrates that $\mathcal{P}$ satisfies condition 2 of Definition 3.

Lemma 17. $r \circ \sigma \in R$ *for each $r \in R$ and each $\sigma \in G$.*

Proof. We need to show that $r \circ \sigma$ satisfies both conditions from Definition 8. We will do it separately.

1. Assume that $a \in S$. We will show that $(r \circ \sigma)(a) \in V(a)$. Indeed, $(r \circ \sigma)(a) = r(\sigma(a)) \in V(\sigma(a))$, hence, by Lemma 15, $(r \circ \sigma)(a) \in V(a)$.
2. We will now show that $\bigcap_{a \in S} \mu_a(r \circ \sigma(a)) \neq \varnothing$. Indeed, by Definition 8, there is a set X such that $X \in \bigcap_{a \in S} \mu_a(r(a))$. Hence, $X \in \mu_a(r(a))$ for each $a \in S$. Thus,

$$(\sigma \circ \mu_{\sigma^{-1}(a)} \circ \mu_a^{-1})X \in (\sigma \circ \mu_{\sigma^{-1}(a)} \circ \mu_a^{-1})\mu_a(r(a)),$$

for each $a \in S$. Hence,

$$(\sigma \circ \mu_{\sigma^{-1}(a)} \circ \mu_a^{-1})X \in \sigma(\mu_{\sigma^{-1}(a)}(r(a))), \tag{8}$$

for each $a \in S$. Note now that $(\sigma \circ \mu_{\sigma^{-1}(a)} \circ \mu_a^{-1})(a) = (\sigma \circ \mu_{\sigma^{-1}(a)})(\hat{a}) = \sigma(\sigma^{-1}(a)) = a$ by the choice of $\hat{a}$ and μ_a. Thus, $\sigma \circ \mu_{\sigma^{-1}(a)} \circ \mu_a^{-1} \in G_a$. Hence, by Lemma 14, $(\sigma \circ \mu_{\sigma^{-1}(a)} \circ \mu_a^{-1})X \sim_a X$. Then, due to (8),

$$X \in \sigma(\mu_{\sigma^{-1}(a)}(r(a))),$$

for each $a \in S$. Thus,

$$\sigma^{-1}(X) \in \sigma^{-1}(\sigma(\mu_{\sigma^{-1}(a)}(r(a)))),$$

for each $a \in S$. Then,

$$\sigma^{-1}(X) \in \mu_{\sigma^{-1}(a)}(r(a)),$$

for each $a \in S$. Hence,

$$\sigma^{-1}(X) \in \bigcap_{a \in S} \mu_{\sigma^{-1}(a)}(r(a)).$$

Then, by Lemma 16,

$$\sigma^{-1}(X) \in \bigcap_{a \in S} \mu_a(r(\sigma(a))).$$

Therefore, $\bigcap_{a \in S} \mu_a(r \circ \sigma(a)) \neq \varnothing$.

$\square$

Definition 9. *For any $a \in S$, any $X \in \mathbb{X}$, and any $p \in P_a$, let $Tr([X]_{\hat{a}}, p)$ be true if $p \in \bigcap \mu_a([X]_{\hat{a}})$.*

The next lemma confirms that $\mathcal{P}$ satisfies condition 3 of Definition 3.

Lemma 18. *For any $a \in S$, any $p \in P_a$, any $\sigma \in G$, and any $X \in \mathbb{X}$, if $p \in \bigcap \mu_a([X]_{\hat{a}})$, then $\sigma(p) \in \bigcap \mu_{\sigma(a)}([X]_{\hat{a}})$.*

Proof. It will be sufficient to show that $\bigcap \mu_a([X]_{\hat{a}}) \subseteq \sigma^{-1}(\bigcap \mu_{\sigma(a)}([X]_{\hat{a}}))$. To demonstrate the latter, we will prove that $\mu_a(Y) \sim_{\hat{a}} \sigma^{-1}(\mu_{\sigma(a)}(Y))$ for each $Y \in \mathbb{X}$. Indeed, by the definition of μ_a and μ_{σ_a}, we have $\mu_{\sigma(a)}^{-1}(\sigma(\mu_a(\hat{a}))) = \hat{a}$. Hence, $\mu_{\sigma(a)}^{-1} \circ \sigma \circ \mu_a \in G_{\hat{a}}$. Thus, $\mu_{\sigma(a)}^{-1}(\sigma(\mu_a(Y)) \sim_{\hat{a}} Y$, by Lemma 14. Therefore, $\mu_a(Y) \sim_{\hat{a}} \sigma^{-1}(\mu_{\sigma(a)}(Y))$.

$\square$

We have now shown that $\mathcal{P}$ is a protocol over signature Σ. The next lemma is a variation of the standard induction lemma in proofs of completeness.

Lemma 19. *For any $r \in R$, any formula $\psi \in \Phi(\Sigma)$, and any $X \in \bigcap_{a \in S} \mu_a(r(a))$,*

$$r \Vdash \psi \quad \text{if and only if} \quad \psi \in X.$$

Proof. Induction on structural complexity of formula ψ. If $\psi \equiv \bot$, then the required follows from Definition 4 and consistency of the set X.

Assume that $\psi \equiv p \in P_{a_0}$. $(\Rightarrow)$: If $r \Vdash p$, then, by Definition 4, $Tr(r(a_0), p)$. Hence, by Definition 9, $p \in \bigcap \mu_{a_0}(r(a_0))$. Recall that $X \in \bigcap_{a \in S} \mu_a(r(a))$. Thus, $X \in \mu_{a_0}(r(a_0))$. Therefore, $p \in X$. $(\Leftarrow)$: If $p \in X$, then $\Box_{a_0} p \in X$ due to maximality of X and the Self-Awareness axiom. Thus, by Definition 6, $\Box_{a_0} p \in Y$ for each Y such that $X \sim_{a_0} Y$. Hence, due to maximality of Y and the Reflexivity axiom, $p \in Y$ for each Y such that $X \sim_{a_0} Y$. Then, $p \in \bigcap \mu_{a_0}(r(a_0))$ because $X \in \mu_{a_0}(r(a_0))$. Hence, by Definition 9, $Tr(r(a_0), p)$. Therefore, by Definition 4, $r \Vdash p$.

Let $\psi \equiv \Box_{a_0} \omega$.

$(\Rightarrow)$: Suppose that $\Box_{a_0} \omega \notin X$. Thus, by Lemma 11, there is $Y \sim_{a_0} X$ such that $\omega \notin Y$. Let $r'(a) = [\mu_a^{-1}(Y)]_{\hat{a}}$ for each $a \in S$. We will show $r' \in R$ using Definition 8. Indeed,

$$\bigcap_{a \in S} \mu_a(r'(a)) = \bigcap_{a \in S} \mu_a([\mu_a^{-1}(Y)]_{\hat{a}}) = \bigcap_{a \in S} [Y]_a \ni Y.$$

We will now show that $r'(a_0) = r(a_0)$. Indeed, $X \in \bigcap_{a \in S} \mu_a(r(a))$ by the assumption of the lemma. Hence, $X \in \mu_{a_0}(r(a_0))$. Thus, $\mu_{a_0}^{-1}(X) \in \mu_{a_0}^{-1}(\mu_{a_0}(r(a_0)))$. In other words, $\mu_{a_0}^{-1}(X) \in r(a_0)$. Recall now that $X \sim_{a_0} Y$. Hence, by Lemma 13, $\mu_{a_0}^{-1}(X) \sim_{\hat{a_0}} \mu_{a_0}^{-1}(Y)$. Thus, $\mu_{a_0}^{-1}(Y) \in r(a_0)$. Therefore, $r'(a_0) = [\mu_{a_0}^{-1}(Y)]_{\hat{a_0}} = r(a_0)$.

Finally, recall that $\omega \notin Y$. Thus, by the Induction Hypothesis, $r' \nVdash \omega$. Therefore, by Definition 4, $r \nVdash \Box_{a_0} \omega$.

$(\Leftarrow)$: Suppose that $\Box_{a_0} \omega \in X$. Consider any $r' \in R$ such that $r'(a_0) = r(a_0)$. It will be sufficient to show that $r' \Vdash \omega$. Indeed, by Definition 8, there is $X' \in \bigcap_{a \in S} \mu_a(r'(a))$. In particular, $X' \in \mu_{a_0}(r'(a_0))$. Thus, $X' \in \mu_{a_0}(r(a_0))$. Recall that $X \in \bigcap_{a \in S} \mu_a(r(a))$. Hence, $X \in \mu_{a_0}(r(a_0))$. Thus, both X' and X belong to the same equivalence class $\mu_{a_0}(r(a_0))$. Then, $X \sim_{a_0} X'$. Thus, $\Box_{a_0} \omega \in X'$ by the assumption $\Box_{a_0} \omega \in X$ and Definition 6. Hence, $\omega \in X'$, by the Reflexivity axiom and the maximality of the set X'. Therefore, by the Induction Hypothesis, $r' \Vdash \omega$.

The case $\psi \equiv \psi_1 \to \psi_2$ follows from Definition 4 and maximality and consistency of the set X in the standard way. $\qquad \Box$

To finish the proof of the completeness theorem, consider $r_0(a) = [\mu_a^{-1}(X_0)]_{\hat{a}}$ as a function of argument a. We will show that $r_0 \in R$. Indeed, $r_0(a) \in V(a)$ because $[X_0]_a \in \mathbb{X}_a$ and $[\mu_a^{-1}(X_0)]_{\hat{a}} \in \mathbb{X}_{\hat{a}} = V(a)$. In addition, $\bigcap_{a \in S} \mu_a(r_0(a)) \neq \varnothing$ because

$$\bigcap_{a \in S} \mu_a(r_0(a)) = \bigcap_{a \in S} \mu_a([\mu_a^{-1}(X_0)]_{\hat{a}}) = \bigcap_{a \in S} [X_0]_a \ni X_0. \tag{9}$$

We now finish the proof of the completeness theorem by showing that $r_0 \nVdash \varphi$. Indeed, recall that $\neg\varphi \in X_0$. By Lemma 19 and due to Statement (9), $r_0 \Vdash \neg\varphi$. Therefore, by Definition 4, $r_0 \nVdash \varphi$. $\qquad \Box$

8   Conclusion

In this paper we introduced a modal logical system for reasoning about knowledge in symmetric protocols and proved soundness and completeness of this system.

The modal language described in this paper can be generalized to distributed knowledge [7] modality $\square_A$, where A is a subset of S. Informally, statement $r \Vdash \square_A \varphi$ means that any agent who knows all values in set A on run r will be able to conclude φ. Formally, the last part of Definition 4 can be changed to

4. $r \Vdash \square_A \psi$ if $r' \Vdash \psi$ for all $r' \in R$ such that $r'(a) = r(a)$ for each $a \in A$.

Axioms of our logical system can be trivially re-written to handle distributed knowledge. For example, the Stability axiom generalizes to $\square_A \sigma(\varphi) \to \square_A \varphi$, where $\sigma \in \bigcap_{a \in A} G_a$. However, to be natural, such generalization will have to allow atomic propositions to express properties of values of any subset of S. For example, proposition $p_{\{a,b\}}$ could state that $a = b$. The proof of completeness presented in this paper does not work in this new setting because it is not clear how $\hat{A}$ should be defined so that it can be used in the generalized Definition 9. Complete axiomatization of epistemic logic of distributed knowledge for symmetric protocols remains an open problem.

References

1. Kane, J., Naumov, P.: Epistemic logic for communication chains. In: 14th conference on Theoretical Aspects of Rationality and Knowledge (TARK 2013), Chennai, India, pp. 131–137 (January 2013)
2. Hintikka, J.: Knowledge and Belief - An Introduction to the Logic of the Two Notions. Contemporary philosophy. Cornell University Press, Ithaca (1962)
3. Murtagh, F.: Symmetry in data mining and analysis: A unifying view based on hierarchy. Proceedings of the Steklov Institute of Mathematics 265, 177–198 (2009)
4. Miller, A., Donaldson, A.F., Calder, M.: Symmetry in temporal logic model checking. ACM Comput. Surv. 38(3) (2006)
5. Kane, J., Naumov, P.: Symmetry in information flow. Annals of Pure and Applied Logic (to appear)
6. Armstrong, W.W.: Dependency structures of data base relationships. In: Information Processing 1974 (Proc. IFIP Congress, Stockholm), pp. 580–583. North-Holland, Amsterdam (1974)
7. Fagin, R., Halpern, J.Y., Moses, Y., Vardi, M.Y.: Reasoning about knowledge. MIT Press, Cambridge (1995)

Accumulative Knowledge under Bounded Resources

Wojciech Jamroga[1,2] and Masoud Tabatabaei[1]

[1] Interdisciplinary Centre for Security and Trust, University of Luxembourg
[2] Computer Science and Communication, University of Luxembourg
{wojtek.jamroga,masoud.tabatabaei}@uni.lu

Abstract. A possible purpose of performing an action is to collect information. Such informative actions are usually resource-consuming. The resources needed for performing them can be for example time or memory, but also money, specialized equipment etc. In this work, we propose a formal framework to study how the ability of an agent to improve its knowledge changes as a result of changing the available resources. We introduce a model for resource-consuming informative actions, and show how the process of accumulating knowledge can be modelled. Based on this model, we propose a modal logic for reasoning about the epistemic abilities of agents. We present some validities of the logic, and show that the model checking problem sits in the first level of polynomial hierarchy. We also discuss the connection between our framework and classical information theory. More specifically, we show that the notion of uncertainty given by Hartley measure can be seen as a special case of an agent's ability to improve its knowledge using informative actions.

1 Introduction

Performing actions is an intrinsic feature of agents. In the real world, execution of an action requires resources. The resources may be time, money, memory, space, etc. Therefore, the abilities ascribed to an agent depend on the amount of available resources. Reasoning about realistic agents should take into account the limitations imposed by resource bounds.

In this work, we are mostly interested in reasoning about the abilities of agents to change their view of the situation. More specifically, we want to capture the way agents with bounded resources, modify their knowledge about the environment by performing informative actions, such as sensing and observing. Building knowledge by performing informative actions is in many cases essential for an intelligent agent. One example of an agent that performs (resource consuming) observations in order to refine its knowledge is a robot in a rescue mission that tries to obtain knowledge about the type of danger and the location of people in the danger zone. Another example is a real-time classifier with the task of classifying a given picture within a short time, and with several classification algorithms at hand. We believe that a logic to reason about accumulating knowledge by use of resource consuming informative actions can help in modelling and analysing the behaviour of agents in many similar scenarios.

J. Leite et al. (Eds.): CLIMA XIV, LNAI 8143, pp. 206–222, 2013.
© Springer-Verlag Berlin Heidelberg 2013

1.1 Related Work

The inspiration for this work can be traced back to Herbert A. Simon who introduced the term of bounded rationality [27]. More recently, several approaches, such as the works of Halpern [19,15], Rantala [25] and Konolige [22], have been introduced to dealing with the so called omniscience problem, and enable reasoning about agents who are not necessarily perfect reasoners themselves. Reasoning about agents' abilities under bounded resources has also become a major topic in the community of temporal and strategic logic, cf. the works by Alechina and Logan [3,4,5,6,7,8] and Bulling and Farwer [11,10]. We review the most relevant approaches below, but it is fair to say that none of them includes both a notion of quantitatively restricted reasoning *and* a semantic representation of the knowledge owned or gained by agents.

In the syntactic approach to knowledge [14,24,22], the known sentences are explicitly listed for each possible world. This approach enables to capture an agent's limited ability to gain knowledge in a given condition. However, such model cannot capture changes in epistemic abilities of an agent when the available resources change. For each new amount of available resource, a new model must be built to reason about the new situation. The same applies to the awareness approach [15], impossible worlds [25], and algorithmic knowledge [19]. On the other hand, the accumulation of knowledge is at the focus of Dynamic Epistemic Logic [28] and its extensions [1]. However, DEL takes into account neither limited observational resources nor imperfections of reasoning by real agents.

In [3,4], a notion of delayed belief was introduced. That approach assumes that the agent is a perfect reasoner in an arbitrary decidable logic, but only derives the consequences of its beliefs after some delay. An advantage of delayed belief is that we can represent situations where an agent does not yet know a property, but it can learn the property by using some action(s). Still, there is no notion of quantitative resource in this approach. So, e.g., we cannot reason about the effect of changing the available resources on the epistemic state of an agent. Likewise, Timed Reasoning Logic [5] allows to capture the dynamics of agents' knowledge, but it lacks the explicit notion of resources (although it is possible to reason about the time consumed when performing actions).

Another group of approaches was proposed in the agent logics community. RTL [10,11] is a resource bounded extension to the Computation Tree Logic (CTL) which models the temporal evolution of a system as a tree-like structure in which the future is not determined. In RTL, each transition between states can consume some resources and produce other resources. The logic RTL includes the notion of resource, and enables reasoning about changes of abilities of agents due to changes of available resources. However, it has no semantic representation of knowledge. In order to reason about the evolution of knowledge, one would have to define new propositions to capture the knowledge of agents, and find out (by using other methods) what an agent knows in each state in order to determine the valuation of these propositions. The same applies to several other logics for resource bounded agents, such as Coalition Logic for Resource Games [6], Resource Bounded Alternating-time Temporal Logic [7], Priced Resource

Bounded ATL [12], and Resource Bounded Coalition Logic [8]. The main focus is reasoning about how agents use actions to achieve their goals under resource bounds, with no specific machinery to capture information flow.

Reasoning about the outcome of accumulated observations has been also studied in belief revision and AI planning. Classical belief revision is syntactic in nature [2], though there are also formalizations based on possible worlds [17]. Still, both strands focus on inference by perfect reasoners using cost-free informative actions. AI planning approaches that take into account epistemic actions are also mostly based on the syntactic approach to knowledge. For instance, the C-BURIDAN planner [13] represents each state by the set of propositions that hold in it. An informative action does not change the propositions, but adds some labels to the state. These labels represent the observations that the agent has has collected, and can later be used to block application of other actions. Although C-BURIDAN and similar planners capture informative actions, they do not include a notion of resource. One can set preconditions for actions, and by this restrict the availability of an action in a state, but there is no way of representing the amount of resources needed to perform the action. Also, the main concern in AI planning is to find a sequence of actions that transforms the initial state of the world to an "objective" goal state, and not to a given *epistemic* state. Outcomes of observations can be used to find out the needed sequence of actions, but cannot define the goal itself.

Variants of AI planning which come much closer to our approach are belief planning [26] and dynamic epistemic planning [9]. They are both based on Kripke semantics, and focus on goals formulated in terms of epistemic states. Still, they lack the notion of quantitative resource, and do not address the impact of available resources on the outcome of plans (nor the on the outcome of planning).

In summary, some existing frameworks allow for reasoning about information flow and epistemic change, albeit in a purely qualitative way. Other approaches capture epistemic limitations of agents under bounded resources, but do not include the concept of resource, and do not facilitate reasoning about the relationship between agents' ability to gain knowledge, and changes in the resources. Yet another group includes the notion of resource and supports reasoning about resource-dependent abilities of agents, but lacks a semantic representation of knowledge and its dynamics. In this paper, we propose a logic-based approach that on the one hand relates epistemic abilities to resources, and on the other hand represents the process of refining knowledge in a semantically sensible way.

2   Resource Bounded Model for Accumulative Knowledge

In this section we develop a model that formalizes scenarios in which agents build their knowledge by using resource-consuming actions. We explain the ideas behind our approach with the following motivating example.

Example 1 (Medical agent). Consider a medical assistant agent. The agent is to help diagnosing patients in areas where there are not enough general practitioners. The process of helping a patient starts when the patient informs the agent about his symptoms. The agent then generates a list of all possible diseases consistent with the symptoms. Among the diseases, some are considered as being serious. The agent's duty is finding out whether the patient's disease is serious or not. If it is found out that the disease is not serious, the agent prescribes appropriate medications. Otherwise the agent sends the patient to a medical centre. A set of medical tests is available to determine the seriousness of the disease. Each medical test takes some specific time. Depending on the result of the test, the agent can rule out some of the diseases, and so on.

In principle, the process should continue until the agent finds out if the disease is serious. However, there are some important questions that an intelligent agent might consider before even starting. What are the relevant medical tests for a patient with the given symptoms? If the supply of test kits is limited, is the agent able to find out the seriousness of the disease with the available kits? If, among the possible diseases, there is one that should be diagnosed quickly, is there a sequence of tests that will make the agent certain about this very disease before the condition of the patient gets critical?

2.1 Observation-Based Certainty Model

We will use *possible worlds models* [23] to formalize this and similar scenarios. Each world corresponds to a possible state of affairs. If an agent cannot distinguish between two worlds, this is represented by the corresponding modal accessibility relation. For instance, for the medical agent, the set of possible worlds can consist of all possible diagnoses (i.e., diseases). The agent knows that a given property holds if and only if it holds in all the accessible worlds. For example, if all the possible diseases consistent with the symptoms are caused by infection, then we say that the agent *knows* that the patient has an infection.

An agent may refine its knowledge by performing informative actions. In this work, we refer to all informative actions as *observations*. The medical agent can, e.g., check the temperature of the patient. Performing an observation may refine the knowledge of an agent by ruling out some of the possible worlds. For example, after learning that the patient does not have high temperature, the medical agent rules out all the diseases that include high temperature. The agent needs resources (time, memory, space, money, etc.) to perform observations. Thus, in order to analyse the agent's ability to gain the required knowledge, we need to take into account the cost of the observations and the available resources.

We formalize the intuitions as follows, drawing inspiration from modal epistemic logic and dynamic epistemic logic.

Definition 1 (Observation-based certainty model). *Having a set of atomic propositions P and a set of agents A, an observation based certainty model is a tuple $M = \langle S, R, V, Obs, obs, cost, cover \rangle$ where:*

- *S is a set of states (possible worlds).*
- *$R \subseteq A \times S \times S$ is the accessibility relation which represents the worlds that are accessible for each agent. We will write $s_1 \sim_a s_2$ instead of $(a, s_1, s_2) \in R$. Each binary relation $R(a, \cdot, \cdot)$ is an equivalence relation.*

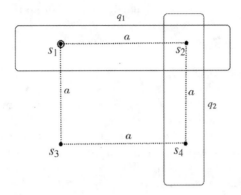

Fig. 1. A model of simple medical diagnosis. The epistemic accessibility relation for agent a is represented by the dotted lines (modulo transitivity). q_1, q_2 are the available observations; their covering sets are depicted by the rectangles. Moreover, we assume that $cost(q_1) = 1$ and $cost(q_2) = 2$.

- $V : P \rightarrow 2^S$ is a valuation propositions that shows which propositions are true in which worlds.
- Obs is a set of labels for binary observations.
- $obs : A \rightarrow 2^{Obs}$ defines availability of observations to agents.
- $cover : Obs \rightarrow 2^S$ is the coverage function. It specifies the set of worlds that correspond to the "positive" outcome of an observation. We call $cover(q)$ the covering set of the observation q.
- $cost : Obs \rightarrow C$ is the cost function that specifies the amount of resources needed to make the observation. The set of cost values C depends on the context. For example, when the resource in question is time, C can be the set of positive real numbers. For memory usage, costs can be conveniently represented by natural numbers. In case of multiple resources consumption, the cost can be a vector of numbers, such that each number represents the consumption of a different type of resource. To simplify the presentation, we will assume that $C = \mathbb{N} \cup \{0\}$ throughout the paper.

An example model is shown in Figure 1, and discussed in detail in Example 2.

2.2   Queries and Updates

Definition 2 (Update by an observation). *Let* $m \subseteq S$ *be a subset of worlds (e.g., the ones considered possible by the agent at some moment), $q \in Obs$ an observation, and $s \in m$ a state. The update of m by observation q in state s is defined as follows:*

$$m|_q^s = \begin{cases} m \cap cover(q) & \text{if } s \in cover(q) \\ m \setminus cover(q) & \text{if } s \notin cover(q). \end{cases}$$

Definition 3 (Query). *A query is a finite sequence of observations, i.e., a tuple $l = \langle q_1, \ldots, q_k \rangle$ where each q_i is an observation.*

Definition 4 (Update by a query). *An update of a subset of worlds $m \subseteq S$ by a query $l = \langle q_1, q_2, \ldots q_k \rangle$ in state s is defined recursively as follows:*

$$m|_l^s = m|_{q_1, q_2, \ldots, q_k}^s = \left(m|_{q_1, \ldots, q_{k-1}}^s \right)|_{q_k}^s$$

After updating the initial set m by the first observation in the sequence, the updated set of worlds is the new set of worlds that is used to be updated by next observation in the sequence. This process continues until updating by the last observation in the sequence is done.

Example 2. Consider the medical agent scenario. In Figure 1, the set of possible worlds $m = \{s_1, s_2, s_3, s_4\}$ represents the diseases consistent with the symptoms of the patient (say, pneumonia, meningitis, leukaemia, and chronic kidney disease). The available medical tests for the medical agent a in this example are the observations q_1 and q_2, which respectively correspond to checking the temperature of the patient and checking her blood pressure. The covering set of the observation q_1 is $\{s_1, s_2\}$, i.e., the diseases with high temperature, and the covering set of q_2 is $\{s_2, s_4\}$, that is, the diseases characterized by high blood pressure. Suppose that that the actual disease is s_1 and the medical agent first checks the temperature and then the blood pressure. It means that we would like to find the update of the set m in state s_1 by the observations q_1 and q_2. Checking the temperature tells the agent whether the actual state is in the covering set of q_1 or not. Here the answer is "yes", and thus we have $m|_{q_1}^{s_1} = m \cap cover(q_1) = \{s_1, s_2\}$. Checking the blood pressure after this corresponds to updating the result of the previous update $\{s_1, s_2\}$ by observation q_2. In state s_1, the final result is $\{s_1\}$, so the agent knows precisely that the disease is pneumonia.

Definition 5 (Cost of a query). *Let $\oplus : \mathcal{C} \times \mathcal{C} \to \mathcal{C}$ be a fixed additive aggregation function [18]. The cost of a query is the aggregation of the costs of its observations:* $cost(\langle q_1, \ldots, q_k \rangle) = cost(q_1) \oplus \cdots \oplus cost(q_k)$.

The aggregation function $\oplus$ is context-dependent, and can be defined in various ways. For example, if the resource is time and observations are made sequentially then the aggregate cost is simply the sum of individual costs. If the observations are applied in parallel, the time needed for the whole query is the maximum of the costs, and so on. In this paper, we assume that $cost(\langle q_1, \ldots, q_k \rangle) = cost(q_1) + \cdots + cost(q_k)$, and leave the general case for future work.

Definition 6 (Relevant observation). *The observation q is called relevant to a set $m \subseteq S$ iff $m \cap cover(q) \neq \emptyset$ and $m \cap cover(q) \neq m$.*

If m is the set of worlds that the agent considers possible, a relevant observation is one that brings new information to the agent. In other words, when an observation is not relevant, the agent knows the result of updating even before applying the observation.

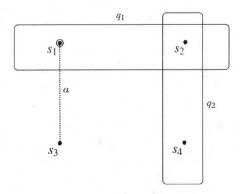

Fig. 2. A model of diagnosis for a more knowledgeable medical agent

Example 3. Consider the model in Figure 2. The set $m = \{s_1, s_3\}$ collects the diseases that the medical agent takes into account. It is easy to see that q_2 in not relevant because the agent already knows that the patient does not have high blood pressure. In other words an update of m by q_2 is equal to m itself. But the agent does not know the result of checking the temperature, therefore q_1 is a relevant observation.

Definition 7 (Relevant query). *Let $a \in A$ and $s \in S$. A query $l = \langle q_1, \ldots, q_k \rangle$ is relevant for agent a in state s iff: (1) $q_i \in obs(a)$ for all i, (2) q_1 is relevant to $\{s'|s\sim_a s'\}$, and (3) q_i is relevant to $\{s'|s\sim_a s'\}|^s_{q_1,\ldots,q_{i-1}}$ for all $i \geq 2$.*

Note that, while we defined the relevance of an observation with respect to a set of worlds, we use a set *and a state* to define the relevance of a query. This is because in the process of updating a set by a query, in each step, the outcome of the update depends on the actual state. This implies that an agent who does not know what the actual world is, might not know beforehand whether a query is relevant or not. However, the agent knows at each step of updating if the next observation to be applied is relevant or not. Note also that in a state, the same query might be relevant for one agent, and irrelevant for another agent.

Finally, we remark that for practical purposes such an explicit modeling of the outcome of observations (in terms of global states in a Kripke model) can be impractical. This can be overcome by using a higher-level model specification language, for instance one based on interpreted systems [16]. We do not dig deeper into this issue, and discuss only the abstract formulation throughout the paper.

3   A Logic of Accumulative Knowledge

In this section, we introduce a modal language for reasoning about the abilities of agents to refine their knowledge under bounded resources.

3.1   Syntax

The set of formulas of Logic of Accumulative Knowledge (LAcK) is defined by the following grammar:

$$\varphi ::= p \mid \neg\varphi \mid \varphi \vee \psi \mid K_a\varphi \mid \mathfrak{K}_a^l\varphi \mid \Diamond\mathfrak{K}_a^b\varphi \mid \Box\mathfrak{K}_a^b\varphi,$$

where $p \in P$ is an atomic proposition, $a \in A$ is an agent, and $b \in \mathcal{B}$ is a resource bound. Unless explicitly stated, we will assume that the set of bounds is $\mathcal{B} = \mathbb{N}\cup\{0, \infty\}$. The other Boolean operators are defined as usual. Additionally, we define $\mathfrak{K}_a\varphi \equiv K_a\varphi \vee K_a\neg\varphi$.

Formula $K_a\varphi$ says that agent a knows that φ. Consequently, $\mathfrak{K}_a\varphi$ expresses that a has no uncertainty about φ, that is, he *knows the truth value* of φ. The formula $\mathfrak{K}_a^l\varphi$ says that a has *observation-based certainty* about φ through observation l. Formula $\Diamond\mathfrak{K}_a^b\varphi$ reads as "a can *possibly* (or *potentially*) obtain certainty about φ under resource bound b". Finally, $\Box\mathfrak{K}_a^b\varphi$ expresses that a is *guaranteed* to obtain certainty about φ under bound b.

3.2   Semantics

The semantics of LAcK in observation-based certainty models is defined by the following clauses:

- $M, s \models p$ iff $s \in V(p)$, for any $p \in P$.
- $M, s \models \neg\varphi$ iff $M, s \not\models \varphi$.
- $M, s \models \varphi \vee \psi$ iff $M, s \models \varphi$ or $M, s \models \psi$.
- $M, s \models K_a\varphi$ iff $\forall s' \in m_a(s): M, s' \models \varphi$, where $m_a(s) = \{s'|s\sim_a s'\}$ denotes the set of states indistinguishable from s for agent a.
- $M, s \models \mathfrak{K}_a^l\varphi$ where $l = \langle q_1, \ldots, q_k\rangle$, iff firstly for all $1 \leq i \leq k$, we have $q_i \in obs(a)$, and secondly either $\forall s' \in m_a(s)|_l^s: M, s' \models \varphi$ or $\forall s' \in m_a(s)|_l^s: M, s' \models \neg\varphi$. We call such l an answer query for (a, φ) in s.
- $M, s \models \Diamond\mathfrak{K}_a^b\varphi$ iff for some query l, $M, s \models \mathfrak{K}_a^l$ and $cost(l) \leq b$.
  Potential certainty expresses that under a given resource bound, the agent has a way to obtain certainty by applying some relevant observations. Note that this does not guarantee that the agent *will* obtain the certainty, since he may not know exactly what observation is the right one in each step of querying.
- $M, s \models \Box\mathfrak{K}_a^b\varphi$ iff, for all queries l which are relevant for a in s and $cost(l) \leq b$, we have either $M, s \models \mathfrak{K}_a^l\varphi$, or there exists a query l' so that $M, s \models \mathfrak{K}_a^{l \cdot l'}\varphi$ and $cost(l \cdot l') \leq b$.
  Equivalently, we can define guaranteed certainty by saying that $M, s \models \Box\mathfrak{K}_a^b\varphi$ iff, for all relevant queries l for agent a in s, which are maximal under bound b (meaning that adding any observation to the query makes its cost more than b), l is an answer query for φ in s. Guaranteed certainty expresses that the agent, by applying relevant and possible observations in any order, obtains certainty without running out of resource.

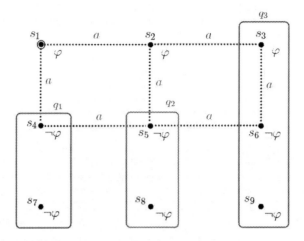

Fig. 3. Observation-based certainty about φ using $\langle q_1, q_2, q_3 \rangle$

3.3   Examples

Example 4. Consider the model in Figure 3. The initial set of possible diseases for the medical agent a is $\{s_1, s_2, \ldots, s_6\}$. Moreover, proposition φ is true in a state if the corresponding disease is dangerous, otherwise it is false. In this example, in some of the possible worlds for the agent the formula φ is true, while in some it is not. Therefore initially the agent is not certain about seriousness of the disease. There are three types of medical tests available, corresponding to observations q_1, q_2 and q_3. After updating its initial set of possible worlds with $l_1 = \langle q_1, q_2, q_3 \rangle$, the agent gets $\{s_1, s_2\}$. Since φ is true in both s_1 and s_2, we have that the agent can use l_1 to become certain about the truth value of φ. We denote this by $M, s_1 \models \mathfrak{K}_a^{l_1} \varphi$. If the agent prescribes only the medical tests q_2 and q_3, then the updated set is $\{s_1, s_2, s_4\}$. As φ is neither true in all elements of this set, nor false in all of them, we have $M, s_1 \not\models \mathfrak{K}_a^{l_2} \varphi$.

Example 5. Now consider the model in Figure 4. As before, the available medical tests are represented with observations q_1, q_2, and q_3. Next to each observation there is a number that shows the cost of applying that medical test. In our example the cost of a test is the time needed to execute it. So, the time needed for test q_1 is 5 hours, and for tests q_2, q_3 it is 2 hours each. The medical agent is not certain about the seriousness of the disease, but it is guaranteed to be certain about it if it has at least 5 hours for doing the tests. To see why, first note that initially all the three observations tests are relevant and their costs are all lower than the bound. Thus, the agent has three choices. If it chooses q_1 as the first test, the updated set is $\{s_1, s_2, s_3\}$. In all the worlds in this set φ is true, So the agent has obtained certainty (in this case, it knows that the disease is dangerous). If the agent chooses q_2 first, the updated set is $\{s_1, s_2, s_3, s_5, s_6\}$.

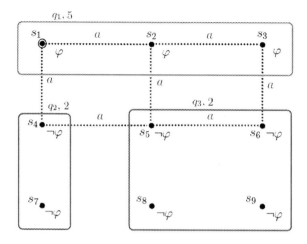

Fig. 4. Guaranteed certainty about φ under bound 5

The agent is not certain yet and has to continue applying observations. The time needed of applying q_2 is 2, so after applying q_2 the agent has $5 - 2 = 3$ hours left, during which it only can apply q_3. After updating by q_3, the updated set is $\{s_1, s_2, s_3\}$. The agent does not need to continue prescribing new tests because the certainty is already gained. The result of applying q_3 first is similar to the previous case, except that this time the second observation is inevitably q_2. So if the agent at each step, chooses any arbitrary observation from the relevant and possible ones, it attains certainty about φ under bound 5. Therefore in this example $M, s_1 \models \Box \mathfrak{K}_a^5 \varphi$.

If the agent had only 3 hours for tests, the only possible choices would be $q2$ and $q3$. But after updating the set of its possible worlds with each of these observations the agent would still be uncertain about the seriousness of the disease and the remaining time would not suffice for applying any more observations. Therefore $M, s_1 \not\models \Diamond \mathfrak{K}_a^3 \varphi$.

Note, finally, that if the actual disease is s_4, the agent is able to obtain certainty within 3 hours. This is possible by choosing observation q_2. On the other hand, a chooses q_3 first, it will not obtain certainty within the same time. Thus, in state s_4, the agent has potential but not guaranteed certainty about φ, i.e., $M, s_4 \models \Diamond \mathfrak{K}_a^3 \varphi \wedge \neg \Box \mathfrak{K}_a^3 \varphi$.

Example 6. Nested formulas refer to an agent's certainty about its own, or another agent's certainty. Consider medical agent a is not sufficiently equipped to become certain about the seriousness of the disease (Figure 5). Instead, a has to decide to which specialized medical center the patient should be sent. The medical centre b specializes in brain diseases, and the medical center c specializes in heart diseases. Test q_1 is a general test and is available for all the agents a, b and c. Test q_2 is only available at the brain centre, and test q_3 is only available at the heart center. So in this model $obs(a) = \{q_1\}$, $obs(b) = \{q_1, q_2\}$ and

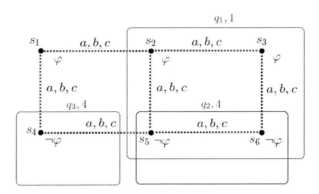

Fig. 5. If $obs(a) = \{q_1\}$, $obs(b) = \{q_1, q_2\}$, and $obs(c) = \{q_1, q_3\}$, then agent a has observation-based certainty about certainty of agents b and c

$obs(c) = \{q_1, q_3\}$. By applying the medical test q_1 the medical agent a is able to determine which specialized center are competent to do the diagnosis in a given time (say, up to 5 hours), and which are not: $M, s_1 \models \mathfrak{K}_a^{\langle q_1 \rangle} \Diamond \mathfrak{K}_b^5 \varphi \wedge \mathfrak{K}_a^{\langle q_1 \rangle} \Diamond \mathfrak{K}_b^5 \varphi$. In consequence, we also have that $M, s_1 \models \Diamond \mathfrak{K}_a^1 \Diamond \mathfrak{K}_b^5 \varphi \wedge \Diamond \mathfrak{K}_a^1 \Diamond \mathfrak{K}_b^5 \varphi$ and $M, s_1 \models \Box \mathfrak{K}_a^1 \Diamond \mathfrak{K}_b^5 \varphi \wedge \Box \mathfrak{K}_a^1 \Diamond \mathfrak{K}_b^5 \varphi$: the agent has bot potential and guaranteed certainty to learn about b and c's epistemic abilities within 1 hour.

4   Some Properties

In this section, we present some interesting properties that can be expressed in LAcK. We begin by listing some validities that capture interesting general properties of accumulative knowledge. Then, in Section 4.2, we show how the basic information-theoretic notion of *Hartley measure* can be characterized in or framework.

4.1   Interesting Validities

Below we list some interesting validities of LAcK. We give only some of the proofs; the others are either straightforward or analogous.

Theorem 1. *The following formulas are valid in LAcK:*

1. $K_a \varphi \rightarrow \mathfrak{K}_a^l \varphi$.
   Certainty cannot be destroyed by observations.
2. $\mathfrak{K}_a^l \varphi \rightarrow \mathfrak{K}_a^{l \cdot l'} \varphi$.
   A more general variant of 1.
3. $\mathfrak{K}_a^l \varphi \wedge \mathfrak{K}_a^l \psi \rightarrow \mathfrak{K}_a^l (\varphi \wedge \psi)$.
   Outcomes of a query combine.
4. $\mathfrak{K}_a^l \varphi \wedge \mathfrak{K}_a^{l'} \psi \rightarrow \mathfrak{K}_a^{l \cdot l'} (\varphi \wedge \psi)$.
   Combining queries yields combined outcomes.

5. $K_a\varphi \to \Diamond\mathfrak{K}_a^b\varphi$ and $K_a\varphi \to \Box\mathfrak{K}_a^b\varphi$.
   A variant of 1 for potential and guaranteed observation-based certainty.
6. $\Diamond\mathfrak{K}_a^b\varphi \to \Box\mathfrak{K}_a^{b+b'}\varphi$ and $\Box\mathfrak{K}_a^b\varphi \to \Box\mathfrak{K}_a^{b+b'}\varphi$.
   Monotonicity of observation-based certainty wrt resource bounds.
7. $\Diamond\mathfrak{K}_a^b\varphi \wedge \Diamond\mathfrak{K}_a^{b'}\psi \to \Diamond\mathfrak{K}_a^{b+b'}(\varphi \wedge \psi)$.
8. $\Diamond\mathfrak{K}_a^b\varphi \vee \Diamond\mathfrak{K}_a^{b'}\psi \to \Diamond\mathfrak{K}_a^{max(b,b')}(\varphi \vee \psi)$.
   Combination rules for potential observation-based certainty.
9. $\Box\mathfrak{K}_a^b\varphi \wedge \Box\mathfrak{K}_a^{b'}\psi \to \Box\mathfrak{K}_a^{max(b,b')}(\varphi \wedge \psi)$.
10. $\Box\mathfrak{K}_a^b\varphi \vee \Box\mathfrak{K}_a^{b'}\psi \to \Box\mathfrak{K}_a^{max(b,b')}(\varphi \vee \psi)$.
    Combination rules for guaranteed observation-based certainty.
11. $\Box\mathfrak{K}_a^b\varphi \to \Diamond\mathfrak{K}_a^b\varphi$.
    Guaranteed certainty implies potential certainty.
12. $\Box\mathfrak{K}_a^\infty\varphi \leftrightarrow \Diamond\mathfrak{K}_a^\infty\varphi$.
    For unlimited resources, the two notions of observation-based uncertainty coincide.

Proof

Ad. 7: From the antecedent, we know that there is an answer query l for (a, φ) such that $cost(l) \leq b$, and there is an answer query l' for (a, ψ) such that $cost(l') \leq b'$. Therefore $l \cdot l'$ is answer query for $(a, \varphi \wedge \psi)$, and $cost(l \cdot l') = cost(l) + cost(l') < b + b'$.

Ad. 9: Assume that $max(b, b') = b$. Then by definition, any relevant maximal query l under bound b is an answer query for (a, φ). Then there exist queries l_1 and l_2 such that $l = l_1 + l_2$ and l_1 is a maximal query under bound b'. From $\Box\mathfrak{K}_a^{b'}\varphi$ we know that l_1 is an answer query for (a, ψ), therefor $l = l_1 + l_2$ is also an answer query for (a, ψ). As l is an answer query both for (a, φ) and for (a, ψ), it is an answer query for $(a, \varphi \wedge \psi)$. The proof is similar in the case that $max(b, b') = b'$.

Ad. 12: Inferring $\Diamond\mathfrak{K}_a^\infty\varphi$ from $\Box\mathfrak{K}_a^\infty\varphi$ is a direct result of the previous property. For proving the other direction, first note that changing the order of the observations in a query does not change the updated set of worlds, and adding some observations to a query cannot make an answer query a non-answer query. Now if we have $\Diamond\mathfrak{K}_a^\infty\varphi$, then there is an answer query l for (a, φ). Therefore any query l' which consists of all the available observations is also an answer query for (a, φ). As the upper limit for the resource is infinity, the agent can choose the observations in any order and it is guaranteed to be certain about φ without running out of recourse, hence $\Box\mathfrak{K}_a^\infty\varphi$.   □

4.2   Relation to Information Theory

In the previous sections we have defined a framework for reasoning about agents that collect information in order to become certain about a given property. In other words, the agents reduce their uncertainty about the property by accumulating observations. There seems to be an intuitive connection to the classical definition of uncertainty, and in particular Hartley measure of uncertainty. In this section, we look at the relationship.

Two most established measures of uncertainty are *Hartley measure* and *Shannon entropy*. Hartley measure is based on possibility theory, whereas Shannon entropy is based on probability theory. Hartley measure quantifies uncertainty in terms of a finite set of possible outcomes. Let X be the set of all alternatives under consideration, out of which only one is considered the *correct one*. Note that this can be seen as corresponding to the set of possible worlds and the actual world, respectively. It was shown by Hartley [20] that the only sensible way to measure the uncertainty about the correct alternative in a set of alternatives X is to use the function:

$$H(X) = \lceil \log_2 |X| \rceil.$$

The unit of uncertainty measured by $H(X)$ is *bit*. The intuition behind Hartley measure is that $\log_2 |X|$ is the minimal number of binary questions that guarantees identifying the correct alternative, provided that the set of questions is rich enough. We will now use the intuition to characterize Hartley measure in LAcK.

Definition 8 (Bisective Observations). *Let $n[i]$ denote the ith bit in the binary unfolding of n. A set of observations O is* bisective *for states S iff there is a bijective ordering of states $ord : S \to \{1, \ldots, |S|\}$ and a bijective mapping $bitno : O \to \{1, \ldots, \lceil \log |S| \rceil\}$ such that $cover(q) = \{s \in S \mid (ord(s))[bitno(q)]\}$ for every $q \in Q$. In other words, we see S as a k-dimensional binary cube, with each $q \in Q$ "cutting across" a different dimension.*

Definition 9 (Distinguishing model). *A possible worlds model M is distinguishing by formulas $\psi_1, \ldots, \psi_k$ iff for every state s_i in M there exists ψ_i which holds exactly in s_i.*

Definition 10 (Hartley model, Hartley formula). *We say that an observation-based certainty model $M = \langle S, R, V, Obs, obs, cost, cover \rangle$ is a Hartley model iff:*

1. *M consists of a single agent a (the "observer"),*
2. *M is distinguishing by some formulas $\psi_1, \ldots, \psi_k$,*
3. *Obs includes a set of bisective observations for S, and*
4. *The cost of every observation is 1.*

The Hartley formula *of M under bound b is defined as: $\chi(M, b) \equiv \bigwedge_{s_i \in S} \Diamond \mathfrak{K}_a^b \psi_i$.*

Intuitively, Hartley formula in a Hartley model expresses that the observer can identify the actual world in at most b steps.

Theorem 2. *Let M be a Hartley model with state space S. Then, for all $s \in S$, we have $M, s \models_{LAcK} \chi(M, H(S))$.*

Proof. Take a query consisting of all the bisective observations in M. Clearly, the query updates any set of indistinguishable states yielding the singleton set containing only the actual state. Moreover, it consists of at most $H(S)$ steps, which concludes the proof.   □

5 Model Checking

In this section, we look at the complexity of verification for accumulative knowledge. Similarly to many problems where agents' uncertainty is involved, it turns out to be **NP**-hard. We also show that the hardness of the problem is due to bounded resources. Finally, we prove that verification becomes tractable in many realistic scenarios where resource bounds are relatively tight.

5.1 General Result

The (local) model checking problem for LAcK is formally defined as follows.

Definition 11 (Model checking for LAcK)
Input: *Observation-based certainty model M, state s in M, LAcK formula φ;*
Output: *yes iff $M, s \models_{\mathsf{LAcK}} \varphi$.*

We will show that the problem sits in the first level of polynomial hierarchy, more precisely between **NP** $\cup$ **coNP** and $\mathbf{\Delta_2^P}$ (where $\mathbf{\Delta_2^P} = \mathbf{NP^{NP}}$ is the class of problems that can be solved in polynomial by a deterministic Turing machine asking adaptive queries to an **NP** oracle). We start by showing the upper bound.

Proposition 1. *Model checking LAcK is in $\mathbf{\Delta_2^P}$.*

Proof. We demonstrate the upper bound by the following algorithm.

$mcheck(M, s, \varphi)$:

Case $\varphi \equiv p$: return($s \in V(p)$);
Cases $\varphi \equiv \neg\psi, \psi_1 \wedge \psi_2, K_a\psi$: standard;
Case $\varphi \equiv \mathfrak{K}_a^l \psi$: $X := \{s' \in S \mid mcheck(M, s', \psi)\}$;
$\quad\quad\quad\quad\quad\quad$ return($m_a(s)|_l^s \subseteq X$ or $m_a(s)|_l^s \subseteq S \setminus X$);
Case $\varphi \equiv \Diamond \mathfrak{K}_a^b \psi$: return($oracle_1(M, s, \psi)$);
Case $\varphi \equiv \Box \mathfrak{K}_a^b \psi$: return(not $oracle_2(M, s, \psi)$);

$oracle_1(M, s, \psi)$:

$X := \{s' \in S \mid mcheck(M, s', \psi)\}$;
guess a query l with no repeated observations;
return$\big(cost(l) \leq b$ and $(m_a(s)|_l^s \subseteq X$ or $m_a(s)|_l^s \subseteq S \setminus X)\big)$;

$oracle_2(M, s, \psi)$:

$X := \{s' \in S \mid mcheck(M, s', \psi)\}$;
guess a query l with no repeated observations;
$maximal := (cost(l) \leq b$ and for all observations $q \notin l$: $cost(lq) > b$;
return$\big(maximal$ and $m_a(s)|_l^s \not\subseteq X$ and $m_a(s)|_l^s \not\subseteq S \setminus X)\big)$; $\square$

To prove the lower bound, we will use an old result by Karp [21].

Definition 12 ([21]). SETCOVERING *is the following decision problem.*
Input: *Domain of elements D, a finite family of finite sets $\mathcal{S} = \{S_1, \ldots, S_n\} \subseteq 2^{2^D}$, and a number $k \in \mathbb{N}$;*
Output: *yes iff there exists a family of k sets $\mathcal{T} = \{T_1, T_2, \ldots, T_k\} \subseteq \mathcal{S}$ such that $\bigcup_j T_j = \bigcup_i S_i$.*

Proposition 2 ([21]). SETCOVERING *is* **NP**-*complete.*

Lemma 1. *Model checking of the LAcK formula $\Diamond \mathfrak{K}_a^b p$ is* **NP**-*complete.*

Proof. Inclusion in **NP** follows from the algorithm in the proof of Proposition 1. The lower bound is obtained by a reduction of SETCOVERING. Let M include:

- $S = D \cup \{s_0\}$ for some $s_0 \notin D$;
- $A = \{a\}$, and $\sim_a = S \times S$;
- $Obs = \{q_1, \ldots, q_n\}$, and $cover(q_i) = \{s_0\} \cup S_i$;
- $cost(q_i) = 1$ for every i;
- single atomic proposition p_0 with $V(p_0) = \{s_0\}$.

Now, SETCOVERING$(D, \{S_1, \ldots, S_n\}, k)$ iff $M, s_0 \models_{\text{LAcK}} \Diamond \mathfrak{K}_a^k$.   □

The following is a straightforward consequence (note that we can use negation to obtain the complement of a problem expressible in LAcK).

Proposition 3. *Model checking LAcK is* **NP**-*hard and* **coNP**-*hard.*

Thus, finally, we obtain the following result.

Theorem 3. *Model checking LAcK is between* (**NP** $\cup$ **coNP**) *and* $\mathbf{\Delta_2^P}$.

5.2   Closer Look

What is the hard part of the verification problem for LAcK? The next result shows that the hardness is due to bounded resources, since with unlimited resources the problem becomes easy.

Proposition 4. *If $\mathcal{B} = \{\infty\}$ then model checking LAcK is in* **P**.

Proof. First, observe that $M, s \models \Diamond \mathfrak{K}_a^\infty \varphi$ iff $M, s \models \mathfrak{K}_a^l \varphi$ for l being the "grand query" collecting all the observations available for a in M. Moreover, $M, s \models \Box \mathfrak{K}_a^\infty \varphi$ iff $M, s \models \Diamond \mathfrak{K}_a^\infty \varphi$ by Theorem 1, point 12. For the other cases, we proceed according to the algorithm in the proof of Proposition 1. It is easy to see that the new algorithm terminates in time $O(|S| \cdot |Obs| \cdot |\varphi|)$.   □

Finally, we want to suggest that the pessimistic view of Theorem 3 is not always justified. True, verification is **NP**-hard in general. However, we argue that it only makes sense to engage in checking $M, s \models \Diamond \mathfrak{K}_a^b \varphi$ or $M, s \models \Diamond \mathfrak{K}_a^b \varphi$ if a's observations are relatively expensive compared to the available resources b. After all, if observations were cheap, a might as well skip deliberation and start observing right away. The following result shows that when the relation between costs and bounds is tight, the model checking problem becomes easy again.

Proposition 5. *Let $\alpha > 1$ be given and fixed. Model checking $\Diamond \mathfrak{K}_a^b p$ and $\Box \mathfrak{K}_a^b p$ in a model such that $\min\{cost(q) \mid q \in Obs\} \geq \frac{b}{\alpha(\log|S|+\log|Obs|+\log b)}$ is in* **P**.

Proof. If $\min\{cost(q) \mid q \in Obs\} \geq \frac{b}{\alpha(\log|S|+\log|Obs|+\log b)}$ then every query that consists of more than $\alpha(\log|S| + \log|Obs| + \log b)$ observations will cost more than b. Thus, it suffices to check the outcome of at most $2^\alpha \cdot b \cdot |S| \cdot |Obs|$ queries, which is polynomial in the size of the model.

Note that, for this result, it is essential that α is not a parameter of the problem, and it makes sense only for relatively small values of α. □

6   Conclusions

Intelligent agents usually choose their actions based on their knowledge about the environment. In order to gain or refine this knowledge, agents may perform informative actions. Informative actions like all other actions require resources. Therefore, the abilities of agents to improve their knowledge are limited by the resources available to them. In this work, we propose a modal approach to modeling, analyzing, and reasoning about agents that build their knowledge by using resource-consuming informative actions.

Our approach is based on several simplifying assumptions, which might not hold in real situations. Nevertheless, we believe the approach to be useful, especially with respect to simple scenarios. In more complex contexts, refinements of the framework could be needed.

Acknowledgements. Wojciech Jamroga acknowledges the support of the FNR (National Research Fund) Luxembourg under project GALOT – INTER/DFG/12/06. Masoud Tabatabaei also acknowledges the support of the National Research Fund, Luxembourg (AFR Code:5884506).

References

1. Ågotnes, T., van Ditmarsch, H.: Coalitions and announcements. In: Proceedings of AAMAS, pp. 673–680 (2008)
2. Alchourrón, C., Gärdenfors, P., Makinson, D.: On the logic of theory change: Partial meet contraction and revision functions. Journal of Symbolic Logic 50(2), 510–530 (1985)
3. Alechina, N., Logan, B.: Logical omniscience and the cost of deliberation. In: Nieuwenhuis, R., Voronkov, A. (eds.) LPAR 2001. LNCS (LNAI), vol. 2250, pp. 100–109. Springer, Heidelberg (2001)
4. Alechina, N., Logan, B.: Ascribing beliefs to resource bounded agents. In: Proceedings of AAMAS, pp. 881–888. ACM (2002)
5. Alechina, N., Logan, B.: A complete and decidable logic for resource-bounded agents. In: Proceedings of AAMAS 2004, pp. 606–613. IEEE Computer Society (2004)

6. Alechina, N., Logan, B., Nga, N., Rakib, A.: Verifying properties of coalitional ability under resource bounds. In: Proceedings of the Logics for Agents and Mobility, LAM (2009)
7. Alechina, N., Logan, B., Nguyen, H., Rakib, A.: Resource-bounded alternating-time temporal logic. In: Proceedings of AAMAS, pp. 481–488 (2010)
8. Alechina, N., Logan, B., Nguyen, H., Rakib, A.: Logic for coalitions with bounded resources. Journal of Logic and Computation 21(6), 907–937 (2011)
9. Bolander, T., Birkegaard Andersen, M.: Epistemic planning for single- and multi-agent systems. Journal of Applied Non-Classical Logics 21(1), 9–34 (2011)
10. Bulling, N., Farwer, B.: Expressing properties of resource-bounded systems: The logics RTL* and RTL. In: Dix, J., Fisher, M., Novák, P. (eds.) CLIMA X. LNCS, vol. 6214, pp. 22–45. Springer, Heidelberg (2010)
11. Bulling, N., Farwer, B.: On the (un-)decidability of model checking resource-bounded agents. In: Proceedings of ECAI. Frontiers in Artificial Intelligence and Applications, vol. 215, pp. 567–572. IOS Press (2010)
12. Della Monica, D., Napoli, M., Parente, M.: On a logic for coalitional games with priced-resource agents. Electron. Notes Theor. Comput. Sci. 278, 215–228 (2011)
13. Draper, D., Hanks, S., Weld, D.: A probabilistic model of action for least-commitment planning with information gathering. In: Proceedings of the Tenth International Conference on Uncertainty in Artificial Intelligence, pp. 178–186. Morgan Kaufmann Publishers Inc. (1994)
14. Eberle, R.A.: A logic of believing, knowing, and inferring. Synthese 26, 356–382 (1974)
15. Fagin, R., Halpern, J.Y.: Belief, awareness, and limited reasoning. Artificial Intelligence 34(1), 39–76 (1987)
16. Fagin, R., Halpern, J.Y., Moses, Y., Vardi, M.Y.: Reasoning about Knowledge. MIT Press (1995)
17. Friedman, N., Halpern, J.: A knowledge-based framework for belief change, Part II: Revision and update. In: Proceedings of KR 1994, pp. 190–200 (1994)
18. Grabisch, M., Marichal, J.-L., Mesiar, R., Pap, E.: Aggregation Functions. Cambridge University Press (2009)
19. Halpern, J., Moses, Y., Vardi, M.: Algorithmic knowledge. In: Proceedings of TARK 1994, pp. 255–266 (1994)
20. Hartley, R.: Transmission of information. The Bell System Technical Journal 7(3), 535–563 (1928)
21. Karp, R.: Reducibility among combinatorial problems. In: Miller, R., Thatcher, J. (eds.) Complexity of Computer Computations, pp. 85–103 (1972)
22. Konolige, K.: A Deduction Model of Belief. Morgan Kaufmann Publishers Inc., San Francisco (1986)
23. Kripke, S.: Semantic analysis of modal logic. Zeitschrift fur Mathematische Logik und Grund lagen der Mathematik 9, 67–96 (1963)
24. Moore, R., Hendrix, G.: Computational models of beliefs and the semantics of belief sentences (1979)
25. Rantala, V.: A modal logic for coalitional power in games. Acta Philosophica Fennica 35, 18–24 (1982)
26. Sardiña, S., Giacomo, G.D., Lespérance, Y., Levesque, H.: On the limits of planning over belief states under strict uncertainty. In: Proceedings of KR, pp. 463–471 (2006)
27. Simon, H.: Theories of bounded rationality. In: McGuire, C., Radner, R. (eds.) Decision and Organization, pp. 161–176. North-Holland, Amsterdam (1972)
28. van Ditmarsch, H., van der Hoek, W., Kooi, B.: Dynamic Epistemic Logic. Springer (2007)

Time Is Up! – Norms with Deadlines in Action Languages

Matthias Knorr, Alfredo Gabaldon, Ricardo Gonçalves, João Leite, and Martin Slota

CENTRIA, Universidade Nova de Lisboa, 2829-516 Caparica, Portugal

Abstract. Action Languages are simple logical formalisms to describe the properties of a domain and the behavior of an agent and to reason about it. They offer an elegant solution to the frame problem, but are inapt to reason with norms in which an obligation deadline may require the agent to adapt its behavior even though no action occurred. In this paper we extend the Action Language $\mathcal{A}$ with features that allow reasoning about norms and time in dynamic domains. Unlike previous extensions of Action Languages with norms, our resulting language is expressive enough to represent and reason with different kinds of obligations with deadlines that explicitly refer to time, as well as norm violations and even simple contrary-to-duty obligations resulting from the satisfaction or violation of an agent's obligations.

1 Introduction

Open dynamic systems, e.g., systems interacting on the Web, social systems and open agent communities, have attracted increased attention in recent years. In these systems, constraints on the behavior of the participants cannot be hard-wired in their specification. Instead, desirable properties by *normative systems* [22,8,7,3,10,35]. Norms, when used to govern *autonomous* agents, do not simply act as hard constraints that prevent the agent from adopting some behavior, but rather provide an indication as to how the agent *should* behave which, if not adhered to, can result in the application of sanctions or other normative effects.

In general, *norms* can be seen as a specification of what is expected to follow from a specific state of affairs, e.g., in the form of *obligations*. There are *obligations to-do*, i.e., obligations to execute an action before a deadline—e.g., to reply within one day after receiving a request, or to register before logging in; *obligations to-achieve*, i.e., obligations to bring about, before the deadline, a state of the world in which some proposition holds—e.g., to achieve a certain amount of credits within the academic year; and *obligations to-maintain*, i.e., obligations to maintain a state of the world in which some proposition holds until the deadline—e.g., to keep the contract with your mobile phone company for one year.

One important characteristic of realistic systems of norms is the prominent role of *time* and *deadlines*. Another feature of complex systems of norms are *reparative obligations*, or *contrary-to-duty obligations* [11], i.e., obligations imposed as a consequence of the violation of some other obligation—e.g., to pay a fine within 10 days if the obligation to return an item by a deadline is violated.

J. Leite et al. (Eds.): CLIMA XIV, LNAI 8143, pp. 223–238, 2013.

Action Languages [25] are simple logical formalisms for modeling dynamic systems, with application in *Artificial Intelligence, Robotics* and *Multi-Agent Systems*. A theory of an *Action Language* describes the properties of a domain and the abilities of an agent, compactly specifying a transition diagram containing all possible trajectories of the system. Action Languages provide a simple and elegant solution to the *frame problem* and enable an agent to encode the applicability of actions, their effects, describe complex interrelations between fluents and use automated planning to achieve some goal. Additionally, Action Languages can easily be encoded in the declarative and well studied paradigm of Answer Set Programming [24]—see, e.g., Coala [23]—thus benefiting from existing highly efficient answer set solvers, such as clasp.[1]

The combination of Action Languages and norms has received some attention in the literature. The line of work in [16,5] extends action language $\mathcal{C}+$ [27] for representing norms and institutional aspects of normative societies, focusing on power and count-as rules. In [26], an action language is extended with propositions for specifying defeasible authorization and obligation policies, but only obligations to-do are considered. In [14], the authors introduce the action language InstAL aimed at representing institutions of agents. This approach uses events as deadlines and can represent obligations and violations of obligations and even contrary-to-duty obligations, but, just like the previous ones, it cannot deal with obligations to-achieve or to-maintain. In fact, none of the previous approaches deals with explicit time, deadlines and the different kinds of obligations simultaneously.

As it turns out, existing Action Languages, and their extensions, cannot capture the dynamics of explicit time deadlines because of the fundamental role they assign to physical *actions*, whose execution is in general *the only way* to cause a state change. With the introduction of norms with explicit time deadlines, and obligations introduced by the violation or satisfaction of previous obligations, state change needs to also be triggered literally just by the passage of time, namely by the violation of other obligations, resulting from the expiration of the deadlines, which cannot be encoded in existing Action Languages.[2] The proposal in [15] focuses on policy analysis with the explicit presence of time, but does not admit obligations to-achieve or to-maintain nor obligations introduced by the violation or satisfaction of such obligations.

To address this limitation, in this paper, we extend the Action Language $\mathcal{A}^3$ [25] with features that allow reasoning about norms and time in dynamic domains, resulting in the Normative Action Language $\mathcal{A}_\mathcal{N}$ and a simple query language that can deal with

- *obligations to-do, to-achieve* and *to-maintain*;
- deadlines that explicitly refer to time;
- norm violations and satisfactions;
- simple contrary-to-duty obligations on satisfaction/violation of obligations.

---

[1] http://www.cs.uni-potsdam.de/clasp/

[2] Note that in the action language of [38] and in $\mathcal{C}+$, state change can also be caused by state conditions. E.g., for [38] internal actions, so-called triggered actions, can be executed based only on state conditions. However, this is obviously insufficient for our purposes because explicit time is not present.

[3] We restrict ourselves to $\mathcal{A}$ and focus on explaining the technical details related to norms with explicit time deadlines, leaving more expressive Action Languages for future work.

At the same time, our approach solves the frame problem also for obligations and it is more amenable to implementation than other related work based on more complex formalisms (see related work in Sect. 4). Please note that, commonly, in these formalisms, one deontic modality can be expressed via the other. Due to our simpler semantics, that is not possible, i.e., we focus on obligations, and leave a more extensive treatment including other deontic modalities (e.g., permission and prohibition) for future work.

After introducing, in Sect. 2, the syntax and semantics of our normative Action Language $\mathcal{A_N}$, illustrating its use, and presenting some basic properties, in Sect. 3 we present a query language for $\mathcal{A_N}$, discuss its complexity and equivalence between theories in $\mathcal{A_N}$, before we conclude in Sect. 4.

2 Normative Action Language $\mathcal{A_N}$

We introduce the syntax and semantics of $\mathcal{A_N}$, a simple language for specifying norms, yet expressive enough to handle different kinds of obligations with deadlines, their satisfaction and violation, and simple contrary-to-duty obligations introduced by the satisfaction/violation of other obligations. We start from the deterministic Action Language $\mathcal{A}$ [25] whose semantics builds on transition systems in which nodes correspond to states of the environment and edges correspond to transitions between states and are labeled by the action that causes the transition. To capture the meaning of a set of norms, we extend this transition system by expanding the states with a deontic component, and by adding a temporal dimension to transitions.

2.1 Syntax

Action Languages provide two disjoint, non-empty sets of function-free first-order atoms[4] defined over a given signature $\Sigma = \langle \mathcal{P}, \mathcal{C}, \mathcal{V} \rangle$ of pairwise disjoint sets of predicates ($\mathcal{P}$), constants ($\mathcal{C}$) and variables ($\mathcal{V}$): a set $\mathcal{A}$ of *elementary actions* and a set $\mathcal{F}$ of *physical fluents*. An *action* is a finite, possibly empty subset of $\mathcal{A}$ and can be understood as a set of elementary actions that are executed simultaneously. If convenient, we denote a singleton action $\{\alpha\}$ with the elementary action α. Physical fluents $f \in \mathcal{F}$ and their negations $\neg f$ form the set of *physical literals*, used to represent states of the "world."

To allow for deontic expressions with explicit time deadlines, we extend the signature Σ with a set of *time points* $\mathcal{T}$ and a set of *time variables* $\mathcal{V}_t$, resulting in the deontic signature $\Sigma_d = \langle \mathcal{P}, \mathcal{C} \cup \mathcal{T}, \mathcal{V} \cup \mathcal{V}_t \rangle$. From now on, we assume an arbitrary but fixed deontic signature Σ_d.

Both additions to the signature are related to time, and we explain them in the following. The set of time points $\mathcal{T}$ represents the time domain, and we assume that $\mathcal{T}$ is a countable subset of non-negative real numbers, including 0, such as the set of natural numbers $\mathbb{N}$. The set of time variables $\mathcal{V}_t$ relates specifically to $\mathcal{T}$ in the same standard way as $\mathcal{V}$ relates to $\mathcal{C}$, and we reserve a special time variable $\mathbf{now} \in \mathcal{V}_t$ which we always associate with the time point representing the current time.

---

[4] In [25], only the propositional case is considered. We use function-free first-order atoms here to ease the presentation of our formalization of time.

Both $\mathcal{T}$ and $\mathcal{V}_t$ are used to define *time expressions*, which allow us to shift time points into the future by a specific time interval. The set of *time expressions* $\mathcal{T}^*$ is defined as $\mathcal{T}^* = \mathcal{T} \cup \{ V + c \mid V \in \mathcal{V}_t \wedge c \in \mathcal{T} \}$.[5] Where convenient, we simply abbreviate $V + 0$ by V.

We now introduce *deontic literals* to represent three types of obligations: 1. *obligations to-do*, requiring that an action be executed; 2. *obligations to-achieve*, requiring that a physical literal become true; 3. *obligations to-maintain*, requiring that a physical literal remain true; all three strictly before a specified deadline.[6]

Definition 1 (Deontic literal). *Let $A \subseteq \mathcal{A}$ be a non-empty action, l a physical literal, and $t \in \mathcal{T}^*$, called the* deadline. *An obligation is of the following three forms:*

- obligation to-do $O_t^d\ A$;
- obligation to-achieve $O_t^a\ l$;
- obligation to-maintain $O_t^m\ l$.

Obligations and their negations form the set of deontic literals. *The expression $O_t\ l$ represents both $O_t^a\ l$ and $O_t^m\ l$.*

Note that obligations to-achieve and to-maintain can be understood as dual: the intention for the former is to require that literal l holds for (at least) one time point strictly in between the introduction of the obligation and its deadline, and for the latter that l holds for all time points from the time point of the introduction until (immediately before) the deadline. This will be accordingly reflected in the semantics later, but does not mean that we can reduce one to the other as argued later in this section.

A *literal* is either a physical literal or a deontic literal. A literal is *ground* if it contains no variables. Literals f and $\neg f$ are called *complementary*. The literal complementary to l is denoted by $\bar{l}$.

In Action Language $\mathcal{A}$, only actions can cause state changes, but the introduction of obligations with deadlines should allow a state change to be triggered also by the violation (V) or the satisfaction (S) of obligations, resulting from the expiration of deadlines for obligations an agent currently has. Deontic events accommodate for that.

Definition 2 (Event). *Let d be an obligation. Deontic events are expressions of the form Vd and Sd. An event is an action or a deontic event.*

We recall propositions in $\mathcal{A}$ and at the same time extend them to include norms.

Definition 3 (Norm and normative specification). *Let e be an event, l a deontic or physical literal and C a set of literals. A proposition n takes the following form:*

$$e \textbf{ causes } l \textbf{ if } C \ . \tag{1}$$

---

[5] Here we abuse the set of time points and time variables to also represent *time intervals*. The expression $V + c$ always represents the addition of a time interval to a time point, or of two time intervals.

[6] The restriction to non-inclusive deadlines is an arbitrary decision and it would be reasonable to consider inclusive deadlines instead, or even to introduce both types of deadlines. For simplicity, we consider only non-inclusive deadlines.

We say that e is the event *of n, l its* effect *and C its* condition. *If C is empty, we write n as (e* **causes** *l). If l is a deontic literal, then n is called* norm. *If l is a physical literal, then e is an action, and all literals in the condition are physical literals. A proposition is* safe *if every variable (different from* **now***) appearing in its effect also appears in its event or in an obligation within its condition. A normative specification* $\mathcal{N}$ *is a finite set of safe propositions of the form* (1).

Intuitively, a norm of the form (1) adds or removes the obligation specified by l (depending on whether the obligation is negated or not) if the *event* occurs and the *condition* is satisfied. Also note that a proposition with physical literal l matches a proposition in $\mathcal{A}$ [25] and the rationale for the applied restrictions is that normative information should not affect the physical world. This is indeed the case and in line with the idea that obligations are meant to represent only guidelines of desired behavior for an agent (including penalties for non-compliance), unlike the line of work in which obligations can be used to prohibit the execution of an action (see, e.g., [13]). Finally, safeness of variables occurring in l prevents from the specification of propositions with non-ground effects.[7]

Example 4. Consider a set of norms in a university library scenario:

$$borrow(X) \textbf{ causes } O^d_{now+4} \, ret(X) \textbf{ if } ugrad \tag{2}$$

$$borrow(X) \textbf{ causes } O^d_{now+12} \, ret(X) \textbf{ if } grad \tag{3}$$

$$renew(X) \textbf{ causes } O^d_{T+4} \, ret(X) \textbf{ if } O^d_T \, ret(X) \tag{4}$$

$$renew(X) \textbf{ causes } \neg O^d_T \, ret(X) \textbf{ if } O^d_T \, ret(X) \tag{5}$$

$$VO^d_T \, ret(X) \textbf{ causes } O^d_{now+1} \, pay \tag{6}$$

$$VO^d_T \, ret(X) \textbf{ causes } O^d_{now+1} \, ret(X) \textbf{ if } ugrad \tag{7}$$

$$VO^d_T \, ret(X) \textbf{ causes } O^d_{now+3} \, ret(X) \textbf{ if } grad \tag{8}$$

Norms (2) and (3) specify that borrowing a book creates the obligation to return that book within the period specified depending on the student's status (4 and 12 weeks for undergraduate and graduate students respectively). A book may be renewed for 4 more weeks, which means updating the obligation with the new deadline (4–5). Finally, a contrary-to-duty norm specifies that, if a user fails to return the book on time, a fine has to be paid within one week (6) and the book has to be returned (7–8).

On different domains, an example of a norm with an achievement obligation is that one has the obligation to achieve 30 credits within the academic year, and an example of a norm with a maintenance obligation is that one has the obligation to maintain a contract with a mobile carrier for (at least) 24 months.

$$enterAcademicYear \textbf{ causes } O^a_{now+12} \, sumCredits(30)$$

$$startMobileContract \textbf{ causes } O^m_{now+24} \, mobileContract$$

---

[7] A less restrictive condition could be applied to propositions whose effect is a physical literal, but this would only affect the action language which is not our major concern.

These two norms can also be used to show why it is not possible to only consider obligations to-achieve or to-maintain and express one using the other. For example, we could try to represent the obligation to achieve 30 credits within 12 months as failing the obligation to maintain the sum of achieved credits below 30 during the next 12 months. However, our language has no means to express to "fail to maintain". We could try to express this in our language by $\neg O^m_{now+12} \neg sumCredits(30)$, but, as we will see next, this corresponds to canceling obligation $O^m_{now+12} \neg sumCredits(30)$. Another option would be to try to represent the obligation to maintain the mobile contract for 24 months as the conjunction of obligations to-achieve the mobile contract in each single month: not only would this be cumbersome, it also would be conceptually counterintuitive since achievement is intended to change the state such that a certain literal becomes true, while maintenance requires that the literal is true throughout the considered period of time.

2.2   Semantics

The semantics of Action Language $\mathcal{A}$ is defined as a transition system T modeling the physical environment. A node σ of T represents a possible physical state and a transition $\langle \sigma, A, \sigma' \rangle$ represents that state σ' can be reached from σ by executing action A. We extend such T with deontic features and time to define the semantics of normative specifications as follows. We augment states σ with deontic states δ and we define when literals are satisfied in such a combined state σ/δ. Next, we present a relation that captures how a deontic event is caused by either reaching a deadline or due to an executed action. We proceed by specifying which positive and negative normative effects are triggered in a state σ/δ, i.e., which obligations are introduced and which are canceled, when executing an action A at time t w.r.t. $\mathcal{N}$, using a Boolean function $\rho_{A,t}()$ in the former case to avoid introducing meaningless obligations. This enables us to define a resulting new deontic state and, subsequently, transitions and paths in the resulting transition system $T_{\mathcal{N}}$.

Let $\mathcal{N}$ be a normative specification. The states of the transition system $T_{\mathcal{N}}$ consist of two parts: a set of physical literals representing the physical "world," and a set of obligations representing the deontic state of the agent. Additionally, we require that obligations be part of the state only if they are not immediately satisfied or violated.

Definition 5   (State of $T_{\mathcal{N}}$). *Let σ be a complete and consistent set of ground physical literals, i.e., for each ground physical fluent f, exactly one of f and $\neg f$ belongs to σ, and δ a finite set of ground obligations. Then, σ/δ is a state of the transition system $T_{\mathcal{N}}$ if the following conditions are satisfied for every physical literal l and deadline t: $(O^a_t l \notin \delta$ or $l \notin \sigma)$ and $(O^m_t l \notin \delta$ or $l \in \sigma)$. We call σ the* physical state *and δ the* deontic state.

Note that, unlike σ, δ is not a complete representation of obligations that hold and do not hold, since it would be impractical to require that obligations d or $\neg d$ occur in δ for each d due to the usually infinite set of time points $\mathcal{T}$. This is also why we consider a separate set δ and do not merge δ and σ into one.

To deal with the satisfaction of non-ground literals in a state σ/δ, we introduce a *variable assignment* z as a function mapping variables to constants ($\mathcal{V} \to \mathcal{C}$) and time variables to time points ($\mathcal{V}_t \to \mathcal{T}$). For every time point t, we denote the set of variable assignments z such that $z(\textbf{now}) = t$ by $\mathcal{Z}_t$. Hence, the index t in $\mathcal{Z}_t$ is not merely notation, but defines the value that is assigned to **now**.

For any literal or event λ, we denote by $\lambda|_z$ the literal or event obtained from λ by substituting every variable according to z, and, subsequently, replacing every time expression $t + c$ with the time point t' such that $t' = t + c$. E.g., $O_9^d\,ret(book)$ is the result of $\left(O_{\textbf{now}+4}^d\,ret(X) \right)\big|_{\{X \to book,\,\textbf{now} \to 5\}}$.

Satisfaction for ground literals in a state σ/δ is defined as follows for a physical literal l and a ground obligation d:

$$\sigma/\delta \models l \text{ iff } l \in \sigma \ ,$$
$$\sigma/\delta \models d \text{ iff } d \in \delta \ ,$$
$$\sigma/\delta \models \neg d \text{ iff } d \notin \delta \ .$$

Furthermore, given a variable assignment z and a set of literals L, we define $\sigma/\delta \models L|_z$ iff for $l \in L$, $\sigma/\delta \models l|_z$. Note that the evaluation of deontic literals here is not an evaluation of a complex modal formula, but rather only used to check if an agent currently has a certain obligation.

Each transition of $T_\mathcal{N}$ is a tuple $\langle \sigma/\delta, (A, t), \sigma'/\delta' \rangle$, where A is a ground action and $t \in \mathcal{T}$ a time point, meaning that A occurred at time t, causing the transition from state σ/δ to σ'/δ'. Since the physical effects are independent of the deontic ones, we first define a relation $R_\mathcal{N}$ that, for a given $\mathcal{N}$, associates each physical state σ and ground action A with a new physical state σ':

$$\langle \sigma, A, \sigma' \rangle \in R_\mathcal{N} \text{ iff } \sigma' = (\sigma \cup \mathsf{E}_A(\sigma)) \setminus \{ \bar{l} \mid l \in \mathsf{E}_A(\sigma) \} \ ,$$

where $\mathsf{E}_A(\sigma)$ stands for the set of all physical literals $l|_z$ such that $(e \text{ \textbf{causes} } l \text{ \textbf{if} } C) \in \mathcal{N}$ and there is $z \in \mathcal{Z}_t$ with $\sigma/\delta \models C|_z$ and $e|_z \subseteq A$. If $A = \emptyset$, then $\sigma' = \sigma$, which allows us to handle deontic updates resulting from deadline expirations at time points in which no action occurs. Note that the requirement that σ' be a physical state ensures that $\langle \sigma, A, \sigma' \rangle \notin R_\mathcal{N}$ if A has contradictory effects in state σ.

We proceed by specifying how to obtain a new deontic state. First, we define the conditions for the occurrence of deontic events, which are satisfactions/violations of obligations occurring in the current deontic state δ w.r.t. the new physical state σ'.

Definition 6 (Occurrence of deontic event). *Let σ/δ be a state of $T_\mathcal{N}$, A, B ground actions, $\langle \sigma, A, \sigma' \rangle \in R_\mathcal{N}$ and t, t' time points. The occurrence relation for ground deontic events under action A at time t, $\vdash_{A,t}$, is defined for tuples $\langle \delta, \sigma' \rangle$ as follows:*

$\langle \delta, \sigma' \rangle \vdash_{A,t} \mathsf{VO}_{t'}^d\, B$	*iff*	$O_{t'}^d\, B \in \delta \wedge t \geq t'$
$\langle \delta, \sigma' \rangle \vdash_{A,t} \mathsf{VO}_{t'}^a\, l$	*iff*	$O_{t'}^a\, l \in \delta \wedge t \geq t'$
$\langle \delta, \sigma' \rangle \vdash_{A,t} \mathsf{SO}_{t'}^m\, l$	*iff*	$O_{t'}^m\, l \in \delta \wedge t \geq t'$
$\langle \delta, \sigma' \rangle \vdash_{A,t} \mathsf{SO}_{t'}^d\, B$	*iff*	$O_{t'}^d\, B \in \delta \wedge t < t' \wedge B \subseteq A$
$\langle \delta, \sigma' \rangle \vdash_{A,t} \mathsf{SO}_{t'}^a\, l$	*iff*	$O_{t'}^a\, l \in \delta \wedge t < t' \wedge l \in \sigma'$
$\langle \delta, \sigma' \rangle \vdash_{A,t} \mathsf{VO}_{t'}^m\, l$	*iff*	$O_{t'}^m\, l \in \delta \wedge t < t' \wedge \bar{l} \in \sigma'$

Additionally, $\epsilon_{A,t}(\delta, \sigma') = \{ e \mid \langle \delta, \sigma' \rangle \vdash_{A,t} e \}$.

The above conditions encode the dynamics of violations and satisfactions, and depend on the type of obligation involved. The first three represent events generated by a deadline expiration. The last three represent events that occur before the expiration of the respective deadline. Namely, either action B is executed (as part of the set of elementary actions A) at time t, or a state change affects the literal l to be achieved (or cease to be maintained). We explain the latter case in more detail for an obligation to-achieve l. Such an obligation can only be part of a state σ/δ if $\bar{l} \in \sigma$. If executing action A at time t introduces l, i.e., adds it to the new state σ' (and removes $\bar{l}$), then an event occurs, which (as we will see below) is used to trigger the removal of the corresponding obligation, but also possibly the introduction of new obligations.

Before defining the normative effects of executing action A at time t in state σ/δ, we need to introduce an auxiliary function $\rho_{A,t}(d, \sigma')$ that determines whether, given σ' with $\langle \sigma, A, \sigma' \rangle \in R_{\mathcal{N}}$, an obligation d, which would be introduced to the new deontic state, is *relevant*: $\rho_{A,t}(d, \sigma') = \perp$ if either (1) d is an obligation with deadline $t' \leq t$, (2) $d = O_{t'}^{\mathsf{d}} B \wedge B \subseteq A$, (3) $d = O_{t'}^{\mathsf{a}} l \wedge l \in \sigma'$, or (4) $d = O_{t'}^{\mathsf{m}} l \wedge \bar{l} \in \sigma'$; otherwise $\rho_{A,t}(d, \sigma') = \top$. Condition (1) matches the first part of Def. 6, while (2-4) matches the second. We thus avoid the introduction of obligations that would be satisfied/violated immediately, following the rationale to only consider obligations whose satisfaction can be influenced by the agent's behavior.

We now define the normative effects of executing an action A at time t in a given state σ/δ. We say that an effect of a norm is positive (negative) if it is an obligation (its negation). For each instance of a norm in $\mathcal{N}$ we need to evaluate its condition in σ/δ, check whether the respective event is a subset of action A or a deontic event, and, in case of the positive effects, check if the effect of the norm is an obligation that is relevant (or can be safely ignored). The latter and the check for deontic events occur w.r.t. the new physical state σ' (obtained by executing A on σ) as already indicated.

Definition 7 (Normative effect). *Let σ/δ be a state of $T_{\mathcal{N}}$, $\langle \sigma, A, \sigma' \rangle \in R_{\mathcal{N}}$, t a time point and d an obligation. The set of* positive normative effects $\mathsf{E}_{A,t}^+(\sigma/\delta, \sigma')$ *and the set of* negative normative effects $\mathsf{E}_{A,t}^-(\sigma/\delta, \sigma')$ *are defined as follows:*

$$\mathsf{E}_{A,t}^+(\sigma/\delta, \sigma') = \{\, (d|_z) \mid (e \text{ causes } d \text{ if } C) \in \mathcal{N} \wedge \exists z \in \mathcal{Z}_t :$$
$$\sigma/\delta \models C|_z \wedge (e|_z \subseteq A \vee \langle \delta, \sigma' \rangle \vdash_{A,t} e|_z)$$
$$\wedge\, \rho_{A,t}(d|_z, \sigma') \,\};$$

$$\mathsf{E}_{A,t}^-(\sigma/\delta, \sigma') = \{\, (d|_z) \mid (e \text{ causes } \neg d \text{ if } C) \in \mathcal{N} \wedge \exists z \in \mathcal{Z}_t :$$
$$\sigma/\delta \models C|_z \wedge (e|_z \subseteq A \vee \langle \delta, \sigma' \rangle \vdash_{A,t} e|_z) \,\}.$$

The new deontic state δ' can now be computed from σ/δ by first detecting which deontic events occur (and removing the corresponding obligations), then adding the positive effects of these events and finally removing their negative effects.

Definition 8 (New deontic state). *Let σ/δ be a state of $T_{\mathcal{N}}$, $\langle \sigma, A, \sigma' \rangle \in R_{\mathcal{N}}$, t a time point and d an obligation. We define $\mathsf{G}(\vee d) = \mathsf{G}(\mathsf{S} d) = d$, for any set of deontic events E, $\mathsf{G}(E) = \{\, \mathsf{G}(e) \mid e \in E \,\}$ and the new deontic state*

$$\delta' = \left[(\delta \setminus \mathsf{G}(\epsilon_{A,t}(\delta, \sigma'))) \cup \mathsf{E}_{A,t}^+(\sigma/\delta, \sigma') \right] \setminus \mathsf{E}_{A,t}^-(\sigma/\delta, \sigma').$$

Four consequences follow immediately: first, the definition requires that the update of the physical state has to be computed first, only then can the deontic state be updated; second, if an obligation is introduced and removed simultaneously by different norms, then the removal prevails, following a generalization of the *in dubio pro reo* principle; third, it may happen that the occurrence of a deontic event removes some obligation, which is immediately re-introduced in $E^+_{A,t}()$ if a corresponding norm exists, such as for example if you pay a fine and, at the same time, commit an offense that incurs in the same penalty; and fourth, the frame problem for obligations is trivially solved in this equation—whatever appears in δ and is not removed on purpose, persists in δ'.

We show that σ' and δ' indeed form a state of $T_\mathcal{N}$.

Proposition 9. *Let σ/δ be a state of $T_\mathcal{N}$, $\langle \sigma, A, \sigma' \rangle \in R_\mathcal{N}$, and δ' as defined in Def. 8. Then σ'/δ' is a state of $T_\mathcal{N}$.*

Furthermore, considering the definition of deontic events, whenever a deadline of an existing obligation is reached, a deontic event always takes place. A consequence of this observation is that a transition from σ/δ must not occur at a time point that exceeds the deadline of some obligation in δ. We define this time point as the earliest deadline among the current obligations, or infinity if there are no obligations in δ. Formally, let $d(\delta) = \{ t \in \mathcal{T} \mid O_t\, l \in \delta \text{ or } O^d_t\, B \in \delta \}$. Then, $\mathsf{ltp}(\delta) = \min(d(\delta))$ if $d(\delta) \neq \emptyset$ and $\mathsf{ltp}(\delta) = \infty$ if $d(\delta) = \emptyset$. Note that, since δ is assumed finite, this notion of least time point is well-defined, i.e., if $d(\delta) \neq \emptyset$, then $\mathsf{ltp}(\delta) \in d(\delta)$, which, along with Proposition 9, allows us to define transitions of $T_\mathcal{N}$:

Definition 10 (Transition). *A transition of $T_\mathcal{N}$ is a tuple $\langle \sigma/\delta, (A, t), \sigma'/\delta' \rangle$ where A is a ground action, t is a time point, σ/δ and σ'/δ' are states of $T_\mathcal{N}$ such that $\langle \sigma, A, \sigma' \rangle \in R_\mathcal{N}$ and δ' is defined as in Def. 8. Moreover, t must satisfy the condition: $t = \mathsf{ltp}(\delta)$ if $A = \emptyset$, and $t \leq \mathsf{ltp}(\delta)$ otherwise.*

Example 11. The following are transitions of $T_\mathcal{N}$ for Example 4 in Sect. 2.1.

$$\langle \{ugrad\}/\emptyset, (borrow(b), 1), \{ugrad\}/\{O^d_5\, ret(b)\} \rangle$$
$$\langle \{ugrad\}/\{O^d_5\, ret(b)\}, (ret(b), 4), \{ugrad\}/\emptyset \rangle$$
$$\langle \{ugrad\}/\{O^d_5\, ret(b)\}, (\emptyset, 5), \{ugrad\}/\{O^d_6\, pay, O^d_6\, ret(b)\} \rangle.$$

The tuple $\langle \{ugrad\}/\{O^d_5\, ret(b)\}, (ret(b), 8), \{ugrad\}/\emptyset \rangle$ is not a transition because $\mathsf{ltp}(\{O^d_5\, ret(b)\}) = 5 \ngeq 8$.

We can show that the transition system $T_\mathcal{N}$ is deterministic.

Proposition 12. *$T_\mathcal{N}$ is deterministic, i.e., if $\langle \sigma/\delta, (A, t), \sigma'/\delta' \rangle$ and $\langle \sigma/\delta, (A, t), \sigma''/\delta'' \rangle$ are transitions of $T_\mathcal{N}$, then $\sigma'/\delta' = \sigma''/\delta''$.*

Now, a path is an alternating sequence of states in $T_\mathcal{N}$ and pairs (A, t) corresponding to the transitions of $T_\mathcal{N}$.

Definition 13 (Path). *A path is a sequence of the form*

$$\sigma_0/\delta_0, (A_1, t_1), \sigma_1/\delta_1, \ldots, (A_n, t_n), \sigma_n/\delta_n \, , \tag{9}$$

where σ_j/δ_j is a state of $T_{\mathcal{N}}$ for every $0 \le j \le n$, $\langle \sigma_j/\delta_j, (A_{j+1}, t_{j+1}), \sigma_{j+1}/\delta_{j+1} \rangle$ is a transition of $T_{\mathcal{N}}$ for every $0 \le j < n$, and $t_j < t_{j+1}$ for every $1 \le j < n$.

The last condition states the assumption that the time points in a path are ordered.

The satisfaction of an obligation to-do or to-achieve and the violation of an obligation to-maintain always indicate some relevant change w.r.t. the previous state.

Proposition 14. *Let P be a path of the form (9).*

$$\text{If } \langle \delta_{j-1}, \sigma_j \rangle \vdash_{A_j, t_j} \mathsf{SO}_t^{\mathsf{d}} B, \text{ then } B \not\subseteq A_{j-1} \text{ and } B \subseteq A_j;$$
$$\text{if } \langle \delta_{j-1}, \sigma_j \rangle \vdash_{A_j, t_j} \mathsf{SO}_t^{\mathsf{a}} l, \text{ then } l \notin \sigma_{j-1} \text{ and } l \in \sigma_j;$$
$$\text{if } \langle \delta_{j-1}, \sigma_j \rangle \vdash_{A_j, t_j} \mathsf{VO}_t^{\mathsf{m}} l, \text{ then } l \in \sigma_{j-1} \text{ and } l \notin \sigma_j.$$

A symmetric result for the other three deontic events does not hold, simply because these occur due to a deadline that is reached with the progress of time.

3   Query Language and Equivalence

We now define a query language for $\mathcal{A}_{\mathcal{N}}$ that can be used to check whether a certain literal/event occurs in a specific time interval given a normative specification and a description of the initial state. We consider decidability and complexity of answering queries. Then, we also discuss equivalence between different normative specifications.

3.1   Syntax of the Query Language

A query language in the case of action languages usually consists of statements describing initial conditions and statements to query the domain description w.r.t. these initial conditions. We adapt the notion of axioms for our purpose.

Definition 15 (Axiom). *Let $\mathcal{N}$ be a normative specification and l a ground physical literal or a ground obligation. An* axiom *is of the form* **initially** *l. Given a set of axioms Γ, a physical state σ in $T_{\mathcal{N}}$* satisfies *Γ if, for every physical literal l, ($\textbf{initially } l$) $\in \Gamma$ implies $l \in \sigma$.*

Let δ be the set of obligations d such that ($\textbf{initially } d$) $\in \Gamma$. A set of axioms Γ is an initial specification *for $\mathcal{N}$ if, for every physical state σ that satisfies Γ, σ/δ forms a state of $T_{\mathcal{N}}$. Such states σ/δ are called* initial w.r.t. *Γ.*

We thus specify that an initial specification for $\mathcal{N}$ aligns with Def. 5, i.e., if Γ contains an axiom for an obligation to achieve (maintain) l, then it must also contain an axiom for $\neg l$ (l). Note that a set of axioms may not *fully specify* the physical state σ, i.e., there may be several states σ that satisfy Γ, hence several initial states.

An *action sequence* is a finite sequence $((A_1, t_1), \dots, (A_k, t_k))$ such that, for all i with $1 \le i \le k$, A_i is a non-empty action, and $t_1, \dots, t_k \in \mathcal{T}$ with $0 < t_1 < \cdots < t_k$. Given an action sequence, queries are defined as follows:

Definition 16 (Query). *Let l be a deontic literal, a deontic event—both without any occurrence of* **now**—*or a physical literal, $t_\alpha, t_\beta \in \mathcal{T}$ with $0 \le t_\alpha \le t_\beta$, and S an action sequence. A* query *is of the form $l : [t_\alpha, t_\beta] : S$.*

Note that even though our query language is quite simple, it is rather versatile and allows for expressive queries due to the usage of variables in queries. Not only may we query for non-ground fluents occurring in a certain time interval, such as whether a user had some book in her possession, but also whether there occurred any obligation or violation in a given time interval without having to specify the deadline.

3.2 Semantics of the Query Language

The semantics of the query language is defined w.r.t. paths of the transition system T_N. First, we establish that a path P of the form (9) *satisfies* an initial specification Γ for N if σ_0/δ_0 is an initial state relative to Γ. The idea is to restrict the paths considered to answer a query to those which match the initial specification.

Next, we link the action sequence in a query to a path by matching each pair (A_i, t_i) in the sequence to exactly one in the path. All other actions in the path have to be empty, i.e., they occur due to deontic events.

Definition 17 (Satisfiability of an Action Sequence). *Let S be an action sequence $(A'_1, t'_1), \ldots, (A'_k, t'_k)$ and P a path of the form (9). P satisfies S if there is an injective mapping $\mu : \{1, \ldots, k\} \mapsto \{1, \ldots, n\}$ (from S to P) such that*

1. *for each i with $1 \leq i \leq k$, $A'_i = A_{\mu(i)}$ and $t'_i = t_{\mu(i)}$,*
2. *for each j with $1 \leq j \leq n$, if $\mu(i) \neq j$ for all i with $1 \leq i \leq k$, then $A_j = \emptyset$.*

Given the definition of action sequences and paths, if such an injective mapping μ exists, then it is clearly unique, and so is the path corresponding to an action sequence for a fixed initial state.

To evaluate whether a certain literal or event holds while executing a sequence of actions, we need to collect all states that fall into the time interval $[t_\alpha, t_\beta]$ given in the query. That is, we collect the state at t_α and all the states inside the interval, or alternatively the final state in the path if the last transition occurs before t_α. In the former case, if there is no action occurring precisely at t_α, then we have to consider the state prior to t_α, because that is then the current state at t_α. Formally, given a path P of the form (9) and time points $t_\alpha \leq t_\beta$, we define the set

$$s(P, [t_\alpha, t_\beta]) = \{\sigma_i/\delta_i \mid t_i < t_\alpha < t_{i+1}\} \cup \{\sigma_i/\delta_i \mid t_\alpha \leq t_i \leq t_\beta\} \cup \{\sigma_n/\delta_n \mid t_n < t_\alpha\}.$$

Additionally, we want to ensure that only those paths are considered that cover the entire interval so that we do not miss any states. Therefore, we define that path P *reaches* time point t if either $t_n \geq t$ or $\mathsf{ltp}(\delta_n) = \infty$.

Finally, we can define how queries are evaluated.

Definition 18 (Query satisfaction). *Let Q be a query of the form $l : [t_\alpha, t_\beta] : S$, N a normative specification and Γ an initial specification for N. Q is a consequence of Γ w.r.t. N, denoted by $\Gamma \models_N Q$, if, for every path P that satisfies Γ and S and that reaches t_β, there exists a variable assignment z such that one of these conditions holds:*

(a) for some $\sigma/\delta \in s(P, [t_\alpha, t_\beta])$, $\sigma/\delta \models l|_z$ if l is a literal;
(b) for some j with $t_\alpha \leq t_j \leq t_\beta$, $\langle \delta_{j-1}, \sigma_j \rangle \vdash_{A_j, t_j} l|_z$ if l is a deontic event.

Note that our definition of query satisfaction implies that if the action sequence is not executable, then the query holds automatically for all paths in the transition system satisfying the conditions, simply because there are none. That is related to the question of consistent action descriptions [39] and also implicit domain constraints [30,37], and we refer to the literature for ways to avoid such problems.

Example 19. Recall Example 4 and $\Gamma = \{\textbf{initially } ugrad\}$:

$$Q_1 = \mathsf{VO}_X^{\mathsf{d}} \, ret(b) : [1,8] : \langle (borrow(b) : 1), (ret(b) : 4) \rangle;$$
$$Q_2 = \mathsf{O}_5^{\mathsf{d}} \, ret(Y) : [0,4] : \langle (borrow(b) : 1) \rangle;$$
$$Q_3 = ugrad : [0,9] : \langle (borrow(b) : 1), (ret(b) : 4) \rangle.$$

We obtain that $\Gamma \not\models_{\mathcal{N}} Q_1$, but $\Gamma \models_{\mathcal{N}} Q_2$ and $\Gamma \models_{\mathcal{N}} Q_3$.

We analyze decidability and computational complexity of answering queries where we measure the input in the size of the set of axioms Γ.

Theorem 20. *Let Q be a query, $\mathcal{N}$ a normative specification and Γ an initial specification for $\mathcal{N}$. If the physical states in $T_{\mathcal{N}}$ are finite, then answering $\Gamma \models_{\mathcal{N}} Q$ is decidable in* coNP. *If Γ additionally fully specifies σ, then answering $\Gamma \models_{\mathcal{N}} Q$ is in* P.

Note that time expressions in the state model do not affect this result nor any potential implementation, since there are only finitely many obligations in each state, and each of them simply contains one element from the time domain only.

3.3   Equivalence

Equivalence is an important problem in the area of normative systems. It can be used, for example, for simplifying normative systems, which usually tend to have redundant norms. In our approach, we define equivalence of normative specifications w.r.t. the answers they provide to queries.

Definition 21 (Equivalence). *We say that normative specifications $\mathcal{N}_1$, $\mathcal{N}_2$ are equivalent if for every set of axioms Γ and every query Q, $\Gamma \models_{\mathcal{N}_1} Q$ if and only if $\Gamma \models_{\mathcal{N}_2} Q$.*

We can show that two normative specifications being equivalent is the same as them having the same transition system.

Theorem 22. *The following conditions are equivalent for any normative specifications $\mathcal{N}_1$, $\mathcal{N}_2$:*

1) $\mathcal{N}_1$, $\mathcal{N}_2$ *are equivalent.*
2) $T_{\mathcal{N}_1} = T_{\mathcal{N}_2}$.
3) The sets of paths of $T_{\mathcal{N}_1}$ and of $T_{\mathcal{N}_2}$ coincide.

A stronger notion of equivalence requires equivalence in the presence of additional norms, important when modularly analyzing subsets of norms of a larger system. Two strongly equivalent subsets of a normative specification can be safely replaced by one another.

Definition 23 (Strong equivalence). *We say that normative specifications* $\mathcal{N}_1$, $\mathcal{N}_2$ *are* strongly equivalent *if for every normative specification* $\mathcal{N}$, $\mathcal{N}_1 \cup \mathcal{N}$ *is equivalent to* $\mathcal{N}_2 \cup \mathcal{N}$.

Strong equivalence implies equivalence but not vice-versa.

Theorem 24. *Let* $\mathcal{N}_1$, $\mathcal{N}_2$ *be normative specifications. If* $\mathcal{N}_1$ *is strongly equivalent to* $\mathcal{N}_2$, *then* $\mathcal{N}_1$ *is also equivalent to* $\mathcal{N}_2$, *but the converse implication does not hold.*

4   Conclusions

We have extended Action Language $\mathcal{A}$ with features that allow reasoning about norms, time and deadlines in dynamic domains. We have shown how our language can be used to express norms involving obligations with deadlines that explicitly refer to time and actions, including obligations to-do, to-achieve and to-maintain but also simple contrary-to-duty situations on violations and satisfactions of obligations, which previous action languages and their extensions to norms did not cover. We have defined a semantics for this language and a simple query language along with its semantics. Moreover, we studied the complexity and equivalence of normative specifications.

Notably, our framework may be useful for introducing norms to other AI action formalisms where norms with explicit time deadlines and such simple contrary-to-duty obligations have received little consideration so far. Interesting examples include the Event Calculus [32], the Situation Calculus [34], the Fluent Calculus [36] and extensions of Dynamic Logic [29] that have a solution to the frame problem [40,41,12,18].

Our query language can be used to define interesting planning problems, such as finding plans which prevent violations, or whose violations are within certain limits. Additionally, our language has important applicability in the development of electronic institutions. Electronic institutions are virtual entities that maintain, promote and enforce a set of norms. They observe agent's actions to determine norm violations (resp. satisfactions), e.g., to enforce sanctions (resp. give rewards). Given its formal semantics, and its strong links to dynamic systems, $\mathcal{A}_{\mathcal{N}}$ can be used as the language to specify and disseminate the norms and the query language used to determine violations and satisfactions.

Related work on normative systems resulted in frameworks that combine obligations and time. The proposals in [19,20,9,6], which combine dynamic, deontic and temporal logic, have a rich language, but they have difficulties in dealing with the frame problem, relevant in the propagation of obligations that have not been fulfilled yet [9], and with dealing with contrary-to-duty obligations. Also, no axiomatization exists for the proposals in [19,20], and hence automatic reasoning is not possible, while the approaches in [9,6] do not deal with actions. In [1], robustness of normative systems is studied building on temporal logic, but neither deadlines nor contrary-to-duty obligations are considered. The work in [28] aims at studying the dynamics of normative violations. However, without an explicit representation of actions, they cannot properly deal with obligations to-do, nor integrate the normative part of the system with the dynamics resulting from the execution of actions provided by Action Languages. In [21] the OperA framework is introduced for representing agent organizations. The normative component of this framework is based on an expressive deontic temporal logic. Although it can deal with contrary-to-duty obligations, it only considers obligations to-achieve and the deadlines can only be state conditions, therefore not allowing the representation of explicit time deadlines. Moreover, since the focus of the framework is the modeling of the organizational structure, non-communicative agent actions are not explicitly represented, since these are seen as internal to the agents. In [31], the authors study the interpretation of security policies from the perspective of obligations based on the concept of accountability, i.e., the property whether all obligations can be fulfilled if the involved agents are diligent. Again, only obligations to-do are considered. Finally, in [17] the focus is set on an operational semantics to be able to modify a normative system during runtime. Yet, there are no time deadlines. Instead, deadlines are state conditions, which may be an interesting extension of our work, but does not cover the expressiveness provided by our formalism.

Our work opens several interesting paths for future research. First of all, we would like to design an implementation. Of course, an encoding in ASP is always possible, but perhaps more efficient solutions exist. The ideas of our paper may then be considered to be applied in MAS architectures, such as [33]. We would also like to extend the language with other deontic constructs such as *prohibition* and *permission*. We already have some notion of prohibition, since an obligation to-maintain $\neg l$ can be seen as a prohibition to bring about l, and some notion of permission, since the removal of an obligation to-maintain $\neg l$ can be seen as a weak permission to bring about l. On the other hand, the counterpart of obligations to-do, forbidden actions, has not been considered here. Accommodating forbidden actions would require a new normative fluent $F_t\, a$ meaning that action a is forbidden until time t. Also interesting is to extend the language in order to allow complex formulas to appear in the scope of deontic operators, as it is allowed in [4] or to allow the combination of ontological and non-monotonic languages [2]. Moreover, we may consider extending our framework to more expressive Action Languages, more complex deadlines, and actions with different durations.

Acknowledgments. We would like to thank the anonymous reviewers whose comments helped to improve the paper.

Matthias Knorr, João Leite and Martin Slota were partially supported by FCT under project "ERRO – Efficient Reasoning with Rules and Ontologies" (PTDC/EIA-CCO/121823/2010). In addition, Matthias Knorr was also partially supported by FCT grant SFRH/BPD/86970/2012 and Ricardo Gonçalves was partially supported by FCT grant SFRH/BPD/47245/2008.

References

1. Ågotnes, T., van der Hoek, W., Wooldridge, M.: Robust normative systems and a logic of norm compliance. Logic Journal of the IGPL 18(1), 4–30 (2010)
2. Alberti, M., Gomes, A.S., Gonçalves, R., Knorr, M., Leite, J., Slota, M.: Normative systems require hybrid knowledge bases. In: van der Hoek, W., Padgham, L., Conitzer, V., Winikoff, M. (eds.) AAMAS, pp. 1425–1426. IFAAMAS (2012)

3. Alechina, N., Dastani, M., Logan, B.: Programming norm-aware agents. In: Proceedings of the 11th International Conference on Autonomous Agents and Multiagent Systems, AAMAS 2012, vol. 2, pp. 1057–1064. IFAAMAS (2012)

4. Alferes, J.J., Gonçalves, R., Leite, J.: Equivalence of defeasible normative systems. Journal of Applied Non-Classical Logics 23(1-2), 25–48 (2013)

5. Artikis, A., Sergot, M., Pitt, J.: Specifying norm-governed computational societies. ACM Trans. Comput. Log. 10(1), 1–42 (2009)

6. Balbiani, P., Broersen, J., Brunel, J.: Decision procedures for a deontic logic modeling temporal inheritance of obligations. Electr. Notes Theor. Comput. Sci. 231, 69–89 (2009)

7. Boella, G., van der Torre, L., Verhagen, H.: Introduction to the special issue on normative multiagent systems. Autonomous Agents and Multi-Agent Systems 17(1), 1–10 (2008)

8. Boella, G., van der Torre, L.W.N.: Regulative and constitutive norms in normative multiagent systems. In: Dubois, D., Welty, C.A., Williams, M.A. (eds.) Principles of Knowledge Representation and Reasoning: Proceedings of the Ninth International Conference (KR 2004), Whistler, Canada, June 2-5, pp. 255–266. AAAI Press (2004)

9. Broersen, J., Brunel, J.: Preservation of obligations in a temporal and deontic framework. In: Durfee, E., Yokoo, M., Huhns, M., Shehory, O. (eds.) Autonomous Agents and Multi-Agent Systems, p. 177 (2007)

10. Bulling, N., Dastani, M.: Verifying normative behaviour via normative mechanism design. In: Proceedings of the Twenty-Second International Joint Conference on Artificial Intelligence, IJCAI 2011, vol. 1, pp. 103–108. AAAI Press (2011)

11. Carmo, J., Jones, A.: Deontic logic and contrary-to-duties. In: Gabbay, D., Guenthner, F. (eds.) Handbook of Philosophical Logic, vol. 8, pp. 265–343. Kluwer Academic Publishers, Dordrecht (2002)

12. Castilho, M.A., Herzig, A., Varzinczak, I.J.: It depends on the context! a decidable logic of actions and plans based on a ternary dependence relation. In: Benferhat, S., Giunchiglia, E. (eds.) NMR, pp. 343–348 (2002)

13. Cholvy, L.: Checking regulation consistency by using SOL-resolution. In: ICAIL, pp. 73–79 (1999)

14. Cliffe, O., De Vos, M., Padget, J.: Specifying and reasoning about multiple institutions. In: Noriega, P., Vázquez-Salceda, J., Boella, G., Boissier, O., Dignum, V., Fornara, N., Matson, E. (eds.) COIN 2006. LNCS (LNAI), vol. 4386, pp. 67–85. Springer, Heidelberg (2007), http://dx.doi.org/10.1007/978-3-540-74459-7_5

15. Craven, R., Lobo, J., Ma, J., Russo, A., Lupu, E., Bandara, A.: Expressive policy analysis with enhanced system dynamicity. In: Proceedings of the 4th International Symposium on Information, Computer, and Communications Security, ASIACCS 2009, pp. 239–250. ACM, New York (2009)

16. Craven, R., Sergot, M.: Agent strands in the action language nC+. J. Applied Logic 6(2), 172–191 (2008)

17. Dastani, M., Meyer, J.J.C., Tinnemeier, N.A.M.: Programming norm change. Journal of Applied Non-Classical Logics 22(1-2), 151–180 (2012)

18. Demolombe, R., Herzig, A., Varzinczak, I.J.: Regression in modal logic. Journal of Applied Non-Classical Logics 13(2), 165–185 (2003)

19. Dignum, F., Kuiper, R.: Combining dynamic deontic logic and temporal logic for the specification of deadlines. In: HICSS (5), pp. 336–346 (1997)

20. Dignum, F., Kuiper, R.: Obligations and dense time for specifying deadlines. In: HICSS (5), pp. 186–195 (1998)

21. Dignum, V.: A model for organizational interaction: based on agents, founded in logic. Ph.D. thesis, Universiteit Utrecht (2004)

22. Esteva, M., Rodríguez-Aguilar, J.-A., Sierra, C., Garcia, P., Arcos, J.-L.: On the formal spec-
    ification of electronic institutions. In: Sierra, C., Dignum, F.P.M. (eds.) Agent Mediated Elec.
    Commerce. LNCS (LNAI), vol. 1991, pp. 126–147. Springer, Heidelberg (2001)
23. Gebser, M., Grote, T., Schaub, T.: Coala: A compiler from action languages to ASP. In: Jan-
    hunen, T., Niemelä, I. (eds.) JELIA 2010. LNCS, vol. 6341, pp. 360–364. Springer, Heidel-
    berg (2010)
24. Gelfond, M., Lifschitz, V.: Classical negation in logic programs and disjunctive databases.
    New Generation Comput. 9(3-4), 365–385 (1991)
25. Gelfond, M., Lifschitz, V.: Action languages. Electron. Trans. Artif. Intell. 2, 193–210 (1998)
26. Gelfond, M., Lobo, J.: Authorization and obligation policies in dynamic systems. In: Gar-
    cia de la Banda, M., Pontelli, E. (eds.) ICLP 2008. LNCS, vol. 5366, pp. 22–36. Springer,
    Heidelberg (2008)
27. Giunchiglia, E., Lee, J., Lifschitz, V., McCain, N., Turner, H.: Nonmonotonic causal theories.
    Artif. Intell. 153(1), 49–104 (2004)
28. Governatori, G., Rotolo, A.: Justice delayed is justice denied: Logics for a temporal account
    of reparations and legal compliance. In: Leite, J., Torroni, P., Ågotnes, T., Boella, G., van
    der Torre, L. (eds.) CLIMA XII 2011. LNCS, vol. 6814, pp. 364–382. Springer, Heidelberg
    (2011)
29. Harel, D.: First-Order Dynamic Logic. Springer-Verlag New York, Inc., Secaucus (1979)
30. Herzig, A., Varzinczak, I.J.: Metatheory of actions: Beyond consistency. Artif. Intell. 171(16-
    17), 951–984 (2007)
31. Irwin, K., Yu, T., Winsborough, W.H.: On the modeling and analysis of obligations. In: Pro-
    ceedings of the 13th ACM Conference on Computer and Communications Security, CCS
    2006, pp. 134–143. ACM, New York (2006)
32. Kowalski, R., Sergot, M.: A logic-based calculus of events. New Generation Computing 4(1),
    67–95 (1986)
33. Leite, J., Soares, L.: Adding evolving abilities to a multi-agent system. In: Inoue, K., Satoh,
    K., Toni, F. (eds.) CLIMA 2006. LNCS (LNAI), vol. 4371, pp. 246–265. Springer, Heidelberg
    (2007)
34. Reiter, R.: The frame problem in the situation calculus: A simple solution (sometimes) and
    a completeness result for goal regression. In: Lifschitz, V. (ed.) Artificial Intelligence and
    Mathematical Theory of Computation, pp. 359–380. Academic Press (1991)
35. Sadiq, W., Governatori, G., Namiri, K.: Modeling control objectives for business process
    compliance. In: Alonso, G., Dadam, P., Rosemann, M. (eds.) BPM 2007. LNCS, vol. 4714,
    pp. 149–164. Springer, Heidelberg (2007)
36. Thielscher, M.: From situation calculus to fluent calculus: State update axioms as a solution
    to the inferential frame problem. Artif. Intell. 111(1), 277–299 (1999)
37. Thielscher, M.: A unifying action calculus. Artif. Intell. 175(1), 120–141 (2011)
38. Tran, N., Baral, C.: Reasoning about triggered actions in AnsProlog and its application to
    molecular interactions in cells. In: Dubois, D., Welty, C.A., Williams, M.A. (eds.) KR, pp.
    554–564. AAAI Press (2004)
39. Zhang, D.-M., Chopra, S., Foo, N.Y.: Consistency of action descriptions. In: Ishizuka, M.,
    Sattar, A. (eds.) PRICAI 2002. LNCS (LNAI), vol. 2417, pp. 70–79. Springer, Heidelberg
    (2002)
40. Zhang, D., Foo, N.Y.: EPDL: A logic for causal reasoning. In: Nebel, B. (ed.) IJCAI, pp.
    131–138. Morgan Kaufmann (2001)
41. Zhang, D.-M., Foo, N.Y.: Interpolation properties of action logic: Lazy-formalization to the
    frame problem. In: Flesca, S., Greco, S., Leone, N., Ianni, G. (eds.) JELIA 2002. LNCS
    (LNAI), vol. 2424, pp. 357–368. Springer, Heidelberg (2002)

External Transaction Logic with Automatic Compensations

Ana Sofia Gomes and José Júlio Alferes*

CENTRIA - Dep. de Informática, Faculdade Ciências e Tecnologias
Universidade Nova de Lisboa

Abstract. External Transaction Logic ($\mathcal{ETR}$) is an extension of logic programming useful to reason about the behavior of agents that have to operate in a two-fold environment in a transactional way: an internal knowledge base defining the agent's internal knowledge and rules of behavior, and an external world where it executes actions and interact with other entities. Actions performed by the agent in the external world may fail, e.g. because their preconditions are not met or because they violate some norm of the external environment. The failure to execute some action must lead, in the internal knowledge base, to its complete rollback, following the standard ACID transaction model. Since it is impossible to rollback external actions performed in the outside world, external consistency must be achieved by executing compensating operations (or repairs) that revert the effects of the initial executed actions.

In $\mathcal{ETR}$, repairs are stated explicitly in the program. With it, every performed external action is explicitly associated with its corresponding compensation or repair. Such user defined repairs provide no guarantee to revert the effects of the original action. In this paper we define how $\mathcal{ETR}$ can be extended to automatically calculate compensations in case of failure. For this, we start by explaining how the semantics of Action Languages can be used to model the external domain of $\mathcal{ETR}$, and how we can use it to reason about the reversals of actions.

1 Introduction and Motivation

Intelligent agents in a multi-agent setting must work and reason over a two-fold environment: an external environment, representing the outside world where the agent acts, and which may include other agents; and an internal environment comprising the information about the agent's rules of behavior, preferences about the outside world, its knowledge and beliefs, intentions, goals, etc. An agent may act on the external environment (external actions), but also on the internal environment (internal actions). Examples of the latter are insertions and deletions in the agent's own knowledge base, updates on its rules of behavior or preferences.

When performing actions, agents must take into account what to do upon an action failure. This is especially relevant inasmuch as the agent has no control over the behavior of the external world. External actions may fail because their preconditions are not met at the time of intended execution or, in norm regimentation, because the execution

---

* The first author was supported by FCT grant SFRH/BD/64038/2009. The work was partially supported by project ERRO (PTDC/EIA-CCO/121823/2010).

J. Leite et al. (Eds.): CLIMA XIV, LNAI 8143, pp. 239–255, 2013.

of the action would cause the violation of some norm (e.g. as allowed by 2OPL [7]), or even by some totally unknown reason to the agent.

The failure of an action should trigger some repair plan. This is especially important when the action is part of a plan, in which case it may be necessary to undo the effects of previous actions that have succeeded. When the action to undo is an internal action, the undo should be trivial. In fact, since the agent has full control over its own internal environment, actions and updates can be made to follow the standard ACID[1] properties of transactions in databases and, as such, the effects made by internal actions are completely discarded. However, since an agent has no control over the external environment, such transactional properties cannot, in general, be guaranteed when undoing external actions.

Example 1 (Medical Diagnosis). Consider an agent in a medical scenario dealing with a two-fold Knowledge Base (KB). An internal KB defining e.g. treatment specifications and history of successful treatments of patients, and an external world where the agent interacts with patients and executes actions. When a patient arrives with a series of symptoms, the agent needs to reason about what should be the treatment applicable to the given patient, but also execute this treatment by possibly giving some medication. In case a patient shows a negative reaction to the medication, thus failing the action of treating the patient, something must be done to counter the possible side-effects of the previous treatment. Moreover, actions and updates in the internal KB need to be executed transactionally, so as to guarantee that the history of successful treatments is not updated with the medication that showed negative effects, which thereby could lead the agent to apply the same treatment again.

In this example, "what to do to counter the side-effects of a previous unsuccessful treatment" is a typical case of a repair plan, something that can be found in agent languages such as 2APL [6] (plan-repair rules) and 3APL [14] (plan-revision rules). In these languages, it is possible to state for each plan, which alternative plan should be performed in case something fails. E.g., in the example, one could say that if some treatment fails, then one should give the patient some alternative medication to counter the effects of the first medication given in the failed treatment.

In this example it is reasonable to assume that the plan (treatment) can only be repaired if the agent's specification explicitly states what are the actions to execute for each failed treatment. In other words, it is reasonable to assume that whoever programmed the agent explicitly included in the program the repair plans for each possible failure. This is e.g. the case in 2APL, where plan-repair rules explicitly include the actions to execute when a given action or plan fails.

However, if one has some knowledge of the external environment, it should be possible for the agent to automatically infer the repair plan in a given failure situation, thus saving the programmer from that task, and from having to anticipate all possible relevant failures.

Example 2 (Supermarket Robot). Imagine a scenario of a robot in a supermarket that has the task to fill up the supermarket's shelves with products. In its internal KB, the

---

[1] where ACID, as usual, stands for Atomicity, Consistency, Isolation and Durability.

agent keeps information about the products' stocks and prices, but also rules on how products should be placed (e.g. "premium" products should be placed in the shelves with higher visibility). Externally, the agent needs to perform the task of putting products in a given shelf, something that can be encoded in a blocks-world manner. In this case, when some action fails in the context of a plan for e.g. arranging the products in some manner, the agent, knowing the effects of the actions in the outside world, should be able to infer what actions to perform in order to restore the external environment to some consistent configuration, upon which some other alternative plan can be started.

Several solutions exist in the literature addressing the problem of reversing actions. E.g. [8] introduces a solution based on Action Languages [9] that reasons about what actions may revert the effects of other actions. For that they define the notions of reverse action, reverse plan and conditional reversals that undo the effects of a given (set of) action(s). These notions may allow the automatic inference of plan repairs.

In this paper we propose a logic programming like language that tackles all the previously mentioned issues. In particular, the language operates over two-fold KBs, with both an internal and an internal environment; it allows for performing actions both in the internal and the external environment; it deals with failure of actions, having a transactional behavior in the actions performed in the internal environment, and executing repair plans in the external environment; it allows to automatically infer repair plans when there is knowledge about the effects of actions.

Our solution is based on External Transaction Logic ($\mathcal{ETR}$) [12,13], an extension of Transaction Logic ($\mathcal{TR}$) [3] for dealing with the execution of external actions. Here, if a transaction fails after external actions are executed in the environment, then external consistency is achieved by issuing compensating actions that revert the effects of the initial executed actions. $\mathcal{ETR}$, as its ancestor $\mathcal{TR}$, is a very general language, that relies on the existence of oracles for querying and updating an internal KB and, in the case of $\mathcal{ETR}$, also for dealing with the external environment. Besides recalling the preliminaries of $\mathcal{ETR}$ (Section 2) and [8] (Section 4), in this paper we:

1. formalize how the external oracle in $\mathcal{ETR}$ can be instantiated using action languages in general, and specifically, with action language $\mathcal{C}$ (Section 3);
2. extend $\mathcal{ETR}$ to deal with repair plans, rather than simply with compensating actions (Section 5);
3. formalize how to automatically infer repair plans when the external environment is expressed as an action language (Section 5);
4. elaborate on the properties of these repair plans (Section 5.3).

2   External Transaction Logic

$\mathcal{ETR}$ [13] is an extension of Transaction Logic [3] to deal with actions performed in an external environment of which an agent has no control. The original Transaction Logic ($\mathcal{TR}$) is a logic to reason about changes in KBs, when these changes are performed as ACID transactions. In a nutshell[2], $\mathcal{TR}$ syntax extends that of first order logic with

---

[2] For lack of space, and since $\mathcal{ETR}$ is a proper extension of $\mathcal{TR}$ (cf. [13]), we do not include here a detailed overview of $\mathcal{TR}$ alone. For the complete details see e.g. [3].

a serial conjunction operator $\otimes$, where $\phi \otimes \psi$ represents the action composed by an execution of ϕ followed by an execution of ψ. Formulas are read as transactions, and they are evaluated over sequences of KB states (*paths*). A formula (or transaction) ϕ is true over a path π iff the transaction successfully executes over that sequence of states. In other words, in $\mathcal{TR}$ truth means successful execution of a transaction. The logic itself makes no particular assumption about the representation of states, or on how states change. For that, $\mathcal{TR}$ requires the existence of two oracles, one abstracting the representation of KB states and used to query them (data oracle $\mathcal{O}^d$), and another abstracting the way the states change (transition oracle $\mathcal{O}^t$).

Besides the concept of a model of a $\mathcal{TR}$ theory, which allows one to prove properties of the theory independently of the paths chosen, $\mathcal{TR}$ also defines the notion of executional entailment. A transaction is entailed by a theory given an initial state, if there is a path starting in that state on which the transaction succeeds. As such, given a transaction and an initial state, the executional entailment determines the path that the KB should follow in order to succeed the transaction in an atomic way. Nondeterministic transactions are possible, in which case several successful paths exist. Transaction Logic Programs [2] are a special class of $\mathcal{TR}$ theories that extend logic programs with serial conjunction. For them, a proof procedure and corresponding implementation exists, which takes into account the ACID execution of transactions.

To deal also with external actions, $\mathcal{ETR}$ operates over a KB including both an internal and an external component. For that, formally $\mathcal{ETR}$ works over two disjoint propositional languages: $\mathcal{L}_P$ (program language), and $\mathcal{L}_O$ (oracles primitives language). Propositions in $\mathcal{L}_P$ denote actions and fluents that can be defined in the program. As usual, fluents are propositions that can be evaluated without changing the state and actions are propositions that cause evolution of states. Propositions in $\mathcal{L}_O$ define the primitive actions and queries to deal with the internal and external KB. $\mathcal{L}_O$ can still be partitioned into $\mathcal{L}_i$ and $\mathcal{L}_a$, where $\mathcal{L}_i$ denotes primitives that query and change the internal KB, while $\mathcal{L}_a$ defines the external actions primitives that can be executed externally. For convenience, it is assumed that $\mathcal{L}_a$ contains two distinct actions failop and nop, respectively defining trivial failure and trivial success in the external domain.

Further, it is also defined $\mathcal{L}_a^*$ as the result of augmenting $\mathcal{L}_a$ with expressions $\text{ext}(a, b)$, called external actions, where $a, b \in \mathcal{L}_a$. Such an expression is used to denote the execution of action a, having action b as compensating action. If b is nop, then we simply write $\text{ext}(a)$ or a. Note that there is no explicit relation between a and b and that it is possible to define different compensating actions for the same action a in the same program. It is thus the programmer's responsibility to determine which is the correct compensation for action a in a given moment.

To construct complex formulas, the language uses the standard connectives $\wedge, \neg$ and $\otimes$ denoting serial conjunction, where $\phi \otimes \psi$ represents the action composed by an execution of ϕ followed by an execution of ψ.

Definition 1 ($\mathcal{ETR}$ **atoms, formulas and programs**). *An $\mathcal{ETR}$ atom is either a proposition in $\mathcal{L}_P$, $\mathcal{L}_i$ or $\mathcal{L}_a^*$ and an $\mathcal{ETR}$ literal is either ϕ or $\neg\phi$ where ϕ is an $\mathcal{ETR}$ atom. An $\mathcal{ETR}$ formula is either a literal, or an expression, defined inductively, of the form $\phi \wedge \psi$, $\phi \vee \psi$ or $\phi \otimes \psi$, where ϕ and ψ are $\mathcal{ETR}$ formulas.*

An $\mathcal{ETR}$ program is a set of rules of the form $\phi \leftarrow \psi$ where ϕ is a proposition in $\mathcal{L}_P$ and ψ is an $\mathcal{ETR}$ formula.

Example 3. Recall Example 1 regarding a medical diagnosis. A possible (partial) encoding of it in $\mathcal{ETR}$ can be expressed by the following rules:

$$sick(X) \leftarrow hasFlu(X)$$
$$hasFlu(X) \leftarrow \mathbf{ext}(hasFever(X)) \otimes \mathbf{ext}(hasHeadache(X)) \otimes nonSerious(X)$$
$$nonSerious(X) \leftarrow \mathbf{ext}(\neg vomiting(X)) \wedge \ldots \wedge \mathbf{ext}(\neg diarrhea(X))$$
$$treatment(X,Y) \leftarrow hasFlu(X) \otimes treatFlu(X,Y) \otimes treatmentHistory(X,Y,Z).ins\otimes$$
$$\mathbf{ext}(goodReaction(X,Y))$$
$$treatFlu(X,Y) \leftarrow \mathbf{ext}(giveMeds(X,p_1), giveMeds(X,c_1))$$
$$treatFlu(X,Y) \leftarrow \mathbf{ext}(giveMeds(X,p_2), giveMeds(X,c_2))$$

In this example, predicate $treatment(X,Y)$ denotes a transaction for treating patient X with treatment Y. Then, one can say, e.g. in the 4th rule, that such a transaction succeeds if a patient X has flue and a medicine Y to treat the flue is given to X (i.e. transaction $treatFlu(X,Y)$ succeeds). Additionally, after a treatment is issued, the medical history of the patient should be updated and the agent needs to check if the patient shows a positive reaction to the treatment in question. In this sense, the formula $treatmentHistory(X,Y,Z).ins \otimes \mathbf{ext}(goodReaction(X,Y))$ denotes the action composed by updating the treatment history of patient X followed by externally asking if the patient X had a good reaction to treatment Y. Moreover, treating a patient with a flue is encoded by the nondeterministic transaction $treatFlu(X,Y)$ (5th and 6th rules) as the external action of giving patient X the medicine p_1 or the medicine p_2. While the action of asking about the reaction of a patient does not need to be repaired, the same is not true for the action of giving a medication. If a failure occurs, the agent has to compensate for it. This is, e.g. expressed by the external action $\mathbf{ext}(giveMeds(X,p_1), giveMeds(X,c_1))$ where c_1 cancels the effects of p_1.

A state in $\mathcal{ETR}$ is a pair (D, E), where D (resp. E) is the internal (resp. external) state identifier taken from a set $\mathcal{D}$ (resp. $\mathcal{E}$). The semantics of states is provided by 3 oracles, which come as a parameter to $\mathcal{ETR}$: a data oracle $\mathcal{O}^d$ that maps elements of $\mathcal{D}$ into transaction formulas; a transition oracle $\mathcal{O}^t$ that maps a pair of elements from $\mathcal{D}$ into transaction formulas; and an external oracle $\mathcal{O}^e$ that maps a pair of elements from $\mathcal{E}$ into transaction formulas. Intuitively $\mathcal{O}^d(D) \models \varphi$ means that, according to the oracle, φ is true in state D, and $\mathcal{O}^t(D_1, D_2) \models \varphi$ (resp. $\mathcal{O}^e(E_1, E_2) \models \varphi)$ that φ is true in the transition of internal (resp. external) states from D_1 to D_2 (resp. E_1 to E_2).

As in $\mathcal{TR}$, $\mathcal{ETR}$ formulas are evaluated in paths (sequence of states). For convenience, as it is necessary in the sequel, paths also include the explicit annotation of the action executed in each transition of states. So $\langle S_1, {}^\varphi S_2 \rangle$ means that action φ occurred in the transition of state S_1 into S_2. Then, interpretations map paths to a Herbrand structures. If $\phi \in M(\pi)$ then, in the interpretation M, path π is a valid execution for the formula ϕ. Moreover, we only consider as interpretations the mappings that comply with the specified oracles:

Definition 2 (Interpretations). *An interpretation is a mapping M assigning a classical Herbrand structure to every path. This mapping is subject to the following restrictions, for all states D_i, E_j and every formula φ:*

1. $\varphi \in M(\langle\langle (D, E) \rangle\rangle)$ iff $\mathcal{O}^d(D) \models \varphi$ for any external state E
2. $\varphi \in M(\langle\langle (D_1, E),^\varphi (D_2, E) \rangle\rangle)$ iff $\mathcal{O}^t(D_1, D_2) \models \varphi$ for any external state E
3. $\varphi \in M(\langle\langle (D, E_1),^\varphi (D, E_2) \rangle\rangle)$ iff $\mathcal{O}^e(E_1, E_2) \models \varphi$ for any internal state D

Satisfaction of $\mathcal{ETR}$ formulas over paths, requires the prior definition of operations on paths. For example, the formula $\phi \otimes \psi$ is true (i.e. successfully executes) in a path that executes ϕ up to some point in the middle, and executes ψ from then onwards. To deal with this:

Definition 3 (Path Splits). A split of a path $\pi = \langle S_1,^{A_1} \ldots,^{A_{i-1}} S_i,^{A_i} \ldots,^{A_{k-1}} S_k \rangle$ of size k (k-path) is any pair of subpaths, π_1 and π_2, such that $\pi_1 = \langle S_1,^{A_1} \ldots,^{A_{i-1}} S_i \rangle$ and $\pi_2 = \langle S_i,^{A_i} \ldots,^{A_{k-1}} S_k \rangle$ for some i $(1 \leq i \leq k)$. In this case, we write $\pi = \pi_1 \circ \pi_2$.

Before we are able to define general satisfaction of formulas, we need two auxiliary relations for constructing compensations. Classical satisfaction is similar to satisfaction in the original $\mathcal{TR}$, and a transaction formula is said to be classically satisfied by an interpretation given a path iff the transaction succeeds in the path without failing any action. A transaction is partially (or partly) satisfied by an interpretation given a path, iff the transaction succeeds in the path up to some point where an action may fail.

Definition 4 (Classical Satisfaction). Let M be an interpretation, π a path and ϕ a formula.

1. **Base Case:** $M, \pi \models_c \phi$ iff $\phi \in M(\pi)$ for any atom ϕ
2. **Negation:** $M, \pi \models_c \neg\phi$ iff it is not the case that $M, \pi \models_c \phi$
3. **"Classical" Conjunction:** $M, \pi \models_c \phi \wedge \psi$ iff $M, \pi \models_c \phi$ and $M, \pi \models_c \psi$.
4. **Serial Conjunction:** $M, \pi \models_c \phi \otimes \psi$ iff $M, \pi_1 \models_c \phi$ and $M, \pi_2 \models_c \psi$ for some split $\pi_1 \circ \pi_2$ of path π.

Definition 5 (Partial Satisfaction). Let M be an interpretation, π a path and ϕ a formula.

1. **Base Case:** $M, \pi \models_p \phi$ iff ϕ is an atom and one of the following holds:
   (a) $M, \pi \models_c \phi$
   (b) $M, \pi \not\models_c \phi$, $\phi \in \mathcal{L}_i$, $\pi = \langle (D, E) \rangle$, $\neg\exists D_i$ s.t. $M, \langle (D, E),^\phi (D_i, E) \rangle \models_c \phi$
   (c) $M, \pi \not\models_c \phi$, $\phi \in \mathcal{L}_a^*$, $\pi = \langle (D, E) \rangle$, $\neg\exists E_i$ s.t. $M, \langle (D, E),^\phi (D, E_i) \rangle \models_c \phi$
2. **Negation:** $M, \pi \models_p \neg\phi$ iff it is not the case that $M, \pi \models_p \phi$
3. **"Classical" Conjunction:** $M, \pi \models_p \phi \wedge \psi$ iff $M, \pi \models_p \phi$ and $M, \pi \models_p \psi$
4. **Serial Conjunction:** $M, \pi \models_p \phi \otimes \psi$ iff one of the following holds:
   (a) $M, \pi \models_p \phi$ and $M, \pi \not\models_c \phi$
   (b) $\exists$ split $\pi_1 \circ \pi_2$ of path π s.t. $M, \pi_1 \models_c \phi$ and $M, \pi_2 \models_p \psi$

With this, we say that a transaction ϕ fails and can be compensated only if $M, \pi \models_p \phi$ but $M, \pi \not\models_c \phi$ where the last state of π stands for the exact point where ϕ fails.

Example 4. Consider and internal KB where a state D is a set of ground atoms and $\mathcal{O}^d(D) = D$. Moreover, for every atom p in D, the transition oracle defines the actions $p.ins$ and $p.del$ respectively denoting insertion and deletion of atom p, and where

$p.ins \in \mathcal{O}^t(D_1, D_2)$ iff $D_2 = D_1 \cup \{p\}$ and $p.del \in \mathcal{O}^t(D_1, D_2)$ iff $D_2 = D_1 - \{p\}$. Furthermore, consider that the external oracle includes $\mathcal{O}^e(E_1, E_2) \models a$, (i.e. the external execution of a in state E_1 succeeds, and makes the external world evolve into E_2), $\mathcal{O}^e(E_1, E_4) \models c$, and that for every state E, $\mathcal{O}^e(E_2, E) \not\models b$ (i.e. the execution of b in state E_2 fails).

Besides these oracles, consider the following rules defining a transaction t:

$$t \leftarrow p.ins \otimes \mathbf{ext}(a, d) \otimes \mathbf{ext}(b, e)$$
$$t \leftarrow q.ins \otimes \mathbf{ext}(c)$$

In this example, the formula $p.ins \otimes \mathbf{ext}(a, d)$ is classically satisfied by all interpretations in the path $\langle(\{\}, E_1), {}^{p.ins}(\{p\}, E_1), {}^{\mathbf{ext}(a,d)}(\{p\}, E_2)\rangle$ while $q.ins \otimes \mathbf{ext}(c)$ is classically satisfied in the path $\langle(\{\}, E_1), {}^{q.ins}(\{q\}, E_1), {}^{\mathbf{ext}(c)}(\{q\}, E_4)\rangle$. Moreover, it is easy to check that $\mathbf{ext}(b, e)$ cannot succeed in any path starting in state E_2 (given the external oracle definition). The idea of partial satisfaction is to identify the path $\langle(\{\}, E_1), {}^{p.ins}(\{p\}, E_1), {}^{\mathbf{ext}(a,d)}(\{p\}, E_2)\rangle$ as one that partly satisfies the complex formula $p.ins \otimes \mathbf{ext}(a, d) \otimes \mathbf{ext}(b, e)$ up to some point, though it eventually fails since the external action $\mathbf{ext}(b, e)$ fails.

When a formula fails in a path after the execution of some external action, we have to say how these actions can be compensated. To define this, we first need to define some auxiliary operations on paths. To start, one has to collect all actions that have been executed in a path and need to be compensated; and to rollback the internal state:

Definition 6 (Rollback Path, and Sequence of External Actions). *Let π be a k-path of the form $\langle(D_1, E_1), {}^{A_1}(D_2, E_2), {}^{A_2}\ldots, {}^{A_{k-1}}(D_k, E_k)\rangle$. The rollback path of π is the path obtained from π by: (1) Replacing all D_is by the initial state D_1; (2) Keeping just the transitions where $A_i \in \mathcal{L}_a^*$.*
The sequence of external actions of π, denoted $\mathrm{Seq}(\pi)$, is the sequence of actions of the form $\mathbf{ext}(a, b)$ that appear in the transitions of the rollback path of π.

$\mathrm{Seq}(\pi)$ only collects the external actions that have the form $\mathbf{ext}(a, b)$. Since this operation aims to compensate the executed actions, then actions without compensations are skipped. With this, a recovery path is obtained from executing each compensation operation defined in $\mathrm{Seq}(\pi)$ in the inverse order.

Definition 7 (Inversion, and Recovery Path). *Let S be a sequence of actions from $\mathcal{L}_a^*$ of the form $\langle\mathbf{ext}(A_1, A_1^{-1}), \ldots \mathbf{ext}(A_n, A_n^{-1})\rangle$. Then, the inversion of S is the transaction formula $\mathrm{Inv}(S) = A_n^{-1} \otimes \ldots \otimes A_1^{-1}$.*
π_r is a recovery path of $\mathrm{Seq}(\pi)$ w.r.t. M iff $M, \pi_r \models_c \mathrm{Inv}(\mathrm{Seq}(\pi))$.

We can now say which paths compensate a formula and define satisfaction.

Definition 8 (Compensating Path for a Transaction). *Let M be an interpretation, π a path and ϕ a formula. $M, \pi \rightsquigarrow \phi$ iff all the following hold:*

1. $\exists \pi_1$ such that $M, \pi_1 \models_p \phi$ and $M, \pi_1 \not\models_c \phi$
2. $\exists \pi_0$ such that π_0 is the rollback path of π_1
3. $\mathrm{Seq}(\pi_1) \neq \emptyset$ and $\exists \pi_r$ such that π_r is a recovery path of $\mathrm{Seq}(\pi_1)$ w.r.t. M
4. π_0 and π_r are a split of π, i.e. $\pi = \pi_0 \circ \pi_r$

Definition 9 (General Satisfaction). *Let M be an interpretation, π a path and ϕ a formula.*

1. **Base Case:** $M, \pi \models \phi$ *if* $\phi \in M(\pi)$ *for any atom* ϕ
2. **Negation:** $M, \pi \models \neg\phi$ *if it is not the case that* $M, \pi \models \phi$
3. **"Classical" Conjunction:** $M, \pi \models \phi \wedge \psi$ *if* $M, \pi \models \phi$ *and* $M, \pi \models \psi$.
4. **Serial Conjunction:** $M, \pi \models \phi \otimes \psi$ *if* $M, \pi_1 \models \phi$ *and* $M, \pi_2 \models \psi$ *for some split* $\pi_1 \circ \pi_2$ *of* π.
5. **Compensating Case:** $M, \pi \models \phi$ *if* $M, \pi_1 \rightsquigarrow \phi$ *and* $M, \pi_2 \models \phi$ *for some split* $\pi_1 \circ \pi_2$ *of* π
6. *For no other* M, π *and* ϕ, $M, \pi \models \phi$.

With this notion of satisfaction, a formula ϕ succeeds if it succeeds classically or, if although an external action failed to be executed, the system can recover from the failure and ϕ can still succeed in an alternative path (point 5). Obviously, recovery only makes sense when external actions are performed before the failure. Otherwise we can just rollback to the initial state and try to satisfy the formula in an alternative branching.

Example 5. Recall example 4 and assume that $\mathcal{O}^e(E_3, E_4) \models c$ and $\mathcal{O}^e(E_2, E_3) \models d$. Then, the rollback path of $\pi = \langle(\{\}, E_1),^{p.ins}(\{p\}, E_1),^{\text{ext}(a,d)}(\{p\}, E_2)\rangle$ is the path $\langle(\{\}, E_1),^{\text{ext}(a,d)}(\{\}, E_2)\rangle$ and $\texttt{Seq}(\pi) = \langle\text{ext}(a,d)\rangle$. Furthermore, the path $\langle(\{\}, E_2),^{a^{-1}}(\{\}, E_3)\rangle$ is a recovery path of $\texttt{Seq}(\pi)$ w.r.t. any interpretation M.

Based on these, the complex formula $(p.ins \otimes \text{ext}(a,d) \otimes \text{ext}(b,e)) \vee (q.ins \otimes \text{ext}(c))$ is satisfied both in the path $\langle(\{\}, E_1),^{q.ins}(\{q\}, E_1),^{\text{ext}(c)}(\{q\}, E_4)\rangle$ – without compensations – but also in the path: $\langle(\{\}, E_1),^{\text{ext}(a,d)}(\{\}, E_2),^{d}(\{\}, E_3),^{q.ins}(\{q\}, E_3),^{\text{ext}(c)}(\{q\}, E_4)\rangle$ – using point 5 above, in this case.

Definition 10 (Models, Logical and Executional Entailment). *Let ϕ and ψ be two $\mathcal{ETR}$ formulas and M be an interpretation. M is a model of ϕ (denoted $M \models \phi$) iff $M, \pi \models \phi$ for every path π. M is a model of a program P iff for every rule $\phi \leftarrow \psi$ in P, if M is a model of ψ then it is also a model of ϕ.*
Then, ϕ logically entails ψ ($\phi \models \psi$) if every model of ϕ is also a model of ψ.
   $P, \langle S_1,^{A_1} \ldots,^{A_{n-1}} S_n \rangle \models \phi$ $(\star)$ iff $M, \langle S_1,^{A_1} \ldots,^{A_{n-1}} S_n \rangle \models \phi$ for every model M of P. We also define $P, S_1- \models \phi$ to be true (and say that ϕ succeeds in P from the state S_1), if there exists a path $S_1,^{A_1} \ldots,^{A_{n-1}} S_n$ that makes $(\star)$ true.

3   Action Languages in $\mathcal{ETR}$

The general $\mathcal{ETR}$ is parametrized by a set of oracles defining the elementary primitives to query and update the internal and external KB. However, to deal with specific problems, these oracles must be defined. For example, to deal with simple internal KBs, one can define a so-called relational oracle, in which: states are defined by sets of atoms; the data oracle simply returns all these formulas, i.e., $\mathcal{O}^d(D) = D$; the transition oracle defines, for each predicate p, two internal actions, $p.ins$ and $p.del$, respectively stating the insertion and deletion of p as $p.ins \in \mathcal{O}^t(D_1, D_2)$ iff $D_2 = D_1 \cup \{p\}$, and $p.del \in \mathcal{O}^t(D_1, D_2)$ iff $D_2 = D_1 - \{p\}$.

If the agent knows nothing about the external environment, the external oracle $\mathcal{O}^e$ can be left open, and whenever the evaluation of an action is required of that oracle, the oracle is called returning either failure or a subsequent successful state (which can be the same state, if the external action is simply a query). However, the agent may have some knowledge about the behavior of the external world. Here we consider the case where the agent's knowledge about the external world can be formalized by Action Languages [9], and show how to define an external oracle for that. Moreover, below we use the external oracle defined in this section to automatically infer repair plans.

Every action language defines a series of *laws* describing actions in the world and their effects. Which laws are possible as well as the syntax and semantics of each law depends on the action language in question. Several solutions like STRIPS, languages $\mathcal{A}, \mathcal{B}, \mathcal{C}$ or $PDDL$, have been proposed in the literature, each with different applications in mind. A set of laws of each language is called an action program description. The semantic of each language is determined by a transition system which depends on the action program description.

Let $\langle \{\texttt{true}, \texttt{false}\}, \mathcal{F}, \mathcal{A} \rangle$ be the signature of an action language, where $\mathcal{F}$ is the set of fluent names and $\mathcal{A}$ is the set of action names in the language. Let $\langle S, V, R \rangle$ be a transition system where S is the set of all possible states, V is the evaluation function from $\mathcal{F} \times S$ into $\{\texttt{true}, \texttt{false}\}$, and finally R is the set of possible relations in the system defined as a subset of $S \times \mathcal{A} \times S$. We assume a function $\mathcal{T}(E)$ that from action program E defines the transition system $\langle S, V, R \rangle$ associated with E, and the previously defined signature. We also define $\mathcal{L}^a = \mathcal{F} \cup \mathcal{A}$.

Equipped with such a function, an $\mathcal{ETR}$ external state is a pair, with the program E describing the external domain and a state of the transition system, and the general external oracle $\mathcal{O}^e$ is (where $\mathcal{T}(E) = \langle S, V, R \rangle$):

1. $\mathcal{O}^e((E, s), (E, s')) \models action$ iff $action \in \mathcal{A} \wedge \langle s, action, s' \rangle \in R$
2. $\mathcal{O}^e((E, s), (E, s)) \models fluent$ iff $fluent \in \mathcal{F} \wedge V(fluent, s) = \texttt{true}$

To be more concrete, let us show one instantiation of this, with action language $\mathcal{C}$ [11]. This language and its extensions like $\mathcal{C}^+$ [10], are known for being traditionally used to represent norms and protocols (e.g. auction, contract formation, negotiation, rules of procedure, communication, etc.) [16,1]

A *state formula* is a propositional combination of fluent names while a *formula* is a propositional combination of fluent names and elementary action names. An external description E is a set of static and dynamic laws. A static law is a law of the form "**caused** F **if** G", where F and G are state formulas. A dynamic law is of the form "**caused** F **if** G **after** U", where F and G are state formulas and U is a formula

An important notion is that actions can be done concurrently. So, in a transition $\langle s_1, A, s_2 \rangle$, A is a subset of $\mathcal{A}$. Intuitively, to execute A from s_1 to s_2 means to execute concurrently the "elementary actions" represented by the action symbols in A changing the state s_1 into s_2. A state is an interpretation of the set of fluents $\mathcal{F}$ that is closed under the static laws. I.e. for every static law "**caused** F **if** G" and every state s, s satisfies F if s satisfies G. Then, the interpretation function V for a state is simply defined as $V(P, s) = s(P)$. To define the set of valid relations R we first need the notion of reduct. For any description E and any transition $\langle s_0, A, s_1 \rangle$ we can define the $E^{\langle s_0, A, s_1 \rangle}$, the reduct of E relative to $\langle s_0, A, s_1 \rangle$, which stands for the set consisting of:

- F for all static laws from E s.t. s_1 satisfies G
- F for all dynamic laws from E s.t. s_1 satisfies G and $s_0 \cup A$ satisfies H

We say that $\langle s_0, A, s_1 \rangle$ is *causally explained* if s_1 is the only state that satisfies the reduct $E^{\langle s_0, A, s_1 \rangle}$. Since the external oracle is defined for elementary actions rather than for sets of actions, we can define the relation R of $\mathcal{T}(E)$ as follows: $\langle s_0, a, s_1 \rangle \in R$ iff $\langle s_0, A, s_1 \rangle$ is causally explained by E and $a \in A$.

4   Reverse Actions in Action Languages

Before defining how to automatically infer repair plans in $\mathcal{ETR}$ plus an external oracle of an action language, we briefly overview [8]'s action reverses, adapting it for the action languages framework defined above.

To start, we need the notion of trajectory of a sequence of actions. Intuitively, we say that a state s_f is the trajectory of a sequence of actions applied to state s_i if there exists a trace from s_i to s_f by executing the given sequence of actions.

Definition 11 (Trajectory of a Sequence of Actions). *We say that s_f is the trajectory of $a_0 \otimes \ldots \otimes a_{m-1}$ when applied to s_0 iff:* $\exists s'_1, \ldots, s'_m$ *s.t.* $\langle s_0, a_0, s'_1 \rangle \in R$ *and* $\langle s'_i, a_i, s'_{i+1} \rangle \in R$ *then* $s'_m = s_f$ *where* $(1 \leq i \leq m - 1)$. *In this case we write* $\mathtt{traj}(s_0; [a_0 \otimes \ldots \otimes a_{m-1}]) = s_f$.

With this we can define the notion of reverse action. An action a^{-1} is a reverse action of a if whenever we execute a^{-1} after we execute a, we always obtain the (initial) state before the execution of a. This is encoded as follows.

Definition 12 (Reverse Action). *Let* a, a^{-1} *be actions in* $\mathcal{A}$. *We say that an action* a^{-1} *reverses* a *iff* $\forall s_1, s_2$ *if* $\langle s_1, a, s_2 \rangle \in R$ *then* $\exists s.\langle s_2, a^{-1}, s \rangle \in R$ *and* $\forall s.\langle s_2, a^{-1}, s \rangle \in R, s = s_1$. *In this case we write* $\mathtt{revAct}(a; a^{-1})$.

Besides the notion of reverse action, the authors of [8] also introduce the notion of reverse plan. Since a single action may not be enough to reverse the effects of another action, the notion of reverse is generalized into a sequence of actions, or *plan*. A reverse plan defines what sequences of actions are able to reverse the effects of one action.

Definition 13 (Reverse Plan). *Let* $a, a_0, \ldots, a_{m-1}$ *be actions in* $\mathcal{A}$. *We say that* $a_0 \otimes \ldots \otimes a_{m-1}$ *is a plan that reverses action* a *iff* $\forall s_1, s_2$ *s.t.* $\langle s_1, a, s_2 \rangle \in R$ *then* $\exists s'$ *s.t.* $\mathtt{traj}(s_2; [a_0 \otimes \ldots \otimes a_{m-1}]) = s'$ *and* $\forall s'$ *s.t.* $\mathtt{traj}(s_2; [a_0 \otimes \ldots \otimes a_{m-1}]) = s'$ *then* $s' = s_1$. *In this case we write* $\mathtt{revPlan}(a; [a_0 \otimes \ldots \otimes a_{m-1}])$.

Intuitively, a reverse plan is a generalization of a reverse action, as every reverse action $\mathtt{revAct}(a, a')$ is a reverse plan of size one: $\mathtt{revPlan}(a, [a'])$.

The previous definitions denote a strong relation between an action and a sequence of actions which holds for *any* state in the set of states defined in the framework. I.e., a sequence of actions is a reverse plan of a given action, if the sequence can always be applied after the execution of a and, in all the transitions defined in the set R, the application of this sequence always leads to the state before the execution of a.

However, some states may prevent the existence of a reverse plan. I.e., an action may have a reverse plan under some conditions, that do not necessarily hold at every reachable state. Thus, we need a weaker notion of reverse that takes into account the information of the states, e.g. values of some fluents obtained by sensing. By restraining the states where the reverse plan is applied, we might get reverse plans that were not applicable before. This is the idea of conditional reversal plan formalized as follows.

Definition 14 (Conditional Reversal Plan). *Let* $a, a_0, \ldots, a_{m-1}$ *be actions in* $\mathcal{A}$. *We say that* $a_0 \otimes \ldots \otimes a_{m-1}$ *is a* $\phi;\psi$-*reverse plan that reverses action* a *back iff:* $\forall s_1, s_2$ *where* $V(s_2, \phi) = V(s_1, \psi) = \mathtt{true}$, *if* $\langle s_1, a, s_2 \rangle \in R$ *then* $\exists s'$ *s.t.* $\mathtt{traj}(s_2; [a_0 \otimes \ldots \otimes a_{m-1}]) = s'$ *and* $\forall s'$ *s.t.* $\mathtt{traj}(s_2; [a_0 \otimes \ldots \otimes a_{m-1}]) = s'$ *then* $s' = s_1$.

5 $\mathcal{ETR}$ with Automatic Compensations

After defining the reversals of actions for action languages, we can show how $\mathcal{ETR}$'s external oracle can be instantiated to use these definitions and automatic infer what is the correct repair plan for each action.

However, we do not need such a strong and generic notion of reverse action as the one defined in [8]. In fact, both reverse actions and reverse plans are defined disregarding the initial state where they are being applied. When defining compensations or repairs of actions in $\mathcal{ETR}$, we already have information about the specific states where the repairs will be applied. This demands for a weaker notion of reverse action and reverse plan, defined for a pair of states rather than for a given action.

Definition 15 (Situated Reverse Action). *We say that an action* a^{-1} *reverses* s_2 *into* s_1 *iff* $\exists s.\langle s_2, a^{-1}, s \rangle \in R$ *and* $\forall s.\langle s_2, a^{-1}, s \rangle \in R, s = s_1$. *In this case we write* $\mathtt{revAct}(s_1, s_2; a^{-1})$.

Intuitively, we say that action a is a reverse action for states s_1 and s_2 iff a can be executed in state s_2 and *all* the transitions that exist in the set of relations R w.r.t. action a applied to state s_2 end in state s_1.

As in [8], instead of only considering singleton actions, we also define the notion of situated reverse plan to specify sequences of actions that are able to reverse the effects of one action. Then, $\mathtt{revPlan}(s_1, s_2; [a_0 \otimes \ldots \otimes a_{m-1}])$ states that the sequence of actions $a_0 \otimes \ldots \otimes a_{m-1}$ always restores s_1 when executed in state s_2. For that, the KB may pass through m arbitrary states necessarily ending in s_2.

Definition 16 (Situated Reverse Plan). *We say that* $a_0 \otimes \ldots \otimes a_{m-1}$ *is a plan that reverses* s_2 *back to* s_1 *iff:* $\exists s_f$ *s.t.* $\mathtt{traj}(s_2; [a_0 \otimes \ldots \otimes a_{m-1}]) = s_f$ *and* $\forall s_f$ *s.t.* $\mathtt{traj}(s_2; [a_0 \otimes \ldots \otimes a_{m-1}]) = s_f$ *then* $s_f = s_1$. *In this case we write* $\mathtt{revPlan}(s_1, s_2; [a_0 \otimes \ldots \otimes a_{m-1}])$

Clearly, several reverse plans may exist restoring s_1 from state s_2. Moreover, there are better reverse plans than others. E.g., imagine that in a state s_i there exists an action a_i that always leads us to the same state s_i, i.e. $\langle s_i, a_i, s_i \rangle \in R$. If a plan exists to restore the system back from s_2 to s_1 passing into state s_i, then there are several plans where the only difference is the amount of times we execute the "dummy" action a_i.

Since recovery is a sensitive operation, in order to minimize the amount of operations to be executed, we define the notion of shorter reverse plans. A shorter reverse plan $\mathtt{revPlan}_s(s_1, s_2; [a_1 \otimes \ldots \otimes a_m])$ is a reverse plan where the number of actions to be executed is minimal (i.e. there is no other $\mathtt{revPlan}(s_1, s_2; [a_1 \otimes \ldots \otimes a_n])$ with $n < m$).

5.1 Goal Reverse Plans

The previous notions define a reverse action or a reverse plan for a pair of states s_1 and s_2, reverting the system from state s_2 back to state s_1, and imposing that the final state obtained is *exactly* s_1. However, it may happen that, for some pair of states, a reverse plan does not exist. Furthermore, if some information is provided (e.g. by the programmer) about the state that we intend to reach, then we might still achieve a state where this condition holds. This is useful for cases where the agent has to find repairs to deal with norm violations. For instance, it may not be possible to return to the exact state before the violation, but it may be possible to reach a consistent state where the agent complies with all the norms.

This corresponds to the notion of goal reverse plans that we introduce here. Based on a state formula ϕ characterizing the state that we want to reach, then $\mathtt{goalRev}(\phi, s_2; [a_0 \otimes \ldots \otimes a_{m-1}])$ says that the sequence $a_0 \otimes \ldots \otimes a_{m-1}$ reverses the system from s_2 into a consistent state s where the state formula ϕ holds.

Definition 17 (Goal Reverse Plan). *We say that $a_0 \otimes \ldots \otimes a_{m-1}$ is a goal plan that reverses s_2 to a state where ϕ holds iff $\exists s'$ s.t. $\mathtt{traj}(s_2; [a_0 \otimes \ldots \otimes a_{m-1}]) = s'$ and $\forall s'$ s.t. $\mathtt{traj}(s_2; [a_0 \otimes \ldots \otimes a_{m-1}]) = s'$ then $V(\phi, s') = \mathtt{true}$. In this case we write $\mathtt{goalRev}(\phi, s_2; [a_0 \otimes \ldots \otimes a_{m-1}])$.*

As before, to preserve efficiency of plans, we define the notion of shorter goal reverse plan. $\mathtt{goalPlan}_s(\phi, s_2; [a_1 \otimes \ldots \otimes a_m])$ holds, if the sequence $a_1 \otimes \ldots \otimes a_m$ is a sequence with minimal length that takes s_2 into a state where ϕ is true.

5.2 External Oracle for Action Languages with Automatic Compensations

We can now make precise how and when repairs are calculated in $\mathcal{ETR}$'s semantics, and what changes of $\mathcal{ETR}$'s language are needed to deal with these automatic repairs.

Besides defining automatically inferred repairs, we want to keep the option of explicitly defining compensations for external actions. The latter are useful in external environments where the agent is not able to automatically infer the repair (see e.g. the repairs in Example 1). However, since more than one action may be required to repair the effects of one external action (e.g., in Example 1 it may be necessary to give the patient a series of medications in order to repair the side-effects of the previously given one), we also extend these explicitly defined compensations to plans.

Consequently, the language of $\mathcal{ETR}$ is extended so that external actions can appear in a program in three different ways: 1) without any kind of compensation associated, i.e. $\mathbf{ext}(a, \mathtt{nop})$, and in this case we write $\mathbf{ext}(a)$ or simply a, where $a \in \mathcal{L}_a$; 2) with a user defined repair plan, written $\mathbf{ext}(a, b_1 \otimes \ldots \otimes b_j)$ where $a, b_i \in \mathcal{L}_a$; 3) with an automatic repair plan, denoted $\mathbf{extA}(a[\phi])$, where $a \in \mathcal{L}_a$, ϕ is an external state formula, and an external state formula is a conjunction of external fluents. Formally:

Definition 18. *An* $\mathcal{ETR}$ atom *is either a proposition in* $\mathcal{L}_P$, $\mathcal{L}_i$ *or an external atom. An external atom is either a proposition in* $\mathcal{L}_a$ *(where* $\mathcal{L}_a = \mathcal{F} \cup \mathcal{A}$*),* $\mathrm{ext}(a, b_1 \otimes \ldots \otimes b_j)$ *or* $\mathrm{ext}\mathbf{A}(a[\phi])$ *where* $a, b_i \in \mathcal{L}_a$ *and* ϕ *is an external state formula. An* $\mathcal{ETR}$ *literal is either* ϕ *or* $\neg\phi$ *where* ϕ *is an* $\mathcal{ETR}$ *atom. An external state formula is a either a literal from* $\mathcal{F}$ *or an expression* $\phi \wedge \psi$ *where* ϕ *and* ψ *are external state formulas. An* $\mathcal{ETR}$ *formula is either a literal, or an expression, defined inductively, of the form* $\phi \wedge \psi$, $\phi \vee \psi$ *or* $\phi \otimes \psi$*, where* ϕ *and* ψ *are* $\mathcal{ETR}$ *formulas. An* $\mathcal{ETR}$ *program is a set of rules of the form* $\phi \leftarrow \psi$ *where* ϕ *is a proposition in* $\mathcal{L}_P$ *and* ψ *is an* $\mathcal{ETR}$ *formula.*

Intuitively, $\mathrm{ext}\mathbf{A}(a[\phi])$ stands for *"execute the external action* a*, and if something fails automatically repair the action's effects either leading to the state just before* a *was executed, or to a state where* ϕ *holds"*. When one wants the repair to restore the system to the very state just before a was executed, one may simply write $\mathrm{ext}\mathbf{A}(a)$ (equivalent to $\mathrm{ext}\mathbf{A}(a[\perp])$).

Example 6. With this extended language one can write, e.g. for the situation described in Example 2, rules like the ones below, plus a specification in $\mathcal{C}$ of the external environment which must include the definition of blocks-world-like actions (omitted here for brevity). Intuitively the rules say that: to place a product one should decrease the stock and then place the product; one can place a product in a better shelf, or in a normal shelf in case the product is not premium. Moreover, moving a product to a given shelf is an external action that can be automatically repaired based on the existing information about the external world. Consequently $\mathrm{ext}\mathbf{A}(move(X, warehouse, betterShelf))$ means that, if something fails after the agent has moved X from the warehouse into a better shelf, then a repair plan will be automatically defined for this action by the semantics.

$$placeProduct(X) \leftarrow decreaseStock(X) \otimes X > 0 \otimes placeOne(X)$$
$$decreaseStock(X) \leftarrow stock(X, S) \otimes stock(X, S).del \otimes stock(X, S-1).ins$$
$$placeOne(X) \leftarrow \mathrm{ext}\mathbf{A}(move(X, warehouse, betterShelf))$$
$$placeOne(X) \leftarrow \neg premium(X) \otimes \mathrm{ext}\mathbf{A}(move(X, warehouse, normalShelf))$$

Note that, the semantics must ensure that the external world is always left consistent by the agent in this example. Particularly, whenever it is not possible to place a non-premium product in the better shelf, a repair plan is executed to put the product back in the warehouse, where after one can try to put the product in the normal shelf; if it is not possible to put the product in either shelf (or to put a premium product in the better shelf), then a repair plan is executed to put the product back in the warehouse, and the stock is rolled back to its previous value (and the transaction fails).

Contrary to the semantics of the original $\mathcal{ETR}$ which is independent of the defined oracles, the semantics of this new language can only be defined given specific oracles that allow the inference of repair plans. For example, for external environments described by action languages, an external state is a pair, with the action program E describing the external domain and a state of the transition system, and the external oracle $\mathcal{O}^e$ is (where $\mathcal{T}(E) = \langle S, V, R \rangle$):

Definition 19 (Action Language Oracle). *Let* f, a *be atoms in* $\mathcal{L}_a$ *s.t.* f *is a fluent in* $\mathcal{F}$ *and* a *is an action in* $\mathcal{A}$*.*

1. $\mathcal{O}^e((E, s_1), (E, s_1)) \models f$ *iff* $V(f, s_1) = \mathtt{true}$

2. $\mathcal{O}^e((E, s_1), (E, s_2)) \models a$ iff $\langle s_1, a, s_2 \rangle \in R$
3. $\mathcal{O}^e((E, s_1), (E, s_2)) \models \textbf{ext}(a, b_1 \otimes \ldots \otimes b_n)$ iff $\langle s_1, a, s_2 \rangle \in R$
4. $\mathcal{O}^e((E, s_1), (E, s_2)) \models \textbf{ext}(a[\phi], a_0^{-1} \otimes \ldots \otimes a_{m-1}^{-1})$ iff one holds:
    (a) $\langle s_1, a, s_2 \rangle \in R \wedge \texttt{revPlan}_s(s_1, s_2; [a_0^{-1} \otimes \ldots \otimes a_{m-1}^{-1}])$; or
    (b) $\langle s_1, a, s_2 \rangle \in R \wedge (\neg \exists a_0^{-1} \otimes \ldots \otimes a_{m-1}^{-1}$ s.t. $\texttt{revPlan}_s(s_1, s_2; [a_0^{-1} \otimes \ldots \otimes a_{m-1}^{-1}])) \wedge \texttt{goalRev}_s(\phi, s_2; [a_0 \otimes \ldots \otimes a_{m-1}])$

Points 3 and 4 above define how the oracle satisfies external actions with compensations. If the agent wants to explicitly define $b_1 \otimes \ldots \otimes b_n$ as the reverse plan for action a, then $\textbf{ext}(a, b_1 \otimes \ldots \otimes b_n)$ is evaluated solely by what the oracle knows about a, holding in a transition iff a holds in that transition of states.

When the agent wants to infer a repair plan for a, then these repairs are calculated based on the notions of reverse plan and goal reverse defined previously. Namely, the formula $\textbf{ext}(a[\phi], a_0^{-1} \otimes \ldots \otimes a_{m-1}^{-1})$ holds, iff a holds in the transition s_1 into s_2, and $a_0^{-1} \otimes \ldots \otimes a_{m-1}^{-1}$ is a shorter reverse plan to repair s_2 back to s_1 or, if $a_0^{-1} \otimes \ldots \otimes a_{m-1}^{-1}$ is a shorter goal plan to repair s_2 into a state where the state formula ϕ holds.

Note that the order of points 4a and 4b is not arbitrary. Goal reverse plans provide an elegant solution to relax the necessary conditions to obtain repairs plans and are specially useful in scenarios where it is not possible to return to the initial state before executing the external action, as e.g. in norms or contracts violations. However, care must be taken when defining the external state formula ϕ of an external action $\textbf{ext}\mathbf{A}(a[\phi])$. In fact, if ϕ provides a very incomplete description of the state that we want to achieve, then we might achieve a state substantially different from the intended one. Particularly, although we constrain the applicability of goal reverse plans to the ones that are shorter, there is no guarantee that the changes of these plans are minimal (w.r.t. the amount of fluents that are different from the previous state). To guarantee such property represents a belief revision problem and is, at this moment, out of scope of this paper.

Finally, compensations can be instantiated by changing the definition of interpretation (Def. 2) which now determines how to deal with automatic repairs.

Definition 20 (Interpretations). *An interpretation is a mapping M assigning a classical Herbrand structure (or $\top$) to every path. This mapping is subject to the following restrictions, for all states D_i, E_j and every formula φ, every external atom a and every state formula ψ:*

1. $\varphi \in M(\langle (D, E) \rangle)$ iff $\mathcal{O}^d(D) \models \varphi$ *for any external state* E
2. $\varphi \in M(\langle (D_1, E), {}^{\varphi}(D_2, E) \rangle)$ iff $\mathcal{O}^t(D_1, D_2) \models \varphi$ *for any external state* E
3. $\varphi \in M(\langle (D, E_1), {}^{\varphi}(D, E_2) \rangle)$ iff $\mathcal{O}^e(E_1, E_2) \models \varphi$ *for any internal state* D
4. $\textbf{ext}\mathbf{A}(a[\psi]) \in M(\langle (D, E_1), {}^{\textbf{ext}(a[\psi], a_0^{-1} \otimes \ldots \otimes a_{m-1}^{-1})}(D, E_2) \rangle)$ iff $\mathcal{O}^e(E_1, E_2) \models \textbf{ext}(a[\psi], a_0^{-1} \otimes \ldots \otimes a_{m-1}^{-1})$ *for any internal state* D

Note that, an external action with automatic repair plans only appears in the program in the form $\textbf{ext}\mathbf{A}(a[\phi])$. With this previous definition, it is the interpretation's responsibility to ask the oracle to instantiate it with the correct repair plan $a_0^{-1} \otimes \ldots \otimes a_{m-1}^{-1}$.

5.3 Properties of Repair Plans

We start by making precise the relation between the concepts presented here, and the definitions from [8]. Specifically, if a goal reverse plan is not considered, then $a_0^{-1} \otimes$

$\ldots \otimes a_{m-1}^{-1}$ is a valid repair plan iff it is a $\phi; \psi$-conditional plan in [8] where the ψ (respectively ϕ) represents the state formula of the initial (resp. final) state s_1 (resp. s_2).

Theorem 1 (Relation with [8]). *Let F_1 and F_2 be formulas that respectively represent completely the states s_1 and s_2. Then, $\mathcal{O}^e((E, s_1), (E, s_2)) \models \text{ext}(a[\bot], a_0^{-1} \otimes \ldots \otimes a_{m-1}^{-1})$ iff $a_0^{-1} \otimes \ldots \otimes a_{m-1}^{-1}$ is a $F_2; F_1$-reversal for a*

Then, we can apply the result on the sufficient condition for the existence of repairs plans from [8] which is based on the notion of involutory actions. An action is said to be involutory if executing the action twice from any state where the action is executable, always results in the starting state, i.e. iff for every s_1, s_2 s.t. $\text{traj}(s_1; [a \otimes a]) = s_2$ then $s_2 = s_1$. An example of an involutory action is a toggle action, as toggling a simple switch twice will always lead the system into the initial state.

Lemma 1. *Let a be an involutory action. For every pair of states s_1, s_2 s.t. $\langle s_1, a, s_2 \rangle \in R$ it holds that $\mathcal{O}^e((E, s_1), (E, s_2)) \models \text{ext}(a[\phi], a)$ for every state formula ϕ.*

Further, we can talk about safety of repairs w.r.t. programs. We say that a program is *repair safe* iff all its external actions have a repair that is guaranteed to succeed.

Theorem 2 (Repair Safety). *Let P be a $\mathcal{ETR}$ program without user defined repair plans of the form $\text{ext}(a, b_1 \otimes \ldots \otimes b_j)$. If for every $\text{extA}(a[\phi])$ defined in P there exists a reverse plan $a_1 \otimes \ldots \otimes a_k$ s.t. $\text{revPlan}(a, [a_1 \otimes \ldots \otimes a_k])$ then P is a repair safe program.*

Note that, although the conditions for a repair safe program are considerably strong, they allow us to reason about the safeness of a program *before* execution. Obviously, we do not want to restrict only to repair safe programs. However, if an agent is defined by a repair safe program, we know that, whatever happens, the agent will always leave the external world in a consistent state.

We can also define a safe property regarding a particular execution of a transaction.

Theorem 3 (Repair Safe Execution). *Let P be a program without user defined repairs, ϕ be a formula, π be a path and M an interpretation where $M \models P$. If $M, \pi \models_p \phi$, $M, \pi \not\models_c \phi$ and $\text{Seq}(\pi) \neq \emptyset$ then $\exists \pi_0, \pi_r$ where π_0 is a rollback path of π, and π_r is a recovery path of π_0 s.t. $\pi' = \pi_0 \circ \pi_r$ and $M, \pi' \rightsquigarrow \phi$*

This result talks about the existence of compensating paths for a given transaction ϕ being executed in a path π. Intuitively, if P does not contain user defined transactions, and π is an execution of ϕ that fails (i.e. $M, \pi \models_p \phi$ but $M, \pi \not\models_c \phi$) after executing some external actions (i.e. if $\text{Seq}(\pi) \neq \emptyset$), then there always exists a path where the execution of ϕ is repaired, i.e. there exists a path π' where $M, \pi' \rightsquigarrow \phi$ holds.

Note that these theorems only provide guarantees for programs where explicit user defined repairs are not presented. The problem with the user defined repairs is that it is impossible to predict, before execution, what will be the resulting state of the external world after their execution, or to guarantee any properties about this resulting state. As such, it may be the case that the existence of user defined repairs jeopardizes the applicability of automatic repair plans. This is as expected: since the user may arbitrarily change the repair of some actions, it may certainly be the case that the specification of the external domain cannot infer any repair plan for other actions in the same sequence. To prevent this, we could preclude the possibility to define user defined repairs. However, this would make $\mathcal{ETR}$ less expressible, making it impossible to use whenever the agent does not possess enough information about the external world.

6   Conclusions and Related Work

We have extended the $\mathcal{ETR}$ language to deal with external environments described by an action language, and to deal with automatically inferred repair plans when some external action fails. The obtained language is able to reason and act in a two-fold environment in a transactional way. By defining a semantics that automatically infers what should be the repairs when something fails in the external world, we ease the programmer's task to anticipate for all the possible failures and write the corresponding correct repair for it. Thus, when enough information is available regarding the external world, $\mathcal{ETR}$ can be used to automatically infer plans to deal with failures. Contrarily, when the agent has no information about the external environment on which she performs actions, then repair plans can be defined explicitly in the agent's program. Though not presented here for lack of space, we have devised a proof procedure for $\mathcal{ETR}$ [13], that readily provides a means for an implementation that is underway.

For dealing with the inference of repair plans, we assumed that the environment is described using the action language $\mathcal{C}$ and based the representation of reversals on the work of [8]. An alternative would be to chose another language for representing changes in the external environment like [17]. [17] defines an action language to represent and reason about commitments in multi-agent domains. In it, it is possible to encode directly in the language which actions are reversible and how. Using this language to represent the external world in $\mathcal{ETR}$ could also be done by changing the external oracle definition, similarly to what we have done here. However, we chose the reversals representation from [8] since its generality makes it applicable to a wider family of action aanguages, like, e.g. the action language $\mathcal{C}$. Since this latter language has several extensions that are already used for norms and protocol representation in multi-agent systems [16,1], by defining an external oracle using this action language $\mathcal{C}$ we provide means to employ such representations together with $\mathcal{ETR}$, extending them with the possibility to describe an agent's behavior in a transactional way. Furthermore, our version of goal reverse plans can be seen as a contribution to the work of [8]'s as it provides means to relax the conditions for the existence of plans, increasing the possibility of achieving a state with some desirable consistent properties.

Several languages to describe an agent's behavior partitioned over an internal and external KB have been proposed in the literature. Jason[4], 2APL[6] and 3APL[14] are successful examples of agent programming languages that deal with environments with both internal updates and external actions. All these language have some way to deal with action failures, and to execute repair plans of some form. However, none of them consider the automatic inference of the repair plans based on the external information available. Moreover, none of them guarantees transactional properties, in particular for actions performed in the internal environment.

Other agent's logic programming based languages exist (e.g. [5,15]) but, to our knowledge, none of them deals with transactions nor with repair plans. The closest might be [15], where the authors mention as future work the definition of transactions. However, the model theory of [15] does not consider the possibility of failure and thus neither the possibility of repairing plans. Contrarily, its operational semantics may react to external events defining failure of actions performed externally, but since no tools are provided to model the external environment, the decision about what to do with the failure is based only on internal knowledge (but which has information about external events). Moreover, since there is no strict distinction between action performed externally and internally, it not clear to see how the semantics would deal with the different levels of atomicity that the combination between internal and external actions demands.

References

1. Artikis, A., Sergot, M.J., Pitt, J.V.: Specifying norm-governed computational societies. ACM Trans. Comput. Log. 10(1) (2009)
2. Bonner, A.J., Kifer, M.: Transaction logic programming. In: ICLP, pp. 257–279 (1993)
3. Bonner, A.J., Kifer, M.: Transaction logic programming (or a logic of declarative and procedural knowledge). Technical Report CSRI-323, University of Toronto (1995)
4. Bordini, R.H., Wooldridge, M., Hübner, J.F.: Programming Multi-Agent Systems in AgentSpeak using Jason. Wiley Series in Agent Technology. John Wiley & Sons (2007)
5. Costantini, S., Tocchio, A.: About declarative semantics of logic-based agent languages. In: Baldoni, M., Endriss, U., Omicini, A., Torroni, P. (eds.) DALT 2005. LNCS (LNAI), vol. 3904, pp. 106–123. Springer, Heidelberg (2006)
6. Dastani, M.: 2apl: a practical agent programming language. Autonomous Agents and Multi-Agent Systems 16(3), 214–248 (2008)
7. Dastani, M., Meyer, J.-J.C., Grossi, D.: A logic for normative multi-agent programs. J. Log. Comput. 23(2), 335–354 (2013)
8. Eiter, T., Erdem, E., Faber, W.: Undoing the effects of action sequences. J. Applied Logic 6(3), 380–415 (2008)
9. Gelfond, M., Lifschitz, V.: Action languages. Electron. Trans. Artif. Intell. 2, 193–210 (1998)
10. Giunchiglia, E., Lee, J., Lifschitz, V., McCain, N., Turner, H.: Nonmonotonic causal theories. Artif. Intell. 153(1-2), 49–104 (2004)
11. Giunchiglia, E., Lifschitz, V.: An action language based on causal explanation: Preliminary report. In: AAAI/IAAI, pp. 623–630. AAAI, The MIT Press (1998)
12. Gomes, A.S., Alferes, J.J.: Transaction logic with external actions. In: Delgrande, J.P., Faber, W. (eds.) LPNMR 2011. LNCS, vol. 6645, pp. 272–277. Springer, Heidelberg (2011)
13. Gomes, A.S., Alferes, J.J.: Extending transaction logic with external actions. Theory and Practice of Logic Programming, On-line Supplement (to appear, 2013)
14. Hindriks, K.V., de Boer, F.S., van der Hoek, W., Meyer, J.-J.C.: Agent programming in 3apl. Autonomous Agents and Multi-Agent Systems 2(4), 357–401 (1999)
15. Kowalski, R.A., Sadri, F.: Abductive logic programming agents with destructive databases. Ann. Math. Artif. Intell. 62(1-2), 129–158 (2011)
16. Sergot, M.J., Craven, R.: The deontic component of action language $n\mathcal{C}+$. In: Goble, L., Meyer, J.-J.C. (eds.) DEON 2006. LNCS (LNAI), vol. 4048, pp. 222–237. Springer, Heidelberg (2006)
17. Son, T.C., Pontelli, E., Sakama, C.: Formalizing commitments using action languages. In: Sakama, C., Sardina, S., Vasconcelos, W., Winikoff, M. (eds.) DALT 2011. LNCS, vol. 7169, pp. 67–83. Springer, Heidelberg (2012)

Perceiving Rules under Incomplete and Inconsistent Information*

Barbara Dunin-Kęplicz and Alina Strachocka

Institute of Informatics, University of Warsaw, Poland

Abstract. The overall goal of this research program is a construction of a paraconsistent model of agents' communication, comprising two building blocks: speaking about facts and speaking about reasoning rules. To construct complex dialogues, such as persuasion, deliberation, information seeking, negotiation or inquiry, the speech acts theory provides the necessary building material. This paper extends the implementation of the speech act *assert* in the paraconsistent framework, presented in our previous paper, by providing means for agents to perceive and learn not only facts, but also rules. To this end the *admissibility criterion* for a rule to be accepted has been defined and the Algorithm for Perceiving Assertions About Rules has been proposed. A natural four-valued model of interaction yields multiple new cognitive situations. *Epistemic profiles* encode the way agents reason, and therefore also deal with inconsistent or lacking information. *Communicative relations* in turn comprise various aspects of communication and allow for the fine-tuning of applications.

The particular choice of a rule-based, $\text{DATALOG}^{\neg\neg}$-like query language 4QL as a four-valued implementation framework ensures that, in contrast to the standard two-valued approaches, tractability of the model is maintained.

1 Communication under Uncertain and Inconsistent Information

The traditional approaches to modeling Agent Communication Languages settled for the two-valued logics despite their natural modeling limitations: inability to properly deal with lacking and inconsistent information. This work continues the subject-matter of the paraconsistent approach to formalizing dialogues in multiagent systems in a more realistic way [5]. The underpinning principle of this research is the adequate logical modeling of the dynamic environments in which artifacts like agents are situated. Agents, viewed as heterogenous and autonomous information sources, may perceive the surrounding reality differently while building their informational stance. Even though consistency of their belief structures is a very desirable property, in practice it is hard to achieve: inevitably, all these differences result in the lack of consistency of their beliefs. However, instead of making a reasoning process trivial, we view inconsistency as a first-class citizen trying to efficiently deal with it.

There is a vast literature on logical systems designed to cope with inconsistency (see for example [28,33]). However none of them turned out to be suitable in all cases. As inconsistency is an immanent property of realistic domains, we lean towards a more pragmatic and flexible solution. Assuming that we have various disambiguation methods

---

* Supported by the Polish National Science Centre grants 2011/01/B/ST6/02769 and CORE 6505/B/T02/2011/40.

J. Leite et al. (Eds.): CLIMA XIV, LNAI 8143, pp. 256–272, 2013.

at hand, the flexible approach allows for an application-, situation- or context-specific choice that does not have to be made a priori. Furthermore, there might be a benefit from postponing the related decision as long as possible, as the new information may come up or the agent being the cause of the conflict may change its mind.

We base our solution on a four-valued logic [12] and the ideas underlying the 4QL query language [11,12] which major win is that queries can be computed in polynomial time. Tractability of 4QL stands in stark contrast to the usual two-valued approaches to group interactions, where EXPTIME completeness of satisfiability problems is a common hindrance [7,8]. This way an important shift in perspective takes place: rather than drawing conclusions from logical theories we reason from paraconsistent knowledge bases. As a great benefit, the belief revision methods turned out to be dramatically simplified. 4QL was designed in such a way that the inconsistency is tamed and treated naturally in the language. The application developer has a selection of uniform tools to adequately deal with inconsistencies in their problem domain.

Building upon the 4-valued logic of 4QL, we deal with four types of situations:

- fact a holds,
- fact a does not hold,
- it is not known whether a holds,
- information about a is inconsistent.

They are confined in the four logical values: t, f, u and i, respectively (Sec. 3). In such settings, maintaining truth or falsity of a proposition, in the presence of multiple information sources, is challenging. Furthermore, the two additional logical values allow to model complex interactions between agents in a more intuitive and subtle manner.

The way the individual agents deal with conflicting or lacking information is encoded in their *epistemic profile* (Sec. 4) which embodies their reasoning capabilities, embracing the diversity of agents and providing a complete agent's characteristics. Moreover, epistemic profiles specify agents' communicative strategies realized with regard to the three communicative relations between the agents involved: *communication with authority*, *peer to peer communication* and *communication with subordinate* as proposed in [5]. These in turn influence the agent's reasoning processes and finally affect the agents' *belief structures*, i.e., their informational stance [6] (Sec. 4). In principle, various agents may reason in completely different ways, as well as apply diverse methods of information disambiguation.

The ultimate aim of our research program is a paraconsistent model of agents' communication. To construct complex dialogues, such as persuasion, deliberation, information seeking, negotiation or inquiry (see [18]), the speech acts theory provides the necessary building material. We initiated our research program [5], by proposing a paraconsistent framework for perceiving new facts via four different speech acts: *assert*, *concede*, *request* and *challenge*. They enable the agents to discuss their informational stance, i.e.,:

- inform one another about their valuations of different propositions via *assertions*,
- ask for other agents' valuations via *requests*,
- acknowledge the common valuations via *concessions* and
- question the contradictory valuations via *challenges*.

In the current paper the next step is taken. We allow the agents to perceive not only new facts but also reasoning rules, which make up the epistemic profiles. To our best knowledge, approaches to modeling communication in MAS, as a legacy of Austin and Searle, settled for frameworks where propositions were the only valid content of speech acts. On the other hand, argumentation about reasoning rules has been well studied in the legal reasoning domain (see for example [26, 27, 34]). Here we intend to bring together these two worlds by leveraging the legal argumentation theory in our paraconsistent communication framework and therefore by allowing the agents to discuss their reasoning rules. We attack this complex problem from analyzing how agents react to perceiving assertions about reasoning rules: should they adopt, reject, ignore or maybe challenge the new rule? Consequently, the paramount issue here is the formulation of the admissibility criterion of the incoming rule (Sec. 5) as a basis to formulate the Algorithm for Perceiving Assertions about Rules.

As we view complex dialogues as communicative games between two or more agents, the dialogue participants, being independent information sources, try to expand, contract, update, and revise their beliefs through communication [25]. The great advantage of our approach is the possibility to revise the belief structures in a very straightforward way, what will be presented in the sequel.

The paper is structured as follows. First, in Section 2, we introduce the building blocks of our approach. Section 3 is devoted to a four-valued logic which is used throughout the paper and to basic information on 4QL. Section 4 introduces epistemic profiles and belief structures, whereas Section 5 outlines the communicative relations and rule admissibility conditions. Section 6 discusses the main technical contribution of the paper, followed by an example in Section 7. Finally, Section 8 concludes the paper.

2   Perceiving Rules

Our goal is to allow agents to communicate flexibly in the paraconsistent world. We will equip agents with various dialogical tools for conversing about rules: from informing or requesting information about a rule head or body, through challenging legitimacy of a rule, to rejecting or conceding acceptance of a new rule. These all can be performed with the use of dedicated speech acts: *assert*, *request*, *challenge*, *reject* and *concede* respectively and later will be used to construct complex dialogues.

In this paper, we take the first basic step, namely, how should agents react upon perceiving assertions ($\mathtt{assert}_{S,R}$) regarding rules ($l :- b$) of inference. As these are "actions that make you change your mind" [25], we explain the process of adopting the new rules and specifically put a spotlight on the easiness of the belief revision phase in our approach. Therefore we ask:

- **In what cases can the rules be added to the agent's epistemic profile without harming the existing structures?**
- **How does the agent's belief structure change in response?**

The merit of the rule base update in traditional approaches lies in solving inconsistency that the new rule might introduce to the logical program. When creating 4QL, the biggest effort was to ease the way we deal with inconsistency. We will exploit this when defining the *admissibility criterion* for a rule to be accepted. Informally, it is meant to express compatibility of the rule conclusions with the current belief structure. This compatibility is founded on the special ordering of truth values, by which we try to achieve two goals:

- protect true and false propositions from being flooded by inconsistency and
- protect already possessed knowledge from unknown.

The execution of the admissibility criterion is the heart of the Algorithm for Perceiving Assertions About Rules, a generalized 4-step procedure, realized via: *filtering*, *parsing*, *evaluation* and *belief revision*. In a perfect case, agents communicate successfully, extending and enriching their knowledge. In more realistic scenarios, some communicative actions fail, calling for a system consistency ensuring mechanism. Also, at each stage of the algorithm, agents must know how to proceed in the lack of response.

3   A Paraconsistent Implementation Environment

In order to deal with perceiving rules, we need to introduce several definitions (in Sections 3, 4 and 5):

- the 4-valued logic we build upon,
- the implementation tool: a rule-based query language 4QL,
- the notions of *epistemic profiles* and *belief structures*, which embody the agents' informational stands and reasoning capabilities,
- the preserving knowledge truth ordering,
- the rule admissibility criterion.

In what follows all <u>sets are finite</u> except for sets of formulas. We deal with the classical first-order language over a given vocabulary without function symbols. We assume that *Const* is a fixed set of constants, *Var* is a fixed set of variables and *Rel* is a fixed set of relation symbols. A *literal* is an expression of the form $R(\bar\tau)$ or $\neg R(\bar\tau)$, with $\bar\tau \in (Const \cup Var)^k$, where k is the arity of R. *Ground literals over Const*, denoted by $\mathcal{G}(Const)$, are literals without variables, with all constants in *Const*. If $\ell = \neg R(\bar\tau)$ then $\neg\ell \stackrel{\text{def}}{=} R(\bar\tau)$. Let $v : Var \longrightarrow Const$ be a *valuation of variables*.

For a literal ℓ, by $\ell(v)$ we mean the ground literal obtained from ℓ by substituting each variable x occurring in ℓ by constant $v(x)$. The semantics of propositional connectives is summarized in Table 1.

Table 1. Truth tables for $\wedge$, $\vee$, $\rightarrow$ and $\neg$ (see [11, 12, 17]).

$\wedge$	f	u	i	t		$\vee$	f	u	i	t		$\rightarrow$	f	u	i	t		$\neg$	
f	f	f	f	f		f	f	u	i	t		f	t	t	t	t		f	t
u	f	u	u	u		u	u	u	i	t		u	t	t	t	t		u	u
i	f	u	i	i		i	i	i	i	t		i	f	f	t	f		i	i
t	f	u	i	t		t	t	t	t	t		t	f	f	t	t		t	f

Definition 3.1. The *truth value* of a literal ℓ w.r.t. a set of ground literals L and valuation v, denoted by $\ell(L, v)$, is defined as follows:

$$\ell(L, v) \stackrel{\text{def}}{=} \begin{cases} \mathbf{t} \text{ if } \ell(v) \in L \text{ and } (\neg \ell(v)) \notin L; \\ \mathbf{i} \text{ if } \ell(v) \in L \text{ and } (\neg \ell(v)) \in L; \\ \mathbf{u} \text{ if } \ell(v) \notin L \text{ and } (\neg \ell(v)) \notin L; \\ \mathbf{f} \text{ if } \ell(v) \notin L \text{ and } (\neg \ell(v)) \in L. \end{cases}$$ ◁

For a formula $\alpha(x)$ with a free variable x and $c \in \textit{Const}$, by $\alpha(x)_c^x$ we understand the formula obtained from α by substituting all free occurrences of x by c. Definition 3.1 is extended to all formulas in Table 2, where α denotes a first-order formula, v is a valuation of variables, L is a set of ground literals, and the semantics of propositional connectives appearing at righthand sides of equivalences is given in Table 1. Observe that the definitions of $\wedge$ and $\vee$ reflect minimum and maximum w.r.t. the ordering

$$\mathbf{f} < \mathbf{u} < \mathbf{i} < \mathbf{t}. \tag{1}$$

Table 2. Semantics of first-order formulas

> - if α is a literal then $\alpha(L, v)$ is defined in Definition 3.1;
> - $(\neg \alpha)(L, v) \stackrel{\text{def}}{=} \neg(\alpha(L, v))$;
> - $(\alpha \circ \beta)(L, v) \stackrel{\text{def}}{=} \alpha(L, v) \circ \beta(L, v)$, where $\circ \in \{\vee, \wedge, \rightarrow\}$;
> - $(\forall x \alpha(x))(L, v) = \min_{a \in \textit{Const}} (\alpha_a^x)(L, v)$,
>   where min is the minimum w.r.t. ordering (1);
> - $(\exists x \alpha(x))(L, v) = \max_{a \in \textit{Const}} (\alpha_a^x)(L, v)$,
>   where max is the maximum w.r.t. ordering (1).

From several languages designed for programming BDI agents (for a survey see, e.g., [13]), none directly addresses belief formation, in particular nonmonotonic or defeasible reasoning techniques. 4QL enjoys tractable query computation and captures all tractable queries. It supports a modular and layered architecture, providing simple, yet powerful constructs for expressing nonmonotonic rules reflecting default reasoning, autoepistemic reasoning, defeasible reasoning, the local closed world assumption, etc. [11]. The openness of the world is assumed, which may lead to lack of knowledge. Negation in rule heads may lead to inconsistencies.

Definition 3.2. By a *rule* we mean any expression of the form:

$$\ell :- b_{11}, \ldots, b_{1i_1} \mid \ldots \mid b_{m1}, \ldots, b_{mi_m}. \tag{2}$$

where $\ell, b_{11}, \ldots, b_{1i_1}, \ldots, b_{m1}, \ldots, b_{mi_m}$ are (negative or positive) literals and ',' and '|' abbreviate conjunction and disjunction, respectively. Literal ℓ is called the *head* of the rule and the expression at the righthand side of :– in (2) is called the *body* of the rule. By a *fact* we mean a rule with an empty body. Facts '$\ell :- .$' are abbreviated to '$\ell.$'. A finite set of rules is called a *program*.   ◁

Definition 3.3. Let a set of constants, *Const*, be given. A set of ground literals L with constants in *Const* is a *model of a set of rules* S iff for each rule (2) and any valuation v mapping variables into constants in *Const*, we have that:

$$\left(\left(\left(b_{11} \wedge \ldots \wedge b_{1i_1}\right) \vee \ldots \vee \left(b_{m1} \wedge \ldots \wedge b_{mi_m}\right)\right) \to \ell\right)(L, v) = \mathsf{t},$$

where it is assumed that the empty body takes the value t in any interpretation.   ◁

To express nonmonotonic/defeasible rules we need the concept of modules and external literals. In the sequel, *Mod* denotes the set of *module names*.

Definition 3.4. An *external literal* is an expression of one of the forms:

$$M.R, -M.R, M.R \text{ IN } T, -M.R \text{ IN } T, \tag{3}$$

where $M \in Mod$ is a module name, R is a positive literal, '$-$' stands for negation and $T \subseteq \{\mathsf{f}, \mathsf{u}, \mathsf{i}, \mathsf{t}\}$. For literals of the form (3), module M is called the *reference module*. ◁

The intended meaning of "$M.R$ IN T" is that the truth value of $M.R$ is in the set T. External literals allow one to access values of literals in other modules. If R is not defined in the module M then the value of $M.R$ is assumed to be u.

Assume a strict tree-like order $\prec$ on *Mod* dividing modules into layers. An external literal with reference module M_1 may appear in rule bodies of a module M_2, provided that $M_1 \prec M_2$.

The semantics of 4QL is defined by well-supported models generalizing the idea of [9]. Intuitively, a model is *well-supported* if all derived literals are supported by a reasoning that is grounded in facts. It appears that for any set of rules there is a unique well-supported model and this can be computed in polynomial time.

4   Epistemic Profiles and Belief Structures

An essential question is how to realize heterogeneity of agents in multiagent systems. Clearly, being different, when seeing the same thing, agents may perceive it differently and then may draw different conclusions. In order to define the way an agent reasons (e.g., by the use of rules) and to express the granularity of their reasoning (e.g., by varying the level of certain attributes or accuracy of rules expressing the modeled phenomena) we introduce a notion of *epistemic profile*. Epistemic profiles also characterize the manner of dealing with conflicting or lacking information by combining various forms of reasoning (also "light" forms of nonomonotonic reasoning), including belief fusion, disambiguation of conflicting beliefs or completion of lacking information. Especially dealing with inconsistency is important for us. Particular agents may adopt different general methods of the disambiguation (like minimal change strategy) or just implement their own local, application-specific methods via rules encoding knowledge on an expert in the field. This way the flexibility of dealing with inconsistency is formally implemented.

As inconsistency is one of the four logical values, it naturally appears on different reasoning levels. It may be finally disambiguated when the necessary information is in place. This is an intrinsic property of 4QL supported by its modular architecture. As an example, consider a rescue agent trying to save people from the disaster region. However it cannot work in high temperatures. Suppose it has inconsistent information about the temperature there. In the classical approach it would stop him from acting immediately, while in our approach, it may proceed till the moment the situation is clarified.

Tough decisions about conflicting or missing information may be solved by the system designer (application developer) based on their expert knowledge. For instance a rule might say that if some external literal is inconsistent or unknown ($M.l \in \{\mathbf{u}, \mathbf{i}\}$) a specific authority source should be consulted (alternatively, the rule cannot be applied).

The following definitions are adapted from [6], where more intuition, explanation and examples can be found. If S is a set then by $\text{FIN}(S)$ we understand the set of all finite subsets of S.

Definition 4.1. Let $\mathbb{C} \overset{\text{def}}{=} \text{FIN}(\mathcal{G}(Const))$ be the set of all finite sets of ground literals over the set of constants $Const$. Then:
- by a *constituent* we understand any set $C \in \mathbb{C}$;
- by an *epistemic profile* we understand any function $\mathcal{E} : \text{FIN}(\mathbb{C}) \longrightarrow \mathbb{C}$;
- by a *belief structure over an epistemic profile* $\mathcal{E}$ we mean $\mathcal{B}^{\mathcal{E}} = \langle \mathcal{C}, F \rangle$, where:
  - $\mathcal{C} \subseteq \mathbb{C}$ is a nonempty set of constituents;
  - $F \overset{\text{def}}{=} \mathcal{E}(\mathcal{C})$ is the *consequent* of $\mathcal{B}^{\mathcal{E}}$.   ◁

We alternate between the notions of the set of consequents and well-supported models. Epistemic profile is realized via 4QL program, which may consist of several modules.

Definition 4.2. Let $\mathcal{E}$ be an epistemic profile. The *truth value of formula* α w.r.t. belief structure $\mathcal{B}^{\mathcal{E}} = \langle \mathcal{C}, F \rangle$ and valuation v, denoted by $\alpha(\mathcal{B}^{\mathcal{E}}, v)$, is defined by:[1]

$$\alpha(\mathcal{B}^{\mathcal{E}}, v) \overset{\text{def}}{=} \alpha(\bigcup_{C \in \mathcal{C}} C, v).$$ ◁

5   Communicative Relations and Rule Admissibility Conditions

In multiagent domains many different aspects of inter-agent relations have been studied, e.g., trust, reputation, norms, commitments. They all have a greater scope of influence than just communication. The communicative relations we propose below, can be viewed as selective lens, through which we can see only these parts of the relations involved, which affect communication. They were introduced in [5] for guarding agents' informational stance. Now we extend our perspective to cover also reasoning rules:

1. *communication with authority*: an agent (receiver) is willing to evaluate the interlocutor's (sender, authority) rules even if they contain unknown premises or unknown conclusions,
2. *peer to peer communication*: both parties are viewed as equally credible and important information sources, therefore nobody's opinion prevails a priori. Unknown premises should be resolved before checking the admissibility of the rule. Whereas to recognize unknown conclusions, different application-specific solutions might be applied (see Algorithm 1).

---

[1] Since $\bigcup_{C \in \mathcal{C}} C$ is a set of ground literals, $\alpha(\mathcal{S}, v)$ is well-defined by Table 2.

3. *communication with subordinate*: when dealing with a less reliable source of information, the receiver with an authority would not be willing to risk his beliefs' and epistemic profile consistency. He would evaluate the new rule only when the conclusions are known (i.e. he would not learn new concepts from the subordinates).

In all cases, whenever the rule makes through to Evaluation and the admissibility criterion holds, the agents accept the new rule regardless the communicative relation. Otherwise, when the rule is not admissible, the interested agents engage in conflict resolution via challenge. Recall, that during the complex communication processes, we intend to protect the already possessed knowledge from unknown and ensure that true or false propositions are abandoned for good reasons solely. This is reflected in the knowledge preserving ordering $\leq_k$ on the truth values (Fig. 1).

Fig. 1. Knowledge ordering $\leq_k$

Dealing with unknown information is a delicate matter. Indeed, accepting rules with unknown literals is risky for the receiver. If the valuation of the unknown literal is finally established as the sender intended, the receiver's resulting belief structure might no longer be compatible. We solve this problem on a meta-level utilizing the communication relations: rules containing unknown premises are evaluated only when the sender is an authority. Otherwise, the unknown premises need to be resolved first.

As epistemic profiles are 4QL programs, adding a rule to an epistemic profile amounts to adding that rule to the specific module in the program.

Definition 5.1. We define an operation of *adding a rule* $M_i.\ell :\!- b$ to an epistemic profile $\mathcal{E} = \{M_1, ..., M_n\}$ as follows:

$$\mathcal{E}' = \mathcal{E} \cup \{M_i.\ell :\!- b\} = \{M_1, ..., M_{i-1}, M_i \cup \ell :\!- b, M_{i+1}, ..., M_n\}$$

Definition 5.2. Let v be a valuation, l a literal, $\mathcal{C}_i$ the set of constituents, F_i the set of consequents, $\mathcal{E}_i$ the epistemic profile and $\mathcal{B}_i$ the belief structure for $i \in \{a, b\}$. Belief structure $\mathcal{B}_b^{\mathcal{E}_b} = \langle \mathcal{C}_b, F_b \rangle$ is *compatible* with belief structure $\mathcal{B}_a^{\mathcal{E}_a} = \langle \mathcal{C}_a, F_a \rangle$ iff.

$$\forall \ell \in F_a \cap F_b \; \ell(\mathcal{B}_a^{\mathcal{E}_a}, v) \leq_k \ell(\mathcal{B}_b^{\mathcal{E}_b}, v).$$

Definition 5.3. Let $\mathcal{C}$ be a set of constituents, F, F' sets of consequents, $\mathcal{E}, \mathcal{E}'$ the epistemic profiles. Rule $\ell :\!- b$ is *compatible* with belief structure $\mathcal{B}^{\mathcal{E}} = \langle \mathcal{C}, F \rangle$, where $F = \mathcal{E}(\mathcal{C})$ iff. belief structure $\mathcal{B}^{\mathcal{E}}$ is compatible with belief structure $\mathcal{B}^{\mathcal{E}'} = \langle \mathcal{C}, F' \rangle$, such that: $\mathcal{E}' = \mathcal{E} \cup \{\ell :\!- b\}$, $F' = \mathcal{E}'(\mathcal{C})$.

We will allow for a rule to be added into agent's epistemic profile only if it is compatible with the agent's current belief structure.

6   Perceiving Assertions about Rules: The Algorithm

In our framework we deal with five different speech acts: *assert, concede, request, reject* and *challenge* (see Table 3), which allow us to characterize the way the 4QL agents communicate. Below, we present the Algorithm of Perceiving Assertions About Rules. The algorithm, viewed as a complex action, determines what move should an agent make after perceiving an assertion about a reasoning rule. It comprises four phases: *filtering* (Subsection 6.1), *parsing* (Subsection 6.2), *evaluation* (Subsection 6.3) and *belief revision* (Subsection 6.4). Filtering restricts the amount of incoming information, Parsing, in addition, provides means for investigating the message's content. In Evaluation the new rule is examined against the admissibility criterion and in Belief Revision, the resulting belief structure is computed on the basis of the new set of rules.

Filtering and Parsing are more tied to a specific application. In the case of Filtering, the implementations may vary from no filtering at all, to advanced solutions where both properties of the message and the current beliefs of the agent are considered. In the Parsing phase we intended to accent the general concepts, like the importance of the proper treatment of the unknown literals, and leave some space to application dependent decisions. In this spirit we have investigated rules in four conceptual groups depending on the location of the unknown literals in the rule head or body, and proposed a specific solution for dealing with unknown with the use of communicative relations.

In the case of Evaluation and Belief Revision, the solution has a general flavor. As explained in Section 5, the special truth ordering serves as a means to adequately identify possible conflicts or threats to the system, which the new rule might introduce. Thanks to the properties of 4QL, the evaluation of the admissibility criterion is straightforward and the conflicting region can be easily determined by comparing the original and the resulting belief structures. Then, the agent knows if it can harmlessly add the new rule or whether it should engage in a conflict resolution dialogue. Finally, the Belief Revision, as advocated before, is also a general procedure that, based on the Evaluation result, should generate a new belief structure, compatible with the previous one.

Table 3. Speech acts and their intended meaning

$\text{assert}_{S,R}(l :- b)$	Sender S tells the Receiver R the rule $l :- b$
$\text{concede}_{S,R}(l :- b)$	Sender S tells the Receiver R that it agrees with the rule $l :- b$
$\text{reject}_{S,R}(l :- b)$	Sender S tells the Receiver R that it could not accept the rule $l :- b$
$\text{challenge}_{S,R}(l :- b)$	Sender S tells the Receiver R that it disagrees with the rule $l :- b$ and asks for its justification
$\text{request}_{S,R}(l)$	Sender S asks the Receiver R information about l

6.1   Filtering

The aim of the filtering phase is to restrict the amount of incoming information and to guard its significance. During this step, the agent filters out noise, unimportant, resource-consuming, or harmful messages. To this end, different properties of the perceived message play a role: the sender, the type of the speech act, the context of the message, etc. Accordingly, different filtering mechanisms can be implemented in 4QL as separate modules, e.g., a module for communicative-relations-based filtering.

If a message makes through Filtering barrier to the Parsing phase, that means it is relevant and significant enough for the agent to consume its resources for handling it.

6.2 Parsing

The goal of parsing is to dissolve a rule into literals and to identify the unknown literals. Then, the receiver's reaction depends both on the communicative relation with the sender and on the rule itself, distinguishing the cases presented below.

Rule Head Is Unknown, Rule Body Is Known. This means, that the agent recognizes all the premises separately: all the literals in the rule body are either true, false or inconsistent. The novel assembly of literals leads to a new, unknown beforehand conclusion and may be viewed as <u>learning the new concept.</u>

Example 6.1. Let module Tom contain only the following facts: use(hammer, nail), nail, hammer, painting, and a rule: hanger :– nail, hammer, use(hammer, nail). In other words, Tom has a nail, a hammer and a painting, and he can use the hammer and the nail. The rule signifies that Tom can make a hanger if he has a nail and a hammer and he can use them. Suppose Bob has uttered a new rule:

hangingPainting :– hanger, painting.

The rule states that that one can achieve a hanging painting if he has a painting and a hanger. For Tom, the rule body is known (literals painting and hanger are true in Tom's belief structure), but the rule head is unknown. If Tom accepts the new rule he would learn how to hang a painting.

Rule Head Is Known, Rule Body Is Unknown. This situation relates to the case when some of the premises are unknown, but the conclusion is known. That may be described as <u>widening the knowledge,</u> or making it more detail. Depending on the communication relation, the unknown literals in the rule body can be treated as a possible threat to the consistency of the agent's beliefs (if the sender is a peer or a subordinate) and therefore need further investigation. Alternatively, in case of communication with an authority, the unknowns need not to be resolved a priori (the sender might for example want to communicate some regulations regarding upcoming events, for which some literals' valuations cannot be known beforehand). Here we follow the philosophy of exploiting communicative relations as explained in Section 5.

Example 6.2. Continuing the example from above, the module now contains the following two rules (one known before, one just learnt):
hanger :– nail, hammer, use(hammer, nail).

hangingPainting :– hanger, painting.

Suppose Bob has uttered another rule:
hanger :– nail, hammer | borrow(hammer), use(hammer, nail).

The rule states, that in order to build a hanger one must have a nail, must know how to use the hammer and the nail, as well as must have a hammer or borrow one. In this case, the rule head is known (hanger is true), but the rule body is not known (borrow(hammer)). If Tom accepts this rule, he would learn another way to build a hanger.

Rule Head Is Known, Rule Body Is Known. Philosophically, such situation pertains to two different cases: the incoming rule is known already, or the incoming rule combines previously known literals as premises (*Eureka!*). That may be described as knowledge discovery.

Example 6.3. If Bob says: hammer :− hanger, nail, use(hammer, nail), both the head and the body of the rule are known to Tom, which of course does not mean Tom should adopt this rule immediately.

Rule Head Is Unknown, Rule Body Is Unknown. In that case, the agent is overburdened with new information and, when communicating with a peer or subordinate, should start from resolving the unknown premises first. However, if the sender was an authority, such a rule may get through Parsing to Evaluation.

Example 6.4. If Bob says: pancake :− flour, egg, milk, pan, stove, Tom does not know any of the literals.

Searching for the meaning of the unknown premises requires a sort of information seeking phase (dialogue). This in turn may fail, leading to the rejection of the rule in question. In the course of dialogue the belief structures could evolve, calling for a repetition of the whole procedure, for example, when the sender turned out to be unreliable it is important to perform filtering anew.

If a message makes through Parsing to Evaluation, that means, the agent has all the means to properly evaluate the rule in its belief structure.

6.3   Evaluation

The evaluation stage is the one when the decision about adopting the new rule is made. The agent needs to verify if it can harmlessly add the rule in question to its epistemic profile. The outcome of this process can be twofold:

- if the rule provides conclusions compatible with current beliefs: admit it,
- if the rule provides conclusions incompatible with current beliefs: if possible, try to resolve the contradictions and otherwise reject the rule.

The rule is compatible with the current beliefs, if when added to agent's current epistemic profile, makes the resulting belief structure compatible with the current structure (see Definition5.3). Thus, all literals that were true or false, remain true or false, respectively. Literals that were inconsistent may become true, false, or remain inconsistent. Literals that were unknown may become true, false, inconsistent or remain unknown.

Similarly to the Filtering phase, the possibility of challenging the sender about the rule in question opens the doors for failures. In case of communication problems, or system-specific parameters such as timeouts, the challenge might fail forcing the agent to reject the rule in question. However, a successful completion of a challenge is always a one-side victory:

- either the challenging agent won (the receiver of the rule), and therefore the rule was not legitimate to accept,

– or the opponent won (the sender of the rule) and the receiver has been convinced to accept the rule.

The messages exchanged in this process might have changed the belief structures of communicating agents. In case the challenging agent won, it may terminate the process, even without explicitly rejecting the rule, as the opponent is perfectly clear of the defeat. In case the challenging agent lost, it means that for its new belief structure the rule in question is no longer incompatible. It may proceed to the Belief Revision phase. Challenges about the rules are subject of the upcoming article, but see [5].

If a message makes through Evaluation to Belief Revision, it means the admissibility criterion is met.

6.4 Belief Revision

The aim of belief revision stage is to update the belief structure according to the rule and type of speech act. In case of assertions, agent's individual beliefs as well as shared beliefs must be refreshed. For concessions, only the shared belief base gets updated.

We do not present a new semantics for belief revision[2]. It is rather a technical means to verify to what extent do the new rules interfere with the previously obtained belief structures. When computing the new belief structures, still the information might be lacking and the inconsistencies may occur. In fact this is the merit of our approach. Later on the modular architecture of 4QL allows for dealing with inconsistencies differently on various layers. Afterwards the update of the rule base is almost trivial: if suffices to compute the new well-supported model, which is in P-Time. Of course, there is space for improvement, for instance by examining only the fragments of the previous well-supported model, which would provide better results. However in the worst case still no better than P-Time can be achieved.

In the case of a successful belief revision, an acknowledgement in form of the concession speech act must be sent, in order to notify the sender about the agreement about the rule. A failure at this stage is a very rare incident, however, might happen (if for example the program running the agent is manually killed) and would cause a fatal error, for which to recover from, special means are needed.

If a message makes through Belief Revision, that means, that the rule has been successfully integrated with the current knowledge and the appropriate acknowledgement has been sent to whom it may concern.

6.5 The Algorithm

The Perceiving Assertions About Rules Algorithm takes the following input parameters:

– $\ell :\!- b$. A rule with a body $b = b_{11}, \ldots, b_{1i_1} \mid \ldots \mid b_{m1}, \ldots, b_{mi_m}$ and a head ℓ, wrapped up in a speech act `assert`.
– S. The sender of the message.
– R. The receiver of the message.
– $\mathcal{E}$. Agent's R epistemic profile.
– $\mathcal{B}_R^{\mathcal{E}} = \langle \mathcal{C}_R, F_R \rangle$. Agent's R belief structure.
– `applicationType`. Application type.

---

[2] For literature see [29–32].

Algorithm 1. Perceiving Assertions About Rules Algorithm

```
 1: procedure PERCEIVE(S, R, ℓ, b, ε, B_R^ε, applicationType)
 2: [Filtering]
 3:     if FilteringModule.allow(speechAct=SA, sender=S, ...) IN{f} then
 4:         go to [End]
 5:     end if
 6: [Parsing]
 7: [Case 1]                                                          ▷ rule head and body recognized
 8:     if l ∈ F_R ∧      ∀         b_{j_k} ∈ F_R then                           ▷ l, b_{j_k} ∈ {t, f, i}
                     j ∈ 1..m, k ∈ 1..i_m
 9:         go to [Evaluation]
10: [Case 2]                                                              ▷ only rule body recognized
11:     else if      ∀       b_{j_k} ∈ F_R then                              ▷ l = u, b_{j_k} ∈ {t, f, i}
                j ∈ 1..m, k ∈ 1..i_m
12:         switch applicationType do
13:             case "exploratory":
14:                 ⟨B_{R_1}^ε, result⟩ ← InformationSeekingAbout( l )
15:                 if result ==success then restart(B_{R_1}^ε)              ▷ possibly new belief structure
16:                 else plug-in custom solutions here
17:                 end if
18:             case "real time": go to [Evaluation]
19:             case "other": send(reject_{R,S}(ℓ :- b)
20: [Case 3]                                                              ▷ only rule head recognized
21:     else if l ∈ F_R then                                               ▷ l ∈ {t, f, i}, b_{j_k} = u
22:         if communicativeRelation(S) == "authority" then
23:             go to [Evaluation]
24:         else
25:             for all j, k : b_{j_k} = u do                                      ▷ execute in parallel
26:                 ⟨B_{R_2}^ε, result⟩ ← send(request_{R,S}(b_{j_k}))
27:                 if result ==success then restart(B_{R_2}^ε)                    ▷ new belief structure
28:                 else send(reject_{R,S}(ℓ :- b))
29:                 end if
30:             end for
31:         end if
32: [Case 4]                                                     ▷ rule head and rule body unknown
33:     else                                                                        ▷ l, b = u
34:         go to [Case 3]                                                  ▷ resolve the body first
35:     end if
36: [Evaluation]
37:     if l ∈ F_R then                               ▷ rule head known: check if the rule is admissible
38:         ε_TEST ← ε ∪ {ℓ :- b}                             ▷ add the rule to a candidate epistemic profile
39:         F_{R_TEST} ← ε_TEST(C)
40:         B_{R_TEST}^ε ← ⟨C_R, F_{R_TEST}⟩                         ▷ compute the candidate belief structure
41:         if incompatible(B_{R_TEST}^ε, B_R^ε) then                        ▷ try to resolve the problem
42:             ⟨B_{R_3}^ε, result, winner⟩ ← send(challenge_{R,S}(ℓ :- b))
43:             if result ==success then
44:                 if winner == R then                                      ▷ the rule was not admissible
45:                     go to [End]
46:                 else restart(B_{R_3}^ε)              ▷ the opponent won, restart with the new belief structure
47:                 end if
48:             else send(reject_{R,S}(ℓ :- b))
49:             end if
50:         else go to [BeliefRevision]                               ▷ belief structures compatible
51:         end if
52:     else                                                                   ▷ rule head unknown
53:         switch communicativeRelation(S) do
54:             case "authority": go to [BeliefRevision]
55:             case "peer": plug-in custom solutions here
56:             case "subordinate": go to [End]
57:     end if
```

Algorithm 2. Perceiving Rules Algorithm (continued)

```
58: [BeliefRevision]
59:    E ← E ∪ {ℓ :– b}                           ▷ add the rule to the epistemic profile
60:    F_R ← E_ℓ(C)
61:    B_R^E ← ⟨C_R, F_R⟩                          ▷ compute the new belief structure
62:    send(concede_{R,S}(ℓ :– b))
63: [End]
64: end procedure
```

7   Example

Let us present a more thorough example demonstrating some of the cases described above. Recall, that Tom is an agent realized[3] via 4QL program outlined in Figure 2.

```
module tom:
    relations:   a(literal), use(literal, literal), borrow(literal).
    rules:
        a(hanger) :- a(nail), a(hammer), use(hammer, nail).
        a(X) :- borrow(X).
    facts:
        a(nail).
        a(hammer).
        a(painting).
        use(hammer, nail).
end.
```

Fig. 2. Example of a 4QL program realizing agent Tom

Tom's epistemic profile consist of four facts (hammer, painting, use(hammer, nail), nail), and two rules: one, describing his ability to borrow things and the other, depicting how to make a hanger. Tom's belief structure (the well-supported model) is:

$$B_T = \{\texttt{nail}, \texttt{hammer}, \texttt{painting}, \texttt{use(hammer, nail)}, \texttt{hanger}\}$$

Suppose Bob has uttered the following rule (see Section 2):

$$\texttt{assert}_{B,T}(\texttt{hangingPainting} :– \texttt{hanger}, \texttt{painting}.)$$

The rule head is unknown to Tom (it is absent from his belief structure: B_T) but the rule body is recognized: both literals are in the belief structure (but notice that hanger is not a fact from the epistemic profile). According to the algorithm, Tom needs to exercise the admissibility criterion for the new rule. He adds the rule to his candidate epistemic profile and computes the new belief structure:

$$B_T' = \{\texttt{nail}, \texttt{hammer}, \texttt{painting}, \texttt{use(hammer, nail)}, \texttt{hanger}, \texttt{hangingPainting}\}$$

Now, B_T' is compatible with B_T, because all literals that were true remained true and one literal which was unknown is now true. Tom concludes that he can add the rule

---

[3] For modeling and for computing well-supported models we use the 4QL interpreter, developed by P. Spanily. It can be downloaded from http://www.4ql.org/.

to his epistemic profile permanently. In this way, Tom learnt how to achieve something from already available means.

Another interesting case concerns agents' ability to learn alternative ways of achieving goals. In Figure 3 the new module Tom, equipped with the newly learnt rule is presented. Consider now the case that Tom does not have the hammer at hand (fact `hammer` is false). Tom's new belief structure is the following:

$$B_T'' = \{\mathtt{nail}, \neg\mathtt{hammer}, \mathtt{painting}, \mathtt{use(hammer, nail)}\}$$

```
module tom:
    relations:    a(literal), use(literal, literal), borrow(literal).
    rules:
        a(hangingPainting) :- a(hanger), a(painting).
        a(hanger) :- a(nail), a(hammer), use(hammer, nail).
        a(X) :- borrow(X).
    facts:
        a(nail).
        -a(hammer).
        a(painting).
        use(hammer, nail).
end.
```

Fig. 3. Tom with a new rule added, but without the hammer

Suppose Bob has uttered the following rule, providing another way to achieve a hanger:

hanger :- nail, hammer | borrow(hammer), use(hammer, nail).

All literals are known to Bob, so the candidate belief structure B_T''' can be computed:

$$B_T''' = \{\mathtt{nail}, \neg\mathtt{hammer}, \mathtt{painting}, \mathtt{use(hammer, nail)}\}$$

The new rule can be safely added to Tom's epistemic profile. Notice that if Tom borrowed the hammer (a fact `borrow(hammer)` was added to Tom's epistemic profile), he would achieve `hangingPainting` now (see $B_{T'''_{borrowed}}$). It would have been impossible without the new rule from Bob (compare with $B_{T''_{borrowed}}$):

$$B_{T'''_{borrowed}} = \{\mathtt{nail}, \mathtt{hammer}, \neg\mathtt{hammer}, \mathtt{borrow(hammer)}, \mathtt{painting}, \mathtt{use(hammer, nail)},$$
$$\mathtt{hanger}, \mathtt{hangingPainting}\}$$

$$B_{T''_{borrowed}} = \{\mathtt{nail}, \mathtt{hammer}, \neg\mathtt{hammer}, \mathtt{borrow(hammer)}, \mathtt{painting}, \mathtt{use(hammer, nail)}\}$$

8 Discussion and Conclusions

This paper aligns with our ultimate research goal, namely, a paraconsistent model of agents' communication. In order to construct complex dialogues, the speech acts theory provides the necessary building material. We initiated our research program by proposing a paraconsistent framework for perceiving new facts via four different speech acts: assert, concede, request and challenge [5]. In this work we make a second step by allowing the agents to perceive assertions about reasoning rules as well.

The application of Speech Acts theory to communication in MAS dates back to late 20th century [19]. Since then it proved to be a practical tool for creating various agent communication languages such as KQML and FIPA ACL [10] as well as formal models of dialogues [1, 14, 15, 24].

Perceiving new information, whether it is some previously unknown fact, a new valuation of a proposition, or a reasoning rule, typically requires belief revision [21]. Our implementation tool of choice, the rule-base query language 4QL was designed in such a way that the inconsistency is tamed and treated naturally in the language. As a great benefit, belief revision turned out to be dramatically simplified and obtained in P-Time.

In this paper we focus on the case, when the information in question reflects the procedural component on the agents' epistemic profile, namely: the rules. This subject has hitherto received little attention. Even though in [22], a cooperative rule learning approach for exchanging sets of rules among agents has been presented and in [23], a formalism has been proposed that allows for discussing inference rules acceptability by agents, none of the approaches deals explicitly with unknown and possibly inconsistent information. Trying to fill this gap in [5] and our recent paper, the next step will concern challenging rules. In this context the aspect of validity and sensibility of the rules themselves, which wasn't treated here, will be vital.

References

1. Atkinson, K., Bench-Capon, T., McBurney, P.: Computational representation of practical argument. Synthese 152, 157–206 (2005)
2. Austin, J.L.: How to Do Things with Words, 2nd edn. Clarendon Press, Oxford (1975) Edited by J. O. Urmson, M. Sbisa
3. de Amo, S., Pais, M.: A paraconsistent logic approach for querying inconsistent databases. International Journal of Approximate Reasoning 46, 366–386 (2007)
4. Dignum, F., Dunin-Kęplicz, B., Verbrugge, R.: Creating collective intention through dialogue. Logic Journal of the IGPL 9, 145–158 (2001)
5. Dunin-Kęplicz, B., Strachocka, A., Szałas, A., Verbrugge, R.: Perceiving Speech Acts under Incomplete and Inconsistent Information. In: KES AMSTA. Frontiers of Artificial Intelligence and Applications, vol. 252, pp. 255–264. IOS Press (2013)
6. Dunin-Kęplicz, B., Szałas, A.: Epistemic profiles and belief structures. In: Jezic, G., Kusek, M., Nguyen, N.-T., Howlett, R.J., Jain, L.C. (eds.) KES-AMSTA 2012. LNCS, vol. 7327, pp. 360–369. Springer, Heidelberg (2012)
7. Walther, D., Lutz, C., Wolter, F., Wooldridge, M.: ATL satisfiability is indeed EXPTIME-complete. Journal of Logic and Computation 16(6), 765–787 (2006)
8. Dziubiński, M., Verbrugge, R., Dunin-Kęplicz, B.: Complexity issues in multiagent logics. Fundamenta Informaticae 75(1-4), 239–262 (2007)
9. Fages, F.: Consistency of Clark's completion and existence of stable models. Methods of Logic in Computer Science 1, 51–60 (1994)
10. FIPA (2002), http://www.fipa.org/
11. Małuszyński, J., Szałas, A.: Living with Inconsistency and Taming Nonmonotonicity. In: de Moor, O., Gottlob, G., Furche, T., Sellers, A. (eds.) Datalog 2010. LNCS, vol. 6702, pp. 384–398. Springer, Heidelberg (2011)
12. Małuszyński, J., Szałas, A.: Partiality and Inconsistency in Agents' Belief Bases. In: KES-AMSTA. Frontiers of Artificial Intelligence and Applications, vol. 252, pp. 3–17. IOS Press (2013)

13. Mascardi, V., Demergasso, D., Ancona, D.: Languages for programming BDI-style agents: an overview. In: Corradini, F., De Paoli, F., Merelli, E., Omicini, A. (eds.) WOA 2005 - Workshop From Objects to Agents, pp. 9–15 (2005)
14. Parsons, S., McBurney, P.: Argumentation-based dialogues for agent coordination. Group Decision and Negotiation 12, 415–439 (2003)
15. Prakken, H.: Formal systems for persuasion dialogue. The Knowledge Engineering Review 21(2), 163–188 (2006)
16. Searle, J.R.: Speech Acts. Cambridge University Press, Cambridge (1969)
17. Vitória, A., Małuszyński, J., Szałas, A.: Modeling and reasoning with paraconsistent rough sets. Fundamenta Informaticae 97(4), 405–438 (2009)
18. Walton, D., Krabbe, E.: Commitment in Dialogue: Basic Concepts of Interpersonal Reasoning. State University of New York Press, Albany (1995)
19. Cohen, P.R., Levesque, H.J.: Rational interaction as the basis for communication. Technical Report 433, SRI International, Menlo Park, CA (1988)
20. Kaiser, M., Dillmann, R., Rogalla, O.: Communication as the basis for learning in multi-agent systems. In: ECAI 1996 Workshop on Learning in Distributed AI Systems (1996)
21. Paglieri, F., Castelfranchi, C.: Revising beliefs through arguments: Bridging the gap between argumentation and belief revision in MAS. In: Rahwan, I., Moraïtis, P., Reed, C. (eds.) ArgMAS 2004. LNCS (LNAI), vol. 3366, pp. 78–94. Springer, Heidelberg (2005)
22. Costantini, S.: Learning by knowledge exchange in logical agents. In: WOA 2005, Dagli (2005)
23. Mcburney, P., Parsons, S.: Tenacious Tortoises: A formalism for argument over rules of inference. In: Computational Dialectics (ECAI 2000 Workshop) (2000)
24. Singh, M.: A semantics for speech acts. Annals of Mathematics and Artificial Intelligence, pp. 47–71. Springer, Netherlands (1993) Print ISSN: 1012-2443
25. Linder, B., Hoek, W., Meyer, J.-J. C.: Actions that make you change your mind. In: KI 1995: Advances in Artificial Intelligence, vol. 98, pp. 185–196 (1995)
26. Prakken, H.: Modelling Reasoning about Evidence in Legal Procedure. In: Proceedings of the Eighth International Conference on Artificial Intelligence and Law, pp. 119–128 (2001)
27. Bench-Capon, T.J.M., Prakken, H.: Using Argument Schemes for Hypothetical Reasoning in Law. Artificial Intelligence and Law 18(2), 153–174 (2010)
28. Gabbay, D., Hunter, A.: Making Inconsistency Respectable: A Logical Framework for Inconsistency in Reasoning, Part I - A Position Paper. In: Jorrand, P., Kelemen, J. (eds.) FAIR 1991. LNCS, vol. 535, pp. 19–32. Springer, Heidelberg (1991)
29. Winslett, M.: Updating logical databases. Cambridge University Press (1990)
30. van Harmelen, F., Lifschitz, V., Porter, B.: Handbook of Knowledge Representation. Elsevier Science (2007)
31. Alferes, J.J., Leite, J.A., Pereira, L.M., Przymusinska, H., Przymusinski, T.C.: Dynamic Logic Programming. In: Procs. of the Sixth International Conference on Principles of Knowledge Representation and Reasoning, Trento, Italy, pp. 98–109 (1998)
32. Alferes, J.J., Brogi, A., Leite, J., Moniz Pereira, L.: Evolving Logic Programs. In: Flesca, S., Greco, S., Leone, N., Ianni, G. (eds.) JELIA 2002. LNCS (LNAI), vol. 2424, pp. 50–61. Springer, Heidelberg (2002)
33. Béziau, J.-Y., Carnielli, W.A., Gabbay, D.M.: Handbook of paraconsistency. College publications (2007)
34. Walton, D., Reed, C., Macagno, F.: Argumentation Schemes. Cambridge University Press (2008)

Using Agent JPF to Build Models
for Other Model Checkers

Louise A. Dennis, Michael Fisher, and Matt Webster

Department of Computer Science, University of Liverpool, UK
L.A.Dennis@liverpool.ac.uk

Abstract. We describe an extension to the AJPF agent program model-checker so that it may be used to generate models for input into other, non-agent, model-checkers. We motivate this adaptation, arguing that it improves the efficiency of the model-checking process and provides access to richer property specification languages.

We illustrate the approach by describing the export of AJPF program models to SPIN and PRISM. In the case of SPIN we also investigate, experimentally, the effect the process has on the overall efficiency of model-checking.

1 Introduction

Agent Java Pathfinder (AJPF) [1] is a program model-checker for programs written in a range of Belief–Desire–Intention (BDI) agent programming languages. It is built on top of Java Pathfinder (JPF), an explicit state program model-checker for Java programs [2], and checks the execution of Java based interpreters for BDI languages. AJPF has a property specification language based upon Linear Temporal Logic (LTL) extended with descriptions of beliefs, intentions, etc.

AJPF (and JPF) are "program" model-checkers, meaning that they work directly on the program code, rather than on a mathematical model of the program's execution (as is typical for model-checking). In fact, these program model-checkers utilise *symbolic execution* to internally build a model to be analysed. Thus, using a *program* model-checker gives the advantage that results derived apply directly to the program under consideration. However, AJPF is slow when compared to traditional model-checkers and, in general, it is the internal generation of the program model (created by executing all possible paths through the Java program) that causes a significant bottleneck.

Hunter et al. [3] suggested the use of JPF to generate models of agent programs that could then be checked in other model-checkers. We expand upon this idea showing how AJPF can be adapted to output models in the input languages of both SPIN and PRISM tools. While such model generation remains slow, there are still efficiency gains, especially when the property becomes more complex. More importantly, such translations give access to a wider range of property specification languages. This means that AJPF can be used as an automated link between programs written in BDI languages and a range of model-checkers appropriate for verifying properties of those programs.

J. Leite et al. (Eds.): CLIMA XIV, LNAI 8143, pp. 273–289, 2013.

The key advantages of this approach are potential improvements in the efficiency and scope of model checking; and access to a richer set of logics for specifying program properties.

2   Background

2.1   AJPF

Java PathFinder (JPF) is an explicit state program model-checker for Java programs [2]. This means that it takes as input an executable Java program rather than a model of a Java program. It then explores all possible execution paths through this program to ensure that some property holds. For example, using JPF, it is possible to explore all possible thread scheduling options for a multi-threaded program to ensure that deadlock between threads never occurs.

AJPF [1] is a program model-checker for linear temporal logic (LTL) built on top of JPF. AJPF is specially designed for model-checking programs for rational agents, that is agents that use the BDI paradigm (see [4]) and whose execution can be described in terms of rational, goal-directed behaviour.

AJPF extends JPF with an LTL model-checking algorithm based on [7,6][1]. The property specification language contains shallow modalities for agent concepts such as belief ($\mathcal{B}$), goal ($\mathcal{G}$), intention ($\mathcal{I}$), etc., as well as the standard LTL modalities ($\Diamond$ (eventually), $\Box$ (always), etc., but not $\bigcirc$ (next)[2]). The agent concepts are mapped to specific data structures in the Java program, and allow properties such as the following to be verified:

$$\Box \Diamond \mathcal{B}_{a} \text{ reached(destination)}$$

This property states that *it is always the case that, eventually, agent a believes it has reached its destination.*

AJPF is intended for use with BDI agent programming languages which have an explicit operational semantics. The language's operational semantics is implemented in the *Agent Infrastructure Layer* (AIL): a set of Java classes that support AJPF allowing the rapid construction of interpreters for BDI agent programming languages [1]. The AIL also provides support for the Belief, Goal and Intention modalities used by the property specification language. The property specification language is discussed more fully in [1] and summarised in Fig. 1.

There are two key (and related) advantages to using a program model-checker such as AJPF instead of one with a specialised modelling language for input. Firstly, it avoids the need for the programmer (or designer) to create a separate

---

[1] JPF does not currently support LTL model-checking, focusing instead on searching for deadlocks and exception freedom. However it has had LTL support in the past and work is currently in progress to re-instate this support.

[2] $\bigcirc$ was omitted partly because it isn't straightforward to determine the correct semantics for "next step" in a BDI program execution and partly because it complicates the model checking algorithm.

AJPF *Property Specification Language Syntax* The syntax for property formulæ ϕ is as follows, where ag is an "agent constant" referring to a specific agent in the system, and f is a ground first-order atomic formula:

$$\phi ::= \mathcal{B}_{ag}\, f \mid \mathcal{G}_{ag} f \mid \mathcal{A}_{ag} f \mid \mathcal{I}_{ag} f \mid \mathcal{P}(f) \mid \phi \vee \phi \mid \neg\phi \mid \phi\,\mathcal{U}\phi \mid \phi\mathcal{R}\phi$$

Here, $\mathcal{B}_{ag}\, f$ is true if ag believes f to be true, $\mathcal{G}_{ag} f$ is true if ag has a goal to make f true, and so on (with $\mathcal{A}$ representing actions, $\mathcal{I}$ representing intentions, and $\mathcal{P}$ representing percepts, i.e., properties that are true in the environment).

AJPF *Property Specification Language Semantics* We summarise those aspects of the semantics of property formulæ relevant to this paper. Consider a program, P, describing a multi-agent system and let MAS be the state of the multi-agent system at one point in the run of P. MAS is a tuple consisting of the local states of the individual agents and of the environment. Let $ag \in MAS$ be the state of an agent in the MAS tuple at this point in the program execution. Then

$$MAS \models_{MC} \mathcal{B}_{ag}\, f \quad \text{iff} \quad ag \models \mathcal{B}_{ag}\, f$$

where $\models$ is logical consequence as implemented by the agent programming language. The semantics of $\mathcal{G}_{ag}f$ and $\mathcal{I}_{ag}f$ similarly refer to internal implementations of the language interpreter. The interpretation of $\mathcal{A}_{ag}f$ is:

$$MAS \models_{MC} \mathcal{A}_{ag}f$$

if, and only if, the last action changing the environment was action f taken by agent ag. Finally, the interpretation of $\mathcal{P}(f)$ is given as:

$$MAS \models_{MC} \mathcal{P}(f)$$

if, and only if, f is a percept that holds true in the environment.

The other operators in the AJPF property specification language have standard PLTL semantics [5] and are implemented as Büchi Automata as described in [6,7]. Thus, the classical logic operators are defined by:

$$MAS \models_{MC} \varphi \vee \psi \text{ iff } MAS \models_{MC} \varphi \text{ or } MAS \models_{MC} \psi$$
$$MAS \models_{MC} \neg\phi \text{ iff } MAS \not\models_{MC} \phi.$$

The temporal formulæ apply to runs of the programs in the JPF model checker. A run consists of a (possibly infinite) sequence of program states MAS_i, $i \geq 0$ where MAS_0 is the initial state of the program (note, however, that for model checking the number of *different* states in any run is assumed to be finite). Let P be a multi-agent program, then

$$MAS \models_{MC} \quad \varphi\,\mathcal{U}\psi \quad \text{iff} \quad$$ in all runs of P there exists a state MAS_j such that $MAS_i \models_{MC} \varphi$ for all $0 \leq i < j$ and $MAS_j \models_{MC} \psi$

$$MAS \models_{MC} \varphi\mathcal{R}\psi \quad \text{iff} \quad$$ either $MAS_i \models_{MC} \varphi$ for all i or there exists MAS_j such that $MAS_i \models_{MC} \varphi$ for all $0 \leq i \leq j$ and $MAS_j \models_{MC} \varphi \wedge \psi$

The common temporal operators $\Diamond$ (eventually) and $\Box$ (always) are, in turn, derivable from $\mathcal{U}$ and $\mathcal{R}$ in the usual way [5].

Fig. 1. Overview of the the AJPF Property Specification Language (Syntax and Semantics)

model of the implementation for verification. Secondly, in cases where certification of the program is required (e.g., [8,9]), it increases the value of the evidence submitted to the certification authority since it provides direct information about the system that will be deployed, rather than some idealised model.

These advantages come at a cost, however. The main disadvantage of program model-checking, particularly in AJPF, is that it is very slow in comparison with existing specialised model-checkers such as SPIN [10]. This has been (and continues to be) mitigated through updates to AJPF which have decreased the amount of time taken for model-checking. However, the fact remains that programs tend to be more complex than models of programs and this causes program model-checking to be much slower. Typically, to verify a program using AJPF requires minutes, hours or even days in extreme cases.

AIL-based implementations of well-known agent programming languages (e.g., GOAL [11]) are separate from the interpreters generally associated with those languages. Since, in theory, both interpreters use the same operational semantics, choosing an AIL based interpreter instead of the standard interpreter should be similar to choosing between different C compilers and an AIL interpreter can be preferred where certification is an issue. In practice, the standard interpreters are often more efficient, user-friendly and up-to-date.

One issue to consider is whether it is preferable to use just JPF to verify agent programs given that most standard interpreters are written in Java. This approach is certainly feasible, although the interpreters would probably need significant modification to work with JPF. For example, adaptations would be needed to access the AJPF Property Specification Language (or create something similar). Also, in order to minimize the state space explored by JPF careful use of Java data structures is necessary (e.g., all sets must be stored in a canonical form for state matching).

2.2   Spin

SPIN [10] is a popular model-checking tool originally developed by Bell Laboratories in the 1980s. It has been in continuous development for over thirty years and is widely used in both industry and academia (e.g., [12,13,14]). SPIN uses an input language called PROMELA. Typically a model of a program and the property (as a "never claim" – a sequence of transitions that should never occur) are provided in PROMELA, but SPIN also provides tools to convert formulae written in LTL into never claims for use with the model-checker. SPIN works by automatically generating programs written in C which carry out the exploration of the model relative to an LTL property. SPIN's use of compiled C code makes it very quick in terms of execution time, and this is further enhanced through other techniques like partial order reduction.

2.3   Prism

PRISM [15] is a probabilistic symbolic model-checker developed primarily at the Universities of Birmingham and Oxford since 1999. PRISM provides broadly similar functionality to SPIN but also allows for the model-checking of probabilistic models, i.e., models whose behaviour can vary depending on probabilities built into the model. Developers can use PRISM to create a probabilistic model (written in the PRISM language) which can then be model-checked using PRISM's own probabilistic property specification language, which subsumes several well-known probabilistic logics including PCTL, probabilistic LTL, CTL, and PCTL*. PRISM has been used to formally verify a variety of systems in which reliability and randomness play a role, including communication protocols, cryptographic protocols and biological systems [16].

2.4   Related Work

Hunter et al. [3] first suggested using JPF to generate models of programs that could then be used with alternative model-checkers. Their work targets the Brahms [17] agent programming language. They implemented a simulator for Brahms in Java and used JPF to produce a PROMELA model of a Brahms program. They used this system to investigate examples in air traffic control and health-care and demonstrated that it is feasible to use JPF as a model building tool. Their work did not, however, directly address the key BDI concepts of beliefs, intentions, etc., and it was a customised tool specifically aimed at the verification of Brahms programs.

The work reported here takes the ideas from Hunter et al. [3] as a starting point and aims to use them within AJPF's more generic framework in order to provide a general tool in which BDI programs, and BDI concepts can be verified in a wide range of model-checkers.

3   Exporting Models from AJPF

JPF is implemented as a specialised Java virtual machine which stores, among other things, backtracking points which allow the program model-checking algorithm to explore the entire execution space of a Java program. It is highly customisable providing numerous hooks for *listeners* that monitor and control the progress of model-checking. In what follows we will refer to the specialised Java virtual machine used by JPF as the *JPFJVM*. JPF is implemented in Java itself, therefore the JPFJVM is a program that executes in some underlying native Java virtual machine. We refer to this native virtual machine as *NatJVM*. Listeners execute in the NatJVM.

AJPF's checking process is constructed using a JPF listener. As JPF executes, it labels each state explored by the JPFJVM with a number. The AJPF listener tracks these numbers as well as the transitions between them and uses this information to construct a Kripke structure in the NatJVM. The LTL model-checking algorithm is then executed on this Kripke structure. This is partly for reasons of efficiency (the NatJVM naturally executes much faster than the JPFJVM) and also to account for the need for LTL to explore states in the

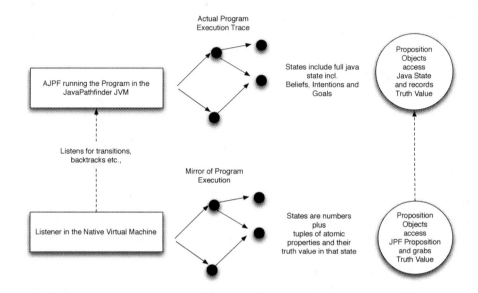

Fig. 2. The operation of AJPF wrt. the two Java Virtual Machines

model several times if the model contains a looping path and an *until expression* (e.g., **true** $\mathcal{U}$ p) exists in the LTL[3] property (see [7] and [6] for details).

In order to determine whether the agents in the original program have particular beliefs, goals, etc., it is necessary for the LTL model-checking algorithm to have access to these. However, they are not stored in the state graph of the Kripke structure accessible to the NatJVM. At the start of a model-checking run AJPF analyses the property being verified in order to produce a list of propositions that are needed for checking that property (e.g., *agent 1 believes it has reached its destination, agent 2 intends to win the auction* etc.). AJPF creates objects representing each of these propositions in both the JPFJVM and NatJVM. In the JPFJVM these propositional objects can access the state of the multi-agent system and explicitly check that the relevant propositions hold (e.g., that the Java object representing agent 1 contains, in its belief set, an object representing the formula *reached(destination)*).

Every time the interpreter for the agent programming language executes one step[4], all of the proposition objects are updated with their current truth value. In the NatJVM, propositional objects are created that track those in the JPFJVM. It is moderately straightforward to access an object in the JPFJVM from the

---

[3] "$a\mathcal{U}p$" means that "a is true continuously up until b becomes true".

[4] The meaning of a "step" in the semantics — as in the next point of interest to verification — is determined by the person implementing the semantics. Typically this is either the application of a single rule from the semantics, or of a whole reasoning cycle. This issue is discussed further in [1].

NatJVM[5]. Once an object has been accessed, inspecting the values of its fields is similarly straightforward providing they contain values of a primitive data type (such as `bool` or `int`). All this is done using JPF's Model Java Interface (MJI) interface [18] (the precise details of this implementation are specific to JPF and MJI). The implementation itself is available via the SourceForge distribution for AJPF (`http://mcapl.sourceforge.net`). The process allows, however, the modal agent properties (i.e., those related to beliefs, desires, intentions, etc.) that can be determined in the JPFJVM to be converted into state labels in the Kripke structure stored in the NatJVM. When the listener detects that a new state has been generated in the JPFJVM, the state in the Kripke structure in the NatJVM is annotated with the truth value of all the required propositions.

The process of adapting this system to produce a model for use with an alternative model checker now involves: (i) bypassing the LTL model-checking algorithm[6] but continuing to generate and maintain a set of propositional objects in order to label states in the Kripke structure, and (ii) exporting the Kripke structure in a format that can be used by another model checker.

3.1   Advantages

Ideally, a program is only model-checked once against a full set of requirements consisting of a conjunction of many properties. However, it is our experience that it is more common to check programs several times against smaller properties. For AJPF, this results in the program model being generated from the Java bytecode for each property. Our experiences with AJPF suggested that the most computationally complex part of the model-checking was in the generation of this program model, and that this was the chief cause of the slow performance of AJPF compared with other model-checkers. (This is unsurprising since in AJPF the generation of a transition in the program model can involve the symbolic execution of significant amounts of Java bytecode.)

The first advantage of the approach described above, therefore, is that exporting the program model prior to model-checking allows us to generate the program model only once, and thereafter we can use the far more compact Kripke structure representation, meaning that the time to model-check each property is reduced (on average).

The second advantage is that other model-checkers (such as SPIN) have many years of development invested in an accurate and efficient implementation of LTL model-checking. Compared to model-checkers like SPIN, there is a much weaker level of assurance that the LTL model-checking implemented in AJPF is correct (although it has been tested against well-known "gotchas"). Also, the

---

[5] The documentation for this mechanism is somewhat opaque and the process itself is complicated, but conceptually is it a simple matter of identifying the current object in the JPFJVM stack in order to obtain a reference for it. This can then be stored for future use in the NatJVM.

[6] This is not strictly necessary but it increases the speed of model generation, and avoids the pruning of some model states based on the property under consideration.

AJPF LTL model-checking algorithm is not highly optimised, being a direct adaptation of the algorithms in [7,6]. Consequently, it seems desirable, both for reasons of confidence and efficiency, to use a more well-developed implementation of model-checking (such as SPIN) where possible.

The third advantage is that this technique will allow us to use richer specification languages than LTL. For instance when verifying hybrid systems, probabilistic values frequently appear both in terms of the reliability of sensors, and the chances that an action will achieve the expected outcome. Exporting an AJPF program model into a probabilistic model-checker such as PRISM will allow us to verify properties stated in more expressive logics, such as probabilistic computation tree logic (PCTL).

3.2   Disadvantages

While there are advantages to using AJPF just for model generation, there are some disadvantages as well.

Firstly, it is arguable that the direct link between the implemented program and the system being verified described in Section 2.1 has been lost. However, the LTL model-checking algorithm used in AJPF was already operating upon an automatically-generated abstraction of the system stored in the NatJVM. Therefore taking this abstracted model and exporting it to a different system does not, in our view, have a significant effect on the correctness of any verification result. However it has introduced a further step into the process which could cause an issue with software certification concerning *tool qualification*. Specifically, we have introduced another tool (SPIN) to the existing verification system (AJPF) which would mean that both tools would now need to be qualified separately, and possibly again as a combined tool, with additional associated costs (tool qualification can be very costly in terms of time and finance). We do, nevertheless, provide a fully automatic route from implemented code, through an abstraction of that code, to a formal verification result, which itself is preferable to systems in which the abstraction from the implementation must be done "by hand."

Secondly, the opportunity to exploit features of the property under test in order to prune model-checking has been lost. In particular, when checking liveness properties (of the form "eventually p will happen", or $\Diamond p$) it is possible to prune the LTL model-checking search tree as soon as p occurs. It would obviously still be possible to do this, if the user were confident that only this property will be checked on the resulting model. Where the model may be used to check a number of properties such pruning is no longer a possibility and the entire program state space must be explored. Similarly, although we have not explored techniques such as property-based slicing [19] in AJPF these would also be difficult to exploit if a full model were to be exported. However, it is likely that in many cases where there are more than a few properties to be checked the additional time taken to produce a complete model will be offset by the time saved in not having to reproduce this model each time a new property needs to be verified. Similarly, the fact that we export the model as a Kripke Structure, means that we may not be able to exploit potential optimisations available within the target model checker. It should be noted, however, that some optimisations such as partial order reduction will already have been applied by JPF.

4   Exporting AJPF Models to Promela/Spin

In this section we describe the process used to translate AJPF models to PROMELA for verification in the SPIN model-checker, and some results of SPIN verification of the PROMELA models generated.

4.1   Translation Details

Both SPIN and AJPF's LTL algorithm operate on Kripke structures so translating between the two is straightforward.

As mentioned above, within AJPF's NatJVM each state is assigned a number, e.g, 12. This is converted to state12 in the SPIN input file. Then the list of propositional objects is examined recursively. Each proposition is converted into a simple string (without spaces or brackets), and assigned either the value true or false, depending upon its value in the state. The transitions in the AJPF model graph are kept separately from the states while PROMELA represents them as goto statements attached to states.

Example. Fig. 3 shows the NatJVM model of a very simple agent program with one property (agent 1 believes "bad") compared to the result of exporting this model in PROMELA.

```
Model States:
=============

0:
    B(ag1,bad()) = false;

1:
    B(ag1,bad()) = false;

2:
    B(ag1,bad()) = false;

Model Edges:
=============

0-->1
1-->2
```

```
bool bag1bad

active proctype JPFModel()
{
state0:
        bag1bad = false;
        goto state1;
state1:
        bag1bad = false;
        goto state2;
state2:
        bag1bad = false;
        printf("end state\n");
}
```

Fig. 3. Equivalent program models in AJPF (left) and PROMELA (right)

4.2 Results

We tested our SPIN implementation on the verification of a simple "leader" agent intended to coordinate a formation of satellites as described in [20]. This program was implemented in a version of the GWENDOLEN language [21]. We implemented a non-deterministic environment for the agent in which messages from the satellite agents randomly arrived (or not) each time the agent took an action. This caused model-checking to explore all possible combinations of messages that the leader agent could receive. The agent was designed to assign positions to four satellites and then wait for responses. Since our hypothesis was that we would see gains in performance as the LTL property to be checked became more complex we tested the system against a sequence of properties:

1. $\Box \neg \mathcal{B}_{lead} \, bad$
   (The agent never believes something bad has happened).
2. $(\Box(\mathcal{B}_{lead} \, informed(ag1) \rightarrow \Diamond \mathcal{B}_{lead} \, maintaining\_pos(ag1))) \rightarrow \Box \neg \mathcal{B}_{lead} \, bad$
   (If it is always the case that when the leader has informed agent 1 of its position then eventually the leader will believe agent 1 is maintaining that position, then it is always the case that the leader does not believe something bad has happened).
3. $(\Box(\mathcal{B}_{lead} \, informed(ag2) \rightarrow \Diamond \mathcal{B}_{lead} \, maintaining\_pos(ag2))) \wedge$
   $\Box(\mathcal{B}_{lead} \, informed(ag1) \rightarrow \Diamond \mathcal{B}_{lead} \, maintaining\_pos(ag1))) \rightarrow \Box \neg \mathcal{B}_{lead} \, bad$
4. $(\Box(\mathcal{B}_{lead} \, informed(ag3) \rightarrow \Diamond \mathcal{B}_{lead} \, maintaining\_pos(ag3))) \wedge$
   $\Box(\mathcal{B}_{lead} \, informed(ag2) \rightarrow \Diamond \mathcal{B}_{lead} \, maintaining\_pos(ag2)) \wedge$
   $\Box(\mathcal{B}_{lead} \, informed(ag1) \rightarrow \Diamond \mathcal{B}_{lead} \, maintaining\_pos(ag1))) \rightarrow \Box \neg \mathcal{B}_{lead} \, bad$
5. $(\Box(\mathcal{B}_{lead} \, informed(ag4) \rightarrow \Diamond \mathcal{B}_{lead} \, maintaining\_pos(ag4)) \wedge$
   $\Box(\mathcal{B}_{lead} \, informed(ag3) \rightarrow \Diamond \mathcal{B}_{lead} \, maintaining\_pos(ag3)) \wedge$
   $\Box(\mathcal{B}_{lead} \, informed(ag2) \rightarrow \Diamond \mathcal{B}_{lead} \, maintaining\_pos(ag2)) \wedge$
   $\Box(\mathcal{B}_{lead} \, informed(ag1) \rightarrow \Diamond \mathcal{B}_{lead} \, maintaining\_pos(ag1))) \rightarrow \Box \neg \mathcal{B}_{lead} \, bad$
6. $(\Box(\mathcal{B}_{lead} \, informed(ag4) \rightarrow \Diamond \mathcal{B}_{lead} \, maintaining\_pos(ag4)) \wedge$
   $\Box(\mathcal{B}_{lead} \, informed(ag3) \rightarrow \Diamond \mathcal{B}_{lead} \, maintaining\_pos(ag3)) \wedge$
   $\Box(\mathcal{B}_{lead} \, informed(ag2) \rightarrow \Diamond \mathcal{B}_{lead} \, maintaining\_pos(ag2)) \wedge$
   $\Box(\mathcal{B}_{lead} \, informed(ag1) \rightarrow \Diamond \mathcal{B}_{lead} \, maintaining\_pos(ag1))) \wedge$
   $\Box(\mathcal{B}_{lead} \, formation(square) \rightarrow \Diamond \mathcal{B}_{lead} \, informed(ag1))) \rightarrow \Box \neg \mathcal{B}_{lead} \, bad$

This sequence of increasingly complex properties was constructed so that each property had the form $P_1 \wedge \ldots \wedge P_n \rightarrow Q$ for some $n \geq 0$ and each P_i was of the form $(\Box(P_i' \rightarrow \Diamond Q_i))$. With the addition of each such logical antecedent the property automata became considerably more complex. Furthermore, the antecedents were chosen so that we were confident that on at least some paths through the program P_i' would be true at some point, necessitating that the LTL checker explore the product automata for $\Diamond Q_i$. We judged that this sequence of properties provided a good test for the way each model-checker's performance scaled as the property under test became more complicated.

SPIN model-checking requires a sequence of steps to be undertaken: the LTL property must be translated to a "never claim" (effectively representing the automaton corresponding to the negation of the required property), then it is compiled together with the PROMELA description into C, which is then compiled again before being run as a C program. We used the LTL3BA tool [22] to compile the LTL property into a never claim since this is more efficient than the built-in SPIN compiler. In our results we present the total time taken for all SPIN operations (SPIN Time) and the total time taken overall including generation of the model in AJPF.

Table 1. Results Comparing AJPF with and without SPIN Model Checking

Property	AJPF	SPIN		
		AJPF model generation	SPIN Time	Total Overall Time
1	5m25s	5m17s	1.972s	5m19s
2	5m54s	5m50s	3.180s	5m53s
3	7m9s	6m28s	4.369s	6m32s
4	8m50s	7m34s	6.443s	7m40s
5	9m22s	8m27s	10.015s	8m37s
6	—	8m51s	22.361s	9m13s

Table 1 shows the running times for model-checking the six properties on a 2.8 GHz Intel Core i7 Macbook running MacOS 10.7.4 with 8 GB of memory. Fig. 4 shows the same information as a graph. There is no result for AJPF model-checking of the final property since the system suffered a stack overflow error when attempting to build the property automata.

The results show that as the LTL property becomes more complex, model-checking using the AJPF to PROMELA/SPIN translation tool is marginally more efficient than using AJPF alone. It should be noted that in the SPIN case, where AJPF is not performing LTL model-checking, and is using a simple list of propositions (rather than an LTL property) the time to generate the model still increases as the property becomes more complex. This is explained by the overhead involved in tracking the proposition objects in the JPFJVM and the NatJVM: as more propositions are involved this time increases.

If only one AJPF model were to be generated then SPIN would give considerable time savings overall. (NB. In this case it would need to be the AJPF model with all relevant propositions, i.e., the one taking nearly 9 minutes to generate.)

We note that the simple fact that AJPF cannot generate a property automata for property 6 is a compelling argument that combining AJPF with SPIN or some other model-checker is sometimes necessary. It also illustrates the point that SPIN is well optimised for working with LTL where AJPF is not.

5   Exporting AJPF Models to Prism

5.1   Translation Details

Both AJPF's NatJVM and SPIN operate on Kripke structures so it was a straightforward process to translate between them. The PRISM input language

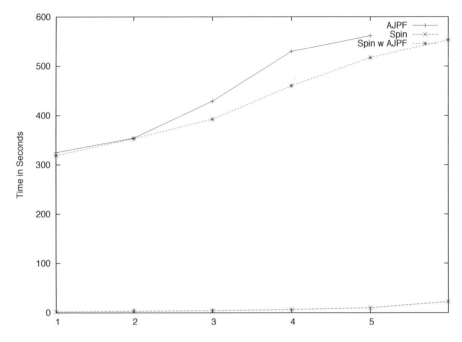

Fig. 4. Results of AJPF against SPIN

is based on probabilistic timed automata. In the examples we are particularly interested in exploring, we can consider the model to be a Kripke structure enhanced by labels on the transitions representing probabilities.

We therefore needed to make some alterations to AJPF. JPF, and hence AJPF, is able to branch the search space when a random element is selected from a finite set. However the system does not record the probabilities of each branch created in a manner accessible to the NatJVM. We developed a new class `Choice` in Java which represented a probabilistic choice from a finite set of options. This class provided a method `pickChoice` which would perform a choice on a probabilistic basis. If this class was used in programming at the JPFJVM level, then a NatJVM *native peer* could detect invocations of methods in this class, intercept such invocations and use a customised *choice generator*, to branch the search space in the JPFJVM while annotating the edges of the model graph in the NatJVM with the appropriate probabilities. The use of native peers and choice generators are standard JPF customisation processes for controlling and recording search in model-checking (see [18] for a discussion of their use). In short, programming with the `Choice` class, in the normal execution of the program, simply picks an element from a set based on some probability distribution. When executed within AJPF, the `Choice` class causes the system to explore all possible choices and label each branch with its probability.

After this the process of translating these models into PRISM's input language is straightforward.

1. First we initialise the model: We input it as a discrete time Markov chain (`dtmc`); We list the numbers of all states and state the initial state (0); We list all the properties initialise them to false.
2. We then iterate through the states in the AJPF model. For each state we:
    (a) Print out `state = num` where `num` is the state number.
    (b) Iterate over all its outgoing edges, for each edge:
        i. Print out the probability of that edge being traversed
        ii. Print out the state number, and values of the properties for the state at the far end of the edge.

As an example we consider a simple program based on [8] in which an unmanned aerial vehicle (UAV) must detect potential collisions. The UAV's radar is only 90% reliable, so it does not always perform an 'evade' maneouvre when a collision is possible. The agent controlling the UAV is implemented in GWENDOLEN which does not contain any probabilistic aspects. However the agent was placed in an environment programmed in Java and we used the `Choice` class to represent the unreliability of the sensor when the agent requested incoming perceptions[7].

The model is tracking two properties $\mathcal{P}(collision)$ which means *a potential collision is perceptible in the environment* and $\mathcal{A}_{uav}evade$ which means *the last action performed was the uav agent taking an evade maneouvre*. The agent was programmed to make evade maneouvres when it believed there would be a collision. It only believed there would be a collision if a potential collision was perceptible and the sensor conveyed that information to the agent.

A fragment of the AJPF model for this program, adapted to show the probability of transitions is shown in Fig. 5 alongside the full model exported to the PRISM input language[8]. Fig. 6 gives a brief outline of some key features of PRISM's property specification language, its full semantics can be found in [23].

5.2 Results

We do not provide performance results since AJPF and PRISM are incomparable using, as they do, different input languages (AJPF does not support probabilistic reasoning and PRISM does not support non-probabilistic LTL model checking). We model-checked the above program in PRISM against the property

$$\text{P}^{=?}\Box(\mathcal{P}(collision) \rightarrow \Diamond\mathcal{A}_{uav}evade)$$

to establish that the probability that the UAV would evade a collision, if one were possible, was 90%.

We also investigated a more complex model, again based on [8], in which the probability of a potential collision arising was also 90% (where it was certain

---

[7] We would also be able to investigate properties of BDI programming languages with probabilistic features, providing their AIL implementation used the `Choice` class — see Further Work.

[8] Note that the nature of rounding in Java means that 0.1 is, in several places, represented as 0.09999999999999998.

AJPF Model

```
Model States:
=============

....

3:
    A(uav,evade()) = false;
    P(collision()) = false;

4:
    A(uav,evade()) = false;
    P(collision()) = true;

5:
    A(uav,evade()) = true;
    P(collision()) = false;

6:
    A(uav,evade()) = true;
    P(collision()) = false;

7:
    A(uav,evade()) = true;
    P(collision()) = true;

...
```

```
Model Edges:
============

...

0.9 ::: 3-->4
0.09999999999999998 ::: 3-->12
1.0 ::: 4-->5
1.0 ::: 5-->6
0.9 ::: 6-->7
0.09999999999999998 ::: 6-->10
```

PRISM Model

```
dtmc

module jpfModel
state : [0 ..13] init 0;
auavevade: bool init false;
pcollision: bool init false;
[] state = 1 -> 1.0:(state'=2) & (auavevade'= false) & (pcollision'= false);
[] state = 2 -> 1.0:(state'=3) & (auavevade'= false) & (pcollision'= false);
[] state = 3 -> 0.9:(state'=4) & (auavevade'= false) & (pcollision'= false)
    + 0.09999999999999998:(state'=12) & (auavevade'= false) & (pcollision'= true);
[] state = 4 -> 1.0:(state'=5) & (auavevade'= true) & (pcollision'= false);
[] state = 5 -> 1.0:(state'=6) & (auavevade'= true) & (pcollision'= false);
[] state = 6 -> 0.9:(state'=7) & (auavevade'= true) & (pcollision'= true)
    + 0.09999999999999998:(state'=10) & (auavevade'= true) & (pcollision'= true);
[] state = 7 -> 1.0:(state'=8) & (auavevade'= false) & (pcollision'= false);
[] state = 8 -> 1.0:(state'=9) & (auavevade'= false) & (pcollision'= false);
[] state = 10 -> 1.0:(state'=11) & (auavevade'= false) & (pcollision'= false);
[] state = 11 -> 1.0:(state'=9) & (auavevade'= false) & (pcollision'= false);
[] state = 12 -> 1.0:(state'=13) & (auavevade'= false) & (pcollision'= false);
[] state = 13 -> 1.0:(state'=9) & (auavevade'= false) & (pcollision'= false);
endmodule
```

Fig. 5. Comparison of Models for AJPF and PRISM

The syntax of the fragment of the PRISM property specification language relevant here is given by the following grammar:

$$\phi ::= \texttt{true} \mid \texttt{a} \mid \phi \wedge \phi \mid \neg\phi \mid \texttt{P}^{\bowtie p}[\psi]$$
$$\psi ::= \phi \texttt{U} \phi$$

where a is an atomic proposition, $\bowtie \in \{\leq, <, \geq, >\}$, $p \in \mathbb{Q}_{\geq 0}$, and $k \in \mathbb{N}$.

The semantics of the propositional logic statements and the CTL until operator are standard and allow $\square$ (always) and $\lozenge$ (eventually) to be defined. P is a probabilistic operator and indicates the probability that some property is true along all paths from some state s where the operator is evaluated. For instance $\texttt{P}^{\geq 0.98}\psi$ means "the probability that ψ is satisfied by the paths from state s is greater than 0.98".

It is also possible to take a quantitative approach so $\texttt{P}^{=?}\psi$ will return a value for the probability that ψ is satisfied for all paths from state s.

Fig. 6. The PRISM Property Specification language

in the simple model above) and the UAV had to interact with an air traffic control agent, and go through take off procedures. The environment contained a navigation manager which, on a probabilistic basis, would either tell the UAV to change its current heading or land. In this situation the probability of the UAV making an evade maneuvre when a collision was perceptible (rather than landing, or spontaneously changing its heading following an instruction from the navigation manager) dropped to 30%.

6   Further Work

One of our primary motivations in performing this work was to enable the probabilistic model-checking of BDI agents, particularly in practical health-care and hybrid systems scenarios. We intend therefore to explore more sophisticated and realistic examples in which an implemented BDI based agent program is executed in AJPF and then model-checked in PRISM. Our interest is in producing results about the overall reliability of systems based on probabilistic analyses of the reliability of sensors and actuators derived through testing.

We are also interested in exploring the verification of multi-agent properties involving strategies. This would involve both adapting our output format for an ATL model-checker, such as MCMAS [24], and adapting the internal models so that transitions are labelled with actions. We may also wish to extend the AIL so that agents can explicitly reason about their own strategies. We would also like to investigate the verification of properties of BDI programming languages that incorporate probabilistic features, something which will likely require that their AIL implementation uses the Choice class.

It would also be possible to adapt AJPF to save and then re-import its own models, avoiding the model generation bottleneck while retaining the entire verification process within a single system. While this would lose some of the benefits (e.g., assurance and efficiency), it would provide a simpler tool and might be more attractive in certification situations.

7   Conclusion

We have shown how the ideas of Hunter et. al [3] for the use of JPF to generate models of Brahms programs for export into SPIN, can be generalised and integrated within the AJPF tool for model-checking BDI programs.

This provides a generic tool for generating models of agent programs implemented in a wide range of BDI languages. These models can then be exported into the input languages of the model-checker of choice. Where such a model-checker operates on Kripke structures there is a direct translation from AJPF's own internal model to that of the target model-checker. For model-checkers using richer input structures it is still relatively easy, using the customisation options available with JPF, to enrich AJPF's models so that they can be exported appropriately. We provided an example of one such adaptation allowing BDI programs to be probabilistically model-checked via the PRISM model-checker.

Acknowledgments. Work partially funded by EPSRC through the "Trustworthy Robotic Assistants", and "Reconfigurable Autonomy" projects, and by the ERDF/NWDA-funded Virtual Engineering Centre.

References

1. Dennis, L.A., Fisher, M., Webster, M., Bordini, R.H.: Model Checking Agent Programming Languages. Automated Software Engineering 19(1), 5–63 (2012)
2. Visser, W., Havelund, K., Brat, G.P., Park, S., Lerda, F.: Model Checking Programs. Automated Software Engineering 10(2), 203–232 (2003)
3. Hunter, J., Raimondi, F., Rungta, N., Stocker, R.: A Synergistic and Extensible Framework for Multi-Agent System Verification. In: Ito, T., Jonker, C., Gini, M., Shehory, O. (eds.) Proc. 13th International Conference on Autonomous Agents and Multiagent Systems (AAMAS). IFAAMAS (2013)
4. Wooldridge, M.: Reasoning about Rational Agents. The MIT Press (2000)
5. Emerson, E.A.: Temporal and Modal Logic. In: van Leeuwen, J. (ed.) Handbook of Theoretical Computer Science, pp. 996–1072. Elsevier (1990)
6. Gerth, R., Peled, D., Vardi, M.Y., Wolper, P.: Simple on-the-fly automatic verification of linear temporal logic. In: Proc. 15th IFIP WG6.1 International Symposium on Protocol Specification, Testing and Verification XV, pp. 3–18. Chapman & Hall, Ltd., London (1996)
7. Courcoubetis, C., Vardi, M., Wolper, P., Yannakakis, M.: Memory-efficient Algorithms for the Verification of Temporal Properties. In: Formal Methods in System Design, pp. 275–288 (1992)
8. Webster, M., Fisher, M., Cameron, N., Jump, M.: Formal Methods for the Certification of Autonomous Unmanned Aircraft Systems. In: Flammini, F., Bologna, S., Vittorini, V. (eds.) SAFECOMP 2011. LNCS, vol. 6894, pp. 228–242. Springer, Heidelberg (2011)

9. Webster, M., Cameron, N., Jump, M., Fisher, M.: Generating Certification Evidence for Autonomous Unmanned Aircraft Using Model Checking and Simulation. Journal of Aerospace Computing, Information, and Communication (2013)

10. Holzmann, G.: The Spin Model Checker: Primer and Reference Manual. Addison-Wesley (2004)

11. Hindriks, K.V., de Boer, F.S., van der Hoek, W., Meyer, J.-J.C.: Agent Programming with Declarative Goals. In: Castelfranchi, C., Lespérance, Y. (eds.) ATAL 2000. LNCS (LNAI), vol. 1986, pp. 228–243. Springer, Heidelberg (2001)

12. Havelund, K., Lowry, M., Park, S., Pecheur, C., Penix, J., Visser, W., White, J.L.: Formal Analysis of the Remote Agent Before and After Flight. In: Proc. 5th NASA Langley Formal Methods Workshop, Virginia, USA (2000)

13. Kars, P.: The Application of Promela and Spin in the BOS Project (Abstract) (1996), http://spinroot.com/spin/Workshops/ws96/Ka.pdf (accessed May 30, 2013)

14. Kirsch, M.T., Regenie, V.A., Aguilar, M.L., Gonzalez, O., Bay, M., Davis, M.L., Null, C.H., Scully, R.C., Kichak, R.A.: Technical Support to the National Highway Traffic Safety Administration (NHTSA) on the Reported Toyota Motor Corporation (TMC) Unintended Acceleration (UA) Investigation. NASA Engineering and Safety Center Technical Assessment Report (January 2011)

15. Kwiatkowska, M., Norman, G., Parker, D.: PRISM: Probabilistic Symbolic Model Checker. In: Field, T., Harrison, P.G., Bradley, J., Harder, U. (eds.) TOOLS 2002. LNCS, vol. 2324, pp. 200–204. Springer, Heidelberg (2002)

16. PRISM: Probabilistic Symbolic Model Checker, http://www.prismmodelchecker.org/ (accessed May 31, 2013)

17. Sierhuis, M., Clancey, W.J.: Modeling and Simulating Work Practice: A Method for Work Systems Design. IEEE Intelligent Systems 17(5), 32–41 (2002)

18. JPF... the Swiss Army Knife of Java^{TM} verification, http://babelfish.arc.nasa.gov/trac/jpf/ (accessed June 9, 2013)

19. Bordini, R.H., Fisher, M., Wooldridge, M., Visser, W.: Property-based slicing for agent verification. J. Log. and Comput. 19(6), 1385–1425 (2009)

20. Lincoln, N.K., Veres, S.M., Dennis, L.A., Fisher, M., Lisitsa, A.: Autonomous Asteroid Exploration - Agent Based Control for Autonomous Spacecraft in Complex Environments. IEEE Computational Intelligence Magazine, Special Issue on Computational Intelligence for Space Systems and Operations (to appear)

21. Dennis, L.A., Farwer, B.: Gwendolen: A BDI Language for Verifiable Agents. In: Proc. AISB Workshop on Logic and the Simulation of Interaction and Reasoning, AISB (2008)

22. Babiak, T., Křetínský, M., Řehák, V., Strejček, J.: LTL to Büchi Automata Translation: Fast and More Deterministic. In: Flanagan, C., König, B. (eds.) TACAS 2012. LNCS, vol. 7214, pp. 95–109. Springer, Heidelberg (2012)

23. Norman, G., Parker, D., Sproston, J.: Model checking for probabilistic timed automata. Formal Methods in System Design, 1–27 (2012)

24. Lomuscio, A., Qu, H., Raimondi, F.: MCMAS: A model checker for the verification of multi-agent systems. In: Bouajjani, A., Maler, O. (eds.) CAV 2009. LNCS, vol. 5643, pp. 682–688. Springer, Heidelberg (2009)

Reasoning about the Beliefs of Agents in Multi-agent Domains in the Presence of State Constraints: The Action Language mAL

Chitta Baral[1], Gregory Gelfond[1], Enrico Pontelli[2], and Tran Cao Son[2]

[1] Arizona State University, Tempe, AZ 85281
[2] New Mexico State University, Las Cruces, NM 88011

Abstract. Reasoning about actions forms the basis of many tasks such as prediction, planning, and diagnosis in a dynamic domain. Within the reasoning about actions community, a broad class of languages called *action languages* has been developed together with a methodology for their use in representing dynamic domains. With a few notable exceptions, the focus of these efforts has largely centered around single-agent systems. Agents rarely operate in a vacuum however, and almost in parallel, substantial work has been done within the dynamic epistemic logic community towards understanding how the actions of an agent may affect the knowledge and/or beliefs of his fellows. What is less understood by both communities is how to *represent and reason* about both the *direct and indirect effects* of both ontic and epistemic actions within a multi-agent setting. This paper presents a new action language, $m\mathcal{AL}$, which brings together techniques developed in both communities for reasoning about dynamic multi-agent domains involving both *ontic* and *epistemic* actions, as well as the *indirect effects* that such actions may have on the domain.

1 Introduction

Reasoning about actions and change has been one of the cornerstones of artificial intelligence research ever since McCarthy's description of the "advice taker system" [16]. Since that time, a considerable body of work on a broad class of languages called *action languages* together with a corresponding methodology for their use has been developed [1,10,11]. A distinguishing characteristic of such languages is their simple syntax and semantics which allow for concise and natural representations of huge transition systems, and elegant solutions to the frame problem [3,5,10,15]. With a few notable exceptions, [5,14], the focus of such languages has been on representing an agent's knowledge concerning *sensing* and *ontic actions* (i.e., those which primarily affect the physical environment). Agents rarely operate in isolation, often exchanging information, and consequently almost in parallel, substantial work has been done within the *Dynamic Epistemic Logic (DEL)* community towards understanding *epistemic actions* (i.e., those which primarily affect the knowledge or beliefs of other agents)

J. Leite et al. (Eds.): CLIMA XIV, LNAI 8143, pp. 290–306, 2013.
© Springer-Verlag Berlin Heidelberg 2013

[2,8,7] and, to a lesser extent ontic actions [6]. What is less understood by both communities is how to *represent and reason* about both the *direct and indirect effects* of both classes of actions in a multi-agent setting. In this paper we present a new action language, $m\mathcal{AL}$, which brings together techniques developed in both communities for reasoning about dynamic multi-agent domains involving both ontic and epistemic actions. Unlike prior works of both the action language [4], and dynamic epistemic logic communities [6], $m\mathcal{AL}$ allows for the representation of complex dependencies between fluents and provides a robust solution to the *ramification problem* [17,12,13]. In addition, it is capable of representing domains involving collaboration between agents for both ontic and epistemic actions.

Example 1 (A Multi-Agent "Lin's Briefcase Domain"). Let us consider a multi-agent variant of the "Lin's Briefcase Domain" [13]: Three agents, A, B, and C, are together in a room with a locked briefcase which contains a coin. The briefcase is locked by two independent latches, each of which may be flipped open (or closed) by an agent. Once both latches are open, the briefcase is unlocked and an agent may peek inside to determine which face of the coin is showing. Suppose that the briefcase is locked, and that this fact, together with the fact that none of the agents knows which face of the coin is showing is common knowledge amongst them. Furthermore, let us suppose that all of the agents are paying attention to their surroundings, and that this is common knowledge as well. Lastly, let us suppose that the coin is actually showing heads. How could agent A determine the face of the coin while keeping B aware of his activities but leaving C in the dark? One way could be as follows: A *distracts* C, causing him to look away; once this is done, he *flips* open both latches, thereby unlocking the briefcase; and finally A *peeks* inside.

Note that the domain in Ex. 1 contains both ontic (e.g., flipping the latches) and epistemic (e.g., peeking into the briefcase) actions. In addition, the actions of *signaling/distracting* an agent and *flipping* the latches have two classes of *indirect effects*: those affecting the *frames of reference* (or degrees of awareness) that agents have with respect to subsequent action occurrences, and those affecting the physical properties of the domain. As an example of the former, once C is distracted, he will be unaware of A's subsequent activities. As an example of the latter, flipping a latch open when its counterpart is as well, causes the briefcase to become unlocked.

While the languages of *action and update models* developed within the DEL community [2,6] provide an elegant means for *deriving the direct effects* of both ontic and epistemic actions, they fall short when it comes to solving the ramification problem, and consequently are unable to represent domains such as the one presented in Ex. 1. Furthermore, their graphical nature and unification of the distinct notions of an *action* and *action occurrence*, renders them inadequate from a *knowledge representation* standpoint due to their lack of *elaboration tolerance*. As we hope to show in this paper, both difficulties are overcome by $m\mathcal{AL}$.

2   The Action Language $m\mathcal{AL}$

The action language $m\mathcal{AL}$ incorporates elements from the action languages $\mathcal{AL}$ [11,9] and $m\mathcal{A}+$ [4], adding to $m\mathcal{A}+$ the ability to describe various dependencies between fluents by the inclusion of *state constraints*.

2.1   Syntax

Theories of $m\mathcal{AL}$ are defined over a multi-agent domain $\mathcal{D}$ with a signature $\Sigma = (\mathcal{AG}, \mathcal{F}, \mathcal{A})$ where $\mathcal{AG}$, $\mathcal{F}$, and $\mathcal{A}$, are finite, disjoint, non-empty sets of symbols respectively defining the *names of the agents within the domain*, the *properties of the domain* (or *fluents*), and the *elementary actions* which the agents may perform. $m\mathcal{AL}$ supports two broad classes of actions: *ontic* and *epistemic* actions, the former describing actions which affect the properties of the domain represented by fluents, and the latter describing actions which primarily affect the agents' beliefs. Epistemic actions are further broken into two categories: *sensing* and *communication*. Sensing actions represent actions which an agent may perform in order to learn the value of a fluent, while communication actions are used to represent actions which communicate information between agents. Ontic properties of the domain are represented by fluents, while the various epistemic properties are represented by modal formulae:

Definition 1 (Modal Formula [8]). *Let $\mathcal{D}$ be a multi-agent domain with the signature $\Sigma = (\mathcal{AG}, \mathcal{F}, \mathcal{A})$. The set of* modal formulae *over Σ is defined as follows:*

- *$f \in \mathcal{F}$ is a formula*
- *if φ is a formula, then $\neg\varphi$ is a formula*
- *if φ_1 and φ_2 are formulae, then $\varphi_1 \wedge \varphi_2$, $\varphi_1 \vee \varphi_2$, $\varphi_1 \rightarrow \varphi_2$, and $\varphi_1 \equiv \varphi_2$ are formulae*
- *if $\alpha \in \mathcal{AG}$ and φ is a formula, then $\mathbf{B}_\alpha\varphi$ is a formula*
- *if $\gamma \subseteq \mathcal{AG}$ and φ is a formula, then $\mathbf{E}_\gamma\varphi$ and $\mathbf{C}_\gamma\varphi$ are formulae*

As the modality of discourse is that of *belief*, we adopt the following readings of modal formulae: $\mathbf{B}_\alpha\varphi$, is understood to mean that "agent α believes φ"; formulae of the form $\mathbf{E}_\gamma\varphi$ denote that "every member of γ believes φ", while those of the form $\mathbf{C}_\gamma\varphi$ are read as "every member of γ believes φ, and every member of γ believes that every member of γ believes φ, ad infinitum, (i.e. φ is a commonly held belief amongst the agents of γ)."

The direct effects of ontic actions are described by *dynamic causal laws* which are statements of the form:

$$a \textbf{ causes } \lambda \textbf{ if } \phi \tag{1}$$

where a is an action, λ is a fluent literal, and ϕ is a conjunction of fluent literals. Laws of this form are read as: "performing the action a in a state which satisfies ϕ causes λ to be true." If ϕ is a tautology, then we simply write the following:

$$a \textbf{ causes } \lambda \tag{2}$$

Sensing actions are described by *sensing axioms* which have the form:

$$a \textbf{ determines } f \tag{3}$$

where a is the name of an action, and f is a fluent. Statements of this form are understood to mean: "if an agent performs the action a, he will learn the value of the fluent f." Communication actions are described by *communication axioms* which have the form:

$$a \textbf{ communicates } \varphi \tag{4}$$

where a is the name of an action, and φ is a modal formula. In $m\mathcal{AL}$ only truthful announcements are allowed.

The constructs (1)–(4) only describe the *direct effects* of their respective actions. In general, an agent's actions may indirectly affect the knowledge/beliefs of his fellows, as well as the values of various fluents. As in $m\mathcal{A}+$, indirect effects of the first form are determined by the *frames of reference* (or *levels of awareness*) that the agents have with respect to the action. In general, for any given action occurrence we divide the agents of the domain into three groups: those who are fully aware of both the action occurrence and its effects; those who are aware of the occurrence but not the full consequences of the action; and those agents who are oblivious as to what has transpired. Frames of reference are dynamic in nature and are described by *perspective axioms* which are statements of the form:

$$X \textbf{ observes } a \textbf{ if } \phi \tag{5}$$
$$X \textbf{ aware of } a \textbf{ if } \phi \tag{6}$$

where X is a set of agent names, a is an action, and ϕ is a modal formula. Perspective axioms of the first form (called *observation axioms*) define the set of agents who are fully aware of both the action occurrence and its effects. Those of the second form (called *awareness axioms*) define the set of agents who are aware of the occurrence, but only partially of its effects. By default, we assume that all other agents within the domain are oblivious. As with dynamic causal laws, if ϕ is a tautology, we adopt the following shorthand:

$$X \textbf{ observes } a \tag{7}$$
$$X \textbf{ aware of } a \tag{8}$$

The inclusion of observation axioms allows us to make explicit the assumption that agents are aware of the actions they perform. In $m\mathcal{AL}$, the only assumptions made regarding the frames of reference of the agents are that those who are fully aware of an action occurrence and its effects, as well as those who are aware only of the occurrence, know the frames of reference of all of the agents within the domain.

Unlike $m\mathcal{A}+$, $m\mathcal{AL}$ includes *state constraints* which are statements of the form:

$$\lambda \textbf{ if } \phi \tag{9}$$

where λ is a fluent literal and ϕ is a conjunction of fluent literals. Statements of this form are read as: "if ϕ is true in a state, then λ must also be true in that state." State constraints are used to represent dependencies between fluents and provide a powerful means for representing indirect effects of the second form.

Lastly, *executability conditions*, which are statements of the form:

$$\textbf{impossible } a \textbf{ if } \phi \tag{10}$$

where a is an action and ϕ is a modal formula, are used to describe when actions may not be performed.

Definition 2 (Action Description of $m\mathcal{AL}$). *An action description, Δ, in $m\mathcal{AL}$ is a collection of statements of the form* (1)–(10).

Now that the syntax has been introduced, we present a detailed axiomatization of the multi-agent variant of the Lin's Briefcase Domain from Ex. 1.

Example 2 (Axiomatization of the Multi-Agent "Lin's Briefcase Domain"). Let λ be a variable ranging over the set $\{l_1, l_2\}$ representing the latches governing the briefcase. Similarly, let α, α_1, and α_2, be variables ranging over the set of agents in our domain. We begin our representation by adopting the following domain signature $\Sigma = (\mathcal{AG}, \mathcal{F}, \mathcal{A})$ where:

$$\mathcal{AG} = \{A, B, C\}$$
$$\mathcal{F} = \{open(\lambda), locked, heads, attentive(\alpha)\}$$
$$\mathcal{A} = \{flip(\alpha, \lambda), peek(\alpha), signal(\alpha_1, \alpha_2), distract(\alpha_1, \alpha_2)\}$$

The direct effects of the action $flip(\alpha, \lambda)$ are represented via the following pair of dynamic causal laws:

$$flip(\alpha, \lambda) \textbf{ causes } open(\lambda) \textbf{ if } \neg open(\lambda) \tag{11}$$
$$flip(\alpha, \lambda) \textbf{ causes } \neg open(\lambda) \textbf{ if } open(\lambda) \tag{12}$$

The following state constraint models the indirect effects of the action, $flip(\alpha, \lambda)$, namely that the briefcase is unlocked once both latches are open.

$$\neg locked \textbf{ if } open(l_1) \wedge open(l_2) \tag{13}$$

The agent directly performing the action $flip(\alpha, \lambda)$, as well as any attentive agents are considered to be fully aware of the action occurrence and of its full effects. This information may be encoded by the following pair of perspective axioms:

$$\{\alpha\} \textbf{ observes } flip(\alpha, \lambda) \tag{14}$$
$$\{\alpha_2\} \textbf{ observes } flip(\alpha_1, \lambda) \textbf{ if } attentive(\alpha_2) \tag{15}$$

The action, $peek(\alpha)$, is an epistemic action — in particular, it is a sensing action. Consequently its direct effects are represented by the following sensing axiom:

$$peek(\alpha) \textbf{ determines } heads \tag{16}$$

The fact that an agent may not peek into a locked briefcase is represented by the following executability condition:

$$\textbf{impossible}\ peek(\alpha)\ \textbf{if}\ locked \tag{17}$$

Unlike the action $flip(\alpha, \lambda)$, only the agent who is peeking is fully aware of the occurrence and its full effects. Agents who are attentive, are only partially aware of the action's effects. This is represented by the following perspective axioms:

$$\{\alpha\}\ \textbf{observes}\ peek(\alpha) \tag{18}$$

$$\{\alpha_2\}\ \textbf{aware of}\ peek(\alpha_1)\ \textbf{if}\ attentive(\alpha_2) \tag{19}$$

Lastly, the actions $signal(\alpha_1, \alpha_2)$ and $distract(\alpha_1, \alpha_2)$ are represented in a similar fashion:

$$signal(\alpha_1, \alpha_2)\ \textbf{causes}\ attentive(\alpha_2) \tag{20}$$

$$\{\alpha_1, \alpha_2\}\ \textbf{observes}\ signal(\alpha_1, \alpha_2) \tag{21}$$

$$\{\alpha\}\ \textbf{observes}\ signal(\alpha_1, \alpha_2)\ \textbf{if}\ attentive(\alpha) \tag{22}$$

$$distract(\alpha_1, \alpha_2)\ \textbf{causes}\ \neg attentive(\alpha_2) \tag{23}$$

$$\{\alpha_1, \alpha_2\}\ \textbf{observes}\ distract(\alpha_1, \alpha_2) \tag{24}$$

$$\{\alpha\}\ \textbf{observes}\ distract(\alpha_1, \alpha_2)\ \textbf{if}\ attentive(\alpha) \tag{25}$$

2.2   Semantics

Before we discuss the semantics of our language, we must first introduce the notions of a *Kripke structure* and *Kripke world*.

Definition 3 (Kripke Structure [8]). *Let $\mathcal{D}$ be a multi-agent domain with signature,* $\Sigma = (\mathcal{AG}, \mathcal{F}, \mathcal{A})$, *where* $\mathcal{AG} = \{\alpha_1, \ldots, \alpha_n\}$. *A Kripke structure, M, is a tuple of the form* $(\Omega, \pi, R_{\alpha_1}, \ldots, R_{\alpha_n})$ *where:*

- Ω *is a nonempty set of* possible worlds
- π *is an* interpretation function *which for each* $\omega \in \Omega$ *gives an interpretation,* $\pi(\omega) : \mathcal{F} \mapsto \{true, false\}$
- *each* R_{α_i} *is a binary relation on Ω called an* accessibility relation for agent α_i

Possible worlds and their respective interpretations describe potential *physical configurations* of the domain, while the accessibility relations represent its various *epistemic properties*. Intuitively, the pair $(\omega_\sigma, \omega_\tau) \in R_{\alpha_i}$ represents the property that from within possible world ω_σ, agent α_i cannot distinguish between ω_σ and ω_τ.

Definition 4 (Kripke World [8]). *A Kripke world is a pair, (M, ω), where M is a Kripke structure, and ω is a possible world of M.*

For a given Kripke world, (M, ω), ω denotes which possible world of M corresponds to the *real physical state of the world* as known to an *impartial external observer*.

Having defined the notions of a Kripke structure and a Kripke world, we can now define the semantics of modal logic.

Definition 5 (Entailment Relation for Modal Formulae). *Let* (M, ω_σ) *be a Kripke world in a multi-agent domain,* $\mathcal{D}$, *with the signature* $\Sigma = (\mathcal{AG}, \mathcal{F}, \mathcal{A})$.

- $(M, \omega_\sigma) \models f$ *where* $f \in \mathcal{F}$ *iff* $M.\pi(\omega_\sigma)(f) = \top$
- $(M, \omega_\sigma) \models \neg\varphi$ *iff* $(M, \omega_\sigma) \not\models \varphi$
- $(M, \omega_\sigma) \models \varphi_1 \wedge \varphi_2$ *iff* $(M, \omega_\sigma) \models \varphi_1$ *and* $(M, \omega_\sigma) \models \varphi_2$
- $(M, \omega_\sigma) \models \varphi_1 \vee \varphi_2$ *iff* $(M, \omega_\sigma) \models \varphi_1$ *or* $(M, \omega_\sigma) \models \varphi_2$
- $(M, \omega_\sigma) \models \mathbf{B}_\alpha\varphi$ *iff* $(M, \omega_\tau) \models \varphi$ *for all* ω_τ *such that* $(\omega_\sigma, \omega_\tau) \in M.R_\alpha$

Let $\mathbf{E}_\gamma^0\varphi$ *be equivalent to* φ *and let* $\mathbf{E}_\gamma^{k+1}\varphi$ *be* $\mathbf{E}_\gamma\mathbf{E}_\gamma^k\varphi$.

- $(M, \omega_\sigma) \models \mathbf{E}_\gamma\varphi$ *iff* $(M, \omega_\sigma) \models \mathbf{B}_\alpha\varphi$ *for each* $\alpha \in \gamma$
- $(M, \omega_\sigma) \models \mathbf{C}_\gamma\varphi$ *iff* $(M, \omega_\sigma) \models \mathbf{E}_\gamma^k\varphi$ *for* $k = 1, 2, 3, \ldots$

As is the case with other action languages, an action description of $m\mathcal{AL}$ defines a transition diagram whose nodes correspond to *states of the domain* — which we model as Kripke worlds — and whose arcs are labeled by *actions*. Within a particular state, the possible worlds comprising the underlying Kripke world correspond to complete consistent sets of fluent literals closed under the state constraints of the action description.

Example 3 (Initial State of the Multi-Agent "Lin's Briefcase Domain"). The initial state, σ_0, of the domain from Ex. 1 corresponds to the Kripke world, (M_0, ω_1), shown in Fig. 1. σ_0 consists of two possible worlds, ω_1 and ω_2, where:

- $M_0.\pi(\omega_1) = \{heads, attentive(A), attentive(B), attentive(C), \neg open(l_1), \neg open(l_2), locked\}$
- $M_0.\pi(\omega_2) = \{\neg heads, attentive(A), attentive(B), attentive(C), \neg open(l_1), \neg open(l_2), locked\}$

A graphical convention that we adopt in this work is to present Kripke structures/worlds as directed graphs whose nodes are drawn as circles with unbroken lines. The possible world(s) designated as pertaining to the real state of the world are marked by a double circle.

The semantics of $m\mathcal{AL}$ is defined via a transition function, $\Phi_\Delta(\sigma, a)$, which when applied to a state, σ, and an action occurrence, a, yields the corresponding successor state(s). The approach taken in this paper combines methods used in defining the semantics of $\mathcal{AL}$ [9], with an approach based on that of [6]. The key intuition behind our semantics is that reasoning about the effects of an action is a two-step process: an agent first reasons about how his fellows may perceive his action, thereby establishing an *epistemic configuration* for the successor state; and then reasons about how his action may actually play out.

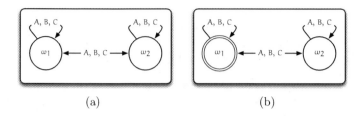

(a)   (b)

Fig. 1. The initial state, σ_0, of the Multi-Agent Lin's Briefcase Domain. 1(a) shows the underlying Kripke structure of σ_0, while 1(b) corresponds to σ_0 itself.

Frames of Reference In order to reason about how his fellows will perceive his actions, an agent must reason about their respective frames of reference; hence the inclusion of perspective axioms, which allow one to dynamically specify the levels of awareness that the agents have with respect to an action occurrence. It must be emphasized, that frames of reference are thought of as *attributes* of an action that differ from one *action occurrence* to another. This is in marked contrast with the approach of [2,6], in which different frames of references yield very different actions.

Definition 6 (Frames of Reference). *Let Δ be an action description of $m\mathcal{AL}$, $\sigma = (M, \omega)$ be a state of the transition diagram defined by Δ, and a be an action. The various* frames of reference *of the agents are defined as follows:*

- *the set of agents who are* fully aware *of a, denoted by $f(\sigma, a)$, is $\{\alpha \in \mathcal{AG} \mid [\alpha$ **observes** a **if** $\phi] \in \Delta \wedge (M, \omega) \models \phi\}$*
- *the set of agents who are* partially aware *of a, denoted by $p(\sigma, a)$, is $\{\alpha \in \mathcal{AG} \mid [\alpha$ **aware of** a **if** $\phi] \in \Delta \wedge (M, \omega) \models \phi\}$*
- *the set of agents who are* oblivious *of a, denoted by $o(\sigma, a)$, is $\mathcal{AG} \setminus f(\sigma, a) \cup p(\sigma, a)$*

Update Schema/Instantiations On a semantic level, an *action occurrence* is represented by an *update schema*[1], which may be thought of as a Kripke structure capturing how the agents in a domain perceive various action occurrences. Rather than possible worlds, an action occurrence is described by a number of *scenarios*, each of which is associated with a necessary *precondition*. What the agents believe about the scenarios is described by their respective *accessibility relations*. This leads to the following definition:

Definition 7 (Update Schema). *Let $\mathcal{L}$ denote the set of all modal formulae that may be defined over the multi-agent domain, $\mathcal{D}$, with signature $\Sigma = (\mathcal{AG} = \{\alpha_1, \ldots, \alpha_n\}, \mathcal{F}, \mathcal{A})$. An* update schema, *$U$, is a tuple of the form $(S_c, R_{\alpha_1}, \ldots, R_{\alpha_n}, pre)$ where:*

---

[1] Update schema/instantiations are analogous to the certain structures described in [2,6], but have been renamed to reflect different intuitions behind their use.

- S_c *is a finite, non-empty set of* scenarios
- *each* R_{α_i} *is a binary relation on* ε *called an* accessibility relation *for agent* α_i
- $pre : S_c \mapsto \mathcal{L}$ *assigns a* precondition function *to each scenario*

An update schema only describes the beliefs of the agents with regards to a particular action occurrence. As with Kripke structures, they do not describe which scenario actually took place. To accomodate this additional information, update schema are *instantiated* by specifying which scenario actually occurred.

Definition 8 (Update Instantiation). *An* update instantiation *is a pair,* (U, ε), *where* U *is an update schema, and* ε *is a scenario of* U.

In the context of $m\mathcal{AL}$, we define three particular *update instantiations*, for ontic, sensing, and communication actions respectively: $\upsilon_o(\sigma, a)$, $\upsilon_s(\sigma, a)$, and $\upsilon_c(\sigma, a)$.

The intuition behind $\upsilon_o(\sigma, a)$ is relatively straightforward: the agents are either aware of the action occurrence or are oblivious. In addition, we make the assumption that those agents who are aware of the action occurrences know which agents are oblivious.

Definition 9 (Ontic Instantiation). *The function* $\upsilon_o(\sigma, a)$ *yields the set of update instantiations represented by the pair* (U, Γ) *where* U *is defined as follows:*

- $U.S_c = \{\varepsilon_p, \varepsilon_i\}$
- $U.R_\alpha = \{(\varepsilon_p, \varepsilon_p), (\varepsilon_i, \varepsilon_i)\}$ *for each agent in* $f(\sigma, a)$
- $U.R_\alpha = \{(\varepsilon_p, \varepsilon_i), (\varepsilon_i, \varepsilon_i)\}$ *for each agent in* $o(\sigma, a)$

Let $\Psi = \{\phi \mid [\textbf{impossible } a \textbf{ if } \phi] \in \Delta\}$.

- $U.pre(\varepsilon_p) = \neg(\bigvee \Psi)$
- $U.pre(\varepsilon_i) = \top$

and $\Gamma = \{\varepsilon_p\}$.

$\upsilon_s(\sigma, a)$ is based on the following intuition: the real value of f is revealed to those agents who are performing the action, causing it to become a commonly held belief amongst them; agents who observe the action learn that the value of f has been revealed to those agents who were directly involved in it; and the beliefs of oblivious agents remain unchanged.

Definition 10 (Sensing Instantiation). *The function* $\upsilon_s(\sigma, a)$ *yields the set of update instantiations represented by the pair* (U, Γ) *where* U *is defined as follows:*

- $U.S_c = \{\varepsilon_p, \varepsilon_n, \varepsilon_i\}$
- $U.R_\alpha = \{(\varepsilon_p, \varepsilon_p), (\varepsilon_n, \varepsilon_n), (\varepsilon_i, \varepsilon_i)\}$ *for each agent in* $f(\sigma, a)$
- $U.R_\alpha = \{(\varepsilon_p, \varepsilon_p), (\varepsilon_n, \varepsilon_n), (\varepsilon_i, \varepsilon_i), (\varepsilon_p, \varepsilon_n), (\varepsilon_n, \varepsilon_p)\}$ *for each agent in* $p(\sigma, a)$
- $U.R_\alpha = \{(\varepsilon_p, \varepsilon_i), (\varepsilon_n, \varepsilon_i), (\varepsilon_i, \varepsilon_i)\}$ *for each agent in* $o(\sigma, a)$

Let f be the fluent determined by the sensing axiom for the action a, and let
$\Psi = \{\phi \mid [\textbf{impossible } a \textbf{ if } \phi] \in \Delta\}$.

- $U.pre(\varepsilon_p) = f \wedge \neg(\bigvee \Psi)$
- $U.pre(\varepsilon_n) = \neg f \wedge \neg(\bigvee \Psi)$
- $U.pre(\varepsilon_i) = \top$

and $\Gamma = \{\varepsilon_p, \varepsilon_n\}$.

The intuition behind $v_c(\sigma, a)$ similar to that of sensing actions: φ becomes a commonly held belief amongst those agents who receive/hear the message; agents who observe the action learn that the value of φ has been revealed to those agents who heard it (they are however unaware of the truth of φ); and lastly, the beliefs of oblivious agents are unchanged.

Definition 11 (Communication Instantiation). *The function $v_c(\sigma, a)$ yields the set of update instantiations represented by the pair (U, Γ) where U is defined as follows:*

- $U.S_c = \{\varepsilon_p, \varepsilon_n, \varepsilon_i\}$
- $U.R_\alpha = \{(\varepsilon_p, \varepsilon_p), (\varepsilon_n, \varepsilon_n), (\varepsilon_i, \varepsilon_i)\}$ *for each agent in* $f(\sigma, a)$
- $U.R_\alpha = \{(\varepsilon_p, \varepsilon_p), (\varepsilon_n, \varepsilon_n), (\varepsilon_i, \varepsilon_i), (\varepsilon_p, \varepsilon_n), (\varepsilon_n, \varepsilon_p)\}$ *for each agent in* $p(\sigma, a)$
- $U.R_\alpha = \{(\varepsilon_p, \varepsilon_i), (\varepsilon_n, \varepsilon_i), (\varepsilon_i, \varepsilon_i)\}$ *for each agent in* $o(\sigma, a)$

Let φ be the formula specified by the communication axiom for the action a, and let $\Psi = \{\phi \mid [\textbf{impossible } a \textbf{ if } \phi] \in \Delta\}$.

- $U.pre(\varepsilon_p) = \varphi \wedge \neg(\bigvee \Psi)$
- $U.pre(\varepsilon_n) = \neg\varphi \wedge \neg(\bigvee \Psi)$
- $U.pre(\varepsilon_i) = \top$

and $\Gamma = \{\varepsilon_p\}$.

Example 4 (Update Instantiations for the Action $distract(A, C)$). Consider an action occurrence $distract(A, C)$. Suppose that agent B is oblivious of the action occurrence. In this case, the corresponding ontic instantiation, is shown in Fig. 2(a). Now consider an occurrence of the action $distract(A, C)$, where all of the agents are fully aware of the action occurrence. This yields a different ontic instantiation, shown in Fig. 2(b). Here we adopt the graphical convention of presenting update schema/instantiations as directed graphs whose nodes are drawn as rounded rectangles with solid lines. Once again, it bears emphasizing that the *action*, $distract(A, C)$, is the same in both instances. Only the attributes corresponding to the agents' frames of reference (which are represented by the respective arcs) differ.

Epistemic Configurations. When reasoning about the effects of an action, an agent first establishes what is called an *epistemic configuration* of the successor state. This is done by the application of what we term an *epistemic update* to a state, and the update instantiation of action occurrence in question.

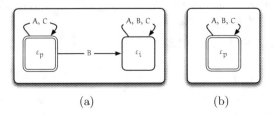

(a)   (b)

Fig. 2. 2(a) shows the ontic instantiation for an occurrence of the action $distract(A, C)$ with A and C fully aware of the occurrence, and agent B oblivious. 2(b) show the ontic instantiation of the same action with all agents fully aware of the occurrence.

An *epistemic configuration* defines the general graphical structure of the successor state. Consequently it is similar to a Kripke structure, but does not include the interpretation function. This intuition leads to the following pair of definitions:

Definition 12 (Epistemic Schema). *Let $\mathcal{D}$ be a multi-agent domain with signature $\Sigma = (\mathcal{AG} = \{\alpha_1, \ldots, \alpha_n\}, \mathcal{F}, \mathcal{A})$. An epistemic schema, $\mathcal{E}$, is a tuple of the form $(S, R_{\alpha_1}, \ldots, R_{\alpha_n})$ where:*

- *S is a nonempty set of* situations
- *each R_{α_i} is a binary relation on S called an* accessibility relation for agent α_i

Definition 13 (Epistemic Configuration). *An epistemic configuration is a pair, $(\mathcal{E}, s)$, where $\mathcal{E}$ is an epistemic schema, and s is a situation of $\mathcal{E}$.*

In order to obtain the epistemic configuration of the successor state, we apply an operation that we call the *epistemic update* operation, which when applied to a state and an update instantiation, defines an *epistemic configuration* for the successor state.

Definition 14 (Epistemic Update Operation). *Given a state, $\sigma = (M, \omega)$, and an update instantiation $\upsilon = (U, \varepsilon)$, such that $\sigma \models U.pre(\varepsilon)$, $\mathbf{Eu}(\sigma, \upsilon)$ defines the epistemic configuration $\mathcal{E}_\mathcal{C} = (\mathcal{E}, (\omega, \varepsilon))$ where:*

- *$\mathcal{E}.S = \{(\omega_j, \varepsilon_j) \mid \omega_j \in M.\Omega, \varepsilon_j \in U.S_c, (M, \omega_j) \models U.pre(\varepsilon_j)\}$*
- *$\mathcal{E}.R_\alpha = \{((\omega_j, \varepsilon_j), (\omega_k, \varepsilon_k)) \mid (\omega_j, \omega_k) \in M.R_\alpha, (\varepsilon_j, \varepsilon_k) \in U.R_\alpha\}$*

Example 5 (Applying the Epistemic Update). Recall from Ex. 1 that A first distracts C. The action $distract(A, C)$ is an ontic action which directly affects the fluent $attentive(C)$ as specified by the dynamic causal law (23). Perspective axioms (24) and (25), together with the fact that the agents are initially attentive, give $f(\sigma_0, distract(A, C)) = \{A, B, C\}$ and $o(\sigma_0, distract(A, C)) = \emptyset$ as the agents' frames of reference. $\upsilon_o(\sigma_0, distract(A, C)))$ is shown in Fig. 3(a) and the epistemic configuration of the successor state resulting from the occurrence of the action $distract(A, C)$ is given by $\mathbf{Eu}(\sigma_0, \upsilon_o(\sigma_0, distract(A, C)))$, and is shown in

Fig. 3(b). For epistemic configurations, we adopt the convention of presenting them as directed graphs whose nodes are drawn as dashed circles (the dashed lines help express the notion that the scenarios are later expanded into possible worlds). Those scenarios which correspond to potential real possible worlds are marked by a double dashed line.

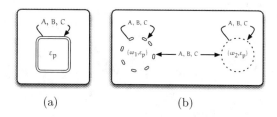

(a)   (b)

Fig. 3. 3(a) shows the update instantiation for an occurrence of the action *distract*(A, C) in σ_0, while Fig. 3(b) shows the epistemic configuration of the successor state resulting from that action occurrence

From Epistemic Configurations to States. The epistemic update only describes how an agent reasons about how his actions are perceived by his fellows. In order to obtain the full successor state, he must then reason about how his actions may actually play out. This is accomplished by abstracting away the presence of other agents, turning the problem into one concerning the effects of an action in a single-agent domain. This is done by applying what we term an *ontic update* operation to the epistemic configuration. Prior to defining the ontic update, we must first describe how to relate an epistemic configuration to the framework for reasoning about the effects of an action from the perspective of $\mathcal{AL}$.

Definition 15 ($\mathcal{AL}(\sigma, w)$). *Let Δ be an action description of $m\mathcal{AL}$ and σ be a state of the transition diagram defined by Δ. Each possible world, w of σ corresponds to a complete consistent set of fluent literals, $\mathcal{AL}(\sigma, w)$, defined as follows:*

$$\{f \mid \sigma.w.\pi(f) = \top\} \cup \{\neg f \mid \sigma.w.\pi(f) = \bot\}$$

Intuitively, an epistemic configuration describes the basic structure of the successor state. Each situation $s = (w, \varepsilon)$ in an epistemic configuration may be read as "scenario ε transpires in the possible world w", and corresponds to possibly multiple possible worlds in the successor state. The possible worlds of the sucessor state within the multi-agent transition diagram are obtained by applying the McCain-Turner equation [15] to the possible worlds defined by $\mathcal{AL}(\sigma, w)$.

Definition 16 (Scenario Expansion). *Let σ be a state of the transition diagram defined by Δ, v be an update instantiation corresponding to the occurrence of an action, a in σ, $\mathcal{E}_C$ be an epistemic configuration defined by $\mathbf{Eu}(\sigma, v)$, and*

$s = (\omega, \varepsilon)$ *be a situation of* $\mathcal{E}_C$. *The expansion of the situation* s *consistent with the state,* σ, *(denoted by* $C(\sigma, s)$), *is defined as follows:*

- *if* $\varepsilon = \varepsilon_i$, *then* $C(\sigma, s) = \{\mathcal{AL}(\sigma, \omega)\}$, *otherwise*
- $C(\sigma, s) = \{\tau(s) \mid \tau(s) = \mathbf{Cn}_\Delta(E(\mathcal{AL}(\sigma, \omega), a) \cup (\mathcal{AL}(\sigma, \omega) \cap \tau(s)))\}$

The expansion of the entire epistemic configuration, $C(\sigma, \mathcal{E}_C)$, *is defined in a straightforward fashion as well:*

$$C(\sigma, \mathcal{E}_C) = \bigcup C(\sigma, s) \text{ for each } s \in \mathcal{E}_C.S$$

Having defined this basic framework, we may now define the *ontic update* operation.

Definition 17 (Ontic Update). *Let* Δ *be an action description of* $m\mathcal{AL}$, σ *be a state of the transition diagram defined by* Δ, *and* $\mathcal{E}_C = (\mathcal{E}, \omega)$ *be an epistemic configuration.* $\mathbf{Ou}_\Delta(\sigma, \mathcal{E}_C)$ *defines a set of Kripke worlds* (M', R_W) *where:*

- $M'.\Omega$ *is the set of new symbols of the form* $\omega_{\tau_i(s)}$ *for each* $\tau_i(s) \in C(\sigma, \mathcal{E}_C)$
- $M'.\pi(\omega_{\tau_i(s)})(f) = \top$ *if* $f \in \tau_i(s)$
- $M'.\pi(\omega_{\tau_i(s)})(f) = \bot$ *if* $\neg f \in \tau_i(s)$
- $M'.R_\alpha = \{(\omega_{\tau_i(s_1)}, \omega_{\tau_j(s_2)}) \mid \omega_{\tau_i(s_1)}, \omega_{\tau_j(s_2)} \in M'.\Omega, \text{ and } (s_1, s_2) \in \mathcal{E}_C.R_\alpha\}$
- $R_W = \{\omega_{\tau_i(s)} \mid \tau_i(s) \in C(\sigma, \omega)\}$

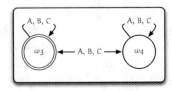

Fig. 4. Successor state, σ_1, resulting from the application of $\mathbf{Ou}_\Delta(\sigma_0, \mathcal{E}_{C0})$

Example 6 (Applying the Ontic Update). Let $\mathcal{E}_{C0}$ denote the epistemic configuration from Ex. 5. Application of the ontic update operation, $\mathbf{Ou}_\Delta(\sigma_0, \mathcal{E}_{C0})$, gives us the successor state, $\sigma_1 = (M_1, \omega_3)$, depicted in Fig. 4. The Kripke structure, M_1, shown in Fig. 4 consists of two possible worlds, $\omega_3 = \omega_{\tau((\omega_1, \varepsilon_p))}$, and $\omega_4 = \omega_{\tau((\omega_2, \varepsilon_p))}$ where:

- $M_1.\pi(\omega_3) = \{heads, locked, \neg open(l_1), \neg open(l_2), attentive(A),$
  $attentive(B), \neg attentive(C)\}$
- $M_1.\pi(\omega_4) = \{\neg heads, locked, \neg open(l_1), \neg open(l_2), attentive(A),$
  $attentive(B), \neg attentive(C)\}$

The Transition Function. As was mentioned previously, the transition function is based on the following intuition: an agent first reasons about how his action is perceived, and then reasons about how it may actually play out. This intuition is realized in the definition of our transition function, $\Phi_\Delta(\sigma, a)$.

Definition 18. *Let Δ be an action description of $m\mathcal{AL}$, σ be a state of the transition diagram defined by Δ, and a be an action. The successor state(s) obtained by performing the action a in the state σ are defined as follows:*

$$\Phi_\Delta(\sigma, a) = \begin{cases} \mathbf{Ou}_\Delta(\sigma, \mathbf{Eu}(\sigma, v_o(\sigma, a))) & \text{ontic action} \\ \mathbf{Ou}_\Delta(\sigma, \mathbf{Eu}(\sigma, v_s(\sigma, a))) & \text{sensing action} \\ \mathbf{Ou}_\Delta(\sigma, \mathbf{Eu}(\sigma, v_c(\sigma, a))) & \text{otherwise} \end{cases}$$

2.3   Properties of the Language

The syntax and semantics of $m\mathcal{AL}$ may be of interest in and of themselves, but of particular interest is the fact that $m\mathcal{AL}$ satisfies certain useful properties - namely that it correctly captures certain intuitions concerning the effects of various types of actions. Space constraints preclude us from including the proofs of the subsequent theorems, which we leave to a future journal paper (the paper is currently in development and will cover $m\mathcal{AL}$ in greater detail, including application of the languages towards modeling collaboration amongst agents for both ontic and epistemic actions).

Theorem 1. *Let Δ be an action description of $m\mathcal{AL}$; $\sigma = (M_\sigma, \omega_\sigma)$ be a state of the transition diagram defined by Δ; a be an ontic action; and $\sigma' = (M_\tau, \omega_\tau) \in \Phi_\Delta(\sigma, a)$. It holds that:*

1. *for every agent $\alpha \in f(\sigma, a)$ and dynamic causal law $[a \textbf{ causes } \lambda \textbf{ if } \phi]$ in Δ, if $(M_\sigma, \omega_\sigma) \models \mathbf{B}_\alpha\phi$ then $(M_\tau, \omega_\tau) \models \mathbf{B}_\alpha\lambda$*
2. *for every agent $\alpha \in f(\sigma, a)$ and state constraint $[\lambda \textbf{ if } \phi]$ in Δ, $(M_\sigma, \omega_\sigma) \models \mathbf{B}_\alpha(\phi \rightarrow \lambda)$*
3. *for each agent $\alpha \in o(\sigma, a)$ and literal, λ, $(M_\tau, \omega_\tau) \models \mathbf{B}_\alpha\lambda$ if and only if $(M_\sigma, \omega_\sigma) \models \mathbf{B}_\alpha\lambda$*

Theorem 2. *Let Δ be an action description of $m\mathcal{AL}$; $\sigma = (M_\sigma, \omega_\sigma)$ be a state of the transition diagram defined by Δ; a be a sensing action described by the axiom $[a \textbf{ determines } f]$ in Δ; and $\sigma' = (M_\tau, \omega_\tau) \in \Phi_\Delta(\sigma, a)$. It holds that:*

1. *$(M_\tau, \omega_\tau) \models \mathbf{C}_{f(\sigma, a)}\lambda$ if and only if $(M_\sigma, \omega_\sigma) \models \lambda$ where $\lambda \in \{f, \neg f\}$*
2. *$(M_\tau, \omega_\tau) \models \mathbf{C}_{p(\sigma, a)}(\mathbf{C}_{f(\sigma, a)}f \vee \mathbf{C}_{f(\sigma, a)}\neg f)$*
3. *for each agent $\alpha \in o(\sigma, a)$ and literal, λ, $(M_\tau, \omega_\tau) \models \mathbf{B}_\alpha\lambda$ if and only if $(M_\sigma, \omega_\sigma) \models \mathbf{B}_\alpha\lambda$*

Theorem 3. *Let Δ be an action description of $m\mathcal{AL}$; $\sigma = (M_\sigma, \omega_\sigma)$ be a state of the transition diagram defined by Δ; a be a communication action described by the axiom $[a \textbf{ communicates } \varphi]$ in Δ; and $\sigma' = (M_\tau, \omega_\tau) \in \Phi_\Delta(\sigma, a)$. It holds that:*

1. *$(M_\tau, \omega_\tau) \models \mathbf{C}_{f(\sigma, a)}\varphi$*
2. *$(M_\tau, \omega_\tau) \models \mathbf{C}_{p(\sigma, a)}(\mathbf{C}_{f(\sigma, a)}\varphi \vee \mathbf{C}_{f(\sigma, a)}\neg\varphi)$*
3. *for each agent $\alpha \in o(\sigma, a)$ and literal, λ, $(M_\tau, \omega_\tau) \models \mathbf{B}_\alpha\lambda$ if and only if $(M_\sigma, \omega_\sigma) \models \mathbf{B}_\alpha\lambda$*

3   Temporal Projection in $m\mathcal{AL}$

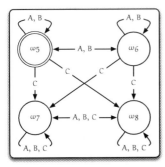

Fig. 5: Successor state, σ_2, resulting from the action sequence $distract(A, C)$, $flip(A, l_1)$

Recall that in Ex. 1 we presented the following sequence of actions by which A might achieve his goal: A *distracts* C, causing him to look away; once this is done, he then *flips* open both latches on the briefcase, thereby unlocking it; and finally A *peeks* inside. Space considerations preclude us from examining the entire trajectory, and consequently we will only show in detail how to obtain the successor state resulting from A flipping open the second latch (represented by the action $flip(A, l_2)$).

Let σ_2, shown in Fig. 5, be the state of the transition diagram resulting from the sequence of actions: $distract(A, C)$, $flip(A, l_1)$.

σ_2 consists of four possible worlds[2], ω_5, ω_6, ω_7, and ω_8 where:

- $M_2.\pi(\omega_5) = \{heads, locked, open(l_1), \neg open(l_2), attentive(A),$
  $attentive(B), \neg attentive(C)\}$
- $M_2.\pi(\omega_6) = \{\neg heads, locked, open(l_1), \neg open(l_2), attentive(A),$
  $attentive(B), \neg attentive(C)\}$
- $M_2.\pi(\omega_7) = \{heads, locked, \neg open(l_1), \neg open(l_2), attentive(A),$
  $attentive(B), \neg attentive(C)\}$
- $M_2.\pi(\omega_8) = \{\neg heads, locked, \neg open(l_1), \neg open(l_2), attentive(A),$
  $attentive(B), \neg attentive(C)\}$

Like its predecessor, $flip(A, l_2)$, is an ontic action, affecting only the values of the fluents of our possible worlds. Consequently, our intuition informs us that the structure of the successor state should essentially be unchanged. σ_2 and observation axioms (14) and (14) give $f(\sigma_2, flip(A, l_2)) = \{A, B\}$ and $o(\sigma_2, flip(A, l_2)) = \{C\}$ as the agents' frames of reference. Being an ontic action, the epistemic configuration, $\mathcal{E}_{C2}$, of the successor state resulting from $flip(A, l_2)$ is given by $\mathbf{Eu}(\sigma_2, \upsilon_o(\sigma_2, flip(A, l_2)))$ and is shown in Fig. 6(a). As we can see, $\mathcal{E}_{C2}$ is structurally similar to σ_2, confirming our aforementioned intuition.

According to the dynamic causal law (11), $flip(A, l_2)$ causes $open(l_2)$. Furthermore, the state constraint (13), informs us that as a consequence of both l_1 and l_2 being open, the briefcase itself should become unlocked (i.e., $\neg locked$ must now be true). The expansions of the scenarios in $\mathcal{E}_{C2}$, that are consistent with σ_2:

- $C(\sigma_2, (\omega_5, \varepsilon_p)) = \{\{heads, \neg locked, open(l_1), open(l_2), attentive(A),$
  $attentive(B), \neg attentive(C)\}\}$
- $C(\sigma_2, (\omega_6, \varepsilon_p)) = \{\{\neg heads, \neg locked, open(l_1), open(l_2), attentive(A),$
  $attentive(B), \neg attentive(C)\}\}$

---

[2] The labels of the possible worlds have been abbreviated for legibility purposes.

- $C(\sigma_2, (\omega_7, \varepsilon_i)) = \{\{heads, locked, \neg open(l_1), \neg open(l_2), attentive(A),$ $attentive(B), \neg attentive(C)\}\}$
- $C(\sigma_2, (\omega_8, \varepsilon_i)) = \{\{\neg heads, locked, \neg open(l_1), \neg open(l_2), attentive(A),$ $attentive(B), \neg attentive(C)\}\}$

confirm our intuition.

Let $\omega_9 = \omega_{\mathcal{T}((\omega_5, \varepsilon_p))}$, $\omega_{10} = \omega_{\mathcal{T}((\omega_6, \varepsilon_p))}$, $\omega_{11} = \omega_{\mathcal{T}((\omega_7, \varepsilon_i))}$, and $\omega_{12} = \omega_{\mathcal{T}((\omega_8, \varepsilon_i))}$. Application of the ontic update operation to σ_2 and $\mathcal{E}_{\mathcal{C}2}$, $\mathbf{Ou}_\Delta(\sigma_2, \mathcal{E}_{\mathcal{C}2})$, yields the successor state, σ_3, shown in Fig. 6(b). Careful examination of σ_3 shows that it entails a number of modal formulae, among which is $\mathbf{C}_{\{A,B\}}\neg locked$ – indicating that it is a commonly held belief amongst A and B that the briefcase is unlocked. In addition, σ_3 entails $\mathbf{C}_{\{A,B\}}\neg \mathbf{B}_C\mathbf{B}_A\neg locked$, as well as other formulae illustrating that C is oblivious of all of the events that transpired since he was distracted, and that this is a commonly held belief amongst A and B.

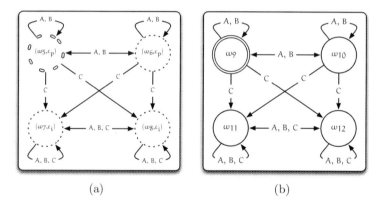

(a)   (b)

Fig. 6. 6(a) shows the epistemic configuration, $\mathcal{E}_{\mathcal{C}2}$, resulting from an occurrence of $flip(A, l_2)$ in σ_2, while 6(b) shows the resulting successor state, σ_3

4   Conclusions and Future Work

In this paper we presented a new multi-agent action language $m\mathcal{AL}$, which extends the language of $m\mathcal{A}+$ [4] with state constraints from the language $\mathcal{AL}$ [9]. The language's application was presented in the context of representing and performing temporal projection in the context of a multi-agent variant of the Lin's Briefcase Domain [13], which heretofore could not be represented in either $m\mathcal{A}+$ or the update model approaches of [2] and [6]. Future work includes a thorough analysis of the language's theoretical properties and formulation of the planning and diagnosis problems within a multi-agent context. Additional extensions to the language such as non-deterministic sensing actions, and false communication are under consideration as well.

References

1. Balduccini, M., Gelfond, M.: The AAA Architecture: An Overview. In: AAAI Spring Symposium 2008 on Architectures for Intelligent Theory-Based Agents (2008)
2. Baltag, A., Moss, L.S.: Logics for Epistemic Programs. Synthese 139(2), 165–224 (2004)
3. Baral, C.: Reasoning About Actions: Non-deterministic Effects, Constraints, and Qualification. In: Proceedings of the 14th International Joint Conferences on Artificial Intelligence, IJCAI 1995, pp. 2017–2023. Morgan Kaufmann (1995)
4. Baral, C., Gelfond, G., Son, T.C., Pontelli, E.: An Action Language for Reasoning about Beliefs in Multi-Agent Domains. In: Proceedings of the 14th International Workshop on Non-Monotonic Reasoning (2012)
5. Baral, C., Gelfond, M.: Reasoning about effects of concurrent actions. Journal of Logic Programming 31, 85–117 (1997)
6. van Benthem, J., van Eijck, J., Kooi, B.: Logics of communication and change. Information and Computation 204(11), 1620–1662 (2006)
7. van Ditmarsch, H., van der Hoek, W., Kooi, B.: Dynamic Epistemic Logic. Springer (2008)
8. Fagin, R., Halpern, J.Y., Moses, Y., Vardi, M.Y.: Reasoning About Knowledge. MIT Press (1995)
9. Gelfond, M.: Answer Sets. In: Handbook of Knowledge Representation, ch. 7. Elsevier (2007)
10. Gelfond, M., Lifschitz, V.: Representing Action and Change by Logic Programs. Journal of Logic Programming 17, 301–322 (1993)
11. Gelfond, M., Lifschitz, V.: Action Languages. Electronic Transactions on AI 3 (1998)
12. Lifschitz, V. (ed.): Formalizing Common Sense – Papers by John McCarthy. Ablex Publishing Corporation (1990)
13. Lin, F.: Embracing Causality in Specifying the Indirect Effects of Actions. In: Proceedings of the 14th International Joint Conferences on Artificial Intelligence, IJCAI 1995. Morgan Kaufmann (1995)
14. Lin, F., Shoham, Y.: Provably correct theories of action. Journal of the ACM 42(2), 293–320 (1995)
15. McCain, N., Turner, H.: A Causal Theory of Ramifications and Qualifications. In: Proceedings of the 14th International Joint Conferences on Artificial Intelligence, IJCAI 1995. Morgan Kaufmann (1995)
16. McCarthy, J.: Programs with common sense. In: Semantic Information Processing, pp. 403–418. MIT Press (1959)
17. McCarthy, J.: Mathematical Logic in Artificial Intelligence. Daedalus 117(1), 297–311 (1988)

A Temporal Argumentation Approach to Cooperative Planning Using Dialogues[*]

Pere Pardo[1,2] and Lluís Godo[1]

[1] Institut d'Investigació en Intel.ligència Artificial (IIIA - CSIC)
08193 Bellaterra, Spain
[2] Dept. de Lògica, Hist. i Filo. Ciència,
Universitat de Barcelona, 08001 Barcelona, Spain
{pardo,godo}@iiia.csic.es

Abstract. In this paper, we study a dialogue-based approach to multi-agent collaborative plan search in the framework of t-DeLP, an extension of DeLP for defeasible temporal reasoning. In t-DeLP programs, temporal facts and defeasible temporal rules combine into arguments, which compare against each other to decide which of their conclusions are to prevail. A backward centralized planning system built on this logical argumentative framework has been already studied in a previous work. In this paper, we consider a distributed collaborative scenario where agents exchange information using suitable dialogues. Agents cooperate to generate arguments and actions (plan steps), and to detect argument threats to plans. We show that the soundness and completeness properties of centralized t-DeLP plan search are preserved.

1 Introduction

The relatively recent area of argumentation [6] has become a focus of attention in AI and multi-agent systems. Argumentation systems provide (human-inspired) frameworks upon which agents can resolve conflicts (attacks) between their claims and arguments, among other applications.

An equally important application of argumentation systems is the area of non-monotonic reasoning, aimed to model common-sense, causal or evidential reasoning (e.g. birds fly, solids fall, etc.). The practical need for a general-purpose criterion of *preference* (between inferences) led in this area to the notion of specificity [20], and later to argumentation systems applying this idea to define the attack relation, e.g. in the defeasible logic programming DeLP system [8]. According to this criterion, a preference can be defined between arguments, by formally comparing their logical structure or informational content (e.g. whether their information pieces are strict –i.e. classical–, or defeasible). Both the DeLP

---

[*] The authors thank the reviewers for their helpful comments. They also acknowledge support of the Spanish CONSOLIDER-INGENIO 2010 project Agreement Technologies (CSD2007-00022), the MINECO project EdeTRI (TIN2012-39348-C02-01) and the Generalitat de Catalunya grant 2009-SGR-1434.

J. Leite et al. (Eds.): CLIMA XIV, LNAI 8143, pp. 307–324, 2013.

system and the criteria of specificity have been recently adapted to temporal reasoning, where arguments contain temporal information explicitly [14], [2], [5] etc. A common motivation for these extensions seems to be common-sense causal reasoning. Finally, several planning systems built upon these logics have been studied, e.g. partial-order planning DeLP-POP [7]; and forward/backward linear planners for t-DeLP [15].

A related motivation to build planners on some non-monotonic logical system are the classical representation problems, some of which affect traditional planners, whose inference simply consist in the update function, or in any case in simple, monotonic inferences. This is due to the use of encapsulated actions, where the effects are contained in the definition of this action –and its fixed set of conditional effects. Despite the simplicity attained in the semantics (e.g. state-transition systems) and the rewrite-based update function, these planning systems prove insufficient for the frame problem (in the broad sense). Indeed, while these systems need not to (costly) compute all the facts that do not change after an action (the narrow frame problem), they cannot address the problems of modeling the indirect effects of actions (the ramification problem), or qualifications on their preconditions as well (the qualification problem).

In this paper we deal with distributed argumentation-based multi-agent planning systems based on t-DeLP, which combine a traditional update function (for temporal actions) with non-monotonic inference (based on t-DeLP temporal argumentation). In particular, we study distributed planning algorithms. These can be seen as distributed versions of some of the planning algorithms studied in [15]. The latter are centralized, so a joint plan for a set of agents is just assigned to them by a single planner. This prevents one from considering more interesting scenarios with autonomous planner agents, i.e. where each agent is also its own (multi-agent) planner and is initially endowed with a planning domain of its own: its beliefs, abilities and goals; in our case, these are resp.: a t-DeLP logic program, a set of (planning-style) actions, and a set of temporal goals (temporal literals). The present focus is on cooperative scenarios, in the sense that all agents have the same set of goals.

Centralized solutions might incur in massive communication costs, in terms of time, energy or privacy. Instead, we propose a dialogue-based algorithm for distributed t-DeLP planning, where all agents take part in the generation of a joint plan by communicating (only) information which is relevant to the present task. The dialogues consist in agents taking turns and addressing the next agent. Each agent contributes to the generation or evaluation of new plan steps for plans under consideration. The main results are soundness and completeness of the dialogue-based plan search algorithm. In other words, setting complexity issues aside, a set of cooperative agents are as good as a central planner can be (with all their information) for the task of generating a joint plan.

The paper is structured as follows. In Section 2 we briefly review first the t-DeLP temporal defeasible logic programming framework. Then in Section 3, we adapt the basic concepts of planning systems to the present case, including an appropriate update function for t-DeLP, and the notion of planning domain and plan. In Section 4 we propose a distributed algorithm (in the spirit of breadth first search) for the multi-agent t-DeLP planning system based on dialogues; and finally we show that this algorithm is sound and complete.

Notation. We make use of the following conventions. Set-theoretic difference between two sets X, Y is denoted $X \smallsetminus Y$. Sequences are denoted $\langle x_0, \ldots, x_n \rangle$ (general case) or $[x_0, \ldots, x_n]$ (for argumentation lines) or $(x_0, \ldots, x_n)$ (for plans). Given a sequence $\boldsymbol{x} = \langle x_0, \ldots, x_n \rangle$ and an element x, we denote by $\boldsymbol{x} ^\frown \langle x \rangle$ the concatenation of $\boldsymbol{x}$ with x, i.e. the sequence $\langle x_0, \ldots, x_n, x \rangle$ or $[x_0, \ldots, x_n, x]$. If f is a function $f : X \to Y$ and $X' \subseteq X$, we define $f[X'] = \{ f(a) \in Y \mid a \in X' \}$.

2   Preliminaries: Temporal Defeasible Logic Programming

The t-DeLP temporal logic programming framework used by the planning system is briefly presented (see [14] for more details).

The language of t-DeLP builds upon a set of temporal literals and temporal defeasible rules. *Temporal literals* are the form $\langle \ell, t \rangle$, where ℓ is a literal (expressions of the form p or $\sim p$ from a given set of variables $p \in \mathsf{Var}$) and t is a time point (we consider discrete time, so t will take values in the natural numbers), and will denote that ℓ holds at time t. Since the strong negation $\sim$ cannot be nested, we will use the following notation over literals: if $\ell = p$ then $\sim\ell$ will denote $\sim p$, and if $\ell = \sim p$ then $\sim\ell$ will denote p. Time determines if a pair of temporal literals $\langle \ell, t \rangle$ and $\langle \sim\ell, t' \rangle$ contradict each other: only when $t = t'$.

A *temporal defeasible rule* (or simply a *rule*) is an expression δ of the form

$$\langle \ell, t \rangle \;\prec\; \langle \ell_0, t_0 \rangle, \ldots, \langle \ell_n, t_n \rangle \qquad \text{where } t \geq \max\{t_0, \ldots t_n\}$$

$\mathsf{body}(\delta)$ will denote the set of its conditions $\{ \langle \ell_0, t_0 \rangle, \ldots, \langle \ell_n, t_n \rangle \}$ and $\mathsf{head}(\delta)$ its conclusion $\langle \ell, t \rangle$. A defeasible rule δ states that if the premises in $\mathsf{body}(\delta)$ are true, then there is a reason for believing that the conclusion (i.e. $\mathsf{head}(\delta)$) is also true. This conclusion, though, may be later withdrawn when further information is considered, as we will see later. t-DeLP only makes use of future-oriented rules: $\mathsf{head}(\delta)$ cannot occur earlier than any $\langle \ell, t \rangle \in \mathsf{body}(\delta)$. A special subset of defeasible rules is that of *persistence* rules, of the form $\langle \ell, t+1 \rangle \prec \langle \ell, t \rangle$, stating that, unless there exist reasons to the contrary, ℓ is preserved from t to $t + 1$ (if true at t). Such a rule will denoted as $\delta_\ell(t)$.

Given a set of temporal rules and literals Γ, we say a literal $\langle \ell, t \rangle$ *derives from* Γ, denoted $\Gamma \vdash \langle \ell, t \rangle$ or also $\langle \ell, t \rangle \in \mathrm{Cn}(\Gamma)$ iff $\langle \ell, t \rangle \in \Gamma$ or there exists $\delta \in \Gamma$ with $\mathsf{head}(\delta) = \langle \ell, t \rangle$, and such that $\mathsf{body}(\delta)$ is a set of literals that derive from Γ. We say Γ is *consistent* iff no pair $\langle \ell, t \rangle, \langle \sim\ell, t \rangle$ exists in $\mathrm{Cn}(\Gamma)$. In particular, a set of literals is consistent iff it does not contain any such pair. Note that derivability is monotonic: $\mathrm{Cn}(\Gamma) \subseteq \mathrm{Cn}(\Gamma')$ whenever $\Gamma \subseteq \Gamma'$.

Definition 1 (Program). *A t-DeLP program, or t-de.l.p., is a pair (Π, Δ) where Π is a consistent set of temporal literals (also called strict facts), and Δ is a set of temporal defeasible rules.*

Definition 2 (Argument). *Given a t-de.l.p. (Π, Δ), an argument for $\langle \ell, t \rangle$ is a set $\mathcal{A} = \mathcal{A}_\Pi \cup \mathcal{A}_\Delta$, with $\mathcal{A}_\Pi \subseteq \Pi$ and $\mathcal{A}_\Delta \subseteq \Delta$, such that:*

(1) $\mathcal{A}_\Delta \cup \Pi \vdash \langle \ell, t \rangle$,   *(3) $\mathcal{A}_\Delta$ is $\subseteq$-minimal satisfying (1) and (2).*
(2) $\Pi \cup \mathcal{A}_\Delta$ is consistent,   *(4) $\mathcal{A}_\Pi$ is $\subseteq$-minimal satisfying $\mathcal{A}_\Delta \cup \mathcal{A}_\Pi \vdash \langle \ell, t \rangle$*

Given an argument $\mathcal{A}$ for $\langle \ell, t \rangle$, we also define $\mathsf{concl}(\mathcal{A}) = \langle \ell, t \rangle$, $\mathsf{base}(\mathcal{A}) = \mathsf{body}[\mathcal{A}] \setminus \mathsf{head}[\mathcal{A}]$ and $\mathsf{literals}(\mathcal{A}) = (\bigcup \mathsf{body}[\mathcal{A}]) \cup \mathsf{head}[\mathcal{A}]$.

It can be shown that each $\langle \ell_0, t_0 \rangle \in \mathsf{literals}(\mathcal{A})$ induces a unique sub-argument of $\mathcal{A}$, denoted $\mathcal{A}(\langle \ell_0, t_0 \rangle)$, i.e. a subset of $\mathcal{A}$ which is an argument for $\langle \ell_0, t_0 \rangle$.

Given a t-de.l.p. (Π, Δ), let $\mathcal{A}_0$ and $\mathcal{A}_1$ be arguments. We say $\mathcal{A}_1$ *attacks* $\mathcal{A}_0$ iff $\sim\mathsf{concl}(\mathcal{A}_1) \in \mathsf{literals}[\mathcal{A}_0]$, where we use the notation $\sim\langle \ell, t \rangle$ to denote $\langle \sim\ell, t \rangle$. In this case, we also say that $\mathcal{A}_1$ attacks $\mathcal{A}_0$ at the sub-argument $\mathcal{A}_0(\sim\mathsf{concl}(\mathcal{A}_1))$.

Defeat between arguments is depends upon their use of strict information (more is better), or their use of persistence rules (less is better).

Definition 3 (Defeat). *Let $\mathcal{A}_1$ attack $\mathcal{A}_0$ at a sub-argument $\mathcal{B}$, where $\mathsf{concl}(\mathcal{A}_1) = \langle \sim\ell, t \rangle$. We say $\mathcal{A}_1$ is a proper defeater for $\mathcal{A}_0$, denoted $\mathcal{A}_1 \succ \mathcal{A}_0$, iff*

$$\mathsf{base}(\mathcal{A}_1) \not\supseteq \mathsf{base}(\mathcal{B}) \quad or \quad \mathcal{B} = \mathcal{A}_1(\langle \ell, t' \rangle) \cup \{\delta_\ell(t'')\}_{t' \leq t'' < t}, \text{ for some } t' < t.$$

We say $\mathcal{A}_1$ is a blocking defeater for $\mathcal{A}_0$ when $\mathcal{A}_1$ attacks $\mathcal{A}_0$ but $\mathcal{A}_1 \not\succ \mathcal{A}_0$ and $\mathcal{A}_0 \not\succ \mathcal{A}_1$. Blocking defeat relations are denoted $\mathcal{A}_1 \prec\!\succ \mathcal{A}_0$. Finally, a defeater is a proper or a blocking defeater.

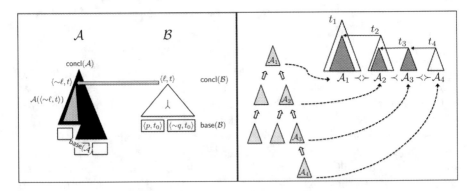

Fig. 1. (Left) Arguments $\mathcal{A}, \mathcal{B}$ are denoted with triangle-like figures. Strict facts from Π in $\mathsf{base}(\mathcal{A}), \mathsf{base}(\mathcal{B})$ are depicted as rectangles. Here, argument $\mathcal{B}$ attacks $\mathcal{A}$ at the sub-argument $\mathcal{A}(\langle \sim, \ell, t \rangle)$, depicted in grey. (Right) An argumentation line $\Lambda = [\mathcal{A}_1, \ldots, \mathcal{A}_4]$ in the dialectical tree for $\mathcal{A}_1$; defeated sub-arguments are depicted in grey. Notice that the time of these attacks is (non-strictly) decreasing: $t_1 > t_2 > t_3 = t_4$.

An argument $\mathcal{B}$ defeating $\mathcal{A}$ can in its turn have its own defeaters $\mathcal{C}, \ldots$ and so on. This gives rise to *argumentation lines*, sequences of arguments where each argument defeats its predecessor (among other conditions). More precisely, if $\mathcal{A}_1$ is an argument in a program (Π, Δ), an *argumentation line* for $\mathcal{A}_1$ is a sequence of arguments $\Lambda = [\mathcal{A}_1, \ldots, \mathcal{A}_n]$ such that:

(i) supporting arguments, i.e. those in odd positions $\mathcal{A}_{2i+1} \in \Lambda$ are jointly consistent with Π, and similarly for interfering arguments $\mathcal{A}_{2i} \in \Lambda$.
(ii) a supporting (interfering) argument is different from the attacked sub-arguments of previous supporting (interfering) arguments: $\mathcal{A}_{i+2k} \neq \mathcal{A}_i(\sim\mathsf{concl}(\mathcal{A}_{i+1}))$.
(iii) $\mathcal{A}_{i+1}$ is a proper defeater for $\mathcal{A}_i$ if $\mathcal{A}_i$ is a blocking defeater for $\mathcal{A}_{i-1}$.

The set of maximal argumentation lines for $\mathcal{A}_1$ can be arranged in the form of a tree, where all paths $[\mathcal{A}_1, \ldots]$ exactly correspond to all the possible maximal argumentation lines for $\mathcal{A}_1$. This *dialectical tree* for $\mathcal{A}_1$ is denoted $\mathcal{T}_{(\Pi,\Delta)}(\mathcal{A}_1)$.

The marking procedure in a dialectical tree $\mathcal{T} = \mathcal{T}_{(\Pi,\Delta)}(\mathcal{A}_1)$ is:
(1) mark all terminal nodes of $\mathcal{T}$ with a U (for undefeated);
(2) mark a node $\mathcal{B}$ with a D (for defeated) if it has a children node marked U;
(3) mark $\mathcal{B}$ with U if all its children nodes are marked D.

Definition 4 (Warrant). *Given a t-de.l.p. (Π, Δ), we say $\langle \ell, t \rangle$ is warranted in (Π, Δ) if there exists an argument $\mathcal{A}$ for $\langle \ell, t \rangle$ in (Π, Δ) such that $\mathcal{A}$ is marked undefeated (U) in the dialectical tree $\mathcal{T}_{(\Pi,\Delta)}(\mathcal{A}_1)$. The set of warranted literals is denoted $\mathsf{warr}(\Pi, \Delta)$.*

One can show t-DeLP enjoys the next logical properties, called Rationality Postulates [4,17], that prevent certain counter-intuitive results occur:

(P1) *Sub-arguments*: if $\mathcal{A}$ is undefeated in $\mathcal{T}_{(\Pi,\Delta)}(\mathcal{A})$, then any sub-argument $\mathcal{A}'$ of $\mathcal{A}$ is also undefeated in $\mathcal{T}_{(\Pi,\Delta)}(\mathcal{A}')$.
(P2) *Direct Consistency*: $\mathsf{warr}(\Pi, \Delta)$ is consistent.
(P3) *Indirect Consistency*: $\mathsf{warr}(\Pi, \Delta) \cup \Pi$ is consistent.
(P4) *Closure*: $\mathsf{Cn}(\mathsf{warr}(\Pi, \Delta) \cup \Pi) \subseteq \mathsf{warr}(\Pi, \Delta)$,

3   A Centralized Planning System for t-DeLP

After this brief review of t-DeLP, we proceed to introduce a planning system based on t-DeLP logic programming. In this section, we focus on multi-agent planning, where the plan is built by a central planner, with access to any knowledge the agents may possess about the initial state, their abilities, etc.

For the purpose of this paper, in order to simplify the description of the planning system, several assumptions are made on the representation of actions. We assume a finite set of actions A to be given, and for each action $\mathsf{e} \in A$ we assume the language contains a variable $\mu_{\mathsf{e}} \in \mathsf{Var}$. Each action e, executed at a time $t_{\mathsf{e}} - 1$, has a unique effect, denoted by the temporal literal $\langle \mu_{\mathsf{e}}, t_{\mathsf{e}} \rangle$ which reads as *action e was just executed at* t_{e}, that is exclusive to this action e (not found in nature, or other actions) and cannot be contradicted once it is made true. We also simplify the temporal aspects of actions: the preconditions of e are all about some unique time-point t, and they need only be warranted at t, not during the execution of e; this execution will take 1 time unit, so $t_{\mathsf{e}} = t + 1$. Finally, agents are simplified as follows: (i) the execution of an action e by an agent a, denoted e_a, makes agent a busy during the interval $[t, t_{\mathsf{e}}]$; and (ii) we will also assume that there exist enough agents.

In what follows we will assume a t-DeLP language be given. Let us proceed with the basic definitions of action, planning domain and update.

Definition 5 (Action, Executability). *An* action *is a pair* $e = (\mathsf{pre}(e), \mathsf{post}(e))$, *where* $\mathsf{pre}(e) = \{\langle \ell, t \rangle, \ldots, \langle \ell', t \rangle\}$ *is a consistent set of temporal literals and* $\mathsf{post}(e) = \{\langle \mu_e, t_e \rangle\}$, *with* $t_e = t+1$. *These are called the the* preconditions *and the* (direct) effect *of* e.

An action e *is* executable *in a t-de.l.p. program* (Π, Δ) *iff* $\mathsf{pre}(e) \subseteq \mathsf{warr}(\Pi, \Delta)$. *Given a set of agents (or actuators)* $\mathsf{Ag} = \{a, b, \ldots\}$, *we denote an action* e *available to agent* a *by* e_a. *A set of actions* A *is* non-overlapping *wrt* Ag *iff for any two actions of a same agent* a *in* A, *say* e_a, f_a, *the effect of* e_a *is to occur strictly before the preconditions of* f_a, *or viceversa.*

Definition 6 (Planning Domain). *Given a set of agents* Ag, *we define a* planning domain *as a triple*
$$\mathbb{M} = ((\Pi, \Delta), A, G)$$
where (Π, Δ) *is a t-de.l.p. representing the domain knowledge[1], with* Π *representing (the facts holding true in) the* initial state, G *is a set of literals representing the* goals, *and* A *is a set of actions available to the agents in* Ag.

Definition 7 (Action Update). *The* update *of a t-de.l.p.* (Π, Δ) *by an action* e, *denoted* $(\Pi, \Delta) \diamond e$, *is a another t-de.l.p. defined as follows:*
$$(\Pi, \Delta) \diamond e = \begin{cases} (\Pi \cup \mathsf{post}(e), \Delta), & \text{if } \mathsf{pre}(e) \subseteq \mathsf{warr}(\Pi, \Delta) \\ (\Pi, \Delta), & \text{otherwise.} \end{cases}$$

A *plan* π is essentially determined by a sequence of actions $\langle e_1, \ldots, e_n \rangle$. Actually, since actions are assigned an execution time by their preconditions, it can just be specified by a set of actions $\{e_1, \ldots, e_n\}$, rather than by a sequence. Indeed, it is not difficult to check that, given a t-de.l.p. (Π, Δ) and a pair of simultaneous actions e_i, e_j, the execution order does not matter. That is, given $\mathsf{pre}(e_i) = \{\langle \ell, t_i \rangle, \ldots\}$ and $\mathsf{pre}(e_j) = \{\langle \ell', t_j \rangle, \ldots\}$, then $t_i = t_j$ implies $((\Pi, \Delta) \diamond e_i) \diamond e_j = ((\Pi, \Delta) \diamond e_j) \diamond e_i$. This enables the following definition.

Definition 8 (Plan update). *The* update *of a t-de.l.p.* (Π, Δ) *by a set of actions* A *(given by a plan) is defined as follows,*
$$(\Pi, \Delta) \diamond A = \begin{cases} (\Pi, \Delta), & \text{if } A = \varnothing \\ ((\Pi, \Delta) \diamond e_i) \diamond \{e_1, \ldots, e_{i-1}, e_{i+1}, \ldots, e_n\}, & \text{if } A = \{e_1, \ldots, e_n\} \\ \text{where } t_i \leq t_j \text{ for any } 1 \leq j \leq n \end{cases}$$

A solution is then a plan whose set of actions makes the goals warranted after execution.

Definition 9 (Solution). *Given a set of agents* Ag *and planning domain* $\mathbb{M} = ((\Pi, \Delta), A, G)$, *a set of actions* $A' \subseteq A$ *is a* solution *for* $\mathbb{M}$ *and* Ag *iff*
$$G \subseteq \mathsf{warr}((\Pi, \Delta) \diamond A') \quad \text{and} \quad A' \text{ is non-overlapping w.r.t. } \mathsf{Ag}.$$

From here on, we will also denote a t-de.l.p. as $\mathbb{P} = (\Pi, \Delta)$.

---

[1] The language of (Π, Δ) is assumed to contain a literal μ_e for each action $e \in A$. Moreover, temporal literals $\langle \mu_e, t_e \rangle$ can only occur in the body of the rules of Δ, while those of the form $\langle \sim\mu_e, t_e \rangle$ cannot occur anywhere in Π, Δ, A or G.

Fig. 2. (Left) An argument step $\mathcal{A}$ introduces an action e which triggers an argument threat $\mathcal{B}$ to $\mathcal{A}$. This threat is addressed by a further plan step $\mathcal{C}$. (Right) The dark-grey area represents the provisional tree for $\mathcal{A}_1$ in plan π, which is a sub-tree of the full dialectical tree (outlined area). After a refinement of π with $\mathcal{A}_5$, this plan step and new threats (the light grey area) occur in the new provisional tree for $\mathcal{A}_1$ in $\pi(\mathcal{A}_5)$.

3.1   Algorithms for Backward Planning in t-DeLP

The idea of t-DeLP backward planning is to start enforcing (i.e. solving) the goals with arguments and actions and iteratively enforce their undefeated status or their preconditions, with the help of more arguments (and actions). The plan construction, starting again from the empty plan and consisting of a sequence of (action+argument) refinement steps, terminates when all these arguments and actions are, respectively, undefeated and executable. In our setting, we consider the following two types of refinement steps: *argument steps*, and *threat resolution moves*. An argument step is introduced to solve an open goal and consists of an argument for that goal, together with a set of actions whose effects (and facts from the initial state) support the base of this argument. A threat for an argument step $\mathcal{A}$ is an interfering argument in a maximal argumentation line for some dialectical (sub-)tree for $\mathcal{A}$.

Finally a threat resolution move is like an argument step but defeating a threat rather solving a goal. Figure 2 (left) depicts examples of plan refinements: (1) a goal exists; (2) an argument step $\mathcal{A}$ (with an action e) is added; (3) the new action e plus the initial state Π enable a threat $\mathcal{B}$; this is an interfering argument in the (new) tree for $\mathcal{A}$; (4) this threat motivates another plan step $\mathcal{C}$, a threat resolution move.

A plan π for some planning domain $\mathbb{M} = (\mathbb{P}, A, G)$ will consist of a triple

$$(A(\pi), \mathsf{Trees}(\pi), \mathsf{goals}(\pi))$$

where $A(\pi)$ is the set of actions the plan involves, $\mathsf{Trees}(\pi)$ is a set of dialectical (sub-)trees (one for each argument step) and $\mathsf{goals}(\pi)$ is the set of open goals of π.[2] $\mathsf{Trees}(\pi)$ is used to keep track of threats and threat resolution moves. Note

---

[2] By construction, open goals cannot be strict facts from the set Π in $\mathbb{P} = (\Pi, \Delta)$.

that if a plan π is directly applied to the initial t-de.l.p. $\mathbb{P}$ (i.e. if actions in $A(\pi)$ are assumed executable), it induces a new t-de.l.p. $\mathbb{P} \oplus \pi = (\Pi \cup \mathsf{post}[A(\pi)], \Delta)$ which at its turn induces a *provisional* dialectical tree $\mathcal{T}_{\mathbb{P} \oplus \pi}(\mathcal{A})$ for each existing argument and, in particular, for each argument step $\mathcal{A}$. In order to avoid unnecessary threat resolution moves, the policy of the planner will be to address each threat $\mathcal{A}_k$ with a *single* defeater $\mathcal{A}_{k+1}$ for it. This results in a sub-tree of the former, denoted $\mathcal{T}_{\mathbb{P} \oplus \pi}^*(\mathcal{A})$ or $\mathcal{T}_{(\Pi, \Delta) \oplus \pi}^*(\mathcal{A})$, to be stored in $\mathsf{Trees}(\pi)$.

The formal definition of a plan (given next) for a planning domain $\mathbb{M} = ((\Pi, \Delta), A, G)$ is by induction: the empty plan is a plan, and so is any refinement of a plan with either type of plan step which is applicable to it. The initial *empty plan* for $\mathbb{M}$, called $\pi_\varnothing$ is simply defined by the triple $\pi_\varnothing = (\varnothing, \varnothing, G)$. The plan resulting after refining $\pi_\varnothing$ with n refinement steps $\mathcal{A}_1, \cdots, \mathcal{A}_n$ is denoted $\pi = \pi_\varnothing(\mathcal{A}_1, \ldots, \mathcal{A}_n)$. Moreover, for $1 \leq k \leq n$, we will write $\pi_k = \pi_\varnothing(\mathcal{A}_1, \ldots, \mathcal{A}_k)$. A refinement of a plan π with plan step $\mathcal{A}$ is denoted $\pi(\mathcal{A}) = \pi_\varnothing(\mathcal{A}_1, \ldots, \mathcal{A}_n, \mathcal{A})$.

An **argument step** for a plan π_k is simply an argument $\mathcal{A}$ such that: its conclusion $\mathsf{concl}(\mathcal{A})$ is an element of $\mathsf{goals}(\pi_k)$; its base $\mathsf{base}(\mathcal{A})$ is a subset of $\Pi \cup \mathsf{post}[A]$; moreover, the minimal (and unique) set $A^\star \subseteq A$ of actions e for literals $\langle \mu_e, t_e \rangle \in \mathsf{base}(\mathcal{A})$ is non-overlapping for each agent. The plan $\pi_k(\mathcal{A})$ resulting from this refinement step is as follows: its actions are expanded with A^*, its goals replace $\langle \ell, t \rangle$ by $\mathsf{pre}[A^*]$, and each plan step updates the set of threats for it in the new t-de.l.p. $\Pi \cup \mathsf{post}[A(\pi) \cup A^*]$; finally, $\mathcal{A}$ and its current set of threats $[\mathcal{A}, \mathcal{B}]$ define the new sub-tree for $\mathcal{A}$.

For a given threat $\Lambda = [\mathcal{A}_i, \ldots, \mathcal{B}]$ in the tree $\mathcal{T}_{\mathbb{P} \oplus \pi}^*(\mathcal{A}_i) \in \mathsf{Trees}(\pi)$, a **threat resolution move** $\Lambda^\cap[\mathcal{A}]$ (also denoted $\mathcal{A}$) must satisfy: $\Lambda^\cap[\mathcal{A}]$ is an argumentation line in the tree $\mathcal{T}_{(\Pi \cup \mathsf{post}[A(\pi) \cup A^*], \Delta)}^*(\mathcal{A})$; and the set of actions A^* for $\mathsf{base}(\mathcal{A})$ is again non-overlapping for each agent. The resulting plan is computed similarly to that of argument steps.

Figure 2 (Right) illustrates a refinement by a threat resolution move $\mathcal{A}_5$, the only newly added (grey) argument in an odd position in the dialectical sub-tree. Finally, we provide the formal definition of a plan.

Definition 10 (Plan). π *is a plan for* $\mathbb{M}$ *and* Ag *iff it is obtained from* $\pi_\varnothing$ *after a finite number of applicable argument steps and threat resolution moves.*

Example 1. Let us suppose that the planner, endowed with two agents $\mathsf{Ag} = \{a_1, a_2\}$, wants some table to be lifted, without breaking a vase which lies on the table. The table has two sides (north and south), which can be lifted by either action, say $\mathsf{lift.N} \in A_{a_1}$, $\mathsf{lift.S} \in A_{a_2}$. Consider the next abbreviations:

$b = \mathsf{broken}(\mathsf{vase})$	$h = \mathsf{horizontal}(\mathsf{table})$	$\mu_N = \mu_{\mathsf{lift.N}}$	$l_N = \mathsf{lifted_N}$
$f = \mathsf{falls.off}(\mathsf{vase})$	$o = \mathsf{on}(\mathsf{vase}, \mathsf{table})$	$\mu_S = \mu_{\mathsf{lift.S}}$	$l_S = \mathsf{lifted_S}$

Then, consider the following goals $G = \{\langle l_N, 10 \rangle, \langle l_S, 10 \rangle, \langle \sim b, 10 \rangle\}$, the initial facts $\Pi_{a_1} = \Pi_{a_2} = \{\langle \sim b, 0 \rangle, \langle h, 0 \rangle \langle \sim l_N, 0 \rangle \langle \sim l_S, 0 \rangle \langle o, 0 \rangle\}$, and the set of defeasible rules Δ:

$\delta_1 : \langle \sim h, t \rangle \prec \langle l_N, t \rangle$ $\delta_2 : \langle \sim h, t \rangle \prec \langle l_S, t \rangle$ $\delta_3 : \langle h, t \rangle \prec \langle l_S, t \rangle, \langle l_S, t \rangle$

$\delta_4 : \langle l_N, t \rangle \prec \langle \mu_N, t \rangle$ $\delta_5 : \langle l_S, t \rangle \prec \langle \mu_S, t \rangle$ $\delta_6 : \langle b, t \rangle \prec \langle f, t \rangle$

$\delta_7 : \langle f, t+1 \rangle \prec \langle \sim h, t \rangle, \langle o, t \rangle$ $\delta_8 : \langle \sim o, t \rangle \prec \langle f, t \rangle$

$\delta_\ell(t)$: persistence rules for each literal $\ell \in \{\sim b, o, l_N, l_S, \sim l_N, \sim l_S\}$ and $t < 10$

The arguments depicted in Fig. 3(left), for a given $0 < t < 10$ are:

$\mathcal{A}_1 = \{\delta_{\sim b}(t')\}_{0 \le t' < 10} \cup \{\langle \sim b, 0 \rangle\}$ $\mathcal{B}_1 = \{\delta_o(t')\}_{0 \le t' < t} \cup \{\delta_1, \delta_4, \delta_6, \delta_7, \langle \mu_S, t \rangle\}$

$\mathcal{A}_3 = \{\delta_3, \delta_4, \delta_5, \langle \mu_N, t \rangle, \langle \mu_S, t \rangle\}$ $\mathcal{B}_2 = \{\delta_o(t')\}_{0 \le t' < t} \cup \{\delta_2, \delta_5, \delta_6, \delta_7, \langle \mu_N, t \rangle\}$

$\mathcal{A}_4 = \{\delta_{l_S}(t')\}_{t \le t' < 10} \cup \{\delta_4, \langle \mu_S, t \rangle\}$ $\mathcal{A}_5 = \{\delta_{l_N}(t')\}_{t \le t' < 10} \cup \{\delta_5, \langle \mu_N, t \rangle\}$

Now, the planner can consider the following plan steps:

$\pi_\varnothing$ open goals G; no threats

$\pi_\varnothing(\mathcal{A}_1)$ solves goal $\langle \sim b, 10 \rangle$; no goals are added

$\pi_\varnothing(\mathcal{A}_1, \mathcal{A}_4)$ solves goal $\langle l_S, 10 \rangle$; new threat $[\mathcal{A}_1, \mathcal{B}_1]$

$\pi_\varnothing(\mathcal{A}_1, \mathcal{A}_4, \mathcal{A}_5)$ solves goal $\langle l_N, 10 \rangle$; new threat $[\mathcal{A}_1, \mathcal{B}_2]$

$\pi_\varnothing(\mathcal{A}_1, \mathcal{A}_4, \mathcal{A}_5, [\mathcal{A}_1, \mathcal{B}_1, \mathcal{A}_3])$ solves $[\mathcal{A}_1, \mathcal{B}_1]$

$\pi_\varnothing(\mathcal{A}_1, \mathcal{A}_4, \mathcal{A}_5, [\mathcal{A}_1, \mathcal{B}_1, \mathcal{A}_3], [\mathcal{A}_1, \mathcal{B}_2, \mathcal{A}_3])$ solves $[\mathcal{A}_1, \mathcal{B}_2]$; this plan is a solution

Figure 3(right) also contains the arguments:

$\mathcal{A}_3^+ = \{\delta_3(t+1), \delta_4(t+1), \delta_5(t), \delta_{l_N}(t), \langle \mu_N, t \rangle\}$,

$\mathcal{A}_4^+ = \{\delta_{l_S}(t')\}_{t < t' < 10} \cup \{\delta_4, \langle \mu_S, t+1 \rangle\}$, and

$\mathcal{B}_1^+ = \{\delta_o(t')\}_{0 \le t' < t} \cup \{\delta_1(t+1), \delta_4(t+1), \delta_6(t+1), \delta_7(t+1), \langle \mu_S, t \rangle\}$.

In this case, we have a sequential execution of actions lift.N (at $t-1$) and lift.S (at t). As before, the argument step $\mathcal{A}_1$ in $\pi_\varnothing(\mathcal{A}_1, \mathcal{A}_5)$ is threatened by $\mathcal{B}_2$, since if nothing else happens, lifting one side of the table will result in the vase being broken. In this case, though, $\mathcal{B}_2$ cannot be resolved after the (wrong) refinement: $\pi_\varnothing(\mathcal{A}_1, \mathcal{A}_5, \mathcal{A}_4^+)$; this plan cannot be further refined into a solution. Also note that the threat $\mathcal{A}_1^+$ of later lifting the other side of the table will not result itself in the vase being broken: in this case, the defeater $\mathcal{A}_3^+$ for $\mathcal{A}_1^+$ would be available for free (given the current actions). In summary, the (action-based) arguments make $\langle \sim b, t \rangle$, $\langle l_N, t \rangle$ and $\langle l_S, t \rangle$ warranted iff agents lift both sides simultaneously –Fig. 3(left)–, or they do nothing.

3.2 Properties of Algorithms for t-DeLP Backward Plan Search

The *space of plans* for a planning domain $\mathbb{M}$ is the graph given by the set of plans (as defined above) and the *"is a refinement of"* relation. Breadth First Search is instantiated by the following algorithm for backward planning:

Data: $\mathbb{M} = ((\Pi, \Delta), A, G)$

Result: π (i.e. the set of actions $A(\pi)$); or fail, if Plans $= \varnothing$

initialization: Plans $= \langle \pi_\varnothing \rangle$ and $\pi = \pi_\varnothing$;

while goals$(\pi) \neq \varnothing$ or   threats$(\pi) \neq \varnothing$ **do**

     delete π from Plans;

     set Plans $=$ Plans $\cap \langle \pi(\mathcal{A}) \mid \pi(\mathcal{A})$ is a refinement of $\pi \rangle$;

     set $\pi =$ the first element of Plans;

end

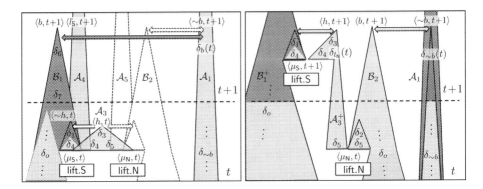

Fig. 3. A representation of arguments related to $\mathcal{A}_1$ in the interval $[t, t+1]$ from both plans in Example 1. Defeated arguments are depicted in dark grey. (Left) A solution plan: both sides are lifted simultaneously at t. The argument $\mathcal{A}_1$ –the vase remains unbroken– is defended by $\mathcal{A}_3$ –the table remains horizontal– from existing threats $\mathcal{B}_1, \mathcal{B}_2$ (only $\mathcal{B}_1$ is shown in detail). (Right) Agent a_1 lifts the table before a_2 does; now $\mathcal{A}_3^+$ cannot defeat the threat $\mathcal{B}_2$. (Note that plan steps $\mathcal{A}_4^+, \mathcal{A}_5$ are not depicted.)

This and many other usual search methods (Depth-First Search, etc.) are sound and complete for backward t-DeLP planning, see [15] for more details.

Theorem 1 (Soundness of BFS plan search.). *Let π be an output of the BFS algorithm in the space of plans for $\mathbb{M}$. Then π is a solution for $\mathbb{M}$.*

Theorem 2 (Completeness of BFS plan search). *Let $\mathbb{M} = ((\Pi, \Delta), A, G)$ be a planning domain and assume some solution $A' \subseteq A$ exists. Then, the BFS search in the space of plans terminates with an output π.*

4   Dialogues for Distributed Planning with Cooperative Agents

After reviewing the necessary elements in the previous sections, we can introduce the dialogue-based planning algorithm for distributed plan search. Recall we assume the agents are cooperative: they share the goals, but their beliefs and actions can widely differ. Also we assume that each agent makes use of single-planner methods from the last section. Agents will generate and discuss different plans during the dialogue. The proposed algorithm is studied in comparison with that of a centralized planner, also defined by the single-planner methods.

In this centralized scenario, agents delegate the planning task to a *central planner*, who is initially supplied with all the information that agents possess. Depending on the size of agents' logic programs in their initial planning domains, centralized planning might involve massive communication costs, only to find that most of the centralized information not relevant at all for the planning problem at hand. By keeping the planning domains distributed, information is only shared by an agent if she believes it might contribute to the present discussion.

Briefly, the dialogue-based algorithm for plan search is as follows. Each agent is initially endowed with a planning domain $\mathbb{M}_a = ((\Pi_a, \Delta_a), A_a, G)$, containing the believed facts and rules (Π_a, Δ_a); a list A_a of available actions (e.g. to agent a) and a set of common goals G. The dialogue consists of an exchange of elements that might be used in some plan refinement, or occur in a threat to a discussed plan. These communicated elements, aimed at generating a new plan step (resp., a threat), are the usual: *rules* to build an argument for some goal (resp., against a plan step), and *initial facts* or *actions* supporting the argument.

During this exchange of suggestions about plans and their threats, agents also keep continuously expanding their planning domains with new beliefs, rules and actions communicated by others, in a kind of shared planning domain $((\mathsf{facts}, \mathsf{rules}), \mathsf{actions}, G)$. These are routinely added to the current planning domain of the agent receiving this information at the present turn. The dialogues considered in the present algorithm consist in agents taking turns to contribute to the plan construction, each agent communicates its present contribution to the next agent in line.

The collaborative tasks of plan generation (the construction of plan steps) and plan evaluation (the discovery of threats) takes place backwards: at the level of the plan (in backward planning, later actions are usually considered first); and also at the level of each plan step or threat in this plan: *within* each plan step or threat: the argument construction starts from the conclusion and ends up with the base; (the reason is that the conclusion determines whether an argument can be a plan step or a threat). Many potential pre-arguments, of course, will not lead to any interesting plan step or threat. But this is the price to pay in order to preserve the completeness of search algorithms under the present distributed approach.

4.1 Distributed and Centralized Planning Domains

We first introduce multiple-planner versions of the definitions found in the Section 3. As we said, each agent $a \in \mathsf{Ag}$ is endowed with an initial planning domain $\mathbb{M}_a$. A sequence of such planning domains $\langle \mathbb{M}_a \rangle_{a \in \mathsf{Ag}}$, with shared goals $G_a = G$, generates a dialogue for the proposal and discussion of plans.

Definition 11 (Multi-planner domain; Union of planning domains; Centralized planning). *Given a set of planner agents* $\mathsf{Ag} = \{a_1, \ldots, a_r\}$, *let* $\mathbb{M}_a = ((\Pi_a, \Delta_a), A_a, G)$ *be a planning domain for each agent* $a \in \mathsf{Ag}$. *Then, we say* $\langle \mathbb{M}_a \rangle_{a \in \mathsf{Ag}}$ *is a* multi-planner domain, *if* $\bigcup_a \Pi_a$ *is a consistent set of literals. We also define the component-wise* union *of two planning domains, say* $\mathbb{M}_1, \mathbb{M}_2$, *as follows*

$$\mathbb{M}_1 \sqcup \mathbb{M}_2 = ((\Pi_1 \cup \Pi_2, \Delta_1 \cup \Delta_2), A_1 \cup A_2, G)$$

More generally, we define the centralized planning domain *induced by* $\langle \mathbb{M}_a \rangle_{a \in \mathsf{Ag}}$, *denoted* $\mathbb{M}_{\mathsf{Ag}}$, *as the n-ary union of this multi-planner domain:*

$$\mathbb{M}_{\mathsf{Ag}} = \bigsqcup_{a \in \mathsf{Ag}} \mathbb{M}_a$$

Note that a more general class of scenarios (altruistic cooperation) could also be considered, where other agents' goals are added to one's list (if jointly consistent). In this case, we would have $\mathbb{M}_1 \sqcup \mathbb{M}_2 = ((\cdot, \cdot), \cdot, G_1 \cup G_2)$, thus making Definition 11 a particular case of it with $G_1 = G_2$.

In any case, the methods of the previous section still apply to each individual planning domain $\mathbb{M}_{\mathsf{Ag}}$ or $\mathbb{M}_a$, and indeed those methods are now used

- to check that dialogue-generated plans are sound (by checking them in $\mathbb{M}_{\mathsf{Ag}}$)
- to contribute to the dialogue: by generating new plans or detecting new threats (agent a checking those plans in her current planning domain $\mathbb{M}_a$)

During the dialogue starting with a given multi-planner domain $\langle \mathbb{M}_a \rangle_{a \in \mathsf{Ag}}$, each agent a passes information to the next agent. This information consists of new possible plans and the elements (facts, rules, actions) needed to fully understand them, according to a. The communication of these latter elements is represented by a (piece-wise) expansion of the addressee's current planning domain.

The most important difference with a single-planner case is caused by the initial differences among agents' planning domains. The problem is that agents need not agree on the following:

- whether a given plan step $\mathcal{A}$ exists,
- whether a sequence of plan steps $\pi = \pi_\varnothing(\mathcal{A}_1, \ldots, \mathcal{A}_n)$ actually defines a plan,
- or which plan does this π define (which threats exist, or open goals remain)

The source of disagreements about a suggested plan $\pi = \pi_\varnothing(\mathcal{A}_1, \ldots, \mathcal{A}_n)$ lies in the fact that this sequence π gives rise to different triples (*actions, trees, goals*) when interpreted from different agents' planning domains. For this reason, from here on we introduce a superscript notation for interpreted plans $\pi^{\mathbb{M}}$ and distinguish between

- a sequence of plan steps $\pi = \pi_\varnothing(\mathcal{A}_1, \ldots, \mathcal{A}_n)$, informally called *plan*, even if a planning domain is not specified, and
- an *interpreted* plan $\pi^{\mathbb{M}}$, denoting the particular result of computing the sequence π in the planning domain $\mathbb{M}$ (only defined if π is actually a plan for $\mathbb{M}$)

$$\pi^{\mathbb{M}} = (A(\pi^{\mathbb{M}}), \mathsf{Trees}(\pi^{\mathbb{M}}), \mathsf{goals}(\pi^{\mathbb{M}}))$$

Definition 12 (Expansion). *Let* $\mathbb{M} = ((\Pi, \Delta), A, G)$ *and* $\mathbb{M}' = ((\Pi', \Delta'), A', G')$ *be planning domains. We say* $\mathbb{M}'$ *is an* expansion *of* $\mathbb{M}$, *denoted* $\mathbb{M} \sqsubseteq \mathbb{M}'$, *iff for each component* $Y \in \{\Pi, \Delta, A, G\}$ *of* $\mathbb{M}$, *its counterpart* Y' *extends* Y, *i.e.* $Y \subseteq Y'$.

Notice in particular that for any pair $\mathbb{M}_1, \mathbb{M}_2$ we have that $\mathbb{M}_1, \mathbb{M}_2 \sqsubseteq \mathbb{M}_1 \sqcup \mathbb{M}_2$.

4.2   Turn-Based Dialogues for Cooperative Planning in t-DeLP

The dialogues will consist in a series of rounds, each agent speaking once each round, and always to the same agent. Starting with turn 1 and agent $a_1 \in \mathsf{Ag}$, the agent speaking at a turn $m > 1$ is $a_{f(m)}$, where $f(m)$ is simply computed as

$$f(m) = \begin{cases} f(m-1)+1 & \text{if } f(m-1) < r \ (= |\mathsf{Ag}|) \\ 1 & \text{if } f(m-1) = r \end{cases}$$

The speaking agent $a_{f(m)}$ then communicates a tuple $\mathsf{turn}(m)$ to the agent next in line $a_{f(m+1)}$. The tuple $\mathsf{turn}(m)$ has the following elements:

$$(\mathsf{Preplans}_m, \ \mathsf{Plans}_m, \ \mathsf{Trueplans}_m, \ \mathsf{Prethreats}_m, \ \mathsf{facts}_m, \ \mathsf{rules}_m, \ \mathsf{actions}_m)$$

The set $\mathsf{Preplans}_m$ is a set of plans together with a pre-refinement step, the latter being an incomplete plan step refining the plan, to be completed by other agents. If a pre-plan is actually a plan for the agent $a_{f(m+1)}$, she will add it to the corresponding set Plans_{m+1}. Other agents can later delete it from this set, if the plan step is found inconsistent with their planning domain (their strict knowledge). Similarly, $\mathsf{Prethreats}_m$ is a set of candidate threats for the current plan under evaluation. Also, when agreement exists among all agents after a whole round that this plan's threats are all known, say at turn $m+k$, the plan is added to the corresponding set $\mathsf{Trueplans}_{m+k}$. Finally, these true plans (if they are not yet solutions) are the targets for further refinements in the next round, where agents can expand them into pre-plans, and the cycle starts again. A formal account of the basic concepts is given next.

Definition 13. *Given a planning domain* $\mathbb{M}$, *a plan* π *for* $\mathbb{M}$, *and a set* $\mathcal{A} \subseteq \Delta$, *we say* $\pi[\mathcal{A}]$ *is a pre-plan for* $\mathbb{M}$ *iff* $\pi(\mathcal{A})$ *is a plan for* $\mathbb{M}' = ((\Pi \cup \mathsf{base}(\mathcal{A}), \Delta), A, G)$. *We also denote by* A^* *the corresponding* $\subseteq$-*minimal set of actions* e *with* $\mathsf{post}(e) \in \mathsf{base}(\mathcal{A})$. *Similarly, we say that* $\mathcal{B} \subseteq \Delta \cup \Pi \cup \mathsf{post}[A(\pi^{\mathbb{M}})]$ *is a pre-threat for some plan step* $\Lambda = [\dots, \mathcal{A}]$ *in* $\pi^{\mathbb{M}}$, *denoted* $(\Lambda^\cap[\mathcal{B}], \pi) \in \mathsf{Prethreats}_m$, *iff* $\mathcal{B}$ *is an argument in the t-de.l.p.* $(\Pi \cup \mathsf{base}(\mathcal{B}) \oplus A(\pi), \Delta)$, $\mathsf{base}(\mathcal{B}) \cap \mathsf{post}[\Lambda] \subseteq \mathsf{post}[A(\pi^{\mathbb{M}})]$ *and* $\sim\mathsf{concl}(\mathcal{B}') \in \mathsf{literals}(\mathcal{A})$.

The remaining sets $\mathsf{facts}_m, \mathsf{rules}_m, \mathsf{actions}_m$ simply store the elements (facts $\langle \ell, t \rangle$, rules δ and actions e) used in plans and pre-plans considered up to the present turn m. In Table 1, we describe how the elements of the tuple $\mathsf{turn}(m+1)$ are computed from the previous turn $\mathsf{turn}(m)$ and the current speaker's planning domain $\mathbb{M}^m_{a_{f(m+1)}}$. Note that, for each turn m and each $a \in \mathsf{Ag}$, we have $\mathbb{M}^m_a \sqsubseteq \mathbb{M}^{m+1}_a$ and $\mathbb{M}^m_a \sqsubseteq \mathbb{M}_{\mathsf{Ag}}$. See also Figure 4 for an illustration of such a dialogue.

Example 2. (Cont'd) We rewrite Example 1 in the form of a multi-planner problem for two planner agents $\mathsf{Ag} = \{a_1, a_2\}$. In $\mathbb{M}_{a_1}, \mathbb{M}_{a_2}$, the goals and initial facts are as in Ex. 1 for both agents. For actions, we have $A_{a_1} = \{\mathsf{lift.N}\}$ and $A_{a_2} = \{\mathsf{lift.S}\}$. The defeasible rules are as in Ex. 1 for $\Delta_{a_1}, \Delta_{a_2}$ except that $\delta_7 \notin \Delta_{a_2}$; i.e., agent a_2 ignores that *objects lying in non-horizontal surfaces tend to fall off*. In the dialogue for this example shown in Table 2, we use the notation $\pi_{mnk+\dots}$ to denote the plan $\pi_\varnothing(\mathcal{A}_m, \mathcal{A}_n, \mathcal{A}_k^+, \dots)$.

Table 1. A definition of the turn-based dialogue. To simplify the notation, we have abbreviated agent subindices in expressions like $\mathbb{M}^m_{f(m+1)}$ to actually denote $\mathbb{M}^m_{a\,f(m+1)}$; the same for Π, Δ and A.

Base Case

$$\mathsf{turn}(0) = (\,\varnothing,\,\varnothing,\,\{\pi_\varnothing\},\,\varnothing,\,\varnothing,\,\varnothing,\,\varnothing\,)$$
$$\mathbb{M}^0_a = \mathbb{M}_a$$

Inductive Case

$$\mathsf{turn}(m+1) = (\,\mathsf{Preplans}_{m+1},\,\mathsf{Plans}_{m+1},\,\mathsf{Trueplans}_{m+1},\,\mathsf{Prethreats}_{m+1},$$
$$\mathsf{facts}_{m+1},\,\mathsf{rules}_{m+1},\,\mathsf{actions}_{m+1}\,)$$

where these elements are defined as follows

$\mathsf{Preplans}_{m+1} = \mathsf{Preplans}_m \cup \{\pi[\mathcal{A}] \mid \pi[\mathcal{A}]$ is a pre-plan in $\mathbb{M}^m_{f(m+1)}\}$

i.e. old pre-plans plus new ones constructible by agent $f(m+1)$

$\mathsf{Plans}_{m+1} = \{\pi(\mathcal{A})$ is a plan for $\mathbb{M}^m_{f(m+1)} \mid \pi[\mathcal{A}] \in \mathsf{Preplans}_{m+1}$ or $\pi(\mathcal{A}) \in \mathsf{Plans}_m\}$

$\mathsf{Trueplans}_{m+1} = \mathsf{Trueplans}_m$ plus the set of plans $\pi \in \mathsf{Plans}_m$ such that

$$\{(\cdot,\pi) : (\cdot,\pi) \in \mathsf{Prethreats}_{m-|\mathsf{Ag}|+1}\} \supseteq \cdots \supseteq \{(\cdot,\pi) : (\cdot,\pi) \in \mathsf{Prethreats}_{m+1}\}$$

$\mathsf{Prethreats}_{m+1} = \{(\Lambda^\cap[\mathcal{B}],\pi) : \pi \in \mathsf{Plans}_{m+1}$ and $\Lambda^\cap[\mathcal{B}]$ is a pre-threat for $\pi^{\mathbb{M}^m_{f(m+1)}}\}$

Auxiliary Defintions

$\mathsf{Newplans}_{m+1} = \bigcup_{m-|\mathsf{Ag}|+1\leq m'\leq m+1} \mathsf{Preplans}_{m'} \cup (\mathsf{Plans}_{m'} \cap \bigcap_{m'<m''\leq m+1} \mathsf{Plans}_{m''})$

i.e. recent (pre)plans (i.e. added during the last round) still in use

$\mathsf{Oldthreats}_{m+1} = \mathsf{Prethreats}_m \setminus \mathsf{Prethreats}_{m+1} \qquad \mathsf{Oldplans}_{m+1} = \mathsf{Plans}_m \setminus \mathsf{Plans}_{m+1}$

Inductive Case (cont'd)

$\mathsf{facts}_{m+1} = \mathsf{facts}_m$ plus those known literals (in Π^m_{f+1}) occurring in plan steps $\mathcal{A}$

with $\pi[\mathcal{A}]$ or $\pi(\mathcal{A}) \in \mathsf{Newplans}_{m+1}$, or in threats $\mathsf{Prethreats}_{m,m+1}$

plus known literals (in $\Pi^m_{f(m+1)}$) whose negations occur in discarded

plan steps $\pi(\mathcal{A}) \in \mathsf{Oldplans}_{m+1}$ or threats $(\mathcal{B},\cdot) \in \mathsf{Oldthreats}_{m+1}$

$\mathsf{rules}_{m+1} = \mathsf{rules}_m$ plus those rules in $\Delta^m_{f(m+1)}$ occurring in the suggested plan

steps $\pi[\mathcal{A}], \pi(\mathcal{A}) \in \mathsf{Newplans}_{m+1}$, or threats $(\Lambda^\cap[\mathcal{B}],\cdot) \in \mathsf{Newthreats}_{m+1}$

$\mathsf{actions}_{m+1} = \mathsf{actions}_m$ plus any $e \in A^m_{f(m+1)}$ supporting plan steps in $\mathsf{Newplans}_{m+1}$

$$\mathbb{M}^{m+1}_a = \begin{cases} \mathbb{M}^m_a & \text{if } a \neq f(m+1) \\ (\,(\Pi^m_{f(m+1)} \cup \mathsf{facts}_{m+1},\, \Delta^m_{f(m+1)} \cup \mathsf{rules}_{m+1}), \\ \qquad\qquad A^m_{f(m+1)} \cup \mathsf{actions}_{m+1},\quad G\,) & \text{if } a = f(m+1) \end{cases}$$

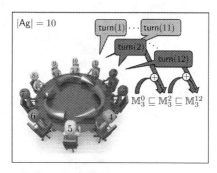

Fig. 4. A representation of the cyclic dialogues for cooperative plan search among a set $Ag = \{a_1, \ldots, a_{10}\}$ of planner agents and an initial multi-planner domain $\langle \mathbb{M}_a^0 \rangle_{a \in Ag}$. Here, agent 1 communicates to agent 2, 2 to 3, etc. and agent 10 to agent 1. This cycle is repeated as needed. Note, for example, that agent 2 speaks at turns $2, 12, 22, \ldots$ The initial planning domain of the next agent, namely $\mathbb{M}_3^0$, is expanded at turn 2 with agent 2's message into $\mathbb{M}_3^2$, and then again at turn(12) into $\mathbb{M}_3^{12}$, and so on.

Table 2. Dialogue corresponding to Exampe 2

speaker	informal dialogue (for Example 2)	formal dialogue
$0, -$	The empty plan $\pi_\varnothing$ is available.	$\pi_\varnothing \in \mathsf{Plans}_0$
$1, a_1$	We might assume the vase will not break.	$\pi_1 \in \mathsf{Plans}_1$
	I might execute lift.N at some $t_{\mathsf{lift.N}} < 10$	$\pi_5, \ldots \in \mathsf{Plans}_1$
$2, a_2$	I might execute lift.S at some $t_{\mathsf{lift.S}} < 10$	$\pi_4, \pi_{4+}, \ldots \in \mathsf{Plans}_2$
	In π_1, if the vase fell off it would break!	$([\mathcal{A}_1, \{\delta_6\}], \pi_1) \in \mathsf{Prethreats}_2$
$\vdots$	$\vdots$	$\vdots$
$4, a_2$	We agree upon our reading of some plans.	$\pi_1, \pi_4, \pi_{4+}, \ldots \in \mathsf{Trueplans}_4$
$5, a_1$	I might execute lift.N at some $t_{\mathsf{lift.N}} < 10$	$\pi_{15}, \pi_{45}, \pi_{4+5} \ldots \in \mathsf{Plans}_5$
$\vdots$	$\vdots$	$\vdots$
$7, a_1$	In π_{15} the vase will fall off!! (a_2 learns δ_7)	$([\mathcal{A}_1, \mathcal{B}_2], \pi_{15}) \in \mathsf{Newthreats}_7$
$\vdots$	$\vdots$	$\vdots$
$9, a_1$	We agree upon our reading of π_{15}.	$\pi_{15} \in \mathsf{Trueplans}_9$
$10, a_2$	I might execute lift.S upon it	$\pi_{154}, \pi_{154+} \in \mathsf{Plans}_{10}$
$11, a_1$	Resp., $[\mathcal{A}_1, \mathcal{B}_1], [\mathcal{A}_1, \mathcal{B}_1^+]$ exist in π_{154}, π_{154+}	$\cdots \in \mathsf{Newthreats}_{11}$
$\vdots$	$\vdots$	$\vdots$
$13, a_1$	We agree upon our reading of π_{154}, π_{154+}.	$\pi_{154}, \pi_{154+} \in \mathsf{Trueplans}_{13}$
$14, a_2$	We can use $[\mathcal{A}_1, \mathcal{B}_2, \mathcal{A}_3]$ to solve $[\mathcal{A}_1, \mathcal{A}_2]$	$\pi_{1543} \in \mathsf{Plans}_{14}$
$\vdots$	$\vdots$	$\vdots$
$16, a_1$	We can use $[\mathcal{A}_1, \mathcal{B}_1, \mathcal{A}_3]$ to solve $[\mathcal{A}_1, \mathcal{B}_1]$	$\pi_{15433} \in \mathsf{Plans}_{16}$
$\vdots$	$\vdots$	$\vdots$
$18, a_2$	We agree that π_{15433} is a solution in $\mathbb{M}^{18}$.	$\pi_{15433} \in \mathsf{Trueplans}_{18}$

Theorem 3 (Soundness). *Let π be the output of the dialogue-based plan search algorithm in Table 1, for some given multi-planner domain $\langle \mathbb{M}_a \rangle_{a \in \mathsf{Ag}}$. Then π is a solution for $\mathbb{M}_{\mathsf{Ag}}$*

Proof sketch: The proof is by induction on the length of the plan $\pi = \pi_\varnothing(\mathcal{A}_1, \ldots, \mathcal{A}_n)$ (the output of the algorithm for $\langle \mathbb{M}_a \rangle_{a \in \mathsf{Ag}}$). In this case, one can show that the shared information at turn m, i.e. the planning domain $\mathbb{M}^m$, suffices to build all the plans π discussed up to that point by other agents. Moreover, it also suffices to show that π is also a plan for any planning domain $\mathbb{M}'$ such that $\mathbb{M}^m \sqsubseteq \mathbb{M}' \sqsubseteq \mathbb{M}_{\mathsf{Ag}}$, and finally, that the interpretation for any such $\mathbb{M}'$ is always the same: $\pi^{\mathbb{M}^m} = \pi^{\mathbb{M}'} = \pi^{\mathbb{M}_{\mathsf{Ag}}}$. The identity among their corresponding sets $\mathsf{Trees}^{(\cdot)}$ is shown by giving upper bounds for the occurrence (turns) of each element of a given threat. $\square$

Theorem 4 (Completeness). *Let $\langle \mathbb{M}_a \rangle_{a \in \mathsf{Ag}}$ be a multi-planner domain with elements of the form $\mathbb{M}_a = (\Pi_a, \Delta_a), A_a, G)$. If a solution $A^\star$ exists for the centralized domain $\mathbb{M}_{\mathsf{Ag}}$, then the dialogue from Table 1 terminates with an output.*

Proof sketch: If a solution $A^\star$ exists, i.e. if $G \subseteq \mathsf{warr}(\mathbb{P}_{\mathsf{Ag}} \diamond A^\star)$, we can assume w.l.o.g. that the solution $A^\star$ is $\subseteq$-minimal. As in Theorem 2, we can extract from $A^\star$ the necessary sets $\mathsf{Lines}, \mathsf{Steps}, \mathsf{Threats}$, and from this a sequence $\pi_\varnothing(\mathcal{A}_1, \ldots, \mathcal{A}_n)$ such that $\mathsf{Steps} = \{\mathcal{A}_1, \ldots, \mathcal{A}_n\}$ addresses all the goals and threats. For each plan step $\mathcal{A}_k$ and each element $\langle \ell, t \rangle$ or δ or e of $\mathcal{A}_k$, we compute a lower bound m for the occurrence of a turn m such that $\pi(\mathcal{A}_k) \in \mathsf{Plans}_m$, $\langle \ell, t \rangle \in \mathsf{facts}_m$, $\delta \in \mathsf{rules}_m$ or $e \in \mathsf{actions}_m$. $\square$

5   Conclusions and Related Work

In this paper we study dialogues for distributed plan search in cooperative planning problems expressible in the t-DeLP planning system. This system, combining a classical update function for temporal planning with an (argumentative) temporal defeasible logical system called t-DeLP. The latter adds non-monotonic temporal reasoning to actions, thus allowing for complex indirect effects. Our contribution is mainly theoretical and consists of showing that the dialogue-based plan search methods are sound and complete for t-DeLP planning. Computational and more practical aspects like the efficiency, applicability and scalability of the approach remain as future work.

Several extensions of classical planning exist in either of the directions taken in the present paper. For example, the literature on temporal planning is quite rich (see e.g. [9], Ch. 14), though mainly based on simple, monotonic reasoning. Also, multi-agent extensions of planning systems for collaborative scenarios have also been studied in a dialogue-based form [22], again built on classical or temporal planners.

The results of the present paper match those from [16], [13], but replacing DeLP [8] by t-DeLP [14], and also the partial order planner of [7] with the temporal linear planner from [15]. While POP planning systems are more flexible, the underlying logic DeLP is less expressive given the implicit time approach. The present paper can also be related to other several proposals found in the literature like multi-agent argumentation, cooperative planning (without defeasible argumentation) and centralized planning. For example, abstract argumentation [6] has been used to reason about conflicting plans and generate consistent sets of goals [1,10,18]. None of these works apply to a multi-agent environment. A proposal for dialogue-based centralized planning is that of [21], but no argumentation is made use of. The work in [3] presents a dialogue based on an argumentation process to reach agreements on plan proposals. Unlike our focus on an argumentative and stepwise construction of a plan, this latter work is aimed at handling the interdependencies between agents' plans. Also, [11] presents an argumentation scheme to propose and justify plans using critical questions.

References

1. Amgoud, L.: A formal framework for handling conflicting desires. In: Nielsen, T.D., Zhang, N.L. (eds.) ECSQARU 2003. LNCS (LNAI), vol. 2711, pp. 552–563. Springer, Heidelberg (2003)
2. Augusto, J., Simari, G.R.: Temporal Defeasible Reasoning. Knowledge and Information Systems 3, 287–318 (2001)
3. Belesiotis, A., Rovatsos, M., Rahwan, I.: Agreeing on plans through iterated disputes. In: Proc. of AAMAS 2010, pp. 765–772 (2010)
4. Caminada, M., Amgoud, L.: On the evaluation of argumentation formalisms. Artificial Intelligence 171, 286–310 (2007)
5. Cobo, M.L., Martinez, D.C., Simari, G.R.: Stable Extensions in Timed Argumentation Frameworks. In: Modgil, S., Oren, N., Toni, F. (eds.) TAFA 2011. LNCS, vol. 7132, pp. 181–196. Springer, Heidelberg (2012)
6. Dung, P.: On the acceptability of arguments and its fundamental role in non-monotonic reasoning, logic programming and n-person games. Artificial Intelligence 77(2), 321–357 (1995)
7. García, D.R., García, A.J., Simari, G.R.: Defeasible Reasoning and Partial Order Planning. In: Hartmann, S., Kern-Isberner, G. (eds.) FoIKS 2008. LNCS, vol. 4932, pp. 311–328. Springer, Heidelberg (2008)
8. García, A.J., Simari, G.R.: Defeasible logic programming: An argumentative approach. Theory and Practice of Logic Programming 4(1-2), 95–138 (2004)
9. Ghallab, M., Nau, D., Traverso, P.: Automated Planning: Theory and Practice. Morgan Kaufmann, San Francisco (2004)
10. Hulstijn, J., van der Torre, L.: Combining goal generation and planning in an argumentation framework. In: Proc. Workshop on Argument, Dialogue and Decision at Non-monotonic Reasoning, NMR 2004 (2004)
11. Medellin-Gasque, R., Atkinson, K., McBurney, P., Bench-Capon, T.: Arguments over co-operative plans. In: Modgil, S., Oren, N., Toni, F. (eds.) TAFA 2011. LNCS, vol. 7132, pp. 50–66. Springer, Heidelberg (2012)
12. Pajares, S., Onaindia, E.: Defeasible argumentation for multi-agent planning in ambient intelligence applications. In: Proc. of AAMAS 2012, pp. 509–516 (2012)
13. Pajares, S., Onaindia, E.: Context-Aware Multi-Agent Planning in intelligent environments. Information Sciences 227, 22–42 (2013)
14. Pardo, P., Godo, L.: t-DeLP: an argumentation-based Temporal Defeasible Logic Programming framework. Annals of Math. and Artif. Intel. Springer (in press)

15. Pardo, P., Godo, L.: An argumentation-based multi-agent temporal planning system built on t-DeLP. In: Proc. of CAEPIA (in Press, 2013)
16. Pardo, P., Pajares, S., Onaindia, E., Godo, L., Dellunde, P.: Multiagent argumentation for cooperative planning in DeLP-POP. In: Proc. AAMAS 2011, pp. 971–978 (2012)
17. Prakken, H.: An abstract framework for argumentation with structured arguments. Argument & Computation 1(2), 93–124 (2010)
18. Rahwan, I., Pasquier, P., Sonenberg, L., Dignum, F.P.M.: On the Benefits of Exploiting Hierarchical Goals in Bilateral Automated Negotiation. In: Rahwan, I., Parsons, S., Reed, C. (eds.) ArgMAS 2007. LNCS (LNAI), vol. 4946, pp. 18–30. Springer, Heidelberg (2008)
19. Simari, G.R., Loui, R.: A mathematical treatment of defeasible reasoning and its implementation. Artificial Intelligence 53, 125–157 (1992)
20. Stolzenburg, F., García, A.J., Chesñevar, C., Simari, G.R.: Computing Generalized Specificity. Journal of Applied Non-Classical Logics 12(1), 1–27 (2002)
21. Tang, Y., Norman, T.J., Parsons, S.: A model for integrating dialogue and the execution of joint plans. In: McBurney, P., Rahwan, I., Parsons, S., Maudet, N. (eds.) ArgMAS 2009. LNCS, vol. 6057, pp. 60–78. Springer, Heidelberg (2010)
22. Torreño, A., Onaindia, E., Sapena, O.: An approach to multi-agent planning with incomplete information. In: Proc. of ECAI 2012, pp. 762–767. IOS Press (2012)

Reconfiguration of Large-Scale Surveillance Systems

Peter Novák and Cees Witteveen

Algorithmics Group, Faculty EEMCS,
Delft University of Technology,
The Netherlands
{P.Novak,C.Witteveen}@tudelft.nl

Abstract. The METIS research project aims at supporting maritime safety and security by facilitating continuous monitoring of vessels in national coastal waters and prevention of phenomena, such as vessel collisions, environmental hazard, or detection of malicious intents, such as smuggling. Surveillance systems, such as METIS, typically comprise a number of heterogeneous information sources and information aggregators. Among the main problems of their deployment lies *scalability* of such systems with respect to a potentially large number of monitored entities. One of the solutions to the problem is continuous and timely adaptation and reconfiguration of the system according to the changing environment it operates in. At any given timepoint, the system should use only a minimal set of information sources and aggregators needed to facilitate cost-effective early detection of indicators of interest.

Here we describe the METIS system prototype and introduce a theoretical framework for modelling scalable information-aggregation systems. We model information-aggregation systems as networks of inter-dependent reasoning agents, each representing a mechanism for justification/refutation of a conclusion derived by the agent. The proposed continuous reconfiguration algorithm relies on standard results from abstract argumentation and corresponds to computation of a grounded extension of the argumentation framework associated with the system.

1 Introduction

The METIS project [4,6] studies techniques supporting development of large-scale dependable systems of systems which aggregate multiple sources of information, analyse them, compute risk factors and deliver assessments to system operators. In this paper we introduce the METIS project's prototype application, which applies the developed concepts to the domain of maritime security and aims to provide advanced situation awareness capabilities for monitoring maritime traffic in national coastal waters. By 'Systems-of-systems' we mean large-scale integrated systems that are heterogeneous and independently operable on their own, but are networked together for a common goal [7]. One of the prominent problems in development of such systems is their *scalability*. Our focus here is on supporting scalability of the system by means of continuous *reconfiguration*, i.e., adaptation to changes in its environment.

The METIS system is a large-scale surveillance system operating in a mixed physical and software environment. It comprises a number of cooperative agents serving as information sources and aggregators. Typically, these would be either situated physical

J. Leite et al. (Eds.): CLIMA XIV, LNAI 8143, pp. 325–339, 2013.

agents, such as cameras, satellites or human patrols, or software components interfacing various public, or proprietary databases, web resources, etc.

In the implemented prototype scenario, METIS aims at detection of ships suspected of smuggling illegal contraband during their approach to the port under surveillance. For every vessel in the zone of its interest, the system accesses the various information sources and subsequently processes the extracted information so as to finally identify vessels which require operator's attention. The available sources provide information about the ships, including their identifications, crew, ports-of-call, various physical characteristics, possibly even digest of news articles reporting on events involving the vessel, or the crew. Quite often, such information would yield inconsistent, or even contradictory information, which needs to be cross-validated and processed in order to infer the most likely values. The resulting information is aggregated by a hierarchy of information aggregators so that the system is ultimately able to determine whether a particular vessel should be considered a smuggling suspect, or it is able to justify that it is innocuous given the available information. In the prototype scenario, the individual aggregators are represented by various information-fusion components operating over a shared data warehouse, but could include also external agents, such as human experts.

METIS should be deployable both on land, as well as on board of independently operating ships. As a consequence, querying individual information sources and subsequent information aggregation could incur non-negligible financial and computational costs. While accessing a publicly available Internet resource via a fixed broadband connection can be relatively cheap, the bandwidth of satellite communication links used on board of maritime vessels is limited and data transfers incur external costs too. Similarly, accessing proprietary industrial databases, or utilisation of physical agents, such as aerial drones, imaging satellites, etc. can incur rather significant costs to the system's operation. Hence, using all available information sources and information fusion components is not always feasible and in turn one of the problems central to development of such a large-scale surveillance multi-agent system is their scalability.

The problem of configuration and dynamic reconfiguration according to the current system's needs can be thus formulated as follows: *Which information sources and aggregators should be active over time so as to maximize the likelihood of early detection of malicious intents in the most cost-efficient manner?*

Here, we propose an approach to (re-)configuration of large-scale information aggregation systems by modelling the interactions between the individual components in terms of an *argumentation framework* [2]. After introducing the basic concepts (Section 2), in Section 3, we present the problems of configuration and reconfiguration of information-aggregation systems to account for changes in their environments. Subsequently, in Section 4, we show that suitable system configurations correspond to the concept of grounded extensions of an associated argumentation framework. The solution concept is closely related to the well-founded semantics of logic programs, so the relationship opens the door for further study of reconfiguration in relation to standard results in logic programming. A discussion of on-going and future work along the presented line of research concludes the paper. Throughout the paper, in a series of expositions, we describe the relevant parts of the METIS system and identify a class of relevant solution concepts.

METIS 1 *In the prototype scenario,* METIS *should continuously monitor vessels in the coastal waters in the* Dutch Exclusive Economic Zone, *source information about them and process it, so as to finally identify vessels which are suspect of smuggling. Upon detection of a suspicion, the system should notify the user, a* Netherlands Coastguard *officer, who then decides on the subsequent course of action. To put the scenario in perspective, note that the monitored area covers more than 63.000 km^2 and typically contains around 3-4.000 vessels at any given moment in time.*

In the system exposure we consider the following simplified fragment of the prototype scenario: Information-sources available to the system comprise a local copy of IHS Fairplay *[5] database and web-portals of* MyShip.com *[11],* MarineTraffic.com *[10] and its* Ports of Call. *There are also three physical sensors: a human* coast-guard patrol *in the field, a receiver for* Automatic Identification System *(AIS) [1] messages, and a* radar *providing kinematic signatures of vessel tracks as interpreted from the readings of the detected spot positions of the vessel over time. Every vessel from a certain size is required to be equipped with an AIS transmitter and regularly broadcast its identity, type, ports of call, etc. Besides cross-validation and and probabilistic inference over the received data, the individual information-processing components also derive meta-information about quality, certainty and trust of the aggregated information.*

2 Preliminaries

An instance of a multi-agent surveillance system such as METIS, comprises a set of *information processing* agents and a *shared database*. *Information source* agents operate in a *dynamic environment* and feed a shared *data store* which is further processed by a set of *information aggregators* agents. The system's objective is to determine the truth value of a set of *distinguished indicators*, information elements corresponding to some non-trivially observable properties of the monitored entities, such as whether a vessel is a smuggling suspect. Below, we introduce the formal framework for modelling information-aggregation systems, together with the related terminology and notation.

2.1 Information-Aggregation System

We model an abstract information-aggregation system as a tuple $S = (A, D, cost)$ comprising a finite set of information-processing agents, a database schema and a cost function respectively. A shared data store of the system is represented by a 3-valued database schema D comprising a finite set of propositional variables over the domain $Dom = \{\top, \bot, \varnothing\}$ representing the truth values *true, false,* and *unknown* respectively. In practice, Dom could include an arbitrary number of distinct crisp values and the METIS system exposure indeed assumes an extended domain of the database schema. Without loss of generality, we also do not distinguish between different interpretations of the unknown value $\varnothing$: *no information* and *value existent, but unknown* [8]. A database snapshot $D : D \to Dom$ of the schema D at a given timepoint is a ground interpretation of variables of D. That is, each variable of D takes a truth value from the domain Dom. $D|x$ denotes the value of the variable x in D. $D_\varnothing$ denotes a database snapshot with all variables valued as unknown, i.e., for all $x \in D$, we have $D_\varnothing|x = \varnothing$. For convenience, we use the term database snapshot interchangeably with the term database.

The information processing agents $\mathcal{A} = \{A_1, \ldots, A_n\}$ of the system are modelled as function objects over interpretations of the schema $\mathcal{D}$, formally $A_i : \mathcal{D} \times Dom \to \mathcal{D} \times Dom$ for each $A \in \mathcal{A}$. That is, given a database snapshot D, an information-processing agent A takes as an input a set of D-valuations of database variables $in_A \subseteq \mathcal{D}$ and produces a set of new valuations for database variables $out_A \subseteq \mathcal{D}$. $D|in_A$ and $D|out_A$ respectively denote value assignments to variables of in_A and out_A corresponding to those in the snapshot D. The sets $D|in_A$ and $D|out_A$ can be seen as partial interpretations of the schema $\mathcal{D}$. Given two snapshots D and D', we denote $A(D|in_A) = D'|out_A$ relying on agents as partial functions over database snapshots. We model information-source agents as standard information-processing agents with an empty set of input variables $in = \emptyset$ and a non-empty set of output variables $out \neq \emptyset$.

The cost function $cost : \mathcal{A} \to \mathbb{R}^+$ models the costs involved in a single computation run of an agent. Without loss of generality we assume that the computation of valuations of the output variables cannot be disentangled and must be carried out as an atomic operation. Informally, the cost of executing an information source agent corresponds to the aggregate cost of sensing its input variable in the environment. Whenever the cost function is irrelevant in the given context, we simply write $\mathcal{S} = (\mathcal{A}, \mathcal{D})$.

A configuration $C \subseteq \mathcal{A}$ of a system $\mathcal{S} = (\mathcal{A}, \mathcal{D}, cost)$ is a set of information processing agents *active* in $\mathcal{S}$ in a given timepoint. Notation for input and output variables of an agent naturally extends to configurations, that is $in_C = \bigcup_{A \in C} in_A$ and $out_C = \bigcup_{A \in C} out_A$. Assuming a single execution of each agent in C, the $cost$ function straightforwardly extends to configurations too: $cost(C) = \sum_{A \in C} cost(A)$.

Given a configuration $C \subseteq \mathcal{A}$ of a system $\mathcal{S} = (\mathcal{A}, \mathcal{D})$ and a database snapshot D of the schema $\mathcal{D}$, we say that a database D' is an *update* of D by C iff for each variable $x \in \mathcal{D}$, such that $D|x \neq D'|x$, there exists an agent $A \in C$, such that $D'|x = A(D|in_A)|x$. That is, each variable modified in the update D' w.r.t. its original value in D, is a result of a computation of some agent from the configuration C. We say that a configuration C is *supported* by a database snapshot D iff for all agents $A \in C$ we have both $A(D|in_A) \subseteq D$, as well as $A(D|out_A) \subseteq D$. That is, the information processing performed by each agent A of the configuration C is reflected in the snapshot D.

$C(D) = D'$ denotes an update D' of D by a configuration C. Note, not all of the outcomes produced by all agents of C need to be reflected in the database update. Alternatively, we say that D' is an update of D by a partial database D_u iff whenever $D|x \neq D_u|x \neq \emptyset$, we have that $D'|x = D_u|x$ and $D'|x = D|x$ otherwise, and we also denote $D' = D \oplus D_u$. We model evolution of a system $\mathcal{S}$ under a configuration $C \subseteq \mathcal{A}$ as a (possibly infinite) sequence of database snapshots $\lambda_{\mathcal{D}} = D_0, \ldots, D_k, \ldots$, such that each $D_{i+1} = C(D_i)$ is an update of D_i for all $i \in \mathbb{N}_0$. Such a $\lambda_{\mathcal{D}}$ is called a *C-evolution* of $\mathcal{S}$ from D_0 on. Finally, note that given a configuration C which is supported by a database snapshot D, every update $C(D)$ equals D. In that case, we say that D is *stable* w.r.t. C.

Evolution of a system strongly depends on both the nature of the active configuration, as well as the particular order in which the agents of the configuration work over the database. We say that a configuration $C \subseteq \mathcal{A}$ of a system $\mathcal{S} = (\mathcal{A}, \mathcal{D})$ is *normal* iff all C-evolutions of $\mathcal{S}$ from every database snapshot D_0 on, eventually *stabilise*, i.e., reach the same stable state regardless of the order of execution of the individual agents in C.

agent	in	out	cost
AIS	∅	aisID*, aisType′	10
FairPlay	∅	fpID*	10
MyShip	∅	myShipID†	200
MarineTraffic	∅	mtID†	300
MarineTraffPorts	∅	portCalls‡	1000
Radar	∅	track′	2000
Patrol	∅	isSpoofingID‡	9500
TrackAnalyser	marked /	vesselType‡	1000
CheckDefault	marked *	isSuspectID†	200
CheckSpoofing	marked †	isSpoofingID‡	800
checkSmuggling	marked ‡	isSmuggling	2000

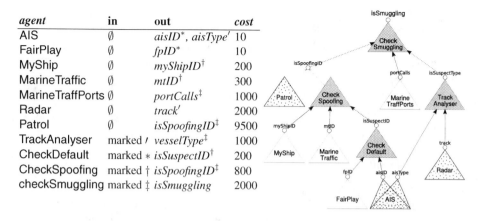

Fig. 1. METIS system agents (left) and their interdependencies (right)

More formally, there is a unique database snapshot $C^*(D_0)$ of the schema $\mathcal{D}$, so that for all C-evolutions $\lambda_{\mathcal{D}} = D_0, \dots, D_k, \dots$ of S from D_0 on, there is an index $k_{\lambda_{\mathcal{D}}} \geq 0$, such that for all $i \geq k_{\lambda_{\mathcal{D}}}$, $D_i = D_{k_{\lambda_{\mathcal{D}}}} = C^*(D_0)$ and C is supported by D_k.

METIS 2 (system structure) *In the prototype scenario (Figure 1),* METIS *features 7 information-source agents (white), including 3 physical sensors (dotted), and three non-trivial information-aggregation agents (grey). The costs of accessing the information sources are only illustrative and estimate the communication bandwidth to access the databases, or the cost of querying the physical sensors. The costlier databases tend to provide richer information about vessels. The cost associated with an information-aggregation agent roughly estimate the computational costs of its execution. In the figure, the dotted lines indicate input-output dependency of information-aggregation agents, while the solid line arrows indicate merely that the agent derives a given variable, otherwise indicated by putting the variable bullet on top of the corresponding agent triangle.*

The CheckDefault *aggregator consults the local physical sensor and cross-validates the self-transmitted vessel identity with those listed in the IHS FairPlay database. Upon a failure to match the identities of the vessel, the system performs a deeper check of the vessel's identity (CheckSpoofing) in order to determine whether it does not actively spoofing it, that is whether it actively lies about its identity. The physical sensor Patrol involves a coast-guard patrol either physically checking the identity of the vessel, or possibly sending an unmanned aircraft to perform the task. Similarly to Check-Spoofing information-aggregator, the Patrol information source is capable to determine whether the vessel is actively spoofing it's identity. It is of course possible that the two inferred valuations of the* isSpoofingID *variable do not match and the conflict needs to be resolved.*

Should the system indeed conclude that the vessel is spoofing its identity, it escalates to the highest-level information-aggregator CheckSmuggling *consulting the most expensive information sources and performing the deepest analysis of the vessel's background so as to assess its potential involvement in smuggling. The* TrackAnalyser *processor matches the vessel's kinematic track signature from the* Radar *sensor to the vessel type retrieved from* AIS. *Should the vessel turn out to be a suspect smuggler according to the* METIS*'s analysis, the valuation of* isSmuggling *information element is communicated to the system operator via a GUI warning. Note, all the involved agents assume a domain of the underlying database extended with enumerations of possible identities, etc. and can also produce the unknown valuation ∅ for each of their output variables.*

2.2 Environment

An information-aggregation system, such as METIS, is situated in a dynamic environment which changes over time. It reads values from it, monitors it, and derives nontrivial information on the basis of the collected evidence. We model an environment as a database schema $\mathcal{E}$ over crisp truth values $\{\top, \bot\}$.

A system $\mathcal{S} = (\mathcal{A}, \mathcal{D})$ can be embedded in an environment $\mathcal{E}$ when the two database schemas coincide in exactly the variables produced by the information-source agents of $\mathcal{S}$. That is, each variable $x \in out_A$ of an agent $A \in \mathcal{A}$ with $in_A = \emptyset$ is included in the environment too, i.e., $x \in \mathcal{E} \cap \mathcal{D}$ and we denote $\mathcal{D}_{in}^{\mathcal{E}} = \mathcal{E} \cap \mathcal{D}$. A variable $x \in \mathcal{D}_{in}^{\mathcal{E}}$ in a database snapshot D of $\mathcal{S}$ *reflects* the state of the environment E iff $D|x \neq \emptyset$ implies $D|x = E|x$. We say that the system $\mathcal{S}$ is *embedded* in E iff computations of all the information-source agents reflect the state of the environment. That is, for all $A \in \mathcal{A}$ with $in_A = \emptyset$ all variables from out_A in the snapshot $A(D)$ reflect E.

The dynamics of the environment is captured by its evolution over time modelled as a (possibly infinite) sequence of database snapshots $\lambda_{\mathcal{E}} = E_0, \ldots, E_k, \ldots$ To ensure correspondence between an evolution $\lambda_{\mathcal{E}}$ of the environment $\mathcal{E}$ and an evolution $\lambda_{\mathcal{D}} = D_0, \ldots, D_l, \ldots$ of a system $\mathcal{S} = (\mathcal{A}, \mathcal{D})$ embedded in $\mathcal{E}$, we require that there exists a sequence of indices $i_0, \ldots, i_m, \ldots \in \mathbb{N}_0$, such that the variables from $\mathcal{D}_{in}^{\mathcal{E}}$ in D_i with $i \in i_j \ldots (i_{j+1} - 1)$ reflect the environment state E_j for $j \geq 0$. That is, at every timepoint, the system is embedded in the current state of the environment.

METIS 3 (evolution example) *A configuration capable to produce the system evolution depicted in Figure 2 could include the agents* AIS, FairPlay, CheckDefault, Radar *and* TrackAnalyser *executed subsequently in that order up to the database snapshot D_4. In the 5th evolution step, the* AIS *agent would produce an unknown valuation ∅ for the* aisID *variable due to a failure to retrieve a crisp information from the environment (e.g., due to a failure of the vessel's AIS transmitter). Subsequently the* CheckDefault *agent would have to produce ∅ also for the* isSuspectID *variable too as one of its inputs is ∅. The total cost of execution of this configuration would be 3420. The environment of the system evolves in a sequence E_0, E_1, E_2 and its changes are reflected in the evolution of the system's database snapshots.*

3 Configuration and Reconfiguration Problems

Assessments of a surveillance information-aggregation systems like METIS could have real-world repercussions. For instance, after deriving that a vessel could be a smuggling

D_0, E_0	D_1	D_2	D_3, E_1	D_4	D_5, E_2	D_6
$aisID^{\mathcal{E}}$	$aisID$	$aisID$	$aisID^{\mathcal{E}}$	$aisID$		
$aisType^{\mathcal{E}}$	$aisType$	$aisType$	$aisType^{\mathcal{E}}$	$aisType$	$aisType^{\mathcal{E}}$	$aisType$
	$fpID$	$fpID$	$fpID$	$fpID$	$fpID$	$fpID$
		$isSuspectID$	$isSuspectID$	$isSuspectID$	$isSuspectID$	
			$track^{\mathcal{E}}$	$track$	$track^{\mathcal{E}}$	$track$
				$isSuspectType$	$isSuspectType$	$isSuspectType$

Fig. 2. An example evolution of the METIS system database. Only variables valued $\top$ are listed. The variables marked $\mathcal{E}$ are read from the corresponding environment update.

suspect, a warning would be indicated to the operator, who might then consider contacting the vessel himself, possibly even sending a patrol to the location. Such actions, however, need to be *justified* in the operational scenario. In consequence, any crisp conclusion computed by the system must be explainable and defensible by inspecting the structure of inferences from basic evidence in the environment. In turn, we are interested in system configurations, which can either crisply answer distinguished queries, such as suspicion of smuggling, or, if that is not possible, the operator needs to be sure that there is no such configuration given the current state of the environment and the system's implementation. In the following, we implicitly assumes that the system is embedded in an environment state reflected in its current (initial) database snapshot.

Problem 1 (configuration problem). Given a tuple $\mathfrak{C} = (\mathcal{S}, \phi, D)$, with $\mathcal{S} = (\mathcal{A}, \mathcal{D}, cost)$ being an information-aggregation system, $\phi \in \mathcal{D}$ a query variable, and D being an initial snapshot of $\mathcal{D}$, the *information-aggregation system configuration problem* is to find a normal configuration C, a solution to $\mathfrak{C}$, such that all evolutions of $\mathcal{S}$ rooted in D stabilise in the snapshot $C^*(D)$ and C satisfies the following:

1. $\phi \in out_C$, i.e., C contains at least one agent $A \in C$ capable to derive ϕ. The resulting *query solution* is a valuation $C^*(D)|\phi$ computed by the configuration C;
2. for each variable $x \in in_C$, we have $x \in out_C$ and $C^*(D)|x \neq \varnothing$; and finally
3. there is no configuration C' with $C \subset C'$ satisfying 1 and 2, such that $C'^*(D)|\phi \neq C^*(D)|\phi$. In that sense, C is maximal.

We say that a configuration C is an *optimal* solution to the reconfiguration problem $\mathfrak{C}$ iff $cost(C)$ is minimal among the solutions of $\mathfrak{C}$.

Condition 1 of the definition above stipulates that the solution configuration indeed provides a valuation of the query, although this can still be valued as unknown $\varnothing$. Condition 2 formalizes the intuition that the query solution can be traced back to the evidence from the environment and computations of a series of crisp variable valuations by the individual agents of the system, that is a justification for the query solution. While theoretically it would acceptable to base computations of a crisp conclusions on unknown valuations of input variables for the interpretation of $\varnothing$ *value existent, but unknown*, it wouldn't be so for inferences based on *no information* valuations. In the former case, the interpretation would behave rather as a kind of a crisp valuation. Consequently, without loss of generality we assume interpretation of $\varnothing$ to equal *no information*. Finally, condition 3 ensures that there is no doubt about the computed query solution.

A solution to configuration problem does not always exist. Consider for instance a system including two agents deriving conflicting values for the same variable, or cyclically dependent agents. In such situations, the system evolution could oscillate and never stabilise. In Section 4 we identify a class of information-aggregation systems for which existence of a solution is always ensured.

Through information-source agents, a dynamic environment serves as the main driver of change within the system. Situating the configuration problem into a changing environment, repeated configuration becomes a means for continuous adaptation of the system to the updates coming from its environment.

Problem 2 (reconfiguration problem). Given a tuple $\mathfrak{R} = (\lambda_{\mathcal{E}}, \mathcal{S}, \phi)$, where $\lambda_{\mathcal{E}} = E_0, \ldots, E_k, \ldots$ is an evolution of an environment $\mathcal{E}$, $\mathcal{S} = (\mathcal{A}, \mathcal{D}, cost)$ is a information aggregation system embedded in $\mathcal{E}$, and $\phi \in \mathcal{D}$ is a query variable, the *information-aggregation reconfiguration problem* is a search for a sequence of configurations $C_0, \ldots, C_l, \ldots$, a solution to $\mathfrak{R}$, such that each C_i is a solution to the configuration problem $\mathfrak{C}_i = (\mathcal{S}, \phi, D_i)$ for $i > 0$, where $D_i = C_{i-1}^*(D_{i-1}) \oplus E_i | \mathcal{D}_{in}^{\mathcal{E}}$ and $D_0 = D_\varnothing \oplus E_0 | \mathcal{D}_{in}^{\mathcal{E}}$. We say that a sequence of configurations $C_0, \ldots, C_l, \ldots$ is a *weak solution* to $\mathfrak{R}$, iff C_i is a solution to $\mathfrak{C}_i = (\mathcal{S}, \phi, D_i)$ if it exists and can be arbitrary otherwise.

Informally, a reconfiguration problem solution is a sequence of configurations producing a database evolution reflecting the changes of the system's environment. The sequence of configurations in a weak solution to the reconfiguration problem captures the intuition that the system tries its best to compute a query solution upon each environment update, which, however, not always exists.

METIS 4 (configuration) *Consider the* METIS *prototype scenario introduced in the previous expositions. An example configuration problem could be* $\mathfrak{C} = (\mathcal{S}_{\text{METIS}}, isSmuggling, D_3)$. *As stated, there is no solution to* $\mathfrak{C}$ *as it is not possible to determine whether the vessel is possibly spoofing it's identity (isSpoofingID) and in turn also whether it is a smuggling suspect (isSmuggling). A solution would exist for a configuration problem over a database including crisp valuations for all the variables produced by information-source agents. Furthermore, the output of the* **Patrol** *agent would have to match that of* **CheckSpoofing** *aggregator. In that case, the solution to* $\mathfrak{C}$ *would comprise all the agents of the system. There would also exist solutions for configuration problems over databases in which the* **Patrol** *information-source produces an unknown for the isSpoofingID variable, but* **CheckSpoofing** *aggregator derives a crisp valuation for it, or vice versa.*

4   Solving Configuration and Reconfiguration Problems

The individual agents of an information-aggregation system perform inference over valuations of their input variables, premises, and thus provide support to the output variables, conclusions. In turn, Dung's theory of abstract argumentation [2] provides a natural model of computation of information-aggregation systems. Here, we propose an approach to solving (re-)configuration problems rooted in sceptical semantics of argumentation. The terminology introduced below is adapted from [2].

Let $S = (A, D)$ be a system and D be a database snapshot of D. We construct a *configuration argumentation framework* $CAF = \langle A, \prec \rangle$ associated with S over D.

Arguments correspond to information-processing agents A and embody a set of interrelations among variables of the schema D. The input variables in_A provide the basis for inferring the conclusions out_A of the argument $A \in A$. We say that an argument is *valid* w.r.t. a database snapshot D iff $A(D|in_A) \subseteq D$ and for all variables $x \in in_A$, we have $D|x \neq \varnothing$. Informally, a valid argument is supported by a given database snapshot in that the input/output characteristics of the internal computation of the agent is truthfully reflected in the database. From now on, we will use the notions of an argument and an agent interchangeably according to the context.

We say that valid argument $A \in A$ *attacks* another argument $A' \in A$ denoted $A' \prec A$, on a variable $x \in out_A \cap out_{A'}$ w.r.t. a given database snapshot D iff $A(D|in_A)|x \neq \varnothing$ and $A(D|in_A)|x \neq A'(D|in_{A'})|x$. That is, the agent A derives a crisp valuation for x which disagrees with the one derived by the agent A'. We also say that A is a *counterargument* to A', or that A is *controversial*. Finally, an argument $A \in A$ attacks a set of arguments $C \subseteq A$ iff there exists $A' \in C$ attacked by A.

Note, the attack relation is defined only for valid arguments supporting their conclusions by crisp valuation of their input. The conclusion, however, does not necessarily need to be crisp itself. Also, the attack relation is not symmetric in that a valid argument supporting a crisp conclusion can attack an argument providing unknown valuation to the same conclusion, but not *vice versa*.

Consider a fixed argumentation framework CAF associated with a system $S = (A, D)$ over a database D. A configuration C is said to be *conflict-free* if there are no agents $A, B \in C$, such that A attacks B w.r.t. CAF. A valid argument $A \in A$ (agent) is *acceptable* to C iff for each $A' \in A$ in the case A' attacks A, then there exists another argument A'' in C, such that A' is attacked by A'' all w.r.t. the database snapshot D.

In security-related information-aggregation systems, such as METIS, computed assessments need to be justified in order to preserve presumption of innocence of the monitored entities. That is, the resulting crisp valuation must be traceable to and justifiable by the evidence coming from the environment. Reasoning of such a systems is sceptical in that only conclusions which the system is sure about can be inferred, given the environment evidence and the system's design. The notion of a grounded extension of an argumentation framework based on a fix-point semantics captures this intuition.

A *grounded extension* of an argumentation framework $CAF = \langle A, \prec \rangle$, denoted GE_{CAF}, is the least fix-point of its *characteristic function* $F_{CAF} : 2^A \to 2^A$ defined as $F_{CAF}(C) = \{A \mid A \in A \text{ is acceptable to } C\}$. GE_{CAF} is *admissible*, i.e., all agents in GE_{CAF} are also acceptable to GE_{CAF} over D, and *complete*, i.e., all agents which are acceptable to GE_{CAF}, also belong to it.

A grounded extension of CAF_C always exists and F_{CAF} is monotonous with respect to set inclusion. In general, an argumentation framework can have multiple grounded extensions, a property undesirable to security-related systems, where assessments should be unambiguous. Dung in [2] shows that argumentation frameworks without infinite chains of arguments $A_1, \ldots, A_n, \ldots$, such that for each i, A_{i+1} attacks A_i, have a unique grounded extension. A way to ensure that property is to consider only *stratified* systems. That is those, for which there exists a stratification, a decomposition into a sequence of *strata* (layers) $\mathfrak{A} = \mathfrak{A}_0, \ldots, \mathfrak{A}_k$, where $\mathfrak{A}_0 = \{A \in \mathcal{A} \mid in_A = \emptyset\}$ and $\mathfrak{A}_i = \{A \in \mathcal{A} \mid in_A \subseteq out_{\bigcup_{j=1..i-1} \mathfrak{A}_j}\}$ for all $i = 1..k$. We say that $\mathfrak{A}$ is the *most compact* stratification of S iff all agents belong the lowest possible layer of $\mathfrak{A}$. Formally, for all stratifications $\mathfrak{A}'$ of S, $A \in \mathfrak{A}_i$ implies $A \in \mathfrak{A}'_j$ with $j \geq i$.

The following proposition establishes the correspondence between solutions to configuration problems for stratified systems and grounded extensions of their configuration argumentation frameworks.

Proposition 1. *Let $\mathfrak{C} = (S, \phi, D)$ be a configuration problem with a stratified system S. Let $C = GE_{\mathfrak{C}}$ be the grounded extension of $CAF_{\mathfrak{C}}$, an argumentation framework associated with S over the database $C^*(D)$. If $\phi \in out_C$, then C is a solution to $\mathfrak{C}$.*

Proof. Let $\mathfrak{A}$ be the most compact stratification of S and let F_{CAF}^i denote the i-th iteration of F_{CAF}, with $F_{CAF}^0 = F_{CAF}(\emptyset)$. Firstly, we show that iteration of F_{CAF} preserves the condition 2 of Problem 1, namely that for each $x \in in_{F_{CAF}^i}$, also $x \in out_{F_{CAF}^i}$ and $C^*(D)|x \neq \emptyset$. The proof proceeds by induction on layers of S.

Initial step: By necessity, $\mathfrak{A}_0$ includes only information-source agents. In turn, $F_{CAF}^0 \subseteq \mathfrak{A}_0$ excludes only those agents, for which there exists a counter-argument (agent) in $\mathfrak{A}_0$. Since $in_{F_{CAF}^0} = \emptyset$, the property is trivially satisfied.

Induction step: Let the property be satisfied for all F_{CAF}^i with $i = 0..k$. $F_{CAF}^{k+1} = F_{CAF}(F_{CAF}^k)$. Firstly, observe that $F_{CAF}^i \setminus F_{CAF}^{i-1} \subseteq \mathfrak{A}_i$ for every i. If that were not the case, there would be an agent A from a higher layer, input of which is computed by agents in the lower layers, or it would belong to a lower stratum. The former cannot be the case since $\mathfrak{A}$ is the most compact stratification of S, since each agent is at its lowest stratum possible. Similarly, the latter can't happen either, since it would be considered for acceptance already in earlier iterations of F_{CAF}. Now either $F_{CAF}^k = F_{CAF}^{k-1}$, the fix-point, and the property is trivially satisfied, or $F_{CAF}^k = F_{CAF}^{k-1} \cup C^k$. In that case, we need to show that for each $A \in C^k$, $in_A \subseteq out_{F_{CAF}^{k-1}}$ and all valuations $C^*(D)|in_A$ are crisp. But since $C^k \subseteq \mathfrak{A}_k$, due to the definition of stratification we have $in_A \subseteq out_{F_{CAF}^{k-1}}$. Finally, each $A \in C^k$ is acceptable to F_{CAF}^{k-1}, hence it also must be valid and in turn all its input variables are crisp.

To conclude, C is a fix-point of F_{CAF}, hence the maximality condition 3 in Problem 1 is straightforwardly satisfied too. Finally, due to the antecedent of Proposition we have that the query ϕ is included in C, hence *C is a solution of $\mathfrak{C}$*.

Proposition 1 can be applied to static databases only. Note, execution of agents considered for acceptance to a candidate solution does not modify the database fragment computed in previous iterations, which also remains stable in further computation. In turn, a naive configuration algorithm utilising Proposition 1 would iteratively proceed in three steps. In the i-th iteration it would i) execute all the agents from stratum $\mathfrak{A}_i$ of the most compact stratification of S, ii) select the non-controversial ones, and finally iii) add them to the candidate solution. To ensure non-validity of arguments from higher strata that utilise controversial inputs derived in this iteration, these should be set to $\emptyset$.

The naive algorithm, while correctly computing a solution to a given configuration problem, is rather inefficient in terms of the overall run-time cost. It targets computation of a grounded extension of the whole framework, instead of only answering the query of the given configuration problem. Firstly, in the initial iteration the algorithm considers and executes all information-source agents. Besides that, it potentially executes also information-processing agents, which do not contribute to answering the query. In both cases it incurs unnecessary run-time cost. In fact, only arguments relevant to derivation of the configuration problem query need to be considered.

Let $S = (\mathcal{A}, \mathcal{D})$ be a stratified system and $\phi \in \mathcal{D}$ be a query. The *agents relevant to* ϕ include $\mathcal{A}_\phi(\emptyset) = \{A \in \mathcal{A} \mid \phi \in out_A\}$. Given a set of agents C relevant to ϕ, all the agents computing the input for those in C are relevant to ϕ too, i.e., $\mathcal{A}_\phi(C) = \{A \in \mathcal{A} \mid out_A \subseteq in_C\}$. The set of all agents relevant to ϕ is the (unique) fix-point of $\mathcal{A}_\phi(\emptyset)$ denoted $\mathcal{A}_\phi^*$. The following proposition formalizes the intuition.

Proposition 2. *Let* $\mathfrak{C} = (S, \phi, D)$, $CAF_\mathfrak{C}$ *and* $GE_\mathfrak{C}$ *be as in Proposition 1. If* $\phi \in out_C$, *then* $C \cap \mathcal{A}_\phi^*$ *is the minimal optimal solution to* $\mathfrak{C}$.

Furthermore, the naive algorithm does not terminate early enough, but rather computes the grounded extension to its full extent, despite the fact that in the course of its computation it might turn out that the query is either derived in a justified manner, or that its computation is hopeless. The former is relatively easy to detect. After all the agents relevant to ϕ were considered for inclusion to the candidate solution, further computation will consider only irrelevant arguments. To detect the latter case, we need to closely inspect the current candidate solution with respect to the interdependencies among the agents of the system. Given a configuration C, let $\overline{\mathcal{A}_\phi}^*(C)$ be the fix-point of the operator $\overline{\mathcal{A}_\phi}(C) = C \cup \{A \in \mathcal{A}_\phi \mid in_A \subseteq out_C \text{ and } in_A \neq \emptyset\}$. $\overline{\mathcal{A}_\phi}^*$ is complementary to $\mathcal{A}_\phi$ in that given a configuration C, it collects all agents dependent solely on the output of C. Consequently, $\overline{\mathcal{A}_\phi}^*(F_{CAF}(C))$ contains C, together with all the arguments which can be still eventually considered for accepting to the candidate solution in future iterations of F_{CAF}. In the case $\phi \in out_{\overline{\mathcal{A}_\phi}^*(C)}$ ceases to hold during computation, the algorithm can terminate, since none of the arguments capable to compute the query solution can be added to C in the future. The following proposition formalizes the relationship between the operator and the structure of the grounded extension.

Proposition 3. *Let* $\mathfrak{C} = (S, \phi, D)$, $CAF_\mathfrak{C}$ *and* $GE_\mathfrak{C}$ *be as in Proposition 1. We have,* $\phi \in out_{GE_\mathfrak{C}}$ *if and only if* $\phi \in out_{\overline{\mathcal{A}_\phi}^*(F_{CAF}(C))}$ *for every* $C \subseteq GE_\mathfrak{C}$.

Finally, the naive algorithm considers arguments for accepting to the candidate solution in sets, subsets of system layers. Considering arguments for acceptance one by one would facilitate even earlier detection of hopeless computations and thus further reduction of run-time costs. It could even consider arguments across strata, however, in that case, in line with the sceptical inference strategy, the accepted arguments can only use input variables which are a part of the already stabilised fragment of the database. An alternative definition of (safe) acceptability of an argument A a conflict-free configuration C is when all its input variables are i) crisply valued, ii) already derived by C, and iii) there are no argument outside of C which can potentially threat the valuations of its input variables. More formally, an argument A is *safely acceptable* to a conflict-free configuration C iff i) there is no $x \in in_A$ with $D|x = \emptyset$, ii) $in_A \subseteq out_C$, and iii) there is no $A' \in \mathcal{A} \setminus C$, such that $in_A \cap out_{A'} \neq \emptyset$. Evaluation of this alternative definition

---

Algorithm 1. Algorithm computing weak-solutions to a reconfiguration problem

---

Require: $\mathfrak{R} = (\lambda_{\mathcal{E}}, \mathcal{S}, \phi)$ with environment evolution $\lambda_{\mathcal{E}} = E_0, \ldots, E_k, \ldots$, a stratified system $\mathcal{S} = (\mathcal{A}, \mathcal{D}, cost)$ and a query $\phi \in \mathcal{D}$

1: $C \leftarrow \emptyset; D = D_\varnothing$
2: **loop** (start with $j = 0$)
3:     $D_\oplus \leftarrow$ the next environment update $E_j | \mathcal{D}_{in}^{\mathcal{E}}$
4:     $(C, D) \leftarrow$ CONFIGURE$(C, D \oplus D_\oplus)$
5:     **if** $\phi \in out_C$ **then** inform operator about ϕ and $D|\phi$
6: **end loop** (increment j)

7: **function** CONFIGURE(C, D) ▷ *returns* $(Configuration, Database)$
8:     $C \leftarrow C \cap F_{CAF}^*(\emptyset)$
9:     **loop**
10:         $C_{acc} \leftarrow \{A \in \mathcal{A}_\phi^* \setminus C \mid A$ is safely acceptable to $C\}$
11:         **if** $C_{acc} = \emptyset$ or $\phi \notin out_{\overline{\mathcal{A}_\phi}^*(C \cup C_{acc})}$ **then return** (C, D)
12:         $A_{min} \leftarrow \arg\min_{A \in C_{acc}} cost(A)$
13:         $D \leftarrow A_{min}(D)$ if $D|in_{A_{min}}$ changed since the last execution of A_{min}
14:         **if** A_{min} attacks $\{A'_1, \ldots, A'_k\} \subseteq C$ **then**
15:             $C \leftarrow C \setminus \{A'_1, \ldots, A'_k\}$ and set all $D|x$ on which A_{min} attacks some A'_i to $\varnothing$
16:         **else** $C \leftarrow C \cup \{A_{min}\}$
17:     **end loop**
18: **end function**

---

of acceptability does not require execution of the agent A and thus can be used in the context of an evolving database, as is the case in METIS.

Algorithm 1 provides a pseudocode for continuous reconfiguration of information-aggregation systems based on the principles embodied in the above analysis. Upon every environment update, in a step j, the algorithm tries to compute the minimal solution to the current configuration problem. Either it succeeds and informs the operator about the query solution, or detects that a solution can't be computed and proceeds. Function CONFIGURE computes the grounded extension of the current configuration problem $\mathfrak{C}_i = (\mathcal{S}, \phi, D \oplus E_i | \mathcal{D}_{in}^{\mathcal{E}})$ restricted to the arguments relevant to ϕ and considers potentially acceptable arguments individually in a greedy manner according to the cost of their execution.

Given a configuration, without executing the agents, the algorithm strips C of all arguments which might need reconsideration (line 8) due to the last environment update (line 4), or because they depend on such arguments. Starting from an empty candidate solution C, in every iteration, the algorithm firstly identifies among the arguments relevant to ϕ (Proposition 2) those potentially acceptable to C (line 10). Before considering their execution, it checks whether a solution can still be computed and should this not be the case, it terminates the procedure. To detect the condition, it exploits the principles presented in Proposition 3. Further, the algorithm selects the cheapest potentially acceptable information-processing agent A_{min} (line 12) and executes it (line 13). In the case A_{min} does not attack the current candidate solution C (line 14), it is accepted to C (line 16). Otherwise, the arguments attacked by A_{min} were previously accepted to C

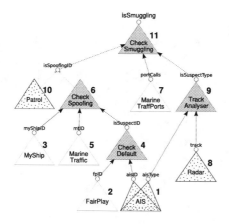

Fig. 3. Ordering of information-aggregation agents as considered by Algorithm 1

prematurely and thus need to be removed. We also need to set the variables on which they disagree to $\varnothing$ so as to ensure that all agents dependent on controversial valuations will be deemed non-valid in the future iterations (line 8). To further reduce the costs incurred by the algorithm, we assume that each agent keeps track of changes to its input, so the algorithm executes it only in the case its re-execution is really needed (line 13).

Algorithm 1 is greedy, in that it always selects the cheapest agent to accept. Hence, although the solutions it computes are optimal it does not always incur the minimal possible run-time cost in terms of the cost of execution of the individual agents. The optimal strategy of selecting the next agent to execute is most likely application-domain dependent.

METIS 5 (configuration) *Consider the example configuration problem* $\mathfrak{C} = (\mathcal{S}_{\text{METIS}},$ *isSmuggling*, $D_\varnothing$)*. In order to compute a solution to the problem, assuming that all the agents produce crisp valuations for their output variables upon their execution, in subsequent iterations Algorithm 1 would execute the agents as depicted in Figure 3. Noteworthy, in step 8, the cheapest agent to consider is the* **TrackAnalyser***, but the algorithm is forced to choose the* **Radar** *agent as that is the cheapest and, unlike* **Track-Analyser***, safely acceptable at the same time. For illustration of detection of hopelessness of configuration computation, consider the agent* **MarineTraffPorts** *producing an unknown valuation for portCalls variable in step 7. The algorithm would immediately detect (line 11) that isSmuggling variable is not computable any more and would stop the computation.*

5   Final Remarks and Outlook

As of spring 2013, the METIS prototype, fragment of which is described here, was implemented and delivered. Figure 4 provides a screenshot of the operator's view in the prototype. It shows several vessels (circular glyphs) in a selected monitored coastal area with indication of the most likely values of their selected attributes. The pop-up

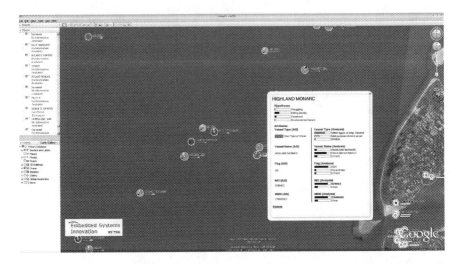

Fig. 4. METIS system screenshot. The background map imagery, courtesy of © 2013 *Google*, © 2013 *Aerodata International Surveys, Data SIO, NOAA, U.S. Navy, NGA* and *GEBCO*.

inspection window shows the likelihoods of the vessel satisfying the target indicators, such as suspicion of a smuggling intent. In the system, the relative size of the vessel glyph corresponds to the cost of the system configuration instantiated for the vessel.

Above, we introduced a formal framework for modelling information-aggregation systems, such as METIS, providing a basis for a rigorous formulation of (re-)configuration problems. We argue that sceptical semantics of argumentation is a natural fit for modelling such systems and paves the way for further study of their properties, as well as development of algorithms for their continuous adaptation on a solid basis of the existing body of research in argumentation theory and logic programming. In our future work we intend to explore these relationships, specifically to study cost- and information-age-constrained reconfiguration of METIS, as well as the relationship of the introduced approach to computation of well-founded models for logic programs [3]. The dynamic nature of the system also invites to study links between their evolution and standard results from theories of evolving knowledge bases (e.g., [9]), logic program updates, belief revision, etc.

Acknowledgements. This work was supported by the Dutch national program COMMIT. The research was carried out as a part of the METIS project under the responsibility of the *TNO-Embedded Systems Innovation*, with *Thales Nederland B.V.* as the carrying industrial partner.

References

1. Automatic Identification System (April 2013),
   http://en.wikipedia.org/wiki/Automatic_Identification_System
2. Dung, P.M.: On the acceptability of arguments and its fundamental role in nonmonotonic reasoning, logic programming and n-person games. Artif. Intell. 77(2), 321–358 (1995)

3. Van Gelder, A., Ross, K.A., Schlipf, J.S.: The well-founded semantics for general logic programs. J. ACM 38(3), 620–650 (1991)
4. Hendriks, T., van de Laar, P.: Metis: Dependable cooperative systems for public safety. Procedia Computer Science 16(0), 542–551 (2013)
5. IHS. IHS Fairplay Bespoke Maritime Data Services (April 2013),
   http://www.ihs.com/products/maritime-information/data/
6. TNO Embedded Systems Innovation. METIS project (April 2013),
   http://www.esi.nl/research/applied-research/
   current-projects/metis/
7. Jamshidi, M.: System of systems engineering - New challenges for the 21st century. IEEE Aerospace and Electronic Systems Magazine 23(5), 4–19 (2008)
8. Klein, H.-J.: Null values in relational databases and sure information answers. In: Bertossi, L., Katona, G.O.H., Schewe, K.-D., Thalheim, B. (eds.) Semantics in Databases 2001. LNCS, vol. 2582, pp. 119–138. Springer, Heidelberg (2003)
9. Leite, J.A.: Evolving Knowledge Bases. Frontiers of Artificial Intelligence and Applications, vol. 81. IOS Press (2003)
10. Maltenoz Limited. MarineTraffic.com (April 2013),
    http://www.marinetraffic.com/
11. MyShip.com. MyShip.com – Mates, Ships, Agencies (April 2013),
    http://myship.com/

An Argumentation-Based Approach
for Automatic Evaluation of Design Debates

Pietro Baroni[1], Marco Romano[1], Francesca Toni[2],
Marco Aurisicchio[2], and Giorgio Bertanza[1]

[1] Università degli Studi di Brescia, Italy
{pietro.baroni,giorgio.bertanza}@ing.unibs.it, marcojulioromano@gmail.com
http://www.unibs.it
[2] Imperial College London, UK
{m.aurisicchio,f.toni}@imperial.ac.uk
http://www.imperial.ac.uk

Abstract. This paper presents a novel argumentation framework to support design debates in an IBIS-based style, by providing an automatic evaluation of the positions put forwards in the debates. It also describes the integration of the proposed approach within the design-VUE software tool along with two case studies in engineering design and their initial evaluation by domain experts.

Keywords: argumentation, design rationale, IBIS.

Engineering design is often described as an information-processing activity based on problem solving within the constraints of bounded rationality [23,22]. It consists of decomposing an initial problem into a range of sub-problems, proposing and assessing partial solutions, and integrating them in a way that they satisfy the overall problem. This process is collaborative and often involves communication between non co-located engineers. The development and communication of design solutions require engineers to form and share their rationale, i.e. the argumentation in favour or against proposed designs.

These aspects of the engineering design process have led to the development of the *Issue Based Information System* (IBIS) method [16], a graph-based formalisation of the decisions made during a design process along with the reasons why they were made. The IBIS method envisions a decision-making process where problems (or issues) are given solutions (or answers) after a thorough debate involving technical, economical, and ethical considerations. It also provides a means to actively develop, communicate and record the argumentation and reasoning behind the design process.

Initially, IBIS has been conceived purely as conceptual information system and its first implementations were paper-based and totally operated by hand. However, over time several software tools have been developed, which provide a means to edit and visualise IBIS graphs [6,3]. One such tool is designVUE [1], an open-source software developed by the Design Engineering Group of the Mechanical Engineering Department at Imperial College London. These tools, including

J. Leite et al. (Eds.): CLIMA XIV, LNAI 8143, pp. 340–356, 2013.
© Springer-Verlag Berlin Heidelberg 2013

designVUE, still leave to the users the burden of actually deriving any conclusion from the argumentative process and, eventually, making a decision. This is a task that, depending on the structure of the graph, may not be trivial.

This paper describes the outcome of a collaborative project, involving experts of *engineering design* and *argumentation theory*, undertaken to overcome the limitation of standard design tools in general, and designVUE in particular. The ultimate goal of this project is to support engineers by providing them with an automated evaluation of alternative design solutions, and quickly identifying the most promising answer to a design issue, given the underlying graph structure developed during the design process.

We have singled out argumentation theory as a promising companion to engineering design towards achieving this goal since one of the main features thereof is evaluating arguments' acceptability (e.g. as in [10,9]) or strength (e.g. as in [8,18,17,12]) within debates and dialogues. For this application area, conventional notions of "binary" acceptability (e.g. the notions in [10]), sanctioning arguments as acceptable or not, are better replaced with notions of numerical strength, as the latter are more fine-grained and allow to distinguish different degrees of acceptability.

This paper presents theoretical and practical results from this project. On the theoretical side, we propose a formal method to assign a numerical score to the nodes of an IBIS graph, starting from a base score provided by users. On the practical side, we describe the implementation of this method within designVUE and its preliminary evaluation in the context of two case studies.

The paper is organised as follows. Section 1 gives the basic notions concerning IBIS and the necessary background on argumentation theory. Section 2 introduces a form of argumentation frameworks abstracting away IBIS graphs and Section 3 defines our approach for evalutating quantitatively arguments in these frameworks. Section 4 describes an implementation of our approach as an extension of designVUE and Section 5 illustrates its application in two engineering domains. Section 6 discusses related work and Section 7 concludes.

1   Background

1.1   Issue Based Information System (IBIS)

IBIS [16] is about proposing answers to issues, and assessing them through arguments. At the simplest level, the IBIS method consists of a structure that can be represented as a directed acyclic graph with four types of node: an *issue* node represents a problem being discussed, namely a question in need of an answer; an *answer* node represents a candidate solution to an issue; a *pro-argument* node represents an approval to a given answer or to another argument; a *con-argument* node represents an objection to a given answer or to another argument. An answer node is always linked to an issue node, whereas pro-argument and con-argument nodes are normally linked to answer nodes or to another argument. Each link is directed, pointing towards the dependent node.

Figure 1 shows an example of IBIS graph, with a concrete illustration of the content of the nodes (labelled A1, A2, P1, C1 and C2) in the design domain of Internal Combustion Engines (ICE). This example graph has three layers: the first layer consists of the issue node, the second layer of the two alternative answers, and the third layer of the arguments.

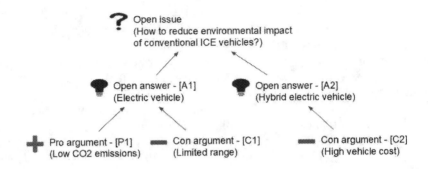

Fig. 1. A simple IBIS graph

An IBIS graph is constructed according to the following rules: (1) an issue is captured; (2) answers are laid out and linked to the issue; (3) arguments are laid out and linked to either the answers or other arguments; (4) further issues may emerge during the process and be linked to either the answers or the arguments.

Conceptually, each addition of an answer or an argument corresponds to a move in the exploration of the design space. In the design domain, IBIS graphs have specific features. First, each IBIS graph concerns a single issue. Second, answers correspond to alternative solutions and compete among them as just one answer can be accepted for an issue.

In some implementations of the IBIS method, the four nodes can have alternative statuses to help users visualise aspects of the decision making process. The precise meaning of these statuses depends on the node type, and is manually assigned by the users. For example, a designer may change the status of an answer from "open" to "accepted", "likely" or "unlikely". In this paper we define a method for automatically, rather than manually, evaluating nodes in (restricted kinds of) IBIS graphs, based on a form of argumentation theory, reviewed next.

1.2   Abstract Argumentation and Argument Valuations

In this work we will make use of Abstract Argumentation [10] and some extensions thereof. We review these briefly here (see the original papers for more details).

Definition 1. *A (finite) abstract argumentation framework (AF) is a pair $\langle \mathcal{X}, \mathcal{D} \rangle$, where $\mathcal{X}$ is a finite set of arguments and $\mathcal{D} \subseteq \mathcal{X} \times \mathcal{X}$ is the attack (or defeat) relation. A pair $\langle x, y \rangle \in \mathcal{D}$ is referred to as 'x is an attacker (or defeater) of y'.*

An AF can be described as a directed graph whose nodes represent arguments and whose edges represent attacks. The nature and underlying structure of the arguments are completely abstracted away and the focus of the theory is essentially on the management of the conflicts represented by the attack relation. In this context an *(argumentation) semantics* is a criterion to identify the *extensions* of an AF, namely those sets of arguments which can "survive the conflict together". In turn, the *justification status* of an argument, according to a given semantics, can be defined in terms of its membership to the extensions prescribed by the semantics. A variety of semantics have been considered in the literature, whose review is beyond the scope of this paper (see [4] for a survey). The only point we remark is that these semantics evaluate arguments based on a binary notion of membership and thus give rise to a discrete set of justification statuses, which may be appropriate when arguments, e.g., are interpreted as logical sentences in a reasoning process, but may be unsuitable in other contexts.

While AFs are focused on conflicts between arguments, other forms of arguments interaction can be considered, in particular a relation of support, which can be incorporated into AFs to give rise to bipolar AFs [9]:

Definition 2. *A (finite) bipolar* AF *(BAF) is a triple* $\langle \mathcal{X}, \mathcal{D}, \mathcal{S} \rangle$, *where* $\langle \mathcal{X}, \mathcal{D} \rangle$ *is a (finite)* AF *and* $\mathcal{S} \subseteq \mathcal{X} \times \mathcal{X}$ *is the support relation. A pair* $\langle x, y \rangle \in \mathcal{S}$ *is referred to as 'x is a supporter of y'.*

The discrete argument evaluation for AFs can be extended to BAFs (see [9]).

Another direction of enhancement of AFs amounts to assigning a numerical evaluation to arguments on a continuous scale. We recall here two proposals in this direction. The first gives a notion of local gradual valuation of a BAF, that can be summarised as follows (see [8] for details):

Definition 3. *Let L be a completely ordered set, L^* be the set of all the finite sequences of elements of L (including the empty sequence), and H_{def} and H_{sup} be two ordered sets. Let $\langle \mathcal{X}, \mathcal{D}, \mathcal{S} \rangle$ be a BAF. Then, a local gradual valuation on $\langle \mathcal{X}, \mathcal{D}, \mathcal{S} \rangle$ is a function $v : \mathcal{X} \rightarrow L$ such that, for a generic argument $a \in \mathcal{X}$, given $\mathcal{D}^-(a) = \{d_1, \ldots, d_n\}$ the set of attackers of a and $\mathcal{S}^-(a) = \{s_1, \ldots, s_p\}$ the set of supporters of a (for $n, p \geq 0$):*
$$v(a) = g(h_{sup}(v(s_1), \ldots, v(s_p)), h_{def}(v(d_1), \ldots, v(d_n)))$$
where $g : H_{sup} \times H_{def} \rightarrow L$ is a function with $g(x, y)$ increasing on x and decreasing on y, and $h_{def} : L^* \rightarrow H_{def}/h_{sup} : L^* \rightarrow H_{sup}$ are functions (valuing the quality of the defeat/support, respectively) satisfying for any $x_1, \ldots, x_n, x_{n+1}$ (here $h = h_{def}$ or h_{sup}): (i) if $x_i \geq x_{i'}$ then $h(x_1, \ldots, x_i, \ldots, x_n) \geq h(x_1, \ldots, x_{i'}, \ldots, x_n)$; (ii) $h(x_1, \ldots, x_n) \leq h(x_1, \ldots, x_n, x_{n+1})$; (iii) $h() \leq h(x_1, \ldots, x_n)$; (iv) $h(x_1, \ldots, x_n)$ is bounded by a limit value β.

Note that the local gradual valuation (LGV in the remainder) of an argument is defined recursively in terms of the valuations of its attackers and supporters.

The second proposal we consider is the Extended Social Abstract Argumentation approach of [12], taking into account, in addition to attackers and supporters, also positive or negative votes on arguments. In a nutshell, the idea is that in a social context (like an Internet-based social network or debate) opinions (arguments) are evaluated by a community of users through a voting process.

Definition 4. *An* Extended Social Abstract Argumentation Framework *(*ESAAF*) is a 4-tuple* $\langle \mathcal{X}, \mathcal{D}, \mathcal{S}, \mathcal{V} \rangle$ *where* $\langle \mathcal{X}, \mathcal{D}, \mathcal{S} \rangle$ *is a (finite)* BAF *and* $\mathcal{V} : \mathcal{X} \to \mathbb{N} \times \mathbb{N}$ *is a function mapping arguments to the number of their positive and negative votes.*

Given an (acyclic) ESAAF, argument evaluation is based on votes and on the attack/support relations. It involves a set of operators (called Semantic Framework) extending the operators of [17], where only attackers were considered:

Definition 5. *A semantic framework is a 7-tuple* $\langle L, \tau, \wedge, \vee, \neg, \odot, \uplus \rangle$ *where* L *is a completely ordered set,* $\tau : \mathbb{N} \times \mathbb{N} \to L$, $\wedge : L \times L \to L$, $\vee : L \times L \to L$, $\neg : L \to L$, $\odot : L \times L \to L$, $\uplus : L \times L \to L$. *Given an* ESAAF $\langle \mathcal{X}, \mathcal{D}, \mathcal{S}, \mathcal{V} \rangle$ *and a semantic framework* $\langle L, \tau, \wedge, \vee, \neg, \odot, \uplus \rangle$, *the valuation of argument* $a \in \mathcal{X}$ *is:*
$$M^+(a) = (\tau(a) \wedge \neg \vee \{M^+a_i : (a_i, a) \in \mathcal{D}\}) \uplus (\tau(a) \odot \vee \{M^+a_i : (a_i, a) \in \mathcal{S}\})$$

Omitting details, informally, the operator τ evaluates the social support for each argument a, based on its accumulated positive and negative votes (given by $\mathcal{V}$), and so assigns an *initial score*, $\tau(a)$, to a. This initial score has no counterpart in LGV seen earlier. Then, as in the case of LGV, the valuation of a is defined recursively in terms of the valuations of its attackers and supporters. The individual valuations of the attackers and of the supporters of a are first aggregated using the $\vee$ operator. Then the aggregated valuations of the attackers and supporters are combined with $\tau(a)$ using the $\wedge$ and $\neg$ operators and the $\odot$ operator respectively. This results in a pair of values which roughly corresponds to the pair $h_{sup}(v(s_1), \ldots, v(s_p)), h_{def}(v(d_1), \ldots, v(d_n))$ in LGV, the main difference being the fact that $\tau(a)$ can be regarded as an additional parameter of these functions. Finally, the $\uplus$ operator maps the above pair of values in a single final evaluation (and so clearly corresponds to the function g in LGV).

2 Quantitative Argumentation Debate Frameworks

In section 1.1 we have seen that design scenarios require IBIS graphs with specific features, and in particular with a single specific (design) issue and answers (linking to that issue) corresponding to different alternative solutions. Whereas IBIS graphs (in general and in design contexts) allow new issues to be brought up during the argumentation, in this paper for simplicity we will disallow this possibility, and focus on design debates that can be represented by IBIS graphs where arguments can only be pointed to by other arguments, although argument nodes may have other argument nodes as children, recursively.

We will define, in Section 3, a method for evaluating arguments and answers in IBIS graphs, and accompanying or replacing the manual evaluation available in some IBIS implementations (see Section 1.1). Examining some design scenarios with the relevant experts (see also Section 5) it emerged that, in their valuations, they typically ascribe different importance to pro- and con-arguments, which entails that a *base score* is required as a starting point for the evaluation. In order to fulfil these requirements, we propose a formal framework as follows:

Definition 6. *A* QuAD (Quantitative Argumentation Debate) *framework is a 5-tuple* $\langle \mathcal{A}, \mathcal{C}, \mathcal{P}, \mathcal{R}, \mathcal{BS} \rangle$ *such that (for scale* $\mathbb{I}=[0,1]$*):*
  $\mathcal{A}$ *is a finite set of* answer arguments*;*
  $\mathcal{C}$ *is a finite set of* con-arguments*;*
  $\mathcal{P}$ *is a finite set of* pro-arguments*;*
  the sets $\mathcal{A}$*,* $\mathcal{C}$*, and* $\mathcal{P}$ *are pairwise disjoint;*
  $\mathcal{R} \subseteq (\mathcal{C} \cup \mathcal{P}) \times (\mathcal{A} \cup \mathcal{C} \cup \mathcal{P})$ *is an acyclic binary relation;*
  $\mathcal{BS} : (\mathcal{A} \cup \mathcal{C} \cup \mathcal{P}) \to \mathbb{I}$ *is a total function;* $\mathcal{BS}(a)$ *is the* base score *of a.*

The framework is referred to as "quantitative" due to the presence of the base score. Ignoring this base score, clearly QuAD graphs are abstractions of (restricted forms of) IBIS graphs, with the issue node omitted since QuAD frameworks are focused on the evaluation of answer nodes for a specific issue. For example, the QuAD graph representation of the IBIS graph in Figure 1 has $\mathcal{A} = \{A1, A2\}$, $\mathcal{C} = \{C1, C2\}$, $\mathcal{P} = \{P1\}$ and $\mathcal{R} = \{(P1, A1), (C1, A1), (C2, A2)\}$.

It is easy to see that a QuAD framework can also be interpreted as a BAF (again ignoring the base score), as notions of attack and support are embedded in the disjoint sets $\mathcal{C}$ and $\mathcal{P}$. This is made explicit by the following definition.

Definition 7. *Let* $\mathcal{F} = \langle \mathcal{A}, \mathcal{C}, \mathcal{P}, \mathcal{R}, \mathcal{BS} \rangle$ *be a QuAD framework and let* $a \in (\mathcal{A} \cup \mathcal{C} \cup \mathcal{P})$*. The set of* direct attackers *of a is defined as* $\mathcal{R}^-(a) = \{b \in \mathcal{C} : (b, a) \in \mathcal{R}\}$*. The set of* direct supporters *of a is defined as* $\mathcal{R}^+(a) = \{b \in \mathcal{P} : (b, a) \in \mathcal{R}\}$*. Then, the* BAF *corresponding to* $\mathcal{F}$ *is* $\langle \mathcal{X}, \mathcal{D}, \mathcal{S} \rangle$ *such that:*
$\mathcal{X} = \mathcal{A} \cup \mathcal{C} \cup \mathcal{P}$*,* $\mathcal{D} = \{(b, a) | b \in \mathcal{R}^-(a), a \in \mathcal{X}\}$*,* $\mathcal{S} = \{(b, a) | b \in \mathcal{R}^+(a), a \in \mathcal{X}\}$*.*

Note that an ESAAF equipped with a semantic framework can give rise to a QuAD framework, with the base score in the QuAD framework given by the initial score τ in the semantic framework for the ESAAF. The semantic framework includes however a recipe for calculating the initial score of arguments, based on votes in the ESAAF, whereas our QuAD framework assumes that the base score is given. Indeed, differently from the application contexts envisaged for ESAAF, design debates do not involve large community of users so the notion of a base score based on votes is not appropriate, rather the base score can be represented as a numerical value directly assessed by experts.

3 Automatic Evaluation in QuAD Frameworks

Given a QuAD framework, in order to support the decision making process by design engineers we need a method to assign a quantitative evaluation, called *final score*, to answer nodes. To this purpose we investigate the definition of a *score function* $\mathcal{SF}$ for arguments of a QuAD framework. The basic idea is that the final score of an argument depends on its base score and on the final scores of its attackers and supporters, so $\mathcal{SF}$ is defined recursively using a *score operator* able to combine these three elements. For a generic argument a, let $(a_1, \ldots, a_n)$ be an arbitrary permutation of the $(n \geq 0)$ attackers in $\mathcal{R}^-(a)$. We denote as $\mathcal{SC}(\mathcal{R}^-(a)) = (\mathcal{SF}(a_1), \ldots, \mathcal{SF}(a_n))$ the corresponding sequence of final scores. Similarly, letting $(b_1, \ldots, b_m)$ be an arbitrary permutation of the $(m \geq 0)$ supporters in $\mathcal{R}^+(a)$, we denote as $\mathcal{SC}(\mathcal{R}^+(a)) = (\mathcal{SF}(b_1), \ldots, \mathcal{SF}(b_m))$ the corresponding sequence of final scores. Then, using the hypothesis (implicitly adopted both in [8] and [12]) of separability of the evaluations concerning attackers and supporters,[1] a generic score function for an argument a can be defined as:

$$\mathcal{SF}(a) = g(\mathcal{BS}(a), \mathcal{F}_{att}(\mathcal{BS}(a), \mathcal{SC}(\mathcal{R}^-(a))), \mathcal{F}_{supp}(\mathcal{BS}(a), \mathcal{SC}(\mathcal{R}^+(a)))) \quad (1)$$

Referring to the example of Figure 1, suppose that $\mathcal{BS}(A1) = \mathcal{BS}(A2) = 0.5$, $\mathcal{BS}(C1) = 0.7$, $\mathcal{BS}(C2) = 0.4$, $\mathcal{BS}(P1) = 0.9$. Then, denoting the empty sequence as $()$, we obtain

$$\mathcal{SF}(A1) = g(0.5, \mathcal{F}_{att}(0.5, \mathcal{SC}((C1))), \mathcal{F}_{supp}(0.5, \mathcal{SC}((P1))));$$
$$\mathcal{SF}(A2) = g(0.5, \mathcal{F}_{att}(0.5, \mathcal{SC}((C2))), \mathcal{F}_{supp}(0.5, ()));$$
$$\mathcal{SF}(C1) = g(0.7, (), ()); \quad \mathcal{SF}(C2) = g(0.4, (), ()); \quad \mathcal{SF}(P1) = g(0.9, (), ()).$$

We identify some basic requirements for the score function. First, if there are neither attackers nor supporters for an argument then its final evaluation must coincide with the base score (in our running example this applies to arguments $C1$, $C2$, and $P1$). For any $v_0 \in \mathbb{I}$, this requirement can be expressed as

$$g(v_0, (), ()) = v_0. \quad (2)$$

Moreover, each attacker (supporter) should have a negative or null (positive or null, respectively) effect on the final scores. Given a generic sequence $S = (s_1, \ldots, s_k) \in \mathbb{I}^k$ and $v \in \mathbb{I}$, let us denote as $S \cup (v)$ the sequence $(s_1, \ldots, s_k, v) \in \mathbb{I}^{k+1}$. The above requirements can then be expressed, for sequences S_1, S_2, as

$$g(v_0, \mathcal{F}_{att}(S_1), \mathcal{F}_{supp}(S_2)) \geq g(v_0, \mathcal{F}_{att}(S_1 \cup (v)), \mathcal{F}_{supp}(S_2)) \quad (3)$$
$$g(v_0, \mathcal{F}_{att}(S_1), \mathcal{F}_{supp}(S_2)) \leq g(v_0, \mathcal{F}_{att}(S_1), \mathcal{F}_{supp}(S_2 \cup (v))) \quad (4)$$

We define $\mathcal{F}_{att}$ (and dually $\mathcal{F}_{supp}$) so that the contribution of an attacker (supporter) to the score of an argument decreases (increases) the argument score by an amount proportional both to (i) the score of the attacker (supporter), i.e. a strong attacker (supporter) has more effect than a weaker one, and (ii) to the previous score of the argument itself, i.e. an already strong argument benefits quantitatively less from a support than a weak one and an already weak argument suffers quantitatively less from an attack than a stronger one. Focusing on the case of a single attacker (supporter) with score v this leads to the following base expressions:[2]

$$f_{att}(v_0, v) = v_0 - v_0 \cdot v = v_0 \cdot (1 - v) \quad (5)$$
$$f_{supp}(v_0, v) = v_0 + (1 - v_0) \cdot v = v_0 + v - v_0 \cdot v \quad (6)$$

---

[1] Here, separability amounts to absence of interaction between attackers and supporters.

[2] The expression of f_{supp} corresponds to the T-conorm operator also referred to as *probabilistic sum* in the literature [15].

The definitions of $\mathcal{F}_{att}$ and $\mathcal{F}_{supp}$ have then the same recursive form. Let $*$ stand for either att or $supp$. Then:

$$\mathcal{F}_*(v_0, ()) = v_0 \tag{7}$$

$$\mathcal{F}_*(v_0, (v)) = f_*(v_0, v) \tag{8}$$

$$\mathcal{F}_*(v_0, (v_1, \ldots, v_n)) = f_*(\mathcal{F}_*(v_0, (v_1, \ldots, v_{n-1})), v_n) \tag{9}$$

Note that this definition directly entails that $\mathcal{F}_{att}(v_0, S) \geq \mathcal{F}_{att}(v_0, S \cup (v))$ and $\mathcal{F}_{supp}(v_0, S) \leq \mathcal{F}_{supp}(v_0, S \cup (v))$. In our running example, we get

$\mathcal{F}_{att}(0.5, \mathcal{SC}((C1))) = \mathcal{F}_{att}(0.5, (0.7)) = f_{att}(0.5, 0.7) = 0.15,$
$\mathcal{F}_{supp}(0.5, \mathcal{SC}((P1))) = \mathcal{F}_{supp}(0.5, (0.9)) = f_{supp}(0.5, 0.9) = 0.95,$
$\mathcal{F}_{att}(0.5, \mathcal{SC}((C2))) = \mathcal{F}_{att}(0.5, (0.4)) = f_{att}(0.5, 0.4) = 0.3,$ and
$\mathcal{F}_{supp}(0.5, ()) = 0.5.$

We now establish some basic properties of $\mathcal{F}_{att}$ and $\mathcal{F}_{supp}$. First, they return values in $\mathbb{I} = [0, 1]$, as required:

Proposition 1. *For any $v_0 \in \mathbb{I}$ and for any sequence $(v_1, \ldots, v_k) \in \mathbb{I}^k$, $k \geq 0$, $\mathcal{F}_{att}(v_0, (v_1, \ldots, v_k)) \in \mathbb{I}$ and $\mathcal{F}_{supp}(v_0, (v_1, \ldots, v_k)) \in \mathbb{I}$.*

Proof. By induction on k. For the base case, trivially the statement holds for $k = 0$ (empty sequence) and $k = 1$ given the definitions of f_{att} and f_{supp}. Assume that the statement holds for a generic sequence of length $k - 1$, i.e. $\mathcal{F}_{att}(v_0, (v_1, \ldots, v_{k-1})) = v_x \in \mathbb{I}$ then, from (9), $\mathcal{F}_{att}(v_0, (v_1, \ldots, v_k)) = f_{att}(v_x, v_k)$. Similarly, letting $\mathcal{F}_{supp}(v_0, (v_1, \ldots, v_{k-1})) = v_y \in \mathbb{I}$ we get $\mathcal{F}_{supp}(v_0, (v_1, \ldots, v_k)) = f_{supp}(v_y, v_k)$. Then, again the statement holds by definition of f_{att} and f_{supp}.

Then, it is of course required that $\mathcal{F}_{att}$ and $\mathcal{F}_{supp}$ produce the same result for any permutation of the same sequence.

Proposition 2. *For any $v_0 \in \mathbb{I}$ and $(v_1, \ldots, v_k) \in \mathbb{I}^k$, $k \geq 0$, let $(v_{1_i}, \ldots, v_{k_i})$ be an arbitrary permutation of $(v_1, \ldots, v_k)$. It holds that $\mathcal{F}_{att}(v_0, (v_1, \ldots, v_k)) = \mathcal{F}_{att}(v_0, (v_{1_i}, \ldots, v_{k_i}))$ and $\mathcal{F}_{supp}(v_0, (v_1, \ldots, v_k)) = \mathcal{F}_{supp}(v_0, (v_{1_i}, \ldots, v_{k_i}))$.*

Proof. $\mathcal{F}_{att}(v_0, (v_1, \ldots, v_k)) = f_{att}(f_{att}(\ldots f_{att}(v_0, v_1)\ldots), v_{k-1}), v_k) = (((v_0 \cdot (1 - v_1)) \cdot (1 - v_2)) \ldots \cdot (1 - v_k)) = v_0 \cdot \prod_{i=1}^{k}(1 - v_i)$. Thus the statement follows directly from commutativity and associativity of the product of the $(1 - v_i)$ factors. As to $\mathcal{F}_{supp}$, $\mathcal{F}_{supp}(v_0, (v_1, \ldots, v_k)) = f_{supp}(f_{supp}(\ldots f_{supp}(v_0, v_1)\ldots), v_{k-1}), v_k)$, the statement follows from the well-known properties of commutativity and associativity of any T-conorm.

Another desirable property of $\mathcal{F}_{att}$ and $\mathcal{F}_{supp}$ is a sort of monotonic behavior with respect to the increasing score of attackers and supporters respectively.

Proposition 3. *For any $v_0 \in \mathbb{I}$ and for any $S = (v_1, \ldots, v_h, \ldots, v_k) \in \mathbb{I}^k$, $k \geq 1$, $1 \leq h \leq k$, let S^+ be a sequence obtained from S by replacing v_h with some $v_l > v_h$. Then $\mathcal{F}_{att}(v_0, S) \geq \mathcal{F}_{att}(v_0, S^+)$ and $\mathcal{F}_{supp}(v_0, S) \leq \mathcal{F}_{supp}(v_0, S^+)$.*

Proof. As to $\mathcal{F}_{att}$ given that for a generic sequence $\mathcal{F}_{att}(v_0, (v_1, \ldots, v_k)) = v_0 \cdot \prod_{i=1}^{k}(1 - v_i)$, we observe that $\mathcal{F}_{att}(v_0, S^+) = \mathcal{F}_{att}(v_0, S) \cdot \frac{1-v_l}{1-v_h}$ and the statement follows from $0 \leq 1 - v_l < 1 - v_h$. As to $\mathcal{F}_{supp}$, from commutativity and associativity of f_{supp}, letting $S^* = (v_1, \ldots, v_{h-1}, v_{h+1}, \ldots, v_k) \in \mathbb{I}^{k-1}$, we get $\mathcal{F}_{supp}(v_0, S) = f_{supp}(\mathcal{F}_{supp}(v_0, S^*), v_h)$ and $\mathcal{F}_{supp}(v_0, S^+) = f_{supp}(\mathcal{F}_{supp}(v_0, S^*), v_l)$ and the statement follows from the well-known monotonicity of T-conorms.

In order to finalise the definition of score function we need to define g. For this we adopted the idea that when the effect of attackers is null (i.e. the base score is left unchanged as far as attackers are concerned) the final score must coincide with the one established on the basis of supporters, and dually when the effect of supporters is null. Clearly, when both are null the final score must coincide with the base score. When both attackers and supporters have an effect, the final score is obtained averaging the two contributions. Formally:

Definition 8. *The operator* $g : \mathbb{I} \times \mathbb{I} \times \mathbb{I} \to \mathbb{I}$ *is defined as follows:*

$$g(v_0, v_a, v_s) = v_a \, if \, v_s = v_0 \tag{10}$$

$$g(v_0, v_a, v_s) = v_s \, if \, v_a = v_0 \tag{11}$$

$$g(v_0, v_a, v_s) = \frac{(v_a + v_s)}{2} \, otherwise \tag{12}$$

Then, the following result directly follows from Propositions 1–3:

Proposition 4. *The score function* $\mathcal{SF}(a)$ *defined by equations (1), (7), (8) and (9) and by Definition 8 satifies properties (2), (3), and (4).*

For our running example, we get $\mathcal{SF}(A1) = g(0.5, 0.15, 0.95) = 0.55$ and $\mathcal{SF}(A2) = g(0.5, 0.3, 0.5) = 0.3$.

Note that, by definition of our operator g, the addition of an attack (support) for an argument previously not attacked (supported, respectively) gives rise to a discontinuity. This in a sense reflects a discontinuity in the underlying debate. Whether this behaviour is suitable in all contexts is an open question, and the definition of different forms of $\mathcal{SF}$ without this discontinuity is an importnat direction for future work.

On the computational side, given that in a QuAD framework the relation $\mathcal{R}$ is acyclic, evaluating $\mathcal{SF}$ for answers nodes (in fact, for any node) is quite easy: given an argument a to be evaluated the score function is invoked recursively on its attackers and supporters to obtain $\mathcal{SC}(\mathcal{R}^-(a))$ and $\mathcal{SC}(\mathcal{R}^+(a))$ which are finally fed to the $\mathcal{SF}$ operator along with the base score $\mathcal{BS}(a)$. The recursion is well-founded given the acyclicity of $\mathcal{R}$, the base being provided by nodes with neither attackers nor supporters whose final score coincides with their base score.

4   Implementation in designVUE

The proposed approach has been implemented within a pre-existing IBIS application known as *design Visual Understanding Environment* (designVUE) [1].

designVUE has been chosen as a platform for the implementation of the proposed approach for various reasons: it is open-source; it has been developed by the Design Engineering Group at Imperial College London; it is receiving increasing interest from academia and industry and as a result has a growing user community. In the following paragraphs we describe in more detail designVUE and its extension with the QuAD framework.

designVUE is an application developed using Java to attain cross-platform portability. Its GUI consists primarily of a main window, which contains the menu bar, the toolbar and the graph canvas.

The main purpose of designVUE is to draw graphs (also referred to as diagrams and maps) mostly consisting of nodes (depicted as boxes) and links (depicted as arrows) among them. The programme does not impose any restriction on the way a graph can be drawn. It is up to the user to confer any meaning to a graph. Among the large variety of graphs that can be drawn, designVUE supports IBIS graphs. These have no special treatment in designVUE and, in particular, there is no support to the evaluation of the argumentative process. In addition to the main window, there are floating windows that can be opened from the *Windows* menu. One of these, called Info Window, presents information about the currently selected node.

The QuAD framework has been implemented in Java and integrated into a customised version of designVUE, forking its existing codebase. The additions and modifications brought to designVUE fit broadly in two categories: those related to the GUI; and those concerning the implementation of the score assignment method. As for the GUI:

- a new pane called *BaseScore Pane* has been added to the *Info Window*: it displays the base score of the currently selected IBIS node and allows the user to edit it (base scores are created with a default value of 0.5);
- a new pane called *Score Pane* has been added to *Info Window*: it displays the final score of the currently selected IBIS node;
- a new menu item labeled *Compute Argumentation on IBIS node* has been added to the *Content* menu: it can be invoked only after selecting an IBIS answer node and triggers the score computation for the selected node (and for all the nodes on which it depends).

As to the algorithm to compute final scores, it has been implemented in a Java class, which basically carries out a depth-first post-order traversal, which acts directly onto the IBIS nodes displayed in the canvas. To enhance performances in complex graphs where some pro and/or con arguments affect many other arguments, the algorithm implements a so-called closed list in order to reuse the scores already computed in previous phases of the graph traversal.

5 Case Studies

The enhanced version of designVUE was evaluated through two case studies. The first, in the domain of civil engineering, concerns the choice of foundations for a multi-storey building to be developed on a brownfield. The second, in the domain of water engineering, focuses on the choice of a reuse technology for sludge produced by wastewater treatment plants.

The first case study was developed in collaboration with a civil engineer with more than ten years of experience in the industry, who was already familiar with the IBIS concept having used it through the Compendium software [6]. Differently, the second case study was developed together with an expert at the University of Brescia, who had neither previous knowledge of the IBIS concept, nor of any tool implementing it.

5.1   Foundations

This case study is based on a design task, which was selected to satisfy the following criteria: the design problem had to be well known to the industry; and the problem solving process had to rely on the application of known and established solution principles. On this basis the task presented in this case study can be considered to be at the boundary between adaptive and variant design [19]. The reason for choosing this type of design task is to adopt a *walk before you run* approach to evaluation.

The case is based on real project experience of the collaborating engineer. However, it was not developed during the actual design process but rather reconstructed retrospectively. Prior to the development of the case, the engineer was introduced to the enhanced version of designVUE and instructed to use it including inputting values for the base scores.

As mentioned earlier, the design problem focuses on the selection of the most appropriate type of foundation for a multi-storey building in a brownfield area. This is the part of urban planning concerning the re-use of abandoned or under-used industrial and commercial facilities. When considering the choice of building foundations in brownfield sites, multiple alternatives are common and multiple considerations have to be made starting from the different kinds of ground and their load bearing capabilities, which are usually different than in greenfield sites.

The starting point of the IBIS graph developed by the engineer is the issue to choose a suitable foundation given the requirements discussed earlier (see Figure 2). Three types of foundation solutions are considered, namely Pad, Raft and Piles, and these are subsequently evaluated using several pro- and con-arguments. After the development of the IBIS graph the engineer executed the score computation on the three solutions under two situations: 1) using default values for the base scores; and 2) using modified values for the base scores. The modified values for the base scores emerged through a three step process involving extraction of the criteria behind each argument (see text in bracket at the bottom of each argument in Figure 2), analysis of the relative importance of the criteria in the context of the selected design task, and assignment of a numerical value between 0 and 1 to each criteria.

The results for the situation with unchanged values indicate that Pad (0.51) is the preferred solution over Raft (0.49) and Piles (0.44). Differently, the results for the situation in which the values were changed suggest that Piles (0.56) is sligthly preferable to Raft (0.55) and considerably preferable to Pad (0.41). As it can be seen, the three alternatives are ranked exactly in the reverse order. Only the results based on the modified values for the base scores were judged by the expert consistent with his conclusions.

On one hand this confirms the importance of weighting pro- and con-arguments with expert-provided base scores in order to get meaningful results. On the other hand, it shows that a purely graphical representation of the pros and cons is typically insufficient to give an account of the reasons underlying the final choice by the experts. In this sense, representing and managing explicitly quantitative valuations enhances transparency and accountability of the decision process.

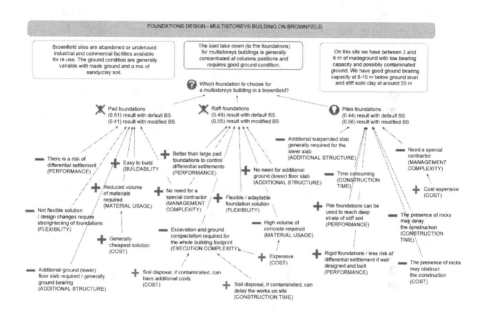

Fig. 2. designVUE graph of the foundation project debate. Note that in designVUE the answer node has multiple statuses. In agreement with the automatic evaluation, the status for the Pad and Raft foundation answers has been manually changed to 'rejected' (red crossed out light bulb icon), while that for the Piles foundation answer to 'accepted' (green light bulb icon).

5.2   Sludge Reuse

Sewage sludge is produced from the treatment of wastewater. Its traditional reuse option (alternative to landfill disposal) had been land application (due to its content of organic carbon and nutrients). Actually, reuse in agriculture is subject to restrictions (since the sludge also contains pollutants), so that other disposal routes, such as wet oxidation, reuse in the cement industry or energy recovery by combustion are considered as viable alternatives. The choice of the best alternative depends on technical (feasibility, applicability, reliability), economic, environmental and social factors whose importance varies from site to site. In this context, the use of the enhanced version of designVUE was proposed to an environmental engineering expert, who had no previous experience with any IBIS support tool.

As a first step, the expert provided a qualitative valuation scheme in tabular form that has been translated into a designVUE graph. Then the expert was asked to assign weights to the pro and con arguments associated with the different options and to compare the system's evaluation of the alternatives with his own one. As for the first request, the expert was able to assign weights to the pro and con arguments associated with each technology without particular problems. As to the second request, he observed that in this context technical experts are not in charge of the final decision since environment related projects are subjected to the approval of public officers or committees, who, taking into account context-specific aspects (e.g. social issues), may ascribe different importance to the technical considerations formulated by the expert. To properly represent this two-phase decision process within designVUE the expert suggested the use of a graph with a characteristic 2-tier structure (see figure 3), where:

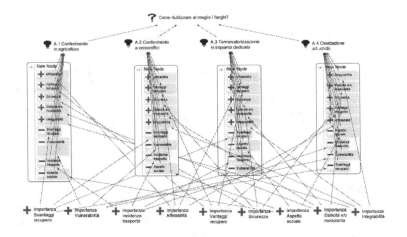

Fig. 3. designVUE graph for the second phase of the sludge reuse project debate. Note that the four answers are in the 'open' status (blue light bulb icon) as a decision has not been made yet.

- the first tier takes into account the technical strengths and weaknesses of every single alternative. These are the pro and con arguments directly linked with the answers, whose base scores are provided by domain experts.
- The second tier involves the final decision-makers and consists of pro arguments attached to the pros and cons expressed by the expert. By assigning the base scores to the arguments of the second tier, the decision-makers

modulate the actual influence of first tier arguments according to context specific considerations. The structure of the 2-tier graph is defined so as to ensure that the same factor gets the same weight in the assessment of all alternatives.

Following this line, designVUE can be used to support a multistep methodology taking explicitly into account different classes of stakeholders. While the study of this methodology is left to future work, the expert expressed a positive judgment about the tool, with particular appreciation for the intuitive visual representation and the traceability of the reasons underlying the final decisions.

6   Related Work

In engineering design, various methods are used to support the evaluation of design alternatives, e.g. decision-matrix [20] and analytic hierarchy process [21]. Among these, the decision-matrix, also known as Pugh method, is the simplest and most commonly adopted. It consists of ranking alternatives by identifying a set of evaluation criteria, weighting their importance, scoring the alternatives against each criteria, multiplying the scores by the weight, and computing the total score for each alternative. Our work differs from the Pugh method in that it aims to extract a quantitative evaluation of alternatives from rich and explicitly captured argumentation rather than systematically assigned and justified scores. Hence, it seems to have the potential to lead to more logically reasoned decisions.

Turning to argumentation literature, the idea of providing a quantitative evaluation of a given position on the basis of arguments in favor and against has been considered in several works.

In [5], in the context of a logic-based approach to argumentation, an argument structure for a logical formula α is (omitting some details) a collection of reasons supporting $(\neg)\alpha$. Each reason is represented as an argument tree, whose root is an argument for $(\neg)\alpha$ and where the children of an argument node are attackers of the node itself. Each argument tree is quantitatively evaluated using a *categoriser*. The results of the evaluation of argument trees for $(\neg)\alpha$ are aggregated separately using an *accumulator* function and then combined. Though this work shows several similarities with our approach at a generic level, we point out some important differences. In [5] the evaluation concerns logical formulas rather than arguments, arguments can only attack (not support) each other, while the notion of support for a formula coincides with the (defeasible) derivation of the formula. Then, differently from our approach, the recursive procedure corresponding to the categoriser concerns attacks only and the notion of support plays a role only in the accumulator. Also, in [5] there is no notion of base score.

The gradual valuation of BAFs [8] (see Section 1.2) is closer to our proposal. In fact, the generic valuation function v of BAFs (see Definition 3) has a similar structure to our $\mathcal{SF}$, with h_{sup}, h_{def} corresponding to our $\mathcal{SC}(\mathcal{R}^+(a))$, $\mathcal{SC}(\mathcal{R}^-(a))$ respectively and satisfying analogous properties. A basic difference concerns the base score, absent in [8] and crucial in our application domain.

The ESAAF approach of [12] (see Section 1.2) has more similarities, as it encompasses an initial score for arguments (obtained from votes) and a recursive evaluation mechanism similar to ours. In fact, the treatment we propose for attackers coincides with the one proposed in [12], while our proposal differs in the treatment of supporters: in [12] supporters are treated as a sort of "negative attacks", while in our approach supporters contribute to increase the base score specularly to the way attackers contribute to decrease it. As a consequence, in ESAAF the operator $\odot$ for the combination of the initial score with the aggregation of supporters' valuations includes the min operator to prevent that the combination exceeds the limit value of 1. This means that the contribution of supporters is subject to a saturation which may be undesirable in some cases.

The approach of [13] also features significant similarities with our proposal. In fact the notion of *real equational network* introduced in [13] uses an evaluation function $f(a)$ from the set of arguments to $[0, 1]$ which is defined recursively, for an argument a, as $f(a) = h_a(f(a_1), \ldots, f(a_k))$ where $a_1, \ldots, a_k$ are the attackers of a. [13] explores several alternatives for the function f with unrestricted graph topology (in the presence of cycles the solution is a fixed point of f) but no notion of base argument score is considered. Note that, assuming a fixed initial score of 1 for any argument, our $\mathcal{F}_{att}$ coincides with the function called $Eq_{inverse}$ in [13]. [13] considers also the presence of a support relation, but treated as a potential "vehicle" for attacks, in the sense that if an argument a supports another argument b, an attacker of a is also considered as an (indirect) attacker of b and contributes to decreasing its score. On the other hand a supporting argument cannot increase the score of the supported argument. This view is coherent with the absence of a base score and is clearly alternative to ours.

Other approaches to quantitative valuation have been proposed in the context of Dung's abstract argumentation where only the attack relation is encompassed. For example, [18] proposes a game-theoretic approach to evaluate argument strength in abstract argumentation frameworks. In a nutshell, the strength of an argument x is the value of a game of argumentation strategy played by the proponent of x. The approach does not encompass a support relations nor base scores: extending this game-theoretic perspective with these notions appears to be a significant direction of future investigation. Also, in weighted argumentation frameworks [11], real valued weights are assigned to attacks (rather than to arguments). These weights are not meant to be a basis for scoring arguments, rather they represent the "amount of inconsistency" carried by an attack. This use of weights is clearly different from ours and, in a sense, complementary. Investigating a combination of these two kinds of valuations (possibly considering also weights for support links) is a further interesting direction of future work.

Our system extends an existing IBIS-based tool, designVUE, already used in the engineering domain and in particular familiar to some of the experts responsible for our case studies. Other IBIS-based system exist in the literature. For example, Cohere and Compendium [7,6] adopt an IBIS methodology to support design rationale in collaborative settings. However, these systems do not incorporate means to automatically evaluate debates. Other examples are the Carneades [14] and the PARMENIDES [2] systems. These adopt a more articulate model of debate as they use argument schemes and critical questions as basic building blocks of the argumentation process. However, they do not incorporate a numerical evaluation of positions in debates. The extension of these other systems to take advantage of our scoring methodology is a possible direction of future work.

7   Conclusions

We presented a novel argumentation-based formal framework for quantitative assessment of design alternatives, its implementation in the designVUE software tool, and its preliminary experimentation in two case studies. Several directions of future work can be considered. On the theoretical side, a more extensive analysis of the properties of the proposed score function is under way, along with the study of alternative score functions exhibiting a different behavior (e.g. concerning the effect of attacks and supports and their balance) while satisfying the same basic requirements. On the implementation side, we plan to integrate the QuAD framework in the web-based debate system www.quaestio-it.com so to gain experience on its acceptability by users in other domains. On the experimentation side, the development of further engineering design case studies (more complex and in other domains) is under way and we intend to carry out a detailed on field comparison with more traditional approaches to the evaluation of design alternatives.

Acknowledgments. The authors thank V. Evripidou and E. Marfisi for their support and cooperation. Aurisicchio and Toni thank the support of a Faculty of Engineering EPSRC Internal Project on 'Engineering design knowledge capture and feedback'. The authors also thank the anonymous reviewers for their detailed and helpful comments.

References

1. designVUE (February 2013),
   http://www3.imperial.ac.uk/designengineering/tools/designvue
2. Atkinson, K., Bench-Capon, T.J.M., McBurney, P.: PARMENIDES: Facilitating deliberation in democracies. Artificial Intelligence and Law 14(4), 261–275 (2006)
3. Aurisicchio, M., Bracewell, R.H.: Capturing an integrated design information space with a diagram based approach. Journal of Engineering Design 24, 397–428 (2013)
4. Baroni, P., Caminada, M., Giacomin, M.: An introduction to argumentation semantics. Knowledge Eng. Review 26(4), 365–410 (2011)
5. Besnard, P., Hunter, A.: A logic-based theory of deductive arguments. Artificial Intelligence 128(1-2), 203–235 (2001)
6. Buckingham Shum, S.J., Selvin, A.M., Sierhuis, M., Conklin, J., Haley, C.B., Nuseibeh, B.: Hypermedia support for argumentation-based rationale: 15 years on from gIBIS and QOC. In: Dutoit, A.H., McCall, R., Mistrik, I., Paech, B. (eds.) Rationale Management in Software Engineering, pp. 111–132. Springer (2006)

7. Buckingham Shum, S.J.: Cohere: Towards web 2.0 argumentation. In: Besnard, P., Doutre, S., Hunter, A. (eds.) Computational Models of Argument: Proceedings of COMMA 2008, Toulouse, France, May 28-30. Frontiers in Artificial Intelligence and Applications, vol. 172, pp. 97–108. IOS Press (2008)

8. Cayrol, C., Lagasquie-Schiex, M.C.: Gradual valuation for bipolar argumentation frameworks. In: Godo, L. (ed.) ECSQARU 2005. LNCS (LNAI), vol. 3571, pp. 366–377. Springer, Heidelberg (2005)

9. Cayrol, C., Lagasquie-Schiex, M.C.: On the acceptability of arguments in bipolar argumentation frameworks. In: Godo, L. (ed.) ECSQARU 2005. LNCS (LNAI), vol. 3571, pp. 378–389. Springer, Heidelberg (2005)

10. Dung, P.M.: On the acceptability of arguments and its fundamental role in non-monotonic reasoning, logic programming and n-person games. Artificial Intelligence 77(2), 321–357 (1995)

11. Dunne, P.E., Hunter, A., McBurney, P., Parsons, S., Wooldridge, M.: Weighted argument systems: Basic definitions, algorithms, and complexity results. Artificial Intelligence 175(2), 457–486 (2011)

12. Evripidou, V., Toni, F.: Argumentation and voting for an intelligent user empowering business directory on the web. In: Proc. of the 6th Int. Conf. on Web Reasoning and Rule Systems (RR 2012), pp. 209–212 (2012)

13. Gabbay, D.M.: Equational approach to argumentation networks. Argument & Computation 3(2-3), 87–142 (2012)

14. Gordon, T.F., Walton, D.: The Carneades argumentation framework - using presumptions and exceptions to model critical questions. In: Dunne, P.E., Bench-Capon, T.J.M. (eds.) Computational Models of Argument: Proceedings of COMMA 2006, Liverpool, UK, September 11-12 (2006)

15. Klement, E.P., Mesiar, R., Pap, E.: Triangular Norms. Kluwer (2000)

16. Kunz, W., Rittel, H.: Issues as elements of information systems. Working Paper 131, Institute of Urban and Regional Development. University of California, Berkeley, California (1970)

17. Leite, J., Martins, J.: Social abstract argumentation. In: Proc. of the 22nd Int. Joint Conf. on Artificial Intelligence (IJCAI 2011), pp. 2287–2292 (2011)

18. Matt, P.-A., Toni, F.: A game-theoretic measure of argument strength for abstract argumentation. In: Hölldobler, S., Lutz, C., Wansing, H. (eds.) JELIA 2008. LNCS (LNAI), vol. 5293, pp. 285–297. Springer, Heidelberg (2008)

19. Pahl, G., Beitz, W.: Engineering design: a systematic approach. Tech. rep., Design Council, London, UK (1984)

20. Pugh, S.: Total Design: Integrated Methods for Successful Product Engineering. Addison-Wesley (1991)

21. Saaty, T.L.: The Analytic Hierarchy Process: Planning, Priority Setting, Resource Allocation. McGraw-Hill (1980)

22. Simon, H.A.: The Sciences of the Artificial, 3rd edn. The MIT Press (1996)

23. Simon, H.A., Newell, A.: Human problem solving: The state of the theory in 1970. American Psychologist 26(2), 145–159 (1971)

Risk Assessment as an Argumentation Game

Henry Prakken[1,2], Dan Ionita[3], and Roel Wieringa[3]

[1] Department of Information and Computing Sciences, Utrecht University,
Utrecht, The Netherlands
h.prakken@uu.nl
[2] Faculty of Law, University of Groningen, Groningen, The Netherlands
[3] Department of Computer Science, University of Twente, Enschede, The Netherlands
d.ionita@student.utwente.nl,r.j.wieringa@ewi.utwente.nl

Abstract. This paper explores the idea that IT security risk assessment can be
formalized as an argumentation game in which assessors argue about how the
system can be attacked by a threat agent and defended by the assessors. A system
architecture plus assumptions about the environment is specified as an $ASPIC^+$
argumentation theory, and an argument game is defined for exchanging arguments
between assessors and hypothetical threat agents about whether the specification
satisfies a given security requirement. Satisfaction is always partial and involves a
risk assessment of the assessors. The game is dynamic in that the players can both
add elements to and delete elements from the architecture specification. The game
is shown to respect the underlying argumentation logic in that for any logically
completed game 'won' by the defender, the security requirement is a justified
conclusion from the architecture specification at that stage of the game.

1 Introduction and Motivation

This paper explores the idea that IT security risk assessment can be formalized as an
argumentation game in which assessors alternate between playing the role of defenders
and attackers of the system, arguing how the system can be defended and attacked,
respectively. Our long-term goal is that such a formalization is used to develop tool
support for human assessors during a risk assessment, to keep track of the arguments for
and against a security architecture. Two characteristics of IT security risk assessment
(RA) as it happens in practice are that the time available for doing the assessment is
limited, and that the resources of the defender to protect a system, and of the attacker to
attack the system, are limited too. Assessors have limited, qualitative information about
the system, its vulnerabilities, and threats. In addition, malice and accident have to be
taken into account [5]. As a consequence, the information involved in risk assessments
is highly defeasible and cannot be easily quantified, which motivates an argumentation
approach to RA instead of, for example, Bayesian or model-checking approaches.

Some current risk assessment frameworks also provide tool support for security discussions, but they are mostly geared toward communication between the stakeholders
and the risk analysts or towards dissemination of the *results* of the risk assessments.
One example is the CORAS tool [8], which uses UML-based diagrams on top of which
several kinds of elements and relationships are defined as to allow a visual representation of the risk assessment. Their "risk diagrams" and "treatment diagrams" describe

J. Leite et al. (Eds.): CLIMA XIV, LNAI 8143, pp. 357–373, 2013.
© Springer-Verlag Berlin Heidelberg 2013

the possible attacks and mitigations that were discussed during the assessment. We ultimately also want to provide support for the *process* of RA, to keep track not only of the final output of an RA but also of the assumptions and design decisions that were made during the assessment. Another reason for supporting the process of RA is the limited time and resources available for the risk assessors. This puts constraints on the assessment process that call for efficient and effective assessment. For this reason we take a dialogue game approach, since dialogue systems for argumentation are recognised in the literature as a way to promote effective and efficient debate [7].

We also want to contribute to the literature by taking a formal but non-quantative approach. Current RA practice is fully informal and uses checklists to assess threats to a system. Current formalizations assume quantitative information, an assumption that is often not warranted. The only approach that uses argumentation, uses Toulmin argument diagrams and is still informal [4, 5]. By formalising the RA argumentation process in state-of the-art AI formalisms, we aim to give a precise semantics to the use of argumentation in RA and to make well-founded computational tools available for the support of the RA process.

In more detail, our idea is that an RA game starts with a defeasible argument by the defenders that the current system architecture is sufficient to guard against attacks; the argument is defeasible because it will make assumptions about the vulnerability of some system components and about capabilities, resources or risk appetite of attackers. In an attacker round, the (assessors playing the role of) attackers defeat some arguments of the (assessors playing the role of) defenders by attacking the defenders' assumptions, rebutting defeasible conclusions or by undercutting a defeasible inference made by the defender. After an attacker round, the architecture of the system may be changed by the defender to falsify some assumptions made by the attacker, and they may change their assumptions about the attackers. Then they will play the defender round again with the new system architecture, by renewing their argument for the security of the system. The renewed argument is still defeasible, for the same reasons as indicated above. The new argument may even contain parts of their old argument that have been undermined, undercut or rebutted by the attacker. This depends on the defenders' risk assessment and risk appetite. If there is time left, more attacker rounds, redesigns and defender's rounds are played. The game ends when time is up, and the goal is to end it in a state where the defenders estimate the arguments of the defense stronger than the arguments of the attackers, given the defender's assumptions about the environment and risk appetite.

Our primary goal in this paper is to test the feasibility of the idea of modelling risk assessment as an argumentation game by giving a first formalization. A special feature of our argumentation game is that the arguments are not simply constructed from a given theory, but that the theory is itself dynamically constructed during the RA: the players can add new elements to the theory (such as descriptions of system elements, preferences or assumptions about the environment) and they can also delete or change elements from the theory (for example, if the system specification has to be changed because of an attack that exposes a risk). This is what risk assessors do in practice and our game can therefore not just be a logical argument game for testing the acceptability status of an argument in a given information state, but must allow for changes in the information state. This is another reason why we take a dialogue game approach to

RA, since dialogue games allow for such dynamics. The logical part of the game will be an instantiation of the $ASPIC^+$ framework of [11, 15]. This choice is in order to profit from the logical consistency and closure properties of $ASPIC^+$ and since the application requires explicit preferences and defeasible rules. The dialogical part of our game combines the framework of [13, 14] with some new elements.

In Section 2 we present the logical background, in the form of an instantiation of the $ASPIC^+$ framework. In Section 3 we sketch how this instantiation can be used to specify an architecture and to express security risk assessment arguments. In Section 4 we present our formal dialogue game and prove a correspondence property with the underlying logic. In Section 5 we illustrate the game with an example, and we conclude with a discussion of related work and future research.

2   The Formal Setting

An *abstract argumentation framework* (AF) is a pair $\langle \mathcal{A}, defeat \rangle$, where $\mathcal{A}$ is a set arguments and $defeat \subseteq \mathcal{A} \times \mathcal{A}$ is a binary relation. The theory of AFs then addresses how sets of arguments (called *extensions*) can be identified which are internally coherent and defend themselves against defeat. A key notion here is that of an argument being *acceptable with respect to*, or *defended by* a set of arguments: $A \in \mathcal{A}$ is defended by $S \subseteq \mathcal{A}$ if for all $A \in S$: if $B \in \mathcal{A}$ attacks A, then some $C \in S$ attacks B. Then relative to a given AF various types of extensions can be defined. In this paper we focus on the grounded extension, which is defined as follows :

- $E \subseteq \mathcal{A}$ is the *grounded extension* if E is the least fixpoint of operator F, where $F(S)$ returns all arguments defended by S.

A proof procedure in the form of a logical argument game between a proponent and an opponent can be used to test whether a given argument is in the grounded extension. Informally, the proponent starts a game with the argument to be tested and then the players take turns, trying to defeat the previous move of the other player. In doing so, the proponent must strictly defeat the opponent's arguments. A game is terminated if the player to move has no arguments to play and a game is won by the player who moves last. Then an argument is proven to be justified if the proponent has a winning strategy for it, that is, if he can make the opponent run out of moves whatever choice the opponent makes. A winning strategy is in fact a tree with as root the argument to be tested and then at even depth all defeaters of the parent node while at odd depth one strict defeater of the parent node.

Our reason for using grounded semantics is that we want to build a logical argument game into our dialogue game for argumentation, since this is a natural way to make the outcome of an argumentation dialogue agree with the underlying logic. Since we ultimately intend to provide support tools for human risk assessors, the tool must be simple and intuitive, and grounded semantics has, as just explained, a particularly simple and intuitive logical argument game. However, in our future research we want to investigate generalisation to other semantics.

$ASPIC^+$ [11, 15] is a general framework for structured argumentation. It defines the notion of an *argumentation system*, which consists of a logical language $\mathcal{L}$ with a binary contrariness relation $^-$ and two sets of inference rules $\mathcal{R}_s$ and $\mathcal{R}_d$ of *strict* and *defeasible inference rules* defined over $\mathcal{L}$, written as $\varphi_1, \ldots, \varphi_n \rightarrow \varphi$ and $\varphi_1, \ldots,$ $\varphi_n \Rightarrow \varphi$. Informally, that an inference rule is strict means that if its antecedents are accepted, then its consequent must be accepted *no matter what*, while that an inference rule is defeasible means that if its antecedents are accepted, then its consequent must be accepted *if there are no good reasons not to accept it*. An argumentation system also contains a function n which for each defeasible rule in $\mathcal{R}_d$ returns a formula in $\mathcal{L}$. Informally, $n(r) \in \mathcal{L}$ expresses that $r \in \mathcal{R}$ is applicable.

In the present paper we assume argumentation systems in which $\mathcal{L}$ consists of first-order predicate-logic literals (i.e., atomic formulas or their negation) and its contrariness relation corresponds to classical negation, and in which the n function should be obvious from the examples.

$ASPIC^+$ arguments chain applications of the inference rules from AS into inference trees, starting with elements from a *knowledge base* $\mathcal{K}$. In this paper we assume that all premises are so-called *axiom premises*, that is, they are not attackable. In what follows, for any argument A, Prem returns all the formulas of $\mathcal{K}$ (*premises*) used to build A, Conc returns A's conclusion, Sub returns all of A's sub-arguments, Rules and DefRules respectively return all rules and all defeasible rules in A, and TopRule(A) returns the last rule applied in A.

Definition 1. *An ASPIC$^+$ argument A on the basis of a knowledge base $\mathcal{K}$ in an argumentation system $(\mathcal{L}, ^-, \mathcal{R}, n)$ is:*

1. φ *if* $\varphi \in \mathcal{K}$ *with:* Prem$(A) = \{\varphi\}$; Conc$(A) = \varphi$; Sub$(A) = \{\varphi\}$; Rules$(A) = \emptyset$; TopRule$(A) = undefined$.
2. $A_1, \ldots A_n \rightarrow/\Rightarrow \psi$ *if* $A_1, \ldots, A_n$ *are finite arguments such that there exists a strict/defeasible rule* Conc$(A_1), \ldots,$ Conc$(A_n) \rightarrow/\Rightarrow \psi$ *in* $\mathcal{R}_s/\mathcal{R}_d$.
   Prem$(A) =$ Prem$(A_1) \cup \ldots \cup$ Prem(A_n), Conc$(A) = \psi$,
   Sub$(A) =$ Sub$(A_1) \cup \ldots \cup$ Sub$(A_n) \cup \{A\}$.
   Rules$(A) =$ Rules$(A_1) \cup \ldots \cup$ Rules$(A_n) \cup \{$Conc$(A_1), \ldots,$ Conc$(A_n) \rightarrow/\Rightarrow \psi\}$,
   DefRules$(A) = \{r | r \in$ Rules$(A), r \in \mathcal{R}_d\}$,
   TopRule$(A) =$ Conc$(A_1), \ldots$ Conc$(A_n) \rightarrow/\Rightarrow \psi$

An argument A is strict *if* DefRules$(A) = \emptyset$ *and* defeasible *if* DefRules$(A) \neq \emptyset$.

Example 1. Consider a knowledge base in an argumentation system with

$\mathcal{R}_s = \{p, q \rightarrow s; \ u, v \rightarrow w\}, \mathcal{R}_d = \{p \Rightarrow t; \ s, r, t \Rightarrow v\}$
$\mathcal{K} = \{q, p, r, u\}$

An argument for w and its subarguments are written as follows:

$A_1: p \quad A_2: q \quad A_5: A_1 \Rightarrow t \qquad A_6: A_1, A_2 \rightarrow s$
$A_3: r \quad A_4: u \quad A_7: A_5, A_3, A_6 \Rightarrow v \quad A_8: A_7, A_4 \rightarrow w$

We have that

Prem$(A_8) = \{p, q, r, u\}$; Conc$(A_8) = w$
Sub$(A_8) = \{A_1, A_2, A_3, A_4, A_5, A_6, A_7, A_8\}$
DefRules$(A_8) = \{p \Rightarrow t; \ s, r, t \Rightarrow v\}$; TopRule$(A_8) = v, u \rightarrow w$

An argumentation system and a knowledge base are combined with an *argument ordering* into an *argumentation theory*. The argument ordering could be defined in any way. In this paper we assume a so-called last-link ordering defined in terms of a total preorder on $\mathcal{R}_d$. Informally, the last-link ordering compares arguments on their last-used defeasible rules. For the formal definition see [11].

Definition 2. *[Argumentation theories] An* argumentation theory *is a triple $AT = (AS, \mathcal{K}, \preceq)$ where AS is an argumentation system, $\mathcal{K}$ is a knowledge base in AS and $\preceq$ is the last-link ordering in the sense of [11] on the set of all arguments that can be constructed on the basis of $\mathcal{K}$ in AS, assuming a total preordering $\leq$ on $\mathcal{R}_d$. That $A \preceq B$ means that B is at least as preferred as A. The symbols $\prec$, $<$ and $\approx$ are defined as usual. All this is likewise for $\leq$.*

In the present instantiation of $ASPIC^+$ arguments can be attacked in two ways: by attacking a conclusion of a defeasible inference (rebutting attack) or by attacking the defeasible inference itself (undercutting attack). To define how a defeasible inference can be attacked, the function n of an AS can be used, which assigns to each element of $\mathcal{R}_d$ a well-formed formula in $\mathcal{L}$. Recall that informally, $n(r)$ (where $r \in \mathcal{R}_d$) means that r is applicable.[1]

Definition 3. *[attacks] A attacks B iff A undercuts or rebuts B, where:*

- *A undercuts argument B (on B') iff $\text{Conc}(A) = -n(r)$ for some $B' \in \text{Sub}(B)$ such that B''s top rule r is defeasible.*
- *A rebuts argument B (on B') iff $\text{Conc}(A) = -\varphi$ for some $B' \in \text{Sub}(B)$ of the form $B_1'', \ldots, B_n'' \Rightarrow \varphi$.*

Example 2. In Example 1 argument A_8 can be (indirectly) rebutted on its subargument A_5 with an argument for $\neg t$ and on its subargument A_7 with an argument for $\neg v$, because both A_5 and A_7 have a defeasible top rule. Whether these rebuttals are symmetric depends on whether the rebutting arguments use a strict or defeasible top rule. If the argument for $\neg t$ uses a defeasible top rule, then it is in turn rebutted by A_5; likewise, if the argument for $\neg v$ uses a defeasible top rule, then it is in turn rebutted by A_7. However, A_8 itself does not rebut these arguments for $\neg t$ and $\neg v$. Note that a direct rebuttal of A_5 indirectly rebuts not just A_8 but also A_7. Note also that A_8 cannot be rebutted (on A_8) with an argument for $\neg w$ or (on A_2) with an argument for $\neg s$, since both A_2 and A_8 have a strict top rule. For the same reason A_8 cannot be undercut on A_2 or A_8. It can be undercut, however, on its subarguments A_5 and A_7, with arguments for, respectively, the conclusions $\neg n(p \Rightarrow t)$ and $\neg n(s, r, t \Rightarrow v)$. Again, an undercutter of A_5 indirectly undercuts not just A_8 but also A_7.

Attacks combined with the preferences defined by an argument ordering yield two kinds of defeat.

Definition 4. *[Successful rebuttal and defeat]*

- *A successfully rebuts B if A rebuts B on B' and $A \not\prec B'$.*

---

[1] Henceforth $--\neg\varphi$ denotes φ, while if φ does not start with a negation, $-\varphi$ denotes $\neg\varphi$.

– *A defeats B iff A undercuts or successfully rebuts B.*

The success of rebutting attacks thus involves comparing the conflicting arguments at the points where they conflict. For undercutting attack no preferences are needed to make it succeed, since undercutters state exceptions to the rule they attack.

$ASPIC^+$ thus defines a set of arguments with a binary relation of defeat, that is, it defines abstract argumentation frameworks in the sense of [3]. Formally:

Definition 5. *[Argumentation framework] An* abstract argumentation framework (AF) corresponding to an argumentation theory AT is a pair $< \mathcal{A}$, Def> *such that:*

– $\mathcal{A}$ *is the set of arguments on the basis of AT as defined by Definition 1,*
– Def *is the relation on $\mathcal{A}$ given by Definition 4.*

Thus any semantics for abstract argumentation can be applied to $ASPIC^+$. As noted above, in this paper we will use grounded semantics. A formula φ from $\mathcal{L}$ is then *justified* on the basis of AT if the grounded extension of the AF corresponding to AT contains an argument with conclusion φ.

3   Architecture Specification in $ASPIC^+$

In this section we present a motivating example and describe how it can be formalized in terms of $ASPIC^+$.

3.1   An Example with a PIN Entry Device

Our running example is a design for a Pin Entry Device (PED) that can be used by merchants in shops and restaurants. Figure 1 shows the architecture of a fixed PED,

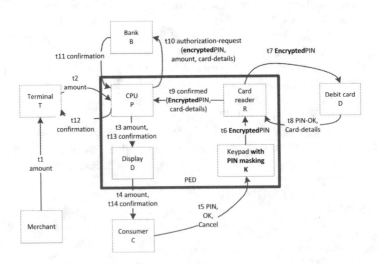

Fig. 1. Architecture of a Pin Entry Device (PED) and its context. The properties in bold are absent from the original architecture and have been added in the second round of the argument game. The labels are for ease of reference.

which is connected to a terminal and receives the amount to be paid from the terminal. The core functional requirement for the PED is

- FR1 Consumers can pay with a PED using a PIN.

Figure 1 shows the architecture of the PED and part of the context. Consider first the architecture without the bold annotations. The top-level informal argument for functional correctness of the architecture is given by tracing the interctions between components through the architecture roughly in the order in which we numbered them. This argument assumes that all components are implemented correctly according to their specification, that all interactions between components are reliable and that no other interactions, invisible in the diagram, occur.

Attackers keep the assumption that all components are implemented correctly, but violate the other two: They will try to change the interactions in the architecture or context (for example by changing the communication with the bank to their advantage) or will try to add additional interactions (for example by reading the PIN remotely). To make this less likely to happen, we require that the PED and its context satisfy the following properties:

SR1 PIN shall remain confidential during payment transactions
SR2 PIN communicated between nodes of the network shall remain accurate during transactions

There is no way to justify that the original architecture of figure 1 satisfies these properties. The defenders now change the architecture a bit (the bold annotations in figure 1) and make additional assumptions about the context (for example that the Consumer keeps PINs secret). The job of satisfying properties SR1 and SR2, and hence the responsibility for mitigating the risk of violating SR1 and SR2, is thus divided over the PED and its context. With the improved architecture and the additional context assumptions, the defenders can refute the argument of the attacker and reason that SR1 and SR2 are now satisfied.

3.2   Formalizing the Example in $ASPIC^+$

We formalize this example as follows. Our general idea is that input-output relations between the components of a system are formalised as defeasible rules, while assumptions about the environment are stated as facts, which for convenience we represent a defeasible rules with empty antecedent. An argument that the system satisfies the security requirement then applies the defeasible rules to the assumptions, and is thus of a hypothetical character.

First, we represent the architecture in $ASPIC^+$ by a set of defeasible rules of the form C1!m $\Rightarrow$ C2?m, meaning that if C1 outputs message m, C2 receives message m. These rules claim that communication in the system is reliable. For example, in figure 1,

(t5): C!PIN $\Rightarrow$ K?PIN.

There is one such rule in $\mathcal{R}_d$ for each labeled interaction in figure 1.

Second, we assume that the assessors share defeasible beliefs about security properties of the communications between the components in the architecture. For example,
in figure 1,

(conf-t5): C!confidentialPIN ⇒ K?confidentialPIN.

This rule says that if a PIN was confidential when sent, it is still confidential when
received by the keypad. These rules cannot be derived from the diagram; it is expert
knowledge based on the diagram and the assessors can use it in their argumentation.

Third, we assume that the experts know the capabilities of each component. For
example,

(K): K?PIN → K!encryptedPIN.

There are many of these rules for each component, and they jointly represent the knowledge that the assessors have of the capabilities of the component. This is a strict rule, as
we (and the attackers) assume that each component is functioning correctly.[2]

Fourth, the experts also know how security properties are handled by each component. For example,

(conf-K): K?confidentialPIN → K!encryptedConfidentialPIN.

This rule says that if the PIN was confidential when entered in the keypad, it is still
confidential after being sent in encrypted form.

Fifth, we assume that the confidentiality requirement SR1 "PIN shall remain confidential during payment transactions" is formalized as SR1

(SR1): confidentialPIN.

In general, any requirement to be verified is represented as the consequent of a defeasible rule in the architecture description and does not occur in the antecedent of any
rule.

The assessors share knowledge about the meaning of the requirement in the form of
a set of strict rules that for each component X,

(CRX): confidentialPIN → X!confidentialPIN.

So any non-confidential PIN transfer will violate the requirement.

Sixth, to prove a requirement, we need assumed facts, which are included in $\mathcal{R}_d$ as a
set of defeasible rules with empty antecedents. Such rules are given the lowest priority
in the ordering on $\mathcal{R}_d$; they are called *assumptions*.

In the first round of the game, defenders argue that the system is functionally correct,
assuming that confidentialPIN is true. Attackers then try to imagine violations of
SR1. For example, from the assumption that the consumer keeps her PIN confidential,

(C-keep-PIN-conf): ⇒ C!confidentialPIN

defenders derive that the PIN received by the keypad is confidential,
K?confidentialPIN using rule (conf-t5).

---

[2] In our formalisation in Section 4 we will also include the so-called transpositions of strict
   rules, in order to inherit the logical closure and consistency results proven in [11, 15] about the
   ASPIC[+] framework.

There are many ways in which the assumed fact (C-keep-PIN-conf) can be violated, one of which is a successful social engineering attack on a consumer [4], for instance, forcing the user to reveal the PIN. Defenders and attackers know that

(Attack-C-SE): `SuccessfulSocialAttack` $\Rightarrow$ `¬C!confidentialPIN`.

Switching to the role of attackers, the assessors now add the assumption

(Successful-attack-C-SE): $\Rightarrow$ `SuccessfulSocialAttack`.

This gives a rebutting attack on the initial proof of PIN confidentiality, and it proves violation of the confidentiality requirement (SR1).

To be able to allocate risk to various actors, we now assume that all users of the PED payment infrastructure support the argument. The assessors can now transfer the responsibility for beating a social engineering attack to the consumer, by simply stating that it does not occur:

(No-successful-attack-C-SE): `¬SuccessfulSocialAttack`.

This is not a change in the architecture but a change in assumptions (this time unattackable) about the environment that reinstates the original security argument.

To illustrate how responsibility for guarding against a security requirement violation can be shifted to the PED, consider the following. In the original architecture, the PED had no PIN masking device (a cover that hides the keypad from view). If this is expressed as an assumption, then in that architecture, the attacker can rebut (conf-t5):

(not-conf-t5-masking): $\Rightarrow$ `¬KwithMasking?confidentialPIN`
(not-K-keep-PIN-conf): `¬KwithMasking?confidentialPIN` $\Rightarrow$ `¬K?confidentialPIN`

Defenders will then change the architecture by adding PIN masking, expressed by adding the following fact to $\mathcal{K}$:

(masking): `KwithMasking?confidentialPIN`

and by changing (conf-t5) into

(conf-t5-masking): `C!confidentialPIN, KwithMasking?confidentialPIN`
$\Rightarrow$ `K?confidentialPIN`.

So far, we have shown that simple security arguments can be represented in an argumentation theory that is partly represented in an architecture model and partly in the knowledge and beliefs of the assessors. To play the risk argumentation game, we need to extend the argumentation theory with a dialogue game. We introduce such a game in the next section.

4   An Argument Game

4.1   Ideas

We now informally sketch a dialogue game for argumentation between a defender and an attacker of a design, who want to test whether a given safety or security requirement SR is satisfied by the design. The players exchange arguments and counterarguments and during the dialogue dynamically build a joint $ASPIC^+$ argumentation theory describing a design and its environment. The defender's task is to ensure that the theory expresses a design that satisfies SR, while the attacker's task is to produce successful attacks on the defender's security arguments. Despite this dialectical setting, the players are cooperative in that they both want a good design that meets the requirements: their real goal is not to win but to collaborate on creating a design by critically discussing its pros and cons. For this reason we will not build rules into our dialogue game that would prevent 'selfish' players from playing moves just to obstruct the other player (such as nonrepetition moves).

The game starts with an initial argumentation theory as described in Section 3. In the first move the defender presents an argument for SR based on the initial theory and assumptions about the world. Then the players take turns after each move. The attacker's task is to defeat defender's 'current' argument for SR, after which the defender must either show that the attacker's attack is flawed (by in turn strictly defeating it) or by modifying the design in such a way that again an undefeated argument can be built that SR is satisfied. The defender can modify a design by deleting existing rules and (if needed) adding new rules as part of a new argument. The attacker cannot delete rules from the theory, because it cannot modify the design, but it can add new rules just as the defender can. Moreover, both players can add new rule priorities to make their rebutting arguments (strictly) defeat their target (but they must in doing so respect that properties of a preorder). Likewise, they can add new rule names to $\mathcal{L}$ to express undercutting defeaters. Another requirement is that each move must succeed in the mover's dialectical goal: after each defender move an argument for SR must be dialogically acceptable or *in* (in a sense to be defined below) while after each attacker move all arguments for SR must be dialogically *out* (also a sense to be defined below).

4.2   The Game Defined

We now define a dialogue game for a single security requirement SR. Throughout this section the logical language $\mathcal{L}$ is assumed fixed but all other elements of an AT can vary. Unless specified otherwise, the following definitions leave implicit that arguments, priorities, rules and rule names belong to some given argumentation theory with logical language $\mathcal{L}$. In our examples $\mathcal{L}$ consists of propositional literals but we stress that our game does not in any way depend on a particular logical language.

Definition 6. *A move is a tuple* $m = (i, A, pr, ns, del, t)$ *where:*

- $i \in \mathbb{N}$ *is the move identifier;*
- *A is an argument;*
- *pr is a set of priority statements about defeasible rules;*
- *ns is a set of ordered pairs* (r, l), *where* $r \in \mathcal{R}_d$ *and* $l \in \mathcal{L}$; *(an assignment of names to defeasible rules, as part of the n function on* $\mathcal{R}_d)^3$
- *del is a set of rules (to be deleted from the 'current' architecture specification)*
- $t \in \mathbb{N}$ *is the move target, that is, the move to which the move replies.*

---

^{3} In the remainder we will for ease of notation represent the n function as a set of ordered pairs.

Below we will leave set elements of a move that are empty implicit. To indicate an element of a move m we will often write $i(m)$, $A(m)$ and so on.

Definition 7. *A* dialogue *is a finite sequence of moves* $m_1, \ldots, m_n$ *such that* $t(m_1) = 0$ *and for all* j *such that* $1 < j \le n$ *it holds that* $i(m_j) = j$ *and* $t(M_j)$ *is some* x *such that* $1 \le x < j$.

Below d_n is shorthand for dialogue $m_1, \ldots, m_n$, where d_0 is the empty dialogue. We call $m_i \in d_n$ a *defender move* if i is odd and an *attacker move* otherwise.

Definition 8. *The* argumentation theory AT_i *relative to a dialogue* d_i *is defined as follows:*

1. *AT_0 is any argumentation theory describing a system architecture where $\mathcal{R}_s^0$ is closed under transposition and $\le = \{r \approx r \mid r \in \mathcal{R}_d\}$.*
2. *AT_i for $i > 0$ is such that:*
   (a) *$\mathcal{R}_s^i = (\mathcal{R}_s^{i-1} \setminus del) \cup Cl_{tr}((\texttt{StrictRules}(A(m_i))))$* [4]
   (b) *$\mathcal{R}_d^i = (\mathcal{R}_d^{i-1} \setminus del) \cup \texttt{DefRules}(A(m_i))$*
   (c) *$\le^i = \le^{i-1} \cup pr \cup \{r < r' \mid r, r' \in \mathcal{R}_d^i$ and r has but r' does not have an empty antecedent$\} \cup \{r \approx r \mid r \in \mathcal{R}_d^i\}$*
   (d) *$n^i = n^{i-1} \cup ns_i$.*
3. *$\mathcal{K}_n^i = \mathcal{K}_n^{i-1} \cup \texttt{Prem}(A(m_i))$*

The 'current winner' of a dialogue can be defined by adapting [13, 14]'s notion of dialogical status of a move:

Definition 9

- *Move m is* in *iff all replies to m are* out*;*
- *Move m is* out *if either it has a retracted rule or it has a reply that is* in*.*

Note that since the reply structure on the game moves induces a tree, the dialogical status of a move is always uniquely defined.

We now adapt [13, 14]'s notion of relevance as follows.

Definition 10. *A defender move m_i is relevant iff exactly one defender move m_j ($j \le i$) such that $\texttt{Conc}(A(m_j) = SR$ is* in*. An attacker move m_i is relevant iff all defender moves m_j ($j \le i$) such that $\texttt{Conc}(A(m_j) = SR$ are* out*.*

We next define when a move is legal in a dialogue.

Definition 11. *A dialogue $d = m_1, \ldots, m_n$ is legal iff for all $m_i \in d$ it holds that m_i is legal in $m_1, \ldots, m_{i-1}$ (or in the empty dialogue if $d = m_1$).*
   A move m_i is legal in dialogue d_{i-1} iff the following conditions are satisfied.

1. *If m_i is a defender (attacker) move, then $t(m_i)$ is an attacker (defender) move.*
2. *m_i is relevant.*
3. *$pr(m_i)$ leaves $\le_i$ a total preorder.*
4. *$ns(m)$ leaves n_i a (partial or total) function from $\mathcal{L}$ to $\mathcal{R}_d^i$.*

---

[4] $Cl_{tr}(S)$ yields for any set S of strict rules its closure under transposition as defined in [11].

5. m_1 is such that
   (a) $\text{Conc}(A(m_1)) = SR$; and
   (b) $\text{Prem}(A(m_1)) \subseteq \mathcal{K}^0$; and
   (c) $\text{StrictRules}(A(m_1)) \subseteq \mathcal{R}_s^0$; and
   (d) $\text{DefRules}(A(m_1)) \subseteq \mathcal{R}_d^0 \cup \{\Rightarrow \varphi \mid \varphi$ is an antecedent of a rule in $\mathcal{R}_s^0$ or $\mathcal{R}_d^0\}$.
6. If $i > 1$ and m_i is an attacker move, then
   (a) $A(m_i)$ defeats $A(t(m_i))$ on the basis of AT_i;
   (b) $del(m_i) = \emptyset$.
7. If $i > 1$ and m_i is a defender move, then
   (a) $A(m_i)$ has a subargument that strictly defeats $A(t(m_i))$ on the basis of AT_i; and
   (b) If $A(m_i)$ does not itself strictly defeat $A(t(m_i))$ on the basis of AT_i, then $\text{Conc}(A(m_i)) = SR$;
   (c) del does not contain rules from arguments in attacker moves in d_{i-1};
   (d) If $t(m_i) \neq i - 1$ then $AT_i = AT_{i-1}$.

Condition 1 states that the players may not respond to their own moves. Condition 2 makes that a dialogue is focussed on what it is meant for, namely, the critical testing whether the design meets requirement SR. Conditions 3-4 are to ensure that the argumentation theory constructed during a dialougue is well-defined, while Condition 5 regulates how the defender can start the game with an argument for SR. Condition 6 says that an attacker move must defeat a defender move without deleting rules.

Condition 7a requires the defender to move an argument with a subargument that strictly defeats the target argument of the attacker. Defeat must here be strict, since the 'burden of proof' is on the defender to show that SR is satisfied. Note that since an argument is a subargument of its own, the defeating subargument of $A(m_i)$ may be $A(m_i)$ itself. Recall that Condition 2 in effect requires that after the defender's move exactly one argument for SR is justified on the basis of AT_i. If m_i does not delete any rules from AT_{i-1} then this argument will be the one that is 'reinstated' by $A(m_i)$'s strict defeat of $A(t(m_i))$, otherwise this argument will be $A(m_i)$ itself. These last observations were illustrated in the final part of Section 3. Condition 7b says that defeating defender arguments can be extended to an argument for SR. The definition of relevance implies that such an extension is only legal if the move does not make an old argument for SR in. Condition 7c forbids the defender from deleting rules from the attackers arguments. This requirement is reasonable since it is defender's responsibility to build and modify the design through his own moves; the attacker does not contribute to the design but only criticises it. Finally, condition 7d says that the defender must always reply to the last move of the attacker, except if the defender makes a move that leaves the argumentation theory unchanged. Such 'logical' backtracking moves must be allowed to ensure that a dialogue can be logically completed.

4.3   Correspondence Result

Definition 12. *A dialogue d_i is logically completed if no legal moves m_{i+1} exist such that $AT_i = AT_{i+1}$.*

In a logically completed dialogue, all logically possible legal moves on the basis of the current argumentation theory have been made. This means that every allowed continuation of the dialogue would change the argumentation theory. We now want for any logically completed dialogue that, if an argument for SR is dialogically *in*, then it is also justified on the basis of the 'current' argumentation theory. We are not so much interested in formal termination criteria for dialogues, since we assume that the players, being in essence cooperative, will agree to terminate a dialogue at a sensible moment. We now prove that our game has this property. The practical value of this result is that, to agree with the underlying logic, we do not need to restart an entire logical argument game after each move (as we would have to do if, for example, the protocol checked after each move whether the current AT justifies SR). Note also that, since all dialogue moves must be relevant, a dialogue will only in exceptional cases not be logically completed. For this reason, the restriction of Theorem 1 to logically completed dialogues is not a severe practical limitation.

Theorem 1. *Let d_i be any logically completed dialogue with a defender move m_i that is in and such that* $\mathrm{Conc}(A(m_i)) = SR$. *Then $A(m_i)$ is justified on the basis of AT_i.*

Proof. The reply relations on the moves in d_i induce a dialogue tree with as root m_1. Let T_i be its subtree with root m_i. Since m_i is *in*, by Proposition 23 of [14] there exists a 'winning part' W_i of T_i in the sense of Definition 22 of [14], i.e., a subtree of T_i that for each set of defender siblings in T_i contains one element and contains all its attacker replies from T_i, and such that all defender moves in W_i are *in* while all attacker moves in W_i are *out*. Now let G_i be the tree obtained from W_i by replacing each move m in W_i with $A(m)$ (below written as A_i). We need to show that G_i is a winning strategy for A_i in the argument game for grounded semantics on the basis of AT_i.

First, all arguments in G_i are constructible on the basis of AT_i: if not, then G_i contains a defender argument A_j with a deleted rule, but then the node m_j in W_i from which it is derived is *out*: contradiction.

Second, it must be shown that G_i contains the correct defeat relations. Note first that by Definition 11(3) for any d_j it holds that $\leq_j$ is a total preorder, so defeat relations are preserved under addition of rule preferences. Then by Definition 11(6a) each argument at even depth defeats its parent. Note next that by definition of relevance of moves and the fact that all defender moves in W_i are *in*, G_i contains exactly one argument for SR, namely, A_i. Then by Definition 11(7a) each argument at odd depth except A_i itself strictly defeats its parent.

Next, since d_i is logically completed and Definition 11 imposes no conditions on logically completing attacker moves other than that their arguments must defeat the argument of their target, all defeaters on the basis of AT_i of any defender argument in G_i are in G_i.

This suffices to show that G_i is a winning strategy for A_i on the basis of AT_i. It follows that A_i is in the grounded extension of AT_i and so is justified.   □

5 Example

We illustrate the definition of the game with the example from Section 3.1. In listing a move we will leave its identifier i obvious from the index of m and we will specify *del* only for defender moves. Moreover, we will leave *ns* obvious from the subscripts of the rules in the moved argument. In specifying AT_i we will, overloading notation, indicate defeasible rules with their names in $\mathcal{L}$, and in specifying $\leq^i$ we will only list the explicitly stated $<$ priorities and leave priorities between assumptions and other rules and priorities that are required to leave $\leq^i$ a total preorder implicit. We will also leave the transpositions of strict rules implicit. Figure 2 shows the state of the following dialogue after move M5.

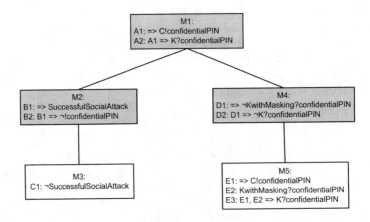

Fig. 2. State of the dialogue after move M5. White boxes are *in* while grey boxes are *out*.

- AT_0 is such that $\mathcal{K} = \mathcal{R}_s = \emptyset$ and $\mathcal{R}_d = \{conf\text{-}t5\}$.

- The defender starts with a move m_1 such that $A(m_1) =$

  $A_1: \Rightarrow_{C-Keep-PIN-conf} \texttt{C!confidentialPIN}$
  $A_2: A_1 \Rightarrow_{conf-t5} \texttt{K?confidentialPIN}$

  Here $pr(m_1) = del(m_1) = \emptyset$ and $t(m_1) = 0$. As a result, AT_1 is such that $\mathcal{K} = \mathcal{R}_s = \emptyset$, $\mathcal{R}_d = \{conf\text{-}t5, C-Keep-PIN-conf\}$. Clearly, M_1 is currently *in* since it has no replies or retracted rules or premises.

- At m_2 the attacker attacks A_2 by directly attacking A_1 with $A(m_2) =$

  $B_1: \Rightarrow_{Successful-attack-C-SE} \texttt{SuccesfulSocialAttack}$
  $B_2: B_1 \Rightarrow_{Attack-C-SE} \neg\texttt{C!confidentialPIN}$

  Here $t(m_2) = 1$. As a result, AT_2 is such that $\mathcal{K} = \mathcal{R}_s = \emptyset$, $\mathcal{R}_d = \{conf\text{-}t5, C-Keep-PIN-conf, Successful\text{-}attack\text{-}C\text{-}SE, Attack\text{-}C\text{-}SE\}$. On the basis of AT_2 we have that B_2 defeats A_2 on A_1, since the last defeasible rule of B_2 is $Attack\text{-}C\text{-}SE$, the last defeasible rule of A_1 is $C-Keep-PIN-conf$ and we have that $C-Keep-PIN-conf < Attack\text{-}C\text{-}SE$ since $C-Keep-PIN-conf$ is an assumption. Moreover, in the game we have that m_2 is *in* since it has no replies, so m_1 is now *out* since it has a reply that is *in*.

- At m_3 the defender moves the following basic argument stating just a fact:

C_1: ¬SuccesfulSocialAttack

where $t(m_3) = 2$ and $pr(m_3) = del(m_3) = \emptyset$. Defender's move M_3 adds fact $No\text{-}successful\text{-}attack\text{-}C\text{-}SE$ to $\mathcal{K}$ and leaves the rest of AT_3 as in AT_2. On the basis of AT_3 we have that C_1 strictly defeats B_2 on B_1, since, unlike B_1, C_1 has no defeasible rules. We now have that m_3 is *in* since it has no replies, so m_2 is now *out* since it has a reply that is *in*: but then m_1 is *in* again since all its replies are *out* and it has no retracted premises or rules. Therefore, m_3 did not need to contain a new argument for SR, since $a(m_1)$ has conclusion SR.

- The attacker move m_4 now backtracks to m_1 (that is, $t(m_4) = 1$), this time attacking argument A_2 by directly attacking it on A_1 with

D_1: $\Rightarrow_{not-conf-t5-masking}$ ¬KwithMasking?confidentialPIN
D_2: $B_1 \Rightarrow_{not-K-keep-PIN-conf}$ ¬K?confidentialPIN

Moreover, the attacker states the priority $pr(m_4) = \{conf\text{-}t5 < not\text{-}K\text{-}keep\text{-}PIN\text{-}conf\}$. As a result, AT_4 is such that $\mathcal{K} = \{No\text{-}successful\text{-}attack\text{-}C\text{-}SE\}$, $\mathcal{R}_s = \emptyset$, $\mathcal{R}_d = \{conf\text{-}t5, C - Keep - PIN - conf, not\text{-}conf\text{-}t5\text{-}masking, Successful\text{-}attack\text{-}C\text{-}SE, not\text{-}K\text{-}keep\text{-}PIN\text{-}conf, Attack\text{-}C\text{-}SE\}$ and $conf\text{-}t5 < not\text{-}K\text{-}keep\text{-}PIN\text{-}conf$. On the basis of AT_4 we have that D_2 defeats A_2 on A_2, since the last defeasible rule of B_2 is $not\text{-}K\text{-}keep\text{-}PIN\text{-}conf$, the last defeasible rule of A_2 is $conf\text{-}t5$ and we have that $conf\text{-}t5 < not\text{-}K\text{-}keep\text{-}PIN\text{-}conf$. In the game we now have that m_4 is *in* so m_1 is now *out* since it has a reply that is *in*.

- At m_5 the defender moves the following argument in reply to m_4:

E_1: $\Rightarrow_{a1}$ C!confidentialPIN
E_2: KwithMasking?confidentialPIN
E_3: $E_1, E_2 \Rightarrow_{conf-t5-masking}$ K?confidentialPIN

Argument E_2 strictly defeats argument D_2 on $D - 1$ since E_2 consists of a fact while D_1 consists of an assumption. Defender's move m_5 adds fact $masking$ to $\mathcal{K}$ and replaces rule $conf\text{-}t5$ in $\mathcal{R}_d$ with $conf\text{-}t5\text{-}masking$. This is effected by making $del(m_5) = \{conf\text{-}t5\}$. So AT_5 is such that $\mathcal{K} = \{No\text{-}successful\text{-}attack\text{-}C\text{-}SE, masking\}$, $\mathcal{R}_s = \emptyset$, $\mathcal{R}_d = \{conf\text{-}t5\text{-}masking, C - Keep - PIN - conf, not\text{-}conf\text{-}t5\text{-}masking, Successful\text{-}attack\text{-}C\text{-}SE, not\text{-}K\text{-}keep\text{-}PIN\text{-}conf, Attack\text{-}C\text{-}SE\}$, and $conf\text{-}t5 < not\text{-}K\text{-}keep\text{-}PIN\text{-}conf$. On the basis of AT_5 we have that argument E_2 strictly defeats argument D_2 on $D - 1$ since E_2 consists of a fact while D_1 consists of an assumption.

Note that m_5 contains a new argument for SR, since the old argument A_2 is not constructible on the basis of AT_5. At this stage M_5 is clearly *in* so M_4 is now *out* since it has a reply that is *in*. However, M_1 remains out for the remainder of the game, since it has a retracted rule.

To illustrate Theorem 1, suppose the attacker makes no new move so that the game terminates. On the basis of AT_5 the attacker would have had no further legal move, so the game is logically completed. Now some move with an argument for the SR is *in*, namely, move M_5 with argument E_3; moreover, E_3 is trivially justified on the basis of AT_5, since it has no defeaters. So the defender's 'winning part' consists of just m_5.

6   Conclusion

This paper shows that it is feasible to reconstruct the security risk assessment dialog of experts as a formal argumentation game in $ASPIC^+$. The game is dynamic in that the players can both add elements to and delete elements from the architecture specification. The game was shown to respect the underlying argumentation logic in that for any logically completed game 'won' by the defender, the security requirement is a justified conclusion from the architecture specification at that stage of the game.

The idea to formalize risk assessment in argumentation logic is not new. Two early papers have suggested the use of argumentation in medical risk assessment [6, 12]. These proposals are preliminary and specific to the medical domain. There is more recent work on the use of argumentation in firewall policy specification and analysis [1, 2]. These papers focus on the logical representation of arguments about whether firewall policies satisfy certain properties and do not focus on dynamic or dialogical aspects. The current paper was based on earlier attempts to use informal Toulmin-style arguments to support IT security risk assessment [4, 5]. Those attempts did not use ideas from defeasible logic dialog games.

This paper raises a number of questions that we will investigate in the near future. An important long-term goal of our research is to provide tool support for argumentation-based risk assessment, and for this it is needed to find informal but precise representations of a risk argumentation game that can be understood by security experts but have a formal grounding in defeasible logic and dialogue games. We therefore want to investigate samples of actual RA dialogues to identify common dialogue patterns that can be exploited by the support tool to give suggestions to the risk assessors. We will here in particular explore the similarity between argumentation trees and attack trees [9], which are a familiar representation and reasoning structure for risk assessors and therefore warrant some confidence that an argumentation-based RA support tool will be natural for them. A further topic for future research is to analyze the role of qualitative risk assessments made in practice, where uncertainty and impact of events are estimated on ordinal scales such as (low, medium, high). Finally, we want to investigate the lifting of our current assumption that rule priorities are uncontroversial. Although in our experience this assumption holds for a fair number of risk assessments, this may not be so in general. One way to deal with this is to replace the current version of $ASPIC^+$ with [10]'s version that allows for argumentation about the argument ordering.

Acknowledgements. We thank the reviewers for their stimulating and useful comments. Roel Wieringa has received funding from the European Union Seventh Framework Programme (FP7/2007-2013) under grant agreement 318003 (TREsPASS). This publication reflects only the author's views and the Union is not liable for any use that may be made of the information contained herein.

References

[1] Applebaum, A., Levitt, K., Rowe, J., Parsons, S.: Arguing about firewall policy. In: Verheij, B., Woltran, S., Szeider, S. (eds.) Computational Models of Argument. Proceedings of COMMA 2012, pp. 91–102. IOS Press, Amsterdam (2012)

[2] Bandara, A.K., Kakas, A.C., Lupu, E.C., Russo, A.: Using argumentation logic for firewall policy specification and analysis. In: State, R., van der Meer, S., O'Sullivan, D., Pfeifer, T. (eds.) DSOM 2006. LNCS, vol. 4269, pp. 185–196. Springer, Heidelberg (2006)

[3] Dung, P.M.: On the acceptability of arguments and its fundamental role in nonmonotonic reasoning, logic programming, and n–person games. Artificial Intelligence 77, 321–357 (1995)

[4] Franqueira, V.N.L., Tun, T.T., Wieringa, R., Nuseibeh, B.: Risk and argument: a risk-based argumentation method for practical security. In: Proceedings of the 19th IEEE International Requirements Engineering Conference, Trento, Italy, pp. 239–248 (2011)

[5] Haley, C., Laney, R., Moffett, J., Nuseibeh, B.: Security requirements engineering: A framework for representation and analysis. IEEE Transactions on Software Engineering 34(1), 133–153 (2008)

[6] Krause, P., Fox, J., Judson, P.: An argumentation-based approach to risk assessment. IMA Journal of Mathematics Applied in Business & Industry 5, 249–263 (1993)

[7] Loui, R.P.: Process and policy: resource-bounded non-demonstrative reasoning. Computational Intelligence 14, 1–38 (1998)

[8] Lund, M.S., Solhaug, B., Stølen, K.: Model-Driven Risk Analysis. The CORAS Approach. Springer, Heidelberg (2011)

[9] Mauw, S., Oostdijk, M.: Foundations of Attack Trees. In: Won, D.H., Kim, S. (eds.) ICISC 2005. LNCS, vol. 3935, pp. 186–198. Springer, Heidelberg (2006)

[10] Modgil, S., Prakken, H.: Reasoning about preferences in structured extended argumentation frameworks. In: Baroni, P., Cerutti, F., Giacomin, M., Simari, G.R. (eds.) Computational Models of Argument. Proceedings of COMMA 2010, pp. 347–358. IOS Press, Amsterdam (2010)

[11] Modgil, S., Prakken, H.: A general account of argumentation with preferences. Artificial Intelligence 195, 361–397 (2013)

[12] Parsons, S., Fox, J., Coulson, A.: Argumentation and risk assessment. In: Proceedings of the AAAI Spring Symposium on Predictive Toxicology (1999)

[13] Prakken, H.: Relating protocols for dynamic dispute with logics for defeasible argumentation. Synthese 127, 187–219 (2001)

[14] Prakken, H.: Coherence and flexibility in dialogue games for argumentation. Journal of Logic and Computation 15, 1009–1040 (2005)

[15] Prakken, H.: An abstract framework for argumentation with structured arguments. Argument and Computation 1, 93–124 (2010)

Assumption-Based Argumentation for Decision-Making with Preferences: A Medical Case Study

Xiuyi Fan[1], Robert Craven[1], Ramsay Singer[2], Francesca Toni[1], and Matthew Williams[1]

[1] Imperial College London, London, UK
[2] University College Hospital, London UK

Abstract. We present a formal decision-making framework, where decisions have multiple attributes and meet goals, and preferences are defined over individual goals and sets of goals. We define decision functions to select 'good' decisions according to an underlying decision criteria. We also define an argumentation-based computational mechanism to compute and explain 'good' decisions. We draw connections between decision-making and argumentation semantics: 'good' decisions are admissible arguments in a corresponding argumentation framework. To show the applicability of our approach, we use medical literature selection as a case study. For a given patient description, we select the most relevant medical papers from the medical literature and explain the selection.

1 Introduction

Argumentation-based decision making has attracted considerable research interest in recent years [1,8,7,10]. In this paper, we give a formal treatment of decision-making with argumentation.

We define *extended decision frameworks*, used to model the agents' knowledge bases, including the agents' preferences. We allow a decision framework to have multiple *decisions* and a set of *goals*, such that each decision can have a number of different *attributes* and each goal can be satisfied by some attributes. We define *preferences* over (sets of) *goals*. We define *extended decision functions* to select 'good' decisions. To compute and explain the selected decisions, we map decision frameworks and decision functions into assumption-based argumentation (ABA) frameworks [3]. We prove that selected decisions with respect to a given decision function are claims of arguments in an admissible extension in the corresponding ABA framework.

We use medical literature selection as a case study for this work. We are given a set of medical research papers and patient descriptions. Each papers contains the results of a clinical trial, and a patient description gives a set of patient properties. The aim of the decision-making process is to select the most relevant papers for a patient. In this way, a specific candidate decision is the use of a given paper. Trial criteria are extracted from each piece of medical

J. Leite et al. (Eds.): CLIMA XIV, LNAI 8143, pp. 374–390, 2013.
© Springer-Verlag Berlin Heidelberg 2013

literature and are used as attributes. Patient properties are collected from patient descriptions and are used as goals. This defines the use of medical literature as a decision-making problem. We show the decision-making framework selects the most relevant papers for the patient and explains the selection.

This paper is organised as follows. Background on ABA is in Section 2. We present extended decision frameworks and decision functions for preference over single goals in Section 3. We show the treatment of preference over combined goals in Section 4. We present the case study on relevant medical literature selection in Section 5. Related work is in Section 6. We conclude in Section 7.

2   Background

An ABA framework [3,5] is a tuple $\langle \mathcal{L}, \mathcal{R}, \mathcal{A}, \mathcal{C} \rangle$ where

- $\langle \mathcal{L}, \mathcal{R} \rangle$ is a *deductive system*, with $\mathcal{L}$ the *language* and $\mathcal{R}$ a set of *rules* of the form $s_0 \leftarrow s_1, \ldots, s_m \ (m \geq 0)$;
- $\mathcal{A} \subseteq \mathcal{L}$ is a (non-empty) set, referred to as the *assumptions*;
- $\mathcal{C}$ is a total mapping from $\mathcal{A}$ into $2^{\mathcal{L}}$, where $\mathcal{C}(\alpha)$ is the *contrary* of $\alpha \in \mathcal{A}$.

When presenting an ABA framework, we omit giving $\mathcal{L}$ explicitly as we assume $\mathcal{L}$ contains all sentences appearing in $\mathcal{R}$, $\mathcal{A}$ and $\mathcal{C}$. Given a rule $s_0 \leftarrow s_1, \ldots, s_m$, we use the following notation: $Head(s_0 \leftarrow s_1, \ldots, s_m) = s_0$ and $Body(s_0 \leftarrow s_1, \ldots, s_m) = \{s_1, \ldots, s_m\}$. As in [3], we enforce that ABA frameworks are *flat*: assumptions do not occur as the heads of rules.

In ABA, *arguments* are deductions of claims using rules and supported by assumptions, and *attacks* are directed at assumptions. Informally, following [3]:

- an *argument for (the claim)* $c \in \mathcal{L}$ *supported by* $S \subseteq \mathcal{A}$ ($S \vdash c$ in short) is a (finite) tree with nodes labelled by sentences in $\mathcal{L}$ or by the symbol τ^1, such that the root is labelled by c, leaves are either τ or assumptions in S, and non-leaves s have as many children as elements in the body of a rule with head s, in a one-to-one correspondence with the elements of this body.
- an *argument* $S_1 \vdash c_1$ *attacks an argument* $S_2 \vdash c_2$ if and only if $c_1 = \mathcal{C}(\alpha)$ for $\alpha \in S_2$.

Attacks between arguments correspond in ABA to attacks between sets of assumptions, where *a set of assumptions A attacks a set of assumptions B* if and only if an argument supported by $A' \subseteq A$ attacks an argument supported by $B' \subseteq B$.

When there is no ambiguity, we also say a sentence b attacks a sentence a when a is an assumption and b is a claim of an argument B such that a is in the support of some argument A and B attacks A.

With argument and attack defined, standard argumentation semantics can be applied in ABA [3]. We focus on the admissibility semantics: *a set of assumptions is admissible* (in $\langle \mathcal{L}, \mathcal{R}, \mathcal{A}, \mathcal{C} \rangle$) if and only if it does not attack itself and it attacks all $A \subseteq \mathcal{A}$ that attack it; *an argument $S \vdash c$ belongs to an admissible extension supported by* $\Delta \subseteq \mathcal{A}$ (in $\langle \mathcal{L}, \mathcal{R}, \mathcal{A}, \mathcal{C} \rangle$) if and only if $S \subseteq \Delta$ and Δ is admissible.

---

[1] As in [3], $\tau \notin \mathcal{L}$ stands for "true" and is used to represent the empty body of rules.

3   Extended Decision Frameworks and Decision Functions

In this paper, we consider the following structure of decision problems: there are a set of possible decisions D, a set of attributes A, and a set of goals G, such that a decision $d \in$ D may *have* some attributes $A \subseteq$ A, and each goal $g \in$ G is *satisfied* by some attributes $A' \subseteq$ A. *Preferences* P are defined as a partial order over *goals*. Decisions are selected based on *extended decision functions*. The relations between decisions, attributes, goals and preferences jointly form an *extended decision framework*, represented as follows:

Definition 1. *[6] An* extended decision framework $\langle$D, A, G, DA, GA, P$\rangle$, *has:*

- *a set of decisions* D $= \{d_1, \ldots, d_n\}, n > 0;$
- *a set of attributes* A $= \{a_1, \ldots, a_m\}, m > 0;$
- *a set of goals* G $= \{g_1, \ldots, g_l\}, l > 0;$
- *a partial order over goals,* P, *representing the preference ranking of goals;*
- *two tables:* DA, *of size* $(n \times m)$, *and* GA, *of size* $(l \times m)$, *such that*
  - *for every* $DA_{i,j}{}^2, 1 \leq i \leq n, 1 \leq j \leq m$, $DA_{i,j}$ *is either 1, representing that decision* d_i *has attributes* a_j, *or 0, otherwise;*
  - *for every* $GA_{i,j}, 1 \leq i \leq l, 1 \leq j \leq m$, $GA_{i,j}$ *is either 1, representing that goal* g_i *is* satisfied *by attribute* a_j, *or 0, otherwise.*

We assume that the column order in both DA *and* GA *is the same, and the indices of decisions, goals, and attributes in* DA *and* GA *are the row numbers of the decision and goals and the column number of attributes in* DA *and* GA, *respectively. We use* $\mathcal{DEC}$ *and* $\mathcal{EDF}$ *to denote the set of all possible decisions and the set of possible extended decision frameworks.*

We represent P as a set of constraints $g_i > g_j$ for $g_i, g_j \in$ G. We illustrate Definition 1 in the following example, adopted from [9].

Example 1. An agent is to choose accommodation in London. DA and GA, are given in Table 1. The preference P is: *near* > *cheap* > *quiet*.

Table 1. DA(left) and GA(right)

	£50	£70	inSK	backSt
jh	0	1	1	1
ic	1	0	1	0

	£50	£70	inSK	backSt
cheap	1	0	0	0
near	0	0	1	0
quiet	0	0	0	1

Decisions (D) are: hotel (jh) and Imperial College Halls (ic). Attributes (A) are: £50, £70, in South Kensington (inSK), and in a backstreet (backSt). Goals

---

^{2} We use $X_{i,j}$ to represent the cell in row i and column j in $X \in \{DA, GA\}$.

(G) are: cheap, near, and quiet. The indices are: 1-jh; 2-ic; 1-cheap; 2-near; 3-quiet; 1-£50; 2-£70; 3-inSK; 4-backSt. The preference order is such that *near* is higher than *cheap* than *quiet*.

In this example, jh is £70, is in South Kensington and is in a backstreet; ic is £50 and is in South Kensington; £50 is cheap, accommodations in South Kensington are near and accommodations in a backstreet are quiet.

We define a decision's *meeting* a goal as the follows:

Definition 2. *[6] Given* $\langle D, A, G, DA, GA, P \rangle$, *a decision* $d \in D$ *with row index* i *in* DA *meets a goal* $g \in G$ *with row index* j *in* GA *if and only if there exists an attribute* $a \in A$ *with column index* k *in both* DA *and* GA, *such that* $DA_{i,k} = 1$ *and* $GA_{j,k} = 1$.

We use $\gamma(d) = S$, *where* $d \in D, S \subseteq G$, *to denote the set of goals met by* d.

Example 2. In Example 1, *jh* meets *near* and *quiet* as *jh* has the attributes *inSK* and *backSt*; and *inSK* fulfils *near* whereas *backSt* fulfils *quiet*. Similarly, *ic* meets *cheap* and *near*.

Extended decision frameworks capture the relations among decisions, goals, attributes, and preferences. We can now define *extended decision function* to select 'good' decisions.

Definition 3. *[6] An* extended decision function *is a mapping* $\psi^E : \mathcal{EDF} \mapsto 2^{\mathcal{DEC}}$, *such that, given* $edf = \langle D, A, G, DA, GA, P \rangle$, $\psi^E(edf) \subseteq D$. *For any* $d, d' \in D$, *if* $\gamma(d) = \gamma(d')$ *and* $d \in \psi^E(df)$, *then* $d' \in \psi^E(df)$. *We say that* $\psi^E(edf)$ *are* selected with respect to ψ^E. *We use* Ψ^E *to denote the set of all extended decision functions.*

Definition 3 gives the basis of an extended decision function. An extended decision function selects a set of decisions from an extended decision framework. When two decisions meet the same set of goals, and one of those decisions belongs to the value of an extended decision function, then the other decision also belongs to the value of the same extended decision function.

We instantiate the basis definition to give the *most-preferred extended decision function*. It selects decisions meeting the more preferred goals that no other decisions meet.

Definition 4. *A* most-preferred extended decision function $\psi^E \in \Psi^E$ *is such that given an extended decision framework* $edf = \langle D, A, G, DA, GA, P \rangle$, *for every* $d \in D$, $d \in \psi^E(edf)$ *if and only if the following holds for all* $d' \in D \setminus \{d\}$:

- *for all* $g \in G$, *if* $g \notin \gamma(d)$ *and* $g \in \gamma(d')$, *then there exists* $g' \in G$, *such that:*
  - $g' > g$ *in* P,
  - $g' \in \gamma(d)$, *and*
  - $g' \notin \gamma(d')$.

We say d *is a* most-preferred *(in edf). We refer to a generic most-preferred decision function as* ψ^E_x.

Table 2. Illustration of the most-preferred extended decision function

	g_1	g_2	g_3	g_4	g_5
d_1	0	1	0	1	1
d_2	0	1	1	0	0

Thus, to select a decision d, we check against all other d' to ensure that: for any g, if d' meets g but d does not, then there exists some g' more preferred than g such that g' is met by d but not d'.

Example 3. Suppose we have two decisions d_1, d_2 and five goals $g_1, g_2, \ldots, g_5$, such that $g_1 > g_2 > \ldots > g_5$. The relations between decisions and goals are illustrated in Table 2. Here, neither d_1 nor d_2 meets the most preferred goal g_1; both of d_1 and d_2 meet g_2, the next preferred goal. Hence, by this point, d_1 and d_2 are considered equally good. However, g_3, the third preferred goal, is only met by d_2, hence d_2 is considered a better decision than d_1. Note that though d_1 meets both g_4 and g_5 where neither is met by d_2, but since they are both less preferred than g_3, d_2 is still considered a better decision here. Definition 4 corresponds to the above intuition as follows. Directly from Definition 4, d_2 is selected as for $d = d_2, d' = d_1$, both g_4 and g_5 meet the conditions $g_4, g_5 \notin \gamma(d_2)$ and $g_4, g_5 \in \gamma(d_1)$ and no other goals meet these two conditions. However, for both g_4 and g_5, there exists g_3 such that $g_3 > g_4$, $g_3 > g_5$, $g_3 \in \gamma(d_2)$ and $g_3 \notin \gamma(d_1)$. d_1 is not selected as for $d = d_1, d' = d_2$, g_3 is the only goal that meets the conditions: $g_1 \notin \gamma(d_1)$ and $g_1 \in \gamma(d_2)$. However, there is no g' meets the 3 conditions: $g' > g$ in P, $g' \in \gamma(d)$, and $g' \notin \gamma(d')$.

Definition 4 gives a criterion for selecting decisions. We construct ABA frameworks to implement this selection, as follows.

Definition 5. *Given an extended decision framework* $edf = \langle D, A, G, DA, GA, P \rangle$, *the* most-preferred *ABA framework corresponds to edf is* $AF = \langle \mathcal{L}, \mathcal{R}, \mathcal{A}, \mathcal{C} \rangle$:

- $\mathcal{R}$ *is such that:*
  for all k, j, i *such that* $1 \leqslant k \leqslant n$, $1 \leqslant j \leqslant m$ *and* $1 \leqslant i \leqslant l$:
    - *if* $DA_{k,i} = 1$ *then* $d_k a_i \leftarrow \in \mathcal{R}$;
    - *if* $GA_{j,i} = 1$ *then* $g_j a_i \leftarrow \in \mathcal{R}$;
    - $d_k g_j \leftarrow d_k a_i, g_j a_i \in \mathcal{R}$;

  for all g_1, g_2 *in* G, *if* $g_1 > g_2 \in P$, *then* $Pg_1 g_2 \leftarrow \in \mathcal{R}$;
  if $1 \leqslant k \leqslant n$, $1 \leqslant r \leqslant n$, $k \neq r$, $1 \leqslant j \leqslant m$: $Nd^k \leftarrow d_r g_j, Nd_k g_j, NX_j^{rk} \in \mathcal{R}$;
  if $1 \leqslant k \leqslant n$, $1 \leqslant r \leqslant n$, $k \neq r$, $1 \leqslant j \leqslant m$, $1 \leqslant t \leqslant m$, $j \neq t$, *then:*
  $X_j^{rk} \leftarrow d_k g_t, Nd_r g_t, Pg_t g_j \in \mathcal{R}$;
  there are no more members of $\mathcal{R}$.
- $\mathcal{A}$ *is such that:*
  if $1 \leqslant k \leqslant n$, *then* $d_k \in \mathcal{A}$;
  if $1 \leqslant k \leqslant n$, $1 \leqslant r \leqslant n$, $k \neq r$, $1 \leqslant j \leqslant m$, *then* $NX_j^{rk} \in \mathcal{A}$;
  if $1 \leqslant k \leqslant n$, $1 \leqslant j \leqslant m$, *then* $Nd_k g_j \in \mathcal{A}$;
  nothing else is in $\mathcal{A}$.

- $\mathcal{C}$ is such that:

  if $1 \leqslant k \leqslant n$, then $\mathcal{C}(d_k) = \{Nd^k\}$;

  if $1 \leqslant k \leqslant n$, $1 \leqslant r \leqslant n$, $k \neq r$, $1 \leqslant j \leqslant m$, then $\mathcal{C}(NX_j^{rk}) = \{X_j^{rk}\}$;

  if $1 \leqslant k \leqslant n$, $1 \leqslant j \leqslant m$, then $\mathcal{C}(Nd_k g_j) = \{d_k g_j\}$.

Here, d_k is read as "select d_k"; $d_k g_j$ is read as "d_k meets g_j"; X_j^{rk} is read as "there is some $g_t, g_t > g_j$, such that d_k meets g_t and d_r does not". All variables starting with N are read as "it is not the case". We illustrate the notion of most-preferred ABA framework in the following example.

Example 4. (Example 1, continued.) The most-preferred ABA framework corresponds to the extended decision framework shown in Example 1 is as follows.[3]

$\mathcal{R}$:

$PNrCp \leftarrow$	$PNrQt \leftarrow$	$PCpQt \leftarrow$
$jh70 \leftarrow$	$jhSK \leftarrow$	$jhBST \leftarrow$
$ic50 \leftarrow$	$icSK \leftarrow$	
$cp50 \leftarrow$	$nrSK \leftarrow$	$qtBST \leftarrow$
$jhCp \leftarrow jh50, cp50$	$jhNr \leftarrow jh50, nr50$	$jhQt \leftarrow jh50, qt50$
$jhCp \leftarrow jh70, cp70$	$jhNr \leftarrow jh70, nr70$	$jhQt \leftarrow jh70, qt70$
$jhCp \leftarrow jhSK, cpSK$	$jhNr \leftarrow jhSK, nrSK$	$jhQt \leftarrow jhSK, qtSK$
$jhCp \leftarrow jhBST, cpBST$	$jhNr \leftarrow jhBST, nrBST$	$jhQt \leftarrow jhBST, qtBST$
$icCp \leftarrow ic50, cp50$	$icNr \leftarrow ic50, nr50$	$icQt \leftarrow ic50, qt50$
$icCp \leftarrow ic70, cp70$	$icNr \leftarrow ic70, nr70$	$icQt \leftarrow ic70, qt70$
$icCp \leftarrow icSK, cpSK$	$icNr \leftarrow icSK, nrSK$	$icQt \leftarrow icSK, qtSK$
$icCp \leftarrow icBST, cpBST$	$icNr \leftarrow icBST, nrBST$	$icQt \leftarrow icBST, qtBST$

$Nd^{jh} \leftarrow icCp, NjhCp, NX_{cheap}^{icjh}$ $Nd^{ic} \leftarrow jhCp, NicCp, NX_{cheap}^{jhic}$

$Nd^{jh} \leftarrow icQt, NjhQt, NX_{quiet}^{icjh}$ $Nd^{ic} \leftarrow jhQt, NicQt, NX_{quiet}^{jhic}$

$Nd^{jh} \leftarrow icNr, NjhNr, NX_{near}^{icjh}$ $Nd^{ic} \leftarrow jhNr, NicNr, NX_{near}^{jhic}$

$X_{cheap}^{icjh} \leftarrow jhNr, NicNr, PnearCp$ $X_{cheap}^{icjh} \leftarrow jhQt, NicQt, PquietCp$

$X_{near}^{icjh} \leftarrow jhCp, NicCp, PcheapNr$ $X_{near}^{icjh} \leftarrow jhQt, NicQt, PquietNr$

$X_{quiet}^{icjh} \leftarrow jhCp, NicCp, PcheapQt$ $X_{quiet}^{icjh} \leftarrow jhNr, NicNr, PnearQt$

$X_{cheap}^{jhic} \leftarrow icNr, NjhNr, PnearCp$ $X_{cheap}^{jhic} \leftarrow icQt, NjhQt, PquietCp$

$X_{near}^{jhic} \leftarrow icCp, NjhCp, PcheapNr$ $X_{near}^{jhic} \leftarrow icQt, NjhQt, PquietNr$

$X_{quiet}^{jhic} \leftarrow icCp, NjhCp, PcheapQt$ $X_{quiet}^{jhic} \leftarrow icNr, NjhNr, PnearQt$

$\mathcal{A}$:

jh	NX_{cheap}^{icjh}	NX_{quiet}^{icjh}	NX_{near}^{icjh}	NX_{cheap}^{jhic}	NX_{quiet}^{jhic}	NX_{near}^{jhic}
ic	$NicCp$	$NicQt$	$NicNr$	$NjhCp$	$NjhQt$	$NjhNr$

$\mathcal{C}$:

$\mathcal{C}(jh) = \{Nd^{jh}\}$ $\mathcal{C}(ic) = \{Nd^{ic}\}$

$\mathcal{C}(NX_{cheap}^{icjh}) = \{X_{cheap}^{icjh}\}$ $\mathcal{C}(NX_{quiet}^{icjh}) = \{X_{quiet}^{icjh}\}$ $\mathcal{C}(NX_{near}^{icjh}) = \{X_{near}^{icjh}\}$

$\mathcal{C}(NX_{cheap}^{jhic}) = \{X_{cheap}^{jhic}\}$ $\mathcal{C}(NX_{quiet}^{jhic}) = \{X_{quiet}^{jhic}\}$ $\mathcal{C}(NX_{near}^{jhic}) = \{X_{near}^{jhic}\}$

$\mathcal{C}(NicCp) = \{icCp\}$ $\mathcal{C}(NicQt) = \{icQt\}$ $\mathcal{C}(NicNr) = \{icNr\}$

$\mathcal{C}(NjhCp) = \{jhCp\}$ $\mathcal{C}(NjhQt) = \{jhQt\}$ $\mathcal{C}(NjhNr) = \{jhNr\}$

---

[3] Nr and nr stand for *near*; Cp and cp stand for *Cheap*; Qt and qt stand for *Quiet*.

Here, $\{ic\} \vdash ic$ is admissible. Though both ic and jh are *near*, ic is cheap but jh is not. A graphical illustration is shown in Figure 1.

$$\{ic\} \vdash ic \qquad\qquad\qquad \{ic\} \vdash ic$$
$$\uparrow \qquad\qquad\qquad\qquad \uparrow$$
$$\{NicCp, NX_{cheap}^{jhic}\} \vdash Nd^{ic} \qquad \{NicQt, NX_{quiet}^{jhic}\} \vdash Nd^{ic}$$
$$\uparrow \qquad\qquad\qquad\qquad \uparrow$$
$$\{\} \vdash icCp \qquad\qquad\qquad \{NjhCp\} \vdash X_{quiet}^{jhic}$$

Fig. 1. Graphical illustration of Example 4. Here, $\{ic\} \vdash ic$ is admissible. The two figures (left & right) show two ways of attacking $\{ic\} \vdash ic$. This figure is read as follows. **Left:** ic should be selected (root argument). ic should not be selected as it is not *cheap* but jh is. Moreover, there is no more preferred goal than *cheap* (middle argument). ic is cheap (bottom argument). **Right:** ic should be selected (root argument). ic should not be selected as it is not *quiet* and there is no more preferred goal than *quiet*, which is met by jh (middle argument). jh is no better than ic as though it is *quiet*, it is not *cheap* and *cheap* is more preferred than *quiet*.

Selected decisions can be found by computing admissible arguments in a corresponding ABA framework, as follows.

Theorem 1. *Given an extended decision framework $edf = \langle \mathsf{D}, \mathsf{A}, \mathsf{G}, \mathsf{DA}, \mathsf{GA}, \mathsf{P} \rangle$, let $AF = \langle \mathcal{L}, \mathcal{R}, \mathcal{A}, \mathcal{C} \rangle$ be the most-preferred ABA framework corresponding to edf. Then, for all $d \in \mathsf{D}$, $d \in \psi_x^E(edf)$ if and only if the argument $\{d\} \vdash d$ belongs to an admissible set in AF.*

Proof. Let d be d_k (k is the index of d in DA).

(**Part I.**) We first prove that if d_k is most-preferred, then $\{d_k\} \vdash d_k$ is in an admissible extension. To show $\{d_k\} \vdash d_k$ is admissible, we need to show:

1. $\{d_k\} \vdash d_k$ is an argument.
2. Using the arguments Δ, $\{d_k\} \vdash d_k$ withstands all attacks.
3. $\{\{d_k\} \vdash d_k\} \cup \Delta$ is conflict-free.

Since d_k is an assumption, $\{d_k\} \vdash d_k$ is an argument. Since $\mathcal{C}(d_k) = \{Nd^k\}$, attackers of $\{d_k\} \vdash d_k$ are arguments with claim Nd^k. Since rules with head Nd^k are of the form $Nd^k \leftarrow d_r g_j, Nd_k g_j, NX_j^{rk}$, attackers of $\{d_k\} \vdash d_k$ are arguments of the form $\{Nd_k g_j, NX_j^{rk}\} \vdash Nd^k$ ($d_r g_j$ is not an assumption and there is no assumption involved in "proving" $d_r g_j$). Hence we need to show for all j, r, $\{d_k\} \vdash d_k$ withstands (with help) attacks from $\{Nd_k g_j, NX_j^{rk}\} \vdash Nd^k$. For fixed j, r, $\{d_k\} \vdash d_k$ withstands attacks from $\{Nd_k g_j, NX_j^{rk}\} \vdash Nd^k$ if $\{Nd_k g_j, NX_j^{rk}\} \vdash Nd^k$ does not withstand attacks towards it. Because NX_j^{rk} is an assumption, if there is an argument $\texttt{Arg}$ for a contrary of NX_j^{rk}, and $\texttt{Arg}$ is not attacked, then $\{Nd_k g_j, NX_j^{rk}\} \vdash Nd^k$ is counterattacked and $\{d_k\} \vdash d_k$ is admissible. We show such $\texttt{Arg}$ exists when d_k is most-preferred.

For all $d_r \in \mathsf{D}, r \neq k$, for $g_j \in \mathsf{G}$ there are two possibilities:

1. it is the case that $g_j \notin \gamma(d_k)$ and $g_j \in \gamma(d_r)$; and
2. it is not the case that $g_j \notin \gamma(d_k)$ and $g_j \in \gamma(d_r)$, i.e., one of the following three sub-cases holds:
    (a) $g_j \notin \gamma(d_k)$ and $g_j \notin \gamma(d_r)$,
    (b) $g_j \in \gamma(d_k)$ and $g_j \in \gamma(d_r)$,
    (c) $g_j \in \gamma(d_k)$ and $g_j \notin \gamma(d_r)$.

In case 1, since d_k is most-preferred, by Definition 4, there exists $g_t \in \mathsf{G} \setminus \{g_j\}$, such that

$$(1) \ g_t > g_j \text{ in P}, \ (2) \ g_t \in \gamma(d_k), \text{ and } (3) \ g_t \notin \gamma(d_r).$$

(i) Since $g_t > g_j$ in P, there is $Pg_tg_j \leftarrow$ in $\mathcal{R}$. (ii) Since $g_t \in \gamma(d_k)$, there is a "proof" for d_kg_t, i.e., $\{\} \vdash d_kg_t$ is an argument. (iii) Since $g_t \notin \gamma(d_r)$, there is no argument for d_rg_t, hence Nd_rg_t is not attacked (the contrary of Nd_rg_t is d_rg_t). Jointly, (i)(ii)(iii), show that there is an argument for X_j^{rk} (by rule $X_j^{rk} \leftarrow d_kg_t, Nd_rg_t, Pg_tg_j$): $\{Nd_rg_t\} \vdash X_j^{rk}$ and this is not attacked. Since the contrary of NX_j^{rk} is X_j^{rk}, $\{Nd_kg_j, NX_j^{rk}\} \vdash Nd^k$ cannot withstand the attack from $\{Nd_rg_t\} \vdash X_j^{rk}$.

In case 2(a), $g_j \notin \gamma(d_r)$, hence there is no attribute $a_i \in \mathsf{A}$ such that d_r has a_i and g_j is fulfilled by a_i. Hence $d_ra_i \leftarrow \notin \mathcal{R}$ or $g_ja_i \leftarrow \notin \mathcal{R}$, or both. Therefore there is no way to "prove" d_rg_j and hence such g_j cannot be used to construct the argument for Nd^k (the only rule with head Nd^k is $Nd^k \leftarrow d_rg_j, Nd_kg_j, NX_j^{rk}$). So no attacks against d_k can be formed in this case.

In case 2(b) and 2(c), $g_j \in \gamma(d_k)$, hence there is $a_i \in \mathsf{A}$ such that d_k has a_i and g_j is fulfilled by a_i. Therefore $\{\} \vdash d_kg_j$ is an argument. Since there is no assumption in the support of $\{\} \vdash d_kg_j$, $\{Nd_kg_j, NX_j^{rk}\} \vdash Nd^k$ cannot withstand the attack from $\{\} \vdash d_kg_j$ (the contrary of Nd_kg_j is d_kg_j).

In case 1 or 2, either $\{Nd_kg_j, NX_j^{rk}\} \vdash Nd^k$ is not an attacking argument or cannot withstand attacks towards it. Hence $\{d_k\} \vdash d_k$ withstands attacks from $\{Nd_kg_j, NX_j^{rk}\} \vdash Nd^k$.

It is easy to see $\{\{d_k\} \vdash d_k\} \cup \Delta$ is conflict-free, as follows. Δ includes all arguments defending $\{d_k\} \vdash d_k$, since attackers of $\{d_k\} \vdash d_k$ are of the form $\{Nd_kg_j, NX_j^{rk}\} \vdash Nd^k$ for $r \neq k$, $\texttt{Arg} \in \Delta$ are either of the form $\{\} \vdash d_kg_j$ or $\{Nd_rg_t\} \vdash X_j^{rk}$, for $r \neq k, j \neq t$. Therefore, assumptions and claims in Δ are of the forms Nd_rg_t and d_kg_j, X_j^{rk}, respectively. Since d_kg_j, X_j^{rk} are not contraries of Nd_rg_t for $r \neq k, j \neq t$, Δ is conflict-free. Similarly, $\{\{d_k\} \vdash d_k\} \cup \Delta$ is conflict-free.

Since $\{d_k\} \vdash d_k$ is an argument and, with help from a conflict-free set of arguments, withstands all attacks towards it, $\{d_k\} \vdash d_k$ belongs to an admissible set of arguments.

(**Part II.**) We show: if $\{d_k\} \vdash d_k$ belongs to an admissible set of arguments, then d_k is most-preferred. To show d_k is most-preferred, we need to show for all $d_r \in \mathsf{D} \setminus \{d_k\}$, the following holds:

382   X. Fan et al.

⋆ for all $g_j \in G$, if $g_j \notin \gamma(d_k)$ and $g_j \in \gamma(d_r)$, then there exists $g_t \in G$ such that: (1) $g_t > g_j$ in P, (2) $g_t \in \gamma(d_k)$, and (3) $g_t \notin \gamma(d_r)$.

Since $\{d_k\} \vdash d_k$ belongs to an admissible set, $\{d_k\} \vdash d_k \cup \Delta$, we know:

1. $\{d_k\} \vdash d_k$ is an argument;
2. with help of Δ, $\{d_k\} \vdash d_k$ withstands all attacks towards it.

Since arguments attacking $\{d_k\} \vdash d_k$ are of the form $\{Nd_k g_j, NX_j^{rk}\} \vdash Nd^k$ (the contrary of d_k is Nd^k and the only rule with head Nd^k is $Nd^k \leftarrow d_r g_j, Nd_k g_j, NX_j^{rk}$), $\{d_k\} \vdash d_k$ withstanding the attack from $\{Nd_k g_j, NX_j^{rk}\} \vdash Nd^k$ means that one of the following three conditions holds:

1. there is no argument for Nd^k for some j, r, i.e., there is no way to "prove" $d_r g_j$, i.e., there is no argument with claim $d_r g_j$ due to the absence of $a_i \in A$, hence either $d_r a_i \leftarrow \notin \mathcal{R}$ or $g_j a_i \leftarrow \notin \mathcal{R}$. This means $g_j \notin \gamma(d_r)$. Therefore part of the antecedent of ⋆, $g_j \in \gamma(d_r)$, is false and ⋆ holds for g_j, d_r;
2. there is an argument Arg for the contrary of $Nd_k g_j$ and Arg withstands all attacks towards it with help from Δ. Since $\mathcal{C}(Nd_k g_j) = \{d_k g_j\}$, having an argument with claim $d_k g_j$ means d_k meets g_j, i.e., $g_j \in \gamma(d_k)$. Therefore the other part of the antecedent of ⋆, $g_j \notin \gamma(d_k)$, is false and ⋆ holds;
3. there is an argument Arg for the contrary of NX_j^{rk} and Arg withstands all attacks towards it. Since $\mathcal{C}(NX_j^{rk}) = \{X_j^{rk}\}$ and $X_j^{rk} \leftarrow d_k g_t, Nd_r g_t, Pg_t g_j$, having Arg with claim X_j^{rk} and Arg withstanding all of attacks towards it means:
   (a) there is an argument for $d_k g_t$;
   (b) $\{Nd_r g_t\} \vdash Nd_r g_t$ withstands all attacks towards it;
   (c) there is an argument for $Pg_t g_j$.

3(a) implies d_k meets g_t, hence $g_t \in \gamma(d_k)$; 3(b) implies d_r does not meet g_t, hence $g_t \notin \gamma(d_r)$; 3(c) implies $g_t > g_j$ in P. Jointly, 3(a) 3(b) and 3(c) imply ⋆.

As ⋆ holds for all cases 1, 2, and 3, and there are no other cases, d_k is most-preferred.

4   Preferences over Combined Goals

Preferences can be expressed over combined goals. For instance it may be that g_1 is preferred to both g_2 and g_3, but g_2 and g_3 together are more preferred than g_1. To model preferences over combined goals, we redefine the preferences P as a partial order over sets of goals, and denote it by P^s.

To save space, we do not repeat Definition 1 but use $\langle D, A, G, DA, GA, P^s \rangle$ to denote an extended decision framework with preferences defined over sets of goals (2^G). Note that the new definition is a generalisation of the earlier one as P are P^s over singletons. We leave Definition 3 unchanged.

To ease the presentation, we define the notion of *comparable goal set* (*comparable set* in short) as follows:

Definition 6. *Given edf* $= \langle \mathsf{D}, \mathsf{A}, \mathsf{G}, \mathsf{DA}, \mathsf{GA}, \mathsf{P}^\mathsf{s} \rangle$, *we let the* comparable goal set, S, *(in edf) be such that:* $\mathsf{S} \subseteq 2^\mathsf{G}$, *and*

- *for every* $s \in \mathsf{S}$, *there is an* $s' \in \mathsf{S}, s \neq s'$, *such that either* $s < s' \in \mathsf{P}^\mathsf{s}$ *or* $s' < s \in \mathsf{P}^\mathsf{s}$;
- *for every* $s \in 2^\mathsf{G} \setminus \mathsf{S}$, *there is no* $s' \in 2^\mathsf{G}$, *such that* $s < s' \in \mathsf{P}^\mathsf{s}$ *or* $s' < s \in \mathsf{P}^\mathsf{s}$.

Example 5. Let G be $\{g_1, g_2, g_3, g_4, g_5\}$, let P^s be:

$$\{g_1\} > \{g_2\} > \{g_4, g_5\} > \{g_3\} > \{g_4\} > \{g_5\}.$$

Then the comparable goal set is: $\{\{g_1\}, \{g_2\}, \{g_3\}, \{g_4\}, \{g_5\}, \{g_4, g_5\}\}$.

We redefine Definition 4 to incorporate the change from P to P^s, as follows.

Definition 7. *A* most-preferred-set extended decision function $\psi^E \in \Psi^E$ *is such that given an extended decision framework edf* $= \langle \mathsf{D}, \mathsf{A}, \mathsf{G}, \mathsf{DA}, \mathsf{GA}, \mathsf{P}^\mathsf{s} \rangle$, *let S be the comparable set in edf, for every* $d \in \mathsf{D}$, $d \in \psi^E(edf)$ *if and only if the following holds for all* $d' \in \mathsf{D} \setminus \{d\}$:

- *for all* $s \in \mathsf{S}$, *if* $s \not\subseteq \gamma(d)$ *and* $s \subseteq \gamma(d')$, *then there exists* $s' \in \mathsf{S}$, *such that:*
  - $s' > s \in \mathsf{P}^\mathsf{s}$,
  - $s' \subseteq \gamma(d)$, *and*
  - $s' \not\subseteq \gamma(d')$.

We say d is a most-preferred-set *(in edf). We refer to a generic most-preferred-set decision function as* ψ^E_s.

Intuitively, Definition 7 is Definition 4 with goals replaced by comparable sets. An informal reading of Definition 7 is: to select a decision d, we check against all other d' to ensure that: for any comparable set of goals s, if d' meets s but d does not, then there exists some s' more preferred than s such that s' is met by d but not d'.

We modify Example 3 to illustrate Definition 7 as follows.

Example 6. As in Example 3, $\gamma(d_1) = \{g_2, g_4, g_5\}$, and $\gamma(g_2) = \{g_2, g_3\}$. Unlike Example 3, we let P^s be the one shown in Example 5. Though g_3 is more preferred than g_4 and g_5 individually, g_4 and g_5 together are more preferred than g_3. It is trivial to see d_1 is more preferred than d_2 as d_1 meets both g_4 and g_5 whereas d_2 does not. Hence, d_1 is a most-preferred-set decision.

Similar to Definition 5, ABA can be used to compute most-preferred-set decisions. We give the corresponding ABA framework as follows.

Definition 8. *Given an extended decision framework edf* $= \langle \mathsf{D}, \mathsf{A}, \mathsf{G}, \mathsf{DA}, \mathsf{GA}, \mathsf{P}^\mathsf{s} \rangle$, *let* $\mathsf{S} = \{s_1, \ldots, s_w\}$ *be the comparable set in edf, the* most-preferred-set *ABA framework corresponds to edf is* $AF = \langle \mathcal{L}, \mathcal{R}, \mathcal{A}, \mathcal{C} \rangle$, *where:*

- $\mathcal{R}$ *is such that:*
  for all k, j *and* i *with* $1 \leqslant k \leqslant n$, $1 \leqslant j \leqslant m$, $1 \leqslant i \leqslant l$:

- *if* $\mathsf{DA}_{k,i} = 1$ *then* $d_k a_i \leftarrow \in \mathcal{R}$;
- *if* $\mathsf{GA}_{j,i} = 1$ *then* $g_j a_i \leftarrow \in \mathcal{R}$;
- $d_k g_j \leftarrow d_k a_i, g_j a_i \in \mathcal{R}$;

for all k *with* $1 \leqslant k \leqslant n$, *all* $s_p \in \mathsf{S}$, *let* $s_p = \{g'_1, g'_2, \ldots, g'_r\}$

- $d_k s_p \leftarrow d_k g'_1, d_k g'_2, \ldots, d_k g'_r \in \mathcal{R}$;

for all $s_1, s_2 \in \mathsf{S}$, *if* $s_1 > s_2 \in \mathsf{P}^{\mathsf{s}}$, *then* $Ps_1s_2 \leftarrow \in \mathcal{R}$;

for all k, r *with* $1 \leqslant k \leqslant n$, $1 \leqslant r \leqslant n$, $k \neq r$, $1 \leqslant j \leqslant w$:
$Nd^k \leftarrow d_r s_j, Nd_k s_j, NX_j^{rk} \in \mathcal{R}$.

for all k, r, j, t *with* $1 \leqslant k \leqslant n$, $1 \leqslant r \leqslant n$, $k \neq r$, $1 \leqslant j \leqslant w$, $1 \leqslant t \leqslant w$,
$j \neq t$: $X_j^{rk} \leftarrow d_k s_t, Nd_r s_t, Ps_t s_j \in \mathcal{R}$;

that is all the rules in $\mathcal{R}$.

- $\mathcal{A}$ *is such that:*

    if $1 \leqslant k \leqslant n$, $d_k \in \mathcal{A}$;

    for all k, r, j *with* $1 \leqslant k \leqslant n$, $1 \leqslant r \leqslant n$, $k \neq r$, $1 \leqslant j \leqslant w$: $NX_j^{rk} \in \mathcal{A}$;

    for all k, j *with* $1 \leqslant k \leqslant n$, $1 \leqslant j \leqslant w$: $Nd_k s_j \in \mathcal{A}$;

    that is all the assumptions.

- $\mathcal{C}$ *is such that:*

    for all k *with* $1 \leqslant k \leqslant n$, $\mathcal{C}(d_k) = \{Nd^k\}$;

    for all k, r, j *with* $1 \leqslant k \leqslant n$, $1 \leqslant r \leqslant n$, $k \neq r$, $1 \leqslant j \leqslant w$: $\mathcal{C}(NX_j^{rk}) = \{X_j^{rk}\}$;

    for all k, j *with* $1 \leqslant k \leqslant n$, $1 \leqslant j \leqslant w$: $\mathcal{C}(Nd_k s_j) = \{d_k s_j\}$.

Definition 8 is given in the same spirit as Definition 5. Instead of checking every individual goal being fulfilled by a decision ($d_k g_j$), using the rule $d_k g_j \leftarrow d_k a_i, g_j a_i$, Definition 8 checks sets of goals $d_k s_j$ fulfilled by a decision using two rules: $d_k s_p \leftarrow d_k g'_1, d_k g'_2, \ldots, d_k g'_r$ and $d_k g_j \leftarrow d_k a_i, g_j a_i$. Hence, a decision meeting a comparable set is the decision meeting all goals in the comparable set. We illustrate this new notion of ABA framework corresponding to extended decision framework with preferences over sets of goals in the next section.

As in Theorem 1, selected decisions are arguments in admissible extensions:

Theorem 2. *Given an extended decision framework* $edf = \langle \mathsf{D}, \mathsf{A}, \mathsf{G}, \mathsf{DA}, \mathsf{GA}, \mathsf{P}^{\mathsf{s}} \rangle$, *let* $AF = \langle \mathcal{L}, \mathcal{R}, \mathcal{A}, \mathcal{C} \rangle$ *be the most-preferred-set ABA framework corresponding to* edf. *Then, for all* $d \in \mathsf{D}$, $d \in \psi_s^E(edf)$ *if and only if the argument* $\{d\} \vdash d$ *belongs to an admissible set in* AF.

The proof of Theorem 2 is very similar to that of Theorem 1. The difference is that a decision meeting a goal is replaced by a decision meeting a comparable sets ($d_k g_j \leftarrow d_k a_i, g_j a_i$ is replaced by $d_k s_p \leftarrow d_k g'_1, d_k g'_2, \ldots, d_k g'_r$). The structure of the proof remains unchanged and the conclusion holds.

5 Selecting Medical Literature as Decision Making

In medical research, one sometimes faces the problem of choosing which medical studies to base a diagnosis on, for a given patient. We view this as a decision making problem and show how our techniques can be used to solve it.

For this case study, we have identified 11 randomised clinical trials on the treatment of brain metastases. The decisions of our model are choices to use a given paper in a diagnosis—they can therefore be represented by names or IDs for the papers themselves. The Arm IDs and PMID Numbers of these literature are given in Table 3. Each literature contains a two-arm trial. We extract a list of representing trial design criteria and patient characteristics from these papers. These criteria and characteristics are considered *attributes* (A) of decisions.

The relations between papers and trial criteria / characteristics are given in Table 4 (DA). Here, a "1" in row k column i should be interpreted as the trial reported in paper p_k has criterion / characteristics i. A blank means the corresponding criterion / characteristics is either not reported or not met by the particular paper. For instance, the first row should be read as: the trial reported in paper p_1 included patients over 18 years old, those with 1 or many brain metastases, with performance status either 0 or 1, and more than 60 percent of the patient sample population included in this trial had primary lung cancer.

Table 3. 11 medical studies on brain metastases

id	ArmID	PMID Number
1	Ayoma Jama 2006	16757720
2	Graham IJROBP 2010	19836153
3	Chang Lancet 2009	1980120
4	Langley ClinOnc 2013	23211715
5	Kocher JCO 2011	21041710
6	Patchell NEJM 1990	2405271
7	Patchell Jama	9809728
8	Mintz Cancer 1996	8839553
9	VechtAnn Neurol 1993	8498838
10	Andrews Lancet 2004	15158627
11	Kondziolka IJROBP 1999	10487566

Since the aim is to find medical papers for a particular patient, we view properties of the given patient as goals (G). In this setting, "good" decisions are medical papers that better match with the particular patient's properties. We present relations between patient's properties and trial characteristics in Table 5 (GA). "1"s in the table represent trial characteristics meeting patient properties. Blanks means otherwise. For instance, the sample patient shown in Table 5 has four properties: being 64 years old, has three metastases, has a performance status 2, and has lung cancer.

We first let the preference (P) be:

$$3mets > Lung > PS2 > Age.$$

Here, the preference order states that: the number of metastases is more important than where the main cancer comes from than the performance status

Table 4. Paper / Trial Characteristics (DA)

	> 18	$1m$	$2m$	$> 2m$	ECD	$PS\ 0,1$	$PS\ 2$	$PS\ 3,4$	$Lung > .6$	$Breast > .6$
p_1	1	1	1	1		1			1	
p_2				1		1	1			
p_3	1	1	1	1		1	1			
p_4	1	1	1	1					1	
p_5	1	1	1	1	1					
p_6	1	1				1				
p_7	1	1				1			1	
p_8		1				1	1	1		
p_9	1	1				1	1			
p_{10}	1	1	1	1	1	1			1	
p_{11}			1	1		1				

Table 5. Patient Properties / Trial Characteristics (GA)

	> 18	$1m$	$2m$	$> 2m$	ECD	$PS\ 0,1$	$PS\ 2$	$PS\ 3,4$	$Lung > .6$	$Breast > .6$
$Age64$	1									
$3met$				1						
$PS\ 2$							1			
$Lung$									1	

than the age of the patient. Thus, we form an extended decision framework $edf = \langle D, A, G, DA, GA, P \rangle$ with decisions $D = \{p_1, \ldots, p_{11}\}$, attributes $A = \{> 18, 1m, 2m, > 2m, ECD, PS\ 0,1, PS\ 2, PS\ 3,4, Lung > .6, Breast > .6\}$, and goals $G = \{Age64, 3\ met, PS\ 2, Lung\}$, GA, DA, and P are given above.

We omit the ABA framework, AF, corresponding to this extended decision framework. We use proxdd[4] to compute the admissible arguments. There, we see that $\{p_{10}\} \vdash p_{10}$ is in an admissible extension in AF, as illustration in Figure 2.

To illustrate preferences over sets of goals, we let P^s be:

$$\{PS2, Age\} > \{3mets\} > \{Lung\} > \{PS2\} > \{Age\}.$$

The comparable goal set is: $\{\{PS2, Age\}, \{3mets\}, \{Lung\}, \{PS2\}, \{Age\}\}$. We insert new rules such as:

- $p1SPS2age \leftarrow p1PS2, p1Age$
- $p1S3mets \leftarrow p13mets$

and so on in the corresponding ABA framework (read as: $p1$ meets the comparable goal set $\{PS2, age\}$ if $p1$ meets $PS2$ and $p1$ meets Age; $p1$ meets the comparable goal set $\{3mets\}$ if $p1$ meets $3mets$, etc.). A graphical illustration of p_3 being a most-preferred-set decision is given in Table 3.

---

[4] http://www.doc.ic.ac.uk/~rac101/proarg/

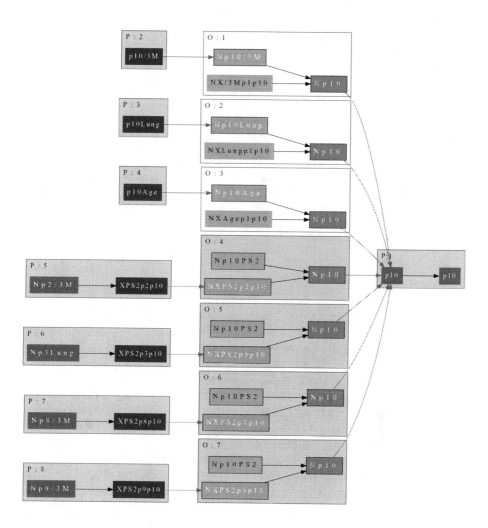

Fig. 2. Graphical illustration of p_{10} being a most-preferred decision. Note that this figure omits opponent arguments which have been counter-attacked by proponent arguments shown in this graph. **Right / Root:** p_{10} is a good paper. **Middle / Opponents:** (attacking the root) p_{10} is not good as it does not meet the *3 metastases* goal and it is not the case that p_{10} meeting some more important goal than *3 metastases*. (O:1) p_{10} is not good as it does not meet the *main cancer from lung* goal and it is not the case that p_{10} meeting some more important goal than *main cancer from lung*. (O:2) Etc. **Left / Support:** (attacking the middle ones) p_{10} meets the *3 metastases* goal (P:2). p_{10} meets the *main cancer from lung* goal (P:3), etc.

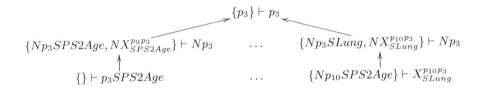

Fig. 3. Graphical illustration of p_3 being a most-preferred-set decision. Note that this figure only shows a small part a debate graph. A reading is follows. **Root:** p_3 is a good paper. **Middle Left:** (attacking the root) p_3 is not good as it does not meet the comparable set $\{PS2, age\}$ and it is not the case that p_3 meeting some more important comparable set than $\{PS2, age\}$. **Bottom Left:** (attacking the middle left) p_3 meets $\{PS2, age\}$. **Middle Right:** (attacking the root) p_3 is not good as it does not meets $\{Lung\}$ and it is not the case that p_3 meeting some more preferred comparable set than p_{10} meeting $Lung$. **Bottom Right:** (attacking the middle right) p_3 meets $\{PS2, age\}$ whereas p_10 does not, and $\{PS2, age\}$ is more preferred than $\{Lung\}$.

6   Related Work

Matt et.al. [9] present an ABA based decision making model. Our work differs from theirs in that we study decision making with preference over goals and sets of goals whereas they focus on decision making without preferences.

Dung et al. [4] present an argumentation-based approach to contract negotiation. Part of that work can be viewed as argumentation-based decision-making with preferences. The main differences are: (1) we give formal definition of decision making frameworks whereas they do not; (2) we study preference over a set of goals whereas they do not; (3) we make explicit connections between 'good' decisions and 'acceptable' arguments whereas they do not.

Fan and Toni [6] present a model of argumentation-based decision-making. Compare to that work, this paper gives a more thorough look at decision making with preferences over goals by examining preferences over individual goals and sets of goals whereas that work has not. Moreover, this work uses a real world example, medical paper selection, as the case study, whereas [6] has not.

Amgoud and Prade [1] present a formal model for making decisions using abstract argumentation. Our work differs from theirs as: (1) they use abstract argumentation whereas we use ABA; (2) they use a pair-wise comparison between decisions to select the "winning" decision whereas we use an unified process to map extended decision frameworks into ABA and then compute admissible arguments.

7   Conclusion

We present an argumentation based decision making model that supports preferences. In our model, we represent knowledge related to decision making in extended decision frameworks in the forms of decisions, attributes, goals and preferences over (sets of) goals. We define extended decision functions to select "good" decisions. We then map both decision frameworks and decision functions into ABA frameworks. In this way, computing selected decisions becomes computing admissible arguments. We obtain sound and complete results such as selected decisions are claims of admissible arguments and vice versa. A benefit of our approach is that it gives an argumentative justification to the selected decisions while computing it. A natural extension of our approach is incorporating defeasibility into our approach to model a form of uncertainty. Comparing with many work in multi-criteria decision making [11], our approach gives a finer granularity in reasoning as not only decisions and goals are considered but also attributes and preferences.

We apply our decision making model to clinical trial selection: given properties of a patient, we select papers that are most relevant to this patient, from a set of papers. We view papers as decisions, trial criteria and characteristics as attributes, patient properties as goals. Hence, "good" decisions are papers best match with patient properties. We show our model gives satisfactory results. Also since our decision model is generic, we can apply it in many other domains. For example, we plan to apply the developed decision making model to select the most suitable treatment for a patient in future.

Although the argumentation frameworks generated are large in comparison with the decision frameworks, the generation is typically quick, and all queries we investigated were answered by proxdd in less than 0.05 seconds. Future work will investigate the complexity and performance evaluation more thoroughly; should the generation of ABA frameworks be found to be expensive, we will look at the possibility of 'lazy' generation, producing relevant inference rules in $\mathcal{R}$ on the fly, as query answering needs them.

Other future directions include studying decision-making with other form of knowledge representation, studying decision-making with conditional preference [2], and studying decision-making in the context of multiple agents sharing potentially conflicting knowledge and preferences.

Acknowledgements. This research was supported by the EPSRC project Transparent Rational Decisions by Argumentation : EP/J020915/1.

References

1. Amgoud, L., Prade, H.: Using arguments for making and explaining decisions. Art. Int. 173(3-4) (2009)
2. Boutilier, C., Brafman, R.I., Domshlak, C., Hoos, H.H., Poole, D.: Cp-nets: A tool for representing and reasoning with conditional ceteris paribus preference statements. JAIR 21, 135–191 (2004)
3. Dung, P.M., Kowalski, R.A., Toni, F.: Assumption-based argumentation. In: Argumentation in AI, pp. 25–44. Springer (2009)
4. Dung, P.M., Thang, P.M., Toni, F.: Towards argumentation-based contract negotiation. In: Proc. COMMA (2008)

5. Dung, P., Kowalski, R., Toni, F.: Dialectic proof procedures for assumption-based, admissible argumentation. AIJ 170, 114–159 (2006)
6. Fan, X., Toni, F.: Decision making with assumption-based argumentation. In: Proc. TAFA (2013)
7. Fox, J., Glasspool, D., Patkar, V., Austin, M., Black, L., South, M., Robertson, D., Vincent, C.: Delivering clinical support services: There is nothing as practical as a good theory. J. of Biom. Inf. 43(5) (2010)
8. Fox, J., Krause, P., Elvang-Gøransson, M.: Argumentation as a general framework for uncertain reasoning. In: Proc. UAI, pp. 428–434 (1993)
9. Matt, P.-A., Toni, F., Vaccari, J.R.: Dominant decisions by argumentation agents. In: McBurney, P., Rahwan, I., Parsons, S., Maudet, N. (eds.) ArgMAS 2009. LNCS, vol. 6057, pp. 42–59. Springer, Heidelberg (2010)
10. Nawwab, F.S., Bench-Capon, T.J.M., Dunne, P.E.: A methodology for action-selection using value-based argumentation. In: Proc. COMMA, pp. 264–275 (2008)
11. Yoon, K.P., Hwang, C.L.: Multiple Attribute Decision Making: An Introduction. Sage Publications Inc. (March 1995)

Author Index